CULTURAL INSIGHTS
ESSAYS ON WESTERN CIVILIZATION

KEVIN MACDONALD

Jewish intellectual and political movements are a powerful force in Western societies. Marxism, Zionism, neoconservatism, psychoanalysis, and multiculturalism have transformed Western self-consciousness, shattered ancient political orders through wars and revolutions, and promoted the ongoing demographic dispossession of European peoples by Third World immigrants. The Jewish role in these movements is often the subject of fierce partisanship, on all sides, but is seldom the subject of careful and dispassionate scientific analysis.

Kevin MacDonald has pioneered the evolutionary analysis of Jewish religious, intellectual, and political movements as strategies for achieving collective survival, advancement, and influence in his trilogy *A People That Shall Dwell Alone: Judaism as a Group Evolutionary Strategy* (1994), *Separation and Its Discontents: Toward an Evolutionary Theory of Anti-Semitism* (1998), and *The Culture of Critique: An Evolutionary Analysis of Jewish Involvement in Twentieth-Century Intellectual and Political Movements* (1998).

In the present volume, MacDonald extends and refines his analyses in chapters on Zionism and the Jewish role in Soviet Communism, neoconservatism, and the promotion of racial integration. MacDonald also devotes chapters to the anti-Semitism of Henry Ford, the psychological basis of ethnocentrism, the unique characteristics of Western civilization, and what Jewish group evolutionary strategies can contribute to its survival.

MacDonald's essays are not only models of scientific rigor, broad research, and deep insight, but of courage, candor, and clarity. They are essential reading not just for scholars and students, but for anyone concerned to understand, and perhaps to alter, the dominant trends of Western civilization.

KEVIN MACDONALD, Professor of Psychology at California State University—Long Beach, holds a Master's degree in evolutionary biology and a Ph.D. in Biobehavioral Sciences from the University of Connecticut. He continued developmental research during a post-doctoral fellowship at the University of Illinois. Since assuming his position at California State University—Long Beach, Dr. MacDonald's research has focused on developing evolutionary perspectives in developmental psychology and personality theory, the origins and maintenance of monogamous marriage in Western Europe, and ethnic relations (human group evolutionary strategies). He is the author of more than 100 scholarly papers and reviews. His books include *Social and Personality Development: An Evolutionary Synthesis* (1988), *Sociobiological Perspectives on Human Development* (ed., 1988), *Parent-Child Play* (1993), and *Evolutionary Perspectives on Human Development* (ed. with Robert Burgess, 2nd ed., 2004). Dr. MacDonald serves on the Editorial Advisory Board of *The Occidental Quarterly*.

CULTURAL INSURRECTIONS:
ESSAYS ON WESTERN CIVILIZATION, JEWISH INFLUENCE, AND ANTI-SEMITISM

KEVIN MACDONALD

THE OCCIDENTAL PRESS
Atlanta
2007

Copyright © 2007 by the Trustees of The Charles Martel Society
All rights reserved

Cover photo © 1988 Owen Franken/CORBIS
Photograph of Kevin MacDonald by Robert Freligh

Published in the United States by
THE OCCIDENTAL PRESS
P.O. Box 8127
Atlanta, GA 31105-8127
USA
http://www.occidentalpress.com/

ISBN 0-9779882-4-4 (numbered cloth edition of 100 copies)
ISBN 0-9779882-2-8 (cloth)
ISBN 0-9779882-3-6 (paper)

First Edition

Library of Congress Cataloguing-in-Publication Data

MacDonald, Kevin B.
　Cultural insurrections : essays on western civilization, Jewish influence, and anti-semitism
/ Kevin MacDonald ; with a foreword by Virginia
Abernethy.
　　p. cm.
　Includes bibliographical references and index.
　ISBN 0-9779882-2-8 (hardcover : alk. Paper) — ISBN 0-9779882-3-6 (softcover : alk. Paper) — ISBN 0-9779882-4-4 (ltd. Ed. Hardcover : alk.
paper)
　1. Jews—Politics and government—20th century. 2. Jews—Intellectual life. 3. Civilization, Western—Jewish influences. I. Title.
　DS143.M156 2007
　323.1192'4—dc22
　　　　　　　　　　　　　2007032934

KEVIN MACDONALD

This book is dedicated to Samuel Francis,
a true warrior whose cultural insurrections continue to reverberate.
He is sorely missed.

Contents

Foreword by Virginia Abernethy...iii

Introduction...1

I. Jewish Influence

1. Background Traits for Jewish Activism................................13

2. Stalin's Willing Executioners...49

3. Zionism and the Internal Dynamics of the Jewish Community......89

4. Neoconservatism as a Jewish Movement.............................120

5. Neoconservative Portraits..159

6. Jews, Blacks, and Race...196

II. Anti-Semitism

7. Henry Ford and the Jewish Question..................................225

8. Enemies of My Enemy..255

III. Western Civilization

9. What Makes Western Culture Unique?................................271

10. Psychology and White Ethnocentrism................................300

11. Biological Roots of Ethnocentrism and Group Conflict............332

12. Immigration and Ethnic Interests......................................342

13. Was the 1924 Immigration Cut-Off "Racist"?......................347

14. Can the Jewish Model Help the West Survive?....................355

Bibliography...365

Index..393

FOREWORD

By Virginia Abernethy

Kevin MacDonald is best known as the author of a trilogy of books on Jews and Judaism and their impact on Western civilization: *A People That Shall Dwell Alone: Judaism as a Group Evolutionary Strategy, Separation and Its Discontents: Toward an Evolutionary Theory of Anti-Semitism,* and *The Culture of Critique: An Evolutionary Analysis of Jewish Involvement in Twentieth-Century Intellectual and Political Movements*. These books are models of scholarly breadth, scientific rigor, and dispassionate objectivity. But they deal with touchy subjects and draw politically incorrect conclusions. Thus the Southern Poverty Law Center branded MacDonald America's "scariest academic." MacDonald has become, to use his own words, a "thought criminal in the academic world."

Evolution and the Construction of Culture

In order to understand the development of MacDonald's thinking, it's important to understand his background. He received his undergraduate degree at the University of Wisconsin as a philosophy major and continued for four years as a graduate student in philosophy at Wisconsin. This was during the period of the cultural revolution of the 1960s when the political and cultural left had such a large influence. MacDonald was deeply affected by this movement and adopted the radical political and cultural beliefs that were so common during the period and continue to shape the world we live in today.

When he finally returned to graduate school in the mid-1970s—this time in the area of evolutionary biology and behavior, the revolution inaugurated by E. O. Wilson's *Sociobiology* was just beginning. Although he could see the power of sociobiological thinking for understanding the behavior of animals and for some important human tendencies, he was skeptical that this body of theory could be easily applied to humans. Like many leftists, he was not attracted to genetic explanations for complex human behavior and culture. And his background in philosophy probably made him more open to the idea that human culture was not reducible to a set of genetic tendencies.

Perhaps surprisingly, his thinking on evolution and culture started out with sex. Robert Trivers' evolutionary theory of sex is the most influential theory in the area of evolutionary explanations of human behavior. The basic idea is that reproduction is very costly for women because of the huge amount of time and energy involved in pregnancy, lactation, and child care. On the other hand, the basic act of reproduction for males is quite inexpensive, requiring only a small amount of time and energy. This means that in the same time period that a female could raise one child, a male could sire a huge number of offspring. Males benefit from having multiple mates because that raises the probability of their leaving many offspring, i.e., of having reproductive success.

It follows, theoretically, that a principal male motive for seeking wealth and power is gaining access to multiple sexual partners. And this has indeed been the pattern throughout the world. From Chinese emperors to African chieftains, males at the top of the social hierarchy were able to mate with many females. Most famously, Sultan Moulay Ismail (the Bloodthirsty) of Morocco sired 888 children with his many wives and concubines.

An anomaly that struck MacDonald is that, at least as early as the Roman period, European cultures developed ideologies and social controls that maintained monogamy as the primary—and ideal—structure for male/female sexual relationships. Even in the face of powerful evolutionary tendencies toward polygyny, marriage of one man to one woman became institutionalized.

MacDonald's solution to this anomaly was to argue that there were conflicts of interest over mating arrangements within human societies. In general, these conflicts of interest are decided in the interests of the wealthy and powerful. However, more egalitarian mating arrangements are also theoretically possible if, for example, lower status males are able to control the behavior of wealthy males by constructing social controls and ideologies that favor monogamy and punish non-monogamous relationships. He then delved into the historical record in order to find support for his hypothesis.

The historical record did indeed support this hypothesis. For example, during the Middle Ages, the Catholic Church developed a powerful ideology for monogamous marriage that it was able to reinforce through various social controls, including rules that prohibited concubinage and prevented bastards from inheriting wealth. At a formal level, the result was to regulate at the group level the sexual behavior of wealthier, more powerful males. *In effect, the social control, or discipline, imposed by the society as a whole was able to compromise the interests of an individual wealthy male and his immediate biological relatives.* This criterion satisfies all the formal requirements for group selection, but the mechanism is not natural selection but the construction of a cultural regime that regulates the behavior of group members in ways that may depart from the interests of at least some group members.

But if sexual behavior can be regulated at the level of the group, then so can anything else. In particular, it suggested to MacDonald that humans would be able to solve the problem of group selection. Group selection is in many ways the fundamental problem of sociobiology—absolutely central to thinking about the social behavior of animals. The basic thinking in evolutionary biology is that natural selection operated at the level of the individual or perhaps at the level of the gene, but there were imposing theoretical reasons to suppose that natural selection at the level of groups was unlikely, except perhaps among closely related family members.

The simplest way to see this is to imagine a group where individuals benefit from group membership (e.g., better protection from predators) but there are also costs to group membership (e.g., the need to warn other group members about approaching predators). Animals are always better off if they attempt to obtain the benefits of group membership without paying the costs. Even if there were a genetic mutation that made some members of the group altruistic, there would be immediate selection against the gene for altruism because an animal with the gene would suffer a cost which would benefit the non-altruists. In the long run, the gene for altruism would tend to disappear. As a result, it's very hard to imagine how groups of altruists could evolve.

Having shown that the sexual behavior of wealthy and powerful males could be regulated by developing social controls on sexual behavior along with a supporting ideology that monogamy was an ideal form of marriage, it was a short step to realize that humans could also create altruistic groups via the same mechanism. From this perspective, the reason that animals are unable to form altruistic groups is that they are unable to monitor group members and enforce group goals by preventing cheating and defection. Humans, however, have no such limitations. Culture is able to accomplish what genetic selection by itself could never bring about.

MacDonald chose to study Judaism because Jews make up a human group that appeared to be related by blood kinship and appeared, as well, to cooperate closely in order to maximize advantage to the in-group in competition with other groups. Jewish groups are able to enforce group goals on individuals by maintaining group discipline—enforcing Jewish monopolies, taxing community members, and punishing Jews who deviate from the group ethic of Judaism.

Most importantly from the standpoint of evolutionary theory, Jews have been able to regulate their own gene pool. For centuries, Ashkenazi and Sephardic Jews engaged in eugenic practices for intelligence. Jewish men who had mastered the voluminous Jewish religious writings were rewarded with good marriages and financial benefits, and this meant that they had more children. The result is that Jews are more intelligent than the people they live among, and this gives them a competitive advantage.

Jews were also able to regulate marriage to prevent the influx of non-Jewish genes. Reviewing the population genetic data, MacDonald shows that Jews have remained genetically distinct from surrounding peoples throughout their history. There were strong controls on marrying within the group. Jews who married outside the group were ostracized, even by their own families. To a great extent these controls are still in place in many Jewish communities, especially in Israel and among the more traditional Jewish sects.

In other words, even though MacDonald emphasized cultural practices in maintaining group boundaries, the result was to enforce genetic segregation from surrounding peoples. This means that competition between Jews and non-Jews was fundamentally an evolutionary story.

But if culture is able to regulate behavior within a group, then it is a short step to realize that there may be conflicts of interest over the construction of culture. Indeed, conflict over the construction of culture is basic to MacDonald's theory of culture beginning with his writings on monogamy. MacDonald's *The Culture of Critique* applied this idea to conflicts of interest between Jews and non-Jews over the construction of culture. Once again, however, even though the conflict is over the construction of culture, there are real evolutionary consequences to the conflict: The basic idea is that Jewish intellectual and political movements have resulted in a very large decline in the political and cultural influence of European Americans and are even leading to a decline of the traditional peoples and culture of Europe.

Obviously, it is massively ironic that MacDonald is now being hounded as a "racist" by organizations such as the Southern Poverty Law Center. His background as a philosopher and as a cultural leftist led him to interpret human behavior as very much influenced by culture. But in reading about Judaism and about the cultural movements that have been so influential in controlling human behavior in recent times, he found that their deep structure was ethnic competition. Over and over again, he calls attention to the deep ethnic commitments of the Jews who were so central, not only for understanding the history of Judaism in traditional societies, but also for understanding the intellectual and political movements that have shaped the Western world at least since the beginning of the twentieth century. MacDonald's "racism" is nothing more than the idea that European-descended peoples have as much right as any other people, including Jews, to preserve their people and their culture.

Cultural Insurrections

The present volume continues many of these themes. It has two foci: Jews and Western civilization. In the first and second sections, MacDonald widens and deepens the analyses of Jewish influence on culture and anti-Semitism that he presented in his trilogy, with essays on the roots of Jewish activism and its manifestations in Soviet Communism, Zionism, neoconservatism, and racial desegregation. MacDonald also offers a balanced reappraisal of Henry Ford's much-maligned *The International Jew*. It is to these sections that readers of the trilogy will probably turn first.

But it is to the third section, on Western civilization, that you will want to return again and again. Readers often remark that they not only learn a great deal about Jews in MacDonald's trilogy, but in the process they learn a great deal about Western civilization as well. Thus it is most welcome to find these insights drawn together and developed in the essay "What Makes Western Civilization Unique?"

However, Western civilization has unique weaknesses as well as strengths, and the greatest of these weaknesses is Western man's relatively low level of ethnocentrism and high tolerance, and even regard, for alien races and civilizations. This strong tendency toward individualism has made Western peoples peculiarly prone to the cultural pressures of political correctness. This is the topic of "Psychology and White Ethnocentrism" and the chapters that follow. The basic project is to show how culture operates at the level of psychology in order to suppress the natural ethnocentric tendencies of Western peoples. These tendencies, although they are illegitimate in today's climate of political correctness, emerge in what he calls "implicit whiteness"—the tendency for a great many European Americans to seek out neighborhoods and cultural forms with ethnically similar others. Because they violate the prohibitions of political correctness, these relatively mild expressions of ethnocentrism cannot be explicit—they cannot speak their name. It goes without saying that he believes that the main sources of the culture of political correctness are the Jewish intellectual and political movements that he describes in *The Culture of Critique* and the present volume.

In section three we can also observe the evolution of Kevin Mac-

Donald's voice as a writer. In "What Make Western Civilization Unique?" MacDonald's tone is as detached as if he were writing about ancient Chinese civilization rather than his own. But in "Psychology and White Ethnocentrism," MacDonald does not just write *about* European peoples, he writes *as* a European person. He writes as someone who has a personal stake in the survival and flourishing of his subject matter.

The facts he adduces are no less factual, the science no less rigorous, but I imagine that MacDonald thought long and hard before adopting this explicitly engaged tone. This is easy to understand in light of the towering edifices of ethnically motivated pseudoscience and deception (conscious and unconscious) that MacDonald explores at length in *The Culture of Critique*. But scientific objectivity does not forbid taking one's own side in an argument, and in particular there is no conflict between scientific objectivity and defending Western civilization, since scientific objectivity is one of the characteristic values and creations of Western civilization.

Kevin MacDonald asks whatever happened to men like Charles Martel and other great defenders of Western civilization. Well one of them is here, in these pages, and it is good to have him on our side.

Virginia Deane Abernethy
Nashville, Tennessee
August 2007

INTRODUCTION

> The symptoms of incipient revolution can be divided into three stages: (1) Destructive criticism of the existing order; (2) revolutionary theorizing and agitation; and (3) revolutionary action. . . . Before the revolutionary onslaught can have any chance of success, the social order must first have been undermined and morally discredited. This is accomplished primarily by the process of *destructive* criticism.
>
> —Lothrop Stoddard, *The Revolt Against Civilization*, 1922[1]

My book *The Culture of Critique*[2] describes the revolutionary onslaught of several influential Jewish intellectual and political movements against the people and culture of the West. This "destructive criticism of the existing order" has now succeeded and has become the intellectual and political establishment—accepted by elite opinion throughout the Western world. The social revolution spawned by this destructive criticism and its political offshoots is having its predictable negative effect on the demographic and cultural dominance of the peoples who once controlled—now precariously—not only their homelands in Europe but also North America, Australia, and New Zealand. No non-Western society has voluntarily put itself at the mercy of an unending invasion by other peoples and cultures. Throughout the rest of the world, the rule by historically dominant peoples is unquestioned and entirely legitimate. Only in Western societies is it common to see the eclipse of their peoples and culture as a moral imperative.

This culture of critique is massively corrupt and is itself due for a thoroughgoing destructive critique. It is massively corrupt because it is rife with double ethical standards—most notably that so many of the advocates of the de-ethnicization of Western peoples themselves retain strong ethnic identifications and a sense of ethnic interests. It is massively corrupt because it systematically fails to honestly address key issues related to ethnic influence—particularly any discussion of Jews as a hostile elite in the West—as well as a great mass of scientific data on human differences related to intelligence and other traits important for

---

[1] Stoddard 1922, 126.
[2] MacDonald 1998/2002. Since *The Culture of Critique* is cited frequently, I will refer to it by title rather than by author name and date.

success in contemporary societies.

There are two major strands to the essays in this volume. First, I broaden and deepen my previous investigations of Jewish influence and anti-Semitism. Second, I attempt to understand why Western cultures are uniquely susceptible to this sort of onslaught.

PART I: JEWISH INFLUENCE

When I finished writing my trilogy on evolutionary strategies, Judaism, anti-Semitism, and Jewish influence, I thought I had written all I ever would on these subjects.[3] Since the beginning of 1992 I had been immersed in studying, analyzing, and describing the interplay of Western civilization and Jewish influence, and I thought it was time to move on to other issues. But any portrait of these issues is a static representation of a constantly changing scene. For one thing, scholarship is an ongoing process, always generating new lenses with which to see the past. Moreover, Jewish movements, such as neoconservatism, that were of little influence when I wrote my trilogy have recently become of critical importance for understanding US foreign policy and events in the Middle East, as well as for understanding the nature of conservative politics in America. My thinking on these issues has also benefited from recent research on ethnocentrism and how it is managed in our current era of political correctness. Part I of this volume collects the essays resulting from further reflection on Jewish issues.

"Background Traits for Jewish Activism" explains why Jews have repeatedly risen to elite status in European societies. I had certainly discussed Jewish influence in my trilogy, and there were bits and pieces of an explanation scattered throughout these books. But nothing really brought these ideas together into a consistent whole. Eventually, ethnocentrism, intelligence and wealth, psychological intensity, and aggressiveness emerged as key explanatory factors. Most of the focus is on ethnocentrism, at least in part because some of the consequences of Jewish hyperethnocentrism are not obvious. In particular, I highlight moral particularism ("Is it good for the Jews?"), the sense of historical grievance and normative hatred of non-Jews and their cultures, Jewish self-deception, and the powerful tendency to coalesce into exclusionary and

---

[3] *The Culture of Critique*, as well as *A People That Shall Dwell Alone: Judaism as a Group Evolutionary Strategy* (MacDonald 1994/2002) and *Separation and Its Discontents: Toward an Evolutionary Theory of Anti-Semitism* (MacDonald 1998/2004). Because these books are cited frequently, I will cite them by title rather than by author name and date.

authoritarian groups under conditions of perceived threat. The fact that Jews form a wealthy, influential elite is not in itself a problem for European peoples. Rather the problem arises from the fact that Jewish elites are hostile to European culture and its peoples and have aggressively supported policies, such as massive non-white immigration, that can be expected to displace European peoples from lands they have long controlled, including Europe itself.

"Stalin's Willing Executioners" examines Yuri Slezkine's book *The Jewish Century*. Slezkine's book is a good example of how recent scholarship can change our views of the past. This book finally brought the issue of Jewish elite status in the Soviet Union to the mainstream academic media. This is a topic that, like so many others, had been mired in charges of anti-Semitism to the point that generations of academic historians had shied away from it. The image of Jews being central to the most murderous regime in European history conflicted with the post-World War II image of Jews as hapless victims, first of the Germans and then of the Arabs. It is an image that is strenuously maintained by Jewish activists of all stripes, inside and outside the academic world.

The conventional wisdom had two parts. The first was that Jews were nothing more than victims of Communism in the USSR—a position that trades on the reality of anti-Semitism in the USSR after World War II. Slezkine's book destroys this myth. I concur with the central thrust of his book—that Jews aggressively removed their competitors for elite status (the pre-revolutionary Russian administrative and entrepreneurial class) and constituted a hostile elite in the USSR, at least until the post-World War II period. The second prong of the propaganda line about Jewish involvement in the USSR was to claim that Jewish Communists were not really Jews, because they had effectively abandoned their religion and their Jewish identification and embraced socialist universalism in their place. This line, which Slezkine repeats and elaborates, provided a fallback position for Jewish activist organizations throughout most of the twentieth century. I demonstrate how and why this position is indefensible. My position has since been bolstered by historian Liliana Riga's paper "Ethnonationalism, Assimilation, and the Social Worlds of the Jewish Bolsheviks in Fin de Siècle Tsarist Russia." For example, in writing about Lazar Kaganovich, Stalin's most notorious mass murderer, Riga notes that Kaganovich distanced himself from his Jewish origins.

> [B]ut it was precisely his Jewishness that was the important motivator for his radicalism. He was a hard-line supporter of the purges, and as Secretary of the Ukrainian Party from 1925 he vigorously pushed

through policies of Ukrainianization and grain requisitioning, for which actions he became the target of anti-Semitic attacks. In many of his appointments and policies he stoked anti-Semitism, but it was clearly something that he did not mind.[4]

Another topic that I hadn't addressed much in my trilogy was Zionism. Because of perceptions of dual loyalty, Zionism certainly contributed to anti-Semitism at certain times and places in the twentieth century. Thus it came up in my book on anti-Semitism (*Separation and Its Discontents*), but it was not at all central to *The Culture of Critique*. Nonetheless, I continued to think about a rather offhand comment of a Jewish historian to the effect that the radicals have always tended to win the day within the Jewish community. If this were correct, such continued radicalization would engender a vicious feed-forward process in which extremists ended up controlling the direction of the Jewish community. It occurred to me that a good contemporary example is the increasing extremism of the Israeli government as the old-line Labor Zionists were replaced by even more radical elements (the Jabotinskyists, the Likud Party, fundamentalists, and West Bank settlers). With a bit more historical research into the history of Zionism as an offshoot of the most radical, religiously fundamentalist Jews of nineteenth century Eastern Europe, the central thesis of "Zionism and the Internal Dynamics of the Jewish Community" took shape: Beginning on the fringes of Jewish society, Zionist activists eventually succeeded in making Zionism a mainstream Jewish movement, due in large part to the sheer force of numbers of the Eastern European vanguard. Over time, the more militant, expansionist Zionists have won the day. They have succeeded in marginalizing less radical Jews, and they have continued to push for territorial expansion within the occupied territories. This has led to conflicts with Palestinians and a widespread belief among Jews that Israel itself is threatened. The result has been a heightened group consciousness among Jews and ultimately support for Zionist extremism among the entire organized American Jewish community.

The reality is that even though Zionism has been a critically important force within the Jewish community at least since the end of World War II, it was of only marginal significance to the United States and the West generally. However, since the end of the Cold War, the politics of Israel and the Middle East have moved to center stage. On the one hand, Israel has continued its expansionist policies at the expense of the Palestinians

---

[4] Riga 2006, 777.

on the West Bank. On the other, the neoconservative movement within the United States assumed great influence to the point that American foreign policy has become captive to the most extreme elements within Israel and their supporters in the United States. When I wrote *The Culture of Critique*, neoconservatism was still of limited influence, but with the arrival of the George W. Bush administration, neoconservatism has achieved a dominant (and disastrous) influence over American foreign policy. The Congressional elections of 2006 may have halted or even reversed that process, but it is far too early to tell.

The essays "Neoconservatism as a Jewish Movement" and "Neoconservative Portraits" therefore constitute a missing chapter from *The Culture of Critique*, necessitated by the turn of events in favor of neoconservative influence. The Jewish identities and pro-Israel commitments of the neocons have become an open secret, especially since the publication of John Mearsheimer and Stephen Walt's work on the Israel lobby.[5] If my essays have anything unique to add, it is in showing similarities to and differences from the other Jewish intellectual and political movements described in *The Culture of Critique*. Most importantly, I explore the commitments and motivations of its key non-Jewish members, such as Henry (Scoop) Jackson and Dick Cheney. Those who dispute the Jewish nature of neoconservatism are quick to point to influential non-Jews in the movement. However, I have documented the long practice whereby non-Jews serve as high-profile members of Jewish intellectual and political movements. This is especially so in a movement, such as neoconservatism, that attempts to influence the wider political process in which Jews are a tiny minority. The chapters highlight additional features of neoconservatism that are seen in other Jewish intellectual and political movements: involvement of prestigious media and academic institutions, and of the organized Jewish community. As I note in the conclusion of "Neoconservatism as a Jewish Movement":

> The rapid rise and immense influence of the neoconservatives make them a remarkable example of Jewish organization and influence. Individuals with strong Jewish identities maintain close ties to Israeli politicians and military figures and to Jewish activist organizations and pro-Israeli lobbying groups while occupying influential policy-making positions in the defense and foreign policy establishment. These same individuals, as well as a chorus of other prominent Jews, have routine access to the most prestigious media outlets in the

---

[5] Mearsheimer and Walt 2006.

United States. People who criticize Israel, however, are routinely vilified and subjected to professional and personal abuse.

A major factor in the ultimate success of the culture of critique in post-World War II America was the powerful moral fervor that surrounded the civil rights movement. There was only a brief discussion of Jewish support for the civil rights movement in *The Culture of Critique*. "Jews, Blacks, and Race" is a chapter in *Race and the American Prospect*, a collection of essays edited by the late Samuel Francis. Jewish efforts on behalf of blacks spanned the entire range from funding and staffing activist organizations, lobbying for legislation with presidents and in Congress, and spearheading intellectual movements that pathologize a sense of ethnic interests and identity among whites. As in "Zionism and the Internal Dynamics of the Jewish Community," I call attention to the peculiar characteristics of the influence of Jewish immigrants from Eastern Europe, whose "teeming fanaticism and passionate ethnocentrism" have had such a great influence on the modern world. I argue that the Jewish-black alliance along with Jewish promotion of massive non-white immigration and multiculturalism must be understood as resulting from Jewish perceptions of their own self-interest, aimed at displacing the previously dominant white Protestant elite.

PART II: ANTI-SEMITISM

The two essays in the section on anti-Semitism also allowed me to expand in new directions. Both deal with anti-Semitism in the United States before World War II. This was a critical period, in which the modern taboo on discussing Jewish interests and influence was created. It was a period in which Jews had not yet attained the position and influence that they achieved in the postwar years. But they had secured a considerable degree of economic and political power, as well as media influence, and the pall of political correctness had not yet fallen over discussing Jewish issues. So it is fascinating to look at attitudes among American elites and how Jews combated some rather high-profile and unflattering attitudes about Jews and their influence.

In researching anti-Semitism for my book *Separation and Its Discontents*, I mentioned Henry Ford in passing, but never really delved into *The International Jew,* the series of articles published in Ford's newspaper, the *Dearborn Independent*, that caused so much controversy during the 1920s. The essay "Henry Ford and the Jewish Question" finds *The International Jew* to be a very flawed work, but of value nonetheless. I conclude that "apart from its fixation on the fictitious *Protocols of the Elders of Zion*, the great majority of its major claims about Jews are correct and have been corroborated by later scholarship. Jews are a relatively closed ethnic group, having vigorously sought to remain separate from the peoples they have lived among throughout their history. They are a very talented group, adept equally at building businesses and lobbying Congress. They have shown a penchant for being able to influence the media, both through ownership but also by economic pressure and by overrepresentation among journalists, writers, and producers of media content. Jews were indeed deeply involved in political radicalism during the 1920s and thereafter, and *The International Jew* was quite correct in emphasizing the importance of Zionism to the later history of Jews and to the world in general."

Indeed, I must credit *The International Jew* for making available a great many details on Jewish activities of the period. For example, one of the things I pointed to in *The Culture of Critique* was the efforts of writers like Horace Kallen to conceptualize the United States as a "proposition nation" lacking in any ethnic or religious identity. It was remarkable to find that the *The International Jew* had already complained of this in 1921.

The International Jew also made me more aware of aggressiveness, psychological intensity, and hatred toward non-Jews as features of Jewish activism, influencing my paper "Background Traits for Jewish Activism." I was particularly interested to find that Jewish campaigns to remove Christianity from the public square were well advanced by 1920 and had already achieved considerable success. I was also struck by passages recounting Jewish hatred for non-Jews over the ages, such as the Jewish massacre of 60,000 Palestinian Christians in 614 A.D. *The International Jew*'s comments on the nascent Zionist movement are also remarkably prescient.

Another portrait of America before the Fall is provided in "Enemies of My Enemy," a review of Joseph Bendersky's *The "Jewish Threat": Anti-Semitic Politics of the U.S. Army*. This essay emphasizes Bendersky's essentially accurate portrayal of elite Americans in the early part of the twentieth century as having a strong racial consciousness and as deeply concerned about the growing influence of newly arrived Jewish immigrants from Eastern Europe. Perhaps the most informative aspect of the book is its documenting the disappearance of race realist rhetoric and explicit statements of racial identification and interests during the 1930s. Attitudes that had been commonplace in the 1920s became taboo. Such views "remained common in the army and elsewhere on the political right, but they were simply not stated publicly. And if they were, heads rolled and careers were ended." This indicates that the origins of political correctness on racial issues are far earlier than usually understood—the result of the successful intellectual and political onslaught on these ideas spearheaded by the Jewish intellectual and political movements discussed in *The Culture of Critique*. As Bendersky notes, a large part of the success of these movements in stifling explicit declarations of racial identity and interest among whites stems from the dominance of Boasian anthropology—a major theme of *The Culture of Critique*.

PART III: WESTERN CIVILIZATION

My writing on Jewish issues, and particularly *The Culture of Critique*, emphasized Jewish influence on the culture of the West. A common comment on my work was to ask why Western culture was so open to the counter-productive influences it described. Would the disastrous effects of the culture of critique be as likely to occur, say, in Muslim societies or in Japan? Why has the Jewish community been so immune to the deluge of cultural criticism directed at it from outsiders?

My essay "What Makes Western Culture Unique?" provides a theory of Western modernization that emphasizes two basic strands: (1) A biologically based tendency toward individualism stemming from prolonged evolution as Northern hunter-gatherers; and (2) the cultural influence of Christianity in combating the interests of the European aristocracy during the medieval period by reinforcing monogamous marriage and combating extensive kinship relationships. The result of these processes has generated the simple household system based on the nuclear family rather than extended kinship systems. It has nurtured the engine of Western progress and modernity, with all the markers that, at least to some degree, distinguish Western culture: individual rights against the state, companionate marriage, representative government, moral universalism, and science.

However, this analysis also implies that Western culture tends to be less ethnocentric than other cultures. Individualistic culture resulted in a society that was freed from internal conflict based on extended kinship groups. Extended kinship groups were eliminated as a necessary prelude to modernization, but this did not eliminate between-group competition entirely. Beginning in the nineteenth century there has been competition between Western individualistic elites and Jews as a collectivist, ethnically conscious group. In this competition, the relative lack of ethnocentrism among Western elites has functioned as a vulnerability.

My paper "Psychology and White Ethnocentrism" continues this analysis, examining how white ethnocentrism is managed in contemporary European societies. Despite being relatively less inclined toward ethnocentrism, Europeans do exhibit ethnocentric tendencies, which are evolved automatic, unconscious mechanisms. I argue that the vestiges of white ethnocentrism generate what I term "implicit white communities" within multicultural America—that is, communities like the Republican Party and NASCAR that reflect white ethnocentrism but that "dare not speak their name": They cannot explicitly state that they are an expression of white ethnocentrism. White ethnocentrism exists at the unconscious level because it is suppressed by cultural programming that takes advantage of some recently evolved cognitive machinery: the conscious processing mechanisms of the human prefrontal cortex. Research shows that prefrontal control mechanisms are able to inhibit and control ethnocentric impulses originating in the older parts of our brain. This is the fundamental mechanism underlying political correctness.

Political correctness involves two general aspects: understanding the penalties for white ethnocentrism, and belief in various scientifically indefensible ideologies of race and ethnicity. I conclude that progress in defending white ethnic interests will happen only by legitimizing explicit assertions of ethnic identity and interests. Several obstacles to this process are discussed, with particular attention paid to understanding the psychological mechanisms underlying white guilt.

Understanding ethnic interests requires an understanding of the psychology of ethnocentrism and group conflict. In "Biological Roots of Ethnocentrism and Group Conflict" I review the scientific data in this area. The clear message of the previous chapter is that white ethnocentrism is alive and well, even if it is being actively suppressed by the institutions of political correctness. In order to build a sense of white identity and interests, we have to know how these mechanisms work. Indeed the forces of political correctness are quite aware of the scientific findings on group conflict and utilize them to serve their purposes. For example, mechanisms that promote group conflict are not necessarily sensitive to genetic differences between groups. Hence, sports teams composed of players of different races tend to de-emphasize race as a form of identity while strengthening identification with the team. Similarly, in the current era, Christian sects aimed at white people typically promote an identification with the religious group rather than the racial or ethnic group.

Nevertheless, it is becoming increasingly clear that science is on the side of defending white interests and identity. Frank Salter's *On Genetic Interests: Family, Ethny, and Humanity in an Age of Mass Migration* is an intellectual breakthrough.[6] As I point out in "Immigration and Ethnic

---

[6] Salter 2003/2006.

Interests," the book demolishes the idea that genetic differences between races and ethnic groups are trivial and therefore of no consequence. When Western countries allow mass immigration of genetically quite different peoples they are undermining not only their gene pool but also the culture it created. Further, many of the groups displacing Europeans have historical grudges against them. Like the ethnic Russians under Bolshevism, becoming dominated by alien hostile elites is likely to lead to disaster.

One of the bulwarks of massive non-white immigration (and other manifestations of political correctness) is disinformation about the past. The idea that the immigration restriction law of 1924 was "racist" has passed into American folklore. Based mainly on chapter 7 in *The Culture of Critique*, my article "Was the 1924 Immigration Cut-Off 'Racist'?" shows that in fact this law was explicitly framed by its advocates as fair because it maintained the ethnic status quo. That is, the law was aimed at maintaining the prevailing ethnic make-up of the United States by keying immigration from Europe to national origins of Americans as reflected in the 1890 census. Its proponents eschewed any claims of racial superiority, but they definitely had a sense that they were defending their ethnic interests against a foreign invasion.

Finally, my paper "Can the Jewish Model Help the West Survive?" describes the features of Jewish groups that must be emulated if European peoples are to reverse the present course of events. Fundamentally, Europeans must develop a racial identity and a sense of having interests that may conflict with those of other groups. Western elites must abandon their individualistic ways and emulate Jewish elites. Jewish elites have an excellent record of ethnic activism in supporting Jewish organizations and in buying media in order to further Jewish interests. For some, individualism is so ingrained that they may not wish to survive without it, and they probably will not. Thus the great question for the survival of European peoples is how we can emulate the more adaptive ways of other peoples while preserving our own uniqueness and sense of what makes life worth living.

To conclude, if there is an overall theme to this volume of essays, it is that they attempt to describe and to analyze the problems faced by Europeans and persons of European descent in developing a sense of their identity and interests. This should neither surprise nor arouse controversy, since it is what every other identifiable human group does. What is truly shocking—if not pathetic—is that a book focused on these issues bears, with good reason, the title *Cultural Insurrections*.

Part I.

Jewish Influence

Chapter 1

Background Traits for Jewish Activism[*]

Jewish populations have always had enormous effects on the societies in which they reside because of several qualities that are central to the Jewish group evolutionary strategy: First and foremost, Jews are ethnocentric and able to cooperate in highly organized, cohesive, and effective groups. Also important is high intelligence, including the usefulness of intelligence in attaining wealth, prominence in the media, and eminence in the academic world and the legal profession. I will also discuss two other qualities that have received less attention: psychological intensity and aggressiveness.

The four background traits of ethnocentrism, intelligence, psychological intensity, and aggressiveness result in Jews being able to produce formidable, effective groups—groups able to have powerful, transformative effects on the peoples they live among. In the modern world, these traits influence the academic world and the world of mainstream and elite media, thus amplifying Jewish effectiveness compared with traditional societies. However, Jews have repeatedly become an elite and powerful group in societies in which they reside in sufficient numbers. It is remarkable that Jews, usually as a tiny minority, have been central to a long list of historical events. Jews were much on the minds of the Church Fathers in the fourth century during the formative years of Christian dominance in the West. Indeed, I have proposed that the powerful anti-Jewish attitudes and legislation of the fourth-century Church must be understood as a defensive reaction against Jewish economic power and enslavement of non-Jews.[1] Jews who had nominally converted to Christianity but maintained their ethnic ties in marriage and commerce were the focus of the 250-year Inquisition in Spain, Portugal, and the Spanish colonies in the New World. Fundamentally, the Inquisition should be seen as a defensive reaction to the economic and political domination of these "New Christians."[2]

---

[*] First published in *The Occidental Quarterly: A Journal of Western Thought and Opinion* 3 (Summer 2003): 1–37. Reprinted in Kevin MacDonald, *Understanding Jewish Influence: A Study in Ethnic Activism* (Augusta, Ga.: Washington Summit Publishers, 2004).

[1] *Separation and Its Discontents*, ch. 3.
[2] *Separation and Its Discontents*, ch. 4.

Jews have also been central to all the important events of the twentieth century. Jews were a necessary component of the Bolshevik revolution that created the Soviet Union, and they remained an elite group in the Soviet Union until at least the post-World War II era. They were an important focus of National Socialism in Germany, and they have been prime movers of the post-1965 cultural and ethnic revolution in the United States, including the encouragement of massive non-white immigration to countries of European origins.[3] In the contemporary world, organized American Jewish lobbying groups and deeply committed Jews in the Bush administration and the media are behind the pro-Israel US foreign policy that is leading to war against virtually the entire Muslim world.

How can such a tiny minority have such huge effects on the history of the West? In this essay, I explore four traits that contribute in large measure to Jewish influence: ethnocentrism, intelligence, psychological intensity, and aggressiveness.

1. JEWS ARE HYPERETHNOCENTRIC

Elsewhere I have argued that Jewish hyperethnocentrism can be traced back to their Middle Eastern origins.[4] Traditional Jewish culture has a number of features identifying Jews with the ancestral cultures of the area. The most important of these is that Jews and other Middle Eastern cultures evolved under circumstances that favored large groups dominated by males.[5] These groups were basically extended families with high levels of endogamy (i.e., marriage within the kinship group) and consanguineous marriage (i.e., marriage to blood relatives), including the uncle-niece marriage sanctioned in the Old Testament. These features are exactly the opposite of Western European tendencies.[6] (See Table 1, on p. 15.)

Whereas Western societies tend toward individualism, the basic Jewish cultural form is collectivism, in which there is a strong sense of group identity and group boundaries. Middle Eastern societies are characterized by anthropologists as "segmentary societies" organized into relatively impermeable, kinship-based groups.[7] Group boundaries are often reinforced through external markers such as hair style or clothing,

---

[3] *The Culture of Critique*, ch. 7.

[4] *A People That Shall Dwell Alone*, ch. 8; *The Culture of Critique*, Preface.

[5] Burton et al. 1996.

[6] See *A People That Shall Dwell Alone*, chs. 3 and 8 for a discussion of Jewish tendencies toward polygyny, endogamy, and consanguineous marriage.

[7] E.g., Coon 1958, 153; Eickleman 1981, 157–74.

as Jews have often done throughout their history. Different groups settle in different areas where they retain their homogeneity alongside other homogeneous groups, as illustrated by the following account from Carleton Coon:

> There the ideal was to emphasize not the uniformity of the citizens of a country as a whole but a uniformity within each special segment, and the greatest possible contrast between segments. The members of each ethnic unit feel the need to identify themselves by some configuration of symbols. If by virtue of their history they possess some racial peculiarity, this they will enhance by special haircuts and the like; in any case they will wear distinctive garments and behave in a distinctive fashion.[8]

TABLE 1
Contrasts between European and Jewish Cultural Forms

	EUROPEAN CULTURAL ORIGINS	JEWISH CULTURAL ORIGINS
Evolutionary History	Northern Hunter-Gatherers	Middle Old World Pastoralists (Herders)
Kinship System	Bilateral; Weakly Patricentric	Unilateral; Strongly Patricentric
Family System	Simple Household	Extended Family; Joint Household
Marriage Practices	Exogamous; Monogamous	Endogamous; Consanguineous; Polygynous
Marriage Psychology	Companionate; Based on Mutual Consent and Affection	Utilitarian; Based on Family Strategizing and Control of Kinship Group
Position of Women	Relatively High	Relatively Low
Social Structure	Individualistic; Republican; Democratic	Collectivistic; Authoritarian; Charismatic Leaders
Ethnocentrism	Relatively Low	Relatively High; "Hyperethnocentrism"
Xenophobia	Relatively Low	Relatively High; "Hyperxenophobia"
Socialization	Stresses Independence, Self-Reliance	Stresses Ingroup Identification, Obligations to Kinship Group
Intellectual Stance	Reason; Science	Dogmatism; Submission to Ingroup Authority and Charismatic Leaders
Moral Stance	Moral Universalism; Morality is Independent of Group	Moral Particularism; Ingroup/Outgroup Morality; "Is it good for the Jews?"

---

[8] Coon 1958, 153.

These societies are by no means blissful paradises of multiculturalism. Between-group conflict often lurks just beneath the surface. For example, in nineteenth-century Turkey, Jews, Christians, and Muslims lived in a sort of superficial harmony, and even inhabited the same areas, "but the slightest spark sufficed to ignite the fuse."[9]

Jews are at the extreme of this Middle Eastern tendency toward hypercollectivism and hyperethnocentrism. I give many examples of Jewish hyperethnocentrism in my trilogy on Jews and Judaism and have suggested in several places that Jewish hyperethnocentrism is biologically based.[10] Middle Eastern ethnocentrism and fanaticism have struck a good many people as extreme, including William Hamilton, perhaps the most important evolutionary biologist of the twentieth century. Hamilton writes:

> I am sure I am not the first to have wondered what it is about that part of the world that feeds such diverse and intense senses of rectitude as has created three of the worlds' most persuasive and yet most divisive and mutually incompatible religions. It is hard to discern the root in the place where I usually look for roots of our strong emotions, the part deepest in us, our biology and evolution.[11]

Referring to my first two books on Jews and Judaism, Hamilton then notes that "even a recent treatise on this subject, much as I agree with its general theme, seems to me hardly to reach to this point of the discussion." If I failed to go far enough in describing or analyzing Jewish ethnocentrism, it is perhaps because the subject seems almost mind-bogglingly deep, with psychological ramifications everywhere. As a pan-humanist, Hamilton was acutely aware of the ramifications of hu-

---

[9] Dumont 1982, 222.

[10] *A People That Shall Dwell Alone*, ch. 8; *Separation and Its Discontents*, ch. 1.

[11] Hamilton 2001, 273. Hamilton likens Judaism to a speciation event in which there is a role for cultural practices such as food preparation: "the main (but moderate) differences from biological situations being that Judaism had come to use a cultural element of inheritance to replace what genes once had been doing more slowly" (p. 271). He also notes that, "In the world of animals, ants perhaps provide *Homo*'s nearest equivalent for typical broadness of niche. If an unspecialized ant species had a Bible, I'd expect to find in it extremely similar injunctions about food, ant genocide, and so forth, as I find in the actual Bible, and I would have no difficulty to suppose these as serving each ant colony well in its struggle for existence" (p. 271).

man ethnocentrism and especially of the Jewish variety. Likening Judaism to the creation of a new human species, Hamilton noted that

> from a humanist point of view, were those "species" the Martian thought to see in the towns and villages a millennium or so ago a good thing? Should we have let their crystals grow; do we retrospectively approve them? As by growth in numbers by land annexation, by the heroizing of a recent mass murderer of Arabs [i.e., Baruch Goldstein, who murdered 29 Arabs, including children, at the Patriarch's Cave in Hebron in 1994], and by the honorific burial accorded to a publishing magnate [Robert Maxwell], who had enriched Israel partly by his swindling of his employees, most of them certainly not Jews, some Israelis seem to favour a "racewise" and unrestrained competition, just as did the ancient Israelites and Nazi Germans. In proportion to the size of the country and the degree to which the eyes of the world are watching, the acts themselves that betray this trend of reversion from panhumanism may seem small as yet, but the spirit behind them, to this observer, seems virtually identical to trends that have long predated them both in humans and animals.[12]

A good start for thinking about Jewish ethnocentrism is the work of Israel Shahak, most notably his co-authored *Jewish Fundamentalism in Israel*.[13] Present-day fundamentalists attempt to re-create the life of Jewish communities before the Enlightenment (i.e., prior to about 1750). During this period the great majority of Jews believed in the Kabbala—the Jewish mystical tradition. Influential Jewish scholars like Gershom Scholem ignored the obvious racialist, exclusivist material in the Kabbalistic literature by using words like "men," "human beings," and "cosmic" to suggest the Kabbala has a universalist message. The actual texts say salvation is only for Jews, while non-Jews have "Satanic souls."[14]

The ethnocentrism apparent in such statements was not only the norm in traditional Jewish society, but remains a powerful current of contemporary Jewish fundamentalism, with important implications for Israeli politics. For example, the Lubavitcher Rebbe, Rabbi Menachem Mendel Schneerson, describing the difference between Jews and non-Jews:

---

[12] Hamilton 2001, 271–72.
[13] Shahak and Mezvinsky 1999.
[14] Shahak and Mezvinsky 1999, 58.

We do not have a case of profound change in which a person is merely on a superior level. Rather we have a case of . . . a totally different species. . . . The body of a Jewish person is of a totally different quality from the body of [members] of all nations of the world. . . . The difference of the inner quality [of the body] . . . is so great that the bodies would be considered as completely different species. This is the reason why the Talmud states that there is an halachic difference in attitude about the bodies of non-Jews [as opposed to the bodies of Jews]: "their bodies are in vain" . . . . An even greater difference exists in regard to the soul. Two contrary types of soul exist, a non-Jewish soul comes from three satanic spheres, while the Jewish soul stems from holiness.[15]

This claim of Jewish uniqueness echoes Holocaust activist Elie Wiesel's claim that "everything about us is different." Jews are "ontologically" exceptional.[16]

The Gush Emunim and other Jewish fundamentalist sects described by Shahak and Mezvinsky are thus part of a long mainstream Jewish tradition which considers Jews and non-Jews completely different species, with Jews absolutely superior to non-Jews and subject to a radically different moral code. Moral universalism is thus antithetical to the Jewish tradition in which the survival and interests of the Jewish people are the most important ethical goal:

Many Jews, especially religious Jews today in Israel and their supporters abroad, continue to adhere to traditional Jewish ethics that other Jews would like to ignore or explain away. For example, Rabbi Yitzhak Ginzburg of Joseph's Tomb in Nablus/Shechem, after several of his students were remanded on suspicion of murdering a teenage Arab girl: "Jewish blood is not the same as the blood of a goy." Rabbi Ido Elba: "According to the Torah, we are in a situation of pikuah nefesh (saving a life) in time of war, and in such a situation one may kill any Gentile." Rabbi Yisrael Ariel writes in 1982 that "Beirut is part of the Land of Israel. [This is a reference to the boundaries of Israel as stated in the Covenant between God and Abraham in Genesis 15: 18–20 and Joshua 1 3–4] . . . our leaders should have entered Lebanon and Beirut without hesitation, and killed every single one of them. Not a memory should have re-

---

[15] In Shahak and Mezvinsky 1999, 59–60.
[16] Wiesel 1985, 153.

mained." It is usually yeshiva students who chant "Death to the Arabs" on CNN. The stealing and corruption by religious leaders that has recently been documented in trials in Israel and abroad continues to raise the question of the relationship between Judaism and ethics.[17]

Moral particularism in its most aggressive form can be seen among the ultranationalists, such as the Gush Emunim, who hold that

> Jews are not, and cannot be a normal people. The eternal uniqueness of the Jews is the result of the Covenant made between God and the Jewish people at Mount Sinai. . . . The implication is that the transcendent imperatives for Jews effectively nullify moral laws that bind the behavior of normal nations. Rabbi Shlomo Aviner, one of Gush Emunim's most prolific ideologues, argues that the divine commandments to the Jewish people "transcend the human notions of national rights." He explains that while God requires other nations to abide by abstract codes of justice and righteousness, such laws do not apply to Jews.[18]

As I argue in chapter 3, "Zionism and the Internal Dynamics of the Jewish Community," it is the most extreme elements within the Jewish community that ultimately give direction to the community as a whole. These fundamentalists and ultranationalists are not tiny fringe groups, mere relics of traditional Jewish culture. They are widely respected by the Israeli public and by many Jews in the Diaspora. They have a great deal of influence on the Israeli government, especially the Likud governments and the recent government of national unity headed by Ariel Sharon. The members of Gush Emunim constitute a significant percentage of the elite units of the Israeli army, and, as expected on the hypothesis that they are extremely ethnocentric, they are much more willing to treat the Palestinians in a savage and brutal manner than are other Israeli soldiers. All together, the religious parties represent about 25 percent of the Israeli electorate[19]—a percentage that is sure to increase because of the high fertility of religious Jews and because intensified troubles with the Palestinians tend to make other Israelis more sympathetic to their cause. Given the factionalism of Israeli politics and

---

[17] Adelman 1999.
[18] Lustick 1987, 123–24.
[19] Shahak and Mezvinsky 1999, 8.

the increasing numbers of the religious groups, it is unlikely that future governments can be formed without their participation. Peace in the Middle East therefore appears unlikely, absent the complete capitulation or expulsion of the Palestinians.

A good discussion of Jewish moral particularism can be found in a 2002 article in *Tikkun*—probably the only remaining liberal Jewish publication. Kim Chernin wonders why so many Jews "have trouble being critical of Israel."[20] She finds several obstacles to criticism of Israel:

> 1. A conviction that Jews are always in danger, always have been, and therefore are in danger now. Which leads to: 2. The insistence that a criticism is an attack and will lead to our destruction. Which is rooted in: 3. The supposition that any negativity towards Jews (or Israel) is a sign of anti-Semitism and will (again, inevitably) lead to our destruction. . . . 6. An even more hidden belief that a sufficient amount of suffering confers the right to violence. . . . 7. The conviction that our beliefs, our ideology (or theology), matter more than the lives of other human beings.

Chernin presents the Jewish psychology of moral particularism:

> We keep a watchful eye out, we read the signs, we detect innuendo, we summon evidence, we become, as we imagine it, the ever-vigilant guardians of our people's survival. Endangered as we imagine ourselves to be; endangered as we insist we are, any negativity, criticism, or reproach, even from one of our own, takes on exaggerated dimensions; we come to perceive such criticism as a life-threatening attack. The path to fear is clear. But our proclivity for this perception is itself one of our unrecognized dangers. Bit by bit, as we gather evidence to establish our perilous position in the world, we are brought to a selective perception of that world. With our attention focused on ourselves as the endangered species, it seems to follow that we ourselves can do no harm. . . . When I lived in Israel I practiced selective perception. I was elated by our little kibbutz on the Lebanese border until I recognized that we were living on land that had belonged to our Arab neighbors. When I didn't ask how we had come to acquire that land, I practiced blindness . . . .

---

[20] Chernin 2002.

The profound depths of Jewish ethnocentrism are intimately tied up with a sense of historical persecution. Jewish memory is a memory of persecution and impending doom, a memory that justifies any response because ultimately it is Jewish survival that is at stake:

> Wherever we look, we see nothing but impending Jewish destruction. . . . I was walking across the beautiful square in Nuremberg a couple of years ago and stopped to read a public sign. It told this story: During the Middle Ages, the town governing body, wishing to clear space for a square, burned out, burned down, and burned up the Jews who had formerly filled up the space. End of story. After that, I felt very uneasy walking through the square, and I eventually stopped doing it. I felt endangered, of course, a woman going about through Germany wearing a star of David. But more than that, I experienced a conspicuous and dreadful self-reproach at being so alive, so happily on vacation, now that I had come to think about the murder of my people hundreds of years before. After reading that plaque I stopped enjoying myself and began to look for other signs and traces of the mistreatment of the former Jewish community. If I had stayed longer in Nuremberg, if I had gone further in this direction, I might soon have come to believe that I, personally, and my people, currently, were threatened by the contemporary Germans eating ice cream in an outdoor cafe in the square. How much more potent this tendency for alarm must be in the Middle East, in the middle of a war zone!

Notice the powerful sense of history here. Jews have a very long historical memory. Events that happened centuries ago color their current perceptions.

This powerful sense of group endangerment and historical grievance is associated with a hyperbolic style of Jewish thought that runs repeatedly through Jewish rhetoric. Chernin's comment that "any negativity, criticism, or reproach, even from one of our own, takes on exaggerated dimensions" is particularly important. In the Jewish mind, all criticism must be suppressed because not to do so would be to risk another Holocaust: "There is no such thing as overreaction to an anti-Semitic incident, no such thing as exaggerating the omnipresent danger. Anyone who scoffed at the idea that there were dangerous portents in American society hadn't learned 'the lesson of the Holocaust.'"[21] Norman Podhoretz,

---

[21] Novick 1999, 178.

editor of *Commentary*, a premier neoconservative journal published by the American Jewish Committee, provides an example:

> My own view is that what had befallen the Jews of Europe inculcated a subliminal lesson. . . . The lesson was that anti-Semitism, even the relatively harmless genteel variety that enforced quotas against Jewish students or kept their parents from joining fashionable clubs or getting jobs in prestigious Wall Street law firms, could end in mass murder.[22]

This is a "slippery slope" argument with a vengeance. The schema is as follows: Criticism of Jews indicates dislike of Jews; this leads to hostility toward Jews, which leads to Hitler and eventually to mass murder. Therefore all criticism of Jews must be suppressed. With this sort of logic, it is easy to dismiss arguments about Palestinian rights on the West Bank and Gaza because "the survival of Israel" is at stake. Consider, for example, the following advertisement distributed by neoconservative publicist David Horowitz:

> The Middle East struggle is not about right versus right. It is about a fifty-year effort by the Arabs to destroy the Jewish state, and the refusal of the Arab states in general and the Palestinian Arabs in particular to accept Israel's existence. . . . The Middle East conflict is not about Israel's occupation of the territories; it is about the refusal of the Arabs to make peace with Israel, which is an expression of their desire to destroy the Jewish state.[23]

"Survival of Israel" arguments thus trump concerns about allocation of scarce resources like water, the seizure of Palestinian land, collective punishment, torture, and the complete degradation of Palestinian communities into isolated, military-occupied, Bantustan-type enclaves. The logic implies that critics of Israel's occupation of the West Bank and Gaza also favor the destruction of Israel and hence the mass murder of millions of Jews.

Similarly, during the debate over selling military hardware to Saudi Arabia in the Carter administration, "the Israeli lobby pulled out all the stops," including circulating books to Congress based on the TV series *The Holocaust*. The American Israel Public Affairs Committee

---

[22] Podhoretz 2000, 148.
[23] Horowitz 2002b.

(AIPAC), the main Jewish lobbying group in Congress, included a note stating, "This chilling account of the extermination of six million Jews underscores Israel's concerns during the current negotiations for security without reliance on outside guarantees."[24] In other words, selling AWACS reconnaissance planes to Saudi Arabia, a backward kingdom with little military capability, is tantamount to collusion in the extermination of millions of Jews.

Jewish thinking about immigration into the United States shows the same logic. Lawrence Auster, a Jewish conservative, describes the logic as follows:

> The liberal notion that "all bigotry is indivisible" [advocated by Norman Podhoretz] implies that all manifestations of ingroup/outgroup feeling are essentially the same—and equally *wrong*. It denies the obvious fact that some outgroups are *more* different from the ingroup, and hence *less* assimilable, and hence *more* legitimately excluded, than other outgroups. It means, for example, that wanting to exclude Muslim immigrants from America is as blameworthy as wanting to exclude Catholics or Jews.
>
> Now when Jews put together the idea that "all social prejudice and exclusion leads potentially to Auschwitz" with the idea that "all bigotry is indivisible," they must reach the conclusion that *any* exclusion of *any* group, no matter how alien it may be to the host society, is a potential Auschwitz.
>
> So there it is. We have identified the core Jewish conviction that makes Jews keep pushing relentlessly for mass immigration, even the mass immigration of their deadliest enemies. In the thought-process of Jews, to keep Jew-hating Muslims out of America would be tantamount to preparing the way to another Jewish Holocaust.[25]

The idea that any sort of exclusionary thinking on the part of Americans—and especially European Americans as a majority group—leads inexorably to a Holocaust for Jews is not the only reason why Jewish organizations still favor mass immigration. I have identified two others as well: the belief that greater diversity makes Jews safer and an intense sense of historical grievance against the traditional peoples and culture of the United States and Europe.[26] These two sentiments also illustrate Jew-

---

[24] In Findley 1989, 102.
[25] Auster 2002.
[26] See *The Culture of Critique*, Preface and ch. 7.

ish moral particularism because they fail to consider the ethnic interests of other peoples in thinking about immigration policy. Recently the "diversity-as-safety" argument was made by Leonard S. Glickman, president and CEO of the Hebrew Immigrant Aid Society, a Jewish group that has advocated open immigration to the United States for over a century. Glickman stated, "The more diverse American society is the safer [Jews] are."[27] At the present time, the HIAS is deeply involved in recruiting refugees from Africa to emigrate to the United States.

The diversity as safety argument and its linkage to historical grievances against European civilization is implicit in a recent statement of the Simon Wiesenthal Center (SWC) in response to former French president Valéry Giscard d'Estaing's argument that Muslim Turkey has no place in the European Union:

> Ironically, in the fifteenth century, when European monarchs expelled the Jews, it was Moslem Turkey that provided them a welcome.... During the Holocaust, when Europe was slaughtering its Jews, it was Turkish consuls who extended protection to fugitives from Vichy France and other Nazi allies.... Today's European neo-Nazis and skinheads focus upon Turkish victims while, Mr. President, you are reported to be considering the Pope's plea that your Convention emphasize Europe's Christian heritage. [The Center suggested that Giscard's new Constitution] underline the pluralism of a multi-faith and multi-ethnic Europe, in which the participation of Moslem Turkey might bolster the continent's Moslem communities—and, indeed, Turkey itself—against the menaces of extremism, hate, and fundamentalism. A European Turkey can only be beneficial for stability in Europe and the Middle East.[28]

Here we see Jewish moral particularism combined with a profound sense of historical grievance—hatred by any other name—against European civilization and a desire for the end of Europe as a Christian civilization with its traditional ethnic base. According to the SWC, the menaces of "extremism, hate, and fundamentalism"—prototypically against Jews—can only be repaired by jettisoning the traditional cultural and ethnic basis of European civilization. Events that happened five hundred years ago are still fresh in the minds of Jewish activists—a phenomenon that should give pause to everyone in an age when Israel

---

[27] Quoted in Cattan 2002.
[28] Simon Wiesenthal Center 2002.

has control of nuclear weapons and long-range delivery systems.[29]

Indeed, a recent article on Assyrians in the United States shows that many Jews have not forgiven or forgotten events of 2,700 years ago, when the Northern Israelite kingdom was forcibly relocated to the Assyrian capital of Nineveh: "Some Assyrians say Jews are one group of people who seem to be more familiar with them. But because the Hebrew Bible describes Assyrians as cruel and ruthless conquerors, people such as the Rev. William Nissan say he is invariably challenged by Jewish rabbis and scholars about the misdeeds of his ancestors."[30]

The SWC inveighs against hate but fails to confront the issue of hatred as a normative aspect of Judaism. Jewish hatred toward non-Jews emerges as a consistent theme throughout the ages, beginning in the ancient world.[31] The Roman historian Tacitus noted that "Among themselves they are inflexibly honest and ever ready to show compassion, though they regard the rest of mankind with all the hatred of enemies."[32] The eighteenth-century English historian Edward Gibbon was struck by the fanatical hatred of Jews in the ancient world:

> From the reign of Nero to that of Antoninus Pius, the Jews discovered a fierce impatience of the dominion of Rome, which repeatedly broke out in the most furious massacres and insurrections. Humanity is shocked at the recital of the horrid cruelties which they committed in the cities of Egypt, of Cyprus, and of Cyrene, where they dwelt in treacherous friendship with the unsuspecting natives; and we are tempted to applaud the severe retaliation which was exercised by the arms of the legions against a race of fanatics, whose dire and credulous superstition seemed to render them the implacable enemies not only of the Roman government, but of human kind.[33]

---

[29] Interview with Dutch-Israeli military historian Martin van Creveld, January 30, 2003: "We possess several hundred atomic warheads and rockets and can launch them at targets in all directions, perhaps even at Rome. Most European capitals are targets for our air force. . . . Our armed forces . . . are not the thirtieth strongest in the world, but rather the second or third. We have the capability to take the world down with us. And I can assure you that that will happen, before Israel goes under" (van Creveld 2003).

[30] Watanabe 2003.

[31] *Separation and Its Discontents*, ch. 2.

[32] Tacitus 1942, 659.

[33] Gibbon 1909, ch. 16, 78.

The nineteenth-century Spanish historian José Amador de los Rios wrote of the Spanish Jews who assisted the Muslim conquest of Spain that "without any love for the soil where they lived, without any of those affections that ennoble a people, and finally without sentiments of generosity, they aspired only to feed their avarice and to accomplish the ruin of the Goths; taking the opportunity to manifest their rancor, and boasting of the hatreds that they had hoarded up so many centuries."[34] In 1913, economist Werner Sombart, in his classic *Jews and Modern Capitalism,* characterized the Jews as "a group by themselves and therefore separate and apart—this from the earliest antiquity. All nations were struck by their hatred of others."[35]

A recent article by Meir Y. Soloveichik, aptly titled "The Virtue of Hate," amplifies this theme of normative Jewish fanatical hatred.[36] "Judaism believes that while forgiveness is often a virtue, hate can be virtuous when one is dealing with the frightfully wicked. Rather than forgive, we can wish ill; rather than hope for repentance, we can instead hope that our enemies experience the wrath of God." Soloveichik notes that the Old Testament is replete with descriptions of horribly violent deaths inflicted on the enemies of the Israelites—the desire not only for revenge but for revenge in the bloodiest, most degrading manner imaginable: "The Hebrew prophets not only hated their enemies, but rather reveled in their suffering, finding in it a fitting justice." In the Book of Esther, after the Jews kill the ten sons of Haman, their persecutor, Esther asks that they be hanged on a gallows.

This normative fanatical hatred in Judaism can be seen by the common use among Orthodox Jews of the phrase *yemach shemo*, meaning, *may his name be erased*. This phrase is used "whenever a great enemy of the Jewish nation, of the past or present, is mentioned. For instance, one might very well say casually, in the course of conversation, 'Thank God, my grandparents left Germany before Hitler, *yemach shemo*, came to power.' Or: 'My parents were murdered by the Nazis, *yemach shemam.*'"[37] Again we see that the powerful consciousness of past suffering leads to present-day intense hatred:

> Another danger inherent in hate is that we may misdirect our odium at institutions in the present because of their past misdeeds. For in-

---

[34] In Walsh 1930, 196.
[35] Sombart 1913/1982, 240.
[36] Soloveichik 2003.
[37] Soloveichik 2003.

stance, some of my coreligionists reserve special abhorrence for anything German, even though Germany is currently one of the most pro-Israel countries in Europe. Similarly, after centuries of suffering, many Jews have, in my own experience, continued to despise religious Christians, even though it is secularists and Islamists who threaten them today, and Christians should really be seen as their natural allies. Many Jewish intellectuals and others of influence still take every assertion of the truth of Christianity as an anti-Semitic attack. After the Catholic Church beatified Edith Stein, a Jewish convert to Christianity, some prominent Jews asserted that the Church was attempting to cover up its role in causing the Holocaust. And then there is the historian Daniel Jonah Goldhagen, who essentially has asserted that any attempt by the Catholic Church to maintain that Christianity is the one true faith marks a continuation of the crimes of the Church in the past. Burning hatred, once kindled, is difficult to extinguish.

Soloveichik could also have included Jewish hatred toward the traditional peoples and culture of the United States. This hatred stems from Jewish memory of the immigration law of 1924, which is seen as having resulted in a greater number of Jews dying in the Holocaust because it restricted Jewish immigration from Eastern Europe during the 1920s and 1930s. Jews are also acutely aware of widespread anti-Jewish attitudes in the United States prior to World War II. The hatred continues despite the virtual disappearance of anti-Jewish attitudes in the United States after World War II and despite the powerful ties between the United States and Israel.[38]

Given the transparently faulty logic and obvious self-interest involved in arguments made by Jewish activists, it is not unreasonable to suppose that Jews are often engaged in self-deception. In fact, self-deception is a very important component of Jewish moral particularism. I wrote an entire chapter on Jewish self-deception in *Separation and Its Discontents*,[39] but it was nowhere near enough. Again, Kim Chernin:

> Our sense of victimization as a people works in a dangerous and seditious way against our capacity to know, to recognize, to name, and to remember. Since we have adopted ourselves as victims we cannot correctly read our own history let alone our present circumstances.

---

[38] See *The Culture of Critique*, Preface.
[39] *Separation and Its Discontents*, ch. 8.

Even where the story of our violence is set down in a sacred text that we pore over again and again, we cannot see it. Our self-election as the people most likely to be victimized obscures rather than clarifies our own tradition. I can't count the number of times I read the story of Joshua as a tale of our people coming into their rightful possession of their promised land without stopping to say to myself, "but this is a history of rape, plunder, slaughter, invasion, and destruction of other peoples." As such, it bears an uncomfortably close resemblance to the behavior of Israeli settlers and the Israeli army of today, a behavior we also cannot see for what it is. We are tracing the serpentine path of our own psychology. We find it organized around a persuasion of victimization, which leads to a sense of entitlement to enact violence, which brings about an inevitable distortion in the way we perceive both our Jewish identity and the world, and involves us finally in a tricky relationship to language.

Political columnist Joe Sobran—who has suffered professionally for expressing his opinions about Israel—exposes the moral particularism of Norman Podhoretz, one of the chorus of influential Jewish voices who advocate restructuring the entire Middle East in the interests of Israel:

Podhoretz has *unconsciously* exposed the Manichaean fantasy world of so many of those who are now calling for war with Iraq. The United States and Israel are "good"; the Arab-Muslim states are "evil"; and those opposed to this war represent "moral relativism," ostensibly neutral but virtually on the side of "evil." This is simply deranged. The ability to see evil only in one's enemies isn't "moral clarity." It's the essence of fanaticism. We are now being counseled to fight one kind of fanaticism with another.[40]

As Sobran notes, the moral particularism is unconscious—an example of self-deception. The world is cut up into two parts, the good and the evil—ingroup-outgroup—as it has been, for Jews, for well over two thousand years. In 2002, Jared Taylor and David Horowitz got into a discussion which touched on Jewish issues. Taylor writes:

Mr. Horowitz deplores the idea that "we are all prisoners of identity

---

[40] Sobran 2002. My emphasis.

politics," implying that race and ethnicity are trivial matters we must work to overcome. But if that is so, why does the home page of FrontPageMag carry a perpetual appeal for contributions to "David's Defense of Israel Campaign"? Why Israel rather than, say, Kurdistan or Tibet or Euskadi or Chechnya? Because Mr. Horowitz is Jewish. His commitment to Israel is an expression of precisely the kind of particularist identity he would deny to me and to other racially-conscious whites. He passionately supports a self-consciously Jewish state but calls it "surrendering to the multicultural miasma" when I work to return to a self-consciously white America. He supports an explicitly ethnic identity for Israel but says American must not be allowed to have one. . . . If he supports a Jewish Israel, he should support a white America.[41]

Taylor is suggesting that Horowitz is self-deceived or inconsistent.

It is interesting that Horowitz was acutely aware of his own parents' self-deception. Horowitz's description of his parents shows the strong ethnocentrism that lurked beneath the noisy universalism of Jewish communists in mid-twentieth century America. In his book, *Radical Son*, Horowitz describes the world of his parents who had joined a "shul" (i.e., a synagogue) run by the Communist Party in which Jewish holidays were given a political interpretation. Psychologically these people might as well have been in eighteenth-century Poland, but they were completely unaware of any Jewish identity. Horowitz writes:

> What my parents had done in joining the Communist Party and moving to Sunnyside was to return to the ghetto. There was the same shared private language, the same hermetically sealed universe, the same dual posturing revealing one face to the outer world and another to the tribe. More importantly, there was the same conviction of being marked for persecution and specially ordained, the sense of moral superiority toward the stronger and more numerous *goyim* outside. And there was the same fear of expulsion for heretical thoughts, which was the fear that riveted the chosen to the faith.[42]

Jews recreate Jewish social structure wherever they are, even when they are completely unaware they are doing so. When asked about their

---

[41] Taylor 2002.
[42] Horowitz 1997, 42.

Jewish commitments, these communists denied having any.[43] Nor were they consciously aware of having chosen ethnically Jewish spouses, although they all married other Jews. This denial has been useful for Jewish organizations and Jewish intellectual apologists attempting to de-emphasize the role of Jews on the radical left in the twentieth century. For example, a common tactic of the ADL beginning in the Red Scare era of the 1920s right up through the Cold War era was to claim that Jewish radicals were no longer Jews because they had no Jewish religious commitments.[44]

Non-Jews run the risk of failing to truly understand how powerful these Jewish traits of moral particularism and self-deception really are. When confronted with his own rabid support for Israel, Horowitz simply denies that ethnicity has much to do with it; he supports Israel as a matter of principle—his commitment to universalist moral principles—and he highlights the relationship between Israel and the West: "Israel is under attack by the same enemy that has attacked the United States. Israel is the point of origin for the culture of the West."[45] This ignores the reality that Israel's treatment of the Palestinians is a major part of the reason why the United States was attacked and is hated throughout the Muslim world. It also ignores the fact that Western culture and its strong strain of individualism are the antithesis of Judaism, and that Israel's Western veneer overlays the deep structure of Israel as an apartheid, ethnically based state.

It's difficult to argue with people who cannot see or at least won't acknowledge the depths of their own ethnic commitments and continue to act in ways that compromise the ethnic interests of others. People like Horowitz (and his parents) can't see their ethnic commitments even when they are obvious to everyone else. One could perhaps say the same of Charles Krauthammer, William Safire, William Kristol, Norman Podhoretz, and the legion of prominent Jews who collectively dominate the perception of Israel presented by the US media. Not surprisingly, Horowitz pictures the United States as a set of universal principles, with no ethnic content. This idea originated with Jewish intellectuals, particularly Horace Kallen, almost a century ago at a time when there was a strong conception that the United States was a European civilization whose characteristics were racially/ethnically based.[46] As

---

[43] See *The Culture of Critique*, ch. 3.
[44] *Separation and Its Discontents*, ch. 6; *The Culture of Critique*, Preface.
[45] Horowitz 2002a.
[46] *The Culture of Critique*, ch. 7

we all know, this world and its intellectual infrastructure have vanished, and I have tried to show that the prime force opposing a European racial/ethnic conception of the United States was a set of Jewish intellectual and political movements that collectively pathologized any sense of European ethnicity or European ethnic interests.[47]

Given that extreme ethnocentrism continues to pervade all segments of the organized Jewish community, the advocacy of the de-ethnicization of Europeans—a common sentiment in the movements I discuss in *The Culture of Critique*—is best seen as a strategic move against peoples regarded as historical enemies. In chapter 8 of *The Culture of Critique*, I call attention to a long list of similar double standards, especially with regard to the policies pursued by Israel versus the policies Jewish organizations have pursued in the United States. These policies include church-state separation, attitudes toward multiculturalism, and immigration policies favoring the dominant ethnic group. This double standard is fairly pervasive. As noted throughout *The Culture of Critique*, Jewish advocates addressing Western audiences have promoted policies that satisfy Jewish (particularist) interests in terms of the morally universalist language that is a central feature of Western moral and intellectual discourse; obviously David Horowitz's rationalization of his commitment to Israel is a prime example of this.

A principal theme of *The Culture of Critique* is that Jewish organizations played a decisive role in opposing the idea that the United States ought to be a European nation. Nevertheless, these organizations have been strong supporters of Israel as a nation of the Jewish people. Consider, for example, a press release of May 28, 1999, by the ADL:

> The Anti-Defamation League (ADL) today lauded the passage of sweeping changes in Germany's immigration law, saying the easing of the nation's once rigorous naturalization requirements "will provide a climate for diversity and acceptance. It is encouraging to see pluralism taking root in a society that, despite its strong democracy, had for decades maintained an unyielding policy of citizenship by blood or descent only," said Abraham H. Foxman, ADL National Director. "The easing of immigration requirements is especially significant in light of Germany's history of the Holocaust and persecution of Jews and other minority groups. The new law will provide a climate for diversity and acceptance in a nation with an onerous legacy of xenophobia, where the concept of 'us versus them' will be

---

[47] *The Culture of Critique, passim*, especially ch. 5.

replaced by a principle of citizenship for all."[48]

There is no mention of analogous laws in place in Israel restricting immigration to Jews, or of the long-standing policy of rejecting the possibility of repatriation for Palestinian refugees wishing to return to Israel or the occupied territories. The prospective change in the "us versus them" attitude alleged to be characteristic of Germany is applauded, while the "us versus them" attitude characteristic of Israel and Jewish culture throughout history is unmentioned. Recently, the Israeli Ministry of Interior ruled that new immigrants who have converted to Judaism will no longer be able to bring non-Jewish family members into the country. The decision is expected to cut by half the number of eligible immigrants to Israel. Nevertheless, Jewish organizations continue to be strong proponents of multiethnic immigration to the United States while maintaining unquestioning support for Israel. This pervasive double standard was noticed by writer Vincent Sheean in his observations of Zionists in Palestine in 1930: "how idealism goes hand in hand with the most terrific cynicism . . . how they are Fascists in their own affairs, with regard to Palestine, and internationalists in everything else."[49] The right hand does not know what the left is doing—self-deception writ large.

Jewish ethnocentrism is well founded in the sense that scientific studies supporting the genetic cohesiveness of Jewish groups continue to appear. Most notable of the recent studies is that of Michael Hammer and colleagues.[50] Based on Y-chromosome data, Hammer et al. conclude that one in 200 matings within Jewish communities were with non-Jews over a 2,000-year period.

Because of their intense ethnocentrism, Jews tend to have great rapport with each other—an important ingredient in producing effective groups. One way to understand this powerful attraction for fellow ethnic group members is J. Philippe Rushton's Genetic Similarity Theory.[51] According to GST, people are attracted to others who are genetically similar to themselves. One of the basic ideas of evolutionary biology is that people are expected to help relatives because they share similar genes. When a father helps a child or an uncle helps a nephew, he is really also helping himself because of their close genetic relation-

---

[48] Anti-Defamation League 1999.
[49] Boyle 2001.
[50] Hammer et al. 2000.
[51] See Rushton 1989; 1999.

ship. (Parents share half their genes with their children; uncles share one-fourth of their genes with nieces and nephews.[52]) GST extends this concept to non-relatives by arguing that people benefit when they favor others who are genetically similar to them even if they are not relatives.

GST has some important implications for understanding cooperation and cohesiveness among Jews. It predicts that people will be friendlier to other people who are genetically more similar to themselves. In the case of Jews and non-Jews, it predicts that Jews would be more likely to make friends and alliances with other Jews, and that there would be high levels of rapport and psychological satisfaction within these relationships.

GST explains the extraordinary rapport and cohesiveness among Jews. Since the vast majority of Jews are closely related genetically, GST predicts that they will be very attracted to other Jews and may even be able to recognize them in the absence of distinctive clothing and hair styles. There is anecdotal evidence for this statement. Theologian Eugene Borowitz writes that Jews seek each other out in social situations and feel "far more at home" after they have discovered who is Jewish.[53] "Most Jews claim to be equipped with an interpersonal friend-or-foe sensing device that enables them to detect the presence of another Jew, despite heavy camouflage." Another Jewish writer comments on the incredible sense of oneness he has with other Jews and his ability to recognize other Jews in public places, a talent some Jews call "J-dar."[54] While dining with his non-Jewish fiancée, he is immediately recognized as Jewish by some other Jews, and there is an immediate "bond of brotherhood" between them that excludes his non-Jewish companion.

Robert Reich, Clinton administration Secretary of Labor, wrote that in his first face-to-face meeting with Federal Reserve Board Chairman Alan Greenspan, "We have never met before, but I instantly know him. One look, one phrase, and I know where he grew up, how he grew up, where he got his drive and his sense of humor. He is New York. He is Jewish. He looks like my uncle Louis, his voice is my uncle Sam. I feel

---

[52] This refers to genes identical because they are inherited from a common ancestor. Uncles and nieces share one-fourth of their genes only on average. Because the relationship is mediated through a sibling relationship, the actual percentage can vary. Siblings may be more or less like one another depending on random processes, but on average they share half their genes.

[53] Borowitz 1973, 136.

[54] *Toronto Globe and Mail*, May 11, 1993.

we've been together at countless weddings, bar mitzvahs, and funerals. I know his genetic structure. I'm certain that within the last five hundred years—perhaps even more recently—we shared the same ancestor."[55] Reich is almost certainly correct that he and Greenspan have a recent common ancestor, and this genetic affinity causes them to have an almost supernatural attraction to each other. Or consider Sigmund Freud, who wrote that he found "the attraction of Judaism and of Jews so irresistible, many dark emotional powers, all the mightier the less they let themselves be grasped in words, as well as the clear consciousness of inner identity, the secrecy of the same mental construction."[56]

Any discussion of Jews and Judaism has to start and probably end with this incredibly strong bond that Jews have among each other—a bond that is created by their close genetic relationship and by the intensification of the psychological mechanisms underlying group cohesion. This powerful rapport among Jews translates into a heightened ability to cooperate in highly focused groups.

To conclude this section: In general, the contemporary organized Jewish community is characterized by high levels of Jewish identification and ethnocentrism. Jewish activist organizations like the ADL, the American Jewish Committee, the Hebrew Immigrant Aid Society, and the neoconservative think tanks are not creations of the fundamentalist and Orthodox, but represent the broad Jewish community, including non-religious Jews and Reform Jews. In general, the more actively people are involved in the Jewish community, the more committed they are to preventing intermarriage and retaining Jewish ethnic cohesion. And despite a considerable level of intermarriage among less committed Jews, the leadership of the Jewish community in the United States is at present not made up of the offspring of intermarried people to any significant extent.

Jewish ethnocentrism is ultimately simple traditional human ethnocentrism, although it is certainly among the more extreme varieties. But what is so fascinating is the cloak of intellectual support for Jewish ethnocentrism, the complexity and intellectual sophistication of the rationalizations for it—some of which are reviewed in *Separation and Its Discontents*[57] and the rather awesome hypocrisy (or cold-blooded deception) of it, given Jewish opposition to ethnocentrism among Europeans.

---

[55] Reich 1997, 79.
[56] In Gay 1988, 601.
[57] *Separation and Its Discontents*, chs. 6–8.

2. Jews Are Intelligent (and Wealthy)

The vast majority of US Jews are Ashkenazi Jews. This is a very intelligent group, with an average IQ of approximately 115 and verbal IQ considerably higher.[58] Since verbal IQ is the best predictor of occupational success and upward mobility in contemporary societies,[59] it is not surprising that Jews are an elite group in the United States. Frank Salter has showed that on issues of concern to the Jewish community (Israel, immigration, ethnic policy in general), Jewish groups have four times the influence of European Americans despite representing approximately 2.5 percent of the population.[60] Recent data indicate that Jewish per capita income in the United States is almost double that of non-Jews, a bigger difference than the black-white income gap.[61] Although Jews make up less than three percent of the population, they constitute more than a quarter of the people on the *Forbes* list of the richest 400 Americans. Jews constitute 45 percent of the top forty of the Forbes 400 richest Americans. Fully one-third of all American multimillionaires are Jewish. The percentage of Jewish households with income greater than $50,000 is double that of non-Jews; on the other hand, the percentage of Jewish households with income less than $20,000 is half that of non-Jews. Twenty percent of professors at leading universities are Jewish, and forty percent of partners in leading New York and Washington D.C. law firms are Jewish.[62]

In 1996, there were approximately 300 national Jewish organizations in the United States, with a combined budget estimated in the range of $6 billion—a sum greater than the gross national product of half the members of the United Nations.[63] For example, in 2001 the ADL claimed an annual budget of over $50 million.[64] There is also a critical mass of very wealthy Jews who are actively involved in funding Jewish causes. Irving Moskowitz funds the settler movement in Israel and pro-Israeli, neoconservative think tanks in Washington D.C., while Charles Bronfman, Ronald Lauder, and Marc Rich fund Birthright Israel, a program to increase ethnic consciousness among Jews by bringing 20,000 young Jews to Israel every year. George Soros finances liberal

---

[58] *A People That Shall Dwell Alone*, ch. 7.
[59] Lynn 1992.
[60] Salter 2002.
[61] Thernstrom and Thernstrom 1997.
[62] Silbiger 2000.
[63] Goldberg 1996, 38–39.
[64] www.adl.org.

immigration policy throughout the Western world and also funds Noel Ignatiev and his "Race Traitor" website dedicated to the abolition of the white race.

So far as I know, there are no major sources of funding aimed at increasing ethnic consciousness among Europeans Americans or at promoting their ethnic interests.[65] Certainly the major conservative foundations in the United States, such as the Bradley and Olin Foundations, are not concerned with European American interests. Indeed, the Bradley Foundation has been a major source of funding for the Jewish-dominated neoconservative movement and for pro-Israel think tanks like the Center for Security Policy.[66]

Paul Findley[67] provides numerous examples of Jews using their financial clout to support political candidates with positions that are to the liking of AIPAC and other pro-Israel activist groups in the United States. This very large financial support for pro-Israel candidates continues into the present—two examples being the campaigns to unseat Cynthia McKinney and Earl Hilliard from Congress in 2002. Because of their predominantly Jewish funding base,[68] Democratic candidates are particularly vulnerable, but all candidates experience this pressure because Jewish support will be funneled to their opponents if there is any hint of disagreement with the pro-Israel lobby.

Intelligence is also important in providing access to the entire range of influential positions, from the academic world, to the media, to business, politics, and the legal profession. In *The Culture of Critique* I describe several influential Jewish intellectual movements developed by networks of Jews who were motivated to advance Jewish causes and interests. These movements were the backbone of the intellectual left in the twentieth century, and their influence continues into the present. Collectively, they call into question the fundamental moral, political, and economic foundations of Western society. These movements have been advocated with great intellectual passion and moral fervor and with a very high level of theoretical sophistication. As with the neoconservative movement, discussed in chapters 4 and 5 below, all of these movements had ready access to prestigious mainstream media sources, at least partly because of the high representation of Jews as owners and producers of mainstream media. All of these movements were strongly

---

[65] Salter 2002.
[66] Vest 2002.
[67] Findley 1989.
[68] Lipset and Raab 1995.

represented at prestigious universities, and their work was published by prestigious mainstream academic and commercial publishers.

Intelligence is also evident in Jewish activism. Jewish activism is like a full court press in basketball: intense pressure from every possible angle. But in addition to the intensity, Jewish efforts are very well organized, well funded, and backed up by sophisticated, scholarly intellectual defenses. A good example is the long and ultimately successful attempt to alter US immigration policy.[69] The main Jewish activist organization influencing immigration policy, the American Jewish Committee, was characterized by "strong leadership, internal cohesion, well funded programs, sophisticated lobbying techniques, well chosen non-Jewish allies, and good timing."[70] The most visible Jewish activists, such as Louis Marshall, were intellectually brilliant and enormously energetic and resourceful in their crusades on behalf of immigration and other Jewish causes. When restrictionist arguments appeared in the media, the American Jewish Committee made sophisticated replies based on at least the appearance of scholarly data, and typically couched in universalist terms as benefiting the whole society. Articles favorable to immigration were published in national magazines, and letters to the editor were published in newspapers. Talented lawyers initiated legal proceedings aimed at preventing the deportation of aliens.

The pro-immigration lobby was also very well organized. Immigration opponents, such as Senator Henry Cabot Lodge, and organizations like the Immigration Restriction League were kept under close scrutiny and pressured by lobbyists. Lobbyists in Washington also kept a daily scorecard of voting tendencies as immigration bills wended their way through Congress, and they engaged in intense and successful efforts to convince Presidents Taft and Wilson to veto restrictive immigration legislation. Catholic prelates were recruited to protest the effects of restrictionist legislation on immigration from Italy and Hungary. There were well-organized efforts to minimize the negative perceptions of immigration by distributing Jewish immigrants around the country and by getting Jewish aliens off public support. Highly visible and noisy mass protest meetings were organized.[71]

Intelligence and organization are also apparent in contemporary Jewish lobbying on behalf of Israel. Les Janka, a US Defense Department

---

[69] *The Culture of Critique*, ch. 7.
[70] Goldstein 1990, 333.
[71] Neuringer 1980.

official, noted that, "On all kinds of foreign policy issues the American people just don't make their voices heard. Jewish groups are the exceptions. They are prepared, superbly briefed. They have their act together. It is hard for bureaucrats not to respond."[72]

Morton A. Klein, national president of the Zionist Organization of America (ZOA), is typical of the highly intelligent, competent, and dedicated Jewish activist. The ZOA website states that Klein had a distinguished career as a biostatistician in academe and in government service in the Nixon, Ford, and Carter administrations. He has received accolades as one of the leading Jewish activists in the United States, especially by media that are closely associated with Likud policies in Israel. For example, the *Wall Street Journal* called the ZOA "heroic and the most credible advocate for Israel on the American Jewish scene today" and added that we should "snap a salute to those who were right about Oslo and Arafat all along . . . including Morton Klein who was wise, brave, and unflinchingly honest. . . . [W]hen the history of the American Jewish struggle in these years is written, Mr. Klein will emerge as an outsized figure." The website boasts of Klein's success "against anti-Israel bias" in textbooks, travel guides, universities, churches, and the media, as well as his work on Capitol Hill." Klein has led successful efforts to block the appointment of Joe Zogby, an Arab American, to the State Department and the appointment of Strobe Talbott, Clinton nominee for Deputy Secretary of State. Klein's pro-Israel articles have appeared in a wide range of mainstream and Jewish media: *New York Times, Washington Post, Los Angeles Times, New Republic, New Yorker, Commentary, Near East Report, Reform Judaism, Moment, Forward, Jerusalem Post, Philadelphia Inquirer, Miami Herald, Chicago Tribune, Ha'aretz* (Jerusalem), *Maariv* (Jerusalem), and the Israeli-Russian paper *Vesti*.

Klein's activism highlights the importance of access to the major media enjoyed by Jewish activists and organizations—a phenomenon that is traceable ultimately to Jewish intelligence. Jews have a very large presence in the media as owners, writers, producers, and editors—far larger than any other identifiable group.[73] In the contemporary world, this presence is especially important with respect to perceptions of Israel. Media coverage of Israel in the United States is dominated by a pro-Israel bias, whereas in most of the world the predominant view is

---

[72] Findley 1989, 164.
[73] *The Culture of Critique*, Preface.

that the Palestinians are a dispossessed people under siege.[74] A critical source of support for Israel is the army of professional pundits "who can be counted upon to support Israel reflexively and without qualification."[75] Perhaps the most egregious example of pro-Israel bias resulting from Jewish media control is the Asper family, owners of CanWest, a company that controls over 33 percent of the English-language newspapers in Canada. CanWest inaugurated an editorial policy in which all editorials had to be approved by the main office. As the Canadian Journalists for Free Expression notes, "the Asper family staunchly supports Israel in its conflicts with Palestinians, and coverage of the Middle East appears to be a particularly sensitive area."[76] CanWest has exercised control over the content of articles related to Israel by editing and spiking articles with pro-Palestinian or anti-Israeli views. Journalists who have failed to adopt CanWest positions have been reprimanded or dismissed.

3. JEWS ARE PSYCHOLOGICALLY INTENSE

I have compared Jewish activism to a full court press—relentlessly intense and covering every possible angle. There is considerable evidence that Jews are higher than average in emotional intensity.[77] Emotionally intense people are prone to intense emotional experience of both positive and negative emotions.[78] Emotionality may be thought of as a behavioral intensifier—an energizer. Individuals high on affect intensity have more complex social networks and more complex lives, including multiple and even conflicting goals. Their goals are intensely sought after.

In the case of Jews, this affects the tone and intensity of their efforts at activism. Among Jews there is a critical mass that is intensely committed to Jewish causes—a sort of 24/7, "pull out all the stops" commitment that produces instant, massive responses on Jewish issues. Jewish activism has a relentless, never-say-die quality. This intensity goes hand in hand with the "slippery slope" style of arguing described above: Jewish activism is an intense response because even the most trivial manifestation of anti-Jewish attitudes or behavior is seen as inevitably leading to mass murder of Jews if allowed to continue.

---

[74] Alterman 2002.
[75] Alterman 2002.
[76] Canadian Journalists for Free Expression 2002.
[77] *A People That Shall Dwell Alone*, ch. 7.
[78] See Larsen and Diener 1987.

Besides its ability to direct Jewish money to its preferred candidates, a large part of AIPAC's effectiveness lies in its ability to rapidly mobilize its 60,000 members. "In virtually every congressional district . . . AIPAC has a group of prominent citizens it can mobilize if an individual senator or representative needs stroking."[79] When Senator Charles Percy suggested that Israel negotiate with the PLO and be willing to trade land for peace, he was inundated with 2,200 telegrams and 4,000 letters, 95 percent against, and mainly from the Jewish community in Chicago.[80] The other side is seldom able to muster a response that competes with the intensity of the Jewish response. When President Eisenhower—the last president to stand up to the pro-Israel lobby—pressured Israel into withdrawing from the Sinai in 1957, almost all the mail opposed his decision. Secretary of State John Foster Dulles complained, "It is impossible to hold the line because we get no support from the Protestant elements in the country. All we get is a battering from the Jews."[81] This pales in comparison to the avalanche of 150,000 letters to President Johnson urging support for Israel when Egypt closed the Strait of Tiran in May 1967. This was just prior to the "Six-Day War," during which the United States provided a great deal of military assistance and actively cooperated in the cover-up of the assault on the USS *Liberty*. Jews had learned from their defeat at the hands of Eisenhower and had redoubled their lobbying efforts, creating by all accounts the most effective lobby in Washington.

Pressure on officials in the State and Defense departments is relentless and intense. In the words of one official, "One has to keep in mind the constant character of this pressure. The public affairs staff of the Near East Bureau in the State Department figures it will spend about 75 percent of its time dealing with Jewish groups. Hundreds of such groups get appointments in the executive branch each year."[82]

Psychological intensity is also typical of Israelis. For example, the Israelis are remarkably persistent in their attempts to obtain US military hardware. The following comment illustrates not only the relentless, intense pressure, but also the aggressiveness of Jewish pursuit of their interests: "They would never take no for an answer. They never gave up. These emissaries of a foreign government always had a shopping list of wanted military items, some of them high technology that no

---

[79] Massing 2002.
[80] Findley 1989.
[81] In Findley 1989, 119.
[82] In Findley 1989, 164.

other nation possessed, some of it secret devices that gave the United States an edge over any adversary."[83] Even though small in number, the effects are enormous. "They never seem to sleep, guarding Israel's interests around the clock."[84] Henry Kissinger made the following comment on Israeli negotiating tactics. "In the combination of single-minded persistence and convoluted tactics the Israelis preserve in the interlocutor only those last vestiges of sanity and coherence needed to sign the final document."[85]

4. JEWS ARE AGGRESSIVE

Being aggressive and "pushy" is part of the stereotype of Jews in Western societies. Unfortunately, there is a dearth of scientific studies on this aspect of Jewish personality. Hans Eysenck, renowned for his research on personality, claims that Jews are indeed rated more aggressive by people who know them well.[86]

Jews have always behaved aggressively toward those they have lived among, and they have been perceived as aggressive by their critics. What strikes the reader of Henry Ford's *The International Jew*, written in the early 1920s, is its portrayal of Jewish intensity and aggressiveness in asserting their interests.[87] As *The International Jew* notes, from Biblical times Jews have endeavored to enslave and dominate other peoples, even in disobedience of divine command. Quoting the Old Testament, "And it came to pass, when Israel was strong, that they put the Canaanites to tribute, and did not utterly drive them out." In the Old Testament the relationship between Israel and foreigners is one of domination. For example, "They shall go after thee, in chains they shall come over; And they shall fall down unto thee. They shall make supplication unto thee" (Isa. 45:14); "They shall bow down to thee with their face to the earth, And lick the dust of thy feet" (49:23). Similar sentiments appear in Trito-Isaiah (60:14, 61:5–6), Ezekiel (e.g., 39:10), and Ecclesiasticus (36:9). The apotheosis of Jewish attitudes of conquest can be seen in the Book of Jubilees, where world domination and great reproductive success are promised to the seed of Abraham:

---

[83] In Findley 1989, 164.
[84] Findley 1989, 328.
[85] In Ball and Ball 1992, 70.
[86] Eysenck 1962, 262.
[87] For more on *The International Jew*, see ch. 7 below, "Henry Ford and the Jewish Question."

I am the God who created heaven and earth. I shall increase you, and multiply you exceedingly; and kings shall come from you and shall rule wherever the foot of the sons of man has trodden. I shall give to your seed all the earth which is under heaven, and they shall rule over all the nations according to their desire; and afterwards they shall draw the whole earth to themselves and shall inherit it for ever. (Jub. 32:18-19)

Elsewhere I have noted that a major theme of anti-Jewish attitudes throughout the ages has been Jewish economic domination.[88] The following petition from the citizens of the German town of Hirschau opposed allowing Jews to live there because Jews were seen as aggressive competitors who ultimately dominate the people among whom they live:

If only a few Jewish families settle here, all small shops, tanneries, hardware stores, and so on, which, as things stand, provide their proprietors with nothing but the scantiest of livelihoods, will in no time at all be superseded and completely crushed by these [Jews] such that at least twelve local families will be reduced to beggary, and our poor relief fund, already in utter extremity, will be fully exhausted within one year. The Jews come into possession in the shortest possible time of all cash money by getting involved in every business; they rapidly become the only possessors of money, and their Christian neighbors become their debtors.[89]

Late nineteenth-century Zionists such as Theodor Herzl were quite aware that a prime source of modern anti-Jewish attitudes was that emancipation had brought Jews into direct economic competition with the non-Jewish middle classes, a competition that Jews typically won. Herzl "insisted that one could not expect a majority to 'let themselves be subjugated' by formerly scorned outsiders whom they had just released from the ghetto."[90] The theme of economic domination has often been combined with the view that Jews are personally aggressive. In the Middle Ages Jews were seen as "pitiless creditors."[91] The philosopher Immanuel Kant stated that Jews were "a *nation* of usurers . . . outwitting

---

[88] *Separation and Its Discontents*, ch. 2.
[89] In Harris 1994, 254.
[90] Kornberg 1993, 183; inner quote from Herzl's diary.
[91] Luchaire 1912, 195.

the people amongst whom they find shelter. . . . They make the slogan 'let the buyer beware' their highest principle in dealing with us."[92]

In early twentieth-century America, the sociologist Edward A. Ross commented on a greater tendency among Jewish immigrants to maximize their advantage in all transactions, ranging from Jewish students badgering teachers for higher grades to Jewish poor attempting to get more than the usual charitable allotment. "No other immigrants are so noisy, pushing, and disdainful of the rights of others as the Hebrews."[93]

> The authorities complain that the East European Hebrews feel no reverence for law as such and are willing to break any ordinance they find in their way. . . . The insurance companies scan a Jewish fire risk more closely than any other. Credit men say the Jewish merchant is often "slippery" and will "fail" in order to get rid of his debts. For lying the immigrant has a very bad reputation. In the North End of Boston "the readiness of the Jews to commit perjury has passed into a proverb."[94]

These characteristics have at times been noted by Jews themselves. In a survey commissioned by the American Jewish Committee's study of the Jews of Baltimore in 1962, "two-thirds of the respondents admitted to believing that other Jews are pushy, hostile, vulgar, materialistic, and the cause of anti-Semitism. And those were only the ones who were willing to admit it."[95]

Jews were unique as an American immigrant group in their hostility toward American Christian culture and in their energetic, aggressive efforts to change that culture. From the perspective of Ford's *The International Jew*, the United States had imported around 3.5 million mainly Yiddish-speaking, intensely ethnocentric Jewish immigrants over the previous forty years. In that very short period, Jews had had enormous effect on American society, particularly in their attempts to remove expressions of Christianity from public life beginning with an attempt in 1899–1900 to remove the word "Christian" from the Virginia Bill of Rights: "The Jews' determination to wipe out of public life

---

[92] In Rose 1992, 7; italics in text.
[93] Ross 1914, 150.
[94] Ross 1914, 150.
[95] Yaffe 1968, 73. Yaffe embeds this comment in a discussion of self-hating Jews—implying that Jews are simply accepting stereotypes that are the fantasies of bigoted non-Jews.

every sign of the predominant Christian character of the United States is the only active form of religious intolerance in the country today."[96]

A prototypical example of Jewish aggressiveness toward American culture has been Jewish advocacy of liberal immigration policies which have had a transformative effect on the United States:

> In undertaking to sway immigration policy in a liberal direction, Jewish spokespersons and organizations demonstrated a degree of energy unsurpassed by any other interested pressure group. Immigration had constituted a prime object of concern for practically every major Jewish defense and community relations organization. Over the years, their spokespersons had assiduously attended congressional hearings, and the Jewish effort was of the utmost importance in establishing and financing such non-sectarian groups as the National Liberal Immigration League and the Citizens Committee for Displaced Persons.[97]

Jewish aggressiveness and their role in the media, in the creation of culture and information in the social sciences and humanities, and in the political process in the United States contrasts with the role of Overseas Chinese.[98] The Chinese have not formed a hostile cultural elite in Southeast Asian countries motivated by historical grievances against the people and culture of their hosts. For example, despite their economic dominance, the Chinese have not been concerned with restrictions on their citizenship rights, which have been common in Southeast Asia.[99] Whereas the Chinese have reacted rather passively to such restrictions, Jews have reacted to any manifestation of anti-Jewish attitudes or behavior with an all-out effort at eradication. Indeed, we have seen that the mainstream Jewish attitude is that even trivial manifestations of anti-Jewish attitudes and behavior must not be ignored because they can and will lead to mass murder. Not only have the Chinese not attempted to remove public displays of symbols of Indonesian nationalism and religion, they have not seriously attempted to change laws in place since the 1960s mandating that there be no public displays of Chinese culture.[100]

---

[96] Ford 1920–1922, 3/21/1920.
[97] Neuringer 1971, 392–93.
[98] *The Culture of Critique*, Preface to the paperback edition.
[99] Coughlin 1960, 169.
[100] *A People That Shall Dwell Alone*, Preface to the first paperback edition.

Besides the normal sorts of lobbying typical of the political process in the United States, perhaps the clearest examples of Jewish aggressiveness are the many examples of intimidation of their opponents—loss of job, death threats, constant harassment, economic losses such as loss of advertising revenue for media businesses, and charges of anti-Semitism—the last being perhaps the greatest sin imaginable against the post-World War II political order. When Adlai Stevenson III was running for governor of Illinois, his record in opposition to Israeli settlement policy and his statement that the PLO was a legitimate voice of the Palestinian people resulted in a whisper campaign that he was an anti-Semite. Stevenson commented:

> There is an intimidating, activist minority of American Jews that supports the decisions of the Israeli government, right or wrong. They do so very vocally and very aggressively in ways that intimidate others so that it's their voice—even though it is a minority—that is heard in American politics. But it still is much louder in the United States than in Israel. In other words, you have a much stronger, more vocal dissent in Israel than within the Jewish community in the United States. The prime minister of Israel has far more influence over American foreign policy in the Middle East than over the policies of his own government generally.[101]

A common tactic has been to charge that critics of Israel are anti-Semites. Indeed, George Ball, a perceptive critic of Israel and its US constituency, maintains that the charge of anti-Semitism and guilt over the Holocaust are the Israeli lobby's most effective weapons—outstripping its financial clout.[102] The utility of these psychological weapons in turn derives from the very large Jewish influence on the US media. Historian Peter Novick notes regarding the importance of the Holocaust in contemporary American life:

> We [i.e., Jews] are not just "the people of the book," but the people of the Hollywood film and the television miniseries, of the magazine article and the newspaper column, of the comic book and the academic symposium. When a high level of concern with the Holocaust became widespread in American Jewry, it was, given the important role that Jews play in American media and opinion-making

---

[101] In Findley 1989, 92.
[102] Findley 1989, 127.

elites, not only natural, but virtually inevitable that it would spread throughout the culture at large.[103]

And, of course, the appeal to the Holocaust is especially compelling for American Jews. When the Mossad wants to recruit US Jews for help in its espionage work, in the words of a CIA agent, "the appeal is a simple one: 'When the call went out and no one heeded it, the Holocaust resulted.'"[104]

Charges of anti-Semitism and guilt over the Holocaust are not the only instruments of Jewish aggressiveness on Israeli issues. Jewish groups intimidate their enemies by a variety of means. People who oppose policies on Israel advocated by Jewish activist organizations have been fired from their jobs, harassed with letters, subjected to intrusive surveillance, and threatened with death. Although there is a great deal of self-censorship in the media on Israel as a result of the major role of Jews in the ownership and production of the media, gaps in this armor are aggressively closed. There are "threats to editors and advertising departments, orchestrated boycotts, slanders, campaigns of character assassination, and personal vendettas."[105] Other examples recounted by Findley include pressure on the Federal Communications Commission to stop broadcast licenses, demands for submission to an oversight committee prior to publication, and the stationing of a Jewish activist in the newsroom of the *Washington Post* in order to monitor the process.

The result of all this intense, well-organized aggression is that

> Those who criticize Israeli policy in any sustained way invite painful and relentless retaliation, and even loss of their livelihood by pressure from one or more parts of Israel's lobby. Presidents fear it. Congress does its bidding. Prestigious universities shun academic programs and buckle under its pressure. Instead of having their arguments and opinions judged on merit, critics of Israel suddenly find their motivations, their integrity, and basic moral values called into question. No matter how moderate their criticism, they may be characterized as pawns of the oil lobby, apologists for Arabs, or even anti-Semitic.[106]

The following quote from Henry Kissinger sums up the aggressive

---

[103] Novick 1999, 12.
[104] *Newsweek* 9/3/1979.
[105] Findley 1989, 296.
[106] Findley 1989, 315.

Israeli attitudes toward US aid:

> Yitzak [Rabin] had many extraordinary qualities, but the gift of human relations was not one of them. If he had been handed the entire "United States Strategic Air Command" as a free gift he would have (a) affected the attitude that at last Israel was getting its due, and (b) found some technical shortcoming in the airplanes that made his accepting them a reluctant concession to us.[107]

But of course by far the most important examples of Israeli aggressiveness have been toward their neighbors in the Middle East. This aggression has been there from the beginning, as Israel has consistently put pressure on border areas with incursions, including the Qibya massacre of 1953 led by Ariel Sharon.[108]

The personal aggressiveness of Israeli society has long been a topic of commentators. Israelis are known for their arrogance, insolence (chutzpah), coldness, roughness, rudeness, and lack of civility. For example, B. Z. Sobel, an Israeli sociologist at the University of Haifa, found that among the motivations for emigrating from Israel was that "there is indeed an edginess [in Israeli society]; tempers flare, and verbal violence is rampant."[109]

CONCLUSION

The current situation in the United States is the result of an awesome deployment of Jewish power and influence. One must contemplate the fact that American Jews have managed to maintain unquestioned support for Israel over the last thirty-five years despite Israel's seizing land and engaging in brutal repression of the Palestinians in the occupied territories—an occupation that will most likely end with expulsion or complete subjugation, degradation, and apartheid. During this same period Jewish organizations in America have been a principal force—in my view the main force—for erecting a state dedicated to suppressing ethnic identification among European Americans, for encouraging massive multi-ethnic immigration into the United States, and for erecting a legal system and cultural ideology that is obsessively sensitive to the complaints and interests of ethnic minorities: the culture of the Holocaust.[110] All this is

---

[107] In Ball and Ball 1992, 70.
[108] See Ball and Ball 1992, 44 and *passim*.
[109] Sobel 1986, 153.
[110] See *The Culture of Critique*, Preface.

done without a whisper of double standards in the aboveground media.

The American Jewish community is well organized and lavishly funded. It has achieved a great deal of power, and it has been successful in achieving its interests.[111] One of the great myths often promulgated by Jewish apologists is that Jews have no consensus and therefore cannot wield any real power. Yet there is in fact a great deal of consensus on broad Jewish issues, particularly in the areas of Israel and the welfare of other foreign Jewries, immigration and refugee policy, church-state separation, abortion rights, and civil liberties.[112] Massive changes in public policy on these issues, beginning with the counter-cultural revolution of the 1960s, coincide with the period of increasing Jewish power and influence in the United States. Indeed, one is hard-pressed to find any significant area where public policy conflicts with the attitudes of mainstream Jewish organizations.

---

[111] Goldberg 1996.
[112] Goldberg 1996, 5.

Chapter 2

STALIN'S WILLING EXECUTIONERS:
JEWS AS A HOSTILE ELITE IN THE USSR[*]

A persistent theme among critics of Jews—particularly those on the pre-World War II right—has been that the Bolshevik revolution was a Jewish revolution and that the Soviet Union was dominated by Jews. This theme appears in a wide range of writings, from Henry Ford's *The International Jew*, to published statements by a long list of British, French, and American political figures in the 1920s (Winston Churchill, Woodrow Wilson, and David Lloyd George), and, in its most extreme form, by Adolf Hitler, who wrote:

> Now begins the last great revolution. By wresting political power for himself, the Jew casts off the few remaining shreds of disguise he still wears. The democratic plebeian Jew turns into the blood Jew and the tyrant of peoples. In a few years he will try to exterminate the national pillars of intelligence and, by robbing the peoples of their natural spiritual leadership, will make them ripe for the slavish lot of a permanent subjugation. The most terrible example of this is Russia.[1]

This long tradition stands in sharp contradiction to the official view, promulgated by Jewish organizations and almost all contemporary historians, that Jews played no special role in Bolshevism and indeed were specifically victimized by it. Yuri Slezkine's *The Jewish Century*[2] provides a much needed resolution to these opposing perspectives. It is an intellectual tour de force, alternately muddled and brilliant, courageous and apologetic.

APOLLONIANS AND MERCURIANS
One of the muddled elements, apparent at the beginning and present

---

[*] First published in *The Occidental Quarterly* 5 (Fall 2005): 65–100.
[1] In Nolte 1965, 406. See Kellogg 2005 for an account of the interactions and influence of White Russian émigrés on the National Socialist movement in Germany.
[2] Yuri Slezkine, *The Jewish Century* (Princeton: Princeton University Press, 2004).

throughout *The Jewish Century,* is Slezkine's claim that the peoples of the world can be classified into two groups. The successful peoples of the modern world, termed Mercurians, are urban, mobile, literate, articulate, and intellectually sophisticated. Distinguished by their ability to manipulate symbols, they pursue "wealth for the sake of learning, learning for the sake of wealth, and both wealth and learning for their own sake" (p. 1). Since Slezkine sees Jews as the quintessential Mercurians, he regards modernization as essentially a process of everyone becoming Jewish. His second group, which he calls Apollonians, is rooted in the land and in traditional agrarian cultures, and prizes physical strength and warrior values.

Slezkine conceptualizes Mercurianism as a worldview, and therefore a matter of psychological choice, rather than as a set of psychological mechanisms, the most important of which is general intelligence. As a result of this false premise, he exaggerates the similarity among Mercurians, underestimates the power of ethnocentrism as a unifying factor in Jewish history, and fails to understand the roots of Western social and economic institutions.

Slezkine views Jews as one of many Mercurian cultures—peoples that dwell alone in Diasporas, living among strangers and often acting as economic middlemen: the Overseas Chinese, Indians, and Lebanese, and the Gypsies and Irish Travelers. Their common denominator, in Slezkine's view (and mine[3]), is their status as strangers to the people they live among—sojourners who, above all else, do not intermarry or socialize with the locals. Their interactions with the local Apollonians involve "mutual hostility, suspicion, and contempt" (p. 20) and a sense of superiority. Moreover, a "common host stereotype of the Mercurians is that they are devious, acquisitive, greedy, crafty, pushy, and crude" (p. 23). The Mercurians possess greater kin solidarity and internal cohesion than the people they live among; they are characterized by extended families and patriarchal social organization.

So far, so good, although I would stress that the family organization of such groups derives more from the long-term adaptation to the culture areas they originate from than from an adaptation to the nomadic, middleman niche.[4] But Slezkine maintains that Mercurians are above all smarter than the people they live among: They are said to possess "cunning intelligence," but it is surely a mistake to consider such disparate groups as Jews (or the Overseas Chinese) and Gypsies (or the Irish

---

[3] See *A People That Shall Dwell Alone* and *Separation and Its Discontents*.

[4] See *A People That Shall Dwell Alone*, Preface to the first paperback edition.

Travelers) as having in common a particular set of intellectual traits. After all, the Jews, as Slezkine shows, have repeatedly become an academic, intellectual, cultural, and economic elite in Western societies, while Gypsies have tended toward illiteracy and are at best an economically marginal group.

Slezkine imagines that the Gypsies and literate middleman groups like the Jews or Overseas Chinese differ not in intelligence but only in whether they express their intelligence through literacy or an oral culture: "Businessmen, diplomats, doctors, and psychotherapists are literate peddlers, heralds, healers, and fortune-tellers" (p. 29)—a formulation that will not stand the test of current psychometric data. In fact, the general patterns of Gypsies are the opposite of Jews: a low-investment, low-IQ reproductive style characterized by higher fertility, earlier onset of sexual behavior and reproduction, more unstable pair bonds, higher rate of single parenting, shorter interval of birth spacing, higher infant mortality rate, and higher rate of survival of low birth weight infants.[5] Intelligence, for Slezkine, is a lifestyle choice, rather than a set of brain processes underlying information processing and strongly influenced by genetic variation. As we shall see, this formulation is very useful to Slezkine as he constructs his argument later in the book.

In his attempt to paint with a very broad brush, Slezkine also ignores other real differences among the Mercurians, most notably, I would argue, the aggressiveness of the Jews compared to the relative passivity of the Overseas Chinese. Both the Jews and the Overseas Chinese are highly intelligent and entrepreneurial, but the Overseas Chinese have not formed a hostile cultural elite in Southeast Asian countries, where they have chiefly settled, and have not been concentrated in media ownership or in the construction of culture. We do not read of Chinese cultural movements disseminated in the major universities and media outlets that subject the traditional culture of Southeast Asians and anti-Chinese sentiment to radical critique, or of Chinese organizations campaigning for the removal of native cultural and religious symbols from public places.[6] Slezkine paints Jews as deeply involved in the construction of culture and in the politics of the host societies, but the role of the Chinese was quite different. The following passage describing the political attitudes of the Overseas Chinese in Thailand could never have applied to Jews in Western societies since the Enlightenment:

---

[5] Bereczkei 1993; Cvorovic 2004.

[6] See discussion in *A People That Shall Dwell Alone*, Preface to the first paperback edition.

But few seem to know or indeed to care about the restrictions on citizenship, nationality rights, and political activities in general, nor are these restrictions given much publicity in the Chinese press. This merely points up the fact, recognized by all observers, that the overseas Chinese are primarily concerned with making a living, or amassing a fortune, and thus take only a passive interest in the formal political life of the country in which they live.[7]

Moreover, Slezkine pictures the middlemen as specializing in "certain dangerous, marvelous, and distasteful" (p. 9), but nevertheless indispensable, pursuits (p. 36)—a formulation that carries a grain of truth, as in places where natives were prohibited from loaning money at interest. However, he ignores, or at least fails to spell out, the extent to which Jews have been willing agents of exploitative elites, not only in Western societies, but in the Muslim world as well.[8] This is the overarching generalization that one can make about Jewish economic behavior over the ages. Their role went far beyond performing tasks deemed inappropriate for the natives for religious reasons; rather they were often tasks at which natives would be relatively less ruthless in exploiting their fellows. This was especially the case in Eastern Europe, where economic arrangements such as tax farming, estate management, and monopolies on retail liquor distribution lasted far longer than in the West:

In this way, the Jewish arendator became the master of life and death over the population of entire districts, and having nothing but a short-term and purely financial interest in the relationship, was faced with the irresistible temptation to pare his temporary subjects to the bone. On the noble estates he tended to put his relatives and co-religionists in charge of the flour-mill, the brewery, and in particular of the lord's taverns where by custom the peasants were obliged to drink. On the church estates, he became the collector of all ecclesiastical dues, standing by the church door for his payment from tithe-payers, baptized infants, newly-weds, and mourners. On the [royal] estates . . . he became in effect the Crown Agent, farming out the tolls, taxes, and courts, and adorning his oppressions with all the dignity of royal authority.[9]

---

[7] Coughlin 1960, 169.
[8] *A People That Shall Dwell Alone*, ch. 5.
[9] Davies 1981, 444; see also Subtelny 1988, 124.

Jewish involvement in the Communist elite of the USSR can be seen as a variation on an ancient theme in Jewish culture rather than a new one sprung from the special circumstances of the Bolshevik Revolution. Rather than being the willing agents of exploitative non-Jewish elites who were clearly separated from both the Jews and the people they ruled, Jews became an entrenched part of an exploitative and oppressive elite in which group boundaries were blurred. This blurring of boundaries was aided by four processes, all covered by Slezkine: shedding overt Jewish identities in favor of a veneer of international socialism in which Jewish identity and ethnic networking were relatively invisible; seeking lower-profile positions in order to de-emphasize Jewish preeminence (e.g., Trotsky); adopting Slavic names; and engaging in a limited amount of intermarriage with non-Jewish elites.[10] Indeed, the "plethora of Jewish wives" among non-Jewish leaders[11] doubtless heightened the Jewish atmosphere of the top levels of the Soviet government, given that everyone, especially Stalin, appears to have been quite conscious of ethnicity.[12] For their part, anti-Semites have accused Jews of having *"implanted those of their own category as wives and husbands for influential figures and officials."*[13]

By emphasizing the necessity and distastefulness of traditional Jewish occupations, Slezkine also ignores the extent to which Jewish competition suppressed the formation of a native middle class in Eastern Europe. (This has also occurred throughout Southeast Asia, because of competition from the Overseas Chinese.) Instead, Slezkine sees Eastern Europeans through stereotypic lenses as quintessential Apollonians, some of whom became Mercurian modernists when forced to by circumstances, rather than as containing elements that would have naturally aspired to and competently performed the economic and cultural functions that instead came to be performed by Jews because of their ability to create ethnic monopolies in goods and services. When Jews won the economic competition in early modern Poland, the result was that the great majority of Poles were reduced to the status of agricultural laborers supervised by Jewish estate managers in an economy in which trade, manufacturing, and artisanry were in large part controlled by Jews.[14] On the other hand, in most of Western Europe Jews had

---

[10] This was also noted by Lindemann 1997.
[11] Vaksberg 1994, 49.
[12] See discussion in *The Culture of Critique*, ch. 3.
[13] In Kostyrchenko 1995, 272; italics in text.
[14] *A People That Shall Dwell Alone*, ch. 5; *Separation and Its Discontents*,

been expelled in the Middle Ages. As a result, when modernization occurred, it was accomplished with an indigenous middle class. If, as in Eastern Europe, Jews had won the economic competition in most of these professions, there would not have been a non-Jewish middle class in England. Whatever one imagines might have been the fortunes and character of England with predominantly Jewish artisans, merchants, and manufacturers, it seems reasonable to suppose that the Christian taxpayers of England made a good investment in their own future when they agreed to pay King Edward I a massive tax of £116,346 in return for expelling two thousand Jews in 1290.[15]

While Slezkine's treatment overemphasizes middlemen as a societal necessity rather than as ethnic outsiders competing for scarce resources, he does note that the rise of the Jews in the USSR came at the expense of the Germans as a Mercurian minority in Russia prior to the Revolution. (Jews were excluded from traditional Russia apart from the Pale of Settlement, which included Ukraine, Lithuania, Byelorussia, Crimea, and part of Poland.) Germans manned the imperial bureaucracy, formed a large percentage of professionals, entrepreneurs, and artisans, were more literate than the Russians, and had a sense of cultural superiority and ethnic solidarity:

> And so they were, *mutatis mutandis*, head to the Russian heart, mind to the Russian soul, consciousness to Russian spontaneity. They stood for calculation, efficiency, and discipline; cleanliness, fastidiousness, and sobriety; pushiness, tactlessness, and energy; sentimentality, love of family, and unmanliness (or absurdly exaggerated manliness). . . . Perhaps paradoxically, in light of what would happen in the twentieth century, Germans were, occupationally and conceptually, the Jews of ethnic Russia (as well as much of Eastern Europe). Or rather, the Russian Germans were to Russia what the German Jews were to Germany—only much more so. So fundamental were the German Mercurians to Russia's view of itself that both their existence and their complete and abrupt disappearance have been routinely taken for granted. (pp. 113–14)

Although the replacement of Germans by Jews was well under way by the time of the Bolshevik Revolution, a key consequence of the Revolution was the substitution of one Mercurian group, the Germans, by an-

---

Introduction to the first paperback edition.
[15] Mundill 1998, 249ff.

other, the Jews. The difference between the Jews and the Germans was that the Jews had a longstanding visceral antipathy, out of past historical grievances, both real and imagined, toward the people and culture they came to administer. Indeed, Russians on the nationalist right admired the Germans, at least up to World War I. For example, a statute of one nationalist organization, Michael the Archangel Russian People's Union, expressed "particular trust in the German population of the Empire,"[16] while its leader, Vladimir Purishkevich, accused the Jews of "irreconcilable hatred of Russia and everything Russian."[17] Jews disliked the Christian religion of the vast majority of Russians because of the antagonistic relationship between Judaism and Christianity over the ages; Jews distrusted the peasants, who "fell from grace" (p. 140) with the intelligentsia after the numerous anti-Jewish pogroms, especially after 1880; and Jews blamed the Tsar for not doing enough to keep the peasants in check and for imposing the various quotas on Jewish advancement that went into place, also beginning in the 1880s—quotas that slowed down but by no means halted Jewish overrepresentation in the universities and the professions. In this respect, the Germans were far more like the Overseas Chinese, in that they became an elite without having an aggressively hostile attitude toward the people and culture they administered and dominated economically. Thus when Jews achieved power in Russia, it was as a hostile elite with a deep sense of historic grievance. As a result, they became willing executioners of both the people and cultures they came to rule, including the Germans.

After the Revolution, not only were the Germans replaced, but there was active suppression of any remnants of the older order and their descendants. Jews have always shown a tendency to rise because their natural proclivities (e.g., high intelligence) and powerful ethnic networking, but here they also benefited from "antibourgeois" quotas in educational institutions and other forms of discrimination against the middle class and aristocratic elements of the old regime that would have provided more competition with Jews. In a letter intercepted by the secret police, the father of a student wrote that his son and their friends were about to be purged from the university because of their class origins. "It is clear that only the Jerusalem academics and the Communist Party members generally are going to stay" (p. 243). The bourgeois elements from the previous regime, including the ethnic Germans, would have no future. Thus the mass murder of peasants and

---

[16] In Kellogg 2005, 41.
[17] In Kellogg 2005, 37.

nationalists was combined with the systematic exclusion of the previously existing non-Jewish middle class. The wife of a Leningrad University professor noted, "in all the institutions, only workers and Israelites are admitted; the life of the intelligentsia is very hard" (p. 243). Even at the end of the 1930s, prior to the Russification that accompanied World War II, "the Russian Federation . . . was still doing penance for its imperial past while also serving as an example of an ethnicity-free society" (p. 276). While all other nationalities, including Jews, were allowed and encouraged to keep their ethnic identities, the revolution remained an anti-majoritarian movement.

Slezkine is aware of the biological reality of kinship and ethnicity, but he steadfastly pursues a cultural determinist model. He argues that biological models of ethnic nepotism are inappropriate because some nomadic groups are not kin groups but rather "quasi-families" like the Sicilian mafia (p. 35). But this is a distinction without a difference: Why are "natural" kinship groups significantly different from groups composed of families that band together? Each is characterized by internal cohesion and external strangeness, the traits Slezkine deems essential, but there are also kinship connections and a genetic divide between themselves and surrounding peoples. Cultural badges of group membership and a culturally generated ideology of kin-group membership are age-old ways of cementing kinship groups and setting up barriers that mark real biological differences—the evolved psychology described by modern research in social identity theory.[18] And in any case, the demonstrable genetic differences between Slezkine's prototypical Mercurians—the Jews, Gypsies, and Overseas Chinese—and the surrounding peoples cry out for a biological analysis.

Moreover, Slezkine underestimates the power of ethnocentrism as a unifying factor in Jewish history. This is most apparent in his discussion of Israel, which he describes as a radical departure from the Jewish tradition, because Israel is a quintessentially Apollonian society. Long after Western societies had rejected ethnic nationalism:

> Israel continued to live in the European 1930s: only Israel still belonged to the eternally young, worshiped athleticism and inarticulateness, celebrated combat and secret police, promoted hiking and scouting, despised doubt and introspection, embodied the seamless unity of the chosen, and rejected most traits traditionally associated with Jewishness. . . . After two thousand years of living as Mercuri-

---

[18] *Separation and Its Discontents*, ch. 1.

ans among Apollonians, Jews turned into the only Apollonians in a world of Mercurians (or rather, the only civilized Apollonians in a world of Mercurians and barbarians). (pp. 327, 328)

But Israelis certainly did not reject traditional Jewish ethnocentrism and sense of peoplehood. Slezkine portrays Israelis as simply choosing to be ethnocentric nationalists, but ethnocentrism (like intelligence) is a biological system, not a lifestyle choice, and traditional Diaspora Jews were certainly deeply and intensely ethnocentric above all else.[19] As I discuss in some detail in chapter 3, there can be little question that Israel and Zionism have been and are promoted and spearheaded by the most ethnocentric elements of the Jewish community.

For Slezkine, as for so many Jews, the moral debt owed to Jews by Western societies justifies the most extreme expressions of Jewish racialism: "The rhetoric of ethnic homogeneity and ethnic deportations, tabooed elsewhere in the West, is a routine element of Israeli political life. . . . It is true that no other European nation is in a condition of permanent war; it is also true that no other European state can have as strong a claim on the West's moral imagination" (pp. 364–65). Slezkine sees the moral taboo on European ethnocentrism, the creation of National Socialism as the epitome of absolute evil, and the consecration of Jews as "the Chosen people of the postwar Western world" (p. 366) as simply the inevitable results of the events of World War II (pp. 365–66). In fact, however, the creation and maintenance of the culture of the Holocaust and the special moral claims of Jews and Israel are the result of Jewish ethnic activism. These claims have a specific historical trajectory, they are fueled by specific key events, and they are sustained by specific forces.[20] For example, the Holocaust was not emphasized as a cultural icon until the late 1960s and early 1970s, when images of the Holocaust were deployed on a large scale in popular culture by Jewish activists specifically to rally support for Israel in the context of its wars of 1967 and 1973.

Similarly, Slezkine sees the United States as a Jewish promised land precisely because it is not defined tribally and "has no state-bearing natives" (p. 369). But the recasting of the United States as a "proposition nation" was importantly influenced by the triumph of several Jewish intellectual and political movements more than it was a natural and

---

[19] *A People That Shall Dwell Alone*, ch. 8; *Separation and Its Discontents*, ch. 7.

[20] Novick 1999; see summary in *The Culture of Critique*, Preface to the first paperback edition.

inevitable culmination of American history.[21] These movements collectively delegitimized cultural currents of the early twentieth century whereby many Americans thought of themselves as members of a very successful ethnic group. For example, the immigration restrictionists of the 1920s unabashedly asserted the right of European-derived peoples to the land they had conquered and settled. Americans of Northern European descent in the United States thought of themselves as part of a cultural and ethnic heritage extending backward in time to the founding of the country, and writers like Madison Grant (*The Passing of the Great Race*) and Lothrop Stoddard (*The Rising Tide of Color against White World Supremacy*) had a large public following. At that time both academia and mainstream culture believed in the reality of race; that there were important differences between the races, including in intelligence and moral character; and that races naturally competed for land and other resources.[22]

JEWISH SUPERIORITY

The assertion that Israel is the only civilized Apollonian society, despite its acknowledged racialism and open discussion of ethnic deportations, reveals Slezkine's belief in Jewish moral and intellectual superiority. Indeed, Slezkine regards both European individualism and the European nation-state as imitations of preexisting Jewish accomplishments: "Europeans imitated Jews not only in being modern [by becoming individualists interacting with strangers], but also in being ancient" [i.e., by developing ethnically based nation-states] (p. 44). So we read condescending passages such as "among the most successful [of the European Mercurians] were Max Weber's Protestants, who discovered a humorless, dignified way to be Jewish" (p. 41). This act of intellectual gymnastics depends on the following analogy: Jews act as an ethnically based tribe within societies, seeing non-Jews as strangers; Europeans establish tribal nation-states while behaving as individualists within their societies (seeing other Europeans as strangers). The sweeping conclusion: Jews are the progenitors therefore of both aspects of modernity: economic individualism and the ethnically based nation-state. The Holocaust then occurred because the European nation-state, although an imitation of Judaism, failed somehow to be sufficiently Jewish: "In the hands of heavily armed, thoroughly bureaucratized, and imperfectly Judaized Apollonians, Mercurian exclusivity and fastidiousness became relentlessly

---

[21] *The Culture of Critique*, chs. 7 and 8.
[22] See Bendersky 2000.

expansive. In the hands of messianically inclined Apollonians, it turned lethal—especially to the Mercurians. The Holocaust had as much to do with tradition as it did with modernity" (p. 46).

But it is a huge stretch to argue from an analogy—and a loose one at that—to actual imitation and influence. (And one just doesn't know what to say about his claim that Europeans perpetrated the Holocaust because they had become imperfect Jews.) Slezkine fails to provide any evidence that there is anything but a hazy and forced logical connection between European individualism and the Jewish role as a Diaspora people living among strangers. The reality is that by becoming individualists, Western Europeans returned to distinctive roots buried in their primeval past,[23] whereas Judaism, because of its deep-seated tribalism, was widely regarded by Enlightenment intellectuals as an outmoded relic. Indeed, several Jewish commentators have noted that the post-Enlightenment forms of Judaism have essentially been responses to the corrosive effects of European civilization, with its emphasis on individualism and ethnic assimilation, on the Jews as an ethnically based collectivist group—what early Zionist Arthur Ruppin described as "the destructive influence of European civilization" on the Jewish community because of its tendency to break down group barriers and lead eventually to assimilation and intermarriage.[24] Moreover, as Slezkine notes, Jews are not really individualists at all. Even in the modern world, the tribal approach of the Jews in economic enterprises employs ethnic kinship as a central component, whereas the individualistic approach of the Europeans sees this as illegitimate (p. 43). The bottom line is that it is ridiculous to claim that Jews are individualists because they treat outsiders as individuals while acknowledging that they retain a powerful ingroup consciousness and are masters of ethnic networking.

It is no stretch at all, however, to show that Jews have achieved a preeminent position in Europe and America, and Slezkine provides us with statistics of Jewish domination only dimly hinted at in the following examples from Europe in the late nineteenth century to the rise of National Socialism. Austria: All but one bank in fin de siècle Vienna was administered by Jews, and Jews constituted 70 percent of the stock exchange council; Hungary: between 50 and 90 percent of all industry was controlled by Jewish banking families, and 71 percent of the most wealthy taxpayers were Jews; Germany: Jews were overrepresented among the economic elite by a factor of 33. Similar massive overrepre-

---

[23] See ch. 9 below on "What Makes Western Culture Unique?"
[24] Ruppin 1973, 339.

sentation was also to be found in educational attainment and among professionals (e.g., Jews constituted 62 percent of the lawyers in Vienna in 1900, 25 percent in Prussia in 1925, 34 percent in Poland, and 51 percent in Hungary). Indeed, "the universities, 'free' professions, salons, coffeehouses, concert halls, and art galleries in Berlin, Vienna, and Budapest became so heavily Jewish that liberalism and Jewishness became almost indistinguishable" (p. 63).

Slezkine documents the well-known fact that, as Moritz Goldstein famously noted in 1912, "We Jews administer the spiritual possessions of Germany." However, he regards Jewish cultural dominance, not only in Germany but throughout Eastern Europe and Austria, as completely benign: "The secular Jews' love of Goethe, Schiller, and the other Pushkins—as well as the various northern forests they represented—was sincere and tender" (p. 68). Their only sin was that their love of cultural icons transcended national and ethnic boundaries in an age of popular nationalism—for example, their promotion of German culture among the Czechs, Latvians, and Romanians. But this is far from the whole story. Jews were not simply lovers of Pushkin and Goethe. A major theme of anti-Jewish attitudes was that Jews were deeply involved in creating a "culture of critique"—that Jewish cultural influence was entirely negative and shattered the social bonds of the peoples among whom they lived. Slezkine cites Heinrich Heine as a prime example of a Jewish intellectual with sincere and tender love for German culture, but the Germans, from Wagner to Treitschke to Chamberlain and Hitler, didn't see it that way. For example, Heinrich von Treitschke, a prominent nineteenth-century German intellectual, complained of Heine's "mocking German humiliation and disgrace following the Napoleonic wars" and Heine's having "no sense of shame, loyalty, truthfulness, or reverence."[25] Nor does he mention Treitschke's comment that "what Jewish journalists write in mockery and satirical remarks against Christianity is downright revolting"; "about the shortcomings of the Germans [or] French, everybody could freely say the worst things; but if somebody dared to speak in just and moderate terms about some undeniable weakness of the Jewish character, he was immediately branded as a barbarian and religious persecutor by nearly all of the newspapers."[26] Such attitudes were prominent among anti-Jewish writers and activists, reaching a crescendo with the National

---

[25] Mosse 1970, 52–53.
[26] In Lindemann 1997, 138–39. Similar complaints were common in Austria (op cit., 193).

Socialists in Germany.

Yet for Slezkine, if Jews did battle against various national cultures—and in the end, he acknowledges that they did—it was only because they realized that their Mercurian worldview was superior: "Did they really want to transform themselves into thick-skulled peasants now that the actual peasants had, for all practical purposes, admitted the error of their ways?" (p. 74). Jews were not recognized as legitimate curators of the national culture, but their lack of acceptance means only that they are truly modern: "Deprived of the comforts of their tribe and not allowed into the new ones created by their Apollonian neighbors, they became the only true moderns" (p. 75)—a statement that accepts at face value the idea that the secular Jews who had become the custodians and main producers of culture had ceased to have a Jewish identification Slezkine fails to provide any evidence at all for this claim, and in fact there is overwhelming evidence that it is false.[27]

The main weapons Jews used against national cultures were two quintessentially modern ideologies, Marxism and Freudianism, "both [of which] countered nationalism's quaint tribalism with a modern (scientific) path to wholeness" (p. 80). Slezkine correctly views both of these as Jewish ideologies functioning as organized religions, with sacred texts promising deliverance from earthly travail. While most of his book recounts the emergence of a Jewish elite under the banner of Marxism in the Soviet Union, his comments on psychoanalysis bear mentioning. Psychoanalysis "moved to the United States to reinforce democratic citizenship with a much-needed new prop. . . . In America, where nationwide tribal metaphors could not rely on theories of biological descent, Freudianism came in very handy indeed" by erecting the "Explicitly Therapeutic State" (pp. 79–80). The establishment of the Explicitly Therapeutic State was much aided by yet another Jewish intellectual movement, the Frankfurt School, which combined psychoanalysis and Marxism.[28] The result was a culture of critique which fundamentally aimed not only at de-legitimizing the older American culture, but even attempted to alter or obliterate human nature itself: "The statistical connection between 'the Jewish question' and the hope for a new species of mankind seems fairly strong" (p. 90).

And when people don't cooperate in becoming a new species, there's always murder. Slezkine describes Walter Benjamin, an icon of the Frankfurt School and darling of the current crop of postmodern intellec-

---

[27] *The Culture of Critique, passim.*

[28] For more on the Frankfurt School, see *The Culture of Critique*, ch. 5.

tuals, "with glasses on his nose, autumn in his soul, and vicarious murder in his heart" (p. 216), a comment that illustrates the fine line between murder and cultural criticism, especially when engaged in by ethnic outsiders. Indeed, on another occasion, Benjamin stated, "Hatred and [the] spirit of sacrifice . . . are nourished by the image of enslaved ancestors rather than that of liberated grandchildren."[29] Although Slezkine downplays this aspect of Jewish motivation, Jews' lachrymose perceptions of their history—their images of enslaved ancestors—were potent motivators of the hatred unleashed by the upheavals of the twentieth century.

Slezkine is entirely correct that Marxism, psychoanalysis, and the Frankfurt School were fundamentally Jewish intellectual movements. However, he fails to provide anything like a detailed account of how these ideologies served specifically Jewish interests, most generally in combating anti-Semitism and subverting ethnic identification among Europeans.[30] Indeed, a major premise of his treatment is that Jewish radicals were not Jews at all.

WERE JEWISH RADICALS JEWS?

Slezkine recounts the vast overrepresentation of Jews in the radical left in Europe and America. His attempts to explain this cover some familiar ground: Jewish intellectual opposition to the status quo resulting from their marginal social status (Thorstein Veblen); Jewish leftism as a secular, universalized form of traditional Jewish messianism and rationalism in which Jewish leftists are descendants of the Old Testament prophets calling for social justice (Lev Shternberg, dean of Soviet anthropologists); Jewish Communists as recreating traditional Jewish culture forms—especially scriptural interpretation and intense teacher-student relationships—in a Communist setting (historian Jaff Schatz). Slezkine's own contribution is to argue that Jewish radicals were in revolt against their families, "rejecting the world of their fathers because it seemed to embody the connection between Judaism and antisocialism (understood as commercialism, tribalism, and patriarchy) . . . the real reason for their common revulsion was the feeling that capitalism and Jewishness were one and the same thing" (pp. 96, 98). "Most Jewish rebels did not fight the state in order to become free Jews; they fought the state in order to become free of Jewishness—and thus Free" (p. 152).

This is a very useful theory, of course—useful because it denies that Jewish radicals were Jews at all, arguing in fact that they were anti-Jews

---

[29] Benjamin 1968, 262.

[30] See *The Culture of Critique*, chs. 3–5 for discussion of these issues.

(if not anti-Semites—and there's the rub). When Slezkine then goes on to recount the Jewish role as an elite in the most murderous regime in European history, we are led to believe that the only connection of those Jews with Jewishness is genealogical: Russian Jewish radicals, lovers of Pushkin and Tolstoy (as their counterparts in Poland, Hungary, and Germany loved Adam Mickiewicz, Sándor Petőfi, and Goethe), idealistically and selflessly set out to fashion a secular utopia of social justice by overcoming Apollonian backwardness even as they rejected their Jewish origins and all things Jewish.

His evidence for this is rather thin, but even in the examples Slezkine uses to illustrate his point it is clear that these Jewish radicals hated everything about their national cultures except for one or two literary figures. The rest would have to go. As Exhibit A, Slezkine presents Georg Lukács, the son of a prominent Jewish capitalist, who describes his profound discontent with his father's way of life. But Lukács also expresses his hatred for "the whole of official Hungary"—how he extended his unhappiness with his father to "cover the whole of Magyar life, Magyar history, and Magyar literature indiscriminately (save for Petőfi)" (p. 97). Ah, yes. Save for Petőfi. All else—the people and the culture—would have to go, by mass murder if necessary. (Lazar Kaganovich, the most prolific Jewish mass murderer of the Stalinist era, is pictured at the end of his life reading Pushkin, Tolstoy, and Turgenev [pp. 97–98].) But rather than see this as an aspect of traditional Jewish hatred for non-Jews and their culture, souped up and rationalized with a veneer of Marxism, Slezkine explains these radicals as enlightened Mercurians who wished to destroy the old culture except for a few classics of modern literature. We may give thanks to know that Shakespeare would have survived the revolution.

Another of Slezkine's examples is Lev Kopelev, a Soviet writer who witnessed and rationalized the Ukrainian famine as "historical necessity" (p. 230). Slezkine states categorically that Kopelev did not identify as a Jew, but his own material indicates the complexity of the matter. Kopelev identified himself on Soviet documents as "Jewish" but claimed that was only because he did not want to be seen as a "'cowardly apostate,' and—after World War II—because he did not want to renounce those who had been murdered for being Jewish" (p. 241). To the external world, Kopelev is a proud Jew, but to his close associates—in his "heart of hearts"—he is only a Communist and Soviet patriot. But of course many of his close associates were ethnic Jews, and he shed no tears for the Ukrainian and Russian peasants and nationalists who were murdered in the name of international socialism even as he mourned the loss of Jews murdered because they were Jews. By World War II he had become a "leading ideologue of Russian patriotism" (p. 279), developing "an acute sense of hurt and injustice on behalf of Russia, Russian history, and the Russian word" (p. 280) as he attempted to rally the Russians to do battle with the Germans. Russian patriotism had suddenly become useful—much as, I would argue, harnessing the patriotism and high regard for military service among Americans has been useful for Jewish neoconservatives eager to rearrange the politics of the Middle East in the interests of Israel. Patriotism is a wonderfully effective instrument in the service of self-deception (or deception).

Probably more typical of the Jewish identity of the Bolsheviks is the account of Vitaly Rubin, a prominent philosopher and an ethnic Jew, who recounted his career at a top Moscow school in the 1930s where over half the students were Jewish:

> Understandably, the Jewish question did not arise there. Not only did it not arise in the form of anti-Semitism, it did not arise at all. All the Jews knew themselves to be Jews but considered everything to do with Jewishness a thing of the past. I remember thinking of my father's stories about his childhood, *heder* [Jewish elementary school], and traditional Jewish upbringing as something consigned to oblivion. None of that had anything to do with me. There was no active desire to renounce one's Jewishness. The problem simply did not exist. (pp. 253–54)

These Jews clearly have a Jewish identity but they have been removed from traditional Jewish religious cultural forms. In such a predominantly Jewish milieu, there was no need to renounce their Jewish identity and no need to push aggressively for Jewish interests because they had achieved elite status. And yet, just prior to World War II, as Russians started replacing Jews among the political elite and National Socialism emerged as an officially anti-Jewish ideology, overt Jewish identity reemerged. Following World War II, Israel began exerting its gravitational pull on Jews, much to the chagrin of a suspicious Stalin. The visit of Golda Meir in 1948 and the outpouring of Jewish support for Zionism that it aroused was a watershed event for Soviet Jewry. Stalin reacted to it by initiating a campaign against public Jews and Yiddish culture.

It is interesting in this regard that the leading Soviet spokesmen on anti-Semitism were both ethnic Jews with non-Jewish sounding names,

Emilian Yaroslavsky (Gubelman) and Yuri Larin (Lurie). Both refer to Jews in the third person (p. 245), as if they themselves were not Jews. But when Larin tried to explain the embarrassing fact that Jews were "preeminent, overabundant, dominant, and so on" (p. 251) among the elite in the Soviet Union, he mentioned the "unusually strong sense of solidarity and a predisposition toward mutual help and support" (p. 252)—ethnic networking by any other name. Obviously, "mutual help and support" require that Jews recognize each other as Jews. Jewish identity may not have been much discussed, but it operated nonetheless, even if subconsciously, in the rarefied circles at the top of Soviet society. An example not presented by Slezkine is recounted in a report of 1950 to the central committee on Jewish activities at an aircraft production facility:

> In a number of extremely important departments of the Central Aero-Hydrodynamic Institute there are workers due to be substituted for political reasons. They gather around themselves people of the same nationality, impose the habit of praising one another (while making others erroneously believe that they are indispensable), and force their protégés through to high posts.[31]

Indeed, there is no other way to explain the extraordinary percentages of Jews throughout elite institutions, which became apparent when the purges began in the late 1940s (see below). High IQ and achievement motivation can only go so far, and cannot explain why, for example, in the late 1940s Jews made up 80 percent of the Soviet Academy of Science Institute of Literature (Pushkin House) (p. 302), 42 percent of the directors of Moscow theaters, over half of Soviet circus directors (p. 301), or eight of the top ten directors of the Bolshoi Theater.[32] In the case of Pushkin House, the opponents of the dominant clique stated that it had been forged "by long-lasting relationships of families and friends, mutual protection, homogeneous (Jewish) national composition, and anti-patriotic (anti-Russian) tendencies."[33]

The reality is that Jewish identity always becomes more salient when Jews feel threatened or feel that their interests as Jews are at stake, but Jewish identity becomes submerged when Jewish interests

---

[31] In Kostyrchenko 1995, 237.

[32] The composition of the board of the Bolshoi is given in Kostyrchenko 1995, 15.

[33] In Kostyrchenko 1995, 171.

coincide with other interests and identities.[34] (This is a human universal and presumably accounts for the fact that the American Founding Fathers felt no need to carefully define the cultural and ethnic parameters of their creation; they assumed the racial and cultural homogeneity of the Republic[35] and perceived no threat to its control by themselves and their descendants.) The relative submergence of Jewish identity within the Jewish milieu in elite circles of the Soviet Union during the 1920s and 1930s is a poor indicator of whether or not these people identified as Jews or would do so when in later years Jewish and Soviet identities began to diverge, when National Socialism reemphasized Jewish identity, or when Israel emerged as a beacon for Jewish identity and loyalty.

As I discuss at some length in chapters 4 and 5 of this volume, a similar stance may be observed among present-day Jewish neoconservatives, who argue that the United States has a deep interest in democratizing the Middle East. The confluence of their interests as Jews in promoting the policies of the Israeli right wing and their construction of American interests allows them to submerge or even deny the relevance of their Jewish identity while posing as American patriots. But if Israeli and American policy began to diverge significantly, Jewish interests would almost certainly control their attitudes and behavior. Indeed, since neoconservative Zionism of the Likud Party variety is well known for promoting a confrontation between the United States and the entire Muslim world, their policy recommendations best fit a pattern of loyalty to their ethnic group, not to America.

In *The Culture of Critique*, I advanced several reasons for supposing that Jews continued to identify as Jews in the USSR, none of which is challenged by Slezkine's treatment: (1) Persons were classified as Jews depending on their ethnic background, at least partly because of residual anti-Jewish attitudes; this would tend to impose a Jewish identity on these individuals and make it difficult to assume an exclusive identity as a member of a larger, more inclusive political group. (2) Many Jewish Bolsheviks, such as those in Evsektsiya (the Jewish section of the Communist Party) and the Jewish Anti-Fascist Committee, aggressively sought to establish a secular Jewish subculture; these phenomena

---

[34] *Separation and Its Discontents*, ch. 9; *The Culture of Critique*, ch. 3.

[35] Weyl and Marina 1971. For example, "The American Negro was deemed [by a national consensus of opinion from George Washington to the end of World War I] an alien presence in American society who could not be assimilated without destroying or largely impairing the homogeneity and national cohesion of the Republic" (p. 377).

are virtually ignored by Slezkine. (3) Very few Jews on the left envisioned a post-revolutionary society without a continuation of the Jewish community; indeed, the predominant ideology among Jewish leftists was that post-revolutionary society would end anti-Semitism because it would end class conflict and the peculiar Jewish occupational profile. (4) The behavior of American Communists shows that Jewish identity and the primacy of Jewish interests over Communist interests were commonplace among individuals who were ethnically Jewish Communists. (5) The existence of Jewish crypsis in other times and places was combined with the possibility that self-deception, identificatory flexibility, and identificatory ambivalence are important components of the Jewish group evolutionary strategy.[36]

And in the end, despite the rationalizations of many Soviet Jews and Slezkine on Jewish identity, it was blood that mattered. By the time of World War II, most Jews, "knew that they were, in some sense, Jews. They may never have been to a synagogue, seen a menorah, heard Yiddish or Hebrew, tasted gefilte fish, or indeed met their grandparents. But they knew they were Jews in the Soviet sense, which was also—in essence—the Nazi sense. They were Jews by blood" (p. 286).

They reemerged as Jews to fight the Nazis and to solicit the support of American Jews to pressure their government to enter the war and provide aid to the Soviet Union. Jewish spokesmen visited New York proclaiming that "the Jewish people—'ethnic' or religious, Communist, Zionist, or traditionalist—were one family" (p. 290).

Moreover, Slezkine leaves out an enormous amount of evidence that conflicts with his Jewish radicalism-as-patricide thesis, evidence indicating that in general Jewish radicals did identify as Jews and acted to promote specific Jewish interests. Certainly Jewish radicals often rejected their fathers' religion and their way of life, but all the evidence points to their identifying in different ways as Jews, not losing their Jewish identity to become de-ethnicized moral crusaders against capitalism. Slezkine uses Franz Boas to illustrate his patricide theory, because Boas was a radical Jew who recognized "the shackles of tradition" (p. 98). But he fails to note that Boas was hardly in rebellion against his own family. Boas was reared in a "Jewish-liberal" family in which the revolutionary ideals of 1848 remained influential,[37] and there is ample evidence of his strong Jewish identification and concern with anti-Semitism.[38]

---

[36] *The Culture of Critique*, ch. 3.
[37] Stocking 1968, 149.
[38] *The Culture of Critique*, ch. 2.

Besides a few individual cases like Lukács and Boas, the only general evidence that Slezkine provides for the patricide thesis comes from Jaff Schatz's study of the generation of Jewish Communists who dominated the Communist movement in Poland beginning in the 1930s. But he provides a mangled account of Schatz's work.[39] These Jews did indeed reject their parents' religion, but the result of their Yiddish upbringing was "a deep core of their identity, values, norms, and attitudes with which they entered the rebellious period of their youth and adulthood. This core was to be transformed in the processes of acculturation, secularization, and radicalization sometimes even to the point of explicit denial. However, it was through this deep layer that all later perceptions were filtered."[40] Most of these individuals spoke Yiddish in their daily lives and had only a poor command of Polish even after joining the party. They socialized entirely with other Jews whom they met in the Jewish world of work, neighborhood, and Jewish social and political organizations. After they became Communists, they dated and married among themselves, and their social gatherings were conducted in Yiddish. Their mentors and principal influences were other ethnic Jews, including especially Luxemburg and Trotsky, and when they recalled personal heroes, they were mostly Jews whose exploits achieved semi-mythical proportions.

In general, Jews who joined the Communist movement did not first reject their ethnic identity, and there were many who "cherished Jewish culture . . . [and] dreamed of a society in which Jews would be equal as Jews."[41] It was common for individuals to combine a strong Jewish identity with Marxism as well as various combinations of Zionism and Bundism (a movement of Jewish socialists). Moreover, the attraction of Polish Jews to Communism was greatly facilitated by their knowledge that Jews had attained high-level positions of power and influence in the Soviet Union and that the Soviet government had established a system of Jewish education and culture. In both the Soviet Union and Poland, Communism was seen as opposing anti-Semitism. In marked contrast, during the 1930s the Polish government enacted policies which excluded Jews from public-sector employment, established quotas on Jewish representation in universities and the professions, and organized boycotts of Jewish businesses and artisans.[42] Clearly, Jews perceived

---

[39] *The Culture of Critique*, ch. 3.
[40] Schatz 1991, 37–38.
[41] Schatz 1991, 48.
[42] Hagen 1996.

Communism as good for Jews, and indeed a major contribution of Slezkine's book is to document that Communism *was* good for Jews: It was a movement that never threatened Jewish group continuity, and it held the promise of Jewish power and influence and the end of state-sponsored anti-Semitism. And when this group achieved power in Poland after World War II, they liquidated the Polish nationalist movement, outlawed anti-Semitism, and established Jewish cultural and economic institutions.

Slezkine also fails to note that in the United States a strong Jewish identification was typical of Jewish radicals and that Jewish support for the left typically waxed and waned depending on specifically Jewish issues, particularly those related to anti-Semitism and support for Israel.[43] The Jewish Old Left was a recognized part of the Jewish community, and American Jewish leftists during the 1960s were the only leftists who didn't reject their parents—they really were "red diaper babies."

It is also remarkable that the revolutionary movement in Tsarist Russia ceased being anti-Jewish when Jews attained highly visible and prominent positions in the movement, even though workers and peasants participated in anti-Jewish pogroms from 1880 to 1905 and continued to harbor anti-Jewish attitudes. As Slezkine himself notes, Jews were the only group that was not criticized by the revolutionary movement (p. 157), even though most Russians, and especially the lower classes whose cause they were supposedly championing, had very negative attitudes toward Jews.[44] When, in 1915, Maxim Gorky, a strong philosemite, published a survey of Russian attitudes toward Jews, the most common response was typified by the comment that "the congenital, cruel, and consistent egoism of the Jews is everywhere victorious over the good-natured, uncultured, trusting Russian peasant or merchant" (p. 159). There were concerns that all of Russia would pass into Jewish hands and that Russians would become slaves of the Jews. In the end, as Slezkine shows, as a result of the Revolution this prediction was not far off the mark. But in any case, one would think that if radical Jews had ceased being Jews, they would have been severely critical of the Jewish role in the pre-Soviet economy.

The other huge lacuna in Slezkine's presentation is that he portrays Jewish radicals as typically the offspring of successful Jewish capitalists—like Georg Lukács—who scorn their fathers and wish for nothing more than to destroy Judaism in order to achieve personal freedom and

---

[43] *The Culture of Critique*, ch. 3.
[44] See also *Separation and Its Discontents*, ch. 2, note 23.

make the world safe for humanity: "Marxism attributed [Jewish patricide] to the proletariat and urged the killing (more or less metaphorical) of the bad fathers, so as to emancipate the world from Judaism and make sure that no sons would have to kill their fathers ever again" (p. 100).

Because he wishes to portray Jews as quintessentially modern Mercurians, Slezkine repeatedly shows how Jews dominated the economy, the universities, and the culture of Eastern Europe—indeed, his book is probably the best, most up-to-date account of Jewish economic and cultural preeminence in Europe (and America) that we have. But that is far from the whole story. A prime force resulting in Jewish radicalism was the grinding poverty of most Jews in Eastern Europe. Jews had overshot their economic niche: The economy was unable to support the burgeoning Jewish population in the sorts of positions that Jews had traditionally filled, with the result that a large percentage of the Jewish population became mired in poverty (along with much higher percentages of the non-Jewish population). The result was a cauldron of ethnic hostility, with governmental restrictions on Jewish economic activity and representation in educational institutions, rampant anti-Jewish attitudes, and increasing Jewish desperation.[45]

The main Jewish response to this situation was an upsurge of fundamentalist extremism that coalesced in the Hasidic movement and, later in the nineteenth century, in political radicalism and Zionism as solutions to Jewish problems. Slezkine devotes one line to the fact that Jewish populations in Eastern Europe had the highest rate of natural increase of any European population in the nineteenth century (p. 115), but this was an extremely important part of Eastern Europe's "Jewish problem." Anti-Semitism and the exploding Jewish population, combined with economic adversity, were of critical importance for producing the great numbers of disaffected Jews who dreamed of deliverance in various messianic movements—the ethnocentric mysticism of the Kabbala and Hasidism, Zionism, or the dream of a Marxist political revolution. Jews emigrated in droves from Eastern Europe, but the problems remained. And in the case of the Marxists, the main deliverance was to be achieved not by killing Judaism, as Slezkine suggests, but by the destruction of the traditional societies of Eastern Europe as a panacea for Jewish poverty and for anti-Semitism.

In fact, the vast majority of Jews in Eastern Europe in the late nine-

---

[45] See ch. 3 below on "Zionism and the Internal Dynamics of the Jewish Community."

teenth and early twentieth centuries were hardly the modern Mercurians that Slezkine portrays them as being. Slezkine does note that well into the twentieth century the vast majority of Eastern European Jews could not speak the languages of the non-Jews living around them, and he does a good job of showing their intense ingroup feeling and their attitudes that non-Jews were less than human.[46] But he ignores their medieval outlook on life, their obsession with the Kabbala (the Jewish mystical tradition), their superstition and anti-rationalism, and their belief in "magical remedies, amulets, exorcisms, demonic possession (*dybbuks*), ghosts, devils, and teasing, mischievous genies."[47] These supposedly modern Mercurians had an attitude of absolute faith in the person of the *tzadik*, their *rebbe*, who was a charismatic figure seen by his followers literally as the personification of God in the world. (Attraction to charismatic leaders is a fundamental feature of Jewish social organization—apparent as much among religious fundamentalists as among Jewish political radicals or elite Jewish intellectuals.)[48]

BOLSHEVISM AS A JEWISH MOVEMENT

Slezkine's main contribution is to summarize previously available data and to extend our understanding of Jewish dominance of the revolutionary movements before 1917 and of Soviet society thereafter. (Oddly, he makes only a passing reference to Albert Lindemann's important *Esau's Tears,* which makes many of the same points.[49]) Not only were Jews vastly overrepresented among revolutionaries, they "were particularly well represented at the top, among theoreticians, journalists, and leaders" (p. 155). Radical Jews, like other Jews, were very talented, highly intelligent, hardworking, and in addition dedicated to creating effective ethnic networks.[50] These traits propelled them to the top of radical organizations and made the organizations themselves more effective.

But if Jews dominated radical and revolutionary organizations, they were immeasurably aided by philosemites like Gorky who, in Albert Lindemann's term, were "jewified non-Jews"—"a term, freed of its ugly connotations, [that] might be used to underline an often overlooked point: Even in Russia there were some non-Jews, whether Bolsheviks

---

[46] See also Vital 1975, 46.
[47] Mahler 1985, 16.
[48] *The Culture of Critique*, 27–28, 127–35, 156, ch. 6.
[49] Lindemann 1997.
[50] See ch. 1 above on "Background Traits for Jewish Activism"; see also *The Culture of Critique*, chs. 1 and 3.

or not, who respected Jews, praised them abundantly, imitated them, cared about their welfare, and established intimate friendships or romantic liaisons with them."[51] (As noted above, many of the non-Jewish elite in the USSR had Jewish wives.)

What united the Jews and philosemites was their hatred for what Lenin (who had a Jewish grandfather) called "the thick-skulled, boorish, inert, and bearishly savage Russian or Ukrainian peasant"—the same peasant Gorky described as "savage, somnolent, and glued to his pile of manure" (p. 163). It was attitudes like these that created the climate that justified the slaughter of many millions of peasants under the new regime.

Philosemites continued to be common among the non-Jewish elite in the USSR, even in the 1950s, when Jews began to be targeted as Jews. One such philosemite was Pavel Sudoplatov, a Slav married to a Jew and with many Jewish friends, who was a high-ranking secret police official with a great deal of blood on his hands. The only murder he unequivocally condemned in his memoirs was that of Paul Mikhoels, a Jewish ethnic activist associated with the Jewish Anti-Fascist Committee.

Figures like Gorky and Sudoplatov were critical to the success of Jews in the Soviet Union. This is a general principle of Jewish political activity in a Diaspora situation: Because Jews tend to constitute a tiny percentage of a society, they need to make alliances with non-Jews whose perceived interests dovetail with theirs. Non-Jews have a variety of reasons for being associated with Jewish interests, including career advancement, close personal relationships with or admiration for individual Jews, and deeply held personal convictions.[52]

Gorky's love for the Jews—what Slezkine terms "the bitter, ardent, and hopeless love of self-described Apollonians for beautiful Mercurians" (p. 165)—was boundless. Gorky saw Jews as possessors of "heroic" idealism, "all-probing, all-scrutinizing"; "this idealism, which expresses itself in their tireless striving to remake the world according to new principles of equality and justice, is the main, and possibly the only, reason for the hostility toward Jews" (quoted on p. 164).

Despite the important role of Jews among the Bolsheviks, most Jews were not Bolsheviks before the revolution. However, Jews were prominent among the Bolsheviks, and once the revolution was under way, the vast majority of Russian Jews became sympathizers and active participants. Jews were particularly visible in the cities and as leaders

---

[51] Lindemann 1997, 433.
[52] See chs. 4 and 5 below on neoconservatism.

in the army and in the revolutionary councils and committees. For example, there were 23 Jews among the 62 Bolsheviks in the All-Russian Central Executive Committee elected at the Second Congress of Soviets in October, 1917.

Jews were the leaders of the movement, and to a great extent they were its public face. Slezkine quotes historian Mikhail Beizer who notes, commenting on the situation in Leningrad, that "Jewish names were constantly popping up in newspapers. Jews spoke relatively more often than others at rallies, conferences, and meetings of all kinds."[53] In general, Jews were deployed in supervisory positions rather than positions that placed them in physical danger. In a Politburo meeting of April 18, 1919, Trotsky urged that Jews be redeployed because there were relatively few Jews in frontline combat units, while Jews constituted a "vast percentage" of the Cheka at the front and in the Executive Committees at the front and at the rear. This pattern had caused "chauvinist agitation" in the Red Army (p. 187).

Jewish representation at the top levels of the Cheka and OGPU (the acronyms by which the secret police was known in different periods) has often been the focus of those stressing Jewish involvement in the revolution and its aftermath. Slezkine provides statistics on Jewish overrepresentation in these organizations, especially in supervisory roles, and agrees with Leonard Schapiro's comment that "anyone who had the misfortune to fall into the hands of the Cheka stood a very good chance of finding himself confronted with and possibly shot by a Jewish investigator" (p. 177). During the 1930s the secret police, then known as the NKVD, "was one of the most Jewish of all Soviet institutions" (p. 254), with 42 of its 111 top officials being Jewish. At this time twelve of the twenty NKVD directorates were headed by ethnic Jews, including those in charge of state security, police, labor camps, and resettlement (i.e., deportation). The Gulag was headed by ethnic Jews from its beginning in 1930 until the end of 1938, a period that encompasses the worst excesses of the Great Terror. They were, in Slezkine's words, "Stalin's willing executioners" (p. 103).

The Bolsheviks continued to apologize for Jewish overrepresentation until the topic became taboo in the 1930s. And it was not until the late 1930s that there was a rise in visibility and assertiveness of "anti-Semites, ethnic nationalists, and advocates of proportional representation" (p. 188). By this time the worst of the slaughters in the Gulag, the purges, and the contrived famines had been completed.

---

[53] Mikhail Beizer, quoted in Slezkine (p. 176).

The prominence of Jews in the Revolution and its aftermath was not lost on participants on both sides, including influential figures such as Winston Churchill, who wrote that the role of Jews in the revolution "is certainly a very great one; it probably outweighs all others."[54] Slezkine highlights similar comments in a book published in 1927 by V. V. Shulgin, a Russian nationalist, who experienced firsthand the murderous acts of the Bolsheviks in his native Kiev in 1919: "We do not like the fact that this whole terrible thing was done *on the Russian back* and that it has cost us unutterable losses. We do not like the fact that you, Jews, a relatively small group within the Russian population, participated in this vile deed *out of all proportion to your numbers*" (p. 181; italics in original). Slezkine does not disagree with this assessment, but argues that Jews were hardly the only revolutionaries (p. 180). This is certainly true, but does not affect my argument that Jewish involvement was a necessary condition, not merely a sufficient condition, for the success of the Bolshevik Revolution and its aftermath.[55] Slezkine's argument clearly supports the Jews-as-necessary-condition claim, especially because of his emphasis on the leadership role of Jews.

However, the claim that Jewish involvement was a necessary condition is itself an understatement because, as Shulgin noted, the effectiveness of Jewish revolutionaries was far out of proportion to the number of Jews. A claim that a group constituting a large proportion of the population was necessary to the success of a movement would be unexceptional. But the critical importance of Jews occurred even though Jews constituted less than 5 percent of the Russian population around the time of the Revolution,[56] and they were much less represented in the major urban areas of Moscow and Leningrad prior to the Revolution because they were prevented from living there by the Pale of Settlement laws. Slezkine is correct that Jews were not the only revolutionaries, but his point only underscores the importance of philosemitism and other alliances Jews typically must make in Diaspora situations in order to advance their perceived interests.

---

[54] Churchill 1920.

[55] *The Culture of Critique*, Preface to the first paperback edition and ch. 3.

[56] The *Jewish Encyclopedia* (http://www.jewishencyclpedia.com) estimates that Jews constituted 3.29 percent of the population of the Russian Empire circa 1900. Slezkine (p. 217) provides data on the Jewish population of Soviet cities before and after the Revolution. Ediev (2001, 294) estimates the population of Russia at around ninety million around the time of the Bolshevik Revolution.

In 1923, several Jewish intellectuals published a collection of essays admitting the "bitter sin" of Jewish complicity in the crimes of the Revolution. In the words of a contributor, I. L. Bikerman, "it goes without saying that not all Jews are Bolsheviks and not all Bolsheviks are Jews, but what is equally obvious is that disproportionate and immeasurably fervent Jewish participation in the torment of half-dead Russia by the Bolsheviks" (p. 183). Many of the commentators on Jewish Bolsheviks noted the "transformation" of Jews: In the words of another Jewish commentator, G. A. Landau, "cruelty, sadism, and violence had seemed alien to a nation so far removed from physical activity." And another Jewish commentator, I. A. Bromberg, noted that:

> the formerly oppressed lover of liberty had turned into a tyrant of 'unheard-of-despotic arbitrariness'.... The convinced and unconditional opponent of the death penalty not just for political crimes but for the most heinous offenses, who could not, as it were, watch a chicken being killed, has been transformed outwardly into a leather-clad person with a revolver and, in fact, lost all human likeness. (pp. 183–84)

This psychological "transformation" of Russian Jews was probably not all that surprising to the Russians themselves, given Gorky's finding that Russians prior to the Revolution saw Jews as possessed of "cruel egoism" and that they were concerned about becoming slaves of the Jews. Gorky himself remained a philosemite to the end, despite the prominent Jewish role in the murder of approximately twenty million of his ethnic kin, but after the Revolution he commented that "*the reason for the current anti-Semitism in Russia is the tactlessness of the Jewish Bolsheviks.* The Jewish Bolsheviks, not all of them but some irresponsible boys, are taking part in the defiling of the holy sites of the Russian people. They have turned churches into movie theaters and reading rooms without considering the feelings of the Russian people."[57] However, Gorky did not blame the Jews for this: "The fact that the Bolsheviks sent the Jews, the helpless and irresponsible Jewish youths, to do these things, does smack of provocation, of course. But the Jews should have refrained" (p. 186).

Those who carried out the mass murder and dispossession of the Russian peasants saw themselves, at least in their public pronounce-

---

[57] The estimate of the number of deaths caused by Communism in the USSR is from Cortois 1999, 4.

ments, as doing what was necessary in pursuit of the greater good. This was the official view not only of the Soviet Union, where Jews formed a dominant elite, but also was the "more or less official view" among Jewish intellectuals in the United States (p. 215) and elsewhere. (It is still far more common for leftist intellectuals to bemoan McCarthyism than the horrors of the USSR.[58])

> It is for the sake of creating a perfect human being—Apollonian in body and Mercurian in mind—that Levinson steels himself for doing what is "necessary," including the requisitioning of a weeping farmer's last pig and the killing of a wounded comrade too weak to be evacuated. . . . [T]he greater the personal responsibility for acts ordinarily considered evil, the more visible the signs of election and the inner strength they bespoke. Demonic as well as Promethean, Bolshevik commissars "carried within them" the pain of historical necessity. (p. 194)

Levinson, a character in A. Fedeev's *The Rout* (1926), a prominent example of socialist realism in the early Soviet period, is not ideologically Jewish, "but there is little doubt that for reasons of both aesthetic and sociological verisimilitude, canonical Jewishness seemed an appropriate expression of the Bolshevik vision of disembodied consciousness triumphing over [peasant] inertia" (p. 193). So it is not surprising that Gorky's mild rebuke of Jewish anti-Christian zealotry was too much for Esther Frumkina, a leader of the Party's Jewish section. Frumkina accused Gorky of attacking "Jewish Communists for their selfless struggle against darkness and fanaticism" (p. 187). In their self-perceptions, Jews are selflessly altruistic even when acting out ancient hatreds.

THE THREE GREAT JEWISH MIGRATIONS OF THE TWENTIETH CENTURY

Slezkine's last and longest chapter describes the three great Jewish migrations of the twentieth century—to Israel, to the United States, and to the urban centers of the Soviet Union. Slezkine perceives all three through the lens of heroic Jewish self-perception. He sees the United States as a Jewish utopia precisely because it had only a "vestigial establishment tribalism" (p. 209) that could not long inhibit Jewish ascendancy: "The United States stood for unabashed Mercurianism, non-

---

[58] *The Culture of Critique*, Preface to the first paperback edition.

tribal statehood, and the supreme sovereignty of capitalism and professionalism. It was—rhetorically—a collection of *homines rationalistici artificiales*, a nation of strangers held together by a common celebration of separateness (individualism) and rootlessness (immigration)" (p. 207). "It was the only modern state . . . in which a Jew could be an equal citizen and a Jew at the same time. 'America' offered full membership without complete assimilation. Indeed, it seemed to require an affiliation with a subnational community as a condition of full membership in the political nation" (p. 207).

Slezkine sees post-World War II America as a Jewish utopia but seems only dimly aware that Jews to a great extent created their own utopia in the United States by undermining nativist sentiments that were common at least until after World War II. Slezkine emphasizes the Jewish role in institutionalizing the therapeutic state, but sees it as completely benign, rather than an aspect of the "culture of critique" that undermined the ethnic identities of white Americans: "By bringing Freudianism to America and by adopting it, briefly, as a salvation religion, [Jews] made themselves more American while making America more therapeutic" (p. 319). There is little discussion of the main antinativist intellectual movements, all of which were dominated by ethnically conscious Jews: Boasian anthropology, Horace Kallen and the development of the theory of America as a "proposition nation," and the Frankfurt School which combined psychoanalysis and Marxism into a devastating weapon against the ethnic consciousness of white Americans. Nor does he discuss the role of Jewish activist organizations in altering the ethnic balance of the United States by promoting large-scale immigration from around the world.

Slezkine also views the Jewish migration to Israel as heroic:

In both Jewish Palestine (the *Yishuv*) and Soviet Russia, brotherhood stood for the full identity of all true believers (always the few against the many) and their complete identification with the cause (ardently desired and genuinely felt by most young Jews in both places). Eventually, both revolutions evolved in the direction of greater hierarchy, institutionalized militarism, intense anxiety about aliens, and the cult of generals, boy soldiers, and elite forces, but between 1917 and the mid-1930s they were overflowing with youthful energy and the spirit of fraternal effort, and self-sacrifice. (p. 212)

The passage is remarkable both for its pinpointing the ingroup/outgroup nature of the psychology of traditional Jewish groups, freed now of the

Torah and the synagogue, and for its description of the ingroup psychology of mass murder (in the USSR) and ethnic cleansing (in the Middle East) as involving valiant self-sacrifice and pride in accomplishment.

But Slezkine spends most of his energy by far in providing a fascinating chronicle of the Jewish rise to elite status in all areas of Soviet society—culture, the universities, professional occupations, the media, and government. In all cases, Jewish overrepresentation was most apparent at the pinnacles of success and influence. To take just the area of culture, Jews were highly visible as avant-garde artists, formalist theorists, polemicists, moviemakers, and poets. They were "among the most exuberant crusaders against 'bourgeois' habits during the Great Transformation; the most disciplined advocates of socialist realism during the 'Great Retreat' (from revolutionary internationalism); and the most passionate prophets of faith, hope, and combat during the Great Patriotic War against the Nazis" (p. 225). And, as their critics noticed, Jews were involved in anti-Christian propaganda. Mikhail Bulgakov, a Russian writer, noticed that the publishers of *Godless* magazine were Jews; he was "stunned" to find that Christ was portrayed as "a scoundrel and a cheat. It is not hard to see whose work it is. This crime is immeasurable" (p. 244).

Some of the juxtapositions are striking and seemingly intentional. On p. 230, Lev Kopelev is quoted on the need for firmness in confiscating the property of the Ukrainian peasants. Kopelev, who witnessed the famine that killed seven to ten million peasants, stated, "You mustn't give in to debilitating pity. We are the agents of historical necessity. We are fulfilling our revolutionary duty. We are procuring grain for our socialist Fatherland. For the Five-Year Plan." Slezkine describes the NKVD as "one of the most Jewish of all Soviet institutions" and recounts the Jewish leadership of the Great Terror of the 1930s (pp. 254 and 255). On p. 256, he writes that in 1937 the prototypical Jew who moved from the Pale of Settlement to Moscow to man elite positions in the Soviet state "probably would have been living in elite housing in downtown Moscow . . . with access to special stores, a house in the country (*dacha*), and a live-in peasant nanny or maid. . . . At least once a year, she would have traveled to a Black Sea sanatorium or a mineral spa in the Caucasus" (p. 256). Slezkine writes long and lovingly detailed sketches of life at the *dachas* of the elite—the "open verandas overlooking small gardens enclosed by picket fences or wildly overgrown yards" (p. 256), but the reader is left to his own imagination to visualize the horrors of the Ukrainian famine and the liquidation of the kulaks.

As Slezkine notes, most of the Soviet elite were not Jews, but Jews were far overrepresented among the elite (and Russians far underrepresented as a percentage of the population). Moreover, the Jews formed a far more cohesive core than the rest of the elite because of their common social and cultural background (p. 236). The common understanding that the new elite had a very large Jewish representation resulted in pervasive anti-Jewish attitudes. In 1926, an Agitprop report noted: "The sense that the Soviet regime patronizes the Jews, that it is 'the Jewish government,' that the Jews cause unemployment, housing shortages, college admissions problems, price rises, and commercial speculation—this sense is instilled in the workers by all the hostile elements. . . . If it does not encounter resistance, the wave of anti-Semitism threatens to become, in the very near future, a serious political question" (p. 244).

Such widespread public perceptions about the role of Jews in the new government led to aggressive surveillance and repression of anti-Jewish attitudes and behavior, including the execution of Russian nationalists who expressed anti-Jewish attitudes. These public perceptions also motivated Jews to adopt a lower profile in the regime, as with Trotsky, who refused the post of commissar of internal affairs because it might lend further ammunition to the anti-Jewish arguments. From 1927 to 1932 Stalin established an ambitious public campaign to combat anti-Semitism that included 56 books published by the government and an onslaught of speeches, mass rallies, newspaper articles, and show trials "aimed at eradicating the evil" (p. 249).

THE DECLINE OF THE JEWS IN THE SOVIET UNION

Jews were able to maintain themselves as an elite until the end of the Soviet regime in 1991—this despite an official push for affirmative action-style programs to open up opportunities for the children of peasants and workers in the 1930s and to blunt the anti-Jewish feelings simmering at the lower levels of Soviet society. Jewish elite status persisted despite the Great Terror of the late 1930s, which disproportionately affected the political elite. On the whole, Jews were underrepresented as victims of the Great Terror. And although the Jewish percentage of the political elite did decline after the purges of the late 1930s and the promotion of former peasants and working class Russians, this did not affect Jewish predominance as a professional, cultural, and managerial elite. Jews also retained their elite status despite Stalin's campaign in the late 1940s against Jewish ethnic and cultural institutions and their spokesmen. Jewish elite status remained even after the purge was expanded to all sectors of the Soviet elite, due at least partly to "the widespread sense [among Russians] that the great victory [in World War II] entitled them to a greater role in decision making" (p. 306). Slezkine shows the very high percentages of Jews in various institutions in the late 1940s, including the universities, the media, the foreign service, and the secret police. For example, the deans of philosophers, historians, and legal scholars were ethnic Jews, and, as already noted, Jews constituted 80 percent of the Soviet Academy of Science Institute of Literature. As for the Jewish role as "vanguard of the working class," Jews still made up 23 percent of the staff at the Trade Union Council's publication *Trud* even after a purge cut their numbers in half.

The campaign against the Jews began only after the apogee of mass murder and deportations in the USSR, and was much less lethal than those mounted against a long list of other ethnic groups, whose typical fate was deportation under the most brutal of circumstances (Cossacks, Chechens, Crimean Tatars, Volga Germans, Moldavians, Kalmyks, Karachai, Balkars, Ingush, Greeks, Bulgars, Crimean Armenians, Meskhetian Turks, Kurds, and Khemshins). The campaign against the Jews was also much less consistent and effective than the Soviet campaigns against the children of the former elite—the factory owners, the Cossack officers, and the middle classes and intelligentsia (p. 308).

Unlike the purges of the 1930s that sometimes targeted Jews as member of the elite (albeit at far less than their percentage of the elite), the anti-Jewish actions of the late 1940s and early 1950s targeted Jews because of their ethnicity. Similar purges were performed throughout Soviet-controlled Eastern Europe (pp. 313–14). "All three regimes [Poland, Romania, Hungary] resembled the Soviet Union of the 1920s insofar as they combined the ruling core of the old Communist underground, which was heavily Jewish, with a large pool of upwardly mobile Jewish professionals, who were, on average, the most trustworthy among the educated and the most educated among the trustworthy" (p. 314). Speaking of the situation in Poland, Khrushchev supported the anti-Jewish purge with his remark that "you have already too many Abramoviches."[59]

Whereas in the 1920s and 1930s children of the pillars of the old order were discriminated against, now Jews were not only being purged because of their vast overrepresentation among the elite, but were being discriminated against in university admissions. Jews, the formerly loyal members of the elite and willing executioners of the bloodiest regime in

---

[59] In Schatz 1991, 272.

history, now "found themselves among the aliens" (p. 310). Rather than rationalize their persecution as resulting from the iron laws of history, some Jews began to feel guilt for their former role. A Jewish woman writes that after her husband was arrested, her maid told her, "You are crying now, but you did not mind when my father was being dekulakized, martyred for no reason at all, and my whole family thrown out in the street" (p. 311).

And so began the exodus of Jews. Stalin died and the anti-Jewish campaign fizzled, but the Jewish trajectory was definitely downhill. Jews retained their elite status and occupational profile until the collapse of the Soviet Union in 1991, but "the special relationship between the Jews and the Soviet state had come to an end—or rather, the unique symbiosis in pursuit of world revolution had given way to a unique antagonism over two competing and incommensurate nationalisms" (p. 330). A response of the Russians was "massive affirmative action" (p. 333) aimed at giving greater representation to underrepresented ethnic groups. Jews were targets of suspicion because of their ethnic status, barred from some elite institutions, and limited in their opportunities for advancement.

The Russians were taking back their country, and it wasn't long before Jews became leaders of the dissident movement and began to seek to emigrate in droves to the United States, Western Europe, and Israel. Despite still possessing elite social status and far fewer disabilities than many groups (e.g., the overwhelming majority of the Soviet population was not allowed to live in cities, and some Christian sects were banned), Jews perceived their situation as "unrelieved humiliation" (p. 339). Overt anti-Semitism was encouraged by the more covert official variety apparent in the limits on Jewish advancement. Under these circumstances, Jews became "in many ways, the core of the antiregime intelligentsia" (p. 340). Jewish dissidents whose parents had run the Gulags, the deportations, and the state-sponsored famines, now led the "urgent call for social justice" (p. 342). Jewish academics with "cult followings" (p. 342)—a familiar Jewish pattern[60]—and close ties to Western Jewish intellectuals became the intellectual vanguard and iconoclasts of the new culture of critique in the Soviet Union.

Applications to leave the USSR increased dramatically after Israel's Six-Day War of 1967, which, as in the United States and Eastern Europe, resulted in an upsurge of Jewish identification and ethnic pride. The floodgates were eventually opened by Gorbachev in the late 1980s,

---

[60] *The Culture of Critique*, 27–28, 127–35, 156, ch. 6.

and by 1994, 1.2 million Soviet Jews had emigrated—43 percent of the total. By 2002, there were only 230,000 Jews left in the Russian Federation, 0.16 percent of the population. These remaining Jews nevertheless exhibit the typical Ashkenazi pattern of high achievement and overrepresentation among the elite, including six of the seven oligarchs who emerged in control of the Soviet economy and media in the period of de-nationalization (p. 362).

Perhaps unsurprisingly, this dénouement did not result in any sense of collective guilt among Soviet Jews (p. 345) or among their American apologists. Indeed, American Jewish media figures who were blacklisted because of Communist affiliations in the 1940s are now heroes, honored by the film industry, praised in newspapers, their work exhibited in museums.[61] At the same time, the cause of Soviet Jews and their ability to emigrate became a critical rallying point for American Jewish activist organizations and a defining feature of neoconservatism as a Jewish intellectual and political movement. (For example, Richard Perle, a key neoconservative, was Senator Henry Jackson's most important security advisor from 1969 to 1979 and organized Congressional support for the Jackson-Vanik Amendment linking US-Soviet trade to the ability of Jews to emigrate from the Soviet Union. The bill was passed over strenuous opposition from the Nixon administration.) Jewish activist organizations and many Jewish historians portray the Soviet Jewish experience as a sojourn in the land of the "Red Pharaohs" (p. 360). The historical legacy is that Jews were the passive, uncomprehending victims of the White armies, the Nazis, the Ukrainian nationalists, and the postwar Soviet state, nothing more.

THE ISSUE OF JEWISH CULPABILITY

Alexander Solzhenitsyn calls on Jews to accept moral responsibility for the Jews who "took part in the iron Bolshevik leadership and, even more so, in the ideological guidance of a huge country down a false path. . . . [and for the Jewish role in the] Cheka executions, the drowning of the barges with the condemned in the White and Caspian Seas, collectivization, the Ukrainian famine—in all the vile acts of the Soviet regime" (quoted on p. 360). But according to Slezkine, there can be no collective guilt because Soviet violence, unlike the Nazi persecution of the Jews, was not tribal violence. Violence of the Soviet sort has "no legitimate heirs—for either the victims or the perpetrators" (p. 345).

---

[61] See discussion in *The Culture of Critique*, Preface to the first paperback edition.

Slezkine acknowledges that Jews were "the most enthusiastic ethnically defined supporters of the Soviet state," but he essentially argues that Jews were not really Jews when they were Communists, at least until World War II caused them to be conscious of their Jewish identities. After all, the legacy of Communism "was almost as strongly committed to cosmopolitanism as it was to mass violence" (p. 346).

Again we see the importance of Slezkine's claims that Jewish Communists lacked a Jewish identity. However, as demonstrated above, there can be little doubt that Soviet Jews thought of themselves as Jews (although they certainly were not religious Jews) and that they worked together on the basis of shared Jewish ethnic identity. Nevertheless, the critical issue for collective guilt is whether the Jewish enthusiasm for the Soviet state and the enthusiastic participation of Jews in the violence against what Slezkine terms "rural backwardness and religion" (p. 346) had something to do with their Jewish identity.

This is a more difficult claim to establish, but the outlines of the argument are quite clear. Even granting the possibility that the revolutionary vanguard composed of Jews like Trotsky that spearheaded the Bolshevik Revolution was far more influenced by a universalist utopian vision than by their upbringing in traditional Judaism, it does not follow that this was the case for the millions of Jews who left the *shtetl* towns of the Pale of Settlement to migrate to Moscow and the urban centers of the new state. The migration of the Jews to the urban centers of the USSR is a critical aspect of Slezkine's presentation, but it strains credulity to suppose that these migrants threw off, completely and immediately, all remnants of the Eastern European *shtetl* culture which, Slezkine acknowledges, had a deep sense of estrangement from non-Jewish culture, and in particular a fear and hatred of peasants resulting from the traditional economic relations between Jews and peasants and exacerbated by the long and recent history of anti-Jewish pogroms carried out by peasants. Traditional Jewish *shtetl* culture also had a very negative attitude toward Christianity, not only as the central cultural icon of the outgroup but as associated in their minds with a long history of anti-Jewish persecution. The same situation doubtless occurred in Poland, where the efforts of even the most "de-ethnicized" Jewish Communists to recruit Poles were inhibited by traditional Jewish attitudes of superiority toward and estrangement from traditional Polish culture.[62]

In other words, the war against "rural backwardness and religion"

---

[62] Schatz 1991, 119.

was exactly the sort of war that traditional Jews would have supported wholeheartedly, because it was a war against everything they hated and thought of as oppressing them. Of course traditional *shtetl* Jews also hated the Tsar and his government due to restrictions on Jews and because they did not think that the government did enough to rein in anti-Jewish violence. There can be little doubt that Lenin's contempt for "the thick-skulled, boorish, inert, and bearishly savage Russian or Ukrainian peasant" was shared by the vast majority of *shtetl* Jews prior to the Revolution and after it. Those Jews who defiled the holy places of traditional Russian culture and published anti-Christian periodicals doubtless reveled in their tasks for entirely Jewish reasons, and, as Gorky worried, their activities not unreasonably stoked the anti-Semitism of the period. Given the anti-Christian attitudes of traditional *shtetl* Jews, it is very difficult to believe that the Jews engaged in campaigns against Christianity did not have a sense of revenge against the old culture that they held in such contempt.

Indeed, Slezkine reviews some of the works of early Soviet Jewish writers that illustrate the revenge theme. The amorous advances of the Jewish protagonist of Eduard Bagritsky's poem "February" are rebuffed by a Russian girl, but their positions are changed after the Revolution when he becomes a deputy commissar. Seeing the girl in a brothel, he has sex with her without taking off his boots, his gun, or his trench coat—an act of aggression and revenge:

> I am taking you because so timid
> Have I always been, and to take vengeance
> For the shame of my exiled forefathers
> And the twitter of an unknown fledgling!
> I am taking you to wreak my vengeance
> On the world I could not get away from!

Slezkine seems comfortable with revenge as a Jewish motive, but he does not consider traditional Jewish culture itself to be a contributor to Jewish attitudes toward traditional Russia, even though he notes that a very traditional part of Jewish culture was to despise the Russians and their culture. (Even the Jewish literati despised all of traditional Russian culture, apart from Pushkin and a few literary icons.) Indeed, one wonders what would motivate the Jewish commissars to revenge apart from motives related to their Jewish identity. Traditional hostility toward non-Jews and their culture forms a central theme in the writings of Israel Shahak and many mainstream Jewish historians, including Slezkine, and I have presented summaries of this material in chapter 1.[63]

An important aspect of Slezkine's general theoretical approach is that relationships between Mercurians and Apollonians involve mutual hostility, suspicion and contempt, and a sense of superiority (p. 20). These traditional attitudes were exacerbated by the increase in tensions between Jews and non-Jews beginning with the pogroms of 1881 and extending, with fits and starts, into the period of the Bolshevik Revolution. Slezkine's argument that Jews were critically involved in destroying traditional Russian institutions, liquidating Russian nationalists, murdering the Tsar and his family, dispossessing and murdering the kulaks, and destroying the Orthodox Church has been made by many other writers over the years, including Igor Shafarevich, a mathematician and member of the prestigious US National Academy of Sciences (NAS). Shafarevich's review of Jewish literary works during the Soviet and post-Soviet period agrees with Slezkine in showing Jewish hatred mixed with a powerful desire for revenge toward pre-revolutionary Russia and its culture.[64] But Shafarevich also suggests that the Jewish "Russophobia" that prompted the mass murder is not a unique phenomenon, but results from traditional Jewish hostility toward the non-Jewish world, considered *tref* (unclean), and toward non-Jews themselves, considered sub-human and as worthy of destruction. Both Shafarevich and Slezkine review the traditional animosity of Jews toward Russia, but Slezkine attempts to get his readers to believe that *shtetl* Jews were magically transformed in the instant of Revolution; although they did carry out the destruction of traditional Russia and approximately twenty million of its people, they did so only out of the highest humanitarian motives and the dream of utopian socialism, only to return to an overt Jewish identity because of the pressures of World War II, the rise of Israel as a source of Jewish identity and pride, and anti-Jewish policies and attitudes in the USSR. This is simply not plausible.

The situation prompts reflection on what might have happened in the United States had American Communists and their sympathizers assumed power. The "red diaper babies" came from Jewish families which "around the breakfast table, day after day, in Scarsdale, Newton, Great Neck, and Beverly Hills have discussed what an awful, corrupt, immoral, undemocratic, racist society the United States is."[65] Indeed,

---

[63] Mahler 1985; Shahak 1994; Shahak and Mezvinsky 1999.

[64] Shafarevich 1989. The NAS asked Shafarevich to resign his position in the academy but he refused (see *Science* 257 [1992]: 743).

[65] Lipset 1988, 393.

hatred toward the peoples and cultures of non-Jews and the image of enslaved ancestors as victims of anti-Semitism have been the Jewish norm throughout history—much commented on, from Tacitus to the present.[66]

It is easy to imagine which sectors of American society would have been deemed overly backward and religious and therefore worthy of mass murder by the American counterparts of the Jewish elite in the Soviet Union—the ones who journeyed to Ellis Island instead of Moscow. The descendants of these overly backward and religious people now loom large among the "red state" voters who have been so important in recent national elections. Jewish animosity toward the Christian culture that is so deeply ingrained in much of America is legendary. As Joel Kotkin points out, "for generations, [American] Jews have viewed religious conservatives with a combination of fear and disdain."[67] And as Elliott Abrams notes, the American Jewish community "clings to what is at bottom a dark vision of America, as a land permeated with anti-Semitism and always on the verge of anti-Semitic outbursts."[68] These attitudes are well captured in Steven Steinlight's charge that the Americans who approved the immigration restriction legislation of the 1920s—the vast majority of the population—were a "thoughtless mob" and that the legislation itself was "evil, xenophobic, anti-Semitic," "vilely discriminatory," a "vast moral failure," a "monstrous policy."[69] In the end, the dark view of traditional Slavs and their culture that facilitated the participation of so many Eastern European *shtetl* Jews in becoming willing executioners in the name of international socialism is not very different from the views of contemporary American Jews about a majority of their fellow countrymen.

There is a certain enormity in all this. The twentieth century was indeed the Jewish century because Jews and Jewish organizations were intimately and decisively involved in its most important events. Slezkine's greatest accomplishment is to set the historical record straight on the importance of Jews in the Bolshevik Revolution and its aftermath, but he doesn't focus on the huge repercussions of the Revolution, repercussions that continue to shape the world of the twenty-first century.

---

[66] See ch. 1 above, "Background Traits for Jewish Activism"; see also *Separation and Its Discontents*, ch. 2; *The Culture of Critique*, ch. 1 and Preface to the first paperback edition; Soloveichik 2003.

[67] Kotkin 2002.

[68] Abrams 1997, 188.

[69] Steinlight 2001.

In fact, for long after the Revolution, conservatives throughout Europe and the United States believed that Jews were responsible for Communism and for the Bolshevik Revolution.[70] The Jewish role in leftist political movements was a common source of anti-Jewish attitudes among a great many intellectuals and political figures. In Germany, the identification of Jews and Bolshevism was widespread in the middle classes and was a critical part of the National Socialist view of the world. As historian Ernst Nolte has noted, for middle-class Germans, "the experience of the Bolshevik revolution in Germany was so immediate, so close to home, and so disquieting, and statistics seemed to prove the overwhelming participation of Jewish ringleaders so irrefutably," that even many liberals believed in Jewish responsibility.[71] Jewish involvement in the horrors of Communism was also an important sentiment in Hitler's desire to destroy the USSR and in the anti-Jewish actions of the German National Socialist government. Jews and Jewish organizations were also important forces in inducing the Western democracies to side with Stalin rather than Hitler in World War II.

The victory over National Socialism set the stage for the tremendous increase in Jewish power in the post-World War II Western world, in the end more than compensating for the decline of Jews in the Soviet Union. As Slezkine shows, the children of Jewish immigrants assumed an elite position in the United States, just as they had in the Soviet Union and throughout Eastern Europe and Germany prior to World War II. This new-found power facilitated the establishment of Israel, the transformation of the United States and other Western nations in the direction of multiracial, multicultural societies via large-scale non-white immigration, and the consequent decline in European demographic and cultural preeminence.[72] The critical Jewish role in Communism has been sanitized, while Jewish victimization by the Nazis has achieved the status of a moral touchstone and is a prime weapon in the push for massive non-European immigration, multiculturalism, and advancing other Jewish causes.

The Jewish involvement in Bolshevism has therefore had an enormous effect on recent European and American history. It is certainly true that Jews would have attained elite status in the United States with or without their prominence in the Soviet Union. However, without the

---

[70] Bendersky 2000; Mayer 1988; Nolte 1965; Szajkowski 1974.

[71] Nolte 1965, 331.

[72] The detailed version of this argument is in *The Culture of Critique*, Preface to the first paperback edition.

Soviet Union as a shining beacon of a land freed of official anti-Semitism where Jews had attained elite status in a stunningly short period, the history of the United States would have been very different. The persistence of Jewish radicalism influenced the general political sensibility of the Jewish community and had a destabilizing effect on American society, ranging from the paranoia of the McCarthy era, to the triumph of the 1960s countercultural revolution, to the conflicts over immigration and multiculturalism that are so much a part of the contemporary political landscape.[73]

It is Slezkine's chief contention that the history of the twentieth century was a history of the rise of the Jews in the West, in the Middle East, and in Russia, and ultimately their decline in Russia. I think he is absolutely right about this. If there is any lesson to be learned, it is that Jews not only became an elite in all these areas, they became a hostile elite—hostile to the traditional peoples and cultures of all three areas they came to dominate. Until now, the greatest human tragedies have occurred in the Soviet Union, but Israel's record as an oppressive and expansive occupying power in the Middle East has made it a pariah among the vast majority of the governments of the world. And Jewish hostility toward the European-derived people and culture of the United States has been a consistent feature of Jewish political behavior and attitudes throughout the twentieth century. In the present, this normative Jewish hostility toward the traditional population and culture of the United States remains a potent motivator of Jewish involvement in the transformation of the United States into a non-European society.[74]

Given this record of Jews as a hostile but very successful elite, I doubt that the continued demographic and cultural dominance of Western European peoples will be retained either in Europe or the United States and other Western societies without a decline in Jewish influence. (Perhaps more obviously, the same might be said vis-à-vis the Palestinians and other peoples in the Middle East.) The lesson of the Soviet Union (and Spain from the fifteenth to seventeenth centuries[75]) is that Jewish influence does wax and wane. Contrary to the utopian ideologies of the nineteenth and twentieth centuries, there is no end to history.

---

[73] *The Culture of Critique*, chs. 7 and 8.
[74] *The Culture of Critique*, ch. 7.
[75] *Separation and Its Discontents*, chs. 4 and 7.

Chapter 3

ZIONISM AND THE INTERNAL DYNAMICS OF THE JEWISH COMMUNITY*

The history of Zionism illustrates a dynamic within the Jewish community in which the most radical elements end up pulling the entire community in their direction. Zionism began among the most ethnocentric Eastern European Jews and had explicitly racialist and nationalist overtones. However, Zionism was viewed as dangerous among the wider Jewish community, especially the partially assimilated Jews in Western countries, because it opened Jews up to charges of disloyalty and because the Zionists' open racialism and ethnocentric nationalism conflicted with the assimilationist strategy then dominant among Western Jews. Zionist activists eventually succeeded in making Zionism a mainstream Jewish movement, due in large part to the sheer force of numbers of the Eastern European vanguard. Over time, the more militant, expansionist Zionists (the Jabotinskyists, the Likud Party, fundamentalists, and West Bank settlers) have won the day and have continued to push for territorial expansion within Israel. This has led to conflicts with the Palestinians and a widespread belief among Jews that Israel itself is threatened. The result has been a heightened group consciousness among Jews and ultimately support for Zionist extremism among the entire organized American Jewish community.

In chapter 1 on "Background Traits for Jewish Activism," I discussed Jewish ethnocentrism as a central trait influencing the success of Jewish activism. In the contemporary world, the most important example of Jewish ethnocentrism and extremism is Zionism. In fact, Zionism is incredibly important. In 2003 the United States destroyed Saddam Hussein's government in Iraq, largely as a result of the influence of neoconservatives in the Bush Administration with strong ties to the Israeli right (see chapters 4 and 5). It is common among influential Jews to advocate war between the United States and virtually the entire Muslim world. Norman Podhoretz, the editor of *Commentary* (an influential

---

* First published as "Zionism and the Internal Dynamics of Judaism," *The Occidental Quarterly* 3 (Fall 2003): 15–44. Reprinted in Kevin MacDonald, *Understanding Jewish Influence: A Study in Ethnic Activism* (Augusta, Ga.: Washington Summit Publishers, 2004).

journal published by the American Jewish Committee), states:

> The regimes that richly deserve to be overthrown and replaced are not confined to the three singled-out members of the axis of evil [i.e., Iraq, Iran, and North Korea]. At a minimum, the axis should extend to Syria and Lebanon and Libya, as well as "friends" of America like the Saudi royal family and Egypt's Hosni Mubarak, along with the Palestinian Authority, whether headed by Arafat or one of his henchmen.[1]

More than anything else, this is a list of countries that Israel doesn't like, and, as I discuss more fully in the following chapters on neoconservatism, intensely committed Zionists with close links to Israel occupy prominent positions in the Bush administration, especially in the Department of Defense and on the staff of Vice President Dick Cheney. The long-term consequence of Zionism is that the United States is on the verge of attempting to completely transform the Arab/Muslim world to produce governments that accept Israel and whatever fate it decides for the Palestinians, and, quite possibly, to set the stage for further Israeli expansionism.

Zionism is an example of an important principle in Jewish history: At all the turning points, it is the more ethnocentric elements—one might term them the radicals—who have determined the direction of the Jewish community and eventually won the day.[2] As recounted in the Books of Ezra and Nehemiah, the Jews who returned to Israel after the Babylonian captivity energetically rid the community of those who had intermarried with the racially impure remnant left behind. Later, during the period of Greek dominance, there was a struggle between the pro-Greek assimilationists and the more committed Jews, who came to be known as Maccabeans.

> At that time there appeared in Israel a group of renegade Jews, who incited the people. "Let us enter into a covenant with the Gentiles round about," they said, "because disaster upon disaster has overtaken us since we segregated ourselves from them." The people thought this a good argument, and some of them in their enthusiasm went to the king and received authority to introduce non-Jewish laws and customs. They built a sports stadium in the gentile style in Jerusalem. They removed their marks of circumcision and repudi-

---

[1] Podhoretz 2002.
[2] Sacks 1993, ix–x.

ated the holy covenant. They intermarried with Gentiles, and abandoned themselves to evil ways.[3]

The victory of the Maccabeans reestablished Jewish law and put an end to assimilation. The Book of Jubilees, written during this period, represents the epitome of ancient Jewish nationalism, in which God represents the national interests of the Jewish people in dominating all other peoples of the world:

> I am the God who created heaven and earth. I shall increase you, and multiply you exceedingly; and kings shall come from you and shall rule wherever the foot of the sons of man has trodden. I shall give to your seed all the earth which is under heaven, and they shall rule over all the nations according to their desire; and afterwards they shall draw the whole earth to themselves and shall inherit it forever.[4]

A corollary of this is that throughout history in times of trouble there has been an upsurge in religious fundamentalism, mysticism, and messianism.[5] For example, during the 1930s in Germany liberal Reform Jews became more conscious of their Jewish identity, increased their attendance at synagogue, and returned to more traditional observance (including a reintroduction of Hebrew). Many of them became Zionists.[6] As I will discuss in the following, every crisis in Israel has resulted in an increase in Jewish identity and intense mobilization of support for Israel.

Today the people who are being rooted out of the Jewish community are Jews living in the Diaspora who do not support the aims of the Likud Party in Israel. The overall argument here is that Zionism is an example of the trajectory of Jewish radicalism. The radical movement begins among the more committed segments of the Jewish community, then spreads and eventually becomes mainstream within the Jewish community; then the most extreme continue to push the envelope (e.g., the settlement movement on the West Bank), and other Jews eventually follow because the more extreme positions come to define the essence of Jewish identity. An important part of the dynamic is that Jewish radicalism tends to result in conflicts with non-Jews, with the result that

---

[3] 1 Maccabees 1:11–15.
[4] Jubilees 32:18–19.
[5] *A People That Shall Dwell Alone*, ch. 3.
[6] Meyer, 1988, 388.

Jews feel threatened, become more group-oriented, and close ranks against the enemy—an enemy seen as irrationally and incomprehensibly anti-Jewish. Jews who fail to go along with what is now a mainstream position are pushed out of the community, labeled "self-hating Jews" or worse, and relegated to impotence.

TABLE 1:
Jewish Radicals Eventually Triumph within the Jewish Community: The Case of Zionism

1. Zionism began among the more ethnocentric, committed segments of the Jewish community (1880s).

2. Then it spread and became mainstream within the Jewish community despite its riskiness (1940s). Supporting Zionism comes to define what being Jewish is.

3. Then the most extreme among the Zionists continued to push the envelope (e.g., the settlement movement on the West Bank; constant pressure on border areas in Israel).

4. Jewish radicalism tends to result in conflicts with non-Jews (e.g., the settlement movement); violence (e.g., intifadas) and other expressions of anti-Jewish sentiment increase.

5. Jews in general feel threatened and close ranks against what they see as yet another violent, incomprehensible manifestation of the eternally violent hatred of Jews. This reaction is the result of psychological mechanisms of ethnocentrism: Moral particularism, self-deception, and social identity.

6. In the United States, this effect is accentuated because committed, more intensely ethnocentric Jews dominate Jewish activist groups.

7. Jews who fail to go along with what is now a mainstream position are systematically marginalized.

ORIGINS OF ZIONISM IN ETHNIC CONFLICT IN EASTERN EUROPE

The origins of Zionism and other manifestations of the intense Jewish dynamism of the twentieth century lie in the Yiddish-speaking world of Eastern Europe in the early nineteenth century. Originally invited in by nobles as estate managers, toll farmers, bankers, and moneylenders, Jews in Poland expanded into commerce and then into artisanry, so that there came to be competition between Jews and non-Jewish butchers, bakers, blacksmiths, shoemakers, and tailors. This produced the typical resource-based anti-Jewish attitudes and behavior so common throughout Jewish history.[7] Despite periodic restrictions and outbursts of hostility, Jews came to dominate the entire economy apart from agricultural labor and the nobility. Jews had an advantage in the competition in trade and artisanry because they were able to control the trade in raw materials and sell at lower prices to coethnics.[8]

This increasing economic domination went along with a great increase in the population of Jews. Jews not only made up large percentages of urban populations, they increasingly migrated to small towns and rural areas. In short, Jews had overshot their economic niche. The economy was unable to support this burgeoning Jewish population in the sorts of positions that Jews had traditionally filled, with the result that a large percentage of the Jewish population became mired in poverty. The result was a cauldron of ethnic hostility, with the government placing various restrictions on Jewish economic activity; rampant anti-Jewish attitudes; and increasing Jewish desperation.

The main Jewish response to this situation was an upsurge of fundamentalist extremism that coalesced in the Hasidic movement and, later in the nineteenth century, into political radicalism and Zionism as solutions to Jewish problems. Jewish populations in Eastern Europe had the highest rate of natural increase of any European population in the nineteenth century, with a natural increase of 120,000 per year in the 1880s and an overall increase within the Russian Empire from one to six million in the course of the nineteenth century.[9] Anti-Semitism and the exploding Jewish population, combined with economic adversity, were of critical importance for producing the sheer numbers of disaffected Jews who dreamed of deliverance in various messianic movements—the ethnocentric mysticism of the Kabbala, Zionism, or the dream of a Marxist political revolution.

Religious fanaticism and messianic expectations have been a typical Jewish response to hard times throughout history.[10] For example, in the eighteenth-century Ottoman Empire there was "an unmistakable picture of grinding poverty, ignorance, and insecurity"[11] among Jews that, in the context of high levels of anti-Semitism, effectively prevented Jewish upward mobility. These phenomena were accompanied by the

---

[7] *A People That Shall Dwell Alone*, ch. 5.
[8] See *Separation and Its Discontents*, Preface to the paperback edition.
[9] Alderman 1983, 112; Frankel 1981, 103; Lindemann 1991, 28–29, 133–35.
[10] E.g., Scholem 1971; *A People That Shall Dwell Alone*, ch. 3.
[11] Lewis 1984, 164.

prevalence of mysticism and a high fertility rate among Jews, which surely exacerbated the problems.

The Jewish population explosion in Eastern Europe in the context of poverty and politically imposed restrictions on Jews was responsible for the generally destabilizing effects of Jewish radicalism in Eastern Europe and Russia up to the revolution. These conditions also had spillover effects in Germany, where the negative attitudes toward the immigrant *Ostjuden* (Eastern Jews) and their foreign, clannish ways contributed to the anti-Semitism of the period.[12] In the United States, radical political beliefs held by a great many Jewish immigrants and their descendants persisted even in the absence of difficult economic and political conditions and have had a decisive influence on US political and cultural history into the present. The persistence of these beliefs influenced the general political sensibility of the Jewish community and has had a destabilizing effect on American society, ranging from the paranoia of the McCarthy era to the triumph of the 1960s countercultural revolution.[13] In the contemporary world, the descendants of these religious fundamentalists constitute the core of the settler movement and other manifestations of Zionist extremism in Israel.

The hypothesis pursued here is that Jewish population dynamics beginning in the nineteenth century resulted in a feed-forward dynamic: Increasing success in economic competition led to increased population. This in turn led to anti-Jewish reactions and eventually to Jewish overpopulation, poverty, and religious fanaticism as a response to external threat. In this regard, Jewish populations are quite the opposite of European populations, in which there is a long history of curtailing reproduction in the face of perceived scarcity of resources.[14] This may be analyzed in terms of the individualism/collectivism dimension, which provides a general contrast between Jewish and European culture:[15] Individualists curtail reproduction in response to adversity in order to better their own lives, whereas a group-oriented culture such as Judaism responds to adversity by strengthening group ties; forming groups with charismatic leaders and a strong sense of ingroup and outgroup; adopting mystical, messianic ideologies; and increasing their fertility—all of which lead to greater conflict.

---

[12] Aschheim 1982.

[13] *The Culture of Critique*, especially ch. 3.

[14] MacDonald 1997 and ch. 9 below, "What Makes Western Culture Unique?"

[15] *The Culture of Critique*, ch. 6.

There is an association between religious or ethnic fanaticism and fertility, and it is quite common for competing ethnic groups to increase their fertility in response to perceived external threats.[16] Ethnic activists respond to the perceived need to increase the numbers of their group in several ways, including exhorting coethnics to reproduce early and often, banning birth control and abortions, curtailing female employment in order to free women for the task of reproducing, and providing financial incentives. In the contemporary world, Jewish activists both within Israel and in the Diaspora have been strong advocates of increasing Jewish fertility, motivated by the threat of intermarriage in the Diaspora, the threat of wars with Israel's neighbors, and as a reaction to Jewish population losses stemming from the Holocaust. Pro-natalism has deep religious significance for Jews as a religious commandment.[17] Within Israel, there is "a nationwide obsession with fertility," as indicated by the highest rate of in-vitro fertilization clinics in the world—one for every 28,000 citizens. This is more than matched by the Palestinians. Originating in the same group-oriented, collectivist culture area as the Jews, the Palestinians have the highest birth rate in the world and have been strongly attracted to charismatic leaders, messianic religious ideology, and desperate, suicidal solutions for their political problems.[18]

For the Jews, the religious fundamentalism characteristic of Eastern Europe from around 1800 to 1940 has been a demographic wellspring for Judaism. Jewish populations in the West have tended to have low fertility. Beginning in the nineteenth century, Western Jewish populations would have stagnated or declined in the absence of "the unending stream of immigrants from Jewish communities in the East."[19] But the point here is that this demographic wellspring created the stresses and strains within this very talented and energetic population that continue to reverberate in the modern world.

These trends can be seen by describing the numerically dominant Hasidic population in early nineteenth-century Galicia, then a province of the Austro-Hungarian Empire; similar phenomena occurred throughout the Yiddish-speaking, religiously fundamentalist culture area of Eastern Europe, most of which came to be governed by the Russian

---

[16] Bookman 1997; Teitelbaum and Winter 1997; Parsons 1998; MacDonald 2000.
[17] Bookman 1997, 89.
[18] Bookman 1997; MacDonald 2000.
[19] Vital 1975, 28.

Empire.[20] Beginning in the late eighteenth century, there were increasing restrictions on Jewish economic activity, such as edicts preventing Jews from operating taverns, engaging in trade, and leasing mills. There were restrictions on where Jews could live, and ghettos were established in order to remove Jews from competition with non-Jews; taxes specific to Jews were imposed; and there were government efforts to force Jewish assimilation, as by requiring the legal documents be in the German language. These laws, even though often little enforced, reflected the anti-Jewish animosity of wider society and undoubtedly increased Jewish insecurity. In any case, a large percentage of the Jewish population was impoverished and doubtless would have remained so even in the absence of anti-Jewish attitudes and legislation. Indeed, the emigration of well over three million Jews to Western Europe and the New World did little to ease the grinding poverty of a large majority of the Jewish population.

It was in this atmosphere that Hasidism rose to dominance in Eastern Europe. The Hasidim passionately rejected all the assimilatory pressures coming from the government. They so cherished the Yiddish language that well into the twentieth century the vast majority of Eastern European Jews could not speak the languages of the non-Jews living around them.[21] They turned to the Kabbala, superstition, and anti-rationalism.[22] Corresponding to this intense ingroup feeling were attitudes that non-Jews were less than human. "As Mendel of Rymanów put it, 'A Gentile does not have a heart, although he has an organ that resembles a heart.'"[23] All nations exist only by virtue of the Jewish people: "Erez Yisreal [the land of Israel] is the essence of the world and all vitality stems from it."[24] Similar attitudes are common among contemporary Jewish fundamentalists and the settler movement in Israel.[25]

The Hasidim had an attitude of absolute faith in the person of the *tzadik*, a charismatic *rebbe* whose followers regarded him as literally the personification of God in the world. The following account of a scene at a synagogue in Galicia in 1903 describes the intense emotionality of the community and its total subordination to its leader:

---

[20] The following relies on Mahler 1985.
[21] Vital 1975, 46.
[22] Mahler 1985, 16.
[23] Mahler 1985, 17.
[24] Mahler 1985, 17.
[25] Shahak and Mezvinsky 1999, 58–60.

There were no benches, and several thousand Jews were standing closely packed together, swaying in prayer like the corn in the wind. When the rabbi appeared the service began. Everybody tried to get as close to him as possible. The rabbi led the prayers in a thin, weeping voice. It seemed to arouse a sort of ecstasy in the listeners. They closed their eyes, violently swaying. The loud praying sounded like a gale. Anyone seeing these Jews in prayer would have concluded that they were the most religious people on earth.[26]

At the end of the service, those closest to the rabbi were intensely eager to eat any food touched by him, and the fish bones were preserved by his followers as relics. Another account notes that "devotees hoping to catch a spark from this holy fire run to receive him."[27] The power of the *tzadik* extends so far "that whatever God does, it is also within the capacity of the *tzadik* to do."[28]

An important role for the *tzadik* is to produce wealth for the Jews, and by taking it from the non-Jews. According to Hasidic doctrine, the non-Jews have the preponderance of good things, but

It was the *tzadik* who was to reverse this situation. Indeed, R. Meir of Opatów never wearied of reiterating in his homilies that the *tzadik* must direct his prayer in a way that the abundance which he draws down from on high should not be squandered during its descent, and not "wander away," that is, outside, to the Gentiles, but that it mainly reach the Jews, the holy people, with only a residue flowing to the Gentiles, who are "the other side" (Satan's camp).[29]

The *tzadiks'* sermons were filled with pleas for vengeance and hatred toward the non-Jews, who were seen as the source of their problems.

These groups were highly authoritarian—another fundamental feature of Jewish social organization.[30] Rabbis and other elite members of the community had extraordinary power over other Jews in traditional societies—literally the power of life and death. Jews who informed the authorities about the illegal activities of other Jews were liquidated on orders of secret rabbinical courts, with no opportunity to defend them-

---

[26] Ruppin 1971, 69.
[27] In Mahler 1985, 8.
[28] In Mahler 1985, 249.
[29] Mahler 1985, 251.
[30] *The Culture of Critique*, ch. 6.

selves. Jews accused of heretical religious views were beaten or murdered. Their books were burned or buried in cemeteries. When a heretic died, his body was beaten by a special burial committee, placed in a cart filled with dung, and deposited outside the Jewish cemetery. In places where the authorities were lax, there were often pitched battles between different Jewish sects, often over trivial religious points such as what kind of shoes a person should wear. In 1838 the governor of Southwestern Russia issued a directive that the police keep tabs on synagogues because "Very often something happens that leaves dead Jews in its wake."[31] Synagogues had jails near the entrance, and prisoners were physically abused by the congregation as they filed in for services.

Not surprisingly, these groups had extraordinary solidarity; a government official observed, "The Hasidim are bound to each other with heart and soul."[32] This solidarity was based not only on the personality of the *rebbe* and the powerful social controls described above, but on the high levels of within-group generosity which alleviated to some extent their poverty. Needless to say, Hasidic solidarity was seen as threatening by outsiders: "How much longer will we tolerate the Hasidic sect, which is united by such a strong bond and whose members help one another."[33]

Hasidism triumphed partly by its attraction for the Jewish masses and partly because of the power politics of the *rebbes*: Opposing rabbis were forced out, so by the early nineteenth century in Galicia, Poland, and the Ukraine, the vast majority of Jews were in Hasidic communities. Their triumph meant the failure of the Jewish Enlightenment (the *Haskalah*) in Eastern Europe. The *Haskalah* movement advocated greater assimilation with non-Jewish society by using vernacular languages, studying secular subjects, and not adopting distinguishing forms of dress, although in other ways their commitment to Judaism remained powerful. These relatively assimilated Jews were the relatively thin upper crust of wealthy merchants and others who were free of the economic and social pressures that fueled Hasidism. They often cooperated with the authorities in attempts to force the Hasidim to assimilate out of fear that Hasidic behavior led to anti-Jewish attitudes.

As noted above, one source of the inward unity and psychological fanaticism of Jewish communities was the hostility of the surrounding

---

[31] Shahak and Mezvinsky 1999, 37.
[32] In Mahler 1985, 21.
[33] In Mahler 1985, 21.

non-Jewish population. Jews in the Russian Empire were hated by all the non-Jewish classes, who saw them as an exploitative class of petty traders, middlemen, innkeepers, store owners, estate agents, and money lenders.[34] Jews "were viewed by the authorities and by much of the rest of population as a foreign, separate, exploitative, and distressingly prolific nation."[35] In 1881 these tensions boiled over into several anti-Jewish pogroms in a great many towns of Southern and Southwestern Russia. It was in this context that the first large-scale stirrings of Zionism emerged.[36] From 1881 to 1884, dozens of Zionist groups formed in the Russian Empire and Romania.

Political radicalism emerged from the same intensely Jewish communities during this period and for much the same reasons.[37] Political radicalism often coexisted with messianic forms of Zionism as well as intense commitment to Jewish nationalism and religious and cultural separatism, and many individuals held various and often rapidly changing combinations of these ideas.[38]

The two streams of political radicalism and Zionism, each stemming from the teeming fanaticism of threatened Jewish populations in nineteenth-century Eastern Europe, continue to reverberate in the modern world. In both England and America the immigration of Eastern European Jews after 1880 had a transformative effect on the political attitudes of the Jewish community in the direction of radical politics and Zionism, often combined with religious orthodoxy.[39] The immigrant Eastern European Jews demographically swamped the previously existing Jewish communities in both countries, and the older community reacted to this influx with considerable trepidation because of the possibility of increased anti-Semitism. Attempts were made by the established Jewish communities to misrepresent the prevalence of radical political ideas and Zionism among the immigrants.[40]

The Zionist and radical solutions for Jewish problems differed, of course, with the radicals blaming the Jewish situation on the economic structure of society and attempting to appeal to non-Jews in an effort to completely restructure social and economic relationships. (Despite at-

---

[34] See summary in *Separation and Its Discontents*, 38–46.
[35] Lindemann 1991, 17.
[36] Vital 1975, 65ff.
[37] Vital 1975, 314.
[38] See Frankel 1981.
[39] Alderman 1983, 47ff; *The Culture of Critique*, ch. 3.
[40] Alderman 1983, 60; *Separation and Its Discontents*, ch. 8.

tempting to appeal to non-Jews, the vast majority of Jewish radicals had a very strong Jewish communal identity and often worked in an entirely Jewish milieu.[41]) Among Zionists, on the other hand, it was common from very early on to see the Jewish situation as resulting from irresoluble conflict between Jews and non-Jews. The early Zionist Moshe Leib Lilienblum emphasized that Jews were strangers who competed with local peoples: "A stranger can be received into a family, but only as a guest. A guest who bothers, or competes with or displaces an authentic member of the household is promptly and angrily reminded of his status by the others, acting out of a sense of self-protection."[42] Later, Theodor Herzl argued that a prime source of modern anti-Semitism was that Jews had come into direct economic competition with the non-Jewish middle classes. Anti-Semitism based on resource competition was rational: Herzl "insisted that one could not expect a majority to 'let themselves be subjugated' by formerly scorned outsiders whom they had just released from the ghetto. . . . I find the anti-Semites are fully within their rights."[43] In Germany, Zionists analyzed anti-Semitism during the Weimar period as "the inevitable and justifiable response of one people to attempts by another to make it share in the formation of its destiny. It was an instinctive response independent of reason and will, and hence common to all peoples, the Jews included."[44]

As was often the case during the period, Zionists had a much clearer understanding of their fellow Jews and the origins of anti-Jewish attitudes. Rabbi Stephen S. Wise, a prominent Zionist and leader of the American Jewish Congress whose membership derived from Eastern European immigrants and their descendants, accused Western European Jews of deception by pretending to be patriotic citizens while really being Jewish nationalists: "They wore the mask of the ruling nationality as of old in Spain—the mask of the ruling religion."[45] Wise had a well-developed sense of dual loyalty, stating on one occasion "I am not an American citizen of Jewish faith. I am a Jew. I am an American. I have been an American 63/64ths of my life, but I have been a Jew for 4,000 years."[46]

---

[41] *The Culture of Critique*, ch. 3; Vital 1975, 313.
[42] Vital 1975, 117.
[43] Kornberg 1993, 183; inner quote from Herzl's diary.
[44] Niewyk 1980, 94.
[45] In Frommer 1978, 118.
[46] In Lilienthal 1953, 165.

Zionists in Western countries were also at the ethnocentric end of the Jewish population. Zionism was seen as a way of combating the assimilatory pressures of Western societies: "Zionist ideologues and publicists argued that in the West assimilation was as much a threat to the survival of the Jewish people as persecution was in the East."[47] Zionism openly accepted a national/ethnic conceptualization of Judaism that was quite independent of religious faith. As Theodor Herzl stated, "We are a people—one people."[48] The Zionist Arthur Hertzberg stated that "the Jews in all ages were essentially a nation and . . . all other factors profoundly important to the life of this people, even religion, were mainly instrumental values."[49] There were a number of Zionist racial scientists in the period from 1890 to 1940, including Elias Auerbach, Aron Sandler, Felix Theilhaber, and Ignaz Zollschan. Zionist racial scientists were motivated by a perceived need to end Jewish intermarriage and preserve Jewish racial purity.[50] Only by creating a Jewish homeland and leaving the assimilatory influences of the Diaspora could Jews preserve their unique racial heritage.

For example, Auerbach advocated Zionism because it would return Jews "back into the position they enjoyed before the nineteenth century—politically autonomous, culturally whole, and racially pure."[51] Zollschan, whose book on "the Jewish racial question" went through five editions and was well known to both Jewish and non-Jewish anthropologists,[52] praised Houston Stewart Chamberlain and advocated Zionism as the only way to retain Jewish racial purity from the threat of mixed marriages and assimilation.[53] Zollschan's description of the phenotypic, and by implication genetic commonality of Jews around the world is striking. He notes that the same Jewish faces can be seen throughout the Jewish world among Ashkenazi, Sephardic, and Oriental Jews. He also remarked on the same mix of body types, head shapes, skin, and hair and eye pigmentation in these widely separated groups.[54]

For many Zionists, Jewish racialism went beyond merely asserting

---

[47] Endelman 1991, 196.
[48] Herzl 1970, 76.
[49] In Neusner 1987, 203.
[50] Efron 1994; Endelman 1991, 196.
[51] Efron 1994, 136.
[52] Efron 1994, 155.
[53] Gilman 1993, 109; Nicosia 1985, 18.
[54] See Efron 1994, 158.

and shoring up the ethnic basis of Judaism, to embrace the idea of racial superiority. Consistent with the anti-assimilationist thrust of Zionism, very few Zionists intermarried, and those who did, such as Martin Buber, found that their marriages were problematic within the wider Zionist community.[55] In 1929 the Zionist leaders of the Berlin Jewish community condemned intermarriage as a threat to the "racial purity of stock" and asserted its belief that "consanguinity of the flesh and solidarity of the soul" were essential for developing a Jewish nation, as was the "will to establish a closed brotherhood over against all other communities on earth."[56]

Assertions of Zionist racialism continued into the National Socialist period, where they dovetailed with National Socialist attitudes. Joachim Prinz, a German Jew who later became the head of the American Jewish Congress, celebrated Hitler's ascent to power because it signaled the end of the Enlightenment values, which had resulted in assimilation and mixed marriage among Jews:

> We want assimilation to be replaced by a new law: *the declaration of belonging to the Jewish nation and the Jewish race*. A state built upon the principle of the purity of nation and race can only be honored and respected by a Jew who declares his belonging to his own kind. . . . For only he who honors his *own* breed and his *own* blood can have an attitude of honor towards the *national will of other nations*.[57]

The common ground of the racial Zionists and their non-Jewish counterparts included the exclusion of Jews from the German *Volksgemeinschaft*.[58] Indeed, shortly after Hitler came to power, the Zionist Federation of Germany submitted a memorandum to the German government outlining a solution to the Jewish question and containing the following remarkable statement. The Federation declared that the Enlightenment view that Jews should be absorbed into the nation state

> . . . discerned only the individual, the single human being freely suspended in space, without regarding the ties of blood and history or spiritual distinctiveness. Accordingly, the liberal state demanded of

---

[55] Norden 1995.
[56] In Niewyk 1980, 129–130.
[57] Prinz 1934; in Shahak 1994, 71–72; italics in text.
[58] Nicosia 1985, 19.

the Jews assimilation [via baptism and mixed marriage] into the non-Jewish environment. . . . Thus it happened that innumerable persons of Jewish origin had the chance to occupy important positions and to come forward as representatives of German culture and German life, without having their belonging to Jewry become visible. Thus arose a state of affairs which in political discussion today is termed "debasement of Germandom," or "Jewification." . . . Zionism has no illusions about the difficulty of the Jewish condition, which consists above all in an abnormal occupational pattern and in the fault of an intellectual and moral posture not rooted in one's own tradition.[59]

ZIONISM AS A "RISKY STRATEGY"

Zionism was a risky strategy—to use Frank Salter's term[60]—because it led to charges of dual loyalty. The issue of dual loyalty has been a major concern throughout the history of Zionism. From the beginnings of Zionism, the vast majority of the movement's activists and supporters, and eventually its leadership, stemmed from Eastern European Jews.[61] In the early decades of the twentieth century, there was a deep conflict within the Jewish communities of Western Europe and the United States, pitting the older Jewish communities originating in Western Europe (particularly Germany) against the new arrivals from Eastern Europe, who eventually overwhelmed them by force of numbers.[62] Thus, an important theme of the history of Jews in America, England, and Germany was the conflict between the older Jewish communities that were committed to some degree of cultural assimilation and the ideals of the Enlightenment, versus the Yiddish-speaking immigrants from Eastern Europe and their commitment to political radicalism, Zionism, and/or religious fundamentalism.

The older Jewish communities were concerned that Zionism would lead to anti-Semitism due to charges of dual loyalty and because Jews would be perceived as a nation and an ethnic group rather than simply as a religion. In England, during the final stages before the issuance of the Balfour Declaration, Edwin Montagu "made a long, emotional appeal to his colleagues [in the British cabinet]: how could he represent the British government during the forthcoming mission to India if the same government declared that his (Montagu's) national home was on

---

[59] In Dawidowicz 1976, 150–52.
[60] Salter 2002b.
[61] Laqueur 1972; Vital 1975.
[62] Frommer 1978; Alderman 1983.

Turkish territory?"⁶³ Similar concerns were expressed in the United States, but by 1937 most American Jews advocated a Jewish state, and the Columbus Platform of the Guiding Principles of Reform Judaism of 1937 officially accepted the idea of a Palestinian homeland and shortly thereafter accepted the idea of political sovereignty for Jews in Israel.⁶⁴

In post-World War I Germany, a major goal of Reform Judaism was to suppress Zionism because of its perceived effect of fanning the flames of anti-Semitism due to charges of Jewish disloyalty.⁶⁵ In *Mein Kampf*, Hitler argued that Jews were an ethnic group and not simply a religion, which was confirmed by his discovery that "among them was a great movement . . . which came out sharply in confirmation of the national character of the Jews: this was the *Zionists*."⁶⁶ Hitler went on to remark that although one might suppose that only a subset of Jews were Zionists and that Zionism was condemned by the great majority of Jews, "the so-called liberal Jews did not reject Zionists as non-Jews, but only as Jews with an impractical, perhaps even dangerous, way of publicly avowing their Jewishness. Intrinsically they remained unalterably of one piece."⁶⁷

Hitler's comments reflect the weak position of the Zionists of his day as a small minority of Jews, but they also show the reality of the worst fears of the German Reform movement during this period: that the publicly expressed ethnocentric nationalism of the Zionists would increase anti-Semitism, because Jews would be perceived not as a religious group but as an ethnic/national entity with no ties to Germany. The existence of Zionism as well as of international Jewish organizations such as the Alliance Israélite Universelle (based in France) and continued Jewish cultural separatism were important sources of German anti-Semitism beginning in the late nineteenth century.

In the Soviet Union, Stalin regarded Jews as politically unreliable after they expressed "overwhelming enthusiasm" for Israel and attempted to emigrate to Israel, especially since Israel was leaning toward the West in the Cold War.⁶⁸ During the fighting in 1948, Soviet Jews

---

⁶³ Laqueur 1972, 196; see also John and Hadawi 1970a, 80.

⁶⁴ Laqueur 1972, 546, 549; Wheatcroft 1996, 98–147; The Columbus Platform: "Guiding Principles of Reform Judaism" (1937); reprinted in Meyer 1988, 389.

⁶⁵ Meyer 1988, 339.

⁶⁶ Hitler 1943, 56.

⁶⁷ Hitler 1943, 56.

⁶⁸ Schatz 1991, 375 n13.

attempted to organize an army to fight in Israel, and there were a great many other manifestations of Soviet-Jewish solidarity with Israel, particularly in the wake of Jewish enthusiasm during Golda Meir's visit to the Soviet Union. Stalin perceived a "psychological readiness on the part of the volunteers to be under the jurisdiction of two states—the homeland of all the workers and the homeland of all the Jews—something that was categorically impossible in his mind."[69] There is also some indication that Stalin, at the height of the Cold War, suspected that Soviet Jews would not be loyal to the Soviet Union in a war with America because many of them had relatives in America.[70]

In the United States, the dual loyalty issue arose because there was a conflict between perceived American foreign policy interests that began with the Balfour Declaration of 1917. The US State Department feared that a British protectorate in Palestine would damage commercial interests in the region and that in any case it was not in the interests of America to offend Turkey or other Middle Eastern states.[71] While President Woodrow Wilson sympathized with the State Department position, he was eventually persuaded by American Zionists, notably Louis Brandeis, to endorse the declaration; it was then quickly approved by the British.

The dual loyalty issue was also raised in Britain, most especially after the Second World War, when the Labour government failed to support the creation of a Jewish state. Many British Jews gave generously to finance illegal activities in the British protectorate of Palestine, including the smuggling of arms and refugees and Jewish attacks on British forces.[72] British losses to Jewish terrorism during this period were not trivial: the bombing of the King David Hotel by future Israeli Prime Minister Menachem Begin and his associates led to the deaths of 83 of the British administrative staff plus five members of the public. These activities led to widespread hostility toward Jews, and the Labour government pointedly refused to outlaw anti-Semitism during this period. During the late 1960s and 1970s, charges of dual loyalty appeared in the House of Commons among Labour MPs, one of whom commented that "it is undeniable that many MPs have what I can only term a dual loyalty, which is to another nation and another nation's interests."[73]

Attitudes ranging from unenthusiastic ambivalence to outright hos-

---

[69] Vaksberg 1994, 197.
[70] Rubenstein 1996, 260.
[71] Sachar 1992, 256ff.
[72] Alderman 1983, 129.
[73] In Alderman 1983, 151.

tility to the idea of a Zionist homeland on the part of presidents, the State Department, Congress, or the American public persisted right up until the establishment of Israel in 1948 and beyond. After World War II, there continued to be a perception in the State Department that American interests in the area would not be served by a Jewish homeland, but should be directed at securing oil and military bases to oppose the Soviets. There was also concern that such a homeland would be a destabilizing influence for years to come because of Arab hostility.[74] Truman's defense secretary, James Forrestal, "was all but obsessed by the threat to [American interests] he discerned in Zionist ambitions. His concern was shared by the State Department and specifically by the Near East Desk."[75] In 1960 Senator J. William Fulbright, chairman of the Senate Foreign Relations Committee, declared in response to attempts to coerce Egypt into agreeing to Israel's use of the Suez Canal, "in recent years we have seen the rise of organizations dedicated apparently not to America, but to foreign states and groups. The conduct of a foreign policy for America has been seriously compromised by this development."[76] Truman himself eventually caved in to Zionist pressure out of desire to ensure Jewish support in the 1948 election, and despite his own personal misgivings about Jewish myopia in pursuit of their own interests.[77]

ZIONIST EXTREMISM BECOMES MAINSTREAM

Since the Second World War, there has been a long evolution such that the American Jewish community now fully supports the settler movement and other right-wing causes within Israel. Zionists made a great deal of progress during the Second World War. They engaged in "loud diplomacy," organizing thousands of rallies, dinners with celebrity speakers (including prominent roles for sympathetic non-Jews), letter-writing campaigns, meetings, lobbying, threats against newspapers for publishing unfavorable items, insertion of propaganda as news items in the press, and giving money to politicians and non-Jewish celebrities in return for their support.[78] By 1944, thousands of non-Jewish associations would pass pro-Zionist resolutions, and both Republican and Democratic platforms included strong pro-Zionist planks, even

---

[74] Goldmann 1978, 31; Lilienthal 1978, 50, 61; Sachar 1992, 580.
[75] Sachar 1992, 597.
[76] In Cohen 1972, 325.
[77] Regarding Truman's attitudes toward Jews, see Dana and Carlson 2003.
[78] Bendersky 2000, 325.

though the creation of a Jewish state was strongly opposed by the Departments of State and War.[79]

A 1945 poll found that 80.5 percent of Jews favored a Jewish state, with only 10.5 percent opposed.[80] This shows that by the end of the Second World War, Zionism had become thoroughly mainstream within the US Jewish community. The triumph of Zionism occurred well before consciousness of the Holocaust came to be seen as legitimizing Israel. (Peter Novick dates the promotion of the Holocaust to its present status as a cultural icon from the 1967 Six-Day War.[81]) What had once been radical and viewed as dangerous had become not only accepted, but seen as central to Jewish identity.

Since the late 1980s, the American Jewish community has not been even-handed in its support of Israeli political factions, but has supported the more fanatical elements within Israel. While wealthy Israelis predominantly support the Labor Party, financial support for Likud and other right-wing parties comes from foreign sources, particularly wealthy US Jews.[82] The support of these benefactors is endangered by any softening of Likud positions, with support then going to the settler movement. "Organized US Jews are chauvinistic and militaristic in their views."[83]

Within Israel, there has been a transformation in the direction of the most radical, ethnocentric, and aggressive elements of the population. During the 1920s-1940s, the followers of Vladimir Jabotinsky (the "Revisionists") were the vanguard of Zionist aggressiveness and strident racial nationalism, but they were a minority within the Zionist movement as a whole. Revisionism had several characteristics typical of influential nineteenth-century Jewish intellectual and political movements—features shared also with other forms of traditional Judaism. Like Judaism itself and the various hermeneutic theories typical of other Jewish twentieth-century intellectual movements, the philosophy of Revisionism was a closed system that offered a complete worldview "creating a self-evident Jewish world."[84] Like the Hasidic movement and other influential Jewish intellectual and political movements, Revisionism was united around a charismatic leader figure, in this case

---

[79] Bendersky 2000, 328; John and Hadawi 1970a, 357.
[80] Wheatcroft 1996, 226.
[81] Novick 1999, 155.
[82] Shahak 1993.
[83] Shahak 1993.
[84] Shavit 1988, 23.

Jabotinsky, who was seen in god-like terms—"Everyone waited for him to speak, clung to him for support, and considered him the source of the one and only absolute truth."[85] There was a powerful sense of "us versus them." Opponents were demonized: "The style of communication . . . was coarse and venomous, aimed at moral delegitimization of the opponent by denouncing him and even 'inciting' the Jewish public against him."[86]

Jabotinsky developed a form of racial nationalism similar to other Zionist racial theorists of the period (see above). He believed that Jews were shaped by their long history as a desert people and that establishment of Israel as a Jewish state would allow the natural genius of the Jewish race to flourish: "These natural and fundamental distinctions embedded in the race are impossible to eradicate, and are continually being nurtured by the differences in soil and climate."[87]

The Revisionists advocated military force as a means of obtaining a Jewish state; they wanted a "maximalist" state that would include the entire Palestine Mandate, including the Transjordan (which became the nation of Jordan in 1946).[88] In the 1940s, its paramilitary wing, the Irgun, under the leadership of Menachem Begin, was responsible for much of the terrorist activity directed against both Arabs and the British forces maintaining the Palestinian Mandate until 1948, including the bombing of the King David Hotel and the massacre at Deir Yasin that was a major factor in terrorizing much of the Palestinian population into fleeing.[89]

Over time, the Labor Party has dwindled in influence, and there has followed the rise and ascendancy of the Likud Party and ultranationalism represented by Begin, who came to power in 1977 and began the process of resurrecting Jabotinsky,[90] by Yitzhak Shamir (commander of LEHI [the Stern Group], another pre-1948 terrorist group), and more recently by the government of Ariel Sharon, whose long record of aggressive brutality is described briefly below. Fundamentalists and other ultranationalists were a relatively weak phenomenon in the 1960s, but have increased to around 25 percent in the late 1990s and were an integral part of Sharon's government. In other words, the more

---

[85] Shavit 1988, 67.
[86] Shavit 1988, 80.
[87] In Shavit 1988, 112.
[88] John and Hadawi 1970a, 249.
[89] John and Hadawi 1970a, 351; John and Hadawi 1970b, 329.
[90] Bruzonsky 1980.

radical Zionists have won out within Israel. (As Noam Chomsky notes, there has been a consensus on retaining sovereignty over the West Bank, so that the entire Israeli political spectrum must be seen as aggressively expansionist.[91] The differences are differences of degree.)

The connections between Jabotinsky and the current Israeli government are more than coincidental: Just before Israel's election in February 2001, Sharon was interviewed seated

> ... symbolically and ostentatiously beneath a large photo of Vladimir Jabotinsky, spiritual father of militant Zionism and Sharon's Likud party. Jabotinsky called for a Jewish state extending from the Nile to the Euphrates. He advocated constant attacks to smash the weak Arab states into fragments, dominated by Israel. In fact, just what Sharon tried to do in Lebanon. Hardly a good omen for the Mideast's future.[92]

Sharon has been implicated in a long string of acts of "relentless brutality toward Arabs," including massacring an Arab village in the 1950s; the "pacification" of the Gaza Strip in the 1970s (involving large-scale bulldozing of homes and deportation of Palestinians); the invasion of Lebanon, which involved thousands of civilian deaths and the massacre of hundreds of Palestinian refugees; and the brutal Israeli response to the second Palestinian intifada.[93] The Kahan Commission, an Israeli board formed to investigate the Lebanese incident, concluded that Sharon was indirectly responsible for the massacre, and it went on to say that Sharon bears personal responsibility.

The intention of the Sharon government was to make life so miserable for the Palestinians that they will voluntarily leave, or, failing that, to simply expel them. Ram HaCohen, an Israeli academic, sums up the situation as of June 2002:

> Step by step, Palestinians have been dispossessed and surrounded by settlements, military camps, by-pass roads and checkpoints, squeezed into sealed-off enclaves. Palestinian towns are besieged by tanks and armed vehicles blocking all access roads. West Bank villages too are surrounded by road blocks, preventing the movement of vehicles in and out: three successive mounds of rubble and earth,

---

[91] Chomsky 1999, 54.
[92] Margolis 2001.
[93] Margolis 2001.

approximately six feet high, with 100 metre gaps between them. All residents wishing to move in and out of the village—old or young, sick or well, pregnant or not—have to climb over the slippery mounds. At present, this policy seems to have been perfected to an extent that it can be further institutionalised by long-term bureaucracy: a permit system, considerably worse than the "pass laws" imposed on blacks in Apartheid South Africa.[94]

Little has changed since this assessment, and this state of affairs has been formalized by the construction of a series of security walls that not only fence in the Palestinians but also result in the effective seizure of land, especially around Jerusalem. The wall encircles and isolates Palestinian villages and divides properties and farmland in ways that make them inaccessible to their owners.[95]

The current state of affairs would have been absolutely predictable simply by paying attention to the pronouncements and behavior of a critical subset of Israeli leaders over the last fifty years. Again, they have been the most radical within the Israeli political spectrum. The clear message is that an important faction of the Israeli political spectrum has had a long-term policy of expanding the state at the expense of the Palestinians, dating from the beginnings of the state of Israel. Expansionism was well entrenched in the Labor Party, centered around David Ben-Gurion, and has been even more central to the Likud coalition under the leadership of Menachem Begin and, more recently, Benjamin Netanyahu and Ariel Sharon. The result is that the Palestinians have been left with little hope of obtaining a meaningful state, despite the current "road map to peace" efforts. The next step may well be expulsion, already advocated by many on the right in Israel, although the strategy of oppression is in fact causing some Palestinians to leave voluntarily.[96] Voluntary emigration has long been viewed as a solution by some, including Prime Minister Yitzhak Rabin (on the more "liberal" end of the Israeli political spectrum), who urged that Israel "create . . . conditions which would attract natural and voluntary migration of the refugees from the Gaza Strip and the West Bank to Jordan."[97]

"Transfer," whether voluntary or involuntary, has long been a fixture of Zionist thought going back to Herzl, Chaim Weizmann, and

---

[94] HaCohen 2002.
[95] Brubacher 2002.
[96] Cockburn 2002.
[97] In Chomsky 1999, 116.

Ben-Gurion.[98] Ben-Gurion wrote in his diary in 1937: "the compulsory transfer of the Arabs from the valleys of the projected Jewish state . . . we have to stick to this conclusion the same way we grabbed the Balfour Declaration, more than that, the same way we grabbed at Zionism itself."[99] A prominent recent proponent of expulsion was Rehavam Ze'evi, a close associate of Sharon and Israel's Minister of Tourism as well as a member of the powerful Security Cabinet until his assassination in October, 2001. Ze'evi described Palestinians as "lice" and advocated the expulsion of Palestinians from Israeli-controlled areas. Ze'evi said Palestinians were living illegally in Israel and, "We should get rid of the ones who are not Israeli citizens the same way you get rid of lice. We have to stop this cancer from spreading within us." There are many examples, beginning no later than the mid-1980s, of leading Israeli politicians referring to the occupied territories on the West Bank as "Judea and Samaria."[100]

The point is that movements that start out on the extreme of the Jewish political spectrum eventually end up driving the entire process, so that in the end not only American Jews but pro-Israeli non-Jewish politicians end up mouthing the rhetoric that was formerly reserved for extremists within the Jewish community. In 2003, at a time when there are well over one hundred Israeli settlements on the West Bank and Gaza filled with fanatic fundamentalists and armed zealots intent on eradicating the Palestinians, it is revealing that Moshe Sharett, Israeli prime minister in the 1950s, worried that the border settlements were composed of well-armed ex-soldiers—extremists who were intent on expanding the borders of Israel. Immediately after the armistice agreement of 1948 Israeli zealots, sometimes within the army and sometimes in the nascent settler movement, began a long string of provocations of Israel's neighbors.[101] An operation of the Israeli army (under the leadership of Ariel Sharon) that demolished homes and killed civilians at Qibya in 1953 was part of a broader plan:

> The stronger the tensions in the region, the more demoralized the Arab populations and destabilized the Arab regimes, the stronger the pressures for the transfer of the concentrations of Palestinian refugees from places near the border away into the interior of the

---

[98] Chomsky 1999, 117; Masalha 1992.
[99] In Masalha 1992, 210.
[100] Aruri 1986.
[101] Chomsky 1999, 101.

Arab world—and the better it was for the preparation of the next war.[102]

At times the army engaged in provocative actions without Prime Minister Sharett's knowledge,[103] as when David Ben-Gurion, Israel's first prime minister, led a raid in 1955 which resulted in a massacre of Arabs in Gaza. When confronted with his actions by an American Jew, Ben-Gurion "stood up. He looked like an angry prophet out of the Bible and got red in the face. He shouted, 'I am not going to let anybody, American Jews or anyone else, tell me what I have to do to provide for the security of my people.'"[104]

The war to occupy the West Bank did not take place until 1967, but Sharett describes plans by the Israeli army to occupy the West Bank dating from 1953. Throughout the period from 1948–1967, "some of the major and persistent accusations" by the Israeli right were that the Labor-dominated governments had accepted the partition of Palestine and had not attempted to "eradicate Palestinian boundaries" during the 1948 war.[105] The annexation of East Jerusalem and the settlement of the West Bank began immediately after the 1967 war—exactly what would be expected on the assumption that this was a war of conquest. Menachem Begin, who accelerated the settlement process when he assumed power in 1977, noted, "In June 1967, we again had a choice. The Egyptian Army concentrations in the Sinai approaches do not prove that [Egyptian President] Nasser was really about to attack us. We must be honest with ourselves. We decided to attack him."[106]

Given the tendency for Jewish radicals to carry the day, it is worth describing the most radical Zionist fringe as it exists now. It is common among radical Zionists to project a much larger Israel that reflects God's covenant with Abraham. Theodor Herzl, the founder of Zionism, maintained that the area of the Jewish state stretches: "From the Brook of Egypt to the Euphrates."[107] This reflects God's covenant with Abraham in Genesis 15: 18-20 and Joshua 1 3-4: "To your descendants I give this land, from the river of Egypt to the great river, the river Euphrates, the land of the Kenites, the Kenizzites, the Kadmonites, the

---

[102] Rokach 1986.
[103] Wheatcroft 1996, 249.
[104] In Findley 1989, 277.
[105] Shavit 1988, 243.
[106] Chomsky 1999, 100.
[107] Herzl 1960, 711.

Hittites, the Perizzites, the Rephaim, the Amorites, the Canaanites, the Girgashites, and the Jebusites." The flexibility of the ultimate aims of Zionism can also be seen by Ben-Gurion's comment in 1936 that:

> The acceptance of partition [of the Palestinian Mandate] does not commit us to renounce Transjordan [i.e., the modern state of Jordan]; one does not demand from anybody to give up his vision. We shall accept a state in the boundaries fixed today. But the boundaries of Zionist aspirations are the concern of the Jewish people and no external factor will be able to limit them.[108]

Ben-Gurion's vision of "the boundaries of Zionist aspirations" included southern Lebanon, southern Syria, all of Jordan, and the Sinai.[109] After conquering the Sinai in 1956, Ben-Gurion announced to the Knesset that, "Our army did not infringe on Egyptian territory. . . . Our operations were restricted to the Sinai Peninsula alone."[110] Or consider Golda Meir's statement that the borders of Israel "are where Jews live, not where there is a line on the map."[111]

These views are common among the more extreme Zionists today—especially the fundamentalists and the settler movement—notably Gush Emunim—who now set the tone in Israel. A prominent rabbi associated with these movements stated: "We must live in this land even at the price of war. Moreover, even if there is peace, we must instigate wars of liberation in order to conquer [the land]."[112] Indeed, in the opinion of Israel Shahak and Norton Mezvinsky, "It is not unreasonable to assume that Gush Emunim, if it possessed the power and control, would use nuclear weapons in warfare to attempt to achieve its purpose."[113] This image of a "Greater Israel" is also much on the minds of activists in the Muslim world. For example, in a 1998 interview Osama bin Laden stated:

> [W]e know at least one reason behind the symbolic participation of the Western forces [in Saudi Arabia] and that is to support the Jewish and Zionist plans for expansion of what is called the Great Israel. . . . Their presence has no meaning save one and that is to offer

---

[108] Chomsky 1999, 161.
[109] In Chomsky 1999, 161.
[110] In Chomsky 1999, 161.
[111] In Chomsky 1999, 50.
[112] In Shahak and Mezvinsky 1999, 73.
[113] In Shahak and Mezvinsky 1999, 73.

support to the Jews in Palestine who are in need of their Christian brothers to achieve full control over the Arab Peninsula which they intend to make an important part of the so-called Greater Israel.[114]

To recapitulate: A century ago Zionism was a minority movement within the Diaspora, with the dominant assimilationist Jews in the West opposing it at least partly because Zionism raised the old dual loyalty issue, which has been a potent source of anti-Semitism throughout the ages. The vast majority of Jews eventually became Zionists, to the point that now not only are Diaspora Jews Zionists, they are indispensable supporters of the most fanatic elements within Israel. Within Israel, the radicals have also won the day, and the state has evolved to the point where the influence of moderates in the tradition of Moshe Sharett is a distant memory. The fanatics keep pushing the envelope, forcing other Jews to either go along with their agenda or to simply cease being part of the Jewish community. Not long ago it was common to talk to American Jews who would say they support Israel but deplore the settlements. Now such talk among Jews is an anachronism, because support for Israel demands support for the settlements. The only refuge for such talk is the increasingly isolated Jewish critics of Israel, such as Israel Shamir and, to a much lesser extent, Michael Lerner's *Tikkun*. The trajectory of Zionism has soared from its being a minority within a minority to its dominating the US Congress, the executive branch, and the entire US foreign policy apparatus.

And because the Israeli occupation and large-scale settlement of the West Bank unleashed a wave of terrorist-style violence against Israel, Jews perceive Israel as under threat. As with any committed group, Jewish commitment increases in times of perceived threat to the community. The typical response of Diaspora Jews to the recent violence has not been to renounce Jewish identity but to strongly support the Sharon government and rationalize its actions. This has been typical of Jewish history in general. For example, during the 1967 and 1973 wars there were huge upsurges of support for Israel and strengthened Jewish identity among American Jews: Arthur Hertzberg, a prominent Zionist, wrote that, "the immediate reaction of American Jewry to the crisis was far more intense and widespread than anyone could have foreseen. Many Jews would never have believed that grave danger to Israel could dominate their thoughts and emotions to the exclusion of everything else."[115]

---

[114] Bin Laden 1998.
[115] Hertzberg 1979, 210.

The same thing is happening now. The typical response to Israel's current situation is for Jews to identify even more strongly with Israel and to exclude Jews who criticize Israel or support Palestinian claims in any way.

This "rallying around the flag" in times of crisis fits well with the psychology of ethnocentrism: When under attack, groups become more unified and more conscious of boundaries, and have a greater tendency to form negative stereotypes of the outgroup. This has happened throughout Jewish history.[116]

Several commentators have noted the void on the Jewish left as the conflict with the Palestinians has escalated under the Sharon government. As noted above, surveys in the 1980s routinely found that half of US Jews opposed settlements on the West Bank and favored a Palestinian state.[117] Such sentiments have declined precipitously in the current climate:

> At a progressive synagogue on Manhattan's Upper West Side, Rabbi Rolando Matalo was torn between his longtime support for Palestinian human rights and his support for an Israel under siege. "There is a definite void on the left," said Matalo. . . . Many American Jewish leaders say Israel's current state of emergency—and growing signs of anti-Semitism around the world—have unified the faithful here in a way not seen since the 1967 and 1973 wars. . . . These feelings shift back and forth, but right now they're tilting toward tribalism.[118]

Note that the author of this article, Josh Getlin, portrays Israel as being "under siege," even though Israel is the occupying power and has killed far more Palestinians than the Palestinians have killed Israelis.

> "I don't recall a time in modern history when Jews have felt so vulnerable," said Rabbi Marvin Hier, dean and founder of the Simon Wiesenthal Center in Los Angeles. . . . This week, the center will be mailing out 600,000 'call to action' brochures that say 'Israel is fighting for her life' and urge American Jews to contact government leaders and media organizations worldwide." . . . Rabbi Mark Diamond, executive vice president of the Board of Rabbis of Southern California, said debate over the West Bank invasion and the attack on the

---

[116] *Separation and Its Discontents*, ch. 1.
[117] Findley 1989, 265.
[118] Getlin 2002.

Palestinian Jenin refugee camp is overshadowed by "a strong sense that Israel needs us, that the world Jewry needs us, that this is our wake-up call." He said he has been overwhelmed in recent weeks by numerous calls from members of synagogues asking what they can do to help or where they can send a check. . . . "I have American friends who might have been moderate before on the issue of negotiating peace, but now they think: 'Our whole survival is at stake, so let's just destroy them all,'" said Victor Nye, a Brooklyn, N.Y., businessman who describes himself as a passionate supporter of Israel.

In this atmosphere, Jews who dissent are seen as traitors, and liberal Jews have a great deal of anxiety that they will be ostracized from the Jewish community for criticizing Israel.[119] This phenomenon is not new. During the 1982 invasion of Lebanon, Richard Cohen of the *Washington Post* criticized the Begin government and was inundated with protests from Jews. "Here dissent becomes treason—and treason not to a state or even an ideal (Zionism), but to a people. There is tremendous pressure for conformity, to show a united front and to adopt the view that what is best for Israel is something only the government there can know."[120] During the same period, Nat Hentoff noted in the *Village Voice*, "I know staff workers for the American Jewish Committee and the American Jewish Congress who agonize about their failure to speak out, even on their own time, against Israeli injustice. They don't, because they figure they'll get fired if they do."[121]

Reflecting the fact that Jews who advocate peace with the Palestinians are on the defensive, funding has dried up for causes associated with criticism of Israel. The following is a note posted on the website of *Tikkun* by its editor, Michael Lerner:

> *TIKKUN Magazine* is in trouble—because we have continued to insist on the rights of the Palestinian people to full self-determination. For years we've called for an end to the Occupation and dismantling of the Israeli settlements. We've called on the Palestinian people to follow the example of Martin Luther King, Jr., Nelson Mandela, and Gandhi—and we've critiqued terrorism against Israel, and insisted on Israel's right to security. But we've also critiqued Israel's house demolitions, torture, and grabbing of land. For years, we had much

---

[119] Getlin 2002.
[120] In Findley 1989, 269.
[121] In Findley 1989, 271.

support. But since Intifada II began this past September, many Jews have stopped supporting us—and we've lost subscribers and donors. Would you consider helping us out?[122]

Another sign that Jews who are "soft" on Israel are being pushed out of the Jewish community is an article by Philip Weiss.[123]

> The refusal of liberal American Jews to make an independent stand has left the American left helpless. American liberalism has always drawn strength from Jews. They are among the largest contributors to the Democratic Party; they have brought a special perspective to any number of social-justice questions, from the advancement of blacks and women to free speech. They fostered multiculturalism. . . .
>
> The Holocaust continues to be the baseline reference for Jews when thinking about their relationship to the world, and the Palestinians. A couple of months ago, I got an e-mail from a friend of a friend in Israel about the latest bus-bombing. "They're going to kill us all," was the headline. (No matter that Israel has one of largest armies in the world, and that many more Palestinians have died than Israelis). Once, when I suggested to a liberal journalist friend that Americans had a right to discuss issues involving Jewish success in the American power structure—just as we examined the WASP culture of the establishment a generation ago—he said, "Well, we know where that conversation ends up: in the ovens of Auschwitz."

Because of Jewish ethnocentrism and group commitment, stories of Jews being killed are seen as the portending of another Holocaust and the extinction of the Jewish people rather than a response to a savage occupation—a clear instance of moral particularism writ large.

The same thing is happening in Canada where Jews are concerned about declining support by Canadians for Israel. "The past three years have been extraordinarily tough on Jews in Canada and around the world," said Keith Landy, national president of the Canadian Jewish Congress. "Every Jew has felt under attack in some form."[124] The response has been increased activism by deeply committed wealthy Jews, including, most famously, the late Israel Asper, executive chairman of CanWest Global Communications Corp. Asper used his media empire to

---

[122] Lerner 2002.
[123] Weiss 2002.
[124] Ross 2003.

promote pro-Likud policies and punished journalists for any deviation from its strong pro-Israel editorial policies.[125] The efforts of these activists are aimed at consolidating Jewish organizations behind "hawkish" attitudes on the Israeli-Palestinian conflict. Older Jewish organizations, such as the Canada-Israel Committee and the Canadian Jewish Congress, would be remodeled or driven out of existence to exclude Jews less committed to these attitudes.

CONCLUSION

An important mechanism underlying all this is that of rallying around the flag during times of crisis, a phenomenon that is well understood by social psychologists. Group identification processes are exaggerated in times of resource competition or other perceived sources of threat,[126] a finding that is highly compatible with an evolutionary perspective.[127] External threat tends to reduce internal divisions and maximize perceptions of common interest among ingroup members, as we have seen among American Jews in response to perceived crises in Israel, ranging from the Six-Day War of 1967 to the unending crises of the 1990s and into the new millennium.[128] Jewish populations also respond to threat by developing messianic ideologies, rallying around charismatic leaders, and expelling dissenters from the community. Traditionally this has taken the form of religious fundamentalism, as among the Hasidim, but in the modern world these tendencies have been manifested in various forms of leftist radicalism, Zionism, and other Jewish intellectual and political movements. Throughout Jewish history, this siege mentality has tended to increase conflict between Jews and non-Jews. In the context of the intense ethnic conflict of nineteenth-century Eastern Europe, the conflict was exacerbated by an enormous increase in the Jewish population.

And in all cases, the leaders of this process are the more ethnocentric, committed Jews. They are the ones who donate to Jewish causes, attend rallies, write letters, join and support activist organizations. As J. J. Goldberg, the editor of *Forward*, notes, Jews who identify themselves as doves feel much less strongly about Israel than those who identify themselves as hawks. "Jewish liberals give to the Sierra Fund. Jewish conservatives are Jewish all the time. That's the whole ball

---

[125] Canadian Journalists for Free Expression 2002.
[126] Hogg and Abrams 1987; Hewstone, Rubin, and Willis 2002.
[127] *Separation and Its Discontents*, chs. 1 and 2.
[128] Alexander 1979.

game. It's not what six million American Jews feel is best—it's what fifty Jewish organizations feel is best."[129] In other words, it's the most radical, committed elements of the Jewish community that determine the direction of the entire community.

As a European in a society that is rapidly becoming non-European, I can sympathize with Jabotinsky's envy of the native Slavic peoples he observed in the early twentieth century:

> I look at them with envy. I have never known, and probably never will know, this completely organic feeling: so united and singular [is this] sense of a homeland, in which everything flows together, the past and the present, the legend and the hopes, the individual and the historical.[130]

> Every nation civilized or primitive, sees its land as its national home, where it wants to stay as the sole landlord forever. Such a nation will never willingly consent to new landlords or even to partnership.[131]

The memory of this rapidly disappearing sense of historical rootedness and the sense of impending dispossession are at the root of the malaise experienced by many Europeans, not only in the United States but elsewhere. The triumph of Zionism took a mere fifty years from Herzl's inspiration to the founding of the state of Israel. There is a tendency to overlook or ignore the powerful ethnocentrism at the heart of Zionism that motivated people like Jabotinsky, especially on the part of the American Jewish community, which has been dedicated throughout the twentieth century to pathologizing and criminalizing the fragile vestiges of ethnocentrism among Europeans.

But the bottom line is that the Zionists were successful. Israel would not have become a state without a great many deeply ethnocentric Jews willing to engage in any means necessary to bring about their dream: a state that would be a vehicle for their ethnic interests. It would not have come about without the most radical among them—people like Jabotinsky, Begin, Shamir, Sharon, and their supporters—a group which now includes the entire organized American Jewish community. The impending dispossession of Europeans will only be avoided if people of their ilk can be found among the political class of Europeans.

---

[129] In Massing 2002.
[130] In Shavit 1988, 116.
[131] In Wheatcroft 1996, 207.

Chapter 4

NEOCONSERVATISM AS A JEWISH MOVEMENT*

In recent years, there has been a torrent of articles on neoconservatism raising (usually implicitly) some difficult issues: Are neoconservatives different from other conservatives? Is neoconservatism a Jewish movement? Is it "anti-Semitic" to say so?

The thesis presented here is that neoconservatism is indeed a Jewish intellectual and political movement. The neoconservatives exemplify the characteristic background traits of Jewish activism: ethnocentrism, intelligence, psychological intensity, and aggressiveness.[1] The ethnocentrism of the neocons has enabled them to create highly organized, cohesive, and effective ethnic networks. Neoconservatives have also exhibited the high intelligence necessary for attaining eminence in the academic world, in the elite media and think tanks, and at the highest levels of government. They have aggressively pursued their goals, not only in purging more traditional conservatives from positions of power and influence, but also in reorienting US foreign policy in the direction of hegemony and empire.

Neoconservatism also illustrates the central theme of the previous chapter: In alliance with virtually the entire organized American Jewish community, neoconservatism is a vanguard Jewish movement with close ties to the most extreme nationalistic, aggressive, racialist, and religiously fanatical elements within Israel.[2]

Neoconservatism also reflects many of the characteristics of Jewish intellectual movements studied in *The Culture of Critique* (see Table 1).

TABLE 1:
Characteristics of Jewish Intellectual Movements

1. A deep concern with furthering specific Jewish interests, such as

---

* First published (in a longer version encompassing ch. 5 below) in *The Occidental Quarterly* 4 (Summer 2004): 7–74. Reprinted in Kevin MacDonald, *Understanding Jewish Influence: A Study in Ethnic Activism* (Augusta, Ga.: Washington Summit Publishers, 2004).

[1] See ch. 1 above on "Background Traits for Jewish Activism."

[2] See ch. 2 above on "Zionism and the Group Dynamics of the Jewish Community."

helping Israel or promoting immigration.
2. Issues are framed in a rhetoric of universalism rather than Jewish particularism.
3. Issues are framed in moral terms, and an attitude of moral superiority pervades the movement.
4. Centered around charismatic leaders (Boas, Trotsky, Freud).
5. Jews form a cohesive, mutually reinforcing core.
6. Non-Jews appear in highly visible roles, often as spokespersons for the movement.
7. A pronounced ingroup/outgroup atmosphere within the movement—dissenters are portrayed as the personification of evil and are expunged from the movement.
8. The movement is irrational in the sense that it is fundamentally concerned with using available intellectual resources to advance a political cause.
9. The movement is associated with the most prestigious academic institutions in the society.
10. Access to prestigious and mainstream media sources, partly as a result of Jewish influence on the media.
11. Active involvement of the wider Jewish community in supporting the movement.

However, neoconservatism also presents several problems to any analysis, the main one being that the history of neoconservatism is relatively convoluted and complex compared to other Jewish intellectual and political movements. To an unusual extent, the history of neoconservatism presents a zigzag of positions and alliances and a multiplicity of influences. This is perhaps inevitable in a fundamentally political movement needing to adjust to changing circumstances and attempting to influence the very large, complex political culture of the United States. The main changes neoconservatives have been forced to confront have been their loss of influence in the Democratic Party and the fall of the Soviet Union. Although there is a remarkable continuity in Jewish neoconservatives' interests as Jews—the prime one being the safety and prosperity of Israel—these upheavals required new political alliances and produced a need for new work designed to reinvent the intellectual foundation of American foreign policy.

Neoconservatism also raises difficult problems of labeling. As described in the following, neoconservatism as a movement derives from the long association of Jews with the left. But contemporary neoconservatism is not simply a term for ex-liberals or leftists. Indeed, in its present incarnation, many second-generation neoconservatives, such as David Frum, Jonah Goldberg, and Max Boot, have never had affiliations with the American left. Rather, neoconservatism represents a fundamentally new version of American conservatism, if it can be properly termed conservative at all. By displacing traditional forms of conservatism, neoconservatism has actually solidified the hold of the left on political and cultural discourse in the United States. The deep and continuing chasm between neocons and more traditional American conservatives—a topic of this and the following chapter—indicates that this problem is far from being resolved.

The multiplicity of influences among neoconservatives requires some comment. The current crop of neoconservatives has at times been described as Trotskyists.[3] As will be seen, in some cases the intellectual influences of neoconservatives can be traced to Trotsky, but Trotskyism cannot be seen as a current influence within the movement. And although the political philosopher Leo Strauss is indeed a guru for some neoconservatives, his influence is by no means pervasive, and in any case provides only a very broad guide to what the neoconservatives advocate in the area of public policy. Indeed, by far the best predictor of neoconservative attitudes, on foreign policy at least, is what the political right in Israel deems in Israel's best interests. Neoconservatism does not fit the pattern of the Jewish intellectual movements described in *The Culture of Critique*, characterized by gurus ("rabbis") and their disciples centered around a tightly focused intellectual perspective in the manner of Freud, Boas, or Marcuse. Neoconservatism is better described in general as a complex interlocking professional and family network centered around Jewish publicists and organizers flexibly deployed to recruit the sympathies of both Jews and non-Jews in harnessing the wealth and power of the United States in the service of Israel. As such, neoconservatism should be considered a semi-covert branch of the massive and highly effective pro-Israel lobby, which includes organizations like the America Israel Public Affairs Committee (AIPAC)—the most powerful lobbying group in Washington—and the Zionist Organization of America (ZOA). Indeed, as discussed below and in the following chapter, prominent neoconservatives have been associated with such overtly pro-Israel organizations as the Jewish Institute for National Security Affairs (JINSA), the Washington Institute for Near East Policy (WINEP), and ZOA. (Acronyms of the main neo-

---

[3] Muravchik (2003) describes and critiques the idea of Trotsky's influence among neoconservatives.

conservative and pro-Israel activist organizations used in this paper are provided in Table 2.)

TABLE 2:
Acronyms of Neoconservative and Pro-Israel Activist Organizations Used in this and the Following Chapter

AEI: American Enterprise Institute—A neoconservative think tank; produces and disseminates books and articles on foreign and domestic policy; www.aei.org.

AIPAC: American Israel Public Affairs Committee—The main pro-Israel lobbying organization in the US, specializing in influencing the US Congress; www.aipac.org.

CSP: Center for Security Policy—Neoconservative think tank specializing in defense policy; formerly headed by Douglas Feith, CSP is now headed by Frank Gaffney; the CSP is strongly pro-Israel and favors a strong US military; www.centerforsecuritypolicy.org.

JINSA: Jewish Institute for National Security Affairs—Pro-Israel think tank specializing in promoting military cooperation between the United States and Israel; www.jinsa.org.

MEF: Middle East Forum—Headed by Daniel Pipes, the MEF is a pro-Israel advocacy organization overlapping with the WINEP but generally more strident; www.meforum.org.

PNAC: Project for the New American Century—Headed by Bill Kristol, the PNAC issues letters and statements signed mainly by prominent neocons and designed to influence public policy; www.newamericancentury.org.

SD/USA: Social Democrats/USA—"Left-neoconservative" political organization advocating pro-labor social policy and pro-Israel, anti-communist foreign policy; www.socialdemocrats.org.

WINEP: Washington Institute for Near East Policy—Pro-Israel think tank specializing in producing and disseminating pro-Israel media material; www.washingtoninstitute.org.

ZOA: Zionist Organization of America—Pro-Israel lobbying organization associated with the more fanatical end of the pro-Israel spectrum in America; www.zoa.org.

Compared with their deep and emotionally intense commitment to Israel, neoconservative attitudes on domestic policy seem more or less an afterthought, and they will not be the main focus here. In general, neoconservatives advocate maintaining the social welfare, immigration, and civil rights policies typical of liberalism (and the wider Jewish community) up to about 1970. Some of these policies represent clear examples of Jewish ethnic strategizing—in particular, the role of the entire Jewish political spectrum and the entire organized Jewish community as the moving force behind the immigration law of 1965, which opened the floodgates to non-white immigration. (Jewish organizations still favor liberal immigration policies. In 2004, virtually all American Jewish public affairs agencies belonged to the National Immigration Forum, the premier open borders immigration-lobbying group.[4]) Since the neocons have developed a decisive influence in the mainstream conservative movement, their support for nonrestrictive immigration policies has perhaps more significance for the future of the United States than their support for Israel.

As always, when discussing Jewish involvement in intellectual movements, there is no implication that all or even most Jews are involved in these movements. As discussed below, the organized Jewish community shares the neocon commitment to the Likud Party in Israel. However, neoconservatism has never been a majority viewpoint in the American Jewish community, at least if being a neoconservative implies voting for the Republican Party. In the 2000 election, 80 percent of Jews voted for Al Gore.[5] This was little changed in the 2004 election, when 76 percent of Jews voted for John Kerry despite the fact that it was well known by then that the top advisors of George W. Bush had very powerful Jewish connections, pro-Likud sympathies, and positive attitudes toward regime change in Arab countries in the Middle East.[6] Jews also voted for Kerry despite the enthusiasm of Jewish pro-Israel activists for President Bush. For example, Bush's May 18, 2004, speech to the national convention of AIPAC:

> . . . received a wild and sustained standing ovation in response to an audience member's call for "four more years." The majority of some 4,500 delegates at the national conference of the American Israel Public Affairs Committee leaped to their feet in support of the president. . . . Anecdotal evidence points to a sea change among Jewish voters, who historically have trended toward the Democratic Party but may

---

[4] Steinlight 2004.
[5] Friedman 2002.
[6] Jewish Vote in Presidential Elections. Jewish Virtual Library. http://www.jewishvirtuallibrary.org/jsource/US-Israel/jewvote.html

be heading to Bush's camp due to his stance on a single issue: his staunch support of Israel.[7]

Quite possibly, Democrats did not lose a substantial number of Jewish voters in 2004 because John Kerry, the Democratic candidate, claimed to have a "100 percent record" for Israel and promised to increase troop strength and retain the commitment to the Iraq War.[8]

The critical issue is not to determine what percentage of Jews support neoconservatism but to determine the extent to which Jews dominate the movement and are a critical component of its success. One must then document the fact that the Jews involved in the movement have a Jewish identity and are motivated by it—that is, that they see their participation as aimed at achieving specific Jewish goals. In the case of neoconservatives, an important line of evidence is to show their deep connections to Israel—their "passionate attachment to a nation not their own," as Patrick Buchanan terms it,[9] and especially to the Likud Party. As indicated above, I will argue that the main motivation for Jewish neoconservatives has been to further the cause of Israel; however, even if that statement is true, it does not imply that all Jews are neoconservatives. I therefore reject the sort of arguments made by Richard Perle, who responded to charges that neoconservatives were predominantly Jews by noting that Jews always tend to be disproportionately involved in intellectual undertakings, and that many Jews oppose the neoconservatives.[10] This is indeed the case, but leaves open

---

[7] Horrigan 2004.
[8] See Buchanan 2004.
[9] Buchanan 2004.
[10] See Ben Wattenberg's interview with Richard Perle (Wattenberg 2002). The entire relevant passage from the interview follows. Note Perle's odd argument that it was not in Israel's interest that the United States invade Iraq because Saddam Hussein posed a much greater threat to Israel than the United States.

> **Ben Wattenberg**: As this argument has gotten rancorous, there is also an undertone that says that these neoconservative hawks, that so many of them are Jewish. Is that valid and how do you handle that?
> **Richard Perle**: Well, a number are. I see Trent Lott there and maybe that's Newt Gingrich, I'm not sure, but by no means uniformly.
> **Ben Wattenberg**: Well, and of course the people who are executing policy, President Bush, Vice President Cheney, Don Rumsfeld, Colin Powell, Connie Rice, they are not Jewish at last report.
> **Richard Perle**: No, they're not. Well, you're going to find a dispropor-

the question of whether neoconservative Jews perceive their ideas as advancing Jewish interests and whether the movement itself is influential. An important point of the following, however, is that the broader organized Jewish community has played a critical role in the success of neoconservatism and in preventing public discussion of its Jewish roots and Jewish agendas.

Non-Jewish Participation in Neoconservatism

As with the other Jewish intellectual and political movements, non-Jews have been welcomed into the movement and often given highly visible roles as the public face of the movement. This of course lessens the perception that the movement is indeed a Jewish movement, and it makes excellent psychological sense to have the spokespersons for any movement resemble the people they are trying to convince. That's why Ahmed Chalabi (a Shiite Iraqi, a student of early neocon theorist Albert Wohlstetter, and a close personal associate of prominent neocons, including Richard Perle) was the neocons' choice to lead postwar Iraq.[11]

---

tionate number of Jews in any sort of intellectual undertaking.

Ben Wattenberg: On both sides.

Richard Perle: On both sides. Jews gravitate toward that, and I'll tell you if you balance out the hawkish Jews against the dovish ones, then we are badly outnumbered, badly outnumbered. But look, there's clearly an undertone of anti-Semitism about it. There's no doubt.

Ben Wattenberg: Well, and the linkage is that this war on Iraq if it comes about would help Israel and that that's the hidden agenda, and that's sort of the way that works.

Richard Perle: Well, sometimes there's an out and out accusation that if you take the view that I take and some others take towards Saddam Hussein, we are somehow motivated not by the best interest of the United States but by Israel's best interest. There's not a logical argument underpinning that. In fact, Israel is probably more exposed and vulnerable in the context of a war with Saddam than we are because they're right next door. Weapons that Saddam cannot today deliver against us could potentially be delivered against Israel. And for a long time the Israelis themselves were very reluctant to take on Saddam Hussein. I've argued this issue with Israelis. But it's a nasty line of argument to suggest that somehow we're confused about where our loyalties are.

Ben Wattenberg: It's the old dual loyalty argument.

[11] Chalabi's status with the neocons is in flux because of doubts about his true allegiances. See Dizard 2004.

There are many examples—including Freud's famous comments on needing a non-Jew to represent psychoanalysis (Carl Jung for a time until Jung balked at the role, and then Ernest Jones). Margaret Mead and Ruth Benedict were the most publicly recognized Boasian anthropologists, and there were a great many non-Jewish leftists and pro-immigration advocates who were promoted to visible positions in Jewish dominated movements—and sometimes resented their role.[12] Albert Lindemann describes non-Jews among the leaders of the Bolshevik revolution as "jewified non-Jews"—"a term, freed of its ugly connotations, [that] might be used to underline an often overlooked point: Even in Russia there were some non-Jews, whether Bolsheviks or not, who respected Jews, praised them abundantly, imitated them, cared about their welfare, and established intimate friendships or romantic liaisons with them."[13]

There was a smattering of non-Jews among the New York Intellectuals, who, as members of the anti-Stalinist left in the 1940s, were forerunners of the neoconservatives. Prominent examples were Dwight Macdonald (labeled by Michael Wrezin "a distinguished goy among the Partisanskies"[14]—i.e., the largely Jewish *Partisan Review* crowd), James T. Farrell, and Mary McCarthy. John Dewey also had close links to the New York Intellectuals and was lavishly promoted by them;[15] Dewey was also allied closely with his former student Sidney Hook, another major figure on the anti-Stalinist left. Dewey was a philosemite, stating: "After all, it was the Christians who made them 'it' [i.e., victims]. Living in New York where the Jews set the standard of living from department stores to apartment houses, I often think that the Jews are the finest product of historical Christianity. . . . Anyway, the finest living man, so far as I know, is a Jew—[humanitarian founder of the International Institute of Agriculture] David Lubin."[16]

This need for the involvement of non-Jews is especially acute for neoconservatism as a political movement: Because neoconservative Jews constitute a tiny percentage of the electorate, they need to make alliances with non-Jews whose perceived interests dovetail with theirs.

---

[12] *The Culture of Critique*, chs. 3 and 7; Klehr 1978, 40; Liebman 1979, 527ff; Neuringer 1980, 92; Rothman and Lichter 1982, 99; Svonkin 1997, 45, 51, 65, 71–72.
[13] Lindemann 1997, 433.
[14] Wrezin 1994.
[15] *The Culture of Critique*, ch. 7; Hollinger 1996, 158.
[16] In Hook 1987, 215.

Non-Jews have a variety of reasons for being associated with Jewish interests, including career advancement, close personal relationships or admiration for individual Jews, and deeply held personal convictions. For example, as described below, Senator Henry Jackson, whose political ambitions were intimately bound up with the neoconservatives, was a strong philosemite due partly to his experiences in childhood; his alliance with neoconservatives also stemmed from his (entirely reasonable) belief that the United States and the Soviet Union were engaged in a deadly conflict and his belief that Israel was a valuable ally in that struggle. Because neoconservatives command a large and lucrative presence in the media, thinktankdom, and political culture generally, it is hardly surprising that complex blends of opportunism and personal conviction characterize participating non-Jews.

UNIVERSITY AND MEDIA INVOLVEMENT

An important feature of the Jewish intellectual and political movements I have studied has been their association with prestigious universities and media sources. The university most closely associated with the current crop of neoconservatives is the University of Chicago, the academic home not only of Leo Strauss, but also of Albert Wohlstetter, a mathematician turned foreign policy strategist, who was mentor to Richard Perle and Paul Wolfowitz, both of whom achieved power and influence in the administration of George W. Bush. The University of Chicago was also home to Strauss disciple Allan Bloom, sociologist Edward Shils, and novelist Saul Bellow among the earlier generation of neoconservatives.

Another important academic home for the neocons has been the School of Advanced International Studies of Johns Hopkins University. Wolfowitz spent most of the Clinton years as a professor at SAIS; the Director of the Strategic Studies Program at SAIS is Eliot Cohen, who has been a signatory to a number of the Project for the New American Century's statements and letters, including the April 2002 letter to President Bush on Israel and Iraq (see the following chapter); he is also an advisor for Frank Gaffney's Center for Security Policy, an important neocon think tank. Cohen is famous for labeling the war against terrorism World War IV. His book, *Supreme Command*, argues that civilian leaders should make the important decisions and not defer to military leaders. This message was understood by Cheney and Wolfowitz as underscoring the need to prevent the military from having too much influence, as in the aftermath of the 1991 Gulf War when Colin Powell as chairman of the Joint Chiefs of Staff had been influential in opposing the removal of Saddam Hussein.[17]

Unlike other Jewish intellectual movements, the neoconservatives have been forced to deal with major opposition from within the academy, especially from Arabs and leftists in academic departments of Middle East studies. As a result, neoconservative activist groups, especially the WINEP and the MEF's Campus Watch, have monitored academic discourse and course content and organized protests against professors, and were behind congressional legislation mandating US government monitoring of programs in Middle East studies (see the following chapter).

Jewish intellectual and political movements also have typically had ready access to prestigious mainstream media outlets, and this is certainly true for the neocons. Most notable are the *Wall Street Journal, Commentary, The Public Interest,* Basic Books (book publishing), and the media empires of Conrad Black and Rupert Murdoch. Murdoch owns the Fox News Channel and the *New York Post*, and is the main source of funding for Bill Kristol's *Weekly Standard*—all major neocon outlets.

A good example illustrating these connections is Richard Perle. Perle is listed as a Resident Fellow of the AEI, and he is on the boards of directors of the *Jerusalem Post* and the Hollinger Corporation, a media company controlled by Conrad Black. Hollinger owns major media properties in the United States (*Chicago Sun Times*), England (the *Daily Telegraph*), Israel (*Jerusalem Post*), and Canada (the *National Post*; 50 percent ownership with CanWest Global Communications, which is controlled by Israel Asper and his family; CanWest has aggressively clamped down on its journalists for any deviation from its strong pro-Israel editorial policies[18]). Hollinger also owns dozens of smaller publications in the United States, Canada, and England. All of these media outlets reflect the vigorously pro-Israel stance espoused by Perle. Perle has written op-ed columns for Hollinger newspapers as well as for the *New York Times*.

Neoconservatives such as Jonah Goldberg and David Frum also have a very large influence on *National Review*, formerly a bastion of traditional conservative thought in the United States. Neocon think tanks such as the AEI have a great deal of cross-membership with Jewish activist organizations such as AIPAC, the main pro-Israel lobbying organization in Washington, and the WINEP. (When President George

---

[17] Mann 2004, 197.
[18] Canadian Journalists for Free Expression 2002.

W. Bush addressed the AEI on Iraq policy, the event was fittingly held in the Albert Wohlstetter Conference Center.) A major goal of the AEI is to promote its fellows as high profile pundits in the mainstream media. A short list would include AEI fellow Michael Ledeen, who is extreme even among the neocons in his lust for war against all Muslim countries in the Middle East. Ledeen is "resident scholar in the Freedom Chair at the AEI," writes op-ed articles for The Scripps Howard News Service and the *Wall Street Journal*, and appears on the Fox News Channel. Michael Rubin, visiting scholar at AEI, writes for the *New Republic* (controlled by staunchly pro-Israel Martin Peretz), the *New York Times*, and the *Daily Telegraph*. Reuel Marc Gerecht, a resident fellow at the AEI and director of the Middle East Initiative at PNAC, writes for the *Weekly Standard* and the *New York Times*. Another prominent AEI member is David Wurmser, who formerly headed the Middle East Studies Program at the AEI until assuming a major role in providing intelligence disinformation in the lead-up to the war in Iraq (see the following chapter). His position at the AEI was funded by Irving Moscowitz, a wealthy supporter of the settler movement in Israel and neocon activism in the United States.[19] At the AEI Wurmser wrote op-ed pieces for the *Washington Times*, the *Weekly Standard*, and the *Wall Street Journal*. His book, *Tyranny's Ally: America's Failure to Defeat Saddam Hussein*, advocated that the United States should use military force to achieve regime change in Iraq. The book was published by the AEI in 1999 with a Foreword by Richard Perle.

Prior to the invasion of Iraq, the *New York Times* was deeply involved in spreading deception about Iraqi weapons of mass destruction and ties to terrorist organizations. Judith Miller's front-page articles were based on information from Iraqi defectors well known to be untrustworthy because of their own interest in toppling Saddam.[20] Many of these sources, including the notorious Ahmed Chalabi, were also touted by the Office of Special Plans of the Department of Defense, which is associated with many of the most prominent Bush administration neocons (see the following chapter). Miller's indiscretions might be chalked up to incompetence were it not for her close connections to prominent neocon organizations, in particular Daniel Pipes's Middle East Forum (MEF), which avidly sought the war in Iraq. The MEF lists Miller as an expert speaker on Middle East issues, and she has published articles in MEF media, including the *Middle East Quarterly* and

---

[19] Bamford 2004, 281.
[20] Moore 2004.

the *MEF Wire*. The MEF also threw a launch party for her book on Islamic fundamentalism, *God Has Ninety-Nine Names*. Miller, whose father is ethnically Jewish, has a strong Jewish consciousness: Her book *One by One: Facing the Holocaust*, "tried to . . . show how each [European] country that I lived and worked in, was suppressing or distorting or politically manipulating the memory of the Holocaust."[21]

The *New York Times* has apologized for "coverage that was not as rigorous as it should have been" but has thus far refused to single out Miller's stories as worthy of special censure.[22] Indeed, the *Times*'s failure goes well beyond Miller:

> Some of the *Times*'s coverage in the months leading up to the invasion of Iraq was credulous; much of it was inappropriately italicized by lavish front-page display and heavy-breathing headlines; and several fine articles by David Johnston, James Risen, and others that provided perspective or challenged information in the faulty stories were played as quietly as a lullaby. Especially notable among these was Risen's "CIA Aides Feel Pressure in Preparing Iraqi Reports," which was completed several days before the invasion and unaccountably held for a week. It didn't appear until three days after the war's start, and even then was interred on Page B10.[23]

As is well known, the *New York Times* is Jewish-owned and has often been accused of slanting its coverage on issues of importance to Jews.[24] It is perhaps another example of the legacy of Jacob Schiff, the Jewish activist/philanthropist who backed Adolph Ochs's purchase of the *New York Times* in 1896 because he believed he "could be of great service to the Jews generally."[25]

INVOLVEMENT OF THE WIDER JEWISH COMMUNITY

Another common theme of Jewish intellectual and political movements has been the involvement and clout of the wider Jewish community. While the prominent neoconservatives represent a small fraction

---

[21] Lamb 1990.

[22] *New York Times* Editors 2002. Okrent (2004) notes that the story was effectively buried by printing it on p. A10.

[23] Okrent 2004.

[24] See examples in *The Culture of Critique*, Preface to the first paperback edition.

[25] Tifft and Jones 1999, 38.

of the American Jewish community, there is little doubt that the organized Jewish community shares their commitment to the Likud Party in Israel and, one might reasonably infer, Likud's desire to see the United States conquer and effectively control virtually all of Israel's enemies.[26] For example, representatives of all the major Jewish organizations serve on the executive committee of AIPAC, the most powerful lobby in Washington. Since the 1980s AIPAC has leaned toward Likud and only reluctantly went along with the Labor government of the 1990s.[27] In October 2002, the Conference of Presidents of Major American Jewish Organizations issued a declaration of support for disarming the Iraqi regime.[28] Jack Rosen, the president of the American Jewish Congress, noted that "the final statement ought to be crystal clear in backing the President having to take unilateral action if necessary against Iraq to eliminate weapons of mass destruction."[29]

The organized Jewish community also plays the role of credential validator, especially for non-Jews. For example, the neocon choice for the leader of Iran following regime change is Reza Pahlavi, son of the former Shah. As is the case with Ahmed Chalabi, who was promoted by the neocons as the leader of post-Saddam Iraq, Pahlavi has proven his commitment to Jewish causes and the wider Jewish community. He has addressed the board of JINSA, given a public speech at the Simon Wiesenthal Center's Museum of Tolerance in Los Angeles, and met with American Jewish communal leaders, and is on friendly terms with Likud Party officials in Israel.[30]

Most important, the main Jewish activist organizations have been quick to condemn those who have noted the Jewish commitments of the neoconservative activists in the Bush administration or seen the hand of the Jewish community in pushing for war against Iraq and other Arab countries. For example, the ADL's Abraham Foxman singled out Pat Buchanan, Joe Sobran, Rep. James Moran, Chris Matthews of MSNBC, James O. Goldsborough (a columnist for the *San Diego Union-Tribune*), columnist Robert Novak, and writer Ian Buruma as subscribers to "a canard that America's going to war has little to do with disarming Saddam, but everything to do with Jews, the 'Jewish lobby'

---

[26] Ch. 3 above, "Zionism and the Internal Dynamics of the Jewish Community"; Massing 2002.
[27] Massing 2002.
[28] Cockburn 2003.
[29] Cockburn 2003.
[30] Massing 2002.

and the hawkish Jewish members of the Bush Administration who, according to this chorus, will favor any war that benefits Israel."[31] Similarly, when Senator Ernest F. Hollings (D-SC) made a speech in the US Senate and wrote a newspaper op-ed piece which claimed the war in Iraq was motivated by "President Bush's policy to secure Israel" and advanced by a handful of Jewish officials and opinion leaders, Abe Foxman of the ADL stated, "when the debate veers into anti-Jewish stereotyping, it is tantamount to scapegoating and an appeal to ethnic hatred. . . . This is reminiscent of age-old, anti-Semitic canards about a Jewish conspiracy to control and manipulate government."[32] Despite negative comments from Jewish activist organizations, and a great deal of coverage in the American Jewish press, there were no articles on this story in any of the major US national newspapers.[33]

These mainstream media and political figures stand accused of anti-Semitism—the most deadly charge that can be imagined in the contemporary world—by the most powerful Jewish activist organization in the United States. The Simon Wiesenthal Center has also charged Buchanan and Moran with anti-Semitism for their comments on this issue.[34] While Foxman feels no need to provide any argument at all, the SWC feels it is sufficient to note that Jews have varying opinions on the war. This of course is a nonissue. The real issue is whether it is legitimate to open up to debate the question of the degree to which the neocon activists in the Bush administration are motivated by their long ties to the Likud Party in Israel and whether the organized Jewish

---

[31] Foxman 2003.

[32] Anti-Defamation League 2004. These sentiments were shortly followed by a similar assessment by the American Board of Rabbis which "drafted a resolution demanding that Senator Hollings immediately resign his position in the Senate, and further demanded that the Democratic Party condemn Hollings' blatant and overt anti-Semitism, as well" (*USA Today*, May 24, 2004); the American Board of Rabbis is an Orthodox Jewish group that regards Sharon's policies as too lenient and advocates assassination of all PLO leaders.

[33] Daily Google-News searches from May 6, 2004 to May 29, 2004. During this period, several articles on the topic appeared in the *Forward*, and there were articles in the *Baltimore Jewish Times* and the *Jewish Telegraphic Agency*. Summary articles written in the *Jerusalem Post* and *Ha'aretz* more than three weeks after the incident focused on anxiety among American Jews that Jews would be blamed for the Iraq war (Zacharia 2004; Guttman 2004). There were no articles on this topic in Hollinger-owned media in the United States.

[34] Simon Wiesenthal Center 2003.

community in the United States similarly supports the Likud Party and its desire to enmesh the United States in wars that are in Israel's interest. (There's not much doubt about how the SWC viewed the war with Iraq; Defense Secretary Rumsfeld invited Rabbi Marvin Hier, dean of the Center, to briefings on the war.)[35]

Of course, neocons in the media—most notably David Frum, Max Boot, Lawrence F. Kaplan, Jonah Goldberg, and Alan Wald[36]—have also been busy labeling their opponents "anti-Semites." An early example concerned a 1988 speech given by Russell Kirk at the Heritage Foundation in which he remarked that "not seldom it has seemed as if some eminent neoconservatives mistook Tel Aviv for the capital of United States"—what Sam Francis characterizes as "a wisecrack about the slavishly pro-Israel sympathies among neoconservatives."[37] Midge Decter, a prominent neocon writer and wife of *Commentary* editor Norman Podhoretz, labeled the comment "a bloody outrage, a piece of anti-Semitism by Kirk that impugns the loyalty of neoconservatives."[38]

Accusations of anti-Semitism have become a common response to suggestions that neoconservatives have promoted the war in Iraq for the benefit of Israel.[39] For example, Joshua Muravchik, whose ties to the neocons are elaborated below and in the following chapter, authored an apologetic article in *Commentary* aimed at denying that neoconservative foreign policy prescriptions are tailored to benefit Israel and that imputations to that effect amount to "anti-Semitism."[40] These accusations are notable for uniformly failing to honestly address the Jewish motivations and commitments of neoconservatives, the topic of a later section.

Finally, the wider Jewish community provides financial support for intellectual and political movements, as in the case of psychoanalysis, where the Jewish community signed on as patients and as consumers of psychoanalytic literature.[41] This has also been the case with neoconservatism, as noted by Gary North:

With respect to the close connection between Jews and neoconser-

---

[35] Morris 2003.
[36] Goldberg 2003; Kaplan 2003; Lind 2003; Wald 2003.
[37] Francis 2004, 9.
[38] In Francis 2004, 9.
[39] Buchanan 2003.
[40] Muravchik 2003.
[41] See *The Culture of Critique*, ch. 4.

vatism, it is worth citing [Robert] Nisbet's assessment of the revival of his academic career after 1965. His only book, *The Quest for Community* (Oxford UP, 1953), had come back into print in paperback in 1962 as *Community and Power*. He then began to write for the neoconservative journals. Immediately, there were contracts for him to write a series of books on conservatism, history, and culture, beginning with *The Sociological Tradition*, published in 1966 by Basic Books, the newly created neoconservative publishing house. Sometime in the late 1960's, he told me: "I became an in-house sociologist for the *Commentary-Public Interest* crowd. Jews buy lots of academic books in America." Some things are obvious but unstated. He could follow the money: book royalties. So could his publishers.[42]

The support of the wider Jewish community and the elaborate neoconservative infrastructure in the media and thinktankdom provide irresistible professional opportunities for Jews and non-Jews alike. I am not claiming that people like Nisbet don't believe what they write in neoconservative publications, but simply that having opinions that are attractive to neoconservatives can be very lucrative and professionally rewarding.

In the remainder of this chapter I will first trace the historical roots of neoconservatism. In the following chapter, I offer portraits of several important neoconservatives that focus on their Jewish identities and their connections to pro-Israel activism.

HISTORICAL ROOTS OF NEOCONSERVATISM: COMING TO NEOCONSERVATISM FROM THE FAR LEFT

All twentieth-century Jewish intellectual and political movements stem from the deep involvement of Jews with the left. However, beginning in the late 1920s, when the followers of Leon Trotsky broke off from the mainstream communist movement, the Jewish left has not been unified. By all accounts the major figure linking Trotsky and the neoconservative movement is Max Shachtman, a Jew born in Poland in 1904 but brought to the United States as an infant. Like other leftists during the 1920s, Shachtman was enthusiastic about the Soviet Union, writing in 1923 that it was "a brilliant red light in the darkness of capitalist gloom."[43] Shachtman began as a follower of James P. Cannon,

---

[42] North 2003.
[43] In Drucker 1994, 25.

who became converted to Trotsky's view that the Soviet Union should actively foment revolution.[44]

The Trotskyist movement had a Jewish milieu as Shachtman attracted young Jewish disciples—the familiar rabbi/disciple model of Jewish intellectual movements: "Youngsters around Shachtman made little effort to hide their New York background or intellectual skills and tastes. Years later they could still hear Shachtman's voice in one another's speeches."[45] To a much greater extent than the Communist Party, which was much larger and was committed to following the Soviet line, the Trotskyists survived as a small group centered around charismatic leaders like Shachtman, who paid homage to the famous Trotsky, who lurked in the background as an exile from the USSR living in Mexico. In the Jewish milieu of the movement, Shachtman was much admired as a speaker because of his ability in debate and in polemics. He became the quintessential rabbinical guru—the leader of a close, psychologically intense group: "He would hug them and kiss [his followers]. He would pinch both their cheeks, hard, in a habit that some felt blended sadism and affection."[46]

Trotskyists took seriously the Marxist idea that the proletarian socialist revolution should occur first in the economically advanced societies of the West rather than in backward Russia or China. They also thought that a revolution only in Russia was doomed to failure because the success of socialism in Russia depended inevitably on the world economy. The conclusion of this line of logic was that Marxists should advocate a permanent revolution that would sweep away capitalism completely rather than concentrate on building socialism in the Soviet Union.

Shachtman broke with Trotsky over defense of the Soviet Union in World War II, setting out to develop his own brand of "third camp Marxism" that followed James Burnham in stressing internal democracy and analyzing the USSR as "bureaucratic collectivism." In 1939–1941, Shachtman battled leftist intellectuals like Sidney Hook, Max Eastman, and Dwight Macdonald, who were rejecting not only Stalinism but also Trotskyism as insufficiently open and democratic; they also saw Trotsky himself as guilty of some of the worst excesses of the

---

[44] Cannon was not Jewish but lived his life in a very Jewish milieu. He was married to Rose Karsner.

[45] Drucker 1994, 43; "A younger, Jewish Trotskyist milieu began to form around him in New York" (p. 35).

[46] In Drucker 1994, 43.

early Bolshevik regime, especially his banning of opposition parties and his actions in crushing the Kronstadt sailors who had called for democracy. Shachtman defended an open, democratic version of Marxism but was concerned that his critics were abandoning socialism—throwing out the baby with the bathwater.

Hook, Eastman, Burnham, and Macdonald therefore constituted a "rightist" force within the anti-Stalinist left; it is this force that may with greater accuracy be labeled as one of the immediate intellectual ancestors of neoconservatism. By 1940, Macdonald was Shachtman's only link to the *Partisan Review* crowd of the New York Intellectuals—another predominantly Jewish group—and the link became tenuous. James Burnham also broke with Shachtman in 1940. By 1941 Burnham rejected Stalinism, fascism, and even the New Deal as bureaucratic menaces, staking out a position characterized by "juridical defense, his criticism of managerial political tendencies, and his own defense of liberty,"[47] eventually becoming a fixture at *National Review* in the decades before it became a neoconservative journal.

Shachtman himself became a Cold Warrior and social democrat in the late 1940s, attempting to build an all-inclusive left while his erstwhile Trotskyist allies in the Fourth International were bent on continuing their isolation in separate factions on the left. During this period, Shachtman saw the Stalinist takeover in Eastern Europe as a far greater threat than US power, a prelude to his support for the Bay of Pigs invasion of Cuba and the US role in Vietnam. By the 1950s he rejected revolutionary socialism and stopped calling himself a Trotskyist.[48] During the 1960s he saw the Democratic Party as the path to social democracy, while nevertheless retaining some commitment to Marxism and socialism. "Though he would insist for the rest of his life that he had found the keys to Marxism in his era, he was recutting the keys as he went along. In the early 1950s he had spoken, written, and acted as a left-wing, though no longer revolutionary, socialist. By the late 1950s he moved into the mainstream of US social democracy"[49] with a strategy of pushing big business and white Southerners out of the Democratic Party (the converse of Nixon's "Southern strategy" for the Republican Party). In the 1960s "he suggested more openly than ever before that US power could be used to promote democracy in the Third World"[50]—a view that aligns him with

---

[47] Francis 1999, 52.
[48] Drucker 1994, 219.
[49] Drucker 1994, 261.
[50] Drucker 1994, 179.

later neoconservatives.

In the 1960s, Michael Harrington, author of the influential *The Other America*, became the best known Shachtmanite, but they diverged when Harrington showed more sympathy toward the emerging multicultural, antiwar, feminist, "New Politics" influence in the Democratic Party while Shachtman remained committed to the Democrats as the party of organized labor and anti-communism.[51] Shachtman became an enemy of the New Left, which he saw as overly apologetic toward the Soviet Union. "As I watch the New Left, I simply weep. If somebody set out to take the errors and stupidities of the Old Left and multiplied them to the *n*th degree, you would have the New Left of today."[52] This was linked to disagreements with Irving Howe, editor of *Dissent*, who published a wide range of authors, including Harrington, although Shachtman followers Carl Gershman and Tom Kahn remained on the editorial board of *Dissent* until 1971–1972.

The main link between Shachtman and the political mainstream was the influence he and his followers had on the AFL-CIO. In 1972, shortly before his death, Shachtman, "as an open anti-communist and supporter of both the Vietnam War and Zionism,"[53] backed Senator Henry Jackson in the Democratic presidential primary. Jackson was a strong supporter of Israel (see below), and by this time support for Israel had become a litmus test for Shachtmanites.[54] Jackson, who was closely associated with the AFL-CIO, hired Tom Kahn, who had become a Shachtman follower in the 1950s. Kahn was executive secretary of the Shachtmanite League for Industrial Democracy, headed at the time by Tom Harrington, and he was also the head of the Department of International Affairs of the AFL-CIO, where he was an "obsessive promoter of Israel"[55] to the point that the AFL-CIO became the world's largest non-Jewish holder of Israel bonds. His department had a budget of around $40 million, most of which was provided by the federally funded National Endowment for Democracy (NED).[56] During the

---

[51] Drucker 1994, 288.

[52] In Drucker 1994, 305.

[53] Vann 2003.

[54] As with everything else, there was an evolution of the Shachtmanites' views on Zionism. The Shachtmanite journal, the *New International*, published two articles by Hal Draper (1956, 1957) that were quite critical of Israel; this journal ceased publication in 1958 when the Shachtmanites merged with the Socialist Party USA.

[55] Brenner 1997.

[56] Massing 1987.

Reagan administration, the AFL-CIO received approximately 40 percent of available funding from the NED, while no other funded group received more than 10 percent. That imbalance has prompted speculation that NED is effectively in the hands of the Social Democrats USA—Shachtman's political heir (see below)—the membership of which today includes both NED president Carl Gershman and a number of AFL-CIO officials involved with the endowment.

In 1972, under the leadership of Carl Gershman and the Shachtmanites, the Socialist Party USA changed its name to Social Democrats/USA.[57] Working with Jackson, SD/USA's members achieved little political power because of the dominance of the New Politics wing of the Democratic Party, with its strong New Left influence from the 1960s. With the election of Ronald Reagan in 1980, however, key figures from SD/USA achieved positions of power and influence both in the labor movement and in the government. Among the latter were Reagan-era appointees such as United Nations Ambassador Jeane Kirkpatrick, Assistant Secretary of State for Inter-American Affairs Elliott Abrams (son-in-law of Podhoretz and Decter), Geneva arms talks negotiator Max Kampelman (aide to Hubert Humphrey and founding member of JINSA; he remains on its advisory board), and Gershman, who was an aide to UN Ambassador Kirkpatrick and head of the NED.[58] Other Shachtmanites in the Reagan administration included Joshua Muravchik, a member of SD/USA's National Committee, who wrote articles defending Reagan's foreign policy, and Penn Kemble, an SD/USA vice-chairman, who headed Prodemca, an influential lobbying group for the Contra opponents of the leftist Sandinistas in Nicaragua. Abrams and Muravchik have continued to play an important role in neocon circles in the George W. Bush administration (see below and the following chapter).

In addition to being associated with SD/USA,[59] Kirkpatrick had strong neocon credentials. She was on the JINSA Board and was a senior fellow at the AEI. She also received several awards from Jewish organizations, including the Defender of Israel Award (New York), given to non-Jews who stand up for the Jewish people (other neocon recipients include Henry Jackson and Bayard Rustin), the Humanitarian Award of B'nai B'rith, and the 50th Anniversary Friend of Zion Award

---

[57] This led to the resignations of many and the eventual reconstruction of the Socialist Party USA with the left wing of the former organization.

[58] Sims 1992, 46ff.; Massing 1987

[59] Sims 1992, 46.

from the prime minister of Israel (1998).[60] Kirkpatrick's husband Evron was a promoter of Hubert Humphrey and long-time collaborator of neocon godfather Irving Kristol.

During the Reagan Administration, Lane Kirkland, the head of the AFL-CIO from 1979 to 1995, was also a Shachtmanite and an officer of the SD/USA. As secretary-treasurer of the AFL-CIO during the 1970s, Kirkland was a member of the Committee on the Present Danger, a group of neoconservatives in which "prominent Jackson supporters, advisers, and admirers from both sides of the aisle predominated."[61] Kirkland gave a eulogy at Henry Jackson's funeral. Kirkland was not a Jew but was married to a Jew and, like Jackson, had very close ties to Jews: "Throughout his career Kirkland maintained a special affection for the struggle of the Jews. It may be the result of his marriage to Irena [née Neumann in 1973—his second marriage], a Czech survivor of the Holocaust and an inspiring figure in her own right. Or it may be because he recognized . . . that the cause of the Jews and the cause of labor have been inseparable."[62]

Carl Gershman remains head of the NED, which supports the US-led invasion and nation-building effort in Iraq.[63] The general line of the NED is that Arab countries should "get over" the Arab-Israeli conflict and embrace democracy, Israel, and the United States. In reporting on talks with representatives of the Jewish community in Turkey, Gershman frames the issues in terms of ending anti-Semitism in Turkey by destroying Al Qaeda; there is no criticism of the role of Israel and its policies in producing hatred throughout the region.[64] During the 1980s, the NED supported nonviolent strategies to end apartheid in South Africa in association with the A. Philip Randolph Institute, headed by longtime civil rights activist and SD/USA neocon Bayard Rustin.[65] Critics of the NED, such as Rep. Ron Paul (R-Texas), have complained that the NED "is nothing more than a costly program that takes US taxpayer funds to promote favored politicians and political parties abroad."[66] Paul suggests that the NED's support of former Communists

---

[60] See Jeane J. Kirkpatrick, American Enterprise Institute biography: www.aei.org/scholars/filter.all,scholarID.32/scholar2.asp.
[61] Kaufman 2000, 296.
[62] *Forward*, August 20, 1999.
[63] Gershman 2003a.
[64] Gershman 2003b.
[65] Massing 1987.
[66] Paul 2003.

reflects Gershman's leftist background.

In general, at the present time SD/USA continues to support organized labor domestically and to take an active interest in using US power to spread democracy abroad. A resolution of January 2003 stated that the main conflict in the world was not between Islam and the West but between democratic and non-democratic governments, with Israel being the only democracy in the Middle East.[67] The SD/USA strongly supports democratic nation building in Iraq.

A prominent member of SD/USA is Joshua Muravchik. A member of the SD/USA National Advisory Council, Muravchik is also a member of the advisory board of JINSA, a resident scholar at the AEI, and an adjunct scholar at WINEP. His book *Heaven on Earth: The Rise and Fall of Socialism*[68] views socialism critically, but advocates a reformist social democracy that falls short of socialism; he views socialism as a failed religion that is relatively poor at creating wealth and is incompatible with very powerful human desires for private ownership.

Another prominent member of SD/USA is Max Kampelman, whose article, posted on the SD/USA website, makes the standard neoconservative complaints about the UN dating from the 1970s, especially regarding its treatment of Israel:

> Since 1964 . . . the UN Security Council has passed 88 resolutions against Israel—the only democracy in the area—and the General Assembly has passed more than 400 such resolutions, including one in 1975 declaring "Zionism as a form of racism." When the terrorist leader of the Palestinians, Arafat, spoke in 1974 to the General Assembly, he did so wearing a pistol on his hip and received a standing ovation. While totalitarian and repressive regimes are eligible and do serve on the UN Security Council, democratic Israel is barred by UN rules from serving in that senior body.[69]

---

[67] Social Democrats, USA 2003.

[68] Muravchik 2002.

[69] Kampelman undated. The article has the following description of Kampelman: Max M. Kampelman was counselor of the State Department; US ambassador to the Conference on Security and Cooperation in Europe; and ambassador and US negotiator with the Soviet Union on Nuclear and Space Arms. He is now chairman emeritus of Freedom House; the American Academy of Diplomacy; and the Georgetown University Institute for the Study of Diplomacy.

NEOCONSERVATISM AS A CONTINUATION OF COLD WAR LIBERALISM'S "VITAL CENTER"

The other strand that merged into neoconservatism stems from Cold War liberalism, which became dominant within the Democratic Party during the Truman administration. It remained dominant until the rise of the New Politics influence in the party during the 1960s, culminating in the presidential nomination of George McGovern in 1972.[70] In the late 1940s, a key organization was Americans for Democratic Action, associated with such figures as Reinhold Niebuhr, Hubert Humphrey, and Arthur M. Schlesinger, Jr., whose book, *The Vital Center* (1947), distilled a liberal anti-communist perspective which combined vigorous containment of communism with "the struggle within our country against oppression and stagnation."[71] This general perspective was also evident in the Congress for Cultural Freedom, whose central figure was Sidney Hook.[72] The CCF was a group of anti-communist intellectuals organized in 1950 and funded by the CIA, and included a number of prominent liberals, such as Schlesinger.

A new wrinkle, in comparison to earlier Jewish intellectual and political movements discussed in *The Culture of Critique,* has been that the central figures, Norman Podhoretz and Irving Kristol, have operated not so much as intellectual gurus in the manner of Freud or Boas or even Shachtman, but more as promoters and publicists of views that they saw as advancing Jewish interests. Podhoretz's *Commentary* (published by the American Jewish Committee) and Kristol's *The Public Interest* became clearinghouses for neoconservative ideas, but many of the articles were written by people with strong academic credentials. For example, in the area of foreign policy Robert W. Tucker and Walter Laqueur appeared in these journals as critics of liberal foreign policy.[73] Their work updated the anti-communist tradition of the "vital center" by taking account of Western weakness apparent in the New Politics liberalism of the Democratic Party and the American left, as well as the anti-Western posturing of the Third World.[74]

---

[70] Ehrman 1995.
[71] Schlesinger 1947, 256.
[72] Hook 1987, 432–60; Ehrman 1995, 47.
[73] Ehrman 1995, 50.
[74] Tucker (1999) later argued that the United States should avoid the temptations of dominion in a unipolar world. It should attempt to spread democracy by example rather than force, and should achieve broad coalitions for its foreign policy endeavors.

This "vital center" intellectual framework typified key neoconservatives at the origin of the movement in the late 1960s, including the two most pivotal figures, Irving Kristol and Norman Podhoretz. In the area of foreign policy, a primary concern of Jewish neoconservatives from the 1960s–1980s was the safety and prosperity of Israel, at a time when the Soviet Union was seen as hostile to Jews within its borders and was making alliances with Arab regimes against Israel.

> As they saw it, the world was gravely threatened by a totalitarian Soviet Union with aggressive outposts around the world and a Third World corrupted by vicious anti-Semitism. . . . A major project of Moynihan, Kirkpatrick, and other neoconservatives in and out of government was the defense of Israel. . . . By the mid-1970s, Israel was also under fire from the Soviet Union and the Third World and much of the West. The United States was the one exception, and the neoconservatives—stressing that Israel was a just, democratic state constantly threatened by vicious and aggressive neighbors—sought to deepen and strengthen this support.[75]

Irving Kristol is quite frank in his view that the United States should support Israel even if it is not in its national interest to do so:

> Large nations, whose identity is ideological, like the Soviet Union of yesteryear and the United States of today, inevitably have ideological interests in addition to more material concerns. . . . That is why we feel it necessary to defend Israel today, when its survival is threatened. No complicated geopolitical calculations of national interest are necessary.[76]

A watershed event in neoconservatism was the statement of November 1975 by UN Ambassador Daniel P. Moynihan in response to the UN resolution equating Zionism with racism. Moynihan, whose work in the UN made him a neocon icon and soon a senator from New York,[77] argued against the "discredited" notion that "there are significant biological differences among clearly identifiable groups, and that

---

[75] Gerson 1996, 161–62.
[76] Kristol 2003.
[77] See Ehrman 1995, 63–96. Moynihan was especially close to Norman Podhoretz, editor of *Commentary*, who was Moynihan's "unofficial advisor and writer" during his stint as UN ambassador (Ehrman 1995, 84).

these differences establish, in effect, different levels of humanity."[78] (In this regard Moynihan may not have been entirely candid, since he appears to have been much impressed by Arthur Jensen's research on race differences in intelligence. As an advisor to President Nixon on domestic affairs, one of Moynihan's jobs was to keep Nixon abreast of Jensen's research.[79]) In his UN speech, Moynihan ascribed the idea that Jews are a race to theorists like Houston Stewart Chamberlain, whose motivation was to find "new justifications . . . for excluding and persecuting Jews" in an era in which religious ideology was losing its power to do so. Moynihan describes Zionism as a "National Liberation Movement," but one with no genetic basis: "Zionists defined themselves merely as Jews, and declared to be Jewish anyone born of a Jewish mother or—and this is the absolutely crucial fact—anyone who converted to Judaism."[80] Moynihan describes the Zionist movement as composed of a wide range of "racial stocks" (quotation marks in original)—"black Jews, brown Jews, white Jews, Jews from the Orient and Jews from the West."

Obviously, there is much to disagree with in these ideas. Jewish racial theorists, among them Zionists like Arthur Ruppin and Vladimir Jabotinsky (the hero of the Likud Party throughout its history), were in the forefront of racial theorizing about Jews from the late nineteenth century onwards.[81] And there is a great deal of evidence that Jews, including most notably Orthodox and Conservative Jews and much of the settler movement that constitutes the vanguard of Zionism today, have been and continue to be vitally interested in maintaining their ethnic integrity.[82] (Indeed, as discussed below, Elliott Abrams has been a prominent neoconservative voice in favor of Jews marrying Jews and retaining their ethnic cohesion.)

Nevertheless, Moynihan's speech is revealing in its depiction of the Jewish community as unconcerned about its ethnic cohesion, and for its denial of the biological reality of race. In general, neoconservatives have been staunch promoters of the racial zeitgeist of post-World War II liberal America. Indeed, as typical Cold War liberals up to the end of the 1960s, many of the older neocons were in the forefront of the racial revolution in the United States. It is also noteworthy that Moynihan's

---

[78] Moynihan 1975/1996.
[79] Miele 2002, 36–38.
[80] Moynihan 1975/1996, 96.
[81] *Separation and Its Discontents*, ch. 5.
[82] *Separation and Its Discontents*, ch. 5.

UN speech is typical of the large apologetic literature by Jewish activists and intellectuals in response to the "Zionism is racism" resolution, of which *The Myth of the Jewish Race* by Raphael Patai and Jennifer Patai is perhaps the best-known example.[83]

The flagship neoconservative magazine *Commentary*, under the editorship of Norman Podhoretz, has published many articles defending Israel. Ruth Wisse's 1981 *Commentary* article "The Delegitimation of Israel" is described by Mark Gerson as "perhaps the best expression" of the neoconservative view that Israel "was a just, democratic state constantly threatened by vicious and aggressive neighbors."[84] Wisse views hostility toward Israel as another example of the long history of anti-Jewish rhetoric that seeks to delegitimize Judaism.[85] This tradition is said to have begun with the Christian beliefs that Jews ought to be relegated to an inferior position because they had rejected Christ. This tradition culminated in twentieth century Europe in hatred directed at secular Jews because of their failure to assimilate completely to European culture. The result was the Holocaust, which was "from the standpoint of its perpetrators and collaborators successful beyond belief."[86] Israel, then, is an attempt at normalization in which Jews would be just another country fending for itself and seeking stability; it "should [also] have been the end of anti-Semitism, and the Jews may in any case be pardoned for feeling that they had earned a moment of rest in history."[87] But the Arab countries never accepted the legitimacy of Israel, not only with their wars against the Jewish state, but also by the "Zionism as racism" UN resolution, which "institutionalized anti-Semitism in international politics."[88] Wisse criticizes *New York Times* columnist Anthony Lewis for criticizing Israeli policies while failing to similarly criticize Arab states that fail to embody Western ideals of freedom of expression and respect for minority rights. Wisse also faults certain American Jewish organizations and liberal Jews for criticizing the policies of the government of Menachem Begin.[89]

---

[83] Patai and Patai 1989. See *Separation and Its Discontents*, ch. 7.
[84] Gerson 1996, 162.
[85] Wisse 1981/1996.
[86] Wisse 1981/1996, 192.
[87] Wisse 1981/1996, 193.
[88] Wisse 1981/1996, 193.
[89] Wisse singles out Arthur Hertzberg as an example of an American Jew critical of Begin's government. Hertzberg continues to be a critic of Israeli policies, especially of the settlement movement. In a *New York Times* op-ed piece "The Price of not Keeping Peace" of August 27, 2003, Hertzberg urges

The article stands out for its cartoonish view that the behavior and attitudes of Jews are completely irrelevant for understanding the history of anti-Semitism. The message of the article is that Jews as innocent victims of the irrational hatred of Europeans have a claim for "a respite" from history that Arabs are bound to honor by allowing the dispossession of the Palestinians. The article is also a testimony to the sea change among American Jews in their support for the Likud Party and its expansionist policies in Israel. Since Wisse's article appeared in 1981, the positive attitudes toward the Likud Party characteristic of the neoconservatives have become the mainstream view of the organized American Jewish community, and the liberal Jewish critics attacked by Wisse have been relegated to the fringe of the American Jewish community.[90]

In the area of domestic policy, Jewish neoconservatives were motivated by concerns that the radicalism of the New Left (many of whom were Jews) compromised Jewish interests as a highly intelligent, upwardly mobile group. Although Jews were major allies of blacks in the civil rights movement, by the late 1960s many Jews bitterly opposed black efforts at community control of schools in New York, because they threatened Jewish hegemony in the educational system, including the teachers' union.[91] Black-Jewish interests also diverged when affirmative action and quotas for black college admission became a divisive issue in the 1970s.[92] It was not only neoconservatives who worried about affirmative action: The main Jewish activist groups—the AJCommittee, the AJCongress, and the ADL—sided with Allan Bakke in a landmark case on racial quota systems in the University of California-Davis medical school, thereby promoting meritocracy, which serves the interests of highly intelligent, upwardly-mobile minorities.[93]

---

the United States to cease funding the expansion of Jewish settlements while also preventing the Palestinians' access to foreign funds used for violence against Israel: "The United States must act now to disarm each side of the nasty things that they can do to each other. We must end the threat of the settlements to a Palestinian state of the future. The Palestinian militants must be forced to stop threatening the lives of Israelis, wherever they may be. A grand settlement is not in sight, but the United States can lead both parties to a more livable, untidy accommodation."

[90] See ch. 3 above on "Zionism and the Internal Dynamics of the Jewish Community."

[91] See Friedman 1995, 257ff.

[92] Friedman 1995, 72.

[93] See ch. 6 below on "Jews, Blacks, and Race." In recent years mainstream Jewish groups such as the AJCommittee have supported some forms of

Indeed, some neoconservatives, despite their record of youthful radicalism and support for the civil rights movement, began to see Jewish interests as bound up with those of the middle class. As Nathan Glazer noted in 1969, commenting on black anti-Semitism and the murderous urges of the New Left toward the middle class:

> Anti-Semitism is only part of this whole syndrome, for if the members of the middle class do not deserve to hold on to their property, their positions, or even their lives, then certainly the Jews, the most middle-class of all, are going to be placed at the head of the column marked for liquidation.[94]

The New Left also tended to have negative attitudes toward Israel, with the result that many Jewish radicals eventually abandoned the left. In the late 1960s, the black Student Non-Violent Coordinating Committee described Zionism as "racist colonialism"[95] which massacred and oppressed Arabs. In Jewish eyes, a great many black leaders, including Stokely Carmichael (Kwame Touré), Jesse Jackson, Louis Farrakhan, and Andrew Young, were seen as entirely too pro-Palestinian. (Young lost his position as UN ambassador because he engaged in secret negotiations with the Palestinians.) During the 1960s, expressions of solidarity with the Palestinians by radical blacks, some of whom had adopted Islam, became a focus of neoconservative ire and resulted in many Jewish New Leftists leaving the movement.[96] Besides radical blacks, other New Left figures, such as I. F. Stone and Noam Chomsky (both Jews), also criticized Israel and were perceived by neocons as taking a pro-Soviet line.[97] The origins of neoconservatism as a Jewish movement are thus linked to the fact that the left, including the Soviet Union and leftist radicals in the United States, had become anti-Zionist.

In 1970 Podhoretz transformed *Commentary* into a weapon against the New Left.[98] In December of that year *National Review* began, warily at first, to welcome neocons into the conservative tent, stating in 1971, "We will be delighted when the new realism manifested in these articles is applied by *Commentary* to the full range of national and in-

---

affirmative action, as in the 2003 University of Michigan case.
[94] Glazer 1969, 36.
[95] Friedman 1995, 230.
[96] Liebman 1979, 561; *The Culture of Critique*, ch. 3.
[97] Ehrman 1995, 38.
[98] Ehrman 1995, 43.

ternational issues."⁹⁹ Irving Kristol supported Nixon in 1972 and became a Republican about ten years before most neocons made the switch. Nevertheless, even in the 1990s the neocons "continued to be distinct from traditional Midwestern and Southern conservatives for their Northeastern roots, combative style, and secularism"[100]—all ways of saying that neoconservatism retained its fundamentally Jewish character.

The fault lines between neoconservatives and paleoconservatives were apparent during the Reagan administration in the battle over the appointment of the head of the National Endowment for the Humanities, eventually won by the neoconservative Bill Bennett. The campaign featured smear tactics and innuendo aimed at M. E. Bradford, an academic literary critic and defender of Southern agrarian culture who was favored by traditional conservatives. After neocons accused him of being a "virulent racist" and an admirer of Hitler, Bradford was eventually rejected as a potential liability to the administration.[101]

The entry of the neoconservatives into the conservative mainstream did not, therefore, proceed without a struggle. Samuel Francis witnessed much of the early infighting among conservatives, won eventually by the neocons. Francis recounts the "catalog of neoconservative efforts not merely to debate, criticize, and refute the ideas of traditional conservatism but to denounce, vilify, and harm the careers of those Old Right figures and institutions they have targeted."[102]

> There are countless stories of how neoconservatives have succeeded in entering conservative institutions, forcing out or demoting traditional conservatives, and changing the positions and philosophy of such institutions in neoconservative directions. . . . Writers like M. E. Bradford, Joseph Sobran, Pat Buchanan, and Russell Kirk, and institutions like *Chronicles*, the Rockford Institute, the Philadelphia Society, and the Intercollegiate Studies Institute have been among the most respected and distinguished names in American conservatism. The dedication of their neoconservative enemies to driving them out of the movement they have taken over and demonizing them as marginal and dangerous figures has no legitimate basis in reality. It is clear evidence of the ulterior aspirations of those behind neoconserva-

---

[99] Ehrman 1995, 46.
[100] Ehrman 1995, 174.
[101] Francis 2004, 7.
[102] Francis 2004, 9.

tism to dominate and subvert American conservatism from its original purposes and agenda and turn it to other purposes. . . . What neoconservatives really dislike about their "allies" among traditional conservatives is simply the fact that the conservatives are conservatives at all—that they support "this notion of a Christian civilization," as Midge Decter put it, that they oppose mass immigration, that they criticize Martin Luther King and reject the racial dispossession of white Western culture, that they support or approve of Joe McCarthy, that they entertain doubts or strong disagreement over American foreign policy in the Middle East, that they oppose reckless involvement in foreign wars and foreign entanglements, and that, in company with the Founding Fathers of the United States, they reject the concept of a pure democracy and the belief that the United States is or should evolve toward it.[103]

Most notably, neoconservatives have been staunch supporters of arguably the most destructive force associated with the left in the twentieth century—massive non-European immigration. Support for massive non-European immigration has spanned the Jewish political spectrum throughout the twentieth century to the present. A principal motivation of the organized Jewish community for encouraging such immigration has involved a deeply felt animosity toward the people and culture responsible for the immigration restriction of 1924–1965—"this notion of a Christian civilization."[104] As neoconservative Ben Wattenberg has famously written, "The non-Europeanization of America is heartening news of an almost transcendental quality."[105] The only exception—thus far without any influence—is that since 9/11 some Jewish activists, including neoconservative Daniel Pipes, head of the MEF, and Stephen Steinlight, senior fellow of the American Jewish Committee, have opposed Muslim—and only Muslim—immigration because of possible effects on pro-Israel sentiment in the United States.[106]

In general, neoconservatives have been far more attached to Jewish interests, and especially the interests of Israel, than to any other identifiable interest. It is revealing that as the war in Iraq has become an expensive quagmire in both lives and money, Bill Kristol has become

---

[103] Francis 2004, 11–12.

[104] *The Culture of Critique*, Preface to the paperback edition and ch. 7.

[105] Wattenberg 1984, 84.

[106] Pipes 2001; see also Pipes' website (www.meforum.org); Steinlight 2001, 2004.

willing to abandon the neoconservatives' alliance with traditional conservatives by allying with John Kerry and the Democratic Party. This is because Kerry has promised to increase troop strength and retain the commitment to Iraq, and because Kerry has declared that he has "a 100 percent record—not a 99, a 100 percent record—of sustaining the special relationship and friendship that we have with Israel."[107] As Pat Buchanan notes, the fact that John Kerry "backs partial birth abortion, quotas, raising taxes, homosexual unions, liberals on the Supreme Court and has a voting record to the left of Teddy Kennedy" is less important than his stand on the fundamental issue of a foreign policy that is in the interest of Israel.[108]

THE FALL OF HENRY JACKSON AND THE RISE OF NEOCONSERVATISM IN THE REPUBLICAN PARTY

The neoconservative takeover of the Republican Party and of American conservatism in general would have been unnecessary had not the Democratic Party shifted markedly to the left in the late 1960s. Henry Jackson is the pivotal figure in the defection of the neocons from the Democratic Party to the Republican Party—the person whose political fortunes most determined the later trajectory of neoconservatism. Jackson embodied the political attitudes and ambitions of a Jewish political network that saw Jewish interests as combining traditionally liberal social policies of the civil rights and Great Society era (but stopping short of advocating quota-type affirmative action policies or minority ethnic nationalism) with a Cold War posture that was at once aggressively pro-Israel and anti-communist at a time when the Soviet Union was perceived as the most powerful enemy of Israel. This "Cold War liberal" faction was dominant in the Democratic Party until 1972 and the nomination of George McGovern. After the defeat of McGovern, the neoconservatives founded the Committee for a Democratic Majority, whose attempt to resuscitate the Cold War coalition of the Democratic Party had a strong representation of Shachtmanite labor leaders as well as people centered around Podhoretz's *Commentary*: Podhoretz; Ben Wattenberg (who wrote speeches for Hubert Humphrey and was an aide to Jackson); Midge Decter; Max Kampelman; Penn Kemble of the SD/USA; Jeane Kirkpatrick (who began writing for *Commentary* during this period); sociologists Daniel Bell, Nathan Glazer, and Seymour Martin Lipset; Michael Novak; Soviet expert

---

[107] In Buchanan 2004.
[108] In Buchanan 2004.

Richard Pipes; and Albert Shanker, president of the American Federation of Teachers. Nevertheless, "by the end of 1974, the neoconservatives appeared to have reached a political dead end. As guardians of vital center liberalism, they had become a minority faction within the Democratic Party, unable to do more than protest the party's leftward drift."[109]

The basic story line is that after failing again in 1976 and 1980 to gain the presidential nomination for a candidate who represented their views, this largely Jewish segment of political activists—now known as neoconservatives—switched allegiance to the Republican Party. The neocons had considerable influence in the Reagan years but less in the George H. W. Bush administration, only to become a critically important force in the foreign policy of the George W. Bush administration where, in the absence of a threat from the Soviet Union, neoconservatives have attempted to use the power of the United States to fundamentally alter the political landscape of the Middle East.

Henry Jackson was an ideal vehicle for this role as champion of Jewish interests. He was a very conscious philosemite: "My mother was a Christian who believed in a strong Judaism. She taught me to respect the Jews, help the Jews! It was a lesson I never forgot."[110] Jackson also had very positive personal experiences with Jews during his youth. During his college years he was the beneficiary of generosity from a Jew who allowed him to use a car to commute to college, and he developed lifelong friendships with two Jews, Stan Golub and Paul Friedlander. He was also horrified after seeing Buchenwald, the World War II German concentration camp, an experience that made him more determined to help Israel and Jews.

Entering Congress in 1940, Jackson was a strong supporter of Israel from its beginnings in 1948. By the 1970s he was widely viewed as Israel's best friend in Congress: "Jackson's devotion to Israel made Nixon and Kissinger's look tepid."[111] The Jackson-Vanik Amendment linking US-Soviet trade to the ability of Jews to emigrate from the Soviet Union was passed over strenuous opposition from the Nixon administration. And despite developing a reputation as the "Senator from Boeing," Jackson opposed the sale of Boeing-made AWACS surveillance aircraft to Saudi Arabia because of the possibility that they might harm the interests of Israel.

---

[109] Ehrman 1995, 62.
[110] In Kaufman 2000, 13.
[111] Kaufman 2000, 263.

Jackson's experience of the Depression made him a liberal, deeply empathetic toward the suffering that was so common during the period. He defined himself as "vigilantly internationalist and anti-communist abroad but statist at home, committed to realizing the New Deal-Fair Deal vision of a strong, active federal government presiding over the economy, preserving and enhancing welfare protection, and extending civil rights."[112] These attitudes of Jackson, and particularly his attitudes on foreign policy, brought him into the orbit of Jewish neoconservatives who held similar attitudes on domestic issues and whose attitudes on foreign policy stemmed fundamentally from their devotion to the cause of Israel:

> Jackson's visceral anti-communism and anti-totalitarianism . . . brought him into the orbit of Jewish neoconservatives despite the subtle but important distinction in their outlook. The senator viewed the threat to Israel as a manifestation of the totalitarian threat he considered paramount. Some neoconservatives viewed Soviet totalitarianism as the threat to Israel they considered paramount.[113]

Jackson had developed close ties with a number of neocons who would later become important. Richard Perle was Jackson's most important national security advisor between 1969 and 1979, and Jackson maintained close relations with Paul Wolfowitz, who began his career in Washington working with Perle in Jackson's office. Jackson employed Perle even after credible evidence surfaced that he had spied for Israel: An FBI wiretap on the Israeli Embassy revealed Perle discussing classified information that had been supplied to him by someone on the National Security Council staff, presumably Helmut ("Hal") Sonnenfeldt. (Sonnenfeldt, who was Jewish, "was known from previous wiretaps to have close ties to the Israelis as well as to Perle. . . . [He] had been repeatedly investigated by the FBI for other suspected leaks early in his career."[114]) As indicated below, several prominent neocons have been investigated on credible charges of spying for Israel: Perle, Wolfowitz, Stephen Bryen, Douglas Feith, and Michael Ledeen. Neocon Frank Gaffney, the non-Jewish president of the CSP, a neocon think tank, was also a Jackson aide. Jackson was also close to Bernard

---

[112] Kaufman 2000, 47.

[113] Kaufman 2000, 295. Kaufman footnotes the last assertion with a reference to an interview with Daniel Patrick Moynihan, July 28, 1996.

[114] Hersh 1982.

Lewis of Princeton University; Lewis is a Jewish expert on the Middle East who has had an important influence on the neocons in the George W. Bush administration as well as close ties to Israel (see the following chapter).[115]

In the 1970s Jackson was involved with two of the most important neocon groups of the period. In 1976 he convened Team B, headed by Richard Pipes (a Harvard University Soviet expert), and including Paul Nitze, Wolfowitz, and Seymour Weiss (former director of the State Department's Bureau of Political-Military Affairs). Albert Wohlstetter, who was Wolfowitz's Ph.D. advisor at the University of Chicago, was a major catalyst for Team B. Jackson was also close to the Committee on the Present Danger. Formed in November 1976, the committee was a Who's Who of Jackson supporters, advisors, confidants, and admirers from both the Democratic and Republican parties, and included several members associated with the SD/USA: Paul Nitze, Eugene Rostow, Jeane Kirkpatrick, Admiral Elmo Zumwalt, Max Kampelman, Lane Kirkland, Richard Pipes, Seymour Martin Lipset, Bayard Rustin, and Norman Podhoretz. CPD was a sort of halfway house for Democratic neocons sliding toward the Republican Party.

The result was that all the important neocons backed Jackson for president in 1972 and 1976. Jackson commanded a great deal of financial support from the Jewish community in Hollywood and elsewhere because of his strong support for Israel, but he failed to win the 1976 Democratic nomination, despite having more money than his rivals. After Jackson's defeat and the ascendance of the leftist tendencies of the Carter administration, many of Jackson's allies went to work for Reagan with Jackson's tacit approval, with the result that they were frozen out of the Democratic Party once Carter was defeated.[116] A large part of the disillusionment of Jackson and his followers stemmed from the Carter administration's attitude toward Israel. Carter alienated American Jews by his proposals for a more evenhanded policy toward Israel, in which Israel would return to its 1967 borders in exchange for peace with the Arabs. Jews were also concerned because of the Andrew Young incident. (Young, the US Ambassador to the UN and an African American, had been fired after failing to disclose to the State Department details of his unauthorized meeting with representatives of the Palestinians. Blacks charged that Jews were responsible for Young's firing.)

---

[115] Kaufman 2000, 172; Waldman 2004.
[116] Z. Brzezinski, in Kaufman 2000, 351.

In October 1977 the Carter administration, in a joint communiqué with the Soviet Union, suggested Israel pull back to the 1967 borders:

> Jackson joined the ferocious attack on the administration that ensued from devotees of Kissinger's incremental approach and from Israel's supporters in the United States. He continued to regard unswerving US support for Israel as not only a moral but a strategic imperative, and to insist that the maintenance of a strong, secure, militarily powerful Israel impeded rather than facilitated Soviet penetration of the Middle East.[117]

Jackson was particularly fond of pointing to maps of Israel showing how narrow Israel's borders had been before its 1967 conquests. For his part, Carter threatened to ask the American people "to choose between those who supported the national interest and those who supported a foreign interest such as Israel."[118]

There was one last attempt to mend the fences between the neocons and the Democrats, a 1980 White House meeting between Carter and major neocons, including Jeane Kirkpatrick, Norman Podhoretz, Midge Decter, Ben Wattenberg, Elliott Abrams (aide to neocon favorite Patrick Moynihan[119]), Max Kampelman, and Penn Kemble. The meeting, which discussed attitudes toward the USSR, did not go well, and "henceforth, their disdain for Carter and dislike of Kennedy would impel the neoconservatives to turn away from the Democratic Party and vote for Reagan."[120] "They had hoped to find a new Truman to rally around, a Democrat to promote their liberal ideas at home while fighting the cold war abroad. Not finding one, they embraced the Republican party and Ronald Reagan as the best alternative."[121]

Perle left Jackson's office in March 1980 to go into business with John F. Lehman (Secretary of the Navy during the Reagan administra-

---

[117] Kaufman 2000, 374. Despite his strong support for Israel, Jackson drew the line at support for the Likud Party, which came into power in 1977 with the election of Menachem Begin. Whereas the Likud policy has been to seize as much of the West Bank as possible and relegate the Palestinians to isolated, impotent Bantustan-like enclaves, Jackson favored full sovereignty for the Palestinians on the West Bank, except for national security and foreign policy.
[118] Kaufman 2000, 375.
[119] Moynihan was expelled from the movement in 1984 because he softened his foreign policy line (Ehrman 1995, 170).
[120] Kaufman 2000, 308.
[121] Ehrman 1995, 95.

tion and, as of 2004, a member of the panel investigating the events of 9/11). Quite a few neocons assumed positions in the Reagan administration in the area of defense and foreign policy: Kirkpatrick as UN ambassador (Kirkpatrick hired Joshua Muravchik, Kenneth Adelman, and Carl Gershman as deputies); Perle as Assistant Secretary of Defense for International Security Policy (Perle hired Frank Gaffney and Douglas Feith); Elliott Abrams as Assistant Secretary of State for Human Rights Affairs; Max Kampelman as US ambassador to the Helsinki human rights conference and later as chief US arms negotiator; Wolfowitz as Assistant Secretary of State for East Asian affairs. Another Jewish neocon, Richard Pipes, was influential in putting together a paper on grand strategy toward the USSR. Nevertheless, Reagan kept the neocons at arm's length and ceased heeding their advice. He favored developing trust and confidence with Soviet leaders rather than escalating tensions by threats of aggressive action.[122]

Bill Clinton courted neocons who had defected to Reagan. Perle, Kirkpatrick, and Abrams remained Republicans, but thirty-three "moderate and neoconservative foreign policy experts" endorsed Clinton in 1992, including Nitze, Kemble, and Muravchik, although Muravchik and several others later repudiated their endorsement, saying that Clinton had returned to the left liberal foreign policy of the Democrats since McGovern.[123] Ben Wattenberg and Robert Strauss remained Democrats "who have not written off the Jackson tradition in their own party."[124] Senator Joseph Lieberman, the Democrats' 2000 vice presidential nominee, is the heir to this tradition.

RESPONDING TO THE FALL OF THE SOVIET UNION

With the end of the Cold War, neoconservatives at first advocated a reduced role for the United States, but this stance switched gradually to the view that US interests required the vigorous promotion of democracy in the rest of the world.[125] This aggressively pro-democracy theme, which appears first in the writings of Charles Krauthammer and then those of Elliot Abrams, eventually became an incessant drumbeat in the

---

[122] Diggins 2004.
[123] Kaufman 2000, 446.
[124] Kaufman 2000, 446.
[125] It's interesting that *Commentary* continued to write of a Soviet threat even after the fall of the Soviet Union, presumably because they feared a unipolar world in which Israel could not be portrayed as a vital ally of the United States (Ehrman 1995, 175–76).

campaign for the war in Iraq.[126] Krauthammer also broached the now familiar themes of unilateral intervention, and he emphasized the danger that smaller states could develop weapons of mass destruction which could be used to threaten world security.[127]

A cynic would argue that this newfound interest in democracy was tailor-made as a program for advancing the interests of Israel. After all, Israel is advertised as the only democracy in the Middle East, and democracy has a certain emotional appeal for the United States, which has at times engaged in an idealistic foreign policy aimed at furthering the cause of human rights in other countries. It is ironic that during the Cold War the standard neocon criticism of President Carter's foreign policy was that it was overly sensitive to human rights in countries that were opposed to the Soviet Union and insufficiently condemnatory of the human rights policies of the Soviet Union. The classic expression of this view was Jeane Kirkpatrick's 1979 *Commentary* article, "Dictatorships and Double Standards." In an essay that would have been excellent reading prior to the invasion of Iraq, Kirkpatrick noted that in many countries political power is tied to complex family and kinship networks resistant to modernization. Nevertheless, "no idea holds greater sway in the mind of educated Americans than the belief that it is possible to democratize governments, anytime, anywhere, under any circumstances."[128] Democracies are said to make heavy demands on citizens in terms of participation and restraint, and developing democracies is the work of "decades, if not centuries."[129] My view is that democracy is a component of the uniquely Western suite of traits deriving from the evolution of Western peoples and their cultural history: monogamy, simple family structure, individual rights against the state, representative government, moral universalism, and science.[130] This social structure cannot easily be exported to other societies, and particularly to Middle Eastern societies whose traditional cultures exhibit traits opposite to these.

It is revealing that, while neocons generally lost interest in Africa, Latin America, and Eastern Europe after these areas were no longer points of contention in the Cold War, there was no lessening of interest in the Middle East.[131] Indeed, neoconservatives and Jews in general

---

[126] Ehrman 1995, 181.
[127] Ehrman 1995, 182.
[128] Kirkpatrick 1979/1996.
[129] Kirkpatrick 1979/1996.
[130] See ch. 9 below, "What Makes Western Culture Unique?"
[131] Ehrman 1995, 192.

failed to support President George H. W. Bush when, in the aftermath of the 1991 Gulf War, his administration pressured Israel to make concessions to the Palestinians and resisted a proposal for $10 billion in loan guarantees for Israel. This occurred in the context of Secretary of State James A. Baker's famous comment, "Fuck the Jews. They didn't vote for us."[132]

CONCLUSION

The rapid rise and immense influence of the neoconservatives make them a remarkable example of Jewish organization and influence. Individuals with strong Jewish identities maintain close ties to Israeli politicians and military figures and to Jewish activist organizations and pro-Israeli lobbying groups while occupying influential policy-making positions in the defense and foreign policy establishment. These same individuals, as well as a chorus of other prominent Jews, have routine access to the most prestigious media outlets in the United States. People who criticize Israel, however, are routinely vilified and subjected to professional and personal abuse.[133]

Perhaps the most telling feature of this entire state of affairs is the surreal fact that in this entire discourse Jewish identity is not mentioned. When Charles Krauthammer, Bill Kristol, Michael Rubin, William Safire, Robert Satloff, or the legions of other prominent media figures write their reflexively pro-Israel pieces in the *New York Times,* the *Wall Street Journal,* or the *Los Angeles Times*, or opine on the Fox News Network, there is never any mention that they are Jewish Americans who have an intense ethnic interest in Israel. When Richard Perle authors a report for an Israeli think tank; is on the board of directors of an Israeli newspaper; maintains close personal ties with prominent Israelis, especially those associated with the Likud Party; has worked for an Israeli defense company; and, according to credible reports, was discovered by the FBI passing classified information to Israel—when, despite all of this, he is a central figure in the network of those pushing for wars to rearrange the entire politics of the Middle East in Israel's favor, and with nary a soul having the courage to mention the obvious overriding Jewish loyalty apparent in Perle's actions, that is indeed a breathtaking display of power.

Above and in the following chapter, I provide a small glimpse of the incredible array of Jewish pro-Israel activist organizations, their fund-

---

[132] Ehrman 1995, 197.

[133] Findley 1989; ch. 1 above, "Background Traits for Jewish Activism."

ing, their access to the media, and their power over the political process. Taken as a whole, neoconservatism is an excellent illustration of the key traits behind the success of Jewish activism: ethnocentrism, intelligence and wealth, psychological intensity, and aggressiveness.[134] Now imagine a similar level of organization, commitment, and funding directed toward changing the US immigration system put into law in 1924 and 1952, or inaugurating the revolution in civil rights, or the post-1965 countercultural revolution: In the case of the immigration laws we see the same use of prominent non-Jews to attain Jewish goals, the same access to the major media, and the same ability to have a decisive influence on the political process by establishing lobbying organizations, recruiting non-Jews as important players, funneling financial and media support to political candidates who agree with their point of view, and providing effective leadership in government.[135] Given this state of affairs, one can easily see how Jews, despite being a tiny minority of the US population, have been able to transform the country to serve their interests. It's a story that has been played out many times in Western history, but the possible effects now seem enormous, not only for Europeans but literally for everyone on the planet, as Israel and its hegemonic ally restructure the politics of the world.

History also suggests that anti-Jewish reactions develop as Jews increase their control over other peoples.[136] As always, it will be fascinating to observe the dénouement.[137]

---

[134] See ch. 1 above on "Background Traits for Jewish Activism."
[135] *The Culture of Critique*, ch. 7.
[136] *Separation and Its Discontents*, ch. 2, esp. 58–60.
[137] I thank the late Sam Francis for his very helpful comments on this paper. Thanks also to Ted O'Keefe for his editorial work on an earlier version of this paper.

Chapter 5

NEOCONSERVATIVE PORTRAITS[*]

Like members of other Jewish intellectual movements, neoconservatives have a history of mutual admiration, close, mutually supportive personal, professional, and familial relationships, and focused cooperation in pursuit of common goals. For example, Norman Podhoretz, the former editor of *Commentary*, is the father of John Podhoretz, a neoconservative editor and columnist. Norman Podhoretz is also the father-in-law of Elliott Abrams, the former head of the Ethics and Public Policy Center (a neoconservative think tank) and the director of Near Eastern affairs at the National Security Council. Norman's wife, Midge Decter, published a hagiographic biography of Secretary of Defense Donald Rumsfeld, whose number-two and number-three deputies at the Pentagon were, respectively, Wolfowitz and Feith. Perle is a fellow at the American Enterprise Institute.[1] He originally helped Wolfowitz obtain a job with the Arms Control and Disarmament Agency in 1973. In 1982, Perle, as Deputy Secretary of Defense for International Security Policy, hired Feith for a position as his Special Counsel, and then as Deputy Assistant Secretary for Negotiations Policy. In 2001, Deputy Secretary of Defense Wolfowitz helped Feith obtain an appointment as Undersecretary for Policy. Feith then appointed Perle as chairman of the Defense Policy Board. This is only the tip of a very large iceberg.

LEO STRAUSS
Leo Strauss is an important influence on several important neoconservatives, particularly Irving and William Kristol. Strauss was a classicist and political philosopher at the University of Chicago. He had a very strong Jewish identity and viewed his philosophy as a means of ensuring Jewish survival in the Diaspora.[2] As Strauss himself noted, "I believe I can say, without any exaggeration, that since a very, very early time the main theme of my reflections has been what is called the

---

[*] First published (as part of a longer version of ch. 4 above) in *The Occidental Quarterly* 4 (Summer 2004): 7–74. Reprinted in Kevin MacDonald, *Understanding Jewish Influence: A Study in Ethnic Activism* (Augusta, Ga.: Washington Summit Publishers, 2004).

[1] Lobe 2003a.
[2] Strauss 1962/1994.

'Jewish Question.'"[3]

Much of Strauss's early writing was on Jewish issues, and a constant theme in his writing was the idea that Western civilization was the product of the "energizing tension" between Athens and Jerusalem—Greek rationalism and the Jewish emphasis on faith, revelation, and religious intensity.[4] Although Strauss believed that religion had effects on non-Jews that benefited Jews, there is little doubt that Strauss viewed religious fervor as an indispensable element of Jewish commitment and group loyalty—ethnocentrism by any other name:

> Some great love and loyalty to the Jewish people are in evidence in the life and works of Strauss. . . . Strauss *was* a good Jew. He knew the dignity and worth of love of one's own. Love of the good, which is the same as love of the truth, is higher than love of one's own, but there is only one road to the truth, and it leads through love of one's own. Strauss showed his loyalty to things Jewish in a way he was uniquely qualified to do, by showing generations of students how to treat Jewish texts with the utmost care and devotion. In this way he turned a number of his Jewish students in the direction of becoming better Jews.[5]

Strauss believed that liberal, individualistic modern Western societies were best for Jews because the illiberal alternatives of both the left (communism) and right (National Socialism) were anti-Jewish. (By the 1950s, anti-Semitism had become an important force in the Soviet Union.) However, Strauss believed that liberal societies were not ideal because they tended to break down group loyalties and group distinctiveness—both qualities essential to the survival of the Jewish community. And he thought that there is a danger that, like the Weimar Republic, liberal societies could give way to fascism, especially if traditional religious and cultural forms were overturned; hence the neoconservative attitude that traditional religious forms among non-Jews are good for Jews.[6] (While

---

[3] Strauss 1962/1994.

[4] Dannhauser 1996, 160.

[5] Dannhauser 1996, 169–70; italics in text. Dannhauser concludes the passage by noting, "I know for I am one of them." Dannhauser poses the Athens/Jerusalem dichotomy as a choice between "the flatland of modern science, especially social science, and the fanaticism in the *Mea Shaarim* section of Jerusalem (incidentally, I would prefer the latter)" (p. 160).

[6] Strauss 1962/1994; Tarcov and Pangle 1987; Holmes 1993, 61–87.

Strauss believed in the importance of Israel for Jewish survival, his philosophy is not a defense of Israel but a blueprint for Jewish survival in a Diaspora in Western societies.)

The fate of the Weimar Republic, combined with the emergence of anti-Semitism in the Soviet Union, had a formative influence on his thinking. As Stephen Holmes writes, "Strauss made his young Jewish-American students gulp by informing them that toleration [secular humanism] was dangerous and that the Enlightenment—rather than the failure of the Enlightenment—led directly to Adolf Hitler."[7] Hitler was also at the center of Strauss's admiration for Churchill—hence the roots of the neocon cult of Churchill: "The tyrant stood at the pinnacle of his power. The contrast between the indomitable and magnanimous statesman and the insane tyrant—this spectacle in its clear simplicity was one of the greatest lessons which men can learn, at any time."[8] I suspect that, given Strauss's strong Jewish identity, a very large part of his admiration of Churchill was not that Churchill opposed tyrants, but that he went to war against an anti-Jewish tyrant at enormous cost to his own people and nation while allied with another tyrant, Joseph Stalin, who had by 1939 already murdered far more people than Hitler ever would.

Strauss has become a cult figure—the quintessential rabbinical guru, with devoted disciples such as Allan Bloom.[9] Strauss relished his role as a guru to worshiping disciples, once writing of "the love of the mature philosopher for the puppies of his race, by whom he wants to be loved in turn."[10] In turn, Strauss was a disciple of Hermann Cohen, a philosopher at the University of Marburg, who ended his career teaching in a rabbinical school; Cohen was a central figure in a school of neo-Kantian intellectuals whose main concern was to rationalize Jewish non-assimilation into German society.

Strauss understood that inequalities among humans were inevitable and advocated rule by an aristocratic elite of philosopher kings forced to pay lip service to the traditional religious and political beliefs of the masses while not believing them.[11] This elite should pursue its vision of

---

[7] Holmes 1993, 63.

[8] In Jaffa 1999, 44.

[9] Himmelfarb 1974, 61: "There are many excellent teachers. They have students. Strauss had disciples." Levine 1994, 354: "This group has the trappings of a cult. After all, there is a secret teaching and the extreme seriousness of those who are 'initiates.'" See also Easton 2000, 38; Drury 1997, 2.

[10] Strauss 1952, 36.

[11] Drury 1997; Holmes 1993; Tarcov and Pangle 1987, 915.

the common good but must reach out to others using deception and manipulation to achieve its goals. As Bill Kristol has described it, elites have the duty to guide public opinion, but "one of the main teachings [of Strauss] is that all politics are limited and none of them is really based on the truth."[12] A more cynical characterization is provided by Stephen Holmes: "The good society, on this model, consists of the sedated masses, the gentlemen rulers, the promising puppies, and the philosophers who pursue knowledge, manipulate the gentlemen, anesthetize the people, and housebreak the most talented young"[13]—a comment that sounds to me like an alarmingly accurate description of the present situation in the United States and elsewhere in the Western world. Given Strauss's central concern that an acceptable political order be compatible with Jewish survival, it is reasonable to assume that Strauss believed that the aristocracy would serve Jewish interests.

Strauss's philosophy is not really conservative. The rule by an aristocratic elite would require a complete political transformation in order to create a society that was "as just as possible":

> Nothing short of a *total transformation* of imbedded custom must be undertaken. To secure this inversion of the traditional hierarchies, the political, social, and educational system must be subjected to a radical reformation. For justice to be possible the founders have to "wipe clean the dispositions of men," that is, justice is possible only if the city and its citizens are *not* what they *are*: the weakest [i.e., the philosophic elite] is supposed to rule the strongest [the masses], the irrational is supposed to submit to the rule of the rational.[14]

Strauss described the need for an external *exoteric* language directed at outsiders, and an internal *esoteric* language directed at ingroup members.[15] A general feature of the movements I have studied is that this Straussian prescription has been followed: Issues are framed in language that appeals to non-Jews rather than explicitly in terms of Jewish interests, although Jewish interests always remain in the background if one cares to look a little deeper. The most common rhetoric used by Jewish intellectual and political movements has been the language of moral universalism and the language of science—languages that appeal

---

[12] Easton 2000, 45, 183.
[13] Holmes 1993, 74.
[14] Levine 1994, 366. Emphasis in original.
[15] Strauss 1952, ch. 2.

to the educated elites of the modern Western world.[16] But beneath the rhetoric it is easy to find statements describing the Jewish agendas of the principal actors. And the language of moral universalism (e.g., advocating democracy as a universal moral imperative) goes hand in hand with a narrow Jewish moral particularism (altering governments that represent a danger to Israel).

It is noteworthy in this respect that the split between the leftist critics of Strauss like Shadia Drury and Stephen Holmes versus Strauss's disciples like Allan Bloom and Harry V. Jaffa comes down to whether Strauss is properly seen as a universalist. The leftist critics claim that the moral universalism espoused by Strauss's disciples is nothing more than a veneer for his vision of a hierarchical society based on manipulation of the masses. As noted, the use of a universalist rhetoric to mask particularist causes has a long history among Jewish intellectual and political movements, and it fits well with Strauss's famous emphasis on esoteric messages embedded in the texts of great thinkers. Moreover, there is at least some textual support for the leftist critique, although there can never be certainty because of the intentionally enigmatic nature of Strauss's writings.

I am merely adding to the leftist critique the idea that Strauss crafted his vision of an aristocratic elite manipulating the masses as a Jewish survival strategy. In doing so, I am taking seriously Strauss's own characterization of his work as centrally motivated by "the Jewish question" and by the excellent evidence for his strong commitment to the continuity of the Jewish people. At a fundamental level, based on my scholarship on Jewish intellectual and political movements, one cannot understand Strauss's well-attested standing as a Jewish guru—as an exemplar of the familiar pattern of an intellectual leader in the manner of Boas or Freud surrounded by devoted Jewish disciples—*unless he had a specifically Jewish message.*

The simple logic is as follows: Based on the data presented here, it is quite clear that Strauss understood that neither communism nor fascism was good for Jews in the long run. But democracy cannot be trusted given that Weimar ended with Hitler. A solution is to advocate democracy and the trappings of traditional religious culture, but managed by an elite able to manipulate the masses via control of the media and academic discourse. Jews have a long history as an elite in Western societies, so it is not in the least surprising that Strauss would advocate an ideal society in which Jews would be a central component of the elite. In my view,

---

[16] *The Culture of Critique*, 86–92.

this is Strauss's esoteric message. The exoteric message is the universalist veneer promulgated by Strauss's disciples—a common enough pattern among Jewish intellectual and political movements.

On the other hand, if one accepts at face value the view of Strauss's disciples that he should be understood as a theorist of egalitarianism and democracy, then Strauss's legacy becomes just another form of leftism, and a rather undistinguished one at that. In this version, the United States is seen as a "proposition nation" committed only to the ideals of democracy and egalitarianism—an ideology that originated with Jewish leftist intellectuals like Horace Kallen.[17] Such an ideology not only fails to protect the ethnic interests of European Americans in maintaining their culture and demographic dominance, it fails as an adequate survival strategy for Jews because of the possibility that, like Weimar Germany, the United States could be democratically transformed into a state that self-consciously opposes the ethnic interests of Jews.

The most reasonable interpretation is that neocons see Strauss's moral universalism as a powerful exoteric ideology. The ideology is powerful among non-Jews because of the strong roots of democracy and egalitarianism in American history and in the history of the West; it is attractive to Jews because it has no ethnic content and is therefore useful in combating the ethnic interests of European Americans—its function for the Jewish left throughout the twentieth century.[18] But without the esoteric message that the proposition nation must be managed and manipulated by a covert, Jewish-dominated elite, such an ideology is inherently unstable and cannot be guaranteed to meet the long-term interests of Jews.

And one must remember that the neocons' public commitment to egalitarianism belies their own status as an elite who were educated at elite academic institutions and created an elite network at the highest levels of the government. They form an elite that is deeply involved in deception, manipulation, and espionage on issues related to Israel and the war in Iraq. They also established the massive neocon infrastructure in the elite media and think tanks. And they have often become wealthy in the process. Their public pronouncements advocating a democratic, egalitarian ideology have not prevented them from having strong ethnic identities and a strong sense of their own ethnic interests; nor have their public pronouncements supporting the Enlightenment ideals of egalitarianism and democracy prevented them from having a thoroughly

---

[17] See *The Culture of Critique*, ch. 7.

[18] *The Culture of Critique, passim*, esp. 86–92,

anti-Enlightenment ethnic particularist commitment to the most nationalistic, aggressive, racialist elements within Israel—the Likud Party, the settler movement, and the religious fanatics. At the end of the day, the only alternative to the existence of an esoteric Straussian message along the lines described here is massive self-deception.

SIDNEY HOOK

Born in 1902, Sidney Hook was an important leader of the anti-Stalinist, non-Trotskyist left. Hook's career is interesting because he illustrates an evolution toward neoconservatism that was in many ways parallel to the Shachtmanites. Indeed, Hook ended up as honorary chairman of the SD/USA during the 1980s.[19] Hook became a socialist at a time when virtually all socialists supported the Bolshevik revolution as the only alternative to the anti-Jewish government of the Tsar.[20] As a professional philosopher, he saw his role as an attempt to develop an intellectually respectable Marxism strengthened with Dewey's ideas. But until the Moscow Trials of the 1930s he was blind to the violence and oppression in the USSR. During a visit to the USSR in 1929, "I was completely oblivious at the time to the systematic repressions that were then going on against noncommunist elements and altogether ignorant of the liquidation of the so-called kulaks that had already begun that summer. I was not even curious enough to probe and pry, possibly for fear of what I would discover."[21] During the 1930s, when the Communist Party exercised a dominant cultural influence in the United States, "the fear of fascism helped to blur our vision and blunt our hearing to the reports that kept trickling out of the Soviet Union."[22] Even the Moscow Trials were dismissed by large sectors of liberal opinion. It was the time of the Popular Front, where the fundamental principle was the defense of the Soviet Union. Liberal journals like the *New Republic* did not support inquiries into the trials, citing *New York Times* reporter Walter Duranty as an authority who believed in the truth of the confessions.

Unlike the Shachtmanites, Hook never accepted Trotsky because of his record of defending "every act of the Soviet regime, until he himself lost power."[23] "To the very end Trotsky remained a blind, pitiless (even when pitiable) giant, defending the right of the minority vanguard of

---

[19] Massing 1987.
[20] Hook 1987, 46.
[21] Hook 1987, 123.
[22] Hook 1987, 179.
[23] Hook 1987, 244.

the proletariat—the Party—to exercise its dictatorship over 'the backward layers of the proletariat'—i.e., those who disagreed with the self-designated vanguard."[24]

Hook became a leader of the anti-Stalinist left in the 1930s and during the Cold War, usually with John Dewey as the most visible public persona in various organizations dedicated to opposing intellectual thought control. His main issue came to be openness versus totalitarianism rather than capitalism versus socialism. Like other neoconservatives, from the 1960s on he opposed the excesses of the New Left, including affirmative action. Sidney Hook received the Presidential Medal of Freedom from Ronald Reagan. Like many neoconservatives, he never abandoned many of his leftist views: In his acceptance speech, Hook stated that he was "an unreconstructed believer in the welfare state, steeply progressive income tax, a secular humanist," and pro-choice on abortion.[25] Sounding much like SD/USA stalwart Joshua Muravchik,[26] Hook noted that socialists like him "never took the problem of incentives seriously enough."[27]

Like Strauss, Hook's advocacy of the open society stemmed from his belief that such societies were far better for Jews than either the totalitarian left or right. Hook had a strong Jewish identification: He was a Zionist, a strong supporter of Israel, and an advocate of Jewish education for Jewish children.[28] Hook developed an elaborate apologia for Jews and against anti-Semitism in the modern world,[29] and he was deeply concerned about the emergence of anti-Semitism in the USSR.[30] The ideal society is thus culturally diverse and democratic:

> No philosophy of Jewish life is required except one—identical with the democratic way of life—which enables Jews who for any reason at all accept their existence as Jews to lead a dignified and significant life, a life in which together with their fellowmen they strive collectively to improve the quality of democratic, secular cultures

---

[24] Hook 1987, 246.
[25] Hook 1987, 598.
[26] Muravchik 2002.
[27] Hook 1987, 600.
[28] Hook 1989.
[29] *The Culture of Critique*, ch. 6.
[30] Hook 1987, 420: Anti-Semitism in the USSR "had a sobering effect upon intellectuals of Jewish extraction, who had been disproportionately represented among dissidents and radicals."

and thus encourage a maximum of cultural diversity, both Jewish and non-Jewish.[31]

STEPHEN BRYEN

Despite his low profile in the George W. Bush administration, Stephen Bryen is an important neocon. Bryen served as executive director of JINSA from 1979 to 1981 and remains on its advisory board. He is also affiliated with the AEI and the CSP. Richard Perle hired Bryen as Deputy Assistant Secretary of Defense during the Reagan administration. At the Pentagon, Perle and Bryen led an effort to extend and strengthen the Export Administration Act to grant the Pentagon a major role in technology transfer policy. This policy worked to the benefit of Israel at the expense of Europe, as Israel alone had access to the most secret technology designs.[32] In 1988 Bryen and Perle temporarily received permission to export sensitive klystron technology, used in antiballistic missiles, to Israel.

> Two senior colleagues in [the Department of Defense] who wish to remain anonymous have confirmed that this attempt by Bryen to obtain klystrons for his friends was not unusual, and was in fact "standard operating procedure" for him, recalling numerous instances when US companies were denied licenses to export sensitive technology, only to learn later that Israeli companies subsequently exported similar (US derived) weapons and technology to the intended customers/governments."[33]

It is surprising that Perle was able to hire Bryen at all given that, beginning in 1978, Bryen was investigated for offering classified documents to the Mossad station chief of the Israeli embassy in the presence of an AIPAC representative.[34] Bryen's fingerprints were found on the documents in question despite his denials that he had ever had the documents in his possession. (Bryen refused to take a polygraph test.) The Bryen investigation was ultimately shut down because of the failure of the Senate Foreign Relations Committee to grant access to the Justice Department to files important to the investigation, and because of the decision by Philip Heymann, the chief of the Justice Department's

---

[31] Hook 1989, 480–81.
[32] Saba 1984.
[33] Green 2004.
[34] Saba 1984; Green 2004.

Criminal Division and later Deputy Attorney General in the Clinton administration, to drop the case.

Heymann is Jewish and had a close relationship with Bryen's lawyer, Nathan Lewin. Heymann's Jewish consciousness can be seen from the fact that he participated in the campaign to free Israeli spy Jonathan Pollard and expunge his record—a major effort by a great many Jewish organizations and Jewish activists such as Alan Dershowitz. There were reports that Heymann was attempting to bypass Attorney General Janet Reno by preparing a Justice Department recommendation for presidential clemency, and that Heymann's behavior may have been a factor in his resignation shortly thereafter.[35]

Despite this history of covert pro-Israeli activism, in 2001 Bryen was appointed, at the urging of Paul Wolfowitz, to the China Commission, which monitors illicit technology transfers to China, a position that requires top secret security clearance.[36] Many of the illicit technology transfers investigated by the commission are thought to have occurred via Israel.

CHARLES KRAUTHAMMER

In his 1995 book, John Ehrman regards Charles Krauthammer as a key neoconservative foreign policy analyst because Krauthammer was on the cutting edge of neocon thinking on how to respond to the unipolar world created by the collapse of the Soviet Union. Krauthammer has consistently urged that the United States pursue a policy to remake the entire Middle East—a view that represents the "party line" among neoconservatives (e.g., Michael Ledeen, Norman Podhoretz, Bill Kristol, David Frum, and Richard Perle[37]). In a speech at the AEI in February 2004, Krauthammer argued for a unilateral confrontation with the entire Arab-Muslim world (and nowhere else) in the interests of "democratic globalism." He advocated a US foreign policy that is not "tied down" by "multilateralism":

> the whole point of the multilateral enterprise: To reduce American freedom of action by making it subservient to, dependent on, constricted by the will—and interests—of other nations. To tie down Gulliver with a thousand strings. To domesticate the most undomes-

---

[35] Dershowitz 1994; Jones 1996.
[36] Green 2004.
[37] Frum and Perle 2003.

ticated, most outsized, national interest on the planet—ours.[38]

Democratic globalism is aimed at winning the struggle with the Arab-Muslim world:

> Beyond power. Beyond interest. Beyond interest defined as power. That is the credo of democratic globalism. Which explains its political appeal: America is a nation uniquely built not on blood, race, or consanguinity, but on a proposition—to which its sacred honor has been pledged for two centuries. . . . Today, post-9/11, we find ourselves in an . . . existential struggle but with a different enemy: not Soviet communism, but Arab-Islamic totalitarianism, both secular and religious. . . . [D]emocratic globalism is an improvement over realism. What it can teach realism is that the spread of democracy is not just an end but a means, an indispensable means for securing American interests. The reason is simple. Democracies are inherently more friendly to the United States, less belligerent to their neighbors, and generally more inclined to peace. Realists are right that to protect your interests you often have to go around the world bashing bad guys over the head. But that technique, no matter how satisfying, has its limits. At some point, you have to implant something, something organic and self-developing. And that something is democracy. But where? The danger of democratic globalism is its universalism, its open-ended commitment to human freedom, its temptation to plant the flag of democracy everywhere. It must learn to say no. And indeed, it does say no. But when it says no to Liberia, or Congo, or Burma, or countenances alliances with authoritarian rulers in places like Pakistan or, for that matter, Russia, it stands accused of hypocrisy. Which is why we must articulate criteria for saying yes. . . . I propose a single criterion: where it counts. . . . And this is its axiom: *We will support democracy everywhere, but we will commit blood and treasure only in places where there is a strategic necessity—meaning, places central to the larger war against the existential enemy, the enemy that poses a global mortal threat to freedom.*
> Where does it count today? Where the overthrow of radicalism and the beginnings of democracy can have a decisive effect in the war against the new global threat to freedom, the new existential enemy, the Arab-Islamic totalitarianism that has threatened us in both its secular and religious forms for the quarter-century since the

---

[38] Krauthammer 2004b.

Khomeini revolution of 1979. . . . There is not a single, remotely plausible, alternative strategy for attacking the monster behind 9/11. It's not Osama bin Laden; it is the cauldron of political oppression, religious intolerance, and social ruin in the Arab-Islamic world—oppression transmuted and deflected by regimes with no legitimacy into virulent, murderous anti-Americanism. It's not one man; it is a condition.[39]

Krauthammer is a Jew, and his Jewish identification and pro-Israel motivation is typical of Jewish neoconservatives, as is his obeisance to the idea that America is a proposition nation, rather than a nation founded by a particular ethnic group—an ethno-cultural creation of Western Europe that should attempt to preserve this heritage. The same attitude can be seen in Irving Kristol's comment that the United States is an "ideological nation" committed to defend Israel independent of national interest (see the previous chapter). This ideology was the creation of leftist Jewish intellectuals attempting to rationalize a multicultural America in which European-Americans were just one of many cultural/ethnic groups.[40]

Krauthammer is a regular columnist for the *Jerusalem Post* and has written extensively in support of hard-line policies in Israel and on what he interprets as a rise in age-old anti-Jewish attitudes in Europe. In 2002 Krauthammer was presented with Bar-Ilan University's annual Guardian of Zion Award at the King David Hotel in Jerusalem. His acceptance speech reveals an observant Jew who is steeped in Jewish history and the Hebrew tradition. The 1993 Oslo Accords are termed "the most catastrophic and self-inflicted wound by any state in modern history"; this disastrous policy was based on "an extreme expression of post-Zionistic messianism."[41] Krauthammer rejected the "secular messianism" of Shimon Peres as more dangerous than the religious messianism of Gush Emunim (a prominent settler group with a message of Jewish racialism and a vision of a "Greater Israel" encompassing the lands promised to Abraham in Genesis—from the Nile to the Euphrates[42]) or of certain followers of the Lubavitcher *rebbe* because of its impact on shaping contemporary Jewish history.

---

[39] Krauthammer 2004b.
[40] See *The Culture of Critique*, chs. 7 and 8.
[41] Krauthammer 2002b.
[42] See ch. 1 above, "Background Traits for Jewish Activism" and ch. 2 above, "Zionism and the Group Dynamics of the Jewish Community."

Krauthammer is also deeply concerned with anti-Semitism:

> What is odd is not the anti-Semitism of today [in Europe], but its relative absence during the last half-century. That was the historical anomaly. Holocaust shame kept the demon corked for that half-century. But now the atonement is passed. The genie is out again. This time, however, it is more sophisticated. It is not a blanket hatred of Jews. Jews can be tolerated, even accepted, but they must know their place. Jews are fine so long as they are powerless, passive, and picturesque. What is intolerable is Jewish assertiveness, the Jewish refusal to accept victimhood. And nothing so embodies that as the Jewish state.[43]

Another barometer of Jewish identification is Krauthammer's take on Mel Gibson's *The Passion of the Christ*. In sentiments similar to those of many other Jewish activists and writers, he terms it a "blood libel," "a singular act of interreligious aggression," a "spectacularly vicious" personal interpretation.[44] Gibson's interpretations "point overwhelmingly in a single direction—to the villainy and culpability of the Jews." The crucifixion is "a history of centuries of relentless, and at times savage, persecution of Jews in Christian lands." One gets the impression of a writer searching as best he can to find the most extreme terms possible to express his loathing of Gibson's account of the Christian gospel.

PAUL WOLFOWITZ

Paul Wolfowitz's background indicates a strong Jewish identity. His father Jacob was a committed Zionist throughout his life and in his later years organized protests against Soviet treatment of Jews.[45] Jacob was deeply concerned about the Holocaust,[46] and, in his own reminiscences of his teenage years, Paul recalls reading books about the Holocaust and traveling to Israel when his father was a visiting professor at an Israeli university. Wolfowitz reads Hebrew, and his sister married an Israeli and lives in Israel.[47] The professors mentioned in his account of his time at the University of Chicago are all Jewish:[48] Albert Wohl-

---

[43] Krauthammer 2002a.
[44] Krauthammer 2004a.
[45] Mann 2004, 23.
[46] Hirsh 2003.
[47] Mann 2004, 23, 30.
[48] Tannenhaus 2003.

stetter, his Ph.D. advisor; Leo Strauss (Wolfowitz's original intent when enrolling at the University of Chicago was to study with Strauss, and he ended up taking two courses from him); Strauss's disciple Alan Bloom, whose *The Closing of the American Mind: How Higher Education Has Failed Democracy and Impoverished the Souls of Today's Students* (1987) is a neocon classic; and Saul Bellow, the novelist.

Also indicative of a strong Jewish identity is a conversation Wolfowitz had with Natan Sharansky, Israeli Cabinet Minister and leader of a right wing, pro-settlement political party, at a conference on Middle East policy in Aspen, Colorado, in 2002. The conference was arranged by Richard Perle under the auspices of the AEI. Wolfowitz and Sharansky walked to a reception, because the latter, as an observant Jew, could not drive on the Sabbath. Sharansky noted that the walk "gave us a chance to talk about everything—Arafat, international terrorism, Iraq and Iran, and, of course, Jewish history, our roots and so on."[49] Wolfowitz is married to Clare Selgin, and they have three children, Sara, David, and Rachel.[50]

Ravelstein is Saul Bellow's fictionalized but essentially accurate description of Alan Bloom and his circle at the University of Chicago.[51] It is of some interest because it recreates the Jewish atmosphere of Wolfowitz's academic environment. Wolfowitz was a member of Bloom's circle at Cornell University and for his graduate training chose the University of Chicago, most likely at the urging of Bloom, because of the presence there of Leo Strauss. Wolfowitz and Bloom maintained a close relationship after Bloom moved to the University of Chicago and during Wolfowitz's later career in the government. Wolfowitz was one of the "favored students" of Bloom described in Robert Locke's comment that, "Favored students of the usually haughty Bloom were gradually introduced to greater and greater intimacies with the master, culminating in exclusive dinner parties with him and Saul [Bellow] in Bloom's lavishly furnished million-dollar apartment."[52]

As depicted by Bellow, Bloom emerges as the quintessential guru, surrounded by disciples—a "father" who attempts not only to direct his disciples' careers but their personal lives as well.[53] His disciples are described as "clones who dressed as he did, smoked the same Marl-

---

[49] Ephron and Lipper 2002.
[50] Curtiss 2003.
[51] Locke 2002.
[52] Locke 2002.
[53] Bellow 2000, 27.

boros";[54] they were heading toward "the Promised Land of the intellect toward which Ravelstein, their Moses and their Socrates, led them."[55] "To be cut off from his informants in Washington and Paris, from his students, the people he had trained, the band of brothers, the initiates, the happy few made him extremely uncomfortable."[56]

Bloom in turn is depicted as a "disciple" of the Strauss character, Felix Davarr: "Ravelstein talked so much about him that in the end I was obliged to read some of his books. It had to be done if I was to understand what [Ravelstein] was all about."[57]

Bloom's Ravelstein is depicted as very self-consciously Jewish. A theme is the contrast between "crude" Jewish behavior and genteel WASP behavior—a theme described beautifully and authoritatively in the writings of John Murray Cuddihy.[58] And there is the acute consciousness of who is a Jew and who isn't; all of Ravelstein's close friends are Jews. There is an intense interest in whether non-Jews dislike Jews or have connections to fascism. And there is a fixation on the Holocaust and when it will happen again: "They kill more than half of the European Jews. . . . There's no telling which corner it will come from next."[59] Ravelstein thought of Jews as displacing WASPs: He "liked to think of living in one of the tony flat buildings formerly occupied by the exclusively WASP faculty."[60]

Following Strauss, Bloom thought of Western civilization as the product of Athens and Jerusalem, and is said to have preferred the former, at least until the end of his life, when Jerusalem loomed large: Bellow's narrator writes, "I could see [Ravelstein/Bloom] was following a trail of Jewish ideas or Jewish essences. It was unusual for him these days, in any conversation, to mention even Plato or Thucydides. He was full of Scripture now"—all connected to "the great evil," the belief during the World War II era "that almost everybody agreed that the Jews had no right to live . . . a vast collective agreement that the world would be improved by their disappearance and their extinction." Ravelstein's conclusion is that "it is impossible to get rid of one's origins, it is impossible not to remain a Jew. The Jews, Ravelstein . . .

---

[54] Bellow 2000, 56.
[55] Bellow 2000, 56.
[56] Bellow 2000, 103.
[57] Bellow 2000, 101.
[58] Cuddihy 1974. See Bellow 2000, 57–58.
[59] Bellow 2000, 174.
[60] Bellow 2000, 61.

thought, following the line laid down by [his] teacher Davarr [Strauss], were historically witnesses to the absence of redemption."[61]

Ravelstein recounts a conversation with the Wolfowitz character, Philip Gorman, which reflects Wolfowitz's well-known desire to invade Iraq in 1991:

> Colin Powell and Baker have advised the President not to send the troops all the way to Baghdad. Bush will announce it tomorrow. They're afraid of a few casualties. They send out a terrific army and give a demonstration of up-to-date high-tech warfare that flesh and blood can't stand up to. But then they leave the dictatorship in place and steal away....[62]

Wolfowitz has had a close relationship with Richard Perle beginning with their service in the office of Senator Henry Jackson.[63] He also has a long record of pro-Israel advocacy. In 1973 he was appointed to the Arms Control and Disarmament Agency (ACDA); Mark Green notes that, "Wolfowitz . . . brought to ACDA a strong attachment to Israel's security, and a certain confusion about his obligation to US national security."[64] In 1978, he was investigated for providing a classified document to the Israeli government through an AIPAC intermediary, but the investigation ended without indictment. (As Paul Findley shows, leakage of classified information to Israel by American Jews is routine within the Departments of State and Defense—so routine that it is accepted as a part of life in these departments, and investigations of the source of leaks are seldom performed.[65]) Later, in 1992, the Department of Defense discovered that Wolfowitz, as Undersecretary of Defense for Policy, was promoting the export to Israel of advanced AIM-9M air-to-air missiles. The sale was canceled because Israel had been caught selling the previous version to the Chinese. Until his appointment as Deputy Secretary of Defense in the Bush administration, Wolfowitz was on the Advisory Board of WINEP, and was a patron of Dennis Ross, who was Ambassador to Israel in the Clinton Administration before becoming director of Policy and Strategic Planning at WINEP.

---

[61] Bellow 2000, 178–79.
[62] Bellow 2000, 58.
[63] Keller 2002.
[64] Green 2004.
[65] Green 2004, 139–64.

Wolfowitz wrote a 1997 *Weekly Standard* article advocating removal of Saddam Hussein, and signed the public letter to President Clinton organized by Bill Kristol's Project for the New American Century urging a regime change in Iraq. Within the George H. W. Bush administration, Wolfowitz was "the intellectual godfather and fiercest advocate for toppling Saddam."[66] Wolfowitz has become famous as a key advocate for war with Iraq rather than Afghanistan in the immediate aftermath of September 11.[67] Richard Clarke recounts an incident on September 12, 2001, in which President Bush asked a group at the White House for any information that Saddam Hussein was involved in the September 11 attacks. After Bush left, a staffer "stared at [Bush] with her mouth open. 'Wolfowitz got to him.'"[68]

Former CIA political analysts Kathleen and Bill Christison note that "One source inside the administration has described [Wolfowitz] frankly as 'over-the-top crazy when it comes to Israel.'"[69] Although they find such an assessment insufficiently nuanced, they acknowledge that zealotry for Israel is a prime motivator for Wolfowitz. Journalist Bill Keller is much more cautious:

You hear from some of Wolfowitz's critics, always off the record, that Israel exercises a powerful gravitational pull on the man. They may not know that as a teenager he spent his father's sabbatical semester in Israel or that his sister is married to an Israeli, but they certainly know that he is friendly with Israel's generals and diplomats and that he is something of a hero to the heavily Jewish neoconservative movement. Those who know him well say this—leaving aside the offensive suggestion of dual loyalty—is looking at Wolfowitz through the wrong end of the telescope. As the Sadat story illustrates, he has generally been less excited by the security of Israel than by the promise of a more moderate Islam.[70]

This is a remarkable statement. "The Sadat story" refers to Wolfowitz's very positive reaction to Egypt's President Anwar Sadat's speech to the Knesset as part of the peace process between Israel and Egypt. Obviously, it is silly to suppose that this event shows Wolfowitz's relative

---

[66] Woodward 2004, 21.
[67] Mann 2004, 302.
[68] Clarke 2004, 32.
[69] Christison and Christison 2003.
[70] Christison and Christison 2003.

disinterest in Israel's security. Moreover, statements linking Wolfowitz to Israel are always off the record, presumably because people fear retaliation for stating the obvious. Thus Bill Keller coyly manages to document the associations between Wolfowitz and Israel while finding assertions of dual loyalty "offensive" rather than a well-grounded probability.

One of Joshua Muravchik's apologetic claims is that "in fact the careers of leading neoconservatives have rarely involved work on Middle East issues."[71] This is false. For example, Wolfowitz wrote his Ph.D. dissertation on nuclear proliferation in the Middle East. During the Carter administration, he prepared the Limited Contingency Study, which emphasized the "Iraqi threat" to the region, and during the Reagan administration he lobbied against selling AWACS to Saudi Arabia and against negotiating with the Palestinians; during the George H. W. Bush administration he was Undersecretary of Defense for Policy, a position where he "would once again have responsibility for arms control, the Middle East and the Persian Gulf, the areas to which he had devoted the early years of his career."[72]

RICHARD PERLE

As with Wolfowitz and the Strauss-Bloom nexus at the University of Chicago, for Perle

> the defining moment in our history was certainly the Holocaust. . . . It was the destruction, the genocide of a whole people, and it was the failure to respond in a timely fashion to a threat that was clearly gathering. . . . We don't want that to happen again . . . when we have the ability to stop totalitarian regimes we should do so, because when we fail to do so, the results are catastrophic.[73]

Richard Perle first came into prominence in Washington as Senator Henry Jackson's chief aide on foreign policy. He organized Congressional support for the 1974 Jackson-Vanik Amendment, which angered Russia by linking bilateral trade issues to freedom of emigration, primarily of Jews from the Soviet Union to Israel and the United States. In 1970 Perle was recorded by the FBI discussing classified information with the Israeli embassy. In 1981 he was on the payroll of an Israeli

---

[71] Muravchik 2003.
[72] Mann 2004, 170; see also 79–81; 113.
[73] Perle interview on BBC's *Panorama*, in Lobe 2003c.

defense contractor shortly before being appointed Assistant Secretary of Defense for International Security Policy, a position responsible for monitoring US defense technology exports.[74] During his tenure in the Reagan administration, Perle recommended purchase of an artillery shell made by Soltan, an Israeli munitions manufacturer. After leaving his position in the Defense Department in 1987, he assumed a position with Soltan. Like many other former government officials, he has also used his reputation and contacts in the government to develop a highly lucrative business career. For example, although he did not personally register as a lobbyist, he became a paid consultant to a firm headed by Douglas Feith that was established to lobby on behalf of Turkey.[75] At the present time, Perle is on the board of directors of Onset Technology, a technology company founded by Israelis Gadi Mazor and Ron Maor with research and development in Israel. Onset Technology has close ties to Israeli companies and investment funds.[76] He was a close personal friend of Israel Prime Minister Ariel Sharon.[77]

Perle was the "Study Group Leader" of a 1996 report titled "A Clean Break: A New Strategy for Securing the Realm" published by the Institute for Advanced Strategic and Political Studies (IASPS), an Israeli think tank. The membership of the study group illustrates the overlap between Israeli think tanks close to the Israeli government, American policy makers and government officials, and pro-Israel activists working in the United States. Other members of this group who accepted positions in the George W. Bush administration or in pro-Israel activist organizations in the United States include Douglas Feith (Deputy Undersecretary of Defense for Policy), David Wurmser (member of IASPS, a protégé of Perle at AEI, and senior advisor in the State Department), Meyrav Wurmser (head of the Hudson Institute, a neocon thinktank), James Colbert of JINSA, and Jonathan Torop (WINEP).

Despite Joshua Muravchik's apologetic claims,[78] the "Clean Break" report was clearly intended as advice for another of Perle's personal friends,[79] Benjamin Netanyahu, who was then the new prime minister of Israel; there is no indication that it was an effort to further US interests in the region. The purpose was to "forge a peace process and strat-

---

[74] Findley 1989, 160; Green 2004.
[75] Hilzenrath 2004.
[76] Oberg 2003.
[77] Brownfield 2003.
[78] Muravchik 2003.
[79] Hilzenrath 2004.

egy based on an entirely *new intellectual foundation*, one that restores strategic initiative and provides the nation the room to engage every possible energy on rebuilding Zionism." Indeed, the report advises the United States to avoid pressure on the Israelis to give land for peace, a strategy "which required funneling American money to repressive and aggressive regimes, was risky, expensive, and very costly for both the US and Israel, and placed the United States in roles it should neither have nor want." The authors of the report speak as Jews and Israelis, not as US citizens: "Our claim to the land—to which we have clung for hope for 2,000 years—is legitimate and noble." Much of the focus is on removing the threat of Syria, and it is in this context that the report notes, "This effort can focus on removing Saddam Hussein from power in Iraq—an important Israeli strategic objective in its own right—as a means of foiling Syria's regional ambitions."[80]

Proposals for regime change, such as found in "A Clean Break," have a long history in Israeli thought. For example, in 1982 Israeli strategist Oded Yinon echoed a long line of Israeli strategists who argued that Israel should attempt to dissolve all the existing Arab states into smaller, less potentially powerful states. These states would then become clients of Israel as a regional imperial power. Neocons have advertised the war in Iraq as a crusade for a democratic, secular, Western-oriented, pro-Israel Iraq—a dream that has a great deal of appeal in the West, for obvious reasons. However, it is quite possible that the long-term result is that Iraq would fracture along ethnic and religious lines (Sunnis, Shiites, Kurds). This would also be in Israel's interests, because the resulting states would pose less of a threat than the Iraqi regime of Saddam Hussein. As Yinon noted, "Iraq, rich in oil on the one hand and internally torn on the other, *is guaranteed as a candidate for Israel's targets*. Its dissolution is even more important for us than that of Syria. Iraq is stronger than Syria. In the short run it is Iraqi power which constitutes the greatest threat to Israel."[81]

Former Ambassador Joseph C. Wilson has suggested that the dissolution of Iraq may well have been a motive for the war:

> A more cynical reading of the agenda of certain Bush advisers could conclude that the Balkanization of Iraq was always an acceptable outcome, because Israel would then find itself surrounded by small Arab countries worried about each other instead of forming a solid

---

[80] Institute for Advanced Strategic and Political Studies 1996.
[81] Yinon 1982.

block against Israel. After all, Iraq was an artificial country that had always had a troublesome history.[82]

And as the Iraqi insurgency has achieved momentum, there is evidence that Israeli military and intelligence units are operating in Kurdish regions of Iraq and that Israel is indeed encouraging the Kurds to form their own state.[83] There is little doubt that an independent Kurdish state would have major repercussions for Syria and Iran, as well as for Israel's ally Turkey, and would lead to continuing instability in the Middle East. A senior Turkish official noted, "If you end up with a divided Iraq, it will bring more blood, tears, and pain to the Middle East, and [the United States] will be blamed. . . . From Mexico to Russia, everybody will claim that the United States had a secret agenda in Iraq: you came there to break up Iraq. If Iraq is divided, America cannot explain this to the world."

ELLIOTT ABRAMS

Some of Elliott Abrams' neoconservative family and professional associations have been described above. In December 2002 Abrams became President Bush's top Middle East advisor. He is closely associated with the Likud Party in Israel and with prominent neocons (Richard Perle, Bill Kristol, Reuel Marc Gerecht, Michael Ledeen, Jeane Kirkpatrick, Paul Wolfowitz) and neocon think tanks (PNAC, AEI, CSP, JINSA).[84] Because of his reputation as a strongly identified Jew, Abrams was tapped for the role of rallying Jews in support of Reagan in the 1980 campaign.[85]

Abrams is also an activist on behalf of Jewish continuity. The purpose of his book *Faith and Fear: How Jews Can Survive in Christian America* is to shore up Jewish religious identification, avoid intermarriage, and avoid secularization in order to assure Jewish continuity. In this regard it is interesting that other prominent neocons have advocated interracial marriage between whites and blacks in the United States. For example, Douglas J. Besharov, a resident scholar at the AEI,

---

[82] Wilson 2004, 484; Wilson suggests that Scooter Libby or Elliott Abrams revealed that his wife, Valerie Plame, was a CIA agent in retaliation for Wilson's failure to find evidence supporting purchase of material for nuclear weapons by Iraq.
[83] Hersh 2004.
[84] Lobe 2002b.
[85] Ehrman 1995, 139.

has written that the offspring of interracial marriages "are the best hope for the future of American race relations."[86]

In *Faith and Fear,* Abrams notes his own deep immersion in the Yiddish-speaking culture of his parents and grandparents. In the grandparents' generation, "all their children married Jews, and [they] kept Kosher homes."[87] Abrams acknowledges that the mainstream Jewish community "clings to what is at bottom a dark vision of America, as a land permeated with anti-Semitism and always on the verge of anti-Semitic outbursts." The result is that Jews have taken the lead in secularizing America, but that has not been a good strategy for Jews, because Jews themselves have become less religious and therefore less inclined to marry other Jews. (This "dark vision of America" is a critical source of the "Culture of Critique" produced by Jewish intellectual movements; it is also a major reason why the Jewish community has been united in favor of large-scale non-white immigration to the United States: Diluting the white majority and lessening their power is seen as preventing an anti-Jewish outburst.[88]) Following Strauss, therefore, Abrams thinks that a strong role for Christianity in America is good for Jews:

> In this century we have seen two gigantic experiments at postreligious societies where the traditional restraints of religion and morality were entirely removed: Communism and Nazism. In both cases Jews became the special targets, but there was evil enough even without the scourge of anti-Semitism. For when the transcendental inhibition against evil is removed, when society becomes so purely secular that the restraints imposed by God on man are truly eradicated, minorities are but the earliest victims.[89]

---

[86] Besharov and Sullivan 1996, 21; Besharov apparently did not take a position as moderator of a debate between Elliott Abrams and Seymour Martin Lipset on whether the American Jewish community could survive only as a religious community (*The Diamondback*, student newspaper at the University of Maryland, College Park, MD, Dec. 9, 1997). Another prominent neocon, Ben Wattenberg, who is a senior fellow at AEI, is very upbeat about interracial marriage and immigration generally—the better to create a "universal nation" (Wattenberg 2001). Wattenberg's article notes, with no apparent concern, that Jews have high rates of intermarriage as well.

[87] Abrams 1997, ix.

[88] See *The Culture of Critique*, Preface to the first paperback edition and ch. 7.

[89] Abrams 1997, 188.

DOUGLAS FEITH

Like most of his cronies, Feith has been suspected of spying for Israel. In 1972 Feith was fired from a position with the National Security Council because of an investigation into whether he had provided documents to the Israeli embassy. Nevertheless, Perle, who was Assistant Secretary for International Security Policy, hired him as his "special counsel," and then as his deputy. Feith worked for Perle until 1986, when he left government service to form a law firm, Feith and Zell, which was originally based in Israel and best known for obtaining a pardon for the notorious Marc Rich during the final days of the Clinton administration. In 2001, Douglas Feith returned to the Department of Defense as Donald Rumsfeld's Undersecretary for Policy, and it was in his office that Abram Shulsky's Office of Special Plans (OSP) was created. It was OSP that originated much of the fraudulent intelligence that Bush, Cheney, and Rumsfeld have used to justify the attack on Iraq. A key member of OSP was David Wurmser who, as indicated above, is a protégé of Richard Perle.[90]

Retired army officer Karen Kwiatkowski describes Feith as knowing little about the Pentagon and paying little attention to any issues except those relating to Israel and Iraq.[91] Feith is deferential to the Israeli military. As Kwiatkowski escorted a group of Israeli generals into the Pentagon:

> The leader of the pack surged ahead, his colleagues in close formation, leaving us to double-time behind the group as they sped to Undersecretary Feith's office on the fourth floor. . . . Once in Feith's waiting room, the leader continued at speed to Feith's closed door. An alert secretary saw this coming and had leapt from her desk to block the door. "Mr. Feith has a visitor. It will only be a few more minutes." The leader craned his neck to look around the secretary's head as he demanded, "Who is in there with him?"

Unlike the usual practice, the Israeli generals did not have to sign in, so there are no official records of their visits.[92] Kwiatkowski describes the anti-Arab, pro-Israel sentiment that pervaded the neocon network at the Department of Defense. Career military officers who failed to go along with these attitudes were simply replaced.

---

[90] Risen 2004.
[91] Kwiatkowski 2004b.
[92] Kwiatkowski 2004a.

Feith has a strong Jewish identity and is an activist on behalf of Israel. While in law school he collaborated with Joseph Churba, an associate and friend of Meir Kahane, founder of the racialist and anti-Western Jewish Defense League. During the late 1980s to early 1990s he wrote pro-Likud op-ed pieces in Israeli newspapers, arguing that the West Bank is part of Israel, that the Palestinians belong in Jordan, and that there should be regime change in Iraq. He also headed the CSP and was a founding member of One Jerusalem, an Israeli organization "determined to prevent any compromise with the Palestinians over the fate of any part of Jerusalem."[93]

He serves as an officer of the Foundation for Jewish Studies, which is "dedicated to fostering Jewish learning and building communities of educated and committed Jews who are conscious of and faithful to the high ideals of Judaism."[94] In 1997 Feith and his father (a member of Betar, the Zionist youth movement founded by Vladimir Jabotinsky) were given awards from the ZOA because of their work as pro-Israel activists. The ZOA is a staunch supporter of the most extreme elements within Israel. Feith's law partner, L. Marc Zell of the firm's Tel Aviv office, is a spokesman for the settler movement in Israel, and the firm itself is deeply involved in legal issues related to the reconstruction of Iraq, a situation that has raised eyebrows because Feith is head of reconstruction in Iraq.[95]

Zell was one of many neocons close to Ahmed Chalabi but abandoned his support because Chalabi had not come through on his prewar pledges regarding Israel—further evidence that aiding Israel was an important motive for the neocons. According to Zell, Chalabi "said he would end Iraq's boycott of trade with Israel, and would allow Israeli companies to do business there. He said [the new Iraqi government] would agree to rebuild the pipeline from Mosul [in the northern Iraqi oil fields] to Haifa [the Israeli port, and the location of a major refinery]."[96] Another partner in the law firm of Feith and Zell is Salem

---

[93] Bamford 2004, 279.
[94] http://rightweb.irc-online.org/profile/1146.
[95] Kamen 2003.
[96] Dizard 2004. Dizard notes:

Why did the neocons put such enormous faith in Ahmed Chalabi, an exile with a shady past and no standing with Iraqis? One word: Israel. They saw the invasion of Iraq as the precondition for a reorganization of the Middle East that would solve Israel's strategic problems, without the need for an accommodation with either the Palestinians or the existing Arab states.

Chalabi, Ahmed Chalabi's nephew. In 2003 Salem Chalabi was appointed General Director of the Iraqi Special Tribunal in charge of the trial of Saddam Hussein and other members of his government.[97]

ABRAM SHULSKY

Abram Shulsky is a student of Leo Strauss, a close friend of Paul Wolfowitz both at Cornell and the University of Chicago,[98] and yet another protégé of Richard Perle. He was an aide to neocon Senators Henry Jackson (along with Perle and Elliot Abrams) and Daniel Patrick Moynihan, and worked in the Department of Defense in the Reagan administration. During the George W. Bush administration, he was appointed head of the Office of Special Plans under Feith and Wolfowitz. The OSP became more influential on Iraq policy than the CIA or the Defense Intelligence Agency,[99] but is widely viewed by retired intelligence operatives as manipulating intelligence data on Iraq in order to influence policy.[100] Reports suggest that the OSP worked closely with Israeli intelligence to paint an exaggerated picture of Iraqi capabilities in unconventional weapons.[101] It is tempting to link the actions of the OSP under Shulsky with Strauss's idea of a "noble lie" carried out by the elite to manipulate the masses, but one doesn't really need Strauss to understand the importance of lying in order to manipulate public opinion on behalf of Israel.

The OSP included other neocons with no professional qualifications

---

Chalabi assured them that the Iraqi democracy he would build would develop diplomatic and trade ties with Israel, and eschew Arab nationalism. Now some influential allies believe those assurances were part of an elaborate con, and that Chalabi has betrayed his promises on Israel while cozying up to Iranian Shia leaders.

[97] "Friends of Israel are turning up in the strangest places," *American Conservative*, May 24, 2004, 19.

[98] Mann 2004, 75.

[99] Kwiatkowski 2004b. Hersh 2003: "'They [the CIA] see themselves as outsiders,' a former CIA expert who spent the past decade immersed in Iraqi-exile affairs said of the Special Plans people."

[100] Lobe 2003c.

[101] Marshall 2004: "Shlomo Brom, a former Israeli intelligence officer now at the Jaffe Center for Strategic Studies at Tel Aviv University, has confirmed that Israeli intelligence played a major role in bolstering the administration's case for attacking Iraq. The problem, Brom maintains, is that the information was not reliable."

in intelligence but long records of service in neoconservative think tanks and pro-Israel activist organizations, especially the Washington Institute for Near East Policy. Examples include Michael Rubin, who is affiliated with AEI and is an adjunct scholar at WINEP, David Schenker, who has written books and articles on Middle East issues published by WINEP and the *Middle East Quarterly* (published by Daniel Pipes' MEF, another pro-Israel activist organization), Elliott Abrams, David Wurmser, and Michael Ledeen. The OSP relied heavily on Iraqi defectors associated with Ahmed Chalabi, who, as indicated above, had a close personal relationship with Wolfowitz, Perle, and other neocons.[102]

MICHAEL LEDEEN

Michael Ledeen's career illustrates the interconnectedness of the neoconservative network. Ledeen was the first executive director of JINSA (1977–1979) and remains on its board of advisors. He was hired by Richard Perle in the Defense Department during the Reagan years, and during the same period he was hired as special advisor by Wolfowitz in his role as head of the State Department Policy Planning Staff. Along with Stephen Bryen, Ledeen became a member of the China Commission during the George W. Bush administration. He was also a consultant to Abram Shulsky's OSP, the Defense Department organization most closely linked with the manufacture of fraudulent intelligence leading up to the Iraq War. The OSP was created by Douglas Feith, who in turn reports to Paul Wolfowitz. As noted above, he is resident scholar in the Freedom Chair at AEI.

Ledeen has been suspected of spying for Israel.[103] During the Reagan years, he was regarded by the CIA as "an agent of influence of a foreign government: Israel," and was suspected of spying for Israel by his immediate superior at the Department of Defense, Noel Koch.[104] While working for the White House in 1984, Ledeen was also accused by National Security Adviser Robert C. McFarlane of participating in an unauthorized meeting with Israeli Prime Minister Shimon Peres that led to the proposal to funnel arms through Israel to Iran in order to free US hostages being held in Lebanon—the origins of the Irangate scandal.[105]

Ledeen has been a major propagandist for forcing change on the

---

[102] E.g., Hersh 2003; Bamford 2004.
[103] See Green 2004.
[104] Green 2004.
[105] Milstein 1991.

whole Muslim world. Ledeen's revolutionary ideology stems not from Trotsky or Marx, but from his favorable view of Italian fascism as a universalist (nonracial) revolutionary movement.[106] His book, *War on the Terror Masters*, is a program for complete restructuring of the Middle East by the United States couched in the rhetoric of universalism and moral concern, not for Israel, but for the Arab peoples who would benefit from regime change. Ledeen is a revolutionary of the right, committed to "creative destruction" of the old social order:

> Creative destruction is our middle name, both within our own society and abroad. We tear down the old order every day, from business to science, literature, art, architecture, and cinema to politics and the law. Our enemies have always hated this whirlwind of energy and creativity, which menaces their traditions (whatever they may be) and shames them for their inability to keep pace. Seeing America undo traditional societies, they fear us, for they do not wish to be undone. They cannot feel secure so long as we are there, for our very existence—our existence, not our politics—threatens their legitimacy. They must attack us in order to survive, just as we must destroy them to advance our historic mission. . . .
>
> Behind all the anti-American venom from the secular radicals in Baghdad, the religious fanatics in Tehran, the minority regime in Damascus, and the multicultural kleptomaniacs in the Palestinian Authority is the knowledge that they are hated by their own people. Their power rests on terror, recently directed against us, but always, first and foremost, against their own citizens. Given the chance to express themselves freely, the Iraqi, Iranian, Syrian, Lebanese, and Palestinian people would oust their current oppressors. Properly waged, our revolutionary war will give them a chance.[107]

BERNARD LEWIS

The main intellectual source for imposing democracy on the Arab world is Bernard Lewis, the Princeton historian who argues that Muslim cultures have an inferiority complex stemming from their relative decline compared to the West over the last three hundred years. (Such arguments minimize the role of Israel and US support for Israel as a source of Arab malaise. However, there is good evidence that the motives of Osama bin Laden and the 9/11 conspirators derive much more

---

[106] Laughland 2003.
[107] Ledeen 2002.

from US support for Israel than a general anti-Western animus.[108]) He contends that Arab societies with their antiquated, kinship-based structure can only be changed by forcing democracy on them.[109] Wolfowitz has used Lewis as the intellectual underpinning of the invasion of Iraq: "Bernard has taught how to understand the complex and important history of the Middle East, and use it to guide us where we will go next to build a better world for generations to come."[110] During the 1970s Lewis was invited by Richard Perle to give a talk to Henry Jackson's group, and, as Perle notes, "Lewis became Jackson's guru, more or less." Lewis also established ties with Daniel Patrick Moynihan and with Jackson's other aides, including Wolfowitz, Abrams, and Gaffney. One of Lewis's main arguments is that the Palestinians have no historical claim to a state because they were not a state before the British Mandate in 1918.

Lewis also argues that Arabs have a long history of consensus government, if not democracy, and that a modicum of outside force should be sufficient to democratize the area—a view that runs counter to the huge cultural differences between the Middle East and the West that stem ultimately from very different evolutionary pressures.[111] Lewis, as a cultural historian, is in a poor position to understand the deep structure of the cultural differences between Europe and the Middle East. He seems completely unaware of the differences in family and kinship structure between Europe and the Middle East, and he regards the difference in attitudes toward women as a mere cultural difference rather than as a marker for an entirely different social structure.[112]

Lewis's flawed beliefs about the Middle East have nevertheless been quite useful to Israel—reflecting the theme that Jewish intellectual movements have often used available intellectual resources to advance a political cause. Not only did he provide an important intellectual rationale for the war against Iraq, he is very close to governmental and academic circles in Israel—the confidant of successive Israeli Prime Ministers from Golda Meir to Ariel Sharon.[113]

---

[108] See Bamford 2004, 96–101, 138–45.
[109] Waldman 2004.
[110] Waldman 2004.
[111] See ch. 9 below on "What Makes Western Culture Unique?"
[112] Lewis 2002.
[113] Waldman 2004.

DICK CHENEY

By several accounts, Vice President Cheney had a "fever" to invade Iraq and transform the politics of the Middle East and was the leading force within the administration convincing President Bush of the need to do so.[114] As with the other Jewish intellectual and political movements I have reviewed, non-Jews have been welcomed into the movement and often given highly visible roles as the movement's public face. Among the current crop in this intellectual lineage, the most important non-Jews are Dick Cheney and Donald Rumsfeld, both of whom have close professional and personal relationships with neoconservatives that long pre-date their present power and visibility. Both Cheney and Rumsfeld have been associated with Bill Kristol's PNAC (which advocated a unilateral war for regime change in Iraq at least as early as 1998)[115] and the CSP, two neocon think tanks; Cheney was presented with the ADL's Distinguished Statesman Award in 1993 and was described by Abraham Foxman as "sensitive to Jewish concerns."[116] When Cheney was a Congressman during the early 1980s, he attended lunches hosted for Republican Jewish leaders by the House leadership. Cheney was described by Marshall Breger, a senior official in the Reagan and George H. W. Bush administrations as "very interested in outreach and engaging the Jewish community."[117] He was also a member of JINSA, a major pro-Israel activist organization, until assuming his office as vice president.

Cheney has also had a close involvement with leading Israeli politicians, especially Natan Sharansky, Secretary of Jerusalem and Diaspora Affairs in the Likud government and the prime architect of the ideology that the key to peace between Israel and the Arab world, including the Palestinians, is Arab acceptance of democracy. When President Bush articulated the importance of Palestinian democracy for the Middle East peace "roadmap" in his June 2002 policy speech,

> Sharansky could have written the speech himself, and, for that matter, may have had a direct hand in its drafting. The weekend prior to the speech, he spent long hours at a conference [organized by Richard Perle and] sponsored by the AEI in Aspen secluded together with Vice President Cheney and Deputy Secretary of Defense Paul

---

[114] Woodward 2004, 416.
[115] Project for the New American Century 1998a, 1998b.
[116] Samber 2000.
[117] Samber 2000.

Wolfowitz. The Bush speech clearly represented a triumph for the Cheney-Rumsfeld-Wolfowitz axis in the administration over the State Department, which was eager to offer the Palestinians a provisional state immediately."[118]

Both Cheney and Rumsfeld have close personal relationships with Kenneth Adelman, a former Ford and Reagan administration official.[119] Adelman wrote op-ed pieces in the *Washington Post* and *Wall Street Journal* in the period leading up to the war, and he, along with Wolfowitz and Irving Lewis "Scooter" Libby (Cheney's chief of staff), were guests of Cheney for a victory celebration in the immediate aftermath of the war (April 13, 2003).[120] Adelman has excellent neocon credentials. He was a member of the Committee on the Present Danger in the 1970s and UN Ambassador during the Reagan Administration, and worked under Donald Rumsfeld on three different occasions. He was a signatory to the April 3, 2002, letter of the Project for the New American Century to President Bush calling for Saddam Hussein's ouster and increased support for Israel. The letter stated, "Israel is targeted in part because it is our friend, and in part because it is an island of liberal, democratic principles—American principles—in a sea of tyranny, in-

---

[118] Rosenblum 2002. See also Milbank 2002. In a later column, Rosenblum (2003) noted,

Now [Sharansky] delivered the same message to Cheney: No matter how many conditions Bush placed on the creation of a Palestinian state under Arafat, any such announcement would constitute a reward for two years of non-stop terror against Israeli civilians. The normally laconic Cheney shot to attention when he heard these words. 'But your own government has already signed off on this,' he told Sharansky, confirming the latter's worst suspicions. Sharansky nevertheless repeated, as Cheney scribbled notes, that without the removal of Arafat and the entire junta from Tunis, the creation of an atmosphere in which Palestinians could express themselves without fear of reprisal, and the cessation of incitement against Israel in the Palestinian schools and media peace is impossible. President Bush's upcoming speech had already undergone 30 drafts at that point. It was about to undergo another crucial shift based on Sharansky's conversation with Cheney. Two days later, on June 24, 2002, President Bush announced at the outset, 'Peace requires a new and different Palestinian leadership.' He did not mention Yasir Arafat once.

[119] Drew 2003.
[120] Woodward 2004, 409–12.

tolerance, and hatred." The advocacy of war with Iraq was linked to advancing Israeli interests:

> If we do not move against Saddam Hussein and his regime, the damage our Israeli friends and we have suffered until now may someday appear but a prelude to much greater horrors. . . . Israel's fight against terrorism is our fight. Israel's victory is an important part of our victory. For reasons both moral and strategic, we need to stand with Israel in its fight against terrorism.[121]

Adelman's wife, Carol, is affiliated with the Hudson Institute, a neoconservative think tank.

Cheney's role in the ascendancy of the neocons in the Bush administration is particularly important: As head of the transition team, he and Libby were able to staff the subcabinet levels of the State Department (John Bolton) and the Defense Department (Wolfowitz, Feith) with key supporters of the neocon agenda. Libby is a close personal friend of Cheney whose views "echo many of Wolfowitz's policies"; he "is considered a hawk among hawks and was an early supporter of military action against terrorism and particularly against Iraq."[122] He is Jewish and has a long history of involvement in Zionist causes and as the attorney for Marc Rich. Libby and Cheney were involved in pressuring the CIA to color intelligence reports to fit with their desire for a war with Iraq.[123] Libby entered the neocon orbit when he was "captivated" while taking a political science course from Wolfowitz at Yale, and he worked under Wolfowitz in the Reagan and the Bush I administrations.[124] He was the coauthor (with Wolfowitz) of the ill-fated draft of the Defense Planning Guidance document of 1992, which advocated US dominance over all of Eurasia and urged preventing any other country from even contemplating

---

[121] Project for the New American Century 2002. Other signatories include William Kristol, Gary Bauer, Jeffrey Bell, William J. Bennett, Ellen Bork, Linda Chavez, Eliot Cohen, Midge Decter, Thomas Donnelly, Nicholas Eberstadt, Hillel Fradkin, Frank Gaffney, Jeffrey Gedmin, Reuel Marc Gerecht, Charles Hill, Bruce P. Jackson, Donald Kagan, Robert Kagan, John Lehman, Tod Lindberg, Rich Lowry, Clifford May, Joshua Muravchik, Martin Peretz, Richard Perle, Daniel Pipes, Norman Podhoretz, Stephen P. Rosen, Randy Scheunemann, Gary Schmitt, William Schneider, Jr., Marshall Wittmann, and R. James Woolsey.

[122] Chicago Model United Nations 2001.

[123] Pincus and Priest 2003; Bamford 2004, 368–70.

[124] Keller 2002; see also Woodward 2004, 48.

challenging US hegemony.[125] (Cheney was Secretary of Defense at that time.) After an uproar, the document was radically altered, but this blueprint for US hegemony remains central to neocon attitudes since the collapse of the Soviet Union.

DONALD RUMSFELD

As noted above, Rumsfeld has deep links with neoconservative think tanks and individual Jews such as Ken Adelman, who began his career working for Rumsfeld when he headed the Office of Economic Opportunity in the Nixon administration. Another close associate is Robert A. Goldwin, a student of Leo Strauss and Rumsfeld's deputy both at NATO and at the Gerald Ford White House; Goldwin is now resident scholar at the AEI.

Rumsfeld also has a long history of appealing to Jewish and Israeli causes. In his 1964 campaign for reelection to Congress as representative from a district on the North Shore of Chicago with an important Jewish constituency, he emphasized Soviet persecution of Jews and introduced a bill on this topic in the House. After the 1967 war, he urged the United States not to demand that Israel withdraw to its previous borders, and he criticized delays in sending US military hardware to Israel.[126] More recently, as Secretary of Defense in the Bush II administration, Rumsfeld was praised by the ZOA for distancing himself from the phrase "occupied territories," referring to them as the "so-called occupied territories."[127]

Despite these links with neoconservatives and Jewish causes, Rumsfeld emerges as less an ideologue and less a passionate advocate for war with Iraq than Cheney. Robert Woodward describes him as lacking the feverish intensity of Cheney, as a dispassionate "defense technocrat" who, unlike Cheney, Wolfowitz, and Feith, would have been content if the United States had not gone to war with Iraq.[128]

---

[125] Lobe 2002a; Mann 2004, 208–10.

[126] Decter 2003, 41–43.

[127] Zionist Organization of America 2002. ZOA National President Morton A. Klein said: "Israel has the greater historical, legal, and moral right to Judea, Samaria, and Gaza. At the very least, those areas should be called disputed territories, not occupied territories, since the term 'occupied' clearly suggests that the 'occupier' has no right to be there. We strongly applaud Secretary Rumsfeld's courageous and principled stance in distancing himself from the 'occupied territory' fallacy."

[128] Woodward 2004, 416.

DANIEL PIPES

Many neoconservatives work mainly as lobbyists and propagandists. Rather than attempt to describe this massive infrastructure in its entirety, I profile Daniel Pipes as a prototypical example of the highly competent Jewish lobbyist. Pipes is the son of Richard Pipes, the Harvard professor who, as noted above, was an early neocon and an expert on the Soviet Union. He is the director of the Middle East Forum and a columnist at the *New York Post* and the *Jerusalem Post,* and appears on the Fox News Channel. Pipes is described as "An authoritative commentator on the Middle East" by the *Wall Street Journal*, according to the masthead of his website.[129] A former official in the Departments of State and Defense, he has taught at the University of Chicago, Harvard University, and the US Naval War College. He is the author of twelve books on the Middle East, Islam, and other political topics; his recent book *Militant Islam Reaches America* (published by W. W. Norton, 2002), a polemic against political Islam, argues that militant Islam is the greatest threat to the West since the Cold War. He serves on the "Special Task Force on Terrorism and Technology" at the Department of Defense, has testified before many congressional committees, and served on four presidential campaigns.

The MEF issues two regular quasi-academic publications, the *Middle East Quarterly* and the *Middle East Intelligence Bulletin*, the latter published jointly with the United States Committee for a Free Lebanon. The *Middle East Quarterly* describes itself as "a bold, insightful, and controversial publication." A recent article on weapons of mass destruction claims that Syria "has more destructive capabilities" than Iraq or Iran. The *Middle East Intelligence Bulletin* "specializes in covering the seamy side of Lebanese and Syrian politics,"[130] an effort aimed at depicting these regimes as worthy of forcible change by the US or Israeli military.

Martin Kramer is the editor of the *Middle East Quarterly*. Kramer is also affiliated with Tel Aviv University's Moshe Dayan Center for Middle Eastern and African Studies. His book, *Ivory Towers on Sand: The Failure of Middle Eastern Studies in America*, has been a major impetus behind the recent effort to prevent criticism of Israel on college campuses. The book was warmly reviewed in the *Weekly Standard*, whose editor, Bill Kristol, is a member of the MEF along with Kramer. Kristol wrote that, "Kramer has performed a crucial service by expos-

---

[129] www.danielpipes.org.
[130] Whitaker 2002.

ing intellectual rot in a scholarly field of capital importance to national well-being."

The MEF also targets universities through its campus speakers bureau, seeking to correct "inaccurate Middle Eastern curricula in American education," by addressing "biases" and "basic errors" and providing "better information" than students can get from the many "irresponsible" professors that it believes lurk in US universities.

The MEF is behind Campus Watch, an organization responsible for repressing academic discussion of Middle East issues at US universities. Campus Watch compiles profiles on professors who criticize Israel: A major purpose is to "identify key faculty who teach and write about contemporary affairs at university Middle East Studies departments in order to analyze and critique the work of these specialists for errors or biases." The MEF also develops "a network of concerned students and faculty members interested in promoting American interests on campus."[131] Again we see the rhetoric of universalism and a concern with "American interests" produced by people who are ethnically Jewish and vitally concerned with the welfare of Israel.

Recently Campus Watch has decided to discontinue its dossiers because over one hundred professors asked to be included in their directory of suspicious people. Nevertheless, Campus Watch continues to print names of people whose views on the Middle East differ from theirs. The MEF, along with major Jewish activist organizations (the American Jewish Committee, the American Jewish Congress, and the Anti-Defamation League), has succeeded in getting the US House of Representatives to overwhelmingly approve a bill that would authorize federal monitoring of government-funded Middle East studies programs throughout US universities. The bill would establish a federal tribunal to investigate and monitor criticism of Israel on American college campuses.

JEWISH INSTITUTE FOR NATIONAL SECURITY AFFAIRS (JINSA)

Rather than profile all of the many neoconservative think tanks and lobbying groups, I will describe JINSA as a prototypical example. JINSA attempts to

> educate the American public about the importance of an effective US defense capability so that our vital interests as Americans can be safeguarded [and to] inform the American defense and foreign affairs

---

[131] www.campus-watch.org.

community about the important role Israel can and does play in bolstering democratic interests in the Mediterranean and the Middle East.[132]

Typical of Jewish intellectual movements, Jewish interests are here cloaked in a rhetoric of American interests and ethical universalism—in this case, the idea that Israel is a beacon of democracy.

In addition to a core of prominent neoconservative Jews (Stephen D. Bryen, Douglas Feith, Max Kampelman, Michael Ledeen, Joshua Muravchik, Richard Perle, Stephen Solarz), JINSA's advisory board includes a bevy of non-Jewish retired US military officers and a variety of non-Jewish political figures (e.g., Dick Cheney) and foreign policy analysts with access to the media (e.g., Jeane Kirkpatrick) who are staunch supporters of Israel. As is typical of Jewish intellectual movements, JINSA is well funded and has succeeded in bringing in high-profile non-Jews who often act as spokesmen for its policies. For example, the former head of the Iraq occupation government, General Jay Garner, signed a JINSA letter stating that, "the Israel Defense Forces have exercised remarkable restraint in the face of lethal violence orchestrated by the leadership of [the] Palestinian Authority."

JINSA reflects the recent trend of American Jewish activist groups not simply to support Israeli policies but to support the Israeli right wing. For JINSA,

> "regime change" by any means necessary in Iraq, Iran, Syria, Saudi Arabia, and the Palestinian Authority is an urgent imperative. Anyone who dissents—be it Colin Powell's State Department, the CIA, or career military officers—is committing heresy against articles of faith that effectively hold there is no difference between US and Israeli national security interests, and that the only way to assure continued safety and prosperity for both countries is through hegemony in the Middle East—a hegemony achieved with the traditional Cold War recipe of feints, force, clientism, and covert action.[133]

Note the exclusionary, us versus them attitude typical of the Jewish intellectual and political movements covered in *The Culture of Critique*.

Part of JINSA's effectiveness comes from recruiting non-Jews who gain by increased defense spending or are willing to be spokesmen in

---

[132] www.jinsa.org.
[133] Vest 2002.

return for fees and travel to Israel. The bulk of JINSA's budget is spent on taking a host of retired US generals and admirals to Israel, where JINSA facilitates meetings between Israeli officials and retired but still-influential US flag officers. These officers then write op-ed pieces and sign letters and advertisements championing the Likudnik line. In one such statement, issued soon after the outbreak of the latest intifada, twenty-six JINSAns of retired flag rank, including many from the advisory board, struck a moralizing tone, characterizing Palestinian violence as a "perversion of military ethics" and holding that, "America's role as facilitator in this process should never yield to America's responsibility as a friend to Israel," because "friends don't leave friends on the battlefield."[134] Sowing seeds for the future, JINSA also takes US service academy cadets to Israel each summer and sponsors a lecture series at the Army, Navy, and Air Force academies.

JINSA also patronizes companies in the defense industry that stand to gain by the drive for total war. "Almost every retired officer who sits on JINSA's board of advisers or has participated in its Israel trips or signed a JINSA letter works or has worked with military contractors who do business with the Pentagon and Israel."[135] For example, JINSA advisory board members Adm. Leon Edney, Adm. David Jeremiah, and Lieut. Gen. Charles May, all retired, have served Northrop Grumman or its subsidiaries as either consultants or board members. Northrop Grumman has built ships for the Israeli Navy and sold F-16 avionics and E-2C Hawkeye planes to the Israeli Air Force, as well as the Longbow radar system to the Israeli Army for use in its attack helicopters. It also works with Tamam, a subsidiary of Israeli Aircraft Industries, to produce an unmanned aerial vehicle.

JINSA is supported not only by defense contractor money but also by deeply committed Zionists, notably Irving Moscowitz, the California bingo magnate who also provides financial support to the AEI. Moscowitz not only sends millions of dollars a year to far-right Israeli West Bank settler groups like Ateret Cohanim, he has also funded land purchases in key Arab areas around Jerusalem. Moscowitz provided the money that enabled the 1996 reopening of a tunnel under the Temple Mount/Haram al-Sharif, which resulted in seventy deaths due to rioting. Also involved in funding JINSA is New York investment banker Lawrence Kadish, who also contributes to Republican causes. Again, we see the effects of the most committed Jews. People like Moscowitz

---

[134] Vest 2002.
[135] Vest 2002.

have an enormous effect because they use their wealth to advance their people's interests, a very common pattern among wealthy Jews.[136]

The integration of JINSA with the US defense establishment can be seen in the program for its 2001 Jackson Award Dinner, an annual event named after Senator Henry Jackson that draws an "A-list" group of politicians and defense celebrities. At the dinner were representatives of US defense industries (the dinner was sponsored by Boeing), as well as the following Defense Department personnel: Under Secretary of Defense Paul Wolfowitz; Under Secretary of Defense Dov Zakheim (an ordained rabbi); Assistant Secretary of the Navy John Young; Dr. William Schneider, the Chairman of the Defense Science Board; the Honorable Mark Rosenker, Senior Military Advisor to the President; Admiral William Fallon, Vice Chief of Naval Operations; General John Keane, Vice Chief of Staff of the Army; General Michael Williams, Vice Commandant of the Marines; Lieutenant General Lance Lord, Assistant Vice Chief of Staff of the Air Force. Also present were a large number of US flag and general officers who were alumni of JINSA trips to Israel, as well as assorted Congressmen, a US Senator, and a variety of Israeli military and political figures. The 2002 Jackson Award Dinner, sponsored by Northrop Grumman, honored Paul Wolfowitz. Dick Cheney was a previous recipient of the award.

JINSA is a good illustration of the point that whatever the deeply held beliefs of the non-Jews who are involved in the neoconservative movement, financial motives and military careerism are also of considerable importance—a testimony to the extent to which neoconservatism has permeated the political and military establishments of the United States. A similar statement could be made about the deep influence of neoconservatism among intellectuals generally.[137]

---

[136] See ch. 1 above, "Background Traits for Jewish Activism."

[137] I thank the late Sam Francis for his very helpful comments on this paper. I am also grateful to an expert on Leo Strauss for his comments, many of which have been incorporated into the section on Strauss. Unfortunately, at his request, he must remain anonymous. Finally, thanks to Ted O'Keefe for his editorial work on an earlier version of this paper.

Chapter 6

JEWS, BLACKS, AND RACE[*]

This essay provides an overview of the history of black-Jewish relationships in the twentieth century. The record shows quite clearly that Jewish organizations as well as a great number of individual Jews contributed enormously to the success of the movement to increase the power of blacks and alter the racial hierarchy of the United States. I also discuss the more difficult question of how to understand Jewish motives in the black-Jewish alliance.

It is important to realize that blacks and Jews are two very different groups. From the ancient world to the present, Jewish populations have repeatedly attained a position of power and influence within Western societies. The Ashkenazi Jews that dominate the American Jewish community have the highest average intelligence of any human group, and they have shown an extraordinary ability to create and participate in highly effective groups in pursuit of their interests.[1] Despite rather widespread anti-Jewish attitudes (although quite mild by historical standards), and despite arriving typically as impoverished immigrants, Jews rapidly achieved social status, wealth, power, and influence in the United States far out of proportion to their numbers. Jewish power was already visible during the public debate on whether to enter World War II on the side of England; indeed, as early as during the immigration debates of the 1920s (although they were not on the winning side). But it increased dramatically after World War II, and since the 1960s, Jewish Americans have become an elite group with a great deal of influence on public policy. Although there are important divisions within the American Jewish community, there has been wide consensus on a number of critical public policy issues, particularly in the areas of support for Israel and the welfare of other foreign Jewries, immigration and refugee policy, church-state separation, abortion rights, and civil liberties.[2]

---

[*] First published in *Race and the American Prospect: Essays on the Racial Realities of our Nation and our Time*, ed. Samuel Francis (Mount Airy, Md.: The Occidental Press, 2006).

[1] See *A People That Shall Dwell Alone* and ch. 1 above "Background Traits for Jewish Activism."

[2] Goldberg 1996, 5.

There was a broad Jewish consensus of sympathy and support for movements that empowered black Americans, at least until the 1970s, when Jewish neoconservatives—a small minority within the Jewish community—began to dissent from some of the more radical forms of legislating black advancement and called for limiting welfare and curtailing some of the more extreme forms of affirmative action and group rights for blacks. In common with the mainstream organized American Jewish community, however, the neoconservatives supported the civil rights revolution of the 1960s.

Blacks have a completely different history and racial profile. In the South, blacks were subjected to slavery, and, following emancipation, racial segregation resulted in a well-defined racial hierarchy. In the North blacks have also been relatively impoverished and powerless, but, when controlled for IQ, blacks have achieved the same level of occupational success as whites since the end of the first phase of the civil rights movement—around 1960. Since that time, controlled for IQ, blacks have been much more likely to be in high-IQ occupations than whites with the same IQ. For example, in a study performed on data from 1990, whites with professional jobs had an average IQ of 114, while blacks holding these jobs had an average IQ of 94.[3] The average black IQ is 85, one standard deviation below the mean for American whites and at least two standard deviations below the mean Jewish-American IQ of 115.[4]

Reflecting this disparity in IQ and achievement, the relationship between blacks and Jews has always been one-sided. Jews have played an important role in organizing, funding, and promoting black causes, but blacks have played no role in running the affairs of the organized Jewish community.[5]

A Brief History of the Black-Jewish Alliance

Jewish activities in support of blacks have involved litigation, legislation, fund-raising, political organizing, and academic movements opposed to the concept of biologically based racial differences.

Jews have played a prominent role in organizing blacks beginning with the founding of the National Association for the Advancement of Colored People (NAACP) in 1909 and, despite increasing black anti-Semitism, continuing into the present. The NAACP was founded by

---

[3] Herrnstein and Murray 1994, 321–22, 488–92.
[4] *A People That Shall Dwell Alone*, ch. 7.
[5] Cruse 1967/1992.

wealthy German Jews, non-Jewish whites, and blacks led by W. E. B. DuBois.[6] The Jewish role was predominant:

> By mid-decade [c. 1915], the NAACP had something of the aspect of an adjunct of B'nai B'rith and the American Jewish Committee, with the brothers Joel and Arthur Spingarn serving as board chairman and chief legal counsel, respectively; Herbert Lehman on the executive committee; Lillian Wald and Walter Sachs on the board (though not simultaneously); and Jacob Schiff and Paul Warburg as financial angels. By 1920, Herbert Seligman was director of public relations, and Martha Gruening served as his assistant.... Small wonder that a bewildered Marcus Garvey stormed out of NAACP headquarters in 1917, muttering that it was a white organization.[7]

Until after World War II, the Jewish-black alliance essentially involved wealthy German Jews aiding black organizations financially and through their organizational abilities; Jewish lawyers also played a prominent role in staffing the legal departments of black activist organizations. Thus the Spingarn brothers were part of this German-Jewish aristocracy. Except for brief periods when he resigned to protest the attitudes of the board, Joel Spingarn was chairman of the NAACP from 1914 to 1934, when the first black assumed the position. Wealthy Jews were important contributors to the National Urban League as well, most notably Jacob Schiff, the premier Jewish activist of the first two decades of the twentieth century, and Julius Rosenwald, whose wealth derived from the Sears, Roebuck Company.[8] Louis Marshall, the most prominent Jewish activist of the 1920s and leader of the American Jewish Committee (AJCommittee), was on the board of directors of the NAACP and was a principal NAACP attorney. Other prominent Jewish attorneys who participated in NAACP lawsuits included Supreme Court Justices Louis Brandeis and Felix Frankfurter, the latter playing a major role in the 1954 Brown v. Board of Education decision. Another Jewish attorney prominent in NAACP affairs was Nathan Margold, described as having "a burning social conscience";[9] Margold developed the plan for the successful assault on the legal basis of segregation. Jack

---

[6] Friedman 1995, 45.
[7] Levering-Lewis 1984, 85
[8] Levering-Lewis 1984, 85
[9] Friedman 1995, 106.

Greenberg, chairman of the NAACP Legal Defense Fund in the 1960s, was also instrumental in the origin of MALDEF, bringing together Mexican activist Pete Tijerina with the Ford Foundation.[10]

Blacks played little role in these efforts until the late 1930s: For example, until 1933 there were no black lawyers in the NAACP legal department, and through the 1930s around half of the NAACP's legal department were Jews.[11] At the height of the black-Jewish alliance, in the 1960s, more than half of the lawyers defending students and other participants in the protest movement in the South were Jews.[12] Heavily Jewish organizations like the National Lawyers Guild, which had ties to the Communist Party,[13] and the American Civil Liberties Union also provided legal talent for these endeavors.

In the post-World War II period the entire gamut of Jewish civil service organizations was involved in black issues, including the AJCommittee, the American Jewish Congress (AJCongress), and the Anti-Defamation League of B'nai B'rith (ADL): "With professionally trained personnel, fully equipped offices, and public relations know-how, they had the resources to make a difference."[14] By the end of the 1940s the ADL had designated the South as particularly in need of change; the ADL monitored instances of racial tension and violence and increasingly sought intervention by the federal government in the affairs of the region, including racial segregation.[15]

Jews contributed from two thirds to three quarters of the money for civil rights groups during the 1960s.[16] The AJCongress, the AJCommittee, and the ADL worked closely with the NAACP to write legal briefs and raise money in the effort to end segregation. Jewish groups, particularly the AJCongress, played a leading role in drafting civil rights legislation and pursuing legal challenges related to civil rights issues mainly benefiting blacks.[17]

> Jewish support, legal and monetary, afforded the civil rights movement a string of legal victories. . . . There is little exaggera-

---

[10] http://www.maldef.org/about/founding.htm.
[11] Friedman 1995, 48, 106.
[12] Friedman 1995, 183.
[13] See Friedman 1995, 182.
[14] Friedman 1995, 135.
[15] Greenberg 1998, 140.
[16] Kaufman 1997, 110.
[17] Svonkin 1997, 79–112.

tion in an American Jewish Congress lawyer's claim that "many of these laws were actually written in the offices of Jewish agencies by Jewish staff people, introduced by Jewish legislators and pressured into being by Jewish voters."[18]

A watershed period in Jewish support for blacks was the aftermath of World War II. Jews emerged from the war in a much more powerful position than before. Anti-Jewish attitudes that had been common before the war declined precipitously, and Jewish organizations assumed a much higher profile in influencing ethnic relations in the United States, not only in the area of civil rights but also in immigration policy. Significantly, this high Jewish profile was spearheaded by the American Jewish Congress and the ADL, both dominated by Jews who had immigrated from Eastern Europe between 1880 and 1920 and their descendants.[19] As indicated below, an understanding of the special character of this Jewish population is critical to understanding Jewish influence in the United States from 1945 to the present. The German-Jewish elite that had dominated Jewish community affairs via the AJCommittee earlier in the century gave way to a new leadership made up of Eastern European immigrants and their descendants. Even the AJCommittee, the bastion of the German-Jewish elite, came to be headed by John Slawson, who had immigrated at the age of seven from the Ukraine. The AJCongress, a creation of the Jewish immigrant community, was headed by Will Maslow, a socialist and a Zionist. Zionism and political radicalism typified the Jewish immigrants from Eastern Europe.[20]

As an indication of the radicalism of the immigrant Jewish community, the 50,000-member Jewish People's Fraternal Order, an affiliate of the AJCongress, was listed as a subversive organization by the US Attorney General. The JPFO was the financial and organizational "bulwark" of the Communist Party USA after World War II and also funded the *Daily Worker*, an organ of the CPUSA, and the *Morning Freiheit*, a Yiddish communist newspaper.[21] Although the AJCongress severed its ties with the JPFO and stated that communism was a threat, it was "at best a reluctant and unenthusiastic participant" in the Jewish effort to develop a public image of anti-communism—a position reflecting the sympathies

---

[18] Levering-Lewis 1984, 94.

[19] Friedman 1995, 133; Greenberg 1998, 136.

[20] *The Culture of Critique*, ch. 3 and ch. 3 above "Zionism and the Internal Dynamics of the Jewish Community."

[21] Svonkin 1997, 166.

of many among its predominantly second- and third-generation Eastern European immigrant membership.[22] Concern that Jewish communists were involved in the civil rights movement centered around the activities of Stanley Levison, a key advisor to Martin Luther King who had very close ties to the Communist Party (as well as to the AJCongress) and may have been acting under communist discipline in his activities with King.[23]

Jews were also instrumental in creating the intellectual context that made possible the revolution in racial relationships in the United States. David Hollinger notes "the transformation of the ethnoreligious demography of American academic life by Jews" in the period from the 1930s to the 1960s,[24] and in *The Culture of Critique*, I have described intellectual and political movements dominated by people who identified as Jews and viewed their efforts as aiding Jewish causes, particularly in ending anti-Semitism. These movements collectively resulted in a decline of evolutionary and biological thinking in the academic world, and they pathologized racial identity among whites.

There were several strands to these intellectual endeavors. Beginning with Horace Kallen, Jewish intellectuals have been at the forefront in developing models of the United States as a culturally and ethnically pluralistic society. This conception that the United States should be organized as a set of separate ethnic-cultural groups was accompanied by an ideology according to which relationships between groups would be cooperative and benign: "Kallen lifted his eyes above the strife that swirled around him to an ideal realm where diversity and harmony coexist."[25]

During the 1930s, the AJCommittee funded the research of Franz Boas, who was instrumental in eradicating the idea that biological race was an important source of differences among people. (While leading this battle, Boas himself never completely rejected the view that there were racial differences in brain size favoring whites. Even at the end of his life, in the 1938 edition of *The Mind of Primitive Man*, Boas advanced the idea that there would be fewer men of high genius among blacks; however, he argued that mean group differences should not be applied to individuals because of variation within each race.[26]) Boasian

---

[22] Svonkin 1997, 132.
[23] See Friedman 1995, 110–11, 117.
[24] Hollinger 1996, 4.
[25] Higham 1984, 209.
[26] See discussion in Williams 1998.

anthropology was a Jewish intellectual movement that by the 1920s came to dominate American anthropology.[27] (As above, by "Jewish intellectual movement" I mean a movement dominated by people who identified as Jews and saw their involvement in the movement as advancing Jewish interests.) Boasian anthropology was enlisted in post–World War II propaganda efforts distributed and promoted by the AJCommittee, the AJCongress, and the ADL, as in the film *Brotherhood of Man*, which depicted all human groups as having equal abilities. In the postwar era, the Boasian ideology denying racial differences, as well as the Boasian ideology of cultural relativism and the belief in the importance of preserving and respecting cultural differences deriving from Horace Kallen, were important ingredients of educational programs sponsored by these Jewish activist organizations and widely distributed throughout the American educational system.[28]

The AJCommittee also supported the efforts of refugee Jewish social scientists who fled Germany in the 1930s, particularly those centered around the Frankfurt School of Social Research (Max Horkheimer, Erich Fromm, T. W. Adorno, Herbert Marcuse). This group combined elements of Marxism and psychoanalysis—both of which are considered Jewish intellectual movements.[29] Fundamentally, *The Authoritarian Personality* and the other works produced by this group (collectively termed the Studies in Prejudice) resulted from a felt need to develop an empirical program of research that would support a politically and intellectually satisfying *a priori* theory of anti-Semitism and other forms of ethnic hostility in order to influence an American academic audience. *The Authoritarian Personality* attempts to show that the group affiliations of non-Jews, and in particular membership in Christian religious sects, nationalism, and close family ties, are indications of psychiatric disorder. At a deep level the work of the Frankfurt School is addressed to altering Western societies in an attempt to make them resistant to anti-Semitism by pathologizing group affiliations of non-Jews.

In 1944 the AJCongress organized the Commission on Community Interrelations under the leadership of Kurt Lewin, a strong advocate of group identity for minority groups. Lewin epitomized the confrontational attitude of the leftist AJCongress in advocating the importance of legislation against discrimination rather than relying on propaganda and

---

[27] *The Culture of Critique*, ch. 2.
[28] Svonkin 1997, 63, 64.
[29] *The Culture of Critique*, chs. 3 and 4.

activist social science alone.[30] The activists/scientists recruited to this group included Kenneth Clark, whose doll study with black children purportedly showing the psychic damage inflicted by segregation was an important component of the landmark 1954 decision in Brown v. Board of Education. Another member was Marie Jahoda, co-author of *Anti-Semitism and Emotional Disorder*, a volume in the Studies in Prejudice published by the AJCommittee.[31] This book consisted of a set of ad hoc psychodynamic proposals whose only similarity is that anti-Semitism involves the projection of some sort of intrapsychic conflict. The book is a good illustration of the usefulness of psychoanalysis in constructing theories of anti-Semitism or other expressions of ethnic hostility as reflecting psychological inadequacy rather than real conflicts of interest.

The general term for this multifaceted effort by Jewish organizations to alter ethnic relations in the United States is the intergroup relations movement.[32] This effort included legal challenges to bias in housing, education, and public employment. Jewish organizations also drafted legislative proposals and attempted to secure their passage into law in state and national legislative bodies. Another prong of the offensive was shaping messages in the media, promoting educational programs for students and teachers, and, as noted above, promoting efforts to reshape the intellectual discourse on race in the academic world. The Anti-Defamation League was centrally involved in these efforts, "utilizing radio and television spots, clever jingles, filmstrips and other media efforts."[33] The ADL recruited celebrities such as Bess Myerson who toured the country with the pitch that "you can't be beautiful, and hate."[34] Hollywood movies such as *Gentleman's Agreement* and *The House I Live In* also disseminated these messages, and the musical *South Pacific*, by Rodgers and Hammerstein, included a theme of interracial marriage and a song stating that children had to be taught to hate. As with Jewish involvement in immigration policy and a great many other instances of Jewish political and intellectual activity in both modern and premodern times, the intergroup relations movement often worked to minimize overt Jewish involvement.[35]

---

[30] Friedman 1995, 144.
[31] Ackerman and Jahoda 1950.
[32] See Svonkin 1997.
[33] Friedman 1995, 140.
[34] In Friedman 1995, 140.
[35] Svonkin 1997, 45, 51, 65, 71–72; *Separation and Its Discontents*, ch. 6.

The ideology of intergroup animosity developed by the intergroup relations movement derived from the Studies in Prejudice series sponsored by the AJCommittee, particularly the Frankfurt School's *The Authoritarian Personality*. This work explicitly viewed manifestations of ethnocentrism or discrimination against outgroups as a mental disease and thus literally a public health problem. The assault on intergroup animosity was likened to the medical assault on deadly infectious diseases, and people with the disease were described by activists as "infected."[36] A consistent theme of the intellectual rationale for this body of ethnic activism emphasized the benefits to be gained by increased levels of intergroup harmony—an aspect of the idealism inherent in Horace Kallen's conceptualization of multiculturalism—without mentioning that some groups, particularly European-derived, non-Jewish groups, would lose economic and political power and decline in cultural influence.[37] Negative attitudes toward groups were viewed not as the result of competing group interests but rather as the result of individual psychopathology.[38] Finally, while ethnocentrism by non-Jews was viewed as a public health problem, the AJCongress fought against Jewish assimilation and was a strong supporter of Israel as a Jewish ethnostate.

The rhetoric of the intergroup relations movement stressed that its goals were congruent with traditional views of America, but this is misleading at best. Their rhetoric emphasized the Enlightenment legacy of individual rights. However, rather than seeing the legacy of individual rights as a unique product of Western culture, the intergroup relations movement interpreted these rights as congruent with Jewish ideals originating with the prophets. This conceptualization ignored the fact that Jewish tradition itself is profoundly collectivist rather than individualist; it also ignored the fact that hostility toward outgroups has always been central to the Jewish group evolutionary strategy.[39] Jewish rhetoric during this period thus relied on an illusory view of the Jewish past that was tailor-made to achieve Jewish objectives in the modern world, where the Enlightenment rhetoric of universalism and individual rights retained considerable intellectual prestige.[40]

The intergroup relations movement either ignored or vilified other

---

[36] Svonkin 1997, 30, 59.
[37] Svonkin 1997, 5.
[38] Svonkin 1997, 75.
[39] Svonkin 1997, 7, 20.
[40] Svonkin 1997.

traditional sources of American identity. There was no mention of the republican strand of American identity as a cohesive, socially homogeneous society.[41] Also ignored or vilified was the idea that America was a Northwestern European culture created by people from a specific ethnic group. This "ethnocultural" strand of American identity as a racial/ethnic group had become quite influential between 1880 and 1920 with the theories of Madison Grant, Lothrop Stoddard, and others. These theories were strongly influenced by Darwinism, and they were the particular target of Boasian anthropology and the other Jewish intellectual movements discussed above.

By the early 1960s an ADL official estimated that one-third of America's teachers had received ADL educational material based on the ideology of the intergroup relations movement.[42] The ADL was also intimately involved in staffing, developing materials, and providing financial assistance for workshops for teachers and school administrators, often with the involvement of social scientists from the academic world—an association that undoubtedly added to the scientific credibility of these exercises. It is ironic, perhaps, that this effort to influence the public school curriculum was carried on by the same groups that were endeavoring to remove overt Christian influences from the public schools. The ADL continues to be a major promoter of diversity education through its A WORLD OF DIFFERENCE® Institute.[43] Since 1985 this institute has trained more than 230,000 elementary and secondary school teachers in diversity education and has conducted workplace diversity training programs for workers and college students in the United States. Teacher training programs have also been instituted in Germany and Russia.

JEWISH MOTIVES IN PROMOTING BLACK CAUSES

It is always difficult to measure influence in complex social transformations such as the enormous changes in ethnic relations that have occurred in the last fifty years. Whatever the exact contribution of Jews and Jewish organizations, one must acknowledge that there was cooperation among mainstream Jewish organizations, black activists, and a vast number of whites who came to internalize the ideological premises of this revolution. Indeed, it is now fair to say that there is a consensus of elite opinion across the political spectrum on the moral foundations of

---

[41] Smith 1988; see *The Culture of Critique*, ch. 8.
[42] Svonkin 1997, 69.
[43] http://www.adl.org/education/.

the revolution in civil rights for blacks. This consensus comes out in stark relief on occasions such as the broad-based censure that followed remarks in December 2002 by Trent Lott that America would not have many of its current problems if Strom Thurmond had been elected president in 1948. Thurmond had run on a segregationist platform.

The evidence reviewed briefly here certainly suggests that Jewish activism was a critical force in leading, organizing, and funding the revolution in ethnic relations that has occurred in the United States since World War II. Even Harold Cruse, a trenchant black critic of the black-Jewish alliance, has noted that, "The truth was (and is) that the American Jewish Committee and its intellectual adherents pioneered in ways never equaled by their white Protestant allies."[44] (A similar statement could be made regarding Jewish involvement in opening up US immigration to all the peoples of the world.[45]) This is not to say that blacks would not have eventually attempted to alter their situation in the absence of an alliance with Jews.

However, it is difficult to believe that these efforts would have been so effective and so quickly successful in the absence of Jewish involvement. After all, at least until the 1960s, blacks had not shown themselves able to develop effective organizations without Jewish input. Blacks, as a low-achieving group, continue to have relatively little power and influence in ethnic relations in the United States and remain underrepresented in all the elite institutions of society. Because of their high intelligence, their high level of mobilization, and their overrepresentation in elite institutions of the government, the media, business, and the academic world, Jewish influence is far out of proportion to their numbers.[46] White non-Jews have relatively little influence compared to Jews because of their lack of mobilization to achieve their ethnic interests.[47]

Moreover, continuing Jewish involvement in the media and in funding black organizations remains an important ingredient in black success, long after the leadership of these organizations passed to blacks. For example, Murray Friedman notes that after 1955 blacks assumed the leadership of the movement: "No longer would Jewish leaders and other outsiders call the shots. They would work behind the scenes, providing

---

[44] Cruse 1987, 122.

[45] See *The Culture of Critique*, ch. 7.

[46] Salter 1998; see also ch. 1 above on "Background Traits for Jewish Activism."

[47] Salter 1998.

money and advice to [Martin Luther] King and his lieutenants, who would head the movement, win the headlines, and endure the jail sentences."

Despite the high profile of Jewish neoconservatives who dissent from some of the more extreme forms of affirmative action and other elements of the black political agenda, the great majority of Jews remain on the left/liberal wing of American politics. Indeed, the effort to turn nondiscrimination in employment into a results-oriented quota system was spearheaded by a heavily Jewish brain trust, most notably Alfred W. Blumrosen, at the Equal Employment Opportunity Commission.[48] Despite representing only 2.5 percent of the population, Jews provide over half of the funding of the Democratic Party, and in the 2000 election, 80 percent of Jews voted for Gore.[49] In general Jewish congressional representatives support liberal programs along with their black colleagues,[50] and Jewish organizations continue to endorse strong, quota-type affirmative action programs, at least if it can be shown that there has been a past history of discrimination.[51]

Jewish support for the Democratic Party appears to be declining. In the 2000 election younger Jews, ages 18–29, voted 59 to 40 percent for Bush. Nevertheless, this portending shift probably does not indicate significant defection of Jews from the achievements of the post-World War II revolution in ethnic affairs. For example, at this writing, support of large-scale multiethnic immigration to the United States characterizes the entire Jewish political spectrum, from the far left to the neoconservative right.[52] Moreover, younger ADL leaders were more likely to endorse a lower threshold for affirmative action policy in which race could be used as a factor in employment and university admissions in the absence of a finding of discrimination.[53] Older Jews tend to view affirmative action through the lens of the quota systems designed to regulate the number of Jews in elite universities in the 1920s and 1930s.

Jewish involvement in altering the racial hierarchy of the United States did not stem from Judaism per se. That is, there is nothing in Judaism as a religion or ethnicity that would dictate that Jews would ally

---

[48] See Graham 1990, 194–96.
[49] Lipset and Raab 1995; Friedman 2002.
[50] Friedman 1995, 351.
[51] See Chanes 1997; discussed below.
[52] *The Culture of Critique*, ch. 7.
[53] Chanes 1997, 307.

with blacks as racial underdogs in European America. Throughout history a common pattern has been for Jews to make alliances with elites, and often with alien and oppressive elites. In the ancient world, in the Muslim world, and in Christian Europe from the Middle Ages to post-World War II Eastern Europe, Jews have allied themselves with rulers and have often been seen as oppressors of the common people.

Indeed, I have argued that an important contrast between Eastern and Western Europe was that exploitative economic systems involving the collaboration between Jews and non-Jewish elites continued far longer in Eastern Europe.[54] There "Jewish estate managers became the master of life and death over the population of entire districts, and having nothing but a short-term and purely financial interest in the relationship, was faced with the irresistible temptation to pare his temporary subjects to the bone."[55] The theme of oppressive Jewish money lending and tax farming was characteristic of anti-Jewish attitudes for centuries.

Moreover, Jewish law condones slavery and elaborates distinctions between the treatment of Jewish and non-Jewish slaves (much to the detriment of the latter). Jews dominated the slave trade in the ancient Roman world,[56] and Jews were involved in financing the African slave trade to the New World as a mercantile elite in Spain, Portugal, and Amsterdam. In the United States, Southern Jews traded and owned slaves,[57] probably at least at levels commensurate with their wealth and their percentage of the population.

Given this history, it is perhaps not surprising that in the United States, Jews in the South were typically reluctant participants in the civil rights movement.[58] The Southern Jewish community was relatively small compared to the much larger Jewish population that came from Eastern Europe between 1880 and 1924, and had relatively little national influence. Southern Jews arrived in the nineteenth century, mainly from Germany, and they tended toward political conservatism, at least compared to their Eastern European brethren. The general perception of Northern Jews and Southern blacks and whites was that Southern Jews had adopted white attitudes on racial issues. Moreover, Southern Jews adopted a low profile because Southern whites often

---

[54] *Separation and Its Discontents*, Preface to the paperback edition.
[55] Davies 1981, 444; see also Subtelny 1988, 124.
[56] *The Culture of Critique*, ch. 3.
[57] Friedman 1995, ch. 1.
[58] Greenberg 1998.

(correctly) blamed Northern Jews as major instigators of the civil rights movement and because of the linkages among Jews, communism, and civil rights agitation during a period when both the NAACP and mainstream Jewish organizations were doing their best to minimize associations with communism.[59] (Jews were the backbone of the Communist Party USA, and the CPUSA agitated on behalf of black causes.[60]) It was common for Southerners to rail against Jews while exempting Southern Jews from their accusations: "We have only the high-type Jew here, not like the kikes in New York."[61]

Jewish businessmen adopted the segregationist mores of the South and often assumed an economic role of exploitation of blacks. A 1946 comment on the ADL Committee on Labor Relations noted: "It must be stated bluntly that with respect to [African Americans] Jews are vulnerable in the South. The only Jew a Negro meets in the city is a pawn broker, grocer, insurance agent, or landlord. The only Jew a sharecropper meets is a storekeeper or tradesman."[62] A journalist reported in 1946 that blacks in the South often had anti-Jewish attitudes; they took a "grim satisfaction from the Nazi persecution of the Jews. They contend that their local Jews have been indistinguishable from the 'crackers' in their attitude toward Negroes."[63] Though there were some exceptions, the vast majority of Southern Jews did not involve themselves in the civil rights movement even after the struggle intensified in the 1950s and 1960s.[64]

Similarly, the great majority of Jews in South Africa cooperated with the apartheid system. Between 1948 and 1970, most Jews gave their political allegiance to the United Party, which "was quite as committed to white supremacy as were the Afrikaner nationalists."[65] By the 1970s Jews were turning more to the Progressive Party, which advocated a gradual dismantling of apartheid, but "there appeared to be a grain of truth in the then current cynical quip that most Jews spoke like Progressives, voted for the United Party, and hoped that the Nationalist

---

[59] Greenberg 1998, 153.
[60] *The Culture of Critique*, ch. 3.
[61] In Greenberg 1998, 126.
[62] In Greenberg 1998, 128.
[63] In Greenberg 1998, 129.
[64] Greenberg 1998, 134. Nevertheless, a 1965 survey of Southern Jews found that they were twice as likely as white Southern Protestants to feel that the end of segregation was inevitable and desirable. Greenberg does not state what the actual percentages were.
[65] Shimoni 2003, 58.

Party would remain in power."[66]

However, the most striking feature of Jewish political behavior under apartheid was that Jews were vastly overrepresented among those banned by the government because of their opposition to apartheid. For example, Jews represented more than half the whites arrested in the Treason Trial of 1956 and almost half of whites suspected of being members of the Communist Party in 1962; in the public mind therefore, "Jews were inordinately prominent in the ranks of those who were attempting to subvert the state."[67]

The best predictor of Jewish participation in radical politics in South Africa was exposure to the political radicalism of the Eastern European Jewish subculture as a child.[68] As indicated below, it is the special character of this Jewish group that has been so critical to the revolution in race relations in the United States since World War II.

In the North, at least through the 1960s, Jews were seen more as exploiters than promoters of blacks because of their role as businessmen in the black community. From Marcus Garvey to Malcolm X, Julius Lester ("We got to take Harlem out of Goldberg's pocket"), Louis Farrakhan, and Khalid Muhammad (Jews were "bloodsuckers of the black nation"), black nationalists have routinely denounced Jews as economic exploiters of blacks because of their role as businessmen in the black community.[69] During the 1930s, as tensions rose with the Great Depression, a black newspaper declared, "If the Jewish merchants in Germany treated German workers as Blumstein's [a Jewish-owned department store] is treating the people of Harlem, then Hitler is right."[70] Perceptions of Jews as exploiters often led to black violence against Jews, as during the Detroit race riots of 1943, when Jewish stores were a prime target of blacks, and in Harlem and Chicago, where black leaders

---

[66] Shimoni 2003, 58.

[67] Shimoni 2003, 60, 61, 62.

[68] Shimoni 2003, 82–94. Most of the South African Jewish community came from Eastern Europe, but from a particular area where Zionism divorced from political radicalism held sway. This was not characteristic of most of Eastern Europe, where both ideologies had powerful influence. Shimoni (p. 94) notes that in general the powerful Zionist commitment of South African Jews did not result in opposition to apartheid, but he notes that some anti-apartheid radicals may have been influenced by the socialist ideas common in the Zionist Youth Movement.

[69] Friedman 1995, 220, 222, 346. Muhammad made his statement in 1994 at Howard University.

[70] In Friedman 1995, 92.

often complained that Jewish-owned stores did not employ blacks.[71] In the 1940s, according to one observer, "to Harlem, it had become a way of life to blame the Jew for discrimination and abuse."[72] Jewish merchants were also targeted in the black riots of the late 1960s and early 1970s; for example, between 1968 and 1972, 22 Jewish merchants were killed by black rioters in Philadelphia and 27 shot or beaten.[73] Charges of rent and price gouging were commonplace.

Nevertheless, although these incidents certainly show that blacks have often perceived Jews negatively, they may be more a symptom of black failure to develop their own businesses than of something uniquely exploitative about Jewish businessmen. In more recent times, blacks targeted Korean-owned stores during the 1993 riots in Los Angeles after Koreans had replaced Jews as owners of businesses serving the black community.

When interviewed about their own motivations, Jews tend to see themselves as altruists in aiding black causes, or they "believe that Jewish concern for black people was 'natural,' growing out of parallel experiences of suffering and oppression."[74] During the high point of the civil rights movements, Jews and Jewish organizations "redefined Judaism as synonymous with liberalism."[75] A commonly expressed attitude was that Jewish work on behalf of civil rights reflected the "universalist ethics" of Judaism.[76] This view ignores the history of the Jewish people as a closed ingroup with a profoundly particularist moral outlook, with very different moral standards for ingroup members and outgroup members.[77]

In the contemporary world the most egregious example of Jewish moral particularism is the reality of Israel as an expansionist apartheid state. Jews in Israel have subjected the Palestinians to a brutal occupation aimed ultimately at expanding their territory to include the land conquered in the 1967 war; American Jews have been strong supporters of Israel, and in recent years the organized American Jewish community has favored Israel's rightist Likud party and its aggressive policies

---

[71] Friedman 1995, 102; see also McDowell 1998; Trotter 1998.
[72] In Friedman 1995, 103.
[73] Friedman 1995, 214.
[74] Diner 1977/1995, xiii.
[75] Greenberg 1998, 162.
[76] E.g., Greenberg 1998, 143.
[77] *A People That Shall Dwell Alone*, ch. 6; *The Culture of Critique*, Preface to the first paperback edition.

toward the Palestinians. Many of the supporters of the Likud are hyper-ethnocentric members of the settler movement and other forms of Jewish fundamentalism.[78]

Another tack has been to acknowledge that Jews furthered their own interests in advancing black causes, but to restrict these interests to a general interest in securing Jewish civil rights. For example, in 1954, Will Maslow, a Jewish activist with the National Jewish Community Relations Advisory Council, wrote that lawsuits brought by the NAACP for black plaintiffs benefited Jews, particularly in ending restrictive housing covenants and the ability to discriminate on the basis of race in hiring decisions.[79] In a 1920 letter, Louis Marshall noted that restrictive housing covenants could be used not only against blacks but "those of every race and of every nationality or origin."[80]

However, the interests of blacks and Jews have increasingly diverged, especially since the high point of the black-Jewish alliance in the 1960s. In the late 1960s Jews bitterly opposed black efforts at community control of schools in New York because they threatened Jewish hegemony in the educational system, including the teachers' union.[81] Black-Jewish issues also diverged when affirmative action and quotas for black college admission became a divisive issue in the 1970s.[82] The main Jewish groups—the AJCommittee, the AJCongress, and the ADL—sided with Bakke in the landmark case on racial quota systems in the University of California–Davis medical school, thereby promoting their own interests as a highly intelligent minority in a meritocracy.

Nevertheless, in recent times Jewish groups have endorsed the use of race as a factor in hiring and university admissions, especially in cases where previous discrimination is demonstrable. In 1995, the ADL rejected a resolution that would have allowed race to be a factor even without "egregious discrimination" or "token presence."[83] During the same period, the AJCongress supported court-ordered goals and timetables "given a finding of discrimination."[84] Major Jewish organizations supported affirmative action in the recent Supreme Court case

---

[78] See ch. 3 above on "Zionism and the Internal Dynamics of the Jewish Community."
[79] Greenberg 1998, 158–59.
[80] In Friedman 1995, 72.
[81] See Friedman 1995, 257ff.
[82] Friedman 1995, 72.
[83] Chanes 1997, 307.
[84] Chanes 1997, 301.

dealing with admissions policy at the University of Michigan. The AJCommittee noted in its amicus brief that, "Diversity not only provides all students with a richer educational experience, but also prepares them for participation in our pluralistic democracy."[85] The ADL favored law school admissions policies that did not assign race a specific point value in admission, declaring that the decision was an "attempt to strike a delicate balance." The ADL further "called upon university admissions offices to recognize that the Court has not authorized the use of race as 'a substitute for individualized consideration of their applicants.'"[86]

Since the 1960s, the Jewish ethnic interest in promoting Israel also conflicted with the views of many radical black activists who saw Israel as a Western colonial power and the Palestinians as a downtrodden Third World Muslim people. For example, in the late 1960s, the Student Non-Violent Coordinating Committee (SNCC) described Zionism as "racist colonialism."[87] In Jewish eyes, a great many black leaders, including the late Stokely Carmichael (Kwame Touré), Jesse Jackson, Louis Farrakhan, and Andrew Young, have been entirely too pro-Palestinian. (Young lost his position as US ambassador to the United Nations as a result of Jewish pressure because he engaged in secret negotiations with the Palestinians.) During the 1960s, expressions of solidarity with the Palestinians by radical blacks, some of whom had adopted the Muslim religion, resulted in many Jewish New Leftists leaving the movement.[88] The origins of neoconservatism are linked partly, if not largely, to the fact that the left, including the Soviet Union and leftist radicals in the United States, had become anti-Zionist and anti-Jewish. Indeed, surveys beginning in the 1960s have consistently found that blacks are more likely to hold anti-Jewish attitudes than whites. The most recent ADL survey, from 1998, found that blacks were nearly four times more likely than whites to have anti-Jewish attitudes (34 percent to 9 percent).[89]

Harold Cruse, a black intellectual, presents a particularly trenchant analysis of the role of Jewish self-interest in their role in Jewish-black coalition: "Jews *know exactly what they want in America.*" Jews want cultural pluralism because of their long-term policy of nonassmilation

---

[85] American Jewish Committee 2003.
[86] Anti-Defamation League 2003.
[87] Friedman 1995, 230.
[88] Liebman 1979, 561; *The Culture of Critique*, ch. 3.
[89] Friedman 1995, 319ff; Anti-Defamation League 1998.

and group solidarity. Cruse notes, however, that the Jewish experience in Europe has shown them that "*two* can play this game" (i.e., develop highly nationalistic ethnocentric groups), and "when that happens, woe be to the side that is short on numbers."[90] Cruse observes that Jewish organizations view white nationalism as their greatest potential threat and that they have tended to support pro-black integration (i.e., assimilationist, individualist) policies for blacks in America, presumably because such policies dilute white power and lessen the possibility of a cohesive, nationalist anti-Jewish white majority. At the same time, Jewish organizations have opposed a black nationalist position while pursuing an anti-assimilationist, nationalist group strategy for their own group.

This suggestion about Jewish motivation must be taken seriously. The Jewish role in black affairs must be seen as part of the broader picture of Jewish strategizing in the period following World War II. We have seen that the central thrust of Jewish activity in the postwar era was the propaganda and political activism of the intergroup relations movement. This "full court press" of educational programs, media messages, legislative initiatives, legal challenges, and protests was aimed at altering the ethnic attitudes and behaviors typical of traditional America. As Stuart Svonkin notes, Jewish activists "saw their commitment to the intergroup relations movement as a preventive measure designed to make sure 'it'—the Nazis' war of extermination against European Jewry—never happened in America."[91]

Besides the movement to alter ethnic relations discussed here, Jewish organizations took the lead in altering US immigration policy in the direction of large-scale multiethnic immigration.[92] Mass multiethnic immigration continues to be a consensus position within the US Jewish community, and several Jewish activists have noted the advantage to be gained by Jews from an America where white political and demographic hegemony has declined and whites are unable to control their own political destiny.[93] Most recently, Leonard S. Glickman, president and CEO of the Hebrew Immigrant Aid Society, stated, "The more diverse American society is, the safer [Jews] are."[94] Having run out of Russian Jews, the HIAS is now deeply involved in recruiting refugees

---

[90] Cruse 1967/1992, 121–22; italics in text.
[91] Svonkin 1997, 10.
[92] *The Culture of Critique*, ch. 7; Graham 2002, 56–57.
[93] See *The Culture of Critique*, ch. 7.
[94] In Cattan 2002.

from Africa—a new twist on the black-Jewish alliance.

Also consistent with this interpretation is that in recent years Jewish organizations have made alliances with other non-white ethnic activist organizations. For example, groups such as the AJCommittee and the Jewish Community Council of Greater Washington have formed coalitions with organizations such as the National Council of La Raza and the League of United Latin American Citizens (LULAC).[95] A prominent aspect of this effort is the Foundation for Ethnic Understanding, cofounded by Rabbi Marc Schneier, president of the North American Boards of Rabbis.[96] The Foundation is closely tied to the World Jewish Congress, which cosponsors the Foundation's Washington, DC office and several of its programs. Typical of the Foundation's efforts was a meeting in August 2003 of the Congressional Black Caucus, the Congressional Hispanic Caucus, the Jewish Congressional Delegation, and the Congressional Asian Pacific American Caucus. The Foundation's many programs include organizing the Congressional Jewish/Black Caucus; the Corporate Diversity Award, given to "a major Fortune 500 company committed to building a diverse work force"; the Annual Latino/Jewish Congressional Awards Ceremony; the Annual Black/Jewish Congressional Awards Ceremony; and the Annual Interethnic Congressional Leadership Forum. The latter project organizes an annual meeting of the NAACP, the National Council of La Raza, the World Jewish Congress, and the National Asian Pacific American Legal Consortium. Quite clearly the various non-European ethnic groups are developing close ties, and Jewish organizations are taking the lead in this effort.

Jewish motivation need not be seen in defensive terms, of course, but rather as aimed at maximizing Jewish power. The reality is that the rise of the Jews in the United States, as well as the rise of their black allies and the millions of post-1965 non-white immigrants, has been accompanied by a consequent decline in the power of the old white Protestant elites. This is motivation enough, certainly, but it leaves out an important psychological component. Throughout this essay I have noted the contrast between the German-Jewish immigrants who came to the United States in the mid- to late nineteenth century and the massive Eastern European Jewish immigration that completely altered the profile of US Jewry in the direction of political radicalism and Zionism. The former group of immigrants rather quickly became an elite group,

---

[95] Amann 2000.
[96] http://www.ffeu.org/index.htm.

and their attitudes, as in Germany, were undoubtedly more liberal than those of similarly situated non-Jews of the time.[97] Nevertheless, they tended toward political conservatism, and, whether living in the North or the South, they did not attempt to radically alter the folkways of the white majority, nor did they engage in radical criticism of non-Jewish society. I rather doubt that in the absence of the massive immigration of Eastern European Jews between 1880 and 1920, the United States would have undergone the radical transformations of the last fifty years.

The Eastern European immigrants and their descendants were and are a quite different group.[98] These immigrants originated in the intensely ethnocentric, religiously fundamentalist *shtetl* communities of Eastern Europe. These groups had achieved a dominant economic position throughout the area, but they were under intense pressure as a result of anti-Jewish attitudes and laws. And because of their high fertility, the great majority of Eastern European Jews were poor. Around 1880 these groups shifted their focus from religious fanaticism to complex mixtures of political radicalism, Zionism, and religious fanaticism, although religious fanaticism was in decline relative to the other ideologies.[99] Their political radicalism often coexisted with messianic forms of Zionism as well as intense commitment to Jewish nationalism and religious and cultural separatism, and many individuals held various and often rapidly changing combinations of these ideas.[100]

The two streams of political radicalism and Zionism, each stemming from the teeming fanaticism and passionate ethnocentrism of threatened Jewish populations in nineteenth-century Eastern Europe, continue to reverberate in the modern world. In both England and America the immigration of Eastern European Jews after 1880 had a transforming effect on the political attitudes of the Jewish communities there in the direction of radical politics and Zionism, often combined with religious orthodoxy.[101] The immigrant Eastern European Jews demographically swamped the previous Jewish communities in both countries, and the older communities grew deeply concerned at the possibility of increased anti-Semitism. Attempts were made by the established

---

[97] See *Separation and Its Discontents*, ch. 5.

[98] See ch. 3 above on "Zionism and the Internal Dynamics of the Jewish Community" for a more complete discussion.

[99] Vital 1975, 314.

[100] See Frankel 1981.

[101] Alderman 1983, 47ff; *The Culture of Critique*, ch. 3.

Jewish communities to misrepresent the prevalence of radical political ideas among the immigrants. However, there is no doubt that immigrant Jews formed the core of the American left at least through the 1960s; as indicated above, Jews continue to be an important force on the left into the present.

One expression of the passionate ethnocentrism of the immigrant Jews and their descendants is hatred directed at the non-Jewish world. In other words, at the conscious level, the Jewish activists who had such a large effect on the history of racial relations in America were motivated to a considerable extent by their hatred for the white power structure of the United States because the white power structure represented the culture of an outgroup. I have tried to describe the intense hatred of Jews toward the non-Jewish social world in several places,[102] but perhaps John Murray Cuddihy says it best:

> From Solomon Maimon to Normon Podhoretz, from Rachel Varnhagen to Cynthia Ozick, from Marx and Lassalle to Erving Goffman and Harold Garfinkel, from Herzl and Freud to Harold Laski and Lionel Trilling, from Moses Mendelssohn to J. Robert Oppenheimer and Ayn Rand, Gertrude Stein, and Reich I and II (Wilhelm and Charles), one dominating structure of an identical predicament and a shared fate imposes itself upon the consciousness and behavior of the Jewish intellectual in *Galut* [exile]: with the advent of Jewish Emancipation, when ghetto walls crumble and the *shtetlach* [small Jewish towns] begin to dissolve, Jewry—like some wide-eyed anthropologist—enters upon a strange world, to explore a strange people observing a strange *halakah* (code). They examine this world in dismay, with wonder, anger, and punitive objectivity. This wonder, this anger, and the vindictive objectivity of the marginal nonmember are recidivist; they continue unabated into our own time because Jewish Emancipation continues into our own time.[103]

Consistent with what we know of the psychology of ethnocentrism, this implies that a fundamental motivation of Jewish intellectuals and activists involved in social criticism has simply been hatred of the non-Jewish power structure, perceived as anti-Jewish and deeply immoral.

---

[102] *The Culture of Critique, passim*; chs. 1 and 3 above "Background Traits for Jewish Activism" and "Zionism and the Internal Dynamics of the Jewish Community."

[103] Cuddihy 1974, 68.

This hatred is typically combined with the specific complaint that the pre-World War II US culture was deeply anti-Jewish. A particular focus of Jewish anger was the Immigration Law of 1924, which closed off immigration of Eastern European Jews to the United States. There is no question that the 1924 law was partly motivated by a consensus in the United States opposed to the political radicalism and clannish ways of the recent Jewish immigrants.[104] The emotional intensity of Jewish involvement in the black-Jewish alliance is mirrored in Jewish involvement in altering US immigration policy; both of these movements had strong overtones of hatred against the entire white, Christian culture of the United States, which was viewed as anti-Jewish and thus immoral.

The Yiddish-speaking Jewish subculture viewed white America through the lens of the Eastern European *shtetl* Jew surrounded by a sea of hostile non-Jews ever ready to ignite an anti-Jewish pogrom. Indeed, in the 1920s and 1930s the Yiddish press routinely referred to lynchings and other manifestations of racial animosity as pogroms or autos-da-fé (i.e., the public penances and executions of secret Jews condemned by the Inquisition for being insincere Catholics).[105] Both terms place the Jew in the position of the black as victim of white aggression. Whites in the American South were seen as no different than marauding Cossacks attacking Jews in eighteenth-century Poland or inquisitors torturing and executing Jews in sixteenth-century Spain—an indication of the profound sense of historical grievance typical of strongly identified Jews.[106]

This deep antipathy toward the non-Jewish world can be seen in the comments of Michael Walzer, a Princeton University sociologist and member of the New York Intellectuals, on the "pathologies of Jewish life." Walzer describes "the sense that 'all the world is against us,' the resulting fear, resentment, and hatred of the *goy*, the secret dreams of reversal and triumph."[107] These emotions were quite apparent in Jewish activities on behalf of blacks after World War II. Walzer himself organized picketing at stores whose Southern branches practiced segregation and marched in the protests of the 1960s; he was also a major donor to the civil rights movement of the 1960s.[108] He notes that Jews involved

---

[104] See *The Culture of Critique*, Preface to the first paperback edition and ch. 7.
[105] Diner 1998, 33.
[106] *Separation and Its Discontents*, ch. 6; 2003a.
[107] Walzer 1994, 6–7.
[108] Friedman 1995, 180–81, 232.

in the civil rights movement were not leftists who happened to be Jews:

> In the civil rights movement, we were emphatically Jewish leftists. Our personal identities, self-knowledge, understanding of our own past, and, most important, our deepest feelings were more engaged in this fight than in any of [the other leftist causes]. . . . We had our own memories of Passover seders [and its theme of Jews as slaves], and we could quote the prophets and tell stories of Jewish persecution. Southern sheriffs with dogs looked to us like Cossacks . . . or Nazis. Things that we didn't think about and didn't talk about in the other movements came easily to mind and tongue in this one. We surprised ourselves with the extent of our identification: of American blacks as Jews, of ourselves as blacks. Civil rights, we thought, was our fight.[109]

Jewish motivation in the black-Jewish alliance must also be seen within the general context of Jewish involvement on the left, a topic I have discussed extensively elsewhere.[110] The following summarizes this discussion:

1. Jews benefited directly from leftist activity by improving their economic situation, as in the black-Jewish alliance, where there were challenges to discrimination in hiring and housing. In Eastern Europe, a great many Jews were impoverished, and Jews benefited from the Bolshevik Revolution because it ended anti-Jewish practices of the government. In their early decades in the United States, Jews involved in the labor movement fought for better economic conditions for Jewish workers.

2. Jews were different from others in the labor movement because of their intense hatred toward the entire social order, which they viewed as anti-Jewish, and the expression of an alien people and culture. This hatred did not change after they achieved upward social mobility in the United States. For example, sociologist Seymour Martin Lipset described typical Jewish "families which around the breakfast table, day

---

[109] Walzer 1997, 402–403. The second ellipsis is in the original. As someone who spent considerable time with Jewish radicals in the 1960s, I can attest to the intense, emotionally charged hatred of Jewish activists toward segregation and other manifestations of white power during the period. I discuss my experiences among Jewish radicals in endnote 83 of *The Culture of Critique*.

[110] *The Culture of Critique*, 79–96.

after day, in Scarsdale, Newton, Great Neck, and Beverly Hills have discussed what an awful, corrupt, immoral, undemocratic, racist society the United States is."[111] For many Jewish New Leftists "the revolution promises to avenge the sufferings and to right the wrongs which have, for so long, been inflicted on Jews with the permission or encouragement, or even at the command of, the authorities in prerevolutionary societies."[112] Interviews with New Left Jewish radicals have shown that many had destructive fantasies in which the revolution would result in "humiliation, dispossession, imprisonment or execution of the oppressors"[113] combined with the belief in their own omnipotence and their ability to create a nonoppressive social order.

3. As noted above, several commentators have remarked that Jews involved in the alliance with blacks saw themselves as altruists and as expressing a universalist ethic deeply embedded in Jewish tradition. In general, studies of Jewish radicals by Jewish social scientists have tended to gratuitously attribute Jewish radicalism to a "free choice of a gifted minority"[114] when economic explanations failed. Leftist ideology did indeed provide a veneer of universalism, but closer examination of Jewish radicals reveals that the great majority had very strong identities as Jews and left the movement when it was seen as compromising Jewish interests. Jewish activists often had a great deal of self-deception regarding their own Jewish commitments. Leftist universalism provided a critique of institutions that promote group ties among non-Jews (such as nationalism and traditional Christian religious associations), while Jews themselves continued to retain a powerful sense of group identity. Jews mouthed universalist sentiments while erecting subtle barriers between themselves and non-Jews:

> [Non-Jewish intellectuals] really are not totally accepted into even the secularist humanist liberal company of their quondam Jewish friends. Jews continue to insist in indirect and often inexplicable ways on their own uniqueness. Jewish universalism in relations between Jews and non-Jews has an empty ring.... Still, we have the anomaly of Jewish secularists and atheists writing their own prayer books. We find Jewish political reformers breaking with their local parties which stress an ethnic style of politics, and ostensibly pressing

---

[111] Lipset 1988, 393.
[112] Cohen 1980, 208.
[113] Cohen 1980, 208.
[114] Rothman and Lichter 1982, 118.

for universal political goals—while organizing their own political clubs which are so Jewish in style and manner that non-Jews often feel unwelcome.[115]

4. Leftist political movements recreated the psychological atmosphere of traditional Jewish society: a strong sense of ingroup pride and moral superiority, messianic fervor aimed at a utopian future, ingroup/outgroup thinking, hierarchical social structure, and exclusion of dissenters.

The above comments apply to the Eastern European immigrants and their descendants who came to dominate the American Jewish community after World War II rather than to the German-Jewish elite of the previous era. The motivations of the German-Jewish elite certainly contained elements of these characteristics. However, Hasia Diner's review of the German-Jewish media of the period shows that they were far more concerned about forms of discrimination against blacks that could also impact Jews, such as restrictive housing covenants, than they were about forms that only applied to blacks, such as segregated public transportation.[116] Their strategy was essentially aimed at securing civil rights via the legal system rather than through the confrontational style that emerged after World War II. Although they undoubtedly had a sense of social marginality and feeling of estrangement from American culture—virtually a defining characteristic of being a Jew[117]—one does not see the intense hatred of the entire non-Jewish social order among them. Political radicalism and Zionism—the twin pillars of the Eastern European Jewish subculture that have had such enormous effects on the modern world—were not characteristic of this group. As an elite, their main concern was to eradicate the civil disabilities that, in their view, limited the horizons of both blacks and Jews.

CONCLUSION

Jews have been the backbone of the left in the United States since early in the century, when the huge wave of Jewish immigration from Eastern Europe was at its crest. At least since the 1940s, the black-Jewish alliance has been an important part of the Jewish involvement on the left. In the present era, the rise of Jewish neoconservatism

---

[115] Liebman 1973, 158.
[116] Diner 1977/1995, 100.
[117] See *Separation and Its Discontents*, ch. 1.

(which accepts the basic principles of the left on racial issues), the anti-Jewish and pro-Palestinian statements of some black activists, and relatively commonplace anti-Jewish attitudes in the black community have not really changed this substantially. I suggest that this is because at a fundamental level the entire Jewish political spectrum, from left/liberal to neoconservative right, continues to view the political and cultural hegemony of white Europeans with hostility and suspicion. Attitudes on immigration are an excellent indication of this. Immigration has already altered the demographics of voting in the United States, and it will result increasingly in the eclipse of the white political and cultural power in the foreseeable future. Jews are united in favor of this result.

Jewish activism played an essential and critical role in the revolution in ethnic relations that has occurred in the last fifty years in the United States. It is a revolution that in its major premises has also been internalized by a large portion of whites in the United States and other Western countries, particularly by the white elite, who have made alliances with Jews and other components of the multiethnic elite. It remains to be seen what the long-term consequences of this revolution will be and whether, in particular, whites will attempt to retain and expand their political and cultural power in the United States and other traditionally Western societies. It should be remembered that there is nothing in the nature of Judaism itself that would imply that the Jewish community would inevitably oppose being a minority in a racially hierarchical society dominated by whites. Jews have often participated in such societies, either as active supporters of the domination of another racial group or at least as passive but willing participants in such a system. One possibility is that Jews might alter their political behavior in this direction as the negative effects of Third World immigration, especially from Muslim countries, begin to take their toll on Jewish sensibilities.[118] Perhaps the neoconservative movement represents the first stirrings of this direction for the Jewish community, although, as it is presently constructed, it remains opposed to the ethnic interests of European Americans.

---

[118] Steinlight (2001) makes this argument. However, to date Jewish organizations have not changed their pro-immigration policies.

Part II.
Anti-Semitism

Chapter 7

HENRY FORD AND THE JEWISH QUESTION[*]

What is one to make of Henry Ford's series of writings on Jews? *The International Jew: The World's Foremost Problem*[1] was first published as a series of weekly articles in Ford's newspaper the *Dearborn Independent*, then compiled into a four volume book that was never copyrighted and has thus been in the public domain for over eighty years. An amalgam of dark speculations on Jewish conspiracy combined with some interesting and, on the whole, accurate information on Jews and perceptions of Jews during the period, *The International Jew* merits a fair and accurate summary.

JEWISH ECONOMIC AND CULTURAL INFLUENCE
The general view of *The International Jew* is that Jews have achieved a great deal of economic, political, and cultural domination in the United States and Europe. At times, *The International Jew* reads as though the US economy was completely dominated by Jews: "In America alone most of the big business, the trusts and the banks, the natural resources and the chief agricultural products, especially tobacco, cotton and sugar, are in the control of Jewish financiers or their agents" (5/22/1920). This undoubtedly exaggerated view of the overarching power of Jewish finance contrasts with discussions of a great many areas describing the extent to which Jews control specific areas of the economy and culture. A later article (6/05/1920) claims several other important industries are under Jewish control in the United States: the

---

[*] First published in *The Occidental Quarterly* 2 (Winter 2002–2003): 53–77.

[1] Henry Ford, *The International Jew: The World's Foremost Problem*, 4 vols. (Dearborn, Mich.: Dearborn Publishing Co. 1920–1922). Citations refer to the original date of publication of each article.

The two people who actually wrote *The International Jew* were Ernest Liebold and Billy Cameron. Liebold was a college-educated bank president before he became Ford's personal secretary and alter-ego. Cameron was a journalist who subscribed to an early version of the Christian identity movement, which holds that the Anglo-Saxons descended from one of the lost tribes of Israel. The main force behind the articles, besides Ford, was Liebold, but he was careful to give credit to Cameron as the person who compiled the data and actually wrote the articles.

motion picture industry, 50 percent of the meat packing industry, "upwards of 60 percent of the shoemaking industry," the clothing industry, distribution and selling of music, jewelry, grain, the Colorado smelting industry, magazine writing, news distribution, the liquor business, and the loan business, "only to name the industries with national and international sweep."

While overly inclined to see Jewish domination of the US economy resulting from Jewish overrepresentation in investment banking, *The International Jew* was essentially correct when it pointed to particular industries that were dominated by Jews. Data from the 1930s indicated that Jews had disproportionate influence in retailing, the garment industry, cosmetics, entertainment, mass media and publishing, investment banking, and the professions.[2] All of these, with the exception of Jewish involvement in the professions, were foci of *The International Jew*, although *The International Jew* did discuss Jewish influence in journalism and the academic world, particularly economics. *The International Jew* is careful to distinguish between investment banking, where Jews had a very strong position, from retail banking, where they did not—a distinction also noted by the Editors of *Fortune*.[3]

All of these industries are given detailed treatment in various places in *The International Jew* (e.g., the liquor business was the focus of three articles appearing in late 1921). In general, *The International Jew* takes a balanced, nuanced approach to Jewish influence in particular areas. For example, in the financial area, *The International Jew* describes a conflict between a nascent Jewish group and a non-Jewish group bent on preventing Jewish influence. "At one time [Jewish influence] threatened to be [paramount], but American financiers have always been silently aware of the International Jewish Financier, and have endeavored quietly to block his game" (11/13/1920). However, *The International Jew* notes that, while presently thwarted, Jewish influence on the stock exchange is increasing rapidly because Jews are willing to pay the highest prices for seats on the New York Stock Exchange as they become available, and no Jew ever sells his seat to a non-Jew: "One outstanding characteristic of the Jewish race is its persistence. What it cannot attain this generation, it will attain next. Defeat it today, it does not remain defeated; its conquerors die, but Jewry goes on, never forgetting, never deviating from its ancient aim of world control in one form or another" (11/13/1920). *The International Jew* gives

---

[2] Editors of *Fortune* 1936; Sachar 1992, 341.
[3] Editors of *Fortune* 1936.

figures for Jewish membership of the NYSE as 60/1,009 in 1872, rising to 106 in 1893 and to 276 in 1919. Jewish control "is struggling to go higher, but has thus far been stopped" (11/13/1920).

Noting the importance of the theater as part of the plan outlined in the *Protocols of the Elders of Zion*, *The International Jew* provides detailed accounts in a series of five articles on Jewish domination of the theater and motion picture industry.

> Not only the "legitimate" stage, so-called, but the motion picture industry—the fifth greatest of all the great industries—is also Jew-controlled, not in spots only, not 50 percent merely, but entirely; with the natural consequence that the world is in arms against the trivializing and demoralizing influences of that form of entertainment as at present managed. As soon as the Jew got control of American Liquor, we had a liquor problem with drastic consequences. As soon as the Jew gained control of the "movies," we had a movie problem, the consequences of which are not yet visible. It is the genius of the race to create problems in whatever business they achieve a majority. . . . Millions of Americans every day place themselves voluntarily within range of Jewish ideas of life, love and labor; within range of Jewish propaganda, sometimes cleverly, sometimes cunningly concealed. (1/01/1921)

> Frivolity, sensuality, indecency, appalling illiteracy and endless platitude are the marks of the American State as it approaches its degeneracy under Jewish control. (1/01/1920)

The International Jew claims that Jewish producers stage plays that provide positive images of Jews and that most of these are not successful despite massive publicity and endorsement by public officialdom. *Ben Hur* is given as a prominent exception, its nineteen-year run explained by the fact that "it is the most successful of all the vehicles for pro-Semitism now on the stage" (1/08/1921).

The International Jew describes the rise during the 1890s of the Jewish-dominated Theatrical Trust, which eclipsed the previous non-Jewish theatrical producers and agents. *The International Jew* states that the Theatrical Trust blacklisted critics who "opposed its methods or pointed out the inferior, coarse and degrading character of the Trust productions." *The International Jew* claims that critics were fired by newspapers threatened by the Trust with loss of advertising revenue (1/08/1921). In turn, the Theatrical Trust became overshadowed by another Jewish company run by the Shubert family (1/22/1921).

Regarding the movies, *The International Jew* reports that 90 percent of the production is in the hands of a few large companies, 85 percent of which "are in the hands of Jews" (2/12/1921). The article appearing on 2/19/1921 discusses the Jews behind the major motion picture companies of the era, going over much the same information as presented in Neal Gabler's *An Empire of Their Own: How the Jews Invented Hollywood*.[4] *The International Jew* is careful to note that its concerns with the moral messages in movies are not idiosyncratic but part of a larger *Kulturkampf* between the movie industry and large segments of the American public: "In almost every state there are movie censorship bills pending, with the old 'wet' and gambling elements against them, and the awakened part of the decent population in favor of them; always, the Jewish producing firms constituting the silent pressure behind the opposition" (2/12/1921). Indeed, the Motion Picture Producers and Distributors of America, headed by Will H. Hays, was created in 1922 in response to movements in over thirty state legislatures to enact strict censorship laws, and the Production Code Administration, headed by Joseph I. Breen, was launched in response to a campaign by the Catholic Legion of Decency.[5] *The International Jew*'s reservations about the moral content of movies were indeed widely shared among the American public.

The International Jew attributes the moral sensibility of the movie industry to the fact that it is dominated by Jews—the contrast between the "Oriental ideal" for culture and the "Anglo-Saxon, the American ideal." The Oriental ideal is, "'If you can't go as far as you like, go as far as you can.' It gravitates naturally to the flesh and its exposure; its natural psychic habitat is among the more sensual emotions." According to *The International Jew*

> Here lies the whole secret of the movies' moral failure: they are not American and their producers are racially unqualified to reproduce the American atmosphere. An influence which is racially, morally and idealistically foreign to America, has been given the powerful projecting force of the motion picture business, and the consequences are what we see. (2/12/1921)

However, *The International Jew* notes that to advocate censorship is construed as anti-Semitism: "Reader, beware! If you so much as resent

---

[4] Gabler 1988.
[5] Gabler 1988.

the filth of the mass of the movies, you will fall under the judgment of anti-Semitism" (2/12/1921).

The International Jew claims that the movies are biased in favor of Judaism and against Christianity. *The International Jew* quotes from a letter from a non-Jewish movie production company submitted during Congressional hearings, stating that Christian plays, such as *Life of the Savior*, have not been produced in order not to offend Jewish sensibilities (2/12/1921).

> You never see a Jewish rabbi depicted on the screen in any but a most honorable attitude. He is clothed with all the dignity of the office and he is made as impressive as can be. Christian clergymen, as any movie fan will readily recall, were subjected to all sorts of misrepresentations, from the comic to the criminal. Now, this attitude is distinctly Jewish. Like many unlabeled influences in our life, whose sources lead back to Jewish groups, the object is to break down as far as possible all respectful or considerate thought about the clergy. The Catholic clergy very soon made themselves felt in opposition to this abuse of their priestly dignity. You never see a priest made light of on the screen. But the Protestant clergyman is still the elongated, sniveling, bilious hypocrite of anti-Christian caricature. . . . You may not depict a Hebrew as owner of a sweatshop—though all sweatshop owners are Hebrews; but you may make a Christian clergyman everything from a seducer to a safe-cracker and get away with it.

The International Jew quotes a movie poster of the period: "'I refuse to live with you any longer. I denounce you as my wife—I will go to HER—my free-lover.' Thus speaks the Rev. Frank Gordon in the greatest of all free-love dramas" (2/19/1921). *The International Jew* then notes pointedly but tentatively

> There may be no connection whatever, but behold what is done, and remembering what is written in the *Protocols*, a question arises. It is written: "We have misled, stupefied and demoralized the youth of the Gentiles by means of education in principles and theories, patently false to us, but which we have inspired." Protocol 9. "We have taken good care long ago to discredit the Gentile clergy." Protocol 17. (2/19/1921)

This typifies the manner in which *The International Jew* refers to the *Protocols* (see also below): Actual events that can be reasonably shown to be due to Jewish influence are shown to fit with the conspiratorial master plan outlined in the *Protocols*. Despite the paranoid logic, the assertions of *The International Jew* are congruent with recent studies indicating that Jews remain in control of the movie industry and that the movies generally portray Christians and Christianity negatively and Jews and Judaism positively.[6]

Finally, there is little doubt that *The International Jew* is correct in its assessment that Jews dominated the music industry in the United States. As Kenneth Kanter notes:

> Both as a business and as an expression of talent and creative artistry, American popular music was in large part shaped and formed by Jews, many of them immigrant newcomers to the American scene. . . . Virtually all the great names that come to mind when one considers popular music—Rodgers and Hammerstein, Irving Berlin, Lorenz Hart, Jerome Kern, George and Ira Gershwin, Irving Caesar, and Charles Harris, for instance, are Jewish names. Jews wrote the songs, Jews sang the songs, and Jews made sure that the songs were circulated to every corner of the country, for they founded and built America's publishing industry. Among the vanguard publishers were M. Witmark, Charles K. Harris, Joseph Stern, Shapiro and Bernstein, Harry von Tilzer, Leo Feist, T. B. Harms, and Irving Berlin [born Israel Baline]. Collectively their publishing firms came to be known as "Tin Pan Alley." . . . It was the Tin Pan Alley ethos, combining the commercial with the aesthetic, that gave our popular music its distinctive character.[7]

JEWISH POLITICAL ACTIVISM IN THE UNITED STATES

Besides the cultural influences described above, *The International Jew* devotes a great deal of attention to the Jewish political campaigns against public expressions of Christianity and for official recognition of the Jewish religion (e.g., recognizing Jewish holidays). "The St. Louis Charity Fair in 1908 planned to remain open on Friday evening; a great outcry; did the managers of that fair mean to insult the Jews; didn't they know that the Jewish Sabbath began on Friday night?" (6/04/1921).

The International Jew presents a history of Jewish activism against

---

[6] E.g., Medved 1992/1993; *The Culture of Critique*, Preface to the paperback edition.

[7] Kanter 1982, ix.

public expressions of Christianity based on Kehillah records, beginning with an attempt in 1899–1900 to remove the word "Christian" from the Virginia Bill of Rights and culminating in 1919–1920:

> In this year the Kehillah was so successful in its New York campaign that it was possible for a Jewish advertiser in New York to say that he wanted Jewish help, but it was not possible for a non-Jewish advertiser to state his non-Jewish preference. This is a sidelight both on Jewish reasonableness and Jewish power. (3/12/1920)

> The Jews' interference with the religion of the others, and the Jews' determination to wipe out of public life every sign of the predominant Christian character of the United States is the only active form of religious intolerance in the country today. (3/21/1920)

Another aspect of Jewish power during the period was the ability to prevent public discussion of Jewish issues as such—an important source of Jewish power with continuing relevance in contemporary times.[8]

> There is a vague feeling that even to openly use the word "Jew," or to expose it nakedly to print, is somehow improper. . . . There is extreme sensitiveness about the public discussion of the Jewish Question on the part of Gentiles. They would prefer to keep it in the hazy borderlands of their thought, shrouded in silence. . . . The principal public Gentile pronouncements upon the Jewish Question are in the manner of the truckling politician or the pleasant after-dinner speaker; the great Jewish names in philosophy, medicine, literature, music and finance are named over, the energy, ability and thrift of the race are dwelt upon, and everyone goes home feeling that a difficult place has been rather neatly negotiated. (6/12/1920)

> Anyone who essays to discuss the Jewish Question in the United States or anywhere else must be fully prepared to be regarded as an Anti-Semite, in high-brow language, or in low-brow language, a Jew-baiter. . . . The press in general is open at this time to fulsome editorials in favor of everything Jewish . . . while the Jewish press, which is fairly numerous in the United States, takes care of the vituperative end. (6/19/1920)

---

[8] *The Culture of Critique*, Preface to the paperback edition; Sobran 1996.

According to *The International Jew*, Jews have succeeded in engaging in ethnic warfare without either side publicly acknowledging that there is indeed a war: "Yes, let it be agreed; if the Jewish idea is the stronger, if the Jewish ability is the greater, let them conquer; let the Anglo-Saxon principles and Anglo-Saxon power go down in ruins before the Tribe of Judah. *But first let the two ideas struggle under their own banners; let it be a fair struggle*" (5/21/1921; emphasis in *The International Jew*).

Based on pronouncements of Jewish organizations and intellectuals, *The International Jew* makes the important point that Jews promote "one of the dangerous doctrines being preached today" that

> the United States is not any definite thing as yet, but that it is yet to be made, and it is still the prey of whatever power can seize it and mold it to its liking. It is a favorite Jewish view that the United States is a great unshapen mass of potentiality, of no particular character which is yet to be given its definite form. . . . We are not making Americans; we are permitting foreigners to be educated in the theory that America is a free-for-all, the prize of whatever fantastic foreign political theory may seize it. (3/05/1921)

This comment on Jewish attitudes fits well with a great deal of evidence that Jews have consistently opposed the notion that the United States has any ethnic overtones or that it is a European or Christian civilization.[9] *The International Jew* also cites a tendency for Jews to be very enthusiastic about the United States because of its potential to serve Jewish interests. As Zionist activist Israel Zangwill noted, "Next to being in a country of their own, there could be no better fate for [Eastern European Jews] than to be together in a land of civil and religious liberty, of whose Constitution Christianity forms no part and where their collective votes would practically guarantee them against future persecution."[10]

A critical component of Jewish attempts to change the United States in conformity with Jewish interests is advocacy of unrestricted immigration. *The International Jew* was well aware that Jewish groups were the main force advocating unrestricted immigration. The article for March 5, 1921, claims that one part of the Jewish program for the United States is unrestricted Jewish immigration from any part of the

---

[9] *The Culture of Critique*, ch. 7.
[10] In Ross 1914, 144.

world: "American Jews have never cared what kind of human riffraff filled the country as long as the Jewish flood was not hindered" (3/21/1921). *The International Jew* notes that the Kehillah yearbook for 1913–1914 stated that the energy of Jewish activists was focused on "preventing the United States from changing the immigration laws in a manner to protect the country from undesirable aliens" (3/21/1920). These comments accord well with the findings of later scholars.[11]

An important technique in opposition to restrictive immigration laws was organizing mass meetings in large cities. *The International Jew* states that the Kehillah is able to organize mass meetings "on a day's notice" in all the major US cities. "It was by Mass Meetings that Congress was coerced into breaking off our commercial treaty with Russia. It was by Mass Meetings that the literacy test [as a criterion for immigration] was defeated. It was by Mass Meetings that every attempt to restrict immigration has been defeated" (3/19/1921).

The International Jew places a great deal of emphasis on Jewish power in the media as a tool of Jewish political activism. *The International Jew* recounts an incident when a professor returned from Russia with a magazine article on the Jewish question in that country. The editor was "deeply impressed with all he learned—but said he could not print the article. The same interest and examination occurred with other magazine editors of the first rank" (6/26/1920). Although Jews had made strides in ownership of the press during this period, *The International Jew* states that ownership of the press is not critical because Jews are able to exert pressure by withholding advertising. A newspaper that reprinted an excerpt of an article on Jews from the *Dearborn Independent* lost a number of Jewish advertising accounts the next day (9/11/1920).

The International Jew also presents an interesting account of resistance to Jewish pressure by James Gordon Bennett, a non-Jew who owned the *New York Herald*, the most prestigious newspaper in the city, until he died in 1918. According to *The International Jew*, the Jewish owners of department stores threatened the city's newspapers with loss of advertising if they failed to back a Jewish candidate for mayor. Bennett published the threatening letter and managed to survive the loss of Jewish advertising. Despite Bennett's victory, Jewish power in journalism increased in New York. The *Herald* died with Bennett, and "Adolph S. Ochs, a Philadelphia Jew, acquired the [*New York*] *Times*. He soon made it into a great newspaper, but one whose bias is to serve the Jews" (2/05/1921). This assessment of the *New York Times* is

---

[11] *The Culture of Critique*, Preface to the paperback edition; Neuringer 1980.

quite reasonable.[12]

The Anti-Defamation League (ADL) also receives some attention from *The International Jew*. The ADL is portrayed as organizing boycotts to achieve its ends, often through its ability to control advertising in newspapers placed by Jewish department store owners. The ADL pressures newspapers to remove negative references to people identified as Jews. This pressure has resulted in Jews with negative press being referred to as Russians or as Englishmen, but never as Jews (3/19/1921; 7/03/1920). *The International Jew* also points to a double standard in this regard: "A Jewish paper may shriek to the skies that Professor So-and-So, or Judge So-and-So, or Senator So-and-So is a Jew; but the secular newspaper that should do that would be visited by an indignant committee bearing threats" (9/11/1920). *The International Jew* also reports that in 1919, the ADL claimed success in getting 150 US cities to exclude *The Merchant of Venice* from public schools.

JEWISH INFLUENCE ON FOREIGN POLICY

The International Jew describes in some detail the 1911 Jewish campaign to abrogate the Russian Trade Agreement. (*The International Jew* was partly motivated out of pique at former President Taft, who was president at the time of the abrogation and who had been recruited by the ADL to release a statement, on November 1, 1920, condemning *The International Jew* "as a foolish pronouncement" [1/15/21].) *The International Jew*'s account of Taft's role in the abrogation of the Russian Trade Agreement agrees with other accounts of the events but adds some interesting personal details. The source of the problem was that the Russian government restricted the freedom of its Jewish citizens to travel and settle within Russia to the so-called Pale of Settlement, an area in Western Russia with a large Jewish population that had been annexed by Russia from Poland at the end of the eighteenth century. (Jews had traditionally been banned from Russia.) Some Jews were getting around these laws by going to the United States, becoming naturalized citizens, and then returning to Russia as US citizens. Russia regarded this as a subterfuge. It continued to view these people as subject to its travel and residence restrictions. The Jewish campaign favored formulations in which the problem was couched as a general *American* problem rather than as a specific problem for American Jews. But the difficulties for American Jews were only a pretext for a larger campaign directed at exerting pressure on Russia to end the Pale of Settlement and

---

[12] See *The Culture of Critique*, Preface to the paperback edition.

thereby change the status of Russian Jews.

A delegation of prominent American Jews, including Jacob Schiff, visited President Taft to discuss this issue as well as the use of literacy tests for immigrants—another important Jewish concern. Taft rebuffed the Jewish delegation on the trade embargo issue, basing his decision on his interpretation of the best interests of the United States, and he also presented the Jewish delegation with a letter from the US Ambassador in Russia giving the Russian point of view on their Jewish subjects and the need to restrict their movements. *The International Jew* does not discuss the contents of this letter, but the official Russian view was that emancipation had resulted in Jews economically dominating and exploiting the Slavic peasants.[13] Jews in Russia "were viewed by the authorities and by much of the rest of population as a foreign, separate, exploitative, and distressingly prolific nation."[14]

Taft's behavior angered the Jewish delegation and particularly Jacob Schiff, who refused to shake the President's hand. The American Jewish Committee began an intense campaign that resulted in victory when, a mere ten months later, "both houses of Congress ordered President Taft to notify Russia that the treaty with Russia would be terminated. . . . Whether this had anything to do with the fact that William Howard Taft became that unusual figure—a one-term President—this chronicle does not undertake to say" (1/15/1921).

The International Jew also presents an interesting account of various descriptions of the anti-Jewish actions in Poland in 1919. The article of November 6, 1920, compares several accounts of the situation in Poland and notes that a very pro-Jewish account by Sir Stuart Samuel, the Jewish head of the British mission to Poland, was widely publicized, including being placed as advertisements in newspapers. On the other hand, accounts by Henry Morgenthau, Sr. (also Jewish, and former US Ambassador to Turkey) and Captain P. Wright (a member of the British mission to Poland) that were less flattering to Jews disappeared from public awareness to the point that copies of them were difficult to obtain.

The International Jew emphasizes Jewish sympathy for communism as an important issue in Polish anti-Semitism: "Whenever Bolshevik Red armies swept across Poland, the Jews met them with welcomes. This is no longer denied, even in the United States: it is explained by the statement that the Bolsheviki are more friendly to the Jews than are

---

[13] Judge 1992, 9, 11.
[14] Lindemann 1991, 17.

the Poles" (11/06/1921). The report by Wright emphasized the successful Jewish demands for group political and legal rights at the Versailles Peace Conference:

> If the Jews of England—after multiplying their numbers by twenty or thirty—demanded that the Jewish Board of Guardians should have extensive powers, including the right to tax for purposes of emigration, and that a separate number of seats should be set aside in the London County Council, the Manchester Town Council, the House of Commons, and the House of Lords, to be occupied only by Jews chosen by Jews; that the president of the board of education should hand over yearly to the Jews sums proportionate to their numbers; if some were to demand the right to have separate Jewish law courts, or at least to be allowed to use Yiddish as well as English in the King's Bench and Chancery Division; if the most advanced even looked forward to a time when Bank of England notes were to be printed in Yiddish as well as in English, then they might well find public opinion, even in England, less well disposed to them.

The International Jew notes the large degree of Jewish influence on Woodrow Wilson: "They formed a solid ring around him." Commenting on the special access to Wilson held by the Jewish journalist David Lawrence, *The International Jew* states, "There was a time when he communicated to the country through no one but a Jew" (12/04/1920). *The International Jew* provides examples of Jews who were involved in corruption during World War I, attributing the crimes to the immense power of Jewish financier Bernard Baruch, who controlled the War Industries Board.

The International Jew states that Simon Wolf, a Jewish lobbyist in Washington, suggested that a Jew be appointed ambassador to Spain "to show Spain that the United States does not approve Spain's act of expulsion back in the fifteenth century. Jews are also suggesting to President Harding that a Jew be appointed Ambassador to Germany to rebuke the Germans' resentment against Jewish control of finance, industry and politics" (3/19/1921). The request for a Jewish ambassador to Spain to protest the expulsion of 1492 is truly remarkable but not at all surprising. It is yet another indication of the intensity and persistence of Jewish memories of anti-Semitism.[15] *The International Jew*

---

[15] *Separation and Its Discontents*, ch. 6; *The Culture of Critique*, Preface to the paperback edition.

also claims that American and British Jews with a Zionist agenda are crowding diplomatic posts in the Middle East, "so that the whole mid-Orient is now under Jewish control, and the Mohammedan World is given to understand that the Jews are merely coming back from their conquest of the white races" (3/19/1921).

All of this paints a picture of enormous Jewish power during this period. However, the limits of Jewish power at the time were also apparent, particularly in the battle over immigration. Unlike the abrogation of the Russian Trade Agreement, immigration aroused intense passions among non-Jews as well, and Jews were on the losing side in the immigration restriction legislation of 1921 and 1924. It was not until 1965 that this immigration policy was overturned despite continued intense Jewish pressure on this issue over the ensuing decades.[16]

ARE JEWS A RACE?

The International Jew takes the view that Jews are a race and understand themselves to be a race but have successfully lobbied to ensure that public references to Judaism refer to it as a religion. (The usage of the term "race" in *The International Jew* reflects the fact that during this period there was no distinction between the major human races and small descent groups, the latter termed "ethnic groups" in today's parlance.) In 1909, Jews successfully pressured Congress to reject a recommendation of the US Census Bureau to have the category of "Jew" for recording immigrants. Jewish lobbyists insisted that Jews were a religion, not a race, despite heated arguments to the contrary by US Senators, including prominent immigration restrictionist Henry Cabot Lodge. As a result, "there are 46 other classifications [of racial/ethnic groups], but none for the Jew," and *The International Jew* quotes a government report stating that classification "by race or people . . . is acceptable to the people of the United States *with one exception*" (10/09/1920; emphasis in *The International Jew*).

The International Jew notes that "at least one indication has appeared in which the Jew has one view to present to the Gentiles, and another which he cherishes among his own people, on this question of Race," i.e., that Jews view themselves as a race but wish non-Jews to regard them only as a religion (10/09/1920). To buttress its claims that Jews are a race—a view that agrees with the results of modern studies of population genetics,[17] *The International Jew* cites comments from a

---

[16] *The Culture of Critique*, ch. 7.
[17] *A People That Shall Dwell Alone*, ch. 2.

number of Jewish scholars and prominent Jews. It quotes a Jewish scholar, Leon Simon, who claimed, "The idea that Jews are a religious sect, precisely parallel to Catholics and Protestants, is nonsense" (10/16/1920). *The International Jew* also quotes the influential proto-Zionist theorist, Moses Hess, that the Jew "belongs to a race; he belongs to a nation; he seeks a kingdom to come on this earth, a kingdom which shall be over all kingdoms, with Jerusalem the ruling city of the world" (10/16/1920). (Given the abundant signs of "the rise of the Jews," to use Albert Lindemann's phrase,[18] it must have seemed ominous to the authors of *The International Jew* to find the prediction of Jewish world supremacy contained not only in ancient Jewish religious writings but also repeated by an influential Jewish intellectual of the modern era.) In the same passage, *The International Jew* also quotes Supreme Court Justice and Zionist Louis Brandeis that "the percentage of foreign blood in the Jews of today is very low. Probably no important European race is as pure." *The International Jew* also cites Jewish scholar Israel Friedlander's statement that the Jewish idea of racial purity stems from the rejection of the Samaritans as Jews recorded in the books of Ezra and Nehemiah in the Old Testament, a view that is common among scholars today.[19] Friedlander writes that "it is enough for us to know that the Jews have always *felt* themselves to be a separate race, sharply marked off from the rest of mankind" (10/16/1920).

The International Jew also points out the irony of Jews claiming to be a religious group in the United States while claiming to be a nationality in Eastern Europe. Jewish groups, including some based in the US, successfully lobbied the post-World War I peace conferences to achieve nationality status in Poland and other Eastern European countries. As several scholars have noted, religious forms of Judaism have acted as a "protective coloring"[20] adopted because "it is a legitimate way to maintain differences when organic ways [i.e., assertions of ethnic peoplehood] are suspect."[21] As Jacob Katz notes, "The definition of the Jewish community as a purely religious unit was, of course, a sham from the time of its conception."[22] John Murray Cuddihy discusses how Judaism came to be considered, along with Protestantism and Catholicism, as one of the three major US religions, although Jews constitute

---

[18] Lindemann 1997.
[19] *A People That Shall Dwell Alone*, ch. 3.
[20] Elazar 1980, 9.
[21] Elazar 1980, 23.
[22] Katz 1986, 32.

only 2 to 3 percent of the population.[23]

THE INTERNATIONAL JEW ON ANTI-SEMITISM

The International Jew takes the view that anti-Semitism results mainly from Jewish behavior and that it can be rationally understood by adducing appropriate evidence. *The International Jew*'s view is that non-Jews who attempt to understand anti-Semitism by attributing blame to the Jews should therefore not be classified as anti-Semites:

> It would seem to be necessary for our Jewish citizens to enlarge their classification of Gentiles to include the class which recognizes the existence of a Jewish Question and still is not anti-Semitic. . . . Anti-Semitism is a term which is bandied about too loosely. It ought to be reserved to denote the real anti-Jewish temper of violent prejudice. . . . Nor is it anti-Semitism to say that the suspicion is abroad in every capital of civilization and the certainty is held by a number of important men that there is active in the world a plan to control the world . . . by control of the machinery of commerce and exchange. It is not anti-Semitism to say that, nor to present the evidence which supports that, nor to bring proof of that. (June 19, 1920)

Anti-Semitism throughout history "has never accomplished anything in behalf of those who used it, and it has never taught anything to the Jews against whom it was used" (6/19/1920). Anti-Semitism "has sometimes broken into murderous violence. . . . There is, of course, no excuse for these outbreaks, but there is sufficient explanation of them" (6/19/1920). Jews tend to over-attribute the Christian religious basis of anti-Semitism: "There is no hesitation in stating that there is no prejudice whatever in the Christian churches against the Jew on account of his religion" (6/19/1920). (Neal Baldwin, the author of *Henry Ford and the Jews: The Mass Production of Hate*, finds the roots of Ford's anti-Jewish attitudes in medieval religious attitudes. He would have benefited by reading this passage.[24])

A common technique of those attempting to criticize Jews is to find Jewish authors who reflect their views. *The International Jew* does this quite often, as in the July 10, 1920, installment where Theodor Herzl is used as a reference supporting the idea that Jews are a nation. "He said, '*We are a people—One people.*'" "Herzl's words are being proved to be true—'when we sink, we become a revolutionary proletariat, *the*

---

[23] Cuddihy 1978.
[24] Baldwin 2001.

subordinate officers of the revolutionary party'" (7/10/1920). The entire passage is quoted as an epigram in the article for July 17, 1920: "*We are a people—One people . . . When we sink, we become a revolutionary proletariat, the subordinate officers of a revolutionary party; when we rise, there rises also our terrible power of the purse.*" *The International Jew* quotes an article by Lord Eustace Perry, republished "apparently with approval" in the Canadian *Jewish Chronicle*, as follows:

> Liberalism and Nationalism, with a flourish of trumpets, threw open the doors of the ghetto and offered equal citizenship to the Jew. The Jew passed out into the Western World, saw the power and the glory of it, used it and enjoyed it, laid his hand indeed upon the nerve centers of civilization, guided, directed and exploited it, and then—refused the offer. . . . Moreover—and this is the remarkable thing—the Europe of nationalism and liberalism, of scientific government and democratic equality is more intolerable to him than the old oppressions and persecutions of despotism. . . . In a world of completely organized territorial sovereignties, he [the Jew] has only two possible cities of refuge: he must either pull down the pillars of the whole national state system or he must create a territorial sovereignty of his own. In this perhaps lies the explanation both of Jewish Bolshevism and Zionism, for at the moment Western Jewry seems to hover uncertainly between the two. In Eastern Europe Bolshevism and Zionism often seem to grow side by side, just as Jewish influence molded Republicanism and Socialist thought throughout the nineteenth century—*not because the Jew cares for the positive side of radical philosophy, not because he desires to be a partaker in Gentile nationalism or Gentile democracy, but because no existing Gentile system of government is ever anything but distasteful to him.* (7/10/1920; emphasis in text)

The International Jew comments: "All that is true, and Jewish thinkers of the more fearless type always recognize it as true. *The Jew is against the Gentile scheme of things*" (7/10/1920; emphasis in text). The passage quoted is in fact remarkably similar to the writings of prominent Zionist Maurice Samuel, especially his *You Gentiles*.[25]

CHARACTERISTICS OF JEWS

Apart from *The International Jew*'s flights into conspiracy theories,

---

[25] Samuel 1924.

especially in the case of the *Protocols*, its view of Jews is reasonably congruent with my account.[26] Jews are a highly talented group: the explanation of their success is in their "vigor, resourcefulness and special proclivities" (5/22/1920). Jews are an aggressive group. According to *The International Jew*, from Biblical times they have endeavored to enslave and dominate other peoples, even in disobedience of divine command, quoting the Old Testament, "And it came to pass, when Israel was strong, that they put the Canaanites to tribute, and did not utterly drive them out."

Throughout history Jews have tended to be unpopular with the people while they have made alliances with elites: "What cared the Jew if the people gnashed their teeth against him, so long as the king and the court were his friends?"[27] Jews have eschewed friendships with non-Jews because of a feeling of racial superiority, and indeed, "the Jew who reflects upon the disparity between his people's numbers and their power may be pardoned if he sees in that fact a proof of their racial superiority" (6/5/1920).

Jews in America separate themselves from others and do not assimilate; "he cultivates by his exclusiveness the feeling that he does not 'belong'" (6/5/1920). "The international Jew . . . rules not because he is rich, but because in a most marked degree he possesses the commercial and masterful genius of his race, and avails himself of a racial loyalty and solidarity the like of which exists in no other human group" (6/12/1920). There is considerable evidence that Jews are indeed highly ethnocentric, what one may even term "hyperethnocentric."

> The contention of certain modernists notwithstanding, the world will go on thinking of the Jew as a member of a race, a race whose persistence has defeated the utmost efforts made for its extermination, a race that has preserved itself in virility and power by the observance of those natural laws the violation of which has mongrelized so many nations. . . . And he will always have the right to feel that to be a Jew is to belong to a superior race. (6/12/1920)

Jews are intent on remaining resolutely separate in America:

> To love a Christian maiden is sinful; this is the theme of all sorts of stories, sketches and editorials appearing these days. But [play-

---

[26] See, especially, *A People That Shall Dwell Alone*.
[27] See *A People That Shall Dwell Alone*, ch. 5, esp. 112–15; *Separation and Its Discontents*, ch. 2.

wright] James Gibbons Huneker, in a sketch extravagantly praised by Jewish critics, shows how deep this idea of separateness is when he makes [his character] Yaankely Ostrowicz say: "As a child I trembled at the sound of music and was taught to put my finger in my ears when *profane music*, Goy music, was played." This is the root idea: All Gentile life and institutions are "profane." It is the Jews' unceasing consciousness of the Goy that constitutes the disease of Judaism, this century-long tradition of separateness. . . . A study of Jewish publications, books, pamphlets, declarations, constitutions and charters, as well as a study of organized Jewish action in this and other countries, indicates that there is a tremendous amount of anti-Goyism, or anti-Gentilism. (3/12/1921)

The International Jew sees Jews as suffering from moral particularism—a tendency to confuse morality with what is good for the Jews.[28] According to *The International Jew*, Jews have a pronounced sense of ingroup-outgroup morality—"the ethics of the stranger," the classic being "unto a stranger thou mayest lend upon usury; but unto thy brother thou shalt not lend upon usury" (5/22/1920). But, according to *The International Jew*, Jewish moral particularism goes beyond that to an inability to see things from the perspective of the other:

Truly, these people are a paradox. They are not fair. They are constituted so that they cannot see the other side of anything. . . . Non-Jews are fair. They are willing to see the other people's point of view. When it was said to us *The Merchant of Venice* was a cruelty upon Jewish school pupils, we said, without investigation, "Out goes the Merchant, then!" (6/04/1921)

The International Jew implores Jews to end their moral particularism and become full participants in society:

The Jew has been too long accustomed to think of himself as exclusively the claimant on the humanitarianism of society; society has a large claim against him that he cease his exclusiveness, that he cease exploiting the world, that he cease making Jewish groups the end of all of his gains, and that he begin to fulfill, in a sense his exclusiveness has never yet enabled him to fulfill, the ancient prophecy that through him all nations of the earth should be blessed.

---

[28] See also *The Culture of Critique*, Preface to the paperback edition.

The International Jew sees Jews as ruthless fanatics who will oppress others if given the chance. The main examples in the contemporary world are said to be Bolshevism and the Jabotinskyists, the fanatic and violent Zionist terrorists in Palestine. However, *The International Jew* also provides a brief history of Jewish violence against Christians and others during antiquity, including the events in Jerusalem in 614 A.D. in which 60,000 Palestinian Christians were massacred by Jews after being purchased as war booty from the conquering Persians. This is indeed an event worth noting. The Israeli archaeologist Ronny Reich writes: "They were probably sold to the highest bidder. According to some sources, the Christian captives at Mamilla Pond were bought by Jews and were then slain on the spot." An eyewitness, Strategius of St. Sabas, was more vivid: "Jews ransomed the Christians from the hands of the Persian soldiers for good money, and slaughtered them with great joy at Mamilla Pool, and it ran with blood. Jews massacred 60,000 Palestinian Christians in Jerusalem alone."[29]

ZIONISM

The International Jew describes a propaganda campaign in the US media in favor of Zionism. *The International Jew* quotes an article from the *Atlantic Monthly* warning that

> ... the information we receive in America comes through the Jewish Telegraph Agency and Zionist Propaganda. "The latter ... with its harrowing stories of pogroms in Europe, and its misrepresentations of the situation in the Near East, has been able to awaken not a little sympathy for the Zionist propaganda." This propaganda of pogroms—"thousands upon thousands of Jews killed"—amounts to nothing except as it illustrates the gullibility of the press. No one believes this propaganda, and governments regularly disprove it. (5/28/1921)

Commenting on Zionist riots against the natives of Palestine ("the 'persecuted' turned persecutor"), *The International Jew* notes that the High Commissioner of Palestine is Sir Herbert Samuel, a Jew, and that all the ministers of the commission are Jews. The British government sentenced militant Zionist Ze'ev Jabotinsky to fifteen years in prison for leading riots against the natives, but "he was released immediately upon the arrival of Sir Herbert Samuel, and is now traveling in state, and is talked of as a possible successor to Sir Herbert, although he is

---

[29] Shamir 2001.

originally one of the Russian Bolsheviki come down to practice the gentle arts of that tribe in Palestine." *The International Jew* takes the view that the long-term intention of Zionism is to establish Israel as a world power: "It begins to be very clear that Jewish nationalism will develop along the line of enmity to the rest of the world. . . . [T]he Jews are thinking of elevating themselves into the military power that shall stand between East and West on that most strategic strip of ground in the world" (5/28/1921). In a comment foreshadowing the expulsion of the Palestinians in 1948 and reminiscent of recent comments by US and Israeli politicians on the status of the West Bank, *The International Jew* quotes Zionist activist Israel Zangwill stating, "Let [the natives] get out! We must gently persuade them to 'trek.' After all, they have all Arabia with its million square miles, and Israel has not a square inch. There is no particular reason for the Arabs to cling to those few kilometers" (5/28/1921).

JEWS AND POLITICAL RADICALISM

The International Jew takes the view that contemporary Communism is an extension of traditional Jewish collectivism:

> The traditional Jewish Kahal [i.e., Jewish self-government] is really the same as the modern Soviet: Under the Kahal or ancient Soviet, the Jews lived by themselves and governed themselves. . . . It was communism in a more drastic form than has been seen in the world outside Russia. Education, taxes, domestic affairs, all were under the absolute control of a few men who constituted the ruling board. . . . All property was in common, which did not prevent the leaders becoming rich. (8/28/1920).

(This last statement is not accurate. Property was not held in common in traditional Jewish communities.)

As was common during the period, *The International Jew* points to the very prominent role of Jews in the Bolshevik government in the USSR (9/25/1920) and in Béla Kun's short-lived communist revolution in Hungary (8/28/1920). *The International Jew* notes the continuation of Hebrew schools in the Soviet Union—an aspect of the Soviet government's well-known encouragement of secular Jewish culture during this period (*Evsektsiya*). *The International Jew* provides a list which claimed that seventeen of the twenty-two members of the "Council of the Commissaries of the People" are Jews. *The International Jew* does not cite its source except to say that it was "smuggled out of the Soviet Union." Many such lists were circulated during the period, and it is impossible to find a consensus on their authenticity or accuracy. Nevertheless, it is certainly true that Jews had a privileged position in the early years of the Soviet government and were a critical part of the ruling elite.[30]

The International Jew states that Jews hailed the victory of Bolshevism at first:

> There was no concealment whatever in the early days of the new regime as to the part which Jewry had in it. Public meetings, interviews, special articles poured forth in which very valuable elements of truth were mingled. There was no attempt at concealment of names. Then the horror of the thing began to take hold upon the world, and for just a breathing space Jewish opinion fell silent. There was a spasmodic denial or two. Then a new burst of glorification. The glorification continues within Judaism itself, but it now carries on the Gentile side of its face a very sad expression labeled "persecution." We have lived to see the day when to denounce Bolshevism is to "persecute the Jews." (9/25/1920)

The International Jew points to an article from *The American Hebrew* of 9/10/1920 that claimed that:

> That achievement [referring to the overthrow of the Tsar] . . . *was largely the outcome of Jewish thinking, of Jewish discontent, of Jewish effort to reconstruct.* This rapid emergence of the Russian revolution from the destructive phase and its entrance into the constructive phase is a conspicuous genius of *Jewish discontent . . . What Jewish idealism and Jewish discontent have so powerfully contributed to accomplish in Russia, the same historic qualities of the Jewish mind and heart ARE TENDING TO PROMOTE IN OTHER COUNTRIES.* (9/25/1920; emphasis provided by *The International Jew*).

The International Jew comments, "Why are 'Jewish idealism' and 'Jewish discontent' always linked together?" Jewish writers have often fancifully linked Jewish radicalism to idealism and moral superiority,[31] but linking it at the same time to Jewish discontent would indeed seem to be the height of self-deception.

The International Jew also cites an article in the London *Jewish*

---

[30] Lindemann 1997; *The Culture of Critique*, ch. 3.
[31] See *The Culture of Critique*, ch. 3.

Chronicle of 1919 stating, "There is much in the fact of Bolshevism itself, in the fact that so many Jews are Bolsheviks, in the fact that the ideals of Bolshevism at many points are consonant with the finest ideals of Judaism" (10/2/1920). The same paper contained an article in 1920 by Israel Zangwill praising "the race which has produced a Beaconsfield [i.e., Disraeli], a Montagu, a Klotz, *a Kurt Eisner* [leader of the short-lived Communist government in Bavaria]*, a Trotsky*" (emphasis in *The International Jew*). *The International Jew* also reproduces part of an article from the newspaper *The Communist*, stating

> Without exaggeration, it may be said that *the great Russian social revolution was indeed accomplished by the hands of the Jews*. Would the dark, oppressed masses of the Russian workmen and peasants have been able to throw off the yoke of the bourgeoisie by themselves? No, *it was precisely the Jews who led the Russian proletariat to the dawn of the Internationale and not only have led, but are now leading the Soviet cause* which remains in their safe hands. ... It is not without reason that during the elections to all Soviet institutions the Jews are winning by an overwhelming majority. (9/25/1920; emphasis provided by *The International Jew*)

The International Jew attributes most of the Jewish support for Bolshevism in the United States to the Jewish trade unions in the garment industry (4/23/1921). *The International Jew* describes the radicalism of the union leaders but also emphasizes their links with the wider Jewish community and particularly their membership in the Kehillah and the links between the Kehillah and the American Jewish Committee. For example, "another big union which makes part of the New York Kehillah is the Amalgamated Clothing Workers of America, whose membership is about 200,000. It is officered by Russian Jews whose pronounced Bolshevism has been widely reported in the Jewish press of New York" (4/23/1921).

Such linkages between radical groups and mainstream Jewish organizations were indeed common at least until the 1950s. For example, the 50,000-member Jewish People's Fraternal Order was an affiliate of the American Jewish Congress and also listed as a subversive organization by the US Attorney General. The JPFO was the financial and organizational "bulwark" of the CPUSA after World War II. The JPFO also funded two major Communist newspapers: the *Daily Worker* and the Yiddish-language *Morning Freiheit*. Although the American Jewish Congress severed its ties with the JPFO and stated that communism was a threat, it was "at best a reluctant and unenthusiastic participant"[32] in the Jewish effort to develop a public image of anti-communism—a position reflecting the sympathies of many among its predominantly second- and third-generation Eastern European immigrant membership.

JEWS AND THE FEDERAL RESERVE SYSTEM

The International Jew is deeply suspicious of the Federal Reserve System enacted into law in 1913 after being proposed originally by Paul Warburg, a German-Jewish immigrant and partner in the Kuhn, Loeb & Co. investment banking firm. Neil Baldwin's account hardly does justice to *The International Jew*'s treatment, stating only that *The International Jew* "mistakenly [accuses] Warburg of advocating only one central bank, when in fact he had pushed from the beginning that the core be tied to diversified branches."[33] *The International Jew* acknowledges that the system is tied to various branches but provides a quotation from Warburg suggesting that this formal structure could be overcome administratively, and it provides data indicating that a vastly disproportionate amount of loans were being made through the New York branch—that the New York branch had become *primus inter pares*.

The International Jew agreed that it was a good idea to have a centralized banking system, but complained that the system actually functioned to funnel money away from agricultural areas, where credit remained tight, to New York, where it was used to further the interests of Jewish financiers who were international in outlook and concerned to promote Jewish interests rather than mainly the interests of the United States. The main suspicion was directed at Kuhn, Loeb & Co. because of Warburg's role in creating the Federal Reserve System and because Warburg had become director of the Federal Reserve Board. *The International Jew* noted that the members of Kuhn, Loeb & Co. had international ties by business and blood to other Jewish banking firms in Europe.

The International Jew provides several examples of the international focus of Kuhn, Loeb & Co. For example, *The International Jew* recounts the well-known fact that Jacob Schiff, a Jewish activist and partner in the firm of Kuhn, Loeb & Co., had financed the Japanese war effort against the Russian Empire in 1905 and had also provided financial support to revolutionary movements within Russia that eventually led to the overthrow of the Tsar. *The International Jew* also noted that

---

[32] Svonkin 1997, 166, 132.
[33] Baldwin 2001, 213–14.

Schiff hated the Tsarist Russian government because of its treatment of its Jewish citizens—certainly an accurate assessment. In other words, *The International Jew* is suggesting that the Federal Reserve might be used to promote the international ethnic interests of Jews rather than the interests of the United States.

The International Jew also points to the internationalism of Paul Warburg's connections by quoting Otto Kahn, another partner in Kuhn, Loeb & Co., to the effect that American money should be put to use in helping build up the French empire, particularly Syria. (In the same passage, *The International Jew* notes the role of international Jewish organizations in getting the French to guarantee Jewish interests in Syria.) Moreover, *The International Jew* asserts that Max Warburg, of the German branch of the banking family, was implicated by a US government document as financing Trotsky's campaign against Russia. *The International Jew* also supports its claim of the internationalism of Jewish bankers by noting that the German Warburgs also made a loan to the city of Paris during World War I: "[T]he international financiers have been so engrossed in world money that the sense of national responsibility sometimes becomes blurred in their minds" (7/09/21).

The International Jew cites figures indicating that the great majority of loans and money are funneled through the New York Fed rather than the eleven other branches located around the country.

> The money is in New York. Go out through the agricultural states, and you will not find it. Go into the districts of silent factories and you will not find it. It is in New York. The Warburg Federal Reserve has deflated the country. . . . The Federal Reserve Idea was doubtless right; if it had not been, it could not have been established. But it has been manipulated. . . . Kuhn, Loeb & Company, the Speyers and the other Jewish money-lenders have money for Mexico, Norway, Germany, and all sorts of commercial companies being organized to do business overseas, and it is American money. The Warburg Federal Reserve System has been badly misused, badly manipulated, and the country is suffering from it. (7/16/1921)

THE *PROTOCOLS*

The discussion of the *Protocols* and references to them throughout the work is definitely the low point of *The International Jew*. Since the *Protocols* were exposed as fraudulent, it has been very easy to discredit the entire enterprise of *The International Jew* because of its extensive use of them, and that is exactly what Baldwin does.[34] The authors of *The International Jew* were well aware of claims that the *Protocols* were forgeries, but rejected them, stating, for example, "This makes the sixth 'final' and 'complete' exposure that the Jews have put forth for public consumption. The Jews have still time to repent and tell the truth. Suppose they make the seventh the whole truth with a true repudiation of the *Protocols*" (10/8/1921).

The *Protocols* present a "theory" in which absolutely every aspect of modernity is explained as the result of a single, centuries-old overarching Jewish conspiracy to subjugate non-Jews. To be charitable, *The International Jew* always presents the *Protocols* as only tentatively authentic. *The International Jew* argues repeatedly that the best evidence for the authenticity of the *Protocols* is that events that have transpired since the *Protocols* were written conform to its predictions. And *The International Jew* acknowledges that, even granted that the predictions have come true, one must also provide actual evidence that Jews have been behind the events forecast by the *Protocols*.

The difficulty is that, while some of the statements from the *Protocols* discussed in *The International Jew* seem fairly straightforward, many are not falsifiable. Moreover, *The International Jew* often fails to provide evidence that Jews are actually behind the events supposedly forecast by the *Protocols*. A general problem with the *Protocols* is that they have too much of a tendency to see any and all actions of Jews as aiming for a common purpose of subjugating non-Jews. While authors like Baldwin apologetically deny any group cohesion to Jews, the *Protocols* err on the opposite side by fitting everything Jews do into an overarching Jewish conspiracy.

The *Protocols* are written in such a way that virtually anything that happens—even anti-Jewish actions—can be seen as part of a Jewish conspiracy. For example, according the *Protocols* and *The International Jew* (7/31/1920), the fact that Jews head labor unions and are prominent capitalists does not show real differences among Jews but only that all the forces of society are run by Jews for a common purpose: to subjugate non-Jews. *The International Jew* approves of Protocol Nine, which states that, "At the present time, if any government raises a protest against us, it is only for the sake of form, it is under our control and it is done by our direction, for *their anti-Semitism is necessary for keeping in order our lesser brothers*" (9/18/1920). The following is intended to give a flavor of *The International Jew*'s use of the *Protocols*.

---

[34] Baldwin 2001.

The International Jew claims that the "World Program" outlined by the *Protocols* has several aspects: financial control; political control; control of education; "trivializing the public mind through a most complete system of allurement"; and "sowing the seeds of disruption everywhere—not the seeds of progress, but of economic fallacies and revolutionary temper" (9/18/1920). *The International Jew* takes the view that acceptance of the *Protocols* is not to be at face value but only as the result of evidence, "if reliable" (7/17/1920). "Whether the method laid down by the Protocols is worth considering or not depends entirely on whether it can be found in actual affairs today" (9/18/1920). The *Protocols* are regarded as the "theory of Jewish World Power rather than the actual operation of that power in the world today," the latter to be discovered by compiling evidence (7/24/1920). For example, "whether the Protocols are of Jewish origin or not, whether they present Jewish interests or not, this [i.e., religious and race hatred] is exactly the state of the world, of the Gentile world, today" (7/31/1920).

The International Jew argues that the idea of a common Jewish plot to rule the world would not be expected to be known by the average Jew and that such a proposal is really no more surprising than to suppose that the Jewish nation has a foreign policy: "There can be little doubt . . . as to the existence of what may be called a 'foreign policy,' that is, a definite point of view and plan of action with reference to the Gentile world. The Jew feels that he is in the midst of enemies, but he also feels that he is a member of a people—'one people' [quoting Zionist pioneer Theodor Herzl]. He must have some policy with regard to the outer world." *The International Jew* states that, "If, in looking about the world, it is possible to see both the established conditions and the strong tendencies to which these *Protocols* allude, it will not be strange if interest in a mere literary curiosity gives way to something like alertness, and it may be alarm" (8/7/1920). In the long run, the goal of the Jews is international control: the *Protocols*: "Then our international rights will eliminate national rights in the narrow sense, and we will govern the governments as they govern their subjects" (8/7/1920).

The *Protocols* and *The International Jew* yearn for a world without division and dissension, presumably a reflection of the traditional Russian society whose ideals the *Protocols* reflect. Both the *Protocols* and *The International Jew* yearn for a world without confusion, where everyone has similar beliefs. Every departure from this homogeneity is seen as the work of the Jews intended to subjugate non-Jews. From the *Protocols*: "People of all opinions and of all doctrines are at our service, restorers of monarchy, demagogues, Socialists, communists, and other Utopians. We have put them all to work" (7/31/1920). All theories, including scientific theories, are part of the plan: There is a "'Jewish' plan to split society by 'ideas'" (8/14/1920). The *Protocols*: "Let *those theories of life which we have induced them to regard as the dictates of science* play the most important role for them. . . . Note the successes we have arranged in *Darwinism, Marxism*, and *Nietzscheism*" (7/31/1920). Racial strife and class antagonism are part of the plan, and *The International Jew* sees the latter fulfilled in Russia where there is "*the spectacle of a Gentile lower class led by Jewish leaders against a Gentile upper class!*" (7/31/1920). "The whole outlook of these *Protocols* upon the world is that the *idea* may be made a most potent poison" (7/31/1920). "*We create* courts." "*We have* taken good care long ago to discredit the Gentile clergy and thereby to destroy their mission" (7/31/1920).

Jews use their influence to corrupt non-Jews, and especially non-Jewish youth. The *Protocols*: "To prevent them from really thinking out anything themselves, we shall deflect their attention to amusements, games, pastimes, excitements and people's palaces." *The International Jew* interprets the following as a fulfillment of the *Protocols*: "Every influence that leads to lightness and looseness in Gentile youth today heads up in a Jewish source" (8/7/1920). "While a certain percentage of the Jewish youth itself is overcome by this social poison, the percentage is almost nothing compared with the results among the youth of the Gentiles" (8/7/1920). The *Protocols*: "To destroy Gentile industry, we shall, as an incentive to this speculation, *encourage among the Gentiles a strong demand for luxuries—all enticing luxuries*" (8/7/1920).

Corresponding to this attempt to corrupt non-Jews, the *Protocols* has a very low estimate of non-Jewish human nature. The *Protocols*:

People in the masses and people of the masses are guided by exceptionally shallow passions, beliefs, customs, traditions, and sentimental theories and are inclined toward party division, a fact which prevents any form of agreement, even when this is founded on a thoroughly logical basis. . . . Our triumph has also been made easier because, in our relations with the people necessary to us, we have always played upon the most sensitive strings of the human mind—on calculation, greed, and the insatiable material desires of men. (7/31/1920)

Reflecting the *Protocols'* tendency to see everything working together to suit Jewish ends, *The International Jew* notes, "Distrust and division are everywhere. And in the midst of the confusion everyone is dimly aware that there is a higher group that is not divided at all, but is getting exactly what it wants by means of the confusion that obtains all around" (7/31/1920).

CONCLUSION

The International Jew is far from ideal as an analysis of Jewish issues. However, apart from its immersion in the *Protocols*, its major claims about Jews are correct and have been corroborated by later scholarship. Jews are indeed an ethnically closed group that has vigorously sought to remain separate from the peoples they have lived among throughout their history. They are a very talented group, adept equally at building businesses and lobbying Congress. They have shown a penchant for being able to influence the media, not only via ownership but also via economic pressure and overrepresentation among journalists, writers, and producers of media content. Jews were indeed deeply involved in political radicalism during the 1920s and thereafter, and *The International Jew* was quite correct to emphasize the importance of Zionism to the later history of Jews and to the world in general.

What strikes the reader of *The International Jew* is its portrayal of Jewish intensity and aggressiveness in asserting their interests. Jews were unique as an American immigrant group in their hostility toward American Christian culture and in their energetic efforts to change that culture.[35] From the perspective of *The International Jew*, the United States had imported around 3.5 million mainly Yiddish-speaking, intensely Jewish immigrants over the previous forty years. In that very short period, Jews had had an enormous effect on American society. The following are, I think, examples of Jewish influence on the United States in which *The International Jew* is essentially accurate:

1. Jews had achieved a great deal of economic success, even to the point of dominating certain important US industries.
2. Jewish organizations had launched highly successful campaigns to remove any references to Christianity from US public culture and to legitimize Judaism as a religion on a par with Protestantism and Catholicism.
3. Jewish organizations had been able to impose their ethnic interests on certain key areas of domestic policy. As *The International Jew*

---

[35] See also *The Culture of Critique*, Preface to the paperback edition.

noted, Jews were the main force behind maintaining the policy of unrestricted immigration; by 1920, unrestricted immigration policy had continued nearly twenty years after US public opinion had turned against it.[36] Jews had also shown the ability to have a great deal of influence in the executive branch of the US government, as indicated by their influence in the Wilson administration.

4. Jews had also been able to impose their ethnic interests in the area of foreign policy despite widespread feelings among the political establishment that the policies advocated by the Jewish community were often not in the best interests of the United States. The main examples highlighted by *The International Jew* were the abrogation of the Russian Trade Agreement in 1911 and post-World War I policy toward Eastern Europe, cases in which Jewish attitudes were entirely dictated by their perceptions of the interests of foreign Jews rather than the economic or political interests of the United States. Jews achieved their goals on these issues despite the views of the Taft administration on the Russian Trade Agreement and the views of a wide range of military and diplomatic figures that the United States should support post-World War I Poland as a bulwark against Bolshevism and that Jewish complaints against Poland were exaggerated.[37]

5. Jews had been a major force behind the success of Bolshevism and its incredibly bloody rein of terror in the Soviet Union and in the abortive Communist revolutions in Hungary (headed by Béla Kun) and Germany (headed by Kurt Eisner).

6. Jews were the main and by far the most energetic component of the radical left in the United States, a movement that advocated a massive political, economic, and cultural transformation of the United States.

7. Jews had attained a substantial influence over the US media via a virtual monopoly on the movie production business, domination of the theater and music businesses, their influence in journalism, ownership of some newspapers, and their ability to apply economic pressure on newspapers because of their importance as advertisers. In turn, the ability of Jews to pressure non-Jewish newspapers depended on Jewish ownership of department stores in major cities. Jews used this media influence to advance their domestic and for-

---

[36] See *The Culture of Critique*, ch. 7.
[37] See Bendersky 2000. See also the discussion of Bendersky in the next chapter.

eign policy agendas, portray Jews and Judaism positively while portraying Christianity negatively, and promote a sexual morality at odds with the traditional culture of the United States.
8. In turn, these consequences stemmed from critical features of the Jewish group evolutionary strategy[38] that were well recognized, if crudely stated, by *The International Jew*: Jews are highly intelligent, and Jews are intensely ethnocentric: "The international Jew . . . rules not because he is rich, but because in a most marked degree he possesses the commercial and masterful genius of his race, and avails himself of a racial loyalty and solidarity the like of which exists in no other human group" (6/12/1920).

The International Jew reported some success in having Jewish issues discussed publicly. For example, the July 17, 1920, article stated that "A great unloosening of speech with reference to the Jewish Question and the Jewish program for world power has occurred in this country since the beginning of this series of articles." The article goes on to quote articles and editorials on Jewish radicalism, including an article in the *Chicago Tribune* ("Trotsky Leads Jew-Radicals to World Rule: Bolshevism only a Tool for His Scheme") and a *Christian Science Monitor* editorial giving credence to the "Jewish peril."

Nevertheless, despite this upsurge in discussion of Jewish issues as a result of the publication of *The International Jew*, public discussions of Jewish issues have remained more or less taboo. Father Charles Coughlin discussed Jewish issues in his widely disseminated radio broadcasts in the 1930s until being effectively shut down in 1940 as a result of a decision by the National Association of Broadcasters to forbid selling airtime to "spokesmen of controversial public issues"[39]—a regulation that was explicitly aimed at keeping Coughlin off the air. In September 1941, Charles Lindbergh had few, if any, defenders in the media when he was subjected to a torrent of abuse for stating a simple fact, that Jews were one of three groups advocating US involvement in World War II against Germany (the others being Britain and the Roosevelt administration). In the long run, *The International Jew* was simply a blip in a long-term trend that continues into the present.

---

[38] *A People That Shall Dwell Alone*, esp. chs. 1 and 8.
[39] Marcus 1973, 176; see also Warren 1996.

Chapter 8

ENEMIES OF MY ENEMY[*]

Since the latter decades of the nineteenth century there has been a remarkable increase in the cultural and political power of Jewish groups and an equally remarkable decline in the cultural and political power of Northern European peoples. In 1880 the vast majority of the Jewish population lived in Eastern Europe, well-removed from the centers of Northern European power. These Jewish populations had expanded dramatically during the nineteenth century—more rapidly than any other European group. This rapid expansion placed enormous strains on both the Jewish and non-Jewish populations of Eastern Europe. As they have in so many traditional societies, Jews had achieved a dominant position in the economies of Eastern Europe.

But there was also a large mass of impoverished Jews who were strongly attracted to messianic religious and political ideologies, especially Zionism and leftist political radicalism. Because of Jewish economic and cultural domination and lack of assimilation, there was also an upsurge in popular and governmental anti-Semitism throughout the area, most famously with the pogroms in Russia beginning in 1881, but extending throughout Eastern and Central Europe. The result was an effort by Jewish organizations to remove Jews from Eastern Europe to other countries, most notably the United States. Between 1880 and 1924, approximately two million Jews immigrated to the United States from Eastern Europe. This event was of momentous importance for the history of the United States in the twentieth century and beyond.

Joseph Bendersky's book *The "Jewish Threat": Anti-Semitic Politics of the U.S. Army*[1] is a history of the conflict between an increasingly powerful Jewish group and a declining Northern European group as revealed in the writings of US Army officers gleaned from the files of the Military Intelligence Division (MID) of the War Department. As recounted by Bendersky, Americans of Northern European descent in the United States thought of themselves as part of a cultural and ethnic heritage extending backward in time to the founding of the country.

---

[*] First published in *The Occidental Quarterly* 1 (Winter 2001): 63–77.

[1] Joseph W. Bendersky, *The "Jewish Threat": Anti-Semitic Politics of the U.S. Army* (New York: Basic Books, 2000).

The Anglo-Saxon heritage of the British Isles was at the center of this self-conception, but Americans of German and Scandinavian descent also viewed themselves as part of this ethnic and cultural inheritance. They had a great deal of pride in their accomplishments. They believed that their civilization was a product of their own unique ingenuity and skills and that it would not survive if other peoples were allowed to play too large a role in it.

Christianity was a deeply embedded aspect of the culture of the Northern Europeans, but it played a remarkably small role in the battles with the emerging Jewish elite. Far more important for framing these battles were Darwinian theories of race. The early part of the twentieth century was the high water mark of Darwinism in the social sciences. It was common at that time to think that there were important differences between the races—that races differed in intelligence and in moral qualities. Not only did races differ, but they were in competition with each other for supremacy. Schooled in the theories of Madison Grant, Lothrop Stoddard, Henry Pratt Fairchild, William Ripley, Gustav Le Bon, Charles Davenport, and William McDougall, this generation of US military officers viewed themselves as members of a particular race and believed that racial homogeneity was the *sine qua non* of every stable nation state. They regarded their racial group as uniquely talented and possessed of a high moral sense.

But, more importantly, whatever the talents and vulnerabilities of their race, they held it in the highest importance to retain control over the lands they had inherited as a result of the exploits of their ancestors who had conquered the continent and tamed the wilderness. And despite the power that their race held at the present, there was dark foreboding about the future, reflected in the titles of some of the classic works of the period: Grant's *The Passing of the Great Race* and Stoddard's *The Rising Tide of Color Against White World Supremacy* and *The Revolt Against Civilization: The Menace of the Under-Man*.

This world of Northern European cultural pride and self-confident hegemony has vanished, and there can be little doubt that the rise of the Jews and the decline of Northern Europeans are causally linked. Bendersky's book is as much a marker of that transformation as it is an extraordinary record of an important arena in the conflict between Jews and Northern Europeans. Bendersky's sense of intellectual and moral superiority and his contempt for his Northern European subjects ooze from every page. The book is a triumphalist history written by a member of a group that won the intellectual and political wars of the twentieth century.

The main thrusts of Jewish activism against Northern European hegemony focused on several critical power centers in the United States: The academic world of information in the social sciences and humanities, the political and legal world where public policy on immigration and other ethnic issues is decided, and the mass media where "ways of seeing" are presented to the public. As recounted in *The "Jewish Threat,"* all of these power centers were important in the battle against the generation of US army officers who came to power after World War I. In focusing on these power centers, these Jewish efforts essentially sidestepped the US military. Their effort was aimed not at achieving an influential position within the officer corps but rather at nullifying the ability of the officer corps to influence public policy. As the old guard retired or died off, it was replaced by a new generation of officers who eventually, as the century wore on, became increasingly steeped in the ideology of the new elite.

One of the advantages of being on the winning side in these intellectual and political battles is that Bendersky can safely assume that any statement by a US military officer that reflects negatively on Jews or Judaism is a reflection of the prejudices and bigotry of the officer and has nothing to do with the actual behavior of Jews or the nature of Judaism. Further, any statement reflecting the Darwinian theories of race differences so prevalent in the early twentieth century can safely be discounted as well because such theories have been shown to be "erroneous" (p. 262). The basic style of the book is simply to catalog the attitudes of US Army officers. To the extent that the attitudes of the officers require any rebuttal at all, Bendersky deems it sufficient simply to cite statements of Jewish activist organizations and his belief that science has placed his ethnic agenda firmly on the side of the angels. In the following discussion, I will try to show that the officers had a basically accurate view of Jews and Judaism for they were quite correct in their fear that Jewish influence would have a disastrous effect on the ability of their race to retain control of the United States.

BELIEFS ABOUT JEWS AND JUDAISM

Jews and Bolshevism

The "Jewish Threat" shows that the commonly held belief in a strong association between Jews and Bolshevism was based on a very wide range of official and unofficial sources spanning a great many countries over the entire period from World War I into the Cold War period after World War II. This information thus buttresses scholarly accounts from other sources of the predominant role of Jews in leftist radicalism.[2] While prone to exaggerations at times—as expected on the basis of psychological theory—the attitudes of US Army officers were basically sound.

Nevertheless, Bendersky ascribes any special attention given to Jews as revealing "the conservative, racial, and nativist perspective of the officers" (p. 51). For example, an agent in Paris reported in 1919 that among Jews there was "a remarkable unanimity of opinion in favor of the Russian Bolshevist movement." Jews were "dazzled by the sudden access to power of their race" (p. 48). Such reports—and there were many like them—should be taken at face value that Jewish policy, in which numerous mainstream Jewish activist organizations were engaged from at least 1880, was to topple the Tsar. Jewish celebration over the success of the revolution is not in the least surprising, if only because the revolution ended Tsarist anti-Jewish policies, and it is well attested by other sources, including some cited by Bendersky.[3] For example, in 1907 Lucien Wolf, a leader of the Jewish community in England, wrote to Louis Marshall of the American Jewish Committee that "the only thing to be done on the whole Russo-Jewish question is to carry on persistent and implacable war against the Russian Government."[4] "Western Jewish leaders actively participated in general actions in favor of the liberal and revolutionary movements in Russia both during the revolution and after its downfall."[5]

In the same way, when Bendersky (pp. 109, 114) reports that MID agents in Riga and Berlin commented that the Soviet embassies were staffed primarily by Jews, I am inclined to believe the agents, not Bendersky's assumption that all of the masses of similar data are the paranoid ravings of racist military officers. Such a finding fits well with the general finding that Jews were massively over-represented in the early Bolshevik governments.

Bendersky also makes it appear that MID reports of Bolshevik atrocities are fantasies. Reports stated that Bolshevik methods included not only seizure and destruction of property but also "barbarism and butchery" (p. xii). Included in the intelligence reports were photographs of "naked bodies with butchered flesh, hanging upside down from trees, while 'the Bolsheviki soldiers were laughing and grinning and

---

[2] See *The Culture of Critique*, chs. 3 and 5.
[3] E.g., Szajkowski 1974.
[4] In Szajkowski 1967, 8.
[5] Szajowski 1967, 9.

standing about'" (p. xiii). Bendersky writes as if such claims are unworthy of being rebutted, yet there is more than enough evidence that such things did happen. Indeed, the *Black Book of Communism* not only documents the horrific slaughter of some twenty million Soviet citizens, the widespread torture, mass deportations, and imprisonment in appalling conditions, but reproduces the photos from 1919 of a naked Polish officer impaled through the anus hanging upside down from trees while Bolshevik soldiers are laughing and grinning and standing about.[6]

Bendersky acknowledges that large numbers of immigrant Jews flocked to leftist movements but faults the MID for not making subtle distinctions among leftists. However, his own findings show that MID placed considerable importance on the fact that American socialist groups, including the Socialist Party, "expressed jubilant support" for Bolshevik Russia (p. 123). Bendersky acknowledges that the great majority of radical leftists were immigrants but states, without support, that the concentration of the MID on Jewish neighborhoods was unwarranted (p. 124). However, MID based their estimates on the numbers of radical meetings in particular ethnic neighborhoods and on their observations at these meetings. The findings of the MID fit well with the general finding that Jews were the only immigrant group that developed an important and influential radical sub-culture, that in fact the immigrant Jewish community in the United States from 1886 to 1920 can best be described as "one big radical debating society."[7]

The idea that the Bolshevik Revolution was part of a coordinated conspiracy is more problematic, but it rested on the widespread intelligence reports that wealthy Jews were important financiers of revolutionary movements—a belief that Bendersky assumes is complete fantasy but for which there is good evidence. In fact, American Jewish capitalists like Jacob Schiff did finance Russian radical movements directed at overthrowing the Tsar and may well have had considerable impact.[8] Schiff, who had already distinguished himself by leading efforts to abrogate a trade agreement between the United States and Russia and had financed the Japanese war effort against Russia in 1905, was repeatedly identified in MID reports as behind the international collusion among wealthy Jews and Jewish revolutionaries. Even then, officers were often remarkably judicious in their appraisal of claims by

---

[6] Courtois et al. 1999, 202–3.
[7] Cohn 1958, 621; see also *The Culture of Critique*, ch. 3.
[8] Goldstein 1990, 26–27; Szajkowski 1967.

informants and agents that there was an international Jewish conspiracy, as in the case of a senior officer who responded to such claims by noting, "I am rather in doubt as to whether the conclusions drawn by this agent are based on observations sufficiently wide to be valuable. However, I am myself convinced that the subject would bear closer investigation and while I am not ready to subscribe entirely to these conclusions, still I am convinced that there may be more than a modicum of truth in them" (p. 49).

Officers were also skeptical about the notorious forgery, *Protocols of the Elders of Zion*, but were nonetheless intrigued by it, not because of evidence of its authenticity but because the *Protocols* seemed to describe actual Jewish behavior. For example, an officer who doubted the authenticity of the *Protocols* stated that "it is a fact that the present activities of Lenin, Trotsky and other Bolsheviks in Russia so correspond to the system as outlined herewith as to lead one to believe that this is actually the basic plan upon which the Bolshevik control functions" (pp. 64–65). Nevertheless, there were examples among the officers of "going too far" in suppositions of Jewish collusion, including fantastic tales of international intrigue among Zionist organizations, Lenin, Jewish media figures in the United States, Jewish infiltrators of the British Secret Service, etc. (p. 136). This "going too far" in finding conspiratorial links among different Jews is a fairly common theme of anti-Semitism[9] but in no way invalidates the strong factual basis of Jewish involvement in Bolshevism and radical leftism generally.

Anti-Semitism

Bendersky touches on all of the themes of anti-Semitism characteristic of the twentieth century. Among the most prominent is that Jews are interested only in what's good for Jews and are only loyal to the countries they reside in to the extent that Jewish interests coincide with national policy (pp. 37–38). In fact there is a great deal of evidence that Jews have often been disloyal to the people among whom they have lived, beginning in the ancient world right up to the current fashionableness of dual loyalty of American Jews to Israel. For example, during World War I, the MID had information that Russian Jews favored the Germans (p. 53)—hardly a surprise given their hatred for the Tsar. Indeed, Russian beliefs that Jewish subjects favored Germany in the war effort resulted in eviction of Jews from the zone of combat.[10]

---

[9] See *Separation and Its Discontents*, ch. 1.
[10] Pipes 1990, 231.

Bendersky repeatedly implies that MID should not have had US interests at heart but Jewish interests. For example, after the Bolshevik revolution, the United States saw Poland as a bulwark against Soviet expansion. But from the Jewish point of view, the Polish government was anti-Jewish, and American Jewish leaders opposed recognizing or giving assistance to the Polish regime until it guaranteed minority rights. The MID was informed that Polish Jews were sympathetic to the Bolsheviks, and this new issue was mixed in with traditional Polish-Jewish animosity related to Jewish separatism, clannishness, economic domination, and disloyalty—all of which have a firm foundation in reality.[11] When the Soviet army was expelled from Vilna in 1919, the Poles attacked Jews who were accused of collaborating with the Soviets and shooting at Polish soldiers. Jewish organizations rallied to the defense of Polish Jews, while the United States tilted toward Poland. The MID had reports, often from multiple sources, that Jews welcomed Soviet troops with flowers or bands, that Jews refused to fight in Polish armies, that Jewish Bolshevik leaders engaged in "unspeakable barbarity," that foreign Jews had stirred up anti-Polish propaganda in Jewish-controlled newspapers by exaggerating the extent of violence against Jews, etc. In fact, these allegations were substantially true. Polish Jews did welcome the 1919 and 1939 Soviet invasions of Poland, because of perceptions of Polish anti-Semitism combined with favorable opinions about the treatment of Jews in the Soviet Union—that in fact Jews were an elite group in the USSR.[12]

Attitudes of MID Officers toward Jews

Bendersky tries to portray the officers as thinking of Jews as a lower race, but his own data belie him. The officers thought Jews were very good in business and disinclined to manual labor (p. 37). Jews were typically seen as very intelligent. In the words of one officer, persecutions over millennia in conjunction with the "desperate, pitiless struggle for existence in occupations requiring sharpened mental qualities . . . [have] made the Jews the keenest race of mankind and the best equipped for a successful struggle for a 'spot in the sun' in our days of liberal laws and equal opportunity for all" (p. 44). Intellectuals who lectured at the Army War College had similar views. For example, Lothrop Stoddard viewed "The Jewish mind [as] instinctively analytical, and sharpened by the dialectic subtleties of the Talmud." Despite

---

[11] See *Separation and Its Discontents*, ch. 2.
[12] Checinski 1982; Schatz 1991.

such statements, Bendersky, echoing the rhetoric of Jewish activist organizations throughout the period, characterizes the 1924 immigration law as directed at "inferior racial types from Southern and Eastern Europe" (p. 154).

Bendersky dismisses the officers' beliefs as resulting from "xenophobic geopolitics, anti-communism, and racial theories" (p. xiii), oftentimes using language that makes the officers seem bizarre and paranoid: "insidious [Jewish] political machinations" (p. 117), "diabolical IWW-Bolshevik scheme" (p. 126); "surreptitious forces" which "officers relentlessly pursued" (p. 129); "paranoid intelligence" (p. 130); "obsession with radicalism and alien forces" (p. 133). US Army officers are described as "racial sentinels" (p. 205) voicing "dire predictions" of the consequences of unrestricted immigration (p. 162) and "the calamitous price of the nation's neglecting the 'racial factor' in history" (p. 167); by enacting the 1924 immigration law, "America had narrowly escaped this disastrous fate [of race mixing]" (p. 181).

Officer Kenyon A. Joyce "described his work as a necessary vigilant struggle against 'subversive' Russian Communism" (p. 201). One wonders why the only word directly quoted from Joyce is "subversive," as if his attitude was weird. The activities of Communists in the United States were indeed subversive, and they were indeed orchestrated from Moscow. It is unconscionable that the attitudes of the officers are ascribed simply to racist paranoia given the findings of Klehr et al. showing that indeed the CPUSA was directed by the Soviet Union and had a high percentage of Jewish members, often above 40 percent.[13] And citing percentages of Jews fails to take account of the personal characteristics of Jewish radicals as a talented, educated, and ambitious group. Leftist sympathies were widespread in the American Jewish Congress—by far the largest organization of American Jews during this period—and Communist-oriented groups were affiliated with the Congress until being reluctantly purged during the McCarthy era.[14]

Bendersky is thus one of a long line of US intellectuals who minimize the threat posed by the CPUSA, minimize Jewish involvement in the CPUSA, and present a nostalgic and exculpatory attitude toward the Jewish Old Left generally. In this version there is never any mention of the twenty million Soviet citizens killed by the actions of their own government, no mention of the very large percentages of Jews who sympathized with the Soviet Union at least until after World War II, no

---

[13] Klehr et al. 1995.
[14] Svonkin 1997, 132, 166.

mention of the intellectuals and media figures who downplayed these atrocities or covered them up completely. Nor is there any acknowledgement of the reality of Soviet subversion of the United States, if for no other reason than that it successfully altered the military balance after World War II.

Bendersky in several places accepts the accounts of Jewish activist organizations' attempts to refute charges against Jews. Two common moves were to argue that Jewish radicals were apostates to Judaism and that most Jews were not radicals. Bendersky makes no attempt to unravel the subtleties of strong Jewish identification, albeit non-religious, among the vast majority of Jewish radicals.[15] Nor is there any acknowledgement that even though most Jews may not have been radical in the period from 1920 to 1950, most radicals were Jews.[16] Nevertheless, it is at least doubtful that most Jews were not sympathetic to radicalism. As noted, leftist sympathies were widespread in the American Jewish Congress until the 1950s. MID also noted the well-known associations between leftist radicalism and Zionism and that prominent Jews (Louis Marshall, Louis Brandeis, Felix Frankfurter) supported Zionism. However, Bendersky does not acknowledge the well-known connection between Zionism and political radicalism among Jews during this period, presumably because it attests to the intense Jewish identification of the great majority of Jewish leftists.

The Threat Represented by Jews

Many officers "feared that 'true Americans' were losing control of something they rightfully possessed by conquest, merit, heritage and even divine providence" (p. 1). There was a tendency to see the decline of their own ethnic group as tantamount to the decline of civilization itself. Were they justified in these attitudes? The view that conquerors control the territory they conquer is hardly a novel idea, since this is exactly what has happened from time immemorial—as applicable to the invading Germanic tribes that overwhelmed the Western Roman Empire at the end of antiquity as to the establishment of Israel in modern times. One might argue that the view that civilization itself depended on Northern Europeans is not credible in light of what we now know about the ability of other human groups to develop advanced technology, art, and literature. However, it was certainly understandable that such an inference would be made early in the twentieth century when Northern Euro-

---

[15] *The Culture of Critique*, chs. 3 and 5.
[16] *The Culture of Critique*, ch. 3; Novick 1999.

pean colonial powers had divided up the rest of the world among themselves, when all of the scientific and technical advances had been made by Northern Europeans, and when there were huge differences in the economic and technical development not only between Europe and the rest of the world but also between Northern and Southern Europe and between Eastern and Western Europe. Such assertions also conform to the normal tendency among humans to glorify their own group and denigrate outsiders. And now that Europeans are slated to be a minority in the United States by 2050 and millions of non-Europeans are living as minorities in European countries, it certainly seems that the officers' fears of "losing control" were indeed prescient.

Part of this sense of losing control came from changes in the media. It is remarkable that people like Lothrop Stoddard and Charles Lindbergh wrote numerous articles for the popular media, including *Collier's*, the *Saturday Evening Post*, and *Reader's Digest* between World War I and World War II (p. 23). In 1920–1921, the *Saturday Evening Post* ran a series of nineteen articles on Eastern European immigration emphasizing Jewish unassimilability and the Jewish association with Bolshevism. At the time, the *Post* was the most widely read magazine in the United States, with a weekly readership of two million.

The tide against the world view of the officers turned with the election of Roosevelt. "Jews served prominently in his administration," (p. 244) including Felix Frankfurter, who had long been under scrutiny by MID as a "dangerous Jewish radical" (p. 244). Jews had also won the intellectual debate: "Nazi racial ideology was under attack in the press as pseudo-science and fanatical bigotry" (p. 244). Jews also had a powerful position in the media, including ownership of several large, influential newspapers (*New York Times*, *New York Post*, *Washington Post*, *Philadelphia Inquirer*, *Philadelphia Record*, and *Pittsburgh Post-Gazette*), radio networks (CBS, the dominant radio network, and NBC, headed by David Sarnoff), and all of the major Hollywood movie studios.

It is remarkable that the word "Nordic" disappeared by the 1930s although the restrictionists still had racialist views of Jews and themselves (p. 245). By 1938 eugenics was "shunned in public discourse of the day" (p. 250). Whereas such ideas were commonplace in the mainstream media in the 1920s, General George van Horn Moseley's 1938 talk on eugenics and its implications for immigration policy caused a furor when it was reported in the newspapers. Moseley was charged with anti-Semitism although he denied referring to Jews in his talk. The incident blew over, but "henceforth, the military determined to protect itself against charges of anti-Semitism that might sully its reputation or cause it political problems. . . . The army projected itself as an institution that would tolerate neither racism nor anti-Semitism" (pp. 252–53).

Moseley himself continued to attack the New Deal, saying it was manipulated by "the alien element in our midst" (p. 253)—obviously a coded reference to Jews. This time he was severely reprimanded, and the press wouldn't let it die. By early 1939, Moseley, who had retired from the army, became explicitly anti-Jewish, asserting that Jews wanted the United States to enter the proposed war in Europe and that the war would be waged for Jewish hegemony. He accused Jews of controlling the media and having a deep influence on the government. His anti-Semitism was crude: In 1939, he testified before the House Un-American Activities Committee on Jewish complicity in Communism and praised the Germans for dealing with the Jews properly (p. 256). But his testimony was beyond the pale by this time. As Bendersky notes, Moseley had only articulated the common Darwinian world view of the earlier generation, and he had asserted the common belief of an association of Jews with Communism. These views remained common in the army and elsewhere on the political right, but they were simply not stated publicly. And if they were, heads rolled and careers were ended.

The new climate can also be seen in the fact that Lothrop Stoddard stopped referring to Jews completely in his lectures to the Army War College in the late 1930s, but continued to advocate eugenics and was sympathetic to National Socialism in the late 1930s because it took the race notion seriously. By 1940, the tables had turned. Anti-Jewish attitudes came to be seen as subversive by the government, and the FBI alerted military intelligence that Lothrop Stoddard should be investigated as a security risk in the event of war (p. 280).

From Bendersky's perspective, these changes are due largely to the triumph of science: "Not only was Stoddard's racial science erroneous, it was—despite his assertions to the contrary—out of step with the major trends in science and scholarship" (p. 262). What Bendersky does not note is that the "scientific" refutation of the ideas of Stoddard and the other Darwinian theorists was entirely due to a political campaign waged in academic social science departments by Franz Boas and his students and sympathizers. The political nature of this shift in intellectual stance and its linkage to Jewish academic ethnic activists has long-been apparent to scholars.[17]

---

[17] Degler 1991; Frank 1997; *The Culture of Critique*, ch. 2; Stocking 1968, 1989.

The racialist, isolationist right viewed World War II as a looming disaster. During the 1930s many officers admired the accomplishments of National Socialism but worried that US national interests would be sacrificed over concerns about National Socialist treatment of Jews. While disapproving of Hitler's Jewish policies, they often sympathized with National Socialist attitudes toward Jews, feeling that the typical complaints had some basis in reality. They wanted to avoid a war with Germany as not in American national interests, distrusted Roosevelt whom they saw as wanting a war, and worried that Jews wanted a war because of their hatred for Hitler and his anti-Jewish policies. Officers often worried that Roosevelt was influenced to be anti-German by his Jewish advisors, Samuel I. Rosenman, Felix Frankfurter, and Henry Morgenthau, Jr., and they worried that Jewish interests and the British would push the United States into a war with Germany. There was often a perception that Jewish-controlled media emphasized National Socialist anti-Jewish actions. William Langer, a Harvard historian, stated in a lecture to the War College that the rising dislike of National Socialist Germany in the United States was due to "Jewish influence."

> You have to face the fact that some of our most important American newspapers are Jewish-controlled, and I suppose if I were a Jew I would feel about Nazi Germany as most Jews feel and it would be most inevitable that the coloring of the news takes on that tinge. As I read the *New York Times*, for example, it is perfectly clear that every little upset that occurs (and after all many upsets occur in a country of seventy million people) is given a great deal of prominence. The other part of it is soft-pedaled or put off with a sneer. So that in a rather subtle way, the picture you get is that there is no good in the Germans whatever. (p. 273)

Although not an officer at that time, Charles Lindbergh was the best-known example of someone with these fears. Lindbergh's thinking was shaped not only by his horror at the destructiveness of modern warfare—the idea that a second World War would be the suicide of European culture—but also by his conviction that it would lead to race suicide, that it would be, in Lindbergh's words, "a war in which the White race is bound to lose." Lindbergh believed that whites should join together to fend off the teeming legions of non-whites who were the real long-term threat. He viewed the Soviet Union as a white bulwark against the Chinese in the East and believed in a racial alliance based on "an English fleet, a German air force, a French army, [and] an

American nation" (p. 276).

Lindbergh made his famous comment of September 11, 1941, that the influence of the Jews was one factor leading the United States into war, but he also noted that, "No person with a sense of dignity of mankind can condone the persecution of the Jewish race in Germany" (p. 285). Nevertheless, despite the truth of Lindbergh's comments and its temperate tone, the speech was greeted with a torrent of abuse and hatred unparalleled for a mainstream public figure in American history. Overnight Lindbergh went from cultural hero to moral pariah. Clearly by the late 1930s or early 1940s at the latest, the tide had turned.

During World War II, anti-Jewish attitudes were common in the officer corps, but "the political climate created by the Roosevelt administration had forced them into silence, particularly concerning Jews and Communists" (p. 301). It became common on the American right to see the Roosevelt administration as influenced greatly by Frankfurter and Morgenthau, as infiltrated by Jews sympathetic to the Soviet Union, and as adopting needlessly harsh policies toward the Germans such as strategic bombing (p. 304). Henry Stimson, Secretary of War, "accused Morganthau and Baruch of succumbing to racial 'impulses,'" calling their behavior "semitism gone wild for vengeance" (p. 313).

One indication of Jewish power at this time is that Jews were able to exert intense pressure on Eisenhower because of accommodations he made with the Vichy French and with Arabs in Morocco in order to facilitate a landing in North Africa. There was fear that lifting anti-Jewish policies in Morocco would set off an Arab riot against Jews. General George C. Patton, who had negative attitudes toward Jews, wrote to Eisenhower: "Arabs don't mind Christians, but they utterly despise Jews. The French fear that the local Jews, knowing how high their side is riding in the US, will try to take the lead here. If they do, the Arabs will murder them and there will be a local state of disorder" (p. 316).

Within the army, long-term thinkers believed in a need to form an alliance with the Moslem world because of oil, and they worried about "the Jew-Arab problem" even before the end of World War II. In 1948, Secretary of State George C. Marshall told Truman that his support for Israel disregarded national interests in order to obtain votes in New York. It was common among the officers to think of Israel as an intensely nationalistic, fascist-like state with a veneer of democracy. For example, during World War II a report described Zionism as "contrary to the very principles for which the Allies fought" (p. 321), noting the intense collectivist tendencies of Zionism, the emphasis on the Hebrew language, and militarism: "the National Socialist outlook of modern Zionism" (p. 322).

Officers commonly believed that there were many anti-German Jews in the US military government after World War II who were bent on de-nazification and revenge.

> Feeling inhibited from speaking publicly by alleged Jewish power, a number of officers, as well as some government officials, complained incessantly in private that Jewish "refugees in American uniforms," together with Jews in the US government, unduly affected American policy toward Germany in a variety of detrimental ways. (p. 364)

Refugee officers (i.e., German Jews returning as members of the US military government) treated Germans brutally, including sadistic beatings and starvation (p. 365). In general, Jews advocated harsh treatment, the concept of collective guilt, and trials for general staff officers. The paradigm for this perspective was the Morgenthau plan, which called for destruction of Germany as an industrial state and which, if implemented, would have resulted in millions of deaths. Bendersky acknowledges that many refugee Jews were in the occupation government and that they were zealous de-Nazifiers, but says only that "some probably agreed with Morgenthau's draconian idea of punishing Germany and preventing its future resurgence" (p. 366). The reputation of these refugee officers was so bad that the Army ended up firing personnel who had entered the United States after 1933.

And thus the saga ends. To be sure there were many officers who retired with their beliefs intact, and some of these, such as Moseley and Albert C. Wedemeyer, became figures on the American right. In the 1970s, Wedemeyer maintained that Zionists controlled Congress and that Jews had huge political and economic power. He also blamed Jews for US entry into World War II. But it was the end of an era. Bendersky, for all of his obvious hatred toward his subjects, tells a compelling story, but, in the end, one just has to believe the officers whose views he chronicles and not their chronicler.

Part III.

WESTERN CIVILIZATION

Chapter 9

WHAT MAKES WESTERN CULTURE UNIQUE?*

In general, cultural uniqueness could derive from either nature or nurture—the same old ageless dichotomy—but I think now we are in a better position to deal with these issues than in times past, and I will be arguing that both are important. Western cultures have experienced certain unique cultural transformations that cannot be predicted by any biological/evolutionary theory, but they also have had a unique evolutionary history. Western culture was built by people who differ genetically from those who have built the other civilizations and cultures of the world. In the following I will argue that Western cultures have a unique cultural profile compared to other traditional civilizations:

1. The Catholic Church and Christianity.
2. A tendency toward monogamy.
3. A tendency toward simple family structure based on the nuclear family.
4. A greater tendency for marriage to be companionate and based on mutual affection of the partners.
5. A de-emphasis on extended kinship relationships and, as a correlative, a relative lack of ethnocentrism.
6. A tendency toward individualism and all of its implications: individual rights against the state, representative government, moral universalism, and science.

THE FIRST EXAMPLE OF WESTERN UNIQUENESS
My background is in the field of evolutionary biology, and one of the first questions that struck me when I was exposed to the evolutionary theory of sex was: "Why are Western cultures monogamous?" The evolutionary theory of sex is quite simple: Females must invest greatly in reproduction—pregnancy, lactation, and often childcare require an extraordinary amount of time. As a result, reproduction by females is highly limited. Even under the best of conditions women could have, say, twenty children. But the act of reproduction is cheap for men. As a result, males benefit from multiple mates, and it is expected that males

---

* First published in *The Occidental Quarterly* 2 (Summer 2002): 9–38.

with wealth and power should use their wealth and power to secure as many mates as possible. In short, intensive polygyny by wealthy, powerful males is an optimal male strategy, i.e., it is behavior that optimizes individual male reproductive success.

This theory is well supported. There are strong associations between wealth and reproductive success in traditional societies from around the world. Wealthy, powerful males are able to control very large numbers of females. The elite males of all of the traditional civilizations around the world, including those of China, India, Muslim societies, the New World civilizations, ancient Egypt, and ancient Israel, often had hundreds and even thousands of concubines. In sub-Saharan Africa, women were generally able to rear children without male provisioning, and the result was low-level polygyny in which males competed to control as many women as possible. In all of these societies, the children from these relationships were legitimate. They could inherit property and were not scorned by the public. The Emperor of China had thousands of concubines, and Sultan Moulay Ismail of Morocco is in the *Guinness Book of World Records* as having fathered 888 children.

To be sure, there are other societies where monogamy is the norm. It is common to distinguish ecologically imposed monogamy from socially imposed monogamy. In general, ecologically imposed monogamy is found in societies that have been forced to adapt to very harsh ecological conditions such as deserts and arctic conditions.[1] Under such harsh conditions, it is impossible for males to control additional females because the investment of each male must be directed to the children of one woman. The basic idea is that under harsh conditions a woman would be unable to rear children by herself but would require provisioning from a male. If these conditions persisted for an evolutionarily significant time, one might expect to find that the population would develop a strong tendency toward monogamy. In fact, one might imagine that the tendency toward monogamy could become so strong that it would result in psychological and cultural tendencies toward monogamy even in the face of altered ecological conditions. Later I will propose that this is exactly what happened in the evolution of Europeans.

Richard Alexander used the term "socially imposed monogamy" (SIM) to refer to situations where monogamy occurs even in the absence of harsh ecological conditions.[2] Harsh conditions imply that men

---

[1] Alexander 1979; see Flinn and Low 1986 and MacDonald 1983 for ethnographic examples.

[2] Alexander 1979.

are needed to directly provision children, but in other situations we expect and generally find that males compete to have as many wives as they can command.

Whereas all of the other economically advanced cultures of the world have been typified by polygyny by successful males, Western societies beginning with the ancient Greeks and Romans and extending up to the present have had a powerful tendency toward monogamy.

Ancient Rome had a variety of political institutions and ideological supports that tended toward monogamy.[3] The origins of socially imposed monogamy in Rome are lost in history, but there were several mechanisms for maintaining monogamy, including laws that lowered the legal status of offspring born outside monogamous marriage, customs opposing divorce, negative social attitudes toward non-conforming sexual behavior, and a religious ideology of monogamous sexual decorum. Variations of these mechanisms have persisted throughout Western history down to the present.

During the period of the Roman Republic, there were also mechanisms that prevented political despotism by any one aristocratic family, including term limits on the consulship and having two consuls concurrently. Legal requirements for the political representation of the lower orders gradually developed, e.g., the Tribune of the Plebes. There were also extensive laws that prevented close relatives from marrying. These laws prevented the concentration of wealth within kinship groups and thus prevented the predominance of any one aristocratic family.[4]

Roman monogamy was far from complete. This was especially so in the Empire when there was a general breakdown of the earlier family functioning due to increases in divorce and a decline in the ideology of monogamous sexual decorum that typified the early Republic. Nevertheless, from a legal point of view, and at least in theory, Roman culture remained monogamous to the end. Polygynous marriage was never sanctioned in law, and children born outside of monogamous marriage had no inheritance rights and took the social and legal status of the mother.

Battles over monogamy became an important feature of the Middle Ages as the Catholic Church attempted to impose monogamy on elite males.[5] The Catholic Church is a unique aspect of Western culture. When Marco Polo visited the Chinese in the thirteenth century and

---

[3] MacDonald 1990.
[4] Corbett 1930; Raaflaub 1986a, 1986b; Watson 1975.
[5] The following is based on MacDonald 1995a.

when Cortez arrived among the Aztecs in 1519, they found a great many similarities with their own society, including a hereditary nobility, priests, warriors, craftsmen, and peasants all living off an agricultural economy. There was thus an overwhelming convergence among the societies. But they did not find societies where the religious establishment claimed to be superior to the secular establishment and was successfully regulating the reproductive behavior of the secular elite. Nor did they find a king like Louis IX (St. Louis) who ruled France while living like a monk with his one wife and went on a Crusade to free the Holy Land.

The Catholic Church was the heir to Roman civilization, where monogamy was ingrained in law and custom, and during the Middle Ages it took it upon itself to impose monogamy on the emerging European aristocracy. To be sure, the level of polygyny found among European aristocrats in the early Middle Ages was quite low compared to the harems of China and the Muslim countries, but that may well have been due partly to the relatively undeveloped economic situation of the early Middle Ages. After all, the emperors of China presided over a vast and populous country with huge surplus economic production. They were much wealthier than the tribal chieftains of early medieval Europe, and they used that wealth and power to obtain vastly more women.

In any case, polygyny did exist in Europe, and during the Middle Ages it became the object of conflict between the Church and the aristocracy. The Church was "the most influential and important governmental institution [of Europe] during the medieval period" and a major aspect of this power over the secular aristocracy involved the regulation of sex and reproduction.[6] The result was that the same rules of sexual conduct were imposed on both rich and poor. The program of the Church "required above all that laymen, especially the most powerful among them, should submit to the authority of the Church and allow it to supervise their morals, especially their sexual morals. It was by this means, through marriage, that the aristocracy could be kept under control. All matrimonial problems had to be submitted to and resolved by the Church alone."[7]

Attempting to understand the behavior of the Church during this period in terms of evolutionary psychology is beyond the scope of this paper.[8] However, one might note that the desire for power is a human

---

[6] Ullman 1970, 1.
[7] Duby 1983, 162.
[8] See MacDonald 1995a.

universal but, like all human desires, it need not be linked with reproductive success. In the same way, people desire sex, but engaging in sex does not necessarily lead to having lots of children, even though Mother Nature designed it that way.

One unique feature of the Church is that its popularity was aided by the image (and reality) that the Church was altruistic. The medieval Church successfully portrayed the image that it was not concerned with controlling women or having a high level of reproductive success. This was not always the case. Before the reforms of the Middle Ages, many priests had wives and concubines. Writing of the French Church in 742, Saint Boniface complained to the Pope about "so-called deacons who have spent their lives since boyhood in debauchery, adultery, and every kind of filthiness, who entered the diaconate with this reputation, and who now, while they have four or five concubines in their beds, still read the gospel."[9]

Nevertheless, reform among the clergy was real. No English prelate of the thirteenth century is known to have had a wife or family. Married clergy even at lower levels were exceptional during this period in England, and low levels of clerical incontinence continued into the Reformation period.

The Church therefore projected the image of chastity and altruism. Its power and wealth were not directed at reproductive success. True reproductive altruism appears to have been a factor in the very widespread attraction of extremely ascetic monastic lifestyles. This asceticism was an important part of the public's perception of the Church during the high Middle Ages. During the eleventh and twelfth centuries thousands of monasteries were founded. Composed of celibate and ascetic males and recruited mainly from the more affluent classes, monasteries "set the tone in the spirituality of the whole church, in education and in art, [and] in the transmission of culture . . ."[10] The image of monastic altruism was also fostered by an ideology in which the prayers of monks were believed to aid all Christians.

These orders provided a very popular public image of the Church. During the thirteenth century, mendicant friars (Dominicans, Franciscans) were instrumental in reforming the Church to extend the power of the Pope over the Church, to enforce rules on clerical celibacy, to prevent nepotism and simony (the buying and selling of Church offices), and to give the Church substantial power over secular powers, including the

---

[9] In Lynch 1972a, 33.
[10] Tellenbach 1993, 101.

ability to regulate sexual relationships. "The voluntary poverty and self-imposed destitution that identified the early Mendicants with the humblest and most deprived sections of the population, in loud contrast to the careerism and ostentation of the secular clergy and the corporate wealth and exclusiveness of the monasteries, moved the conscience and touched the generosity of commercial communities."[11]

> It is one of the most remarkable phenomena in the whole of history that in the high Middle Ages . . . many members of the highest and wealthiest or at least prosperous strata of society, who had the best chances of enjoying earthly pleasures to the full, renounced them. . . . The flow of new candidates was particularly impressive in those places where the rules of monastic life had been restored to their ancient strictness, imposed more rigorously or even redefined more severely. . . . We must assume that the main motive for the choice of a monastic life was always the eschatological ideal of monasticism, even if this may have lost something of its driving force in the course of a long life or was mixed with other motives from the start.[12]

During the thirteenth century, the mendicant friars were typically recruited from the aristocracy, the landed gentry, and other affluent families. Their parents often disapproved of their decision, presumably because, like most parents, they wanted grandchildren. "It was a nightmare for well-to-do families that their children might become friars."[13] These families began to avoid sending their children to universities because of well-founded fears that they would be recruited into a religious life.

At the center of society was an institution with an ideology that people ought to be altruistic, that they ought to be celibate even when they were born to wealth. This explains popular acceptance of the authority of the church in matters of marriage and sex, but it still makes one wonder why these well-off people were entering monasteries and becoming celibate in the first place. Like it or not, whatever else one might say about Western Europe during this period, eugenics was not a part of the picture.

The medieval Church was a unique feature of Western culture, but a

---

[11] Lawrence 1994, 126.
[12] Tellenbach 1993, 103.
[13] Tellenbach 1993, 105.

theme of this paper is that in critical ways it was most un-Western. This is because medieval Europe was a collectivist society with a strong sense of group identification and commitment, and I will be arguing that Western societies are also unique in their commitment to individualism—that in fact individualism is a defining feature of Western civilization.

The collectivism of Western European society in the late Middle Ages was real. There was intense group identification and group commitment to Christianity among all levels of society, as indicated, for example, by the multitudes of pilgrims and the outpouring of religious fervor and ingroup fervor associated with the Crusades to free the Holy Land from Muslim control. The medieval Church had a strong sense of Christian group economic interests *vis-à-vis* the Jews, and often worked vigorously to exclude Jews from economic and political influence and to prevent social intercourse between Christians and Jews.[14]

As described above, there were also high levels of reproductive altruism, particularly among the mendicant friars, many other religious personnel, and eventually the secular elite. Reproductive altruism among the secular elite was mainly the result of coercion, but there are also cases of voluntary restraint, as in the case of Louis IX of France— St. Louis. St. Louis was not only a paragon of proper Christian sexual behavior. He also had a powerful sense of Christian group economic interests *vis-à-vis* the Jews, and he was heavily involved in the Crusades to return the Holy Land to Christian control.[15] Europeans considered themselves part of a Christian ingroup arrayed against non-Christian outgroups (particularly Muslims and Jews) who were seen as powerful and threatening enemies.[16]

There were indeed gaps between the ideal of a unified Christian society based on the power of the Church and sexual restraint among the elite. But these gaps must be balanced by the recognition that many medieval Christians, and especially the central actors in medieval society such as the monastic movements, the mendicant friars, the reforming Popes, the fervent Crusaders, the pious pilgrims, and even many elite aristocrats, saw themselves to be part of a highly unified, supranational collectivity. It is this fundamentally collectivist orientation—so

---

[14] Cohen 1982; Cohen 1994; Jordan 1989; MacDonald 1995b; *Separation and Its Discontents: Toward an Evolutionary Theory of Anti-Semitism*, Preface to the first paperback edition and chs. 3 and 4; Parkes 1976.

[15] Chazan 1973; Gilchrist 1969; Jordan 1989.

[16] Lynch 1992, 161–64.

foreign to contemporary Western life—that renders the high levels of group commitment and altruism characteristic of the medieval period comprehensible in psychological terms.

SOCIAL CONTROLS AND IDEOLOGY MAINTAINING MONOGAMY IN WESTERN EUROPE

In Western Europe the Church adopted an ecclesiastical model of marriage that was diametrically opposed to the reproductive interests of the aristocracy. As a direct result of these efforts, there was a transformation of family structure and the social imposition of monogamy by the Christian Church by the end of the twelfth century. The following factors appear to have been most important in the imposition and maintenance of monogamy:

Prohibitions on Divorce

Wealthy males benefit most by being able to divorce easily because they can more easily remarry. While divorce was common in other Eurasian societies and was legal among the pre-Christian tribes of Europe, the Church's point of view was that marriage was monogamous and indissoluble. Divorce became ever more restricted under the Christian Roman emperors, and between the ninth and the twelfth century the Church engaged in a successful conflict with the aristocracy centering around a series of divorce cases involving the nobility. For example, in the late twelfth century, King Philip II Augustus of France was prevented from divorcing his wife even though he disliked her and she was infertile. The king had to apologize to a group of religious personnel at an abbey in Paris.

At times divorce was allowed, but only if the goal was to obtain a male heir in cases where the first marriage had failed to produce one, e.g., Louis VII and Eleanor of Aquitaine in Medieval France. (But the Pope did not allow Henry VIII to divorce his wife even though they did not produce a son.) Divorce "was virtually impossible except for a handful of the very rich" in England until the reform of 1857. But even then divorce rates remained very low. "In those parts of Europe that had legalized divorce in the sixteenth century, it was three hundred years and more before any line of divorce could be distinguished from the horizontal axis of a graphic depiction of divorce rates." In England the divorce rate remained at less than 0.1/1000 marriages until 1914 and less than 1/1000 until 1943[17]; in 1910 no European country had a

---

[17] Stone 1980.

divorce rate higher than 0.5/1000 population. So far as I know, this powerful tendency in opposition to divorce is unique to Western European civilization.

Penalties for Illegitimacy

From an evolutionary perspective, the most crucial aspect of social controls related to reproduction is the control of concubinage. Controls on illegitimacy oppose the reproductive interests of wealthy males by making concubinage difficult or impossible and by affecting the prospects of illegitimate children by, e.g., preventing them from inheriting property.

The Church was actively opposed to concubinage, especially concubinage in the presence of a legitimate wife. It would appear that social controls on the abilities of illegitimate children to inherit were often effective. The Church held the attitude that legitimate marriage produced legitimate children and that others had no legal standing, although in certain periods bastards had more standing than others (see below). The estates of bastards were subject to confiscation by the Church or the state, so that even if a man wanted to leave property to a bastard his wishes could be thwarted by the authorities. Bastards disappeared from wills altogether during the Puritan era in England.

Besides direct Church influence, there were a variety of other penalties attached to illegitimate birth arising from the secular authorities and public opinion. Being the father and especially the mother of an illegitimate child were causes for ostracism and jail, and it was common for the woman to take every effort to conceal the pregnancy, including leaving the area. These social controls had effects on mortality of illegitimate children. Infant mortality was higher for illegitimate children in both early modern England and France. Women often abandoned illegitimate children. Illegitimate children were often reported as stillborn, indicating infanticide, and women sometimes sought to avoid bearing illegitimate children via abortion.

Controls on Concubinage among the Elite

Controls on concubinage by elite males became increasingly effective during the Middle Ages. The twelfth century thus appears to be pivotal. There are good examples from this period of elite males who were able to avoid social and ideological controls favoring monogamy as well as examples where such individuals were entirely monogamous. The general patterns may be perceived by considering the illegitimate fertility of English kings. Ten of the eighteen kings who ruled England from 1066 to 1485 are known to have taken mistresses, and are known to have fathered 41 illegitimate offspring who can be identified with a fair degree of certainty. Henry I, who ruled from 1100 to 1135, sired twenty of these, and five more are listed as probable. No other medieval king sired more than three, and no certain illegitimate children are recorded for eight of the kings. Henry I is unique in his apparent interest in obtaining large numbers of offspring to further his territorial ambitions. However, Henry treated his illegitimate children far less well than his legitimate children, the latter being pampered, tutored at court, and prepared for life as great nobles. Bastards, on the other hand, were excluded from inheriting the throne, and they were often not offered marriages. Reflecting the general change in attitudes and practices related to marriage occurring in the twelfth century, there is a decline in both the numbers and importance of illegitimate children in the following centuries.

Policing Sexual Behavior in the Middle Ages and Later

One of the prime goals of the medieval Church was to police sexual behavior outside of monogamous marriage. Policing sexual violations was an important function of the ecclesiastical courts beginning in the Middle Ages and extending at least to the end of the seventeenth century. These courts were very active in seventeenth century England prosecuting cases of fornication, adultery, incest, and illicit cohabitation. Although the effectiveness of these ecclesiastical sanctions varied by region and period, there were examples of devastating consequences in which "the victim was hounded by his fellows, deprived of his living by a community boycott, and treated as an outcast."

In the seventeenth century the High Commission of the Ecclesiastical Court system had the ability to impose sanctions, including sanctions for adultery, on the propertied, who could expect to be immune from other judicial processes: "This enforcement of equality before the law did not endear the court to those who mattered in seventeenth-century England."[18] The secular authorities, such as Justices of the Peace, also stood ready to prosecute such offenses. For example, pursuant to Elizabethan statutes, Justices of the Peace in the sixteenth and seventeenth centuries commonly sentenced sexual offenders of both sexes to a public whipping while stripped to waist (the woman "until her back be bloody") and placed in the stocks.[19]

---

[18] Hill 1967, 349.
[19] Marchant 1969, 224.

Ideologies Promoting Monogamy

Although ultimately relying on social controls, the Medieval Church developed elaborate ideologies to promote monogamy and sexual restraint. In general these writings emphasized the moral superiority of celibacy and the sinfulness of extra-marital sex of any kind. All sexual relationships, apart from monogamous marriage, were universally condemned by religious authority throughout the early modern period into contemporary times. Marital sex was viewed as a regrettable and sinful necessity, and excess passion toward one's wife was considered adultery. While there was a relative relaxation of attitudes during the eighteenth century, a powerful anti-hedonist religious sexual ideology rose to prominence in the nineteenth century.

Conclusion

Beginning in the Middle Ages an elaborate system of social controls and ideologies resulted in the more or less complete imposition of monogamy in large areas of Western Europe. "The great social achievement of the early Middle Ages was the imposition of the same rules of sexual and domestic conduct on both rich and poor. The King in his palace, the peasant in his hovel: neither was exempt."[20] Nevertheless, the system was by no means completely egalitarian. There was a positive association between wealth and reproductive success throughout pre-industrial Europe.

In Western Europe there has been a remarkable continuity within a varied set of institutions, which have penalized polygyny and channeled non-monogamous sexuality into non-reproductive outlets or suppressed it altogether. Despite changes in these institutions and despite vast changes in political and economic structures, Western family institutions deriving ultimately from Roman civilization have clearly aimed at the social imposition of monogamy. By and large, this effort has been successful.

EFFECTS OF MONOGAMY

Monogamy is a very central aspect of Western uniqueness with some important effects. Monogamy may well be a necessary condition for the unique European "low-pressure" demographic profile.[21] This demographic profile results from late marriage and celibacy of large percentages of females during times of economic scarcity. The connection with

---

[20] Herlihy 1985, 157.
[21] Wrigley and Schofield 1981.

monogamy is that monogamous marriage results in a situation where the poor of both sexes are unable to mate, whereas in polygynous systems an excess of poor females merely lowers the price of concubines for wealthy males. For example, at the end of the seventeenth century approximately 23 percent of both sexes remained unmarried between ages of forty and 44. But, as a result of altered economic opportunities, this percentage dropped at the beginning of the eighteenth century to 9 percent, and there was a corresponding decline in age of marriage. Like monogamy, this pattern was unique among the stratified societies of Eurasia.[22]

In turn, the low-pressure demographic profile appears to have had economic consequences. Not only was the marriage rate the main damper on population growth, but this response, especially in England, had a tendency to lag well behind favorable economic changes so that there was a tendency for capital accumulation during good times rather than a constant pressure of population on food supply:

> The fact that the rolling adjustment between economic and demographic fluctuations took place in such a leisurely fashion, tending to produce large if gradual swings in real wages, represented an opportunity to break clear from the low-level income trap which is sometimes supposed to have inhibited all pre-industrial nations. A long period of rising real wages, by changing the structure of demand, will tend to give a disproportionately strong boost to demand for commodities other than the basic necessities of life, and so to sectors of the economy whose growth is especially important if an industrial revolution is to occur.[23]

There is therefore some reason to suppose that monogamy, by resulting in a low-pressure demographic profile, was a necessary condition for industrialization. The overall pattern, then, is not one in which there is a constant tendency toward late marriage and/or celibacy in females. Instead, marriage is influenced by economic constraints. In times of prosperity the age of marriage for both sexes declined and fewer females remained non-reproductive. The result was a marriage system which is highly sensitive to resource availability: "An important distinguishing feature of Europe, the pivot upon which the system

---

[22] Hajnal 1965; Hajnal 1983; Laslett 1983; MacFarlane 1986; Wrigley and Schofield 1981.

[23] Wrigley and Schofield 1981, 439; Hajnal 1965; MacFarlane 1986.

turned, was the flexible marital regime, which allowed population to adjust to economy."[24] This suggests that monogamy may indeed be a central aspect of the necessary architecture of Western modernization.

Monogamy and Investment in Children

Polygynous mating systems tend to result in resources being devoted to reproduction and relatively less to investment in children. For a male in a polygynous society it is attractive to invest in another wife or concubine and her low investment offspring.[25] In polygynous societies, investment in additional concubines tends to have a large payoff and requires little investment in children. Offspring of concubines were typically given relatively small inheritances and allowed to descend the social ladder. There is a low sex ratio of offspring among harem women—a preponderance of daughters.[26] In theoretical terms this implies a bias toward low investment offspring because in general it is easier for females to be able to mate.[27] Although the daughters of these concubines will have low social status compared to their father, they will tend to mate. On the other hand, sons of the upper classes were targets of dowry competition for lower status families. In either case, there is little need for fathers to invest time, energy, or money in the offspring of their concubines.

Monogamy, however, restricts the investment of individual males to the offspring of one woman. With the decline in extended kinship relations (see below) and the institutionalization of monogamy on all social classes, support for children came to rest completely upon the independent nuclear family. As described below, this "simple" family was the critical vehicle of Western modernization.

DECLINE OF EXTENDED KINSHIP RELATIONS AND THE RISE OF THE SIMPLE HOUSEHOLD

As in the case of monogamy, the Church also had a role in the decline of extended kinship relationships. In this case, however, Church policy was aided by the rise of strong central governments, which discouraged extended family relationships and replaced the role of the extended family in guaranteeing individual interests.

From an evolutionary perspective one can scarcely overestimate the

---

[24] MacFarlane 1986, 33.
[25] Draper and Harpending 1988.
[26] Guttentag and Secord 1983.
[27] Trivers 1986.

potential importance of kinship relationships. Because of the ties of biological relatedness, kin are expected to have common interests and lower thresholds for cooperation and even self-sacrificing behavior. The Germanic tribes who settled much of Western Europe at the end of the Roman Empire were organized as kinship groups based on biological relatedness among males. The tribes had a strong sense of group solidarity based on these ties of kinship. "Since the early Germans could not rely upon the protection and assistance of a bureaucratic empire when they were threatened with attack or famine, it was incumbent upon each man and woman of the community to adhere to the fundamental sociobiological principle of group survival embodied in the bonds of familial and communal solidarity."[28] It was this world of tribally based kinship groups that the kings and the Church wanted to eradicate.

Forces Opposing Extended Kinship

The eradication of large, powerful kinship groups was in the interests of both the Church and the aristocracy. A higher degree of centralized state power by itself has a tendency to lessen the importance of extended kinship relations, especially if that power protects the interests of individuals. From an evolutionary perspective, extended kinship groups have costs and benefits. The benefits accrue from the protection and support provided by the wider kindred, but these benefits entail costs in terms of: (1) increased demands by kin for reciprocated services; (2) the fact that kin will tend to prevent any individual from rising too much above the others in the kinship group; and (3) the difficulty of establishing oneself in a kinship structure that is far from egalitarian. As a result, individuals are expected to avoid becoming enmeshed in extended kinship groups when their interests are protected by other institutions, i.e., the benefits of extended kinship are removed, but the costs remain. In general individuals tend to seek the protection of the extended kinship group when centralized power fails, and they correspondingly flee the extended kinship group when state power is sufficient to protect their interests.[29]

The picture one gets is the gradual development in the West of an aristocracy based on the simple family and freed from obligations to

---

[28] Russell 1994, 120.

[29] Stone 1977. The protective function of the extended family is a common phenomenon in intermediate level, tribal societies as well as many peasant societies characterized by joint family structure.

collateral kin dominating a peasantry characterized by the simple family and embedded in a society of neighbors and friends, not an extended kinship group. This social structure was an achievement of the late Middle Ages. Extended kinship relations were not important among the peasantry in late Medieval England or France.[30]

Church Policy

For its part, the Church contributed to the eradication of extended kinship ties in Western Europe by opposing consanguineous marriage (marriage of blood relatives) and supporting marriage based solely on consent of the partners. In the case of consanguinity, the Church prohibited marriage between an ever-expanding set of individuals. In the sixth century the prohibition was extended to second cousins and by the eleventh century it was extended to sixth cousins, i.e., individuals with a common great-great-great-great-great grandfather. Clearly these prohibitions on consanguinity go far beyond those predicted by evolutionary theory.[31] Moreover, biological relatedness was not crucial here, since marriage was forbidden to similarly distant affinal relatives (i.e., relatives by marriage) as well as to individuals with spiritual kinship (i.e., relatives of godparents). The effect of the policy was to undermine extensive kinship networks and to create an aristocracy freed from obligations to the wider kin group.

Whatever the rationale given to these prohibitions by the Church, there is evidence that the aristocracy obeyed the ecclesiastical rules. There were very few marriages closer than fourth or fifth cousins among the French nobility of the tenth and eleventh centuries.[32] These practices weakened the extended kinship group, since the expanded range of incestuous marriages prevented the solidarity of extended kinship groups by excluding "the reinforcing of blood with marriage."[33] The result was that biological relatedness was spread diffusely throughout the nobility rather than concentrated at the top. The direct

---

[30] Hanawalt 1986; Barthelemy 1988.

[31] From an evolutionary perspective, marrying close relatives leads to inbreeding depression and an increased risk for genetic diseases caused by recessive genes. Many societies allow first cousin marriage and a few, such as the Jews, allow uncle-niece marriage. As discussed here, Western societies tend to be more exogamous than Near Eastern societies.

[32] Bouchard 1981.

[33] Goody 1983, 145; one effect of this policy, emphasized by Goody, was that families were often without direct heirs and left their property to the Church.

descendents of the family rather than the wider kinship group also benefited: "Men in high secular positions . . . strove to consolidate their fortunes and their families in order to secure as much as possible for their direct descendants to the detriment of wider kin."[34]

In addition to its policy on consanguinity, the Church's doctrine of consent in marriage acted as a force against extended kinship relationships. "The family, the tribe, the clan, were subordinated to the individual. If one wanted to marry enough, one could choose one's own mate and the Church would vindicate one's choice."[35] Marriage came about as a result of consent and was ratified by sexual intercourse. By removing the fundamental nature of marriage from the control of the family and the secular lord to the individuals involved, the Church established its authority against the traditional ties of kinship and family. Freedom of choice of marriage partner was the rule in England throughout the modern period, and parental control was exercised only in the top 1 percent of the population.[36]

AN ETHNIC BASIS FOR WESTERN INDIVIDUALISM

> The Magian [Eastern] man is but *part of a pneumatic "We"* which, descending from above, is one and the same in all members. As body and soul he belongs to himself alone, but something else, something alien and higher, dwells in him, making him with all his glimpses and convictions just a member of a consensus, which, as the emanation of God, excludes all possibility of the self-asserting Ego. Truth is for him something other than for us [i.e., for us of specifically European mentality]. All our epistemological methods, resting upon the *individual* judgment, are for him madness and infatuation and its scientific results a work of the Evil One, who has confused and deceived the spirit as to its true dispositions and purposes. Herein lies the ultimate, for us unapproachable secret of Magian thought in its cavern world—the impossibility of a thinking, believing, and knowing Ego is the presupposition in all the fundamentals of all these religions.
>
> —Oswald Spengler[37]

---

[34] Leyser 1979, 50.
[35] Noonan 1973, 430.
[36] MacFarlane 1986.
[37] Quoted in Campbell 1959, vol. 3, 223–24; bracketed phrase in Campbell.

[Regarding the Faustian soul] Spengler has well said: "In Wolfram von Eschenbach, Cervantes, Shakespeare, and Goethe, the tragic line of the individual life develops from within outward, dynamically, functionally." . . . [The Faustian soul is] willing to question even God if the mask that he shows—or is said to have shown—rings hollow when struck.

—Joseph Campbell[38]

Thus far one might suppose that the creation of the individualistic nuclear family based on consent and love, monogamy, and the decline in the importance of extended kinship is simply the result of the social processes I have mentioned. But the fact is that these changes occurred much more quickly and much more thoroughly than in other parts of the world. The Western world remains the only culture area fundamentally characterized by all of the markers of individualism: monogamy, the conjugal nuclear family, representative government with individual rights against the state, moral universalism, and science. Further, this culture was built on the robust base of Roman civilization, which had several of these features. I suggest, therefore, that these tendencies are unique to the Western European culture area and that they have an ethnic basis. I do not suppose that Western Europeans have any unique biological adaptations, only that we differ in degree in adaptations characteristic of all humans and that the differences are sufficient to enable the evolution of a unique human culture. Similarly, all humans have the distinctively human mental abilities like symbolic representation and language, but races show quantitative differences in IQ sufficient to have major effects on their cultures—perhaps sufficient to result in at least some qualitative differences.

I suggest that over the course of their recent evolution, Europeans have been less subjected to between-group natural selection than Jews and other Middle Eastern populations. This was originally proposed by Fritz Lenz, who suggested that, because of the harsh environment of the Ice Age, the Nordic peoples evolved in small groups and have a tendency toward social isolation.[39] Such a perspective would not imply that Northern Europeans lack collectivist mechanisms for group competition, but only that these mechanisms are relatively less elaborated and/or require a higher level of group conflict to trigger their expression.

This perspective is consistent with ecological theory. Under ecol-

---

[38] In Campbell 1959, vol. 4, 553–54.
[39] Lenz 1931, 657.

ogically adverse circumstances, adaptations are directed more at coping with the adverse physical environment than at competing with other groups, and in such an environment, there would be less pressure for selection for extended kinship networks and highly collectivist groups.[40] Evolutionary conceptualizations of ethnocentrism emphasize the utility of ethnocentrism in group competition. Ethnocentrism would thus be of no importance at all in combating the physical environment, and such an environment would not support large groups.

European groups are part of the North Eurasian and Circumpolar culture area.[41] This culture area derives from hunter-gatherers adapted to cold, ecologically adverse climates. In such climates there is pressure for male provisioning of the family and a tendency toward monogamy because the ecology did not support either polygyny or large groups for an evolutionarily significant period. These cultures are characterized by bilateral kinship relationships which recognize both the male and female lines, suggesting a more equal contribution for each sex as would be expected under conditions of monogamy. There is also less emphasis on extended kinship relationships and marriage tends to be exogamous, i.e., outside the kinship group. All of these characteristics are opposite those found in the Middle Old World culture area, comprising the lower part of Eurasia. This culture group includes Jews and similar Near Eastern groups.

This scenario implies that Northern European peoples are more prone to individualism because they existed for a very long period in an ecological context that did not support large tribal groups based on extended kinship relations. Based on mitochondrial DNA, around 80 percent of European genes are from people who arrived in Europe from the Middle East 30,000–40,000 years ago.[42] These populations persisted through the Ice Ages. Presumably European populations that evolved in the cold and cloudy environments of the North for 40,000 years developed not just blond hair and blue eyes but temperaments and lifestyle preferences to go with them.

These populations were hunters and gatherers, not agriculturalists. Because of the relatively low level of economic production, hunting favors male provision of females.[43] This is because the energetic requirements of the human brain can only be met with a high quality diet.

---

[40] Southwood 1977, 1981.
[41] Burton et al. 1996.
[42] Sykes 2001.
[43] Roebroeks 2001.

The human brain makes up only 2 percent of body mass but requires 20 percent of all energy, 70 percent in the fetal period. This then led to pair bonding—the psychological basis of monogamy—in which there is cooperation between nurturing females and provisioning males beginning around 500,000 years ago. Hunting also required "considerable experience, quality education, and years of intensive practice"[44]—in other words, it requires high-investment parenting. It also pulls for intelligence because hunting for humans relies on cognitive abilities rather than running ability or strength. The hunting scenario is complex and ever changing.[45] Every animal species as well as individuals demonstrate unique behavioral characteristics depending on internal conditions of sex, age, weather, topography, etc. All of these trends are intensified in Northern areas because there is less energy per unit area.

The historical evidence shows that Europeans, and especially Northwest Europeans, were relatively quick to abandon extended kinship networks and collectivist social structures when their interests were protected with the rise of strong centralized governments. There is a general tendency throughout the world for a decline in extended kinship networks with the rise of central authority.[46] But in the case of Northwest Europe this tendency quickly gave rise, at least by the late Middle Ages and probably earlier, to the unique Western European "simple household" type. The simple household type is based on a single married couple and their children. This household style was typical of Scandinavia (except Finland), the British Isles, the Low Countries, German-speaking areas, and Northern France. It contrasts with the joint family structure typical of the rest of Eurasia in which the household consists of two or more related couples, typically brothers and their wives.[47] Before the industrial revolution, the simple household system was characterized by late age of marriage as well as methods of keeping unmarried young people occupied as servants and circulating among the households of the wealthy. The joint household system was characterized by earlier age of marriage for both men and women, a higher birthrate, as well as means of splitting up to form two or more households when the need arises.[48]

---

[44] Roebroeks 2001, 450.
[45] Frison 1998.
[46] Alexander 1979; Goldschmidt and Kunkel 1971; Stone 1977.
[47] Hajnal 1983.
[48] Hajnal 1983; Laslett (1983) further elaborates this basic difference to include four variants ranging from West, West/central or middle, Mediterranean,

This simple household system is a fundamental feature of individualist culture. The individualist family was able to pursue its interests freed from the obligations and constraints of extended kinship relationships and free of the suffocating collectivism of the social structures typical of the rest of the world. Marriage based on individual consent and conjugal affection quickly replaced marriage based on kinship.

This relatively greater proneness to forming a simple household is likely ethnically based. Not only does the simple household make compelling ecological sense for people adapted to harsh climates, but as previously pointed out, this tendency is stronger among the Germanic peoples. It is an intriguing finding that there are major differences within France corresponding to the division between the Germanic peoples who lived northeast of "the eternal line," which connects Saint Malo on the English Channel with Geneva in French-speaking Switzerland. This area developed large-scale agriculture capable of feeding the growing towns and cities, and did so prior to the agricultural revolution of the eighteenth century. It was supported by a large array of skilled craftsmen in the towns, and a large class of medium-sized ploughmen who "owned horses, copper bowls, glass goblets and often shoes; their children had fat cheeks and broad shoulders, and their babies wore tiny shoes. None of these children had the swollen bellies of the rachitics of the Third World."[49] The Northeast became the center of French industrialization and world trade.

The Northeast also differed from the Southwest in literacy rates. In the early nineteenth century, while literacy rates for France as a whole were approximately 50 percent, the rate in the Northeast was close to 100 percent, and differences occurred at least from the seventeenth century. Moreover, there was a pronounced difference in stature, with the Northeasterners being taller by almost two centimeters in an eighteenth-century sample of military recruits. Ladurie notes that the difference in the entire population was probably larger because the army would not accept many of the shorter men from the Southwest. Family historians have noted that the trend toward the economically independent nuclear family was more prominent in the North, while there was a tendency toward joint families as one moves to the South and East.[50]

These findings strongly suggest that ethnic differences are a contributing factor to the geographical variation in family forms within

---

to East.

[49] Ladurie 1987.

[50] E.g., Laslett 1983.

Europe. The findings suggest that the Germanic peoples had a somewhat greater biological tendency toward individualism—a greater tendency toward nuclear family social structure because of selection occurring in a prolonged resource-limited period of their evolution in the North of Europe. These groups were less attracted to extended kinship groups, so that when the context altered with the decline of extended kinship networks, the simple household structure occurred quickly. This simple family structure was adopted relatively easily because this group already had relatively powerful psychological predispositions toward the simple household system resulting from its unique evolutionary history.

Although these differences between the Germanic peoples and other areas of Europe are important, they do not belie the general difference between Western Europe and the rest of Eurasia. Although the trends toward simple households and the demographic transition occurred first in the Northwest of Europe, they spread relatively quickly among all the Western countries.

Another element of Western uniqueness was the custom of placing young people from peasant families as servants in the homes of others in areas of Northwest Europe characterized by the simple family. Between 30 and 40 percent of the youth in pre-industrial England were in service, the largest single occupational group until the twentieth century.[51] The practice of taking in servants went beyond simply providing for one's needs by bringing in outsiders. People would sometimes have their children go to work as servants elsewhere while at the same time taking in unrelated servants.[52] It was not just the children of the poor and landless who became servants, but even large, successful farmers sent their children to be servants elsewhere. In the seventeenth and eighteenth centuries individuals often took in servants early in their marriage, before their own children could help out, and then passed their children to others when the children were older and there was more than enough help.[53]

This suggests a deeply ingrained cultural practice, which resulted in a high level of non-kinship based reciprocity. The practice also bespeaks a relative lack of ethnocentrism because people are taking in non-relatives as household members. These pre-industrial societies are not organized around extended kinship, and it is easy to see that they

---

[51] Laslett 1977.
[52] Hajnal 1983.
[53] Stone 1977.

are pre-adapted to the industrial revolution and modern world generally. In the rest of Eurasia, there was a strong tendency for households to consist of kin.[54]

Interestingly, in a sexually competitive society such as classical China, the female servants would be concubines of the head of the household,[55] so that the resources of the household could be directly translated into reproduction. Thus in the Western European model wealthy males were supporting far more non-relatives than in the sexually competitive societies of Eurasia. It is intriguing that hunter-gatherer societies living in harsh climates often have very elaborate systems of reciprocity aimed at sharing resources such as meat. I suspect that the system of non-kinship based reciprocity so typical of pre-industrial Western Europe was another relic of a prolonged evolution in harsh northern climates.

This establishment of the simple household freed from enmeshment in the wider kinship community was then followed by all the other markers of Western modernization: limited governments in which individuals have rights against the state, capitalist economic enterprise based on individual economic rights, and science as individualist truth seeking. Individualist societies develop republican political institutions and institutions of scientific inquiry that assume that groups are maximally permeable and highly subject to defection when individual needs are not met.

INDIVIDUALISTIC MARRIAGE: CONSENT, LOVE, AND COMPANIONSHIP AS THE BASIS OF MARRIAGE

The rise of the simple household based on consent between the partners meant that personal qualities of the mate became more important compared to the situation where families are enmeshed in extended kinship relationships. In situations where the extended family reigns supreme, marriage is typically consanguineous and affected by family strategizing. In the simple household system, the personal characteristics of the mate become more important, i.e., all those characteristics on which humans choose mates, including intelligence, personality, psychological compatibility, and socioeconomic status.

While collectivist societies emphasize genealogy and degree of genetic relatedness in marriage, individualist societies tend to emphasize

---

[54] Hajnal 1983.
[55] E.g., Ebrey 1986.

personal attraction, e.g., romantic love, common interests.[56] John Money has noted the relatively greater tendency of Northern European groups toward romantic love as the basis of marriage.[57] Frank Salter has suggested that Northern European groups have a number of individualistic adaptations related to sexual behavior, including a greater tendency toward romantic love and genetic rather than social control mechanisms to prevent cuckoldry.[58] At the psychological level, the evolutionary basis of individualism involves mechanisms like romantic love in which adaptive behavior is intrinsically rewarding[59] rather than imposed by family strategizing or coerced, as in collectivist cultures. It is the difference between individual courtship between freely consenting and more or less equal partners, versus institutions like the purdah of Near Eastern civilization where the woman is sequestered and controlled by her male relatives until an arranged marriage is concluded.

There has been a trend, beginning in the Middle Ages, toward companionate marriage based on affection and consent between the partners, eventually affecting even the marriage decisions of the high aristocracy.[60] "Whereas in industrial Western societies the emotional relationship between man and wife is primary, it is not the pivot of social structure in the majority of societies."[61] Indeed, this is a general point of contrast between Eastern and Western stratified societies.[62] The idealization of romantic love as the basis of monogamous marriage has also periodically characterized Western secular intellectual movements, such as the Stoics of late antiquity and nineteenth-century Romanticism.[63] It's not that love and affection between mates do not exist in other societies; it is just that there is greater emphasis on this in Western societies.

Individual consent to marriage, a characteristic of Western marriage since the Middle Ages, is expected to result in individuals weighing more heavily the personal characteristics of a prospective mate. One effect of this is greater age parity in marriage partners. Relative age parity of spouses combined with a late age of marriage is a mark of the

---

[56] Triandis 1990.
[57] Money 1980.
[58] Salter 1994.
[59] MacDonald 1992.
[60] Brundage 1975; Hanawalt 1986; MacFarlane 1986; Stone 1977; Stone 1992.
[61] MacFarlane 1986, 174.
[62] Westermarck 1922.
[63] E.g., Brown 1987; Brundage 1975; Corbin 1990; Porter 1982; Veyne 1987.

Western European system of marriage.[64] The age of marriage for women was higher in Western Europe than elsewhere in Eurasia or Africa, including peasant societies characterized by joint families.[65] Indeed, in a large English sample from 1550–1775 the average age of marriage for females fluctuated around 26 years of age until 1675, when it began a decline to slightly above 24 years of age in 1800.

Another consequence of the simple household was that affection and pair bonding became the basis of marriage. Marriage became much less a matter of political alliance between and within kinship groups or a purely economic affair, or simply an aspect of sexual competition, and became based on interpersonal attraction, including affection. Affection within marriage became a cultural norm with the rise of the simple household. The Western phenomenon of courtship (unique among the cultures of Eurasia and Africa) provided a period in which prospective mates could assess personal compatibility; in Malthus' terms, an opportunity was given for both sexes "of finding out kindred disposition, and of forming those strong and lasting attachments without which the married state is generally more productive of misery than of happiness."[66]

INDIVIDUALISM AND THE DECLINE IN ETHNIC CONSCIOUSNESS AMONG EUROPEANS

Thus far I have sketched a scenario that may be summarized by saying that Western Europeans are relatively non-ethnocentric because of a prolonged period of natural selection in an adverse environment where extended kinship relationships had relatively little utility. Freed from the shackles of extended kinship relationships, Westerners returned to their roots, readily adopting the simple household which set in motion all the other features of modernization: companionate marriage, individual rights against the state, representative government, moral universalism, and science. The result was an extraordinary period of creativity, conquest, and creation of wealth that continues into the present. However, one of the theses of my books on Jews is that individualism is a poor strategy compared to cohesive group strategies. In the West, extended kinship groups were eliminated as a necessary prelude to modernization, but this did not eliminate between-group competition entirely. Beginning in the nineteenth century there has been competi-

---

[64] Laslett 1983.
[65] See Hajnal 1983; MacFarlane 1986; Malthus 1976.
[66] In MacFarlane 1986, 294.

tion between Jews as a collectivist, ethnically conscious group and Western individualistic elites.

Anthropologically, Jews derive from the Middle Old World culture area. This culture area is quite the opposite from the characteristics of Western social organization.[67] Jews are collectivist and highly prone to ethnocentrism, xenophobia, and moral particularism.[68]

A prominent theme appearing in several places in my books on Jews is that individualistic societies are uniquely vulnerable to invasion by cohesive groups. Recent research by evolutionary economists provides fascinating insight on the differences between individualistic cultures versus collectivist cultures. An important aspect of this research is to model the evolution of cooperation among individualistic groups.[69] People will altruistically punish defectors in a "one-shot" game—a game in which participants only interact once and are thus not influenced by the reputations of the people with whom they are interacting. This situation therefore models an individualistic culture because participants are strangers with no kinship ties. The surprising finding was that subjects who made high levels of public goods donations tended to punish people who did not, even though they incurred a cost in doing so. Moreover, the punished individuals changed their ways and donated more in future games even though they knew that the participants in later rounds were not the same as in previous rounds. The researchers suggest that people from individualistic cultures have an evolved negative emotional reaction to free riding that results in their punishing such people even at a cost to themselves—hence the term "altruistic punishment."

Essentially this research provides a model of the evolution of cooperation among individualistic peoples. Their results are most applicable to individualistic groups because such groups are not based on extended kinship relationships and are therefore much more prone to defection. In general, high levels of altruistic punishment are more likely to be found among individualistic, hunter-gatherer societies than in kinship-based societies based on the extended family. Their results are least applicable to Jews or other highly collectivist groups which in traditional societies were based on extended kinship relationships, known kinship linkages, and repeated interactions among members. In such situations, actors know the people with whom they are cooperating and anticipate future

---

[67] See Table 1, p. 15 above.
[68] See *A People That Shall Dwell Alone*.
[69] Fehr and Gächter 2002; Henrich et al. 2001.

cooperation because they are enmeshed in extended kinship networks, or, as in the case of Jews, they are in the same group.

Europeans are thus exactly the sort of groups modeled by this research: They are groups with high levels of cooperation with strangers rather than with extended family members, and they are prone to market relations and individualism.

This suggests the fascinating possibility that the key for a group intending to turn Europeans against themselves is to trigger their strong tendency toward altruistic punishment by convincing them of the moral blameworthiness of their own people. Because Europeans are individualists at heart, they readily rise up in moral anger against their own people once they are seen as free riders and therefore morally blameworthy—a manifestation of their stronger tendency toward altruistic punishment deriving from their evolutionary past as hunter-gatherers. In making judgments of altruistic punishment, relative genetic distance is irrelevant. Free riders are seen as strangers in a market situation, i.e., they have no familial or tribal connection with the altruistic punisher.

As a very interesting and influential European group, the Puritans exemplified this tendency toward altruistic punishment. A defining feature of Puritanism was the tendency to pursue utopian causes framed as moral issues—their susceptibility to utopian appeals to a "higher law" and the belief that government's principal purpose is moral. New England was the most fertile ground for "the perfectibility of man creed," and the "father of a dozen 'isms.'"[70] There was a tendency to paint political alternatives as starkly contrasting moral imperatives, with one side portrayed as evil incarnate—inspired by the devil. Puritan moral intensity can also be seen in their "profound personal piety"[71]—their intensity of commitment to live not only a holy life, but also a sober and industrious life.

Puritans waged holy war on behalf of moral righteousness even against their own genetic cousins. The suggestion is that this is a form of altruistic punishment found more often among cooperative hunter-gatherer groups than among groups based on extended kinship. For example, whatever the political and economic complexities that led to the Civil War, it was the Yankee moral condemnation of slavery that inspired the rhetoric and rendered the massive carnage of closely related Anglo-Americans on behalf of slaves from Africa justifiable in the minds of Puritans. Militarily, the war with the Confederacy rendered

---

[70] Fischer 1989, 357.
[71] Vaughn 1997, 20.

the heaviest sacrifice in lives and property ever made by Americans.[72] Puritan moral fervor and its tendency to justify draconian punishment of evildoers can also be seen in the comments of "the Congregationalist minister at Henry Ward Beecher's Old Plymouth Church in New York [who] went so far as to call for 'exterminating the German people . . . the sterilization of ten million German soldiers and the segregation of the women.'"[73]

Thus the current altruistic punishment so characteristic of contemporary Western civilization: Once Europeans were convinced that their own people were morally bankrupt, any and all means of punishment should be used against them. Rather than see other Europeans as part of an encompassing ethnic and tribal community, fellow Europeans were seen as morally blameworthy and the appropriate target of altruistic punishment. For Westerners, morality is individualistic—violations of communal norms by free riders are punished by altruistic aggression.

On the other hand, group strategies deriving from collectivist cultures, like Jewish culture, are immune to such a maneuver because kinship and group ties come first. Morality is particularistic—whatever is good for the group. There is no tradition of altruistic punishment because the evolutionary history of these groups centers around cooperation of close kin, not strangers.

The best strategy to destroy Europeans, therefore, is to convince the Europeans of their own moral bankruptcy. A major theme of my book, *The Culture of Critique* is that this is exactly what Jewish intellectual movements have done. They have presented Jewish culture as morally superior to European civilization and European civilization as morally bankrupt and the proper target of altruistic punishment. The consequence is that once Europeans are convinced of their own moral depravity, they will destroy their own people in a fit of altruistic punishment. The general dismantling of the culture of the West, and eventually its demise as anything resembling an ethnic entity, will occur as a result of a moral onslaught triggering a paroxysm of altruistic punishment. And thus the intense effort among Jewish intellectuals to continue the ideology of the moral superiority of the Jewish community and its role as undeserving historical victim while at the same time continuing the onslaught on the moral legitimacy of the West.

Individualist societies are therefore an ideal environment for highly collectivist, group-oriented strategies such as Judaism. It is significant

---

[72] Phillips 1999, 477.
[73] In Phillips 1999, 556.

that the problem of immigration of non-European peoples is not at all confined to the United States but represents a severe and increasingly contentious problem in the entire Western world and nowhere else: Only European-derived peoples have opened their doors to the other peoples of the world and now stand in danger of losing control of territory occupied for centuries. And they have done so to a considerable extent as a consequence of a self-perceived moral imperative that was utilized successfully by immigration activists to attain their own ethnic aims.[74]

Western societies have traditions of individualistic humanism that make immigration restriction difficult. In the nineteenth century, for example, the Supreme Court twice turned down Chinese exclusion acts on the basis that they legislated against a group, not an individual.[75] The effort to develop an intellectual basis for immigration restriction was tortuous; by 1920 it was based on the legitimacy of the ethnic interests of Northwestern Europeans and had overtones of racialist thinking. Both these ideas were difficult to reconcile with the stated political, moral, and humanitarian ideology of a republican and democratic society in which, as Jewish pro-immigration activists such as Israel Zangwill emphasized, racial or ethnic group membership had no official intellectual sanction. The replacement of these assertions of ethnic self-interest with an ideology of "assimilability" in the debate over the McCarran-Walter immigration act of 1952 was perceived by its opponents as little more than a smokescreen for "racism." At the end, this intellectual tradition collapsed largely as a result of the onslaught of the intellectual movements reviewed in this volume, and so collapsed a central pillar of the defense of the ethnic interests of European-derived peoples.

One very prominent strategy for Jewish intellectuals has been to promote radical individualism and moral universalism to the point that the entire ethnic basis of the society is undermined. In other words, these movements capitalized on the fact that Western societies had already adopted a paradigm of individualism and moral universalism, and were highly prone to altruistic punishment of their own people. These movements had the collective effect of undermining remaining sources of group cohesion among Europeans while leaving intact a highly cohesive, group-oriented Jewish community. The exemplar of this strategy is the work of the Frankfurt School, but similar comments could be

---

[74] *The Culture of Critique*, ch. 7.
[75] Petersen 1955, 78.

made about leftist political ideology in general and psychoanalysis. At its simplest level, gentile group identifications are regarded as an indication of psychopathology.

Despite the decline of extended kinship and the rise of individualism, Europeans had not entirely shed all sense of being part of a larger community. In the United States, Europeans retained a sense of peoplehood based on race well into the twentieth century. This sense of peoplehood and being a member of a race was buttressed by Darwinian-inspired scholarship, which not only viewed racial differences as well-established scientific findings, but also viewed the white race as uniquely talented. But this final attempt to find a biological sense of peoplehood went into steep decline, and is now widely viewed with horror in the academic establishment, largely because of the intellectual movements I discuss in *The Culture of Critique* and the present volume.

Conclusion

Whether Western individualistic societies are able to defend the legitimate interests of the European-derived peoples remains questionable. The present tendencies lead one to predict that unless individualism is abandoned the end result will be a substantial diminution of the genetic, political, and cultural influence of European peoples. It would be an unprecedented unilateral abdication of such power, and certainly an evolutionist would expect no such abdication without at least a phase of resistance by a significant segment of the population—presumably the more ethnocentric among us. Ironically perhaps, this reaction would emulate Jews by adopting group-serving, collectivist ideologies and social organizations. Whether the decline of the European peoples continues unabated or is arrested, it will constitute a profound impact of the Jewish group evolutionary strategy on the development of Western societies.

Chapter 10

Psychology and White Ethnocentrism[*]

While growing up I would often read accounts of European heroes who had battled for their people and for great causes. William Wallace, Robert the Bruce, and the Scots against the English, Sir Francis Drake leading the battle against the Spanish Armada, Charles Martel and the Franks defending Europe against the Muslims, King Leonidas and the Spartans at Thermopylae, and many others. Those days seem over now. Our political leaders are actually managing the displacement of their own people, and very few white people have the courage to do anything other than vote them back into office. Or they vote for the other party, which simply changes the faces of the managers.

How did it come to this? One might think that evolution would have equipped us with powerful mechanisms of ethnocentrism and group identity that would ensure that such a thing could never happen. We would naturally stand up for our people and fight the good fight, even at great cost. We would willingly die for our people—like William Wallace, whose death is described as follows:

> On 23 August 1305, following the trial, Wallace was taken from the hall, stripped naked and dragged through the city at the heels of a horse to Smithfield Market. He was drawn and quartered—strangled by hanging but released near death, emasculated, eviscerated and his bowels burnt before him, beheaded, then divided into four parts (the four horrors) at the Elms in Smithfield. His preserved head was placed on a pike atop London Bridge. It was later joined by the heads of his brother, John, and Simon Fraser. His limbs were displayed, separately, in Newcastle, Berwick, Stirling and Aberdeen.[1]

But there are no William Wallaces or mass movements of racial defense for Europeans, and the question is why this is so. The even more important question is how we can use our understanding of psychology to chart a path to legitimizing and building a movement of racial defense.

---

[*] First published (in a longer version encompassing ch. 11 below) in *The Occidental Quarterly* 6 (Winter 2006–2007): 7–46.

[1] William Wallace entry in Wikipedia (http://en.wikipedia.org).

This paper begins by describing the two worlds of psychology: the world of automatic, unconscious mechanisms that form our ancient evolutionary heritage, and the world of more recently evolved conscious processing that makes us distinctively human. Ethnocentric tendencies are automatic, unconscious mechanisms, but despite the power of these ancient mechanisms, they can be suppressed or diverted from their original purpose by cultural programming that takes advantage of some recently evolved cognitive machinery: the conscious processing mechanisms of the human prefrontal cortex.

Nevertheless, ethnocentric tendencies continue to influence the behavior of white people. Despite the current cultural programming, white people are gradually coalescing into what I term "implicit white communities" in multicultural America—that is, communities that reflect their ethnocentrism but that "dare not speak their name"—that cannot explicitly state that they are an expression of white ethnocentrism. These implicit white communities are insufficient for ethnic defense, however, and I conclude that progress in defending the ethnic interests of whites will happen only by legitimizing explicit assertions of ethnic identity and interests. Several obstacles to ethnic defense are discussed, with particular attention paid to understanding the psychological mechanisms underlying white guilt.

THE TWO WORLDS OF PSYCHOLOGY

Psychology has reached a consensus that the human mind has two kinds of processing, implicit and explicit (see Table 1). Implicit and explicit mechanisms may be contrasted on a number of dimensions.

TABLE 1:
Characteristics of Implicit and Explicit Cognitive Systems

IMPLICIT SYSTEM	**EXPLICIT SYSTEM**
Unconscious	Conscious
Automatic	Controllable
Fast	Relatively Slow
Evolved Early	Evolved Late
Parallel Processing	Sequential Processing
High Capacity	Limited by Attentional and Working Memory Resources
Effortless	Effortful
Acquisition by Biology or Overlearning	Acquisition by Culture and Formal Tuition

Implicit Processing

Implicit processing is unconscious, automatic, effortless, relatively fast, and involves parallel processing of large amounts of information.[2] Most of the activities going on in our brains in our day-to-day life involve implicit processing. Say you are negotiating with someone about buying a car. Without any conscious effort on your part, your brain is processing an enormous amount of data. It is processing the colors and shapes of the furniture and walls in the room, and it is processing data from your own body to allow you to stand upright without consciously thinking about it. More interestingly, your brain is also processing the facial expressions and posture of the person you are negotiating with, and it is processing the age and sex of this person. If you are a heterosexual man talking to a woman, your brain is assessing the woman's facial attractiveness and her body language as indicators of sexual availability for a long-term or a short-term relationship, even though the conversation is ostensibly about buying a car. And if you are a woman talking to a man, your brain is making calculations that differ from those of a man due to the very different interests that men and women have in sexual relationships, differences that stem from our ancient evolutionary heritage.

Your brain is also assessing how similar this salesperson is to yourself, and, without any conscious awareness on your part, it is making you trust the person more if that person is more like yourself. Furthermore, if the person is from a different race or ethnic group, it is flagging that fact, and it is coloring your interactions with the person by stereotypes—whether negative or positive—that your unconscious mind associates with that race or ethnic group.

You may not be paying conscious attention to these features, but if something seems out of place, your conscious mind may well take notice. Perhaps the other person's facial expression seems shifty, or he blinks too much when he tells you that the car was driven by a little old lady and has only 10,000 miles on it. If so, you may simply feel a vague unconscious unease, or you may actually notice that there is a major conflict between the person's facial expression and what he is telling you. In either case, your brain is telling you that you should back away from the deal.

What's happening here is that a multitude of what psychologist Christof Koch calls "zombie mechanisms" are whirring away deep in the recesses of your mind. They are likened to zombies because we are

---

[2] See, for example, Geary 2005; Stanovich 1999.

completely unconscious of their workings, much like a modern building in which we may be aware that the temperature is a comfortable 72°F but are completely unaware of the complexities of the climate control system that is humming away in the bowels of the building. When we look around the room, our brain is making millions of calculations about the appearance of objects that allow us to perceive the world. We are not aware of these calculations, but we are aware of the product—our visual world. In fact, we are not even consciously aware of most of our visual world, only that to which we are paying attention.

Most of these zombie mechanisms are the result of our evolutionary past. Over thousands and millions of years, our ancestors had to solve the problems of living. These problems were recurrent—they happened over and over again. The result was that natural selection equipped people with a large number of mental mechanisms for coping with these problems—mechanisms for recognizing faces and facial expressions, cooperating with others, interpreting threats, learning language, finding mates, and much else. Without this vast array of evolved modules, we could never do many of the things we do effortlessly and routinely—literally without thinking about it.

But natural selection for modules specialized to solve particular problems is not the only route to implicit processing. Another route is when we learn something so well that we don't have to think about it anymore. When children are learning their multiplication tables, it takes great conscious effort to remember that 3 x 4 = 12. But after a while, the answer to this problem comes automatically, without any conscious effort.

It's the same with driving a car or playing tennis. When one is learning to drive as a teenager, it takes a great deal of conscious effort to monitor the road, watch for crosswalks, pay attention to the dashboard dials, and attempt to coordinate gas pedal and clutch in shifting gears. But after some practice, these activities are performed easily and without much conscious effort. The result is that experienced drivers have no difficulty listening to music or talking with a friend on the cell phone. (Of course, running on autopilot does have its dangers. Talking on a cell phone while driving is illegal in some states.)

Learning multiplication tables, driving a car, and playing tennis are not innate activities. They are learned, but they become overlearned to the point that we don't have to pay much attention to the task when we are performing it. This frees up our limited conscious processing space to do other—often more important—things. As a general rule, the mind makes common mental activities unconscious and automatic so that the limited resources available to the conscious mind can be allocated to tasks requiring attention and cognitive resources.[3] The complicated motor routines involved in driving a car or playing tennis gradually become implicit. In fact, it is part of the folk psychology of tennis that a good way to make players play worse is to have them think about what they are doing. Tennis coaches talk about "muscle memory"—the unconscious, automatic mental processing that allows experienced tennis players to react quickly to situations without having to think about them.

The automaticity resulting from overlearning is important because some of people's unconscious negative racial stereotypes may result from repeated exposure to information on different groups. For example, repeatedly encountering newspaper articles on school failure and dropout by African-American and Latino children would be expected to result in an automatic stereotype of the educational abilities of these children. This stereotype would then be automatically activated when encountering these children or when contemplating sending one's children to a particular school with high percentages of these children. These negative stereotypes may then become implicit and unconscious.

It's important to note that these implicit negative stereotypes may coexist with explicit, conscious beliefs that there are no racial or ethnic differences in academic achievement. As described below, research has shown that there are often conflicts between implicit, unconscious attitudes held by whites on racial issues and consciously asserted explicit attitudes. Explicitly asserted attitudes are much more likely to be "politically correct": That is, they are much more likely to conform to the more or less official racial ideology sanctioned by the media and the academic and political establishment.

Explicit Processing

The opposite of implicit processing is explicit processing. Explicit processing is conscious, controllable, and takes effort. A good example is solving a problem that we haven't encountered before—that is, one that can't be solved automatically like the multiplication tables we learned in the third grade. Say, for example, we are taking an IQ test like the Raven's Progressive Matrices and we encounter the following problem:

---

[3] Bargh and Chartrand 1999.

Raven's Progressive Matrices

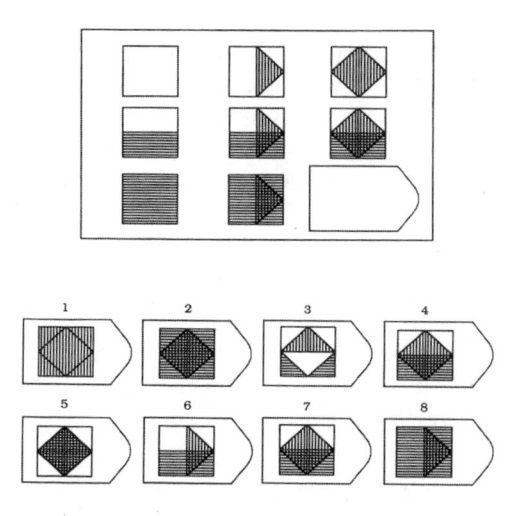

The task is to find which of the eight possible answers fills out the pattern in a logical way. To solve the problem, one has to notice that as you go from the top row to the bottom row, more horizontal lines are being added. So the missing piece must be filled with horizontal lines too—which means either piece 2 or piece 8. You also need to notice that the diamond shape is growing from left to right—from nothing in the left column, to the half-diamond in the middle column, to the full diamond in the right column. Since we already know the right piece must be filled with horizontal lines like piece 2 or piece 8, and the full diamond doesn't appear in piece 8, we know that piece 2 is the right choice.

Solving a problem like this requires that one keep a goal in mind, and it requires that one systematically pay attention to how the patterns change in two dimensions. This takes effort. The solution of the problem also involves processing information in a sequence. Rather than being able to process a vast amount of information in parallel as we do with implicit processing, we approach a problem like this in a sequence, one step at a time. The sequential processing of our conscious mind is always most obvious to me when I am trying to do two things at once, such as reading my e-mail and listening to a comedy routine on TV. It simply can't be done. Focusing on the e-mail means that you really can't pay attention to the jokes.

Whereas implicit mechanisms take in enormous amounts of information and process it very quickly, explicit mechanisms are relatively slow and have very limited capacity. For example, how good one is at solving problems like this (and they can get much harder) depends on working memory capacity. Working memory is the workspace of your mind. People with a strong working memory are better able to focus their attention on problems and ignore interfering information. In general, people with high working memory processing are better at solving these sorts of problems, and they have a higher IQ. But even the smartest human can't really keep very much in mind at once. Most people can remember a number sequence of about seven to nine numbers—far fewer than a computer, and much less information than our modular, implicit mechanisms routinely process effortlessly.

As this example indicates, IQ is a critically important mechanism that involves explicit processing. However, another important explicit processing mechanism is the personality system of Conscientiousness, which will be the focus of this paper.[4] Conscientiousness refers to *"socially prescribed impulse control"*—that is, the ability to control one's behavior to conform to social conventions and to pursue long-term goals.[5] Conscientious people are able to delay gratification and to perform difficult, unpleasant tasks in pursuit of their goals. In general, they behave in a responsible, dependable, and cooperative manner.

Conscientiousness is often labeled effortful control. This emphasizes the fact that Conscientiousness involves explicit, conscious processes. Simply put, conscientious people try hard. In a test of this trait for children, the experimenter places a piece of candy on a child's tongue and asks him to not swallow until instructed to do so. Or the experimenter asks the child not to peek at a gift until the experimenter returns. For most five-year-olds, these are really hard things to do, because their natural tendency is to swallow the candy and look at the gift. In general, girls are more conscientious than boys, and of course Conscientiousness increases with age. It's not surprising that being low on Conscientiousness is a huge risk factor in modern life. Such people do poorly in school and on the job. They are more likely to become impulsive criminals—criminals whose crimes are due to lack of impulse control: murderers who can't control their temper, drug abusers who can't control their cravings, or rapists who can't control their lust.

---

[4] Conscientiousness is capitalized here to indicate that it refers to the personality trait of Conscientiousness as measured by personality tests. It is similar to what people normally think of as conscientiousness.

[5] John and Srivastava 1999, 121.

Notice that being conscientious means that we are better able to control our natural tendencies. Five-year-olds who manage to not peek at the present or eat the candy before the experimenter's okay have to overcome powerful natural urges. We all have a natural attraction to the pleasures of drugs like cocaine (which mimic natural reinforcers) and the attractions of sexual desire. Most of us have had fantasies in which we imagine murdering a rival or enemy.[6] These tendencies are very adaptive, because they motivate us to seek mates and other resources and to move up the social hierarchy.

But conscientious people can control these urges in order to take account of the wider context (for example, going to prison for murder, or becoming a dysfunctional drug addict). They don't allow their urges to interfere with long-term goals (such as inhibiting the desire to party in order to get a good education).

Neurobiological research shows quite clearly how this works. The prefrontal cortex is the seat of conscientiousness. It has inhibitory connections to subcortical regions of the brain responsible for our natural urges (sex, drugs, and rock and roll, as I tell my students). The subcortical parts of the brain process information implicitly, and they are evolutionarily ancient. The prefrontal cortex processes information explicitly and is the crowning achievement of human evolution.

Consider one of evolutionary psychologist David Buss's examples. A man is almost run over by a car; he responds by directing an obscene gesture at the car. The car stops, and men get out and beat him. Suffering the pain and humiliation of being beaten enrages the man, and he responds by getting his gun: "I had stone hatred for him, and I righteously couldn't wait to see the look on his face when I blew him away. As soon as he popped out of the liquor store door, I charged right up to him, rammed the barrel in his chest, and pulled the trigger."[7] This is an example of impulsive aggression—the man is overwhelmed by rage stemming from his subcortex. It is a natural, reflexive reaction. His prefrontal cortex is pretty much out of the loop.

If this man had a stronger Conscientiousness system, things might have happened quite differently. The prefrontal cortex (PFC) takes in information about the wider context of our behavior, and it analyzes the situation explicitly. The subcortical brain is responding in a reflexive, impulsive, angry manner, and the only context it is sensitive to is the fact that another person has inflicted pain. But a person with a strong PFC is

---

[6] Buss 2005.
[7] In Duntley and Buss 2005, 291.

able to control these urges and take account of the wider context. Such a person doesn't simply respond with impulsive aggression; he thinks about the big picture: If I kill this guy, will I get caught? If I kill him with a gun, does it have a serial number that can be traced? Is there any possibility of DNA evidence being left at the scene? If I do get caught, can I plea-bargain it down to manslaughter? Will his friends come and get revenge? Why not just call 911 and let the police deal with the beating?

Most of these issues have become relevant only in modern times and would not have been relevant in the environments in which we evolved. But the explicit processing mechanisms of the PFC allow us to consider them and, if necessary, inhibit our natural tendencies.

Research has shown that children with damage to the PFC have immature, egocentric moral reasoning and are prone to stealing and aggression.[8] Patients with prefrontal damage originating in infancy exhibit a general lack of conscientiousness (lack of dependability, inability to plan for the future, proneness to immediate rewards rather than long-term goals). Their aggression is impulsive rather than planned, and they lack a sense of guilt for transgressions against others.

Adrian Raine of the University of Southern California has shown how this works in the brain by contrasting impulsive murderers with predatory murderers.[9] The brains of both impulsive murderers and predatory murderers have very active areas in the subcortical areas of the brain responsible for aggression. The difference is that predatory murderers also have normal levels of activation in the prefrontal cortex. As a result, they are better able to control their murderous tendencies. Their murders are planned, and because they are planned, it is often quite difficult to catch them. Serial murderers can go for years without being detected, while impulsive murderers are easily caught because they act on the spur of the moment, without the precautions needed to hide their crime.

To sum up, the PFC is able to regulate the more evolutionarily ancient parts of our brain responsible for many of our passions and desires. Another example is sexuality. When male subjects were shown erotic photos, subcortical areas of the brain responsible for sexual arousal were activated.[10] However, when the subjects were told to distance themselves from the erotic stimuli and inhibit their arousal, they were able to do so. The fMRI (Functional Magnetic Resonance Imag-

---

[8] Anderson et al. 1999; Damasio 1994/2000.
[9] Raine et al. 1998.
[10] Beauregard, Lévesque, and Bourgouvin 2001.

ing) pictures of their brains showed that the prefrontal cortex was activated when they inhibited their sexual arousal.

ETHNOCENTRISM AND ITS CONTROL

Why is this important for thinking about psychology and white ethnocentrism? Just as conscientious people can inhibit their natural tendencies toward aggression and sexual arousal, they are able to inhibit their natural tendencies toward ethnocentrism in the same way. The critical point in the following is that cultural information is of vital importance for making people inhibit their ethnocentric tendencies. This cultural information relies on explicit processing and provides the basis for prefrontal inhibitory control of ethnocentrism. The conclusion is that the control of ethnocentrism is a direct consequence of the control of cultural information.

There is good evidence for several different evolved mechanisms related to ethnocentrism: genetic similarity mechanisms,[11] social identity mechanisms,[12] individualism/collectivism,[13] and a human kinds module (see chapter 11 below on "Biological Roots of Ethnocentrism and Group Conflict").[14] In the following, the only assumption is that ethnocentrism exists. It is not important whether ethnocentrism is the result of psychological mechanisms that evolved for group defense or if it is the result of learned negative stereotypes of other groups. The point is that in either case people tend to have negative stereotypes of other races, and they prefer people from their own race. The evidence shows that this includes white people, although as mentioned in the following chapter, there is also evidence that white people are less ethnocentric than other human groups: Western cultures tend toward individualism, whereas most of the rest of the world is much more collectivist in outlook.[15] This implies that the control of ethnocentrism is easier for whites, because the subcortical mechanisms responsible for ethnocentrism are weaker.

Research on ethnocentrism has shown much awareness of the distinction between implicit and explicit processing. Implicit attitudes on race

---

[11] Rushton 1989, 1999.

[12] MacDonald 2001; Tullberg and Tullberg 1997; van der Dennen 1999.

[13] MacDonald 2001.

[14] Hirschfeld 1996.

[15] See above ch. 1, "Background Traits for Jewish Activism" and ch. 9, "What Makes Western Culture Unique?" as well as *The Culture of Critique*, Preface to first paperback edition.

are assessed by tests like the Implicit Attitudes Test. Subjects are presented with photos of blacks and whites in succession and asked to pair positive or negative words (e.g., "intelligent," "law-abiding," "poor," "success") with the photos. Eighty percent of whites take longer to associate positive words with blacks than with whites. This is interpreted as indicating that whites have implicit negative stereotypes of blacks.

On the other hand, explicit attitudes on race are typically assessed by filling out questionnaires.[16] College student populations of whites typically exhibit pro-black attitudes on these tests. For example, one study found that whites scored 1.89 on a six-point scale, with one meaning strongly pro-black, and six being strongly anti-black.[17]

Another way to measure explicit attitudes is by interview. A recent representative sample of 2,000 households found that a surprising 74 percent of whites thought that racial identity was very important (37 percent) or somewhat important (37 percent).[18] In general, people become more racially conscious as they get older—only 53 percent claimed that racial identity was important while growing up. (I have noticed this also as a feature of Jewish identity.[19]) Even more surprising is the finding that 77 percent of whites thought that whites had a culture that should be preserved. However, despite asserting the legitimacy of white ethnic identity, only 4 percent of whites claimed to be a member of an organization based on racial or ethnic identity. And 75 percent of whites state that prejudice and discrimination are important or very important to African-American disadvantage.

This study is therefore compatible with generally pro-black explicit attitudes. In general, blacks and other minorities have much stronger explicit ethnic identities than whites do. For example, this same survey found that 90 percent of blacks thought that racial identity was very important (72 percent) or somewhat important (18 percent), and 91 percent felt that black culture was worth preserving. Blacks also demonstrate a substantially larger explicit ingroup preference than whites.[20]

The main point here is that there is a gap between whites' explicitly

---

[16] For example, the Modern Racism Scale and the Motivation to Respond without Prejudice Scale (see Cunningham, Nezlek, and Banaji 2004).

[17] Phelps et al. 2000.

[18] Croll, Hartmann, and Gerteis 2006.

[19] I describe several cases in my trilogy on Jews, for example, Heinrich Heine (*Separation and Its Discontents*, ch. 2, n. 9).

[20] Nosek, Banaji, and Greenwald 2002; see also Ashburn-Nardo, Knowles, and Monteith 2003.

positive attitudes about blacks and their implicitly negative attitudes. Even white liberals show implicit negative attitudes toward blacks, but their implicit attitudes are less negative than those of conservatives. In fact, white liberals are more hypocritical about race than conservatives: There is a larger gap between implicit attitudes and explicit attitudes toward blacks among white liberals than among white conservatives.[21]

Implicit attitudes on race impact actual behavior. For example, whites' explicit attitudes toward blacks predicted their verbal friendliness and their own perceptions of their behavior when interacting with a black. However, their implicit attitudes were a better predictor of nonverbal friendliness as rated by independent judges (higher rate of blinking and avoidance of eye contact).

The gap between explicit and implicit attitudes is made possible by the inhibitory mechanisms of the prefrontal cortex. Two studies show that prefrontal control is able to inhibit negative implicit attitudes. In one study, subjects were shown photos of blacks and whites while hooked up to an fMRI machine that takes pictures of the brain in action.[22] When the photos were shown for very brief periods—too short to be consciously processed—the fMRI showed that whites had a negative response to the photos of blacks. This procedure therefore measures implicit negative attitudes toward blacks.

However, when the photos of blacks were presented for a much longer period, so that they were consciously experienced, then the difference in reaction to black and white faces decreased. This happened because the prefrontal region was activated. In other words, people who are consciously aware that they are seeing photos of blacks are able to inhibit the negative automatic responses from the subcortex. Subjects who showed the most prefrontal activation showed the lowest subcortical response. This implies that they were better able to inhibit their automatic negative attitudes toward blacks.

Another study had black and white subjects scan photos of blacks and whites. fMRI scans showed subcortical activation when scanning photos of blacks but not when scanning photos of whites. This is interpreted as an implicit fear response because the reaction is involuntary and unconscious. However, when subjects were also given the verbal label "African American" along with the photo of a black person, there was no subcortical fear response. This is interpreted as resulting from prefrontal inhibitory control that suppresses the implicit fear response.

---

[21] Nosek, Banaji, and Greenwald 2002.
[22] Cunningham, Johnson, et al. 2004.

In other words, the moment you start thinking about race in words, you know you're thinking about it and can make decisions. Your prefrontal inhibitory centers have been activated, and the negative thoughts are suppressed.

Both these studies show the importance of prefrontal inhibitory control over automatic negative attitudes of whites toward blacks. White ethnocentrism exists, but it exists in a sort of underground world of unconscious, automatic processing. But ethnocentric attitudes dare not speak their name: As soon as the explicit, conscious processor swings into action, it suppresses the negative implicit attitudes coming from below.

This is nicely illustrated in a study that explains what happens when people confront controversial issues related to race and ethnicity. White subjects were shown pictures of a smiling interracial couple and then told that their response to the photo indicated that they were prejudiced. After being told this, subjects took much longer to respond to later photos. This is interpreted as being due to subjects trying to consciously control their responses to the photos. The photo serves as a "cue for control"—a warning that "the situation is one in which prejudiced responses may occur and that the brakes need to be applied to ongoing behavior."[23]

Young children tend to have unabashedly explicit bias in favor of their own race. Explicit race bias emerges early, as young as age three or four, peaks in middle childhood, and then undergoes a gradual decline through adolescence, and disappears in adulthood.[24] However, there is no such decline in implicit racial preferences, which remain strong into adulthood.[25] There is also a decline in cross-racial friends and companions as children get older. White schoolchildren are much more likely to have white friends than chance expectation would account for, and this trend increases as they get older.[26] This means that at the same time that explicit racial preference in white children is declining, children are becoming less and less likely to actually interact with and form friendships with children from other races. In effect, schools undergo a process of self-segregation. And among adults, whites are significantly less likely than other racial groups to report interracial friendships and contacts.[27]

---

[23] Monteith et al. 2002, 1046.
[24] Aboud 1988; Augoustinos and Rosewarne 2001.
[25] Dunham, Baron, and Banaji 2005.
[26] Moody 2002.
[27] Emerson, Kimbro, and Yancey 2002.

The bottom line, then, is that as children get older they become increasingly aware of the official explicit racial ideology, and they conform to it. Their prefrontal centers of inhibitory control are becoming stronger, so that they are better able to inhibit their relatively positive attitudes about their own group. At the explicit level, they are free from any negative attitudes toward non-white groups and may even be politically liberal or radical. At the same time, however, they are "voting with their feet" by choosing friends and companions of the same race.

And their parents are doing the same thing. I have noted that liberals show a greater gap between explicit attitudes and implicit attitudes and behavior than do conservatives. Indeed, while highly educated white parents tend to have liberal explicit attitudes on racial issues, including the desirability of school integration, a recent study shows that these same highly educated whites seek out schools that are racially segregated and are more likely to live in racially segregated neighborhoods.[28] There is a positive correlation between the average education of white parents and the likelihood that parents will remove their children from public schools as the percentage of black students increases. Michael Emerson, an author of the study, is quite aware of the gap between explicit attitudes and behavior: "I do believe that white people are being sincere when they claim that racial inequality is not a good thing and that they'd like to see it eliminated. However . . . their liberal attitudes about race aren't reflected in their behavior."

The flip side of this is that less affluent whites are more likely to have explicitly illiberal attitudes on racial issues that are condemned by elites. Yet they are also more likely to actually live in racially integrated areas and send their children to racially integrated schools, presumably due to financial constraints.

IMPLICIT WHITE COMMUNITIES

Children's choice of friends and parents' choice of schools and neighborhoods reflect the raw reality of racial hypocrisy in the United States. These children and their parents are acting on their implicit attitudes, and there is a profound gap between their implicit attitudes and their behavior (which show ingroup racial preference), on the one hand, and their explicit attitudes (which express the official racial ideology of egalitarianism), on the other. In effect, they are creating implicit white communities—implicit because even though they are an expression of (implicit) racial preferences, they cannot speak their name: They do not

---

[28] Emerson and Sikkink 2006.

explicitly state that their friendship choices or their choice of neighborhood or school derives from racial preference because that conflicts with their explicit racial attitudes and with the official racial ideology of the wider culture.

My hypothesis is that white Americans are gradually coalescing into a political and cultural affiliation as whites, and that this trend will continue to strengthen in the future. But at present, this political and cultural affiliation is not yet consciously white, at least partly because conscious white affiliation is a cultural taboo.

In the face of overwhelming sanctions on white racial identity in the post-World War II world, whites have adopted a variety of explicit identities which serve as the basis of white association and community. All of these identities exist under the radar of the political correctness enforced by elites in academia, politics, and the media. Considered here are several overlapping explicit white identities: Republican voter, NASCAR racing enthusiast, evangelical Christian, and country music fan. Each of these identities allows white people to associate with other whites and even to form a white political base without any explicit acknowledgement that race plays a role.

Implicit white communities have become an increasingly important part of the American landscape. The most important of these implicit white communities is residential segregation resulting from white flight. As Kevin Kruse notes, "at the dawn of the twenty-first century, America found itself dominated by suburbs and those suburbs dominated by the politics of white flight and urban secession."[29] Part of this phenomenon stems from whites' diminished willingness to contribute to public goods, because the beneficiaries are disproportionately blacks and other non-white minorities: "In the past, the hostility to the federal government, the welfare state, and taxation had been driven by racial resentment, whether in the form of segregationists inside Atlanta or secessionist suburbanites outside it. In the 1990s the new generation of suburban Republicans simply took the politics of white flight to the national stage."[30] As Kruse notes, race is never part of the explicit rhetoric of white flight, which tends to be expressed as opposition to the federal government, the welfare state, taxation, and perceived moral issues like abortion and homosexuality. But at the implicit level, the desire for white communities and the aversion to contributing to public goods for non-whites are the overriding motivations.

---

[29] Kruse 2005, 259.
[30] Kruse 2005, 263.

White flight is part of the fragmented future that lies in store for the United States and other Western countries with high levels of non-European immigration. It is a well-established finding that the more ethnically mixed a population becomes, the greater is its resistance to redistributive policies.[31] For example, a study of donations to the United Way of America charity found that white Americans give less when their communities are more than 10 percent non-white. Sociologist Robert D. Putnam recently showed that the greater the racial diversity of a community, the greater the loss of trust.[32] People living in homogeneous areas like New Hampshire or Montana are more involved with friends, the community, and politics than people in more diverse areas.[33]

At the political level, implicit whiteness is also reflected in Howard Dean's famous comment that the Republican Party is the party of white Christians.[34] In 2004 and 2006, white evangelical or born-again Christians made up a quarter of the electorate, and 78 percent of them voted Republican.[35] In fact, other ethnic groups are coalescing into a non-white voting bloc centered in the Democratic Party to an even greater extent than whites are gravitating to the Republican Party. Over 90 percent of blacks typically vote Democratic, while Latinos vote around 60 to 70 percent Democratic.[36] Non-white ethnic groups tend to vote Democratic even when they have relatively high socioeconomic status—a good indication that this pattern results from identity politics rather than economics. In the 2004 presidential election, John Kerry won first-time Asian votes 78 percent to 20 percent, and among American-born Asians he won by 80 percent to 18 percent.[37] Despite the stridently pro-Israel policies of George W. Bush, around 76 percent of Jews voted for Al Gore in the 2000 presidential election, and Jews continue to form the financial backbone of the Democratic Party.[38] In 2002, only 8 percent of Republican votes came from non-whites, and similar results occurred in 2006.[39]

---

[31] Salter (ed.) 2004.
[32] Lloyd 2006.
[33] Sailer 2007.
[34] Murray 2005.
[35] For 2004: Cooperman 2006. For 2006: Pew Forum on Religion and Public Life (http://pewforum.org).
[36] Sailer 2005c, 2006.
[37] Sailer 2004.
[38] Jewish voting in presidential elections of 2004: Jewish Virtual Library (undated) (www.jewishvirtuallibrary.org); Jews and the Democratic Party: Goldberg 1996.
[39] For 2002: Sailer 2005a, 2005b, 2006. For 2006: Religion vs. race in

Not only are whites voting Republican, but white Republican voters are most likely to be married with children.[40] These are exactly the people for whom white flight to safe neighborhoods, good schools, and predominant white ethnic composition is most compelling. The best correlation with Bush's share of the vote by state in 2004 is the average years married by white women between ages 18 and 44 ($r = .91$). Bush carried 44 percent of single white females but 61 percent of married white females; Bush also won 53 percent of single white men and 66 percent of married white men. Bush carried 25 of the top 26 states in total white fertility, while Kerry won all 16 of the states with the lowest white fertility. The correlation between total white fertility and Bush's share of the vote was 0.86.

The 2006 congressional elections show that white support for Republicans is sensitive to issues such as the disastrous war in Iraq and the abysmal record of the Bush administration—the first neoconservative administration—in actually delivering on white flight political issues. As noted by many, the history of neoconservatism shows a strong support for core liberal issues (including relatively unrestricted immigration) and a stridently pro-Israel foreign policy.[41] Nevertheless, even in 2006, 78 percent of white evangelical Christians—who are the most strongly identified implicit white voting constituency—voted Republican.[42]

Another implicit white community is NASCAR racing, which strongly overlaps with evangelical Christianity, country music, and small town American culture, particularly the culture of the South. A famous Mike Luckovich cartoon that appeared in the *Atlanta Journal-Constitution* shows a black man and a white man talking with a Confederate flag flying in the background. "We need a flag that isn't racist . . . but preserves white southern culture . . ." The next panel shows a NASCAR checkered flag. The implicit/explicit distinction could not be more obvious.

A large part of the attraction of NASCAR is a desire for traditional American culture. NASCAR events are permeated with sentimental patriotism, prayers, military flyovers, and post-race fireworks. As sociologist Jim Wright notes, "just about everything . . . you encounter in a

---

2006 voting and ideology. December 6, 2006 (www.plantingliberally.org).

[40] Sailer 2005a, b.

[41] See ch. 4, "Neoconservatism as a Jewish Movement" and ch. 5, "Neoconservative Portraits," above.

[42] Pew Forum on Religion and Public Life (http://pewforum.org).

day at the track drips with traditional Americana."[43] However, "race is the skeleton in the NASCAR Family closet. On the tracks and in the stands, stock-car racing remains a white-person's sport."[44] The whiteness of NASCAR races can be seen from a comment that, after surveying the crowd at the 1999 Daytona 500, "there were probably about as many Confederate flags here as black people"—i.e., fewer than forty out of a crowd of approximately 200,000.[45] Because the Confederate flag is the ultimate in political incorrectness, their presence at NASCAR events is quite possibly an act of rebellion:

> The near-universal discrediting of the Stars and Bars as a politically incorrect, if not racist, symbol has obviously not yet reached every Winston Cup fan. Either that, or they just don't care. And, as you might imagine, there was no pussyfooting or self-flagellation about the point among fans at the Southern 500, which was adorned by a profusion of Confederate flags the likes of which I had not witnessed at any other track.[46]

Wright stresses the link of NASCAR to traditional small town and rural American culture and its links to outdoor pursuits like hunting, fishing, and camping.[47] There is a large overlap between NASCAR fans and gun ownership. There is also a strong Christian religious atmosphere: Races begin with a benediction and a prayer. There is "a visible Christian fellowship" in NASCAR, including entire teams that identify themselves publicly as Christian teams; many of the drivers actively participate in Christian ministry.[48] Other values in evidence are courage in the face of danger—another throwback to traditional American culture, deriving ultimately from the Scots-Irish culture of the English borderlands: "As we enter the third decade of women's liberation and the second decade of the post communist era, we've come to expect, even demand more sensitivity and empathy in our men than bravado or grit, and the traditional manly virtues of courage, bravery, and 'guts' strike many as anachronistic at best, even dangerous and moronic."[49]

---

[43] Wright 2002, 35.
[44] Wright 2002, 280.
[45] Wright 2002, 83.
[46] Wright 2002, 141.
[47] Wright 2002, 156.
[48] Wright 2002, 37.
[49] Wright 2002, 156.

The only recent scientific survey on NASCAR fans is the Southern Focus Poll of 1998, conducted by the Center for the Study of the South at the University of North Carolina.[50] While 26.1 percent of white Southerners had been to a NASCAR race, compared to 4.4 percent of blacks, in the national sample using the same questions, the percentages were 24.1 and 12.5 percent, respectively. These results undercount the total number of fans of non-NASCAR stock car racing and other forms of auto racing. Furthermore, 18.1 percent of respondents with a high school education had been to a NASCAR race, compared to 22.5 percent of high school graduates, 27 percent with some college, and 18 percent of college graduates. NASCAR also claims 75 million fans in America, 25 percent of the population.[51] NASCAR racing is the fastest growing sport in America, second only to the NFL in sports viewership.[52] This is a very large implicit white community.

Being a NASCAR fan overlaps with other implicit white identities. A 1993 survey carried out by the National Opinion Research Center found a 3:1 ratio in NASCAR attendance between small-town and large-city residents; almost 2:1 for gun owners vs. non-gun owners, 3:1 for hunters vs. non-hunters, and almost 3:1 between people who like country music "very much" and those who hate it (21.3 percent to 7.6 percent).[53] Indeed, one survey found that 49 percent of people who "listen to country music a lot" are fans of NASCAR, compared to 31 percent of all respondents. The biggest disparity is in the other direction: Only 24 percent of people who listen to country music a lot identify themselves as fans of the NBA compared to 47 percent of all respondents.[54]

There is little doubt that country music is an implicit white community: Over 90 percent of country music listeners are white.[55] Although country music remains the most common radio format, it is disappearing from major urban areas where whites are becoming a minority.

While NASCAR is a white sport, the NBA is widely perceived to be a black sport. Whites, especially non-urban whites, are a decreasing

---

[50] Southern Focus Poll: Crosstabs, Non-Southern Sample, 1998. Durham, NC: University of North Carolina Institute for the Study of the American South (ftp://ftp.irss.unc.edu).
[51] Miles 2005.
[52] Wright 2002, 182.
[53] Wright 2002, 167–68.
[54] Edison Media Research: www.crb.org.
[55] Tucker 2007.

audience for the NBA. Since the Michael Jordan era, television ratings for the NBA have been on the decline. In 2005, ratings were down 7 percent on ESPN and TNT, 4 percent on ESPN, and more than 30 percent for the NBA finals.[56] The audience for NASCAR and the NBA are non-overlapping, with the NBA appealing to "a young, multicultural, urban market audience"[57]—the polar opposite of the married, white, Republicans who have adopted implicit white identities.

NASCAR has enjoyed an increasingly dominant television audience position during the portion of the year formerly controlled by the NBA.[58] The NBA culture is seen as African-American, and the response of the NBA has been to attempt to make the NBA look more like white America in order to restore its fan base. Sports writer Gary Peterson notes that

> for decades there has been a racial divide between NBA players (mostly black) and the paying customers (largely white). That divide has become a flashpoint over the past fifteen years. . . . Never before have the players seemed so unlike the fans. This divide is the top concern at the league office—even ahead of declining free throw shooting and baggy shorts. For proof you need look no further than the league-wide dress code NBA commissioner David Stern imposed last season. It was an extraordinary step—he might as well have told the players, "Quit dressing like typical young, urban African-Americans. You're scaring the fans."[59]

Besides banning ostentatious gold chains and mandating business casual attire, the NBA has also handed out draconian penalties for fighting among players, because fighting fits into the image of urban, African-American culture.[60] Another sportswriter, MSNBC's Michael Ventre, opined that "the terms 'NBA' and 'thuggery' have become inextricably linked in the minds of basketball fans the world over."[61]

The point is not that the NBA is more violent than, say, professional

---

[56] *Hollywood Reporter*, July 12, 2005.

[57] Sam Sussman, vp/media director at Starcom, quoted in MediaWeek, July 11, 2005 (www.mediaweek.com).

[58] After increasing seventy percent from 2000 to 2005, NASCAR ratings were flat in 2006 (Tucker 2006).

[59] Peterson 2006.

[60] Peterson 2006.

[61] Ventre 2006.

hockey; it's just that the NBA is conscious of racial stereotyping processes among whites. Part of NASCAR's attraction for whites is that it is an implicit white community. By regulating dress and conduct, the NBA seems to be trying to make itself into an implicit white community despite the racial composition of its players.

MANAGING WHITE ETHNOCENTRISM: THE PROBLEM WITH NON-EXPLICIT WHITE IDENTITY

Thus far the argument has been that white people are gradually coalescing into implicit white communities that reflect their ethnocentrism but "dare not speak their name." They are doing so because of various mechanisms that operate implicitly, below the level of conscious awareness. These white communities cannot assert explicit white identities because the explicit cultural space is deeply committed to an ideology in which any form of white identity is anathema. Explicit culture operates in the conscious prefrontal centers able to control the subcortical regions of the brain.

This implies that the control of culture is of critical importance. The story of how this explicit cultural space came to be and whose interests it serves is beyond the scope of this paper. My view is that these cultural transformations are the result of a complex interaction between preexisting deep-rooted tendencies of Europeans (individualism, moral universalism, and science) and the rise of a Jewish elite hostile to the traditional peoples and culture of Europe.[62] The result has been a "culture of critique" that represents the triumph of the leftist movements that have dominated twentieth-century intellectual and political discourse in the West, especially since World War II. The fundamental assumptions of these leftist movements, particularly as they relate to race and ethnicity, permeate intellectual and political discourse among both liberals and conservatives and define a mainstream consensus among elites in academia, the media, business, and government.

The explicit cultural space can be categorized into two components: social controls and ideology.[63] Social controls include penalties for explicit manifestations of white ethnocentrism (e.g., hate crime statutes, ostracism, loss of livelihood, and the legal infrastructure of massive non-white immigration and affirmative action). While most animals are sensitive only to contexts that have repeatedly occurred in their evolutionary history, we humans are exquisitely sensitive to the complex

---

[62] On this elite, see *The Culture of Critique*.
[63] See MacDonald 1983.

cultural milieu, which includes a variety of subtle and not so subtle penalties for explicitly proclaiming a white identity. Being aware of the wider cultural context of social controls that structure the consequences of behavior requires input to the higher brain centers situated in the prefrontal cortex and, as we have seen, this input may result in inhibiting tendencies toward ethnocentrism originating from lower in the brain.

Ideologies are explicit belief systems that structure attitudes and behavior related to race and ethnicity. Because they are a manifestation of explicit processing, they are products of higher cognitive processes located in the prefrontal cortex. Because of the power of the prefrontal cortex over the lower brain, these ideologies can have important influences on behavior. They include ideologies of race and ethnicity (e.g., race doesn't exist; assertions of white identity and interests are an indication of psychopathology or moral turpitude, while assertions of non-white identities and interests are legitimate and praiseworthy; white achievement and the underachievement of blacks and Latinos are the result of white racism and white privilege; there are no biological differences between the races affecting intelligence and achievement); ideologies promoting massive non-white immigration (e.g., diversity is a strength; America is a country founded on a set of abstract principles with no ethnic identity); counter-stereotypical media images (blacks are more intelligent, wiser, and more responsible parents than whites).

Because implicit ethnocentrism is alive and well among whites and affects their behavior in subtle ways, one might suppose that whites are in fact able to pursue their interests even against the prevailing wind of the explicit culture of powerful anti-white social controls and ideologies. The problem, however, is that white ethnic identity and interests can be managed if they remain only at the implicit level. In general, implicit white communities conform to the official multicultural ideology and adopt conventional attitudes and rhetoric on racial and ethnic issues. This allows them to escape the scrutiny of the cultural elites that enforce conventional attitudes on racial and ethnic issues. However, it renders them powerless to actively promote issues that vitally affect their ethnic interests.

A good example is massive non-white immigration. In recent years, there has been much discussion of illegal immigration that tapped into a very large reservoir of public anger about the lack of control of our borders and, I think, the transformations that immigration is unleashing. Although it was common for proponents of illegal immigration to label their opponents "racists," the fact that illegal immigration is, after all, illegal made it easy for conservatives to oppose it without mentioning their racial interests.

This contrasts with no discussion at all in the mainstream media of the nearly one million legal immigrants who come to the United States every year—no discussion of their effect on the economy, social services, crime, and competition at elite universities; no discussion of their effect on the long-term ethnic composition of the United States and how this will affect the political interests of whites; no discussion of the displacement of native populations in various sectors of the economy; and no discussion of whether most Americans really want all of this. (They don't.)[64] Indeed, it has been quite common for conservative opponents of illegal immigration to assert their support for legal immigration as a means of dodging the charge of "racism." While assertions of ethnic interests by non-whites are a commonplace aspect of the American political and intellectual scene, mainstream explicit assertions of ethnic interests by whites have been missing since the 1920s.[65]

The result is that the leftist ideologies of race and ethnicity have become part of conventional morality and intellectual discourse, even within implicitly white communities. As a result, implicit white communities are impotent in opposing the forces that are changing the country in ways that oppose their long-term interest. Because there is no mainstream attempt by whites to shape the explicit culture in ways that would legitimize white identity and the pursuit of white ethnic interests, implicit white communities become enclaves of retreating whites rather than communities able to consciously pursue white interests.

The creation of an explicit white culture legitimizing white identity and interests is a prerequisite to the successful pursuit of the interests of whites as a group.

Psychological Challenges to Developing an Explicit Culture of White Identity and Interests

My view, then, is that in the absence of changes in the explicit cultural space on issues related to the legitimacy of white racial identity and interests, whites will continue to simply retreat into implicit white communities. There are obviously a great many obstacles to developing such a mainstream culture, the main one being opposition by elites in the media, academia, business, and political cultures. As is well known, there is a major gap between popular and elite opinion on critical issues

---

[64] Francis 2002.
[65] *The Culture of Critique*, ch. 7.

such as massive non-white immigration.[66]

A large part of the problem is that for many in these elites, economic and professional self-interest coincides with support for anti-white policies. Particularly egregious examples are companies that directly benefit from immigration via cheap labor, or companies, such as First Data Corporation, that benefit from remittances sent by immigrants to relatives in other countries.[67] A noteworthy example is Mary Sue Coleman, who in 2006 earned $742,148 as the president of the University of Michigan and has been a leader in attempting to preserve racial preferences and in promoting the educational benefits of diversity.[68]

Another example is the knee-jerk assumption of guilt by faculty and administrators when three Duke University lacrosse players were accused of raping and assaulting a black woman in 2006.[69] Because the leftist political cultural of the university has become conventionalized, expressions deploring the racism and sexism of the players could be counted on as good career moves, even when they turned out to be false. Adopting conventional views on race and ethnicity is a *sine qua non* for a career as a mainstream intellectual or in the political arena.

As Frank Salter has pointed out, whites who fail to attend to the interests of their wider kinship group benefit themselves and their families at the expense of their own ethnic interests.[70] This is especially true for elite whites—people whose intelligence, power, and wealth could make a very large difference in culture and politics. They are in effect sacrificing millions of ethnic kin for the benefit of themselves and their immediate family.

This is a disastrously wrongheaded choice by the standard measures of evolutionary success. However, because our evolved psychology is much more attuned to individual and family interests than to the interests of the ethnic group or race, whites who benefit economically or professionally from adopting conventional views on race and ethnicity are unlikely to feel unease at the psychological level.

Another problem is that part of our evolved psychology is designed to emulate and look up to socially dominant people, especially if they look like us. A critical component of the success of the culture of critique is that it achieved control of the most prestigious and influential

---

[66] Francis 2002.
[67] Guzzardi 2004.
[68] Coleman 2006.
[69] Skube 2006.
[70] Salter 2003/2006.

institutions of the West, and it became a consensus among elites, Jewish and non-Jewish alike.[71] Once this happened, it is not surprising that this culture became widely accepted among people of very different levels of education and among people of different social classes.

Although changing the structure of material benefits is doubtless critical for advancing white ethnic interests, we should also pay attention to the psychological level, because this too plays an important role. Adopting conventional views on race and ethnicity not only confers material benefits, it confers psychological benefits. On the other hand, dissenting from these views carries huge costs. White elites who turn their back on their own ethnic group are likely to be massively reinforced within the contemporary explicit culture, while those who attempt to advance white interests can expect to suffer rather intense psychological costs. The massive social approval University of Michigan president Mary Sue Coleman receives within the culture of the university for her positions on diversity issues is doubtless a positive component of her job.

In large measure, the reason for this lies in the same psychological system discussed previously—Conscientiousness. Thus far, I have stressed the importance of Conscientiousness for inhibiting our natural tendencies in the service of long-term payoffs and fitting into the wider cultural context. However, people who are high on Conscientiousness also tend to be deeply concerned about their reputation.

This is no accident. In fact, developing a good reputation is an important way for conscientious people to get long-term payoffs. Think of it this way. If I cheat someone, I get a short-term gain at the expense of developing a bad reputation. The only way I can continue to survive is to prey on others who don't know my reputation, and that means moving on and interacting with strangers, not friends and allies. On the other hand, if I cooperate with someone we both gain, and I develop a reputation as a cooperator that may last a lifetime. In the long run, therefore, I will be better off. Conscientious people are cooperators, and as a result they are vitally concerned about their reputation. Recent theoretical work has shown that having access to people's reputation is likely to be a necessary condition for the evolution of cooperation.[72]

Information on the reputation of individuals constitutes a collective memory of the past history of individuals and is made possible by lan-

---

[71] See *The Culture of Critique*, ch. 6.
[72] Milinski, Semmann, and Krambeck 2002; Mohtashemi and Mui 2003; Semmann, Krambeck, and Milinski 2005; Smith 2005.

guage—that is, explicit representations of the past history of individuals in cooperative situations.[73] Without such explicit information on reputation, cooperators would be at an evolutionary disadvantage and vulnerable to a strategy of short-term exploitation rather than long-term cooperation with like-minded others. This explicit information on reputation is therefore processed by the higher brain centers located in the prefrontal cortex linked to Conscientiousness.

I am suggesting, therefore, that evolutionary pressure for cooperation is a critical adaptive function accounting for the evolution of Conscientiousness. Psychological research shows that people high in Conscientiousness are responsible, dependable, dutiful, and reliable. Indeed, responsibility emerges as a facet (i.e., subcategory) of Conscientiousness defined as cooperative, dependable, being of service to others, and contributing to community and group projects.[74] These traits are also highly correlated with honesty, morality, and behavior as a moral exemplar.

Thus Conscientiousness not only makes us better able to inhibit natural impulses like ethnocentrism, it also makes us more concerned about our reputation. We want to fit into the community and we want to be known as cooperators, not cheaters. At the opposite end are sociopaths. Sociopaths are at the low end of Conscientiousness. They take advantage of people for short-term gains and care nothing about developing a reputation as honest and trustworthy. After they prey on one victim, they must move on to an area where their reputation is not known.

Obviously, Conscientiousness as defined above is a pillar of human civilization and cultural life. Perhaps paradoxically, this is especially so in the individualistic cultures of the West. Western cultures tend toward individualism, whereas most of the rest of the world is much more collectivist and oriented toward the extended family (see the next chapter). Individualism is associated with all of the markers of modernization in the West—the nuclear family, economic individualism, science, democratic and republican forms of government, and moral universalism.[75] To this set of traits, Francis Fukuyama also adds trust as a critical virtue of individualist societies.[76]

---

[73] Mohtashemi and Mui 2003; see also Panchanathan and Boyd 2003.
[74] Roberts et al. 2005.
[75] See ch. 9 above "What Makes Western Culture Unique?" and *The Culture of Critique*, Preface to the paperback edition.
[76] Fukuyama 1995.

Trust is really a way of emphasizing the importance of moral universalism as a trait of individualist societies. In collectivist, family-oriented societies, trust ends at the border of the family and kinship group. Social organization, whether in political culture or in economic enterprise, tends to be a family affair. Morality is defined as what is good for the group—typically the kinship group (e.g., the notorious line, "Is it good for the Jews?"). This lack of ability to develop a civil society is the fundamental problem of societies in the Middle East and Africa, where divisions into opposing religious and ultimately kinship groups define the political landscape. The movement of the West toward multiculturalism really means the end of individualist Western culture.[77]

In individualist cultures, on the other hand, organizations include non-family members in positions of trust. Morality is defined in terms of universal moral principles that are independent of kinship connections or group membership. Trust therefore is of critical importance to individualist society. And fundamentally trust is about building a trustworthy reputation—for example, a reputation for honest dealing not only with fellow kinsmen, but with others as well. It follows that European-derived people are particularly prone to being concerned with reputation. In the individualistic societies in which they evolved, cooperation (and therefore success) resulted from having a good reputation, not from having extensive kinship relations.

There are obviously great benefits to trust and to the wider psychological system of Conscientiousness. The suite of traits associated with individualism is the basis of Western modernization. Relying on the good reputation of others is a key ingredient to building cooperative civil societies capable of rising above amoral familism.

The downside, however, is that conscientious people become so concerned about their reputations that they become conformists. Once the intellectual and political left had won the day, a large part of its success was that it dominated the moral and intellectual high ground related to issues of race and ethnicity. The culture of critique had become conventionalized and a pillar of the intellectual establishment. People who dissented from this leftist consensus were faced with a disastrous loss of reputation—nothing less than psychological agony.

There are many examples showing the power of this mechanism. Over sixty years ago Anne Morrow Lindbergh became one of the first victims of the modern version of political correctness when her hus-

---

[77] *The Culture of Critique*, ch. 8.

band, Charles Lindbergh, stated that Jews were one of the forces attempting to get the United States to enter World War II. Shortly after his speech, she wrote:

> The storm is beginning to blow up hard. . . . I sense that this is the beginning of a fight and consequent loneliness and isolation that we have not known before. . . . For I am really much more attached to the worldly things than he is, mind more giving up friends, popularity, etc., mind much more criticism and coldness and loneliness. . . . Will I be able to shop in New York at all now? I am always stared at—but now to be stared at with hate, to walk through aisles of hate![78]

What is striking, and perhaps counterintuitive, is that the guilt and shame remain even when she is completely satisfied at an intellectual level that her beliefs are based on good evidence and reasonable inferences, and are morally justifiable. She writes:

> I cannot explain my revulsion of feeling by logic. Is it my lack of courage to face the problem? Is it my lack of vision and seeing the thing through? Or is my intuition founded on something profound and valid? I do not know and am only very disturbed, which is upsetting for him. I have the greatest faith in him as a person   in his integrity, his courage, and his essential goodness, fairness, and kindness—his nobility really. . . . How then explain my profound feeling of grief about what he is doing? If what he said is the truth (and I am inclined to think it is), why was it wrong to state it?

Her reaction is involuntary and irrational—beyond the reach of logical analysis. Charles Lindbergh was exactly right in what he said, but a rational understanding of the correctness of his analysis cannot lessen the psychological trauma to his wife, who must face the hostile stares of others. The trauma is the result of the power of the Conscientiousness system in leading to loss of reputation resulting from breaching the cultural taboo against discussing Jewish influence.

I've had similar experiences, on a much smaller scale, resulting from attacks on me at the university where I work.[79] As with Anne Morrow Lindbergh's concern about going shopping in New York, the

---

[78] Lindbergh 1980, 220–30.
[79] MacDonald 2006b.

most difficult thing is dealing with loss of reputation in my face-to-face world at the university. And it's not just that it's in the face-to-face world of everyday life. It's that the areas of nonconformity on race and ethnicity have huge moral overtones. If one dissents from the reigning theory of macroeconomics or the main influences on nineteenth-century French Romanticism, one may be viewed as a bit eccentric or perhaps none too smart. But one is not likely to be subjected to torrents of moral outrage.

Given that academics tend to be Conscientious types, it's not surprising that academics are generally loath to do or say things that might endanger their reputation. This is at least ironic, because it conflicts with the image of academics as fearless seekers of truth. Unlike politicians, who must continue to curry favor with the public in order to be reelected, and unlike media figures, who have no job protection, academics with tenure have no excuse for not being willing to endure labels such as "anti-Semite" or "racist" in order to pursue truth. Part of the job—and a large part of the rationale for tenure in the first place—is that they are supposed to be willing to take unpopular positions: to forge ahead using all that brain power and expertise to chart new territories that challenge the popular wisdom.

But that image of academia is simply not based in reality. Consider, for example, an article that appeared almost two months after the publication of John Mearsheimer and Stephen Walt's famous essay on the Israel lobby,[80] appropriately titled "A Hot Paper Muzzles Academia."[81]

> Instead of a roiling debate, most professors not only agreed to disagree but agreed to pretend publicly that there was no disagreement at all. At Harvard and other schools, the Mearsheimer-Walt paper proved simply too hot to handle—and it revealed an academia deeply split yet lamentably afraid to engage itself on one of the hottest political issues of our time. Call it the academic Cold War: distrustful factions rendered timid by the prospect of mutually assured career destruction.
>
> Professors refused to take a stand on the paper, either in favor or against. As one Ivy League professor noted, "A lot of [my colleagues] were more concerned about the academic politics of it, and where they should come down, in that sense." Sadly, there is now a great deal of

---

[80] Mearsheimer and Walt 2006.
[81] Fairbanks 2006.

evidence that academics in general are careful to avoid controversy or do much of anything that will create hostility. In fact, some researchers are pointing to this fact to question whether tenure is justified. A recent survey of the attitudes of 1,004 professors at elite universities illustrates this quite clearly.[82] Regardless of their rank, professors rated their colleagues as

> reluctant to engage in activities that ran counter to the wishes of colleagues. Even tenured full professors believed [other full professors] would invoke academic freedom only "sometimes" rather than "usually" or "always"; they chose confrontational options "rarely," albeit more often than did lower ranked colleagues. . . . Their willingness to self-limit may be due to a desire for harmony and/or respect for the criticisms of colleagues whose opinions they value. Thus, the data did not support the depiction of Professorus Americanus as unleashed renegade.

Seen in this context, the reaction to the Mearsheimer and Walt paper makes a lot of sense. As one professor noted, "People might debate it if you gave everyone a get-out-of-jail-free card and promised that afterward everyone would be friends."[83] This intense desire to be accepted and liked by one's colleagues is certainly understandable. Striving for a good reputation is part of our nature, especially for the conscientious among us. Ostracism and moral condemnation from others in one's face-to-face world trigger guilt feelings. These are automatic responses resulting ultimately from the importance of fitting into a group that were developed over evolutionary time. This is especially so in the individualistic cultures of the West, where having a good reputation beyond the borders of the kinship group forms the basis of trust and civil society, and where having a poor reputation would have resulted in ostracism and evolutionary death.

As shown by the example of Anne Morrow Lindbergh, being able to defend rationally the ideas and attitudes that bring moral condemnation is not sufficient to defuse the complex negative emotions brought on by this form of ostracism. One might think that just as the prefrontal control areas can inhibit ethnocentric impulses originating in the subcortex, we should be able to inhibit these primitive guilt feelings. After all, the guilt feelings ultimately result from absolutely normal attitudes of ethnic

---

[82] Ceci et al. 2006.
[83] Fairbanks 2006.

identity and interests that have been delegitimized as a result of the erection of the culture of critique in the West. It should be therapeutic to understand that this culture was instituted by people who typically retained a strong sense of their own ethnic identity and interests. And it should help assuage guilt feelings if we understand that this culture is now maintained by people seeking material advantages and psychological approval at the expense of their own ethnic interests. The guilt feelings are nothing more than the end result of ethnic warfare, pursued at the level of ideology and culture instead of on the battlefield.

Getting rid of guilt and shame, however, is certainly not an easy process. Psychotherapy for white people begins with an explicit understanding of the issues that allows us to act in our interests, even if we can't entirely control the negative feelings engendered by those actions.

Evolutionary theorist Robert Trivers has proposed that the emotion of guilt is a sign to the group that a person will mend his ways and behave in the future. Shame, on the other hand, functions as a display of submission to people higher in the dominance hierarchy. From that perspective, a person who is incapable of shame or guilt even for obvious transgressions is literally a sociopath—someone who has no desire to fit into group norms. As noted above, sociopaths are at the low end of Conscientiousness, and there was doubtless strong selection against sociopathy in the small groups that we evolved in, especially among the individualistic peoples of the West. The trustworthy cooperators with excellent reputations won the day.

CONCLUSION

I think that evolutionists have not been properly sensitive to the enormous gulf between humans and animals resulting from human general intelligence and the Conscientiousness system. At a very broad level, the Conscientiousness system allows our behavior to come under the control of the surrounding culture. We make complex appraisals of how our behavior will affect us given the current cultural milieu. Potential murderers may think about the possibility of leaving DNA evidence and what types of plea bargains might be possible if they are caught. Potential thought criminals must assess the risks to their livelihood and their reputation in their face-to-face world.

But it gets more complicated than that. Modern humans are exposed to an often bewildering array of cultural messages that affect how they see the world. These messages are often directed at the explicit processing system, and they may be influenced by a wide range of competing interests. For example, it is a commonplace that media images have important effects on behavior even though people are often unaware that their behavior is influenced by the images.[84] These images are often engineered by advertisers who are consciously attempting to influence the recipients of the messages in ways that conform to the advertisers' interests, not those of the audience. More important, media messages shape the discussion of issues related to white identity and interests. The culture of critique has become the explicit culture of the West, endlessly repeated in media messages but packaged differently for people of different levels of intelligence and education, and for people with different interests and from different subcultures.[85] The message of this paper is that by programming the higher areas of the brain, this explicit culture is able to control the implicit ethnocentric tendencies of white people. In attempting to find a way out of this morass, therefore, changing the explicit culture is critical. It won't be easy, but I suggest that the first step is a psychological one: Proud and confident explicit assertions of ethnic identity and interests among white people, and the creation of communities where such explicit assertions are considered normal and natural rather than a reason for ostracism. The fact that such assertions appeal to our implicit psychology is certainly an asset. It's always easier to go with a natural tendency than to oppose it. And in this case, opposing our natural ethnocentric tendencies by using our quintessentially human prefrontal inhibitory control against our own ethnic interests is nothing less than collective suicide.

---

[84] Wilson 2002.
[85] *The Culture of Critique*, Preface to first paperback edition.

Chapter 11

BIOLOGICAL ROOTS OF ETHNOCENTRISM AND GROUP CONFLICT[*]

Frank Salter presents a powerful case for the adaptiveness of ethnocentrism.[1] Different human ethnic groups and races have been separated for thousands of years, and during this period they have evolved some genetic distinctiveness. This genetic distinctiveness constitutes a storehouse of genetic interest.

In other words, people have an interest in their ethnic group in exactly the same way that parents have a genetic interest in raising their children: In raising their children, parents ensure that their unique genes are passed on to the next generation. But in defending ethnic interests, people are doing the same thing—ensuring that the genetic uniqueness of their ethnic group is passed into the next generation. When parents of a particular ethnicity succeed in rearing their children, their ethnic group also succeeds because the genetic uniqueness of their ethnic group is perpetuated as part of their child's genetic inheritance. But when an ethnic group succeeds in defending its interests, individual members of the ethnic group also succeed because the genetic uniqueness that they share with other members of the ethnic group is passed on. This is the case even for people who don't have children: A person succeeds genetically when his ethnic group as a whole prospers.

A quick look at the historical record shows that conflict between tribal groups has been common throughout human history. Cooperative defense by tribal peoples is universal and ancient, and it is bound to have boosted the genetic fitness of those who acted to further the interests of their group. Under such circumstances it would be odd indeed if natural selection did not mold the human mind to be predisposed to ethnocentrism. Of course, this fact does not tell us what psychological mechanisms actually evolved to promote ethnocentrism or how these mechanisms can be controlled by inhibitory mechanisms located in the prefrontal cortex. For that, we will have to turn to empirical research.

---

[*] First published (as the Appendix of ch. 10 above) in *The Occidental Quarterly* 6 (Winter 2006–2007): 7–46.
[1] Salter 2003/2006.

GENETIC SIMILARITY THEORY: BIRDS OF A FEATHER FLOCK TOGETHER

J. Philippe Rushton's Genetic Similarity Theory (GST) is a biological/genetic theory aimed at explaining positive assortment on a variety of traits in friendships, marriage, and alliance formation.[2] Friends, spouses, and the other people we make alliances with are more like us than people selected at random. At the psychological level, the same mechanisms that influence these choices may well also be involved in positive attitudes toward people in the same ethnic group.

People not only assort positively for a wide variety of traits, they do so most on traits that are more heritable—that is, the traits that have a relatively strong genetic influence. This means that when you select a genetically similar spouse, your children are more similar to you than they would be if (God forbid!) you had chosen your spouse at random. Moreover, identical twins have more similar spouses and friends than do fraternal twins. Genetic differences therefore influence the tendency to assort with similar others.[3] In other words, some of us are more attracted to genetically similar spouses and friends than others, and this tendency is influenced genetically.

The implication is that when there is a choice to be made, whether in marriage, friendship, or another type of alliance, all things being equal, we are more likely to choose similar others as a way of enhancing the benefits of relationships and lessening the risks. Obviously, being of the same race is a very important basis of similarity. In the previous chapter, I described what I call implicit white communities: communities, such as NASCAR and country music fandom in the United States, where the vast majority of participants are white but not necessarily self-consciously so. That is, white people choose to be among people who are white like themselves, but they don't necessarily think of their choice as resulting from a conscious desire to be part of a white community. At the psychological level, GST is probably the best explanation for this phenomenon.

SOCIAL IDENTITY MECHANISMS: OUR TEAM IS BETTER (AND SMARTER AND MORE MORAL) THAN YOUR TEAM

An early form of social identity theory was stated by William Graham Sumner, a pioneer evolutionary anthropologist, in 1906:

---

[2] Rushton 1989, 1999.
[3] Rushton and Bons 2005.

Loyalty to the group, sacrifice for it, hatred and contempt for outsiders, brotherhood within, warlikeness without—all grow together, common products of the same situation. It is sanctified by connection with religion. Men of an others-group are outsiders with whose ancestors the ancestors of the we-group waged war. . . . Each group nourishes its own pride and vanity, boasts itself superior, exalts its own divinities, and looks with contempt on outsiders. Each group thinks its own folkways the only right ones, and if it observes that other groups have other folkways, these excite its scorn.[4]

Psychological research shows that people are highly prone to identifying themselves with ingroups. And once in a group, people tend to exaggerate the positive traits of ingroup members, and they exaggerate the homogeneity of their ingroup on these positive traits ("we're smart and we have high moral standards"). On the other hand, people tend to have negative stereotypes of the outgroup and are even more likely to exaggerate the extent to which outgroup members share these negative traits ("they're stupid and dishonest").[5] Of course, in some cases, these stereotypes may have a lot of truth to them.

There is good evidence that social identity processes are a psychological adaptation designed by natural selection for competition between groups. William Graham Sumner would not be surprised that modern research shows that these group dynamics are cross-cultural universals. Similar results are found across subjects of different ages, nationalities, and social classes, and can even be seen in very young children.[6] Anthropological evidence indicates the universality of the tendency to view one's own group as superior[7] and to denigrate outgroups. As anthropologist D. L. Horowitz notes, "in one country after another, other ethnic groups are described in unflattering or disparaging terms."[8]

Note that even though social identity processes are an evolutionary adaptation, they do not work by assessing genetic differences between groups. Instead, the important thing is that people be in different groups. A good example would be World War II era intra-service rivalries—as reflected in barroom brawls between soldiers and sailors.

---

[4] Sumner 1906, 13.
[5] For example, Brewer and Brown 1998; Fiske 1998.
[6] Bourhis 1994.
[7] Vine 1987.
[8] Horowitz 1985, 7.

There may be no genetic differences at all between the two teams, or both teams may be a mixture of different ethnic groups, but social identity mechanisms still make us think highly of our team and not so highly of the opposition. In fact, some evolutionary psychologists have proposed using this feature of our psychology to deemphasize the importance of race as a category.[9]

INDIVIDUALISM/COLLECTIVISM: INDIVIDUALISM IS THE BASIS OF WESTERN MODERNIZATION

Even though identifying with groups is a universal tendency, there are some important differences. Western cultures tend toward individualism, whereas most of the rest of the world is much more collectivist in its outlook.[10]

Individualist cultures show little emotional attachment to ingroups. Personal goals are paramount, and socialization emphasizes the importance of self-reliance, independence, individual responsibility, and "finding yourself."[11]

Individualists have more positive attitudes toward strangers and outgroup members and are more likely to behave in a pro-social, altruistic manner to strangers (e.g., white medical missionaries to Africa).[12]

Individualism is linked to a suite of traits that together form the basis of Western modernization: the nuclear family, bilateral kinship patterns, monogamy, moral universalism, civil societies based on trust and reputation rather than kinship connections, relative lack of ethnocentrism and group orientation, and science.[13] Collectivist cultures typical of the Middle East, China, India, and Africa have the opposite suite of traits. Most centrally these societies are based on extended kinship and tribal relationships. An illustrative contrast between individualist and collectivist societies is in the area of moral reasoning. In collectivist societies, morality is defined in terms of whether an action satisfies obligations within the family or kinship group, whereas in individualist societies, morality is thought of as satisfying abstract notions of justice. The moral implications of the individualism/collectivism distinction

---

[9] Cosmides, Tooby, and Kurzban 2003.
[10] See ch. 9 above, "What Makes Western Culture Unique?" and *The Culture of Critique*, Preface to the paperback edition.
[11] Triandis 1991, 82.
[12] Triandis 1990, 61.
[13] See ch. 9 above, "What Makes Western Culture Unique?" and *The Culture of Critique*, Preface to the paperback edition.

can be seen by a study contrasting India (a collectivist culture) and the United States (an individualist culture). Young adults and children are asked what they would do in the following situation:

> Ben was in Los Angeles on business. When his meetings were over, he went to the train station. Ben planned to travel to San Francisco in order to attend the wedding of his best friend. He needed to catch the very next train if he was to be on time for the ceremony, as he had to deliver the wedding rings. However, Ben's wallet was stolen in the train station. He lost all of his money as well as his ticket to San Francisco. Ben approached several officials as well as passengers at the train station and asked them to loan him money to buy a new ticket. But, because he was a stranger, no one was willing to lend him the money he needed. While Ben was sitting on a bench trying to decide what to do next, a well-dressed man sitting next to him walked away for a minute. Looking over at where the man had been sitting, Ben noticed that the man had left his coat unattended. Sticking out of the man's coat pocket was a train ticket to San Francisco. Ben knew that he could take the ticket and use it to travel to San Francisco on the next train. He also saw that the man had more than enough money in his coat pocket to buy another train ticket.[14]

Indian subjects were more than twice as likely to decide to take the ticket in order to fulfill their family obligation (around 80 percent to 40 percent). Children in the United States, on the other hand, tended to say that the man should not steal the train ticket because stealing violates principles of justice that apply to everyone. For children from India, morality is defined by the needs of the family. For children in the United States, morality is defined more by abstract principles of justice.

Individualism forms the basis of Western success, but it also implies that the control of ethnocentrism among white people is relatively easy. As discussed in the previous chapter, this does not imply that white people lack ethnocentrism. But it does imply that controlling ethnocentrism among whites is easier because they are relatively less attached to their people and culture than the vast majority of other humans.

Individualism/collectivism is very likely to have a biological basis because of its widespread ramifications in the areas of kinship relationships, marriage, and the development of civil societies that define Western modernization. My theory is that this suite of traits is the result

---

[14] Miller and Bersoff 1992, 545.

of a long history of evolution in northern climates.[15]

IS THERE A "HUMAN KINDS" MODULE?

People have a natural tendency to place themselves in groups and to think highly of their ingroup and denigrate outgroups. These groups can range from groups that are arbitrarily chosen by psychologists, to bowling leagues, football teams, and religious groups. But in general, some groups seem to have much more of an emotional pull than others. Psychologists may indeed find discrimination against outgroups in arbitrarily composed groups, but people are not going to lay down their lives for an arbitrarily chosen group, not even for their bowling team. College students identify with their college or fraternity and denigrate other colleges and fraternities, but few students would incur a huge cost in doing so. On the other hand, ethnic, religious, and patriotic emotions run deep, and it is not at all uncommon for people to make the ultimate sacrifice on behalf of these groups.

This raises the question of whether race and ethnicity are natural categories. If so, people would have a natural tendency to classify themselves into ingroups and outgroups on the basis of these categories. And they would tend to have stronger allegiance to these groups than, say, their stamp collecting club. These mechanisms would also make these groups more emotionally compelling. People would have more of a tendency to become emotionally involved in these groups than in garden-variety groupings: For example, we would get more psychological satisfaction in being accepted by the racial or ethnic group, and we would be more distressed at the possibility of being ostracized from the racial or ethnic group. The deep and seemingly ineradicable attachments that so many people have to their ethnic groups strongly suggest that there is indeed a human kinds module that automatically places people in racial categories. Such a module might also result in automatic negative emotions toward racial outgroups. As described below, even relatively non-ethnocentric white people have an attachment to their race, albeit rather rudimentary and unconscious.

To date, research has focused on whether race and ethnicity are natural categories. Since the official ideology is that race is nothing more than a social construct, it is not surprising that there is a great deal of controversy on this issue.[16] In fact it often seems that a great deal of politically correct intellectual energy is put into trying to prove that

---

[15] See ch. 9 above, "What Makes Western Culture Unique?"

[16] Discussed in MacDonald 2001.

Mother Nature could not possibly have made race or ethnicity a natural category. Some argue that people could not possibly have a human kinds module, because prior to the modern world of long-distance transportation they would not have come into contact with other races or ethnic groups.[17] In fact, long distance migrations over several generations did indeed bring people with different physical appearance into contact with each other.[18] This sort of repeated contact with outsiders would allow the evolution of a module specialized to detect and respond to racial and ethnic differences.

Another politically correct proposal is that people are "fooled" into thinking that ethnic and racial groups are real because they superficially resemble animal species.[19] Like animal species, ethnic groups marry among themselves and membership is by descent. (One can't just decide to be, say, Japanese.) According to this theory, the mistake is to think that races and ethnic groups really are like animal species.

Another theory argues that there is a human kinds module that evolved for categories like sex and age, but not race. Since all humans would have been exposed to the categories of sex and age over evolutionary time, there would be a module that these categories are essential to people's identity and can't be changed. However, this module is "fooled" into thinking that different races and ethnic groups are also natural human kinds.[20]

But of course, ethnic groups do show genetic differences from each other, and they typically look different from each other. The mistake is to deny the reality of genetically based racial and ethnic differences and to simply dismiss the possibility that humans would have been repeatedly exposed to different groups over evolutionary time so that indeed racial and ethnic differences would be a natural trigger for this module.

My view is that in fact we do have a human kinds module designed not simply to categorize people in terms of a variety of natural categories such as men, women, and children, but to specifically categorize people as belonging to different racial/ethnic groups.[21] Even at very early ages children view race in more essentialist terms than either occupation or body build—that is, they see it as inherited and an impor-

---

[17] For example, Cosmides, Tooby, and Kurzban 2003.

[18] Henry Harpending, Department of Anthropology, University of Utah, personal communication, June 28, 2002.

[19] Gilwhite 2001.

[20] Hirschfeld 1996, 197.

[21] MacDonald 2001.

tant part of a person's identity. We can change our body build or our occupation, but not our race.

Race and ethnicity have all the features of an evolved module. Processing of racial and ethnic differences is rapid, unconscious, and automatic—all characteristics of implicit processing and hallmarks of evolved modules.[22] Social psychology experiments show that subjects respond differently to faces of racial ingroups and outgroups.[23] For example, subjects are better able to recall the faces of people from their own race.[24] Subjects are also quicker to classify pictures of racial outgroup members than ingroup members.[25]

There is good evidence that people have a natural fear of snakes and spiders because of our evolutionary past. So it's interesting that for white people, looking at photos of blacks triggers a fear response in the same way that pictures of snakes and spiders do.[26] The basic procedure is to show, say, a white subject various photos (flowers, black people, white people, snakes, automobiles), some of which are followed by a mild shock. After learning what will happen when the photos are presented, subjects anticipate the shock by showing a fear response as soon as the photo is presented. Then the shock is discontinued. The results are that even after the shock is discontinued white subjects show a fear reaction to photos of blacks and snakes, but not to whites or photos of harmless things like flowers that had been paired with shocks. This is consistent with the theory that whites have a natural fear of blacks (and snakes). The fact that they quickly stop fearing the picture of a flower when it is no longer paired with a shock means that we don't have a natural fear of flowers.

In another study, photos of racial ingroup and outgroup members were assessed by Functional Magnetic Resonance Imaging recordings. The results showed that the photos triggered responses in the amygdala, a subcortical region responsible for fear.[27] For example, white subjects had a stronger amygdala response to photos of blacks than to whites when the photos were presented too fast to be processed consciously. Under these circumstances, the photos are processed unconsciously by triggering the amygdala.

---

[22] Rothbart and Taylor 2001.
[23] Fiske 1998.
[24] Platz and Hosch 1988; Bothwell, Brigham, and Malpass 1989.
[25] Levin 1996; Valentine and Endo 1992.
[26] Olsson et al. 2005.
[27] Cunningham et al. 2004.

These studies are evidence that there is a natural fear of racial outgroups.[28] This evidence is not conclusive because it is conceivable that automatic negative attitudes of whites toward blacks could be learned by repeated bad experiences with blacks or because of repeated negative portrayals of blacks in the media. The mechanism could also work via early socialization: The type of people I see around me early in life are my racial ingroup. In fact, developmental data shows that preference for one's own race occurs by three months, but is not present at one month.[29] Moreover, babies have less of a preference for their own race if they are exposed to other races during this early period. If this is the case, then people would have a same-race preference under typical natural conditions. This mechanism could be "fooled," however, by exposure to other races during early infancy.

CONCLUSION

The evolutionary roots of ethnocentrism are unsettled, but we should be open to the idea that more than one mechanism is relevant.

1. Of the mechanisms reviewed here, Rushton's Genetic Similarity Theory has the most unequivocal empirical support. As indicated above, this mechanism is likely responsible for the implicit white communities discussed in the previous chapter.
2. There is also good evidence that social identity processes are a biological adaptation. But since they don't respond to genetic differences between groups, they are not really of use in ethnic defense unless the groups are already constituted on an ethnic basis.
3. Individualism/collectivism is also very likely to have a biological basis because of its widespread ramifications in the areas of kinship relationships, marriage, and the development of civil societies that define Western modernization. This suite of traits also makes sense as an ecological response of northern hunter-gatherer peoples to the conditions of the Ice Age.
4. The existence of a module sensitive to racial and ethnic ingroups and outgroups remains controversial, but I think the evidence is persuasive that such a module exists. Indeed, I think it's the only way to explain why ethnic emotions and allegiances are so intense and persistent, even in the modern world. The best evidence is that this module is programmed as a result of early experience during infancy.

---

[28] Öhman 2005.
[29] Bar-Haim et al. 2006; Kelly et al. 2005.

In any case, whatever the strength of the mechanisms underlying ethnocentrism reviewed here, these natural ethnocentric tendencies are insufficient to provide for ethnic defense of whites in the contemporary world—the argument made in the previous chapter.

Chapter 12

IMMIGRATION AND ETHNIC INTERESTS[*]

Arguments over immigration are usually limited to cultural or economic factors. Political scientists like Samuel Huntington point out that the culture of the country will change dramatically if there is a continued influx of Spanish-speaking immigrants.[1] And economists like George Borjas have demonstrated that large masses of newcomers depress wages and create enormous demands on the environment and on public services, especially health care and education.[2]

These lines of argument are, of course, legitimate. But there always seems to be an element of timidity present. No one wants to talk about the 800 pound gorilla sitting over there in the corner—the issue of ethnic interests.

Any attempt to bring up the ethnic issue is usually strangled in the cradle. Indeed, other lines of argument are frequently met by assertions that they are masking ethnic concerns. Thus immigration enthusiasts are quick to smear arguments that immigration will harm the environment as "the greening of hate."

This strategy has been highly effective—because, if there is one area where the intellectual left has won a complete and decisive victory, it is in pathologizing any consideration by the European majority of the United States of its own ethnic interests. By "pathologizing" I mean not only that people have been indoctrinated that their commonsense perceptions of race and ethnicity are "illusions," but, further, that the slightest assertion of ethnic self-interest or consciousness by the European majority of the United States is the sign of a grave moral defect—so grave that it is a matter of psychiatric concern.

Of course, this is hypocritical. While assertions of ethnic interest by Europeans are stigmatized, assertions of ethnic interest by other groups are utterly commonplace. Mexican activists loudly advertise their goal of reconquering the Southwestern United States via immigration from Mexico—which would obviously be in the ethnic interests of Mexicans

---

[*] First published as "Immigration and the Unmentionable Question of Ethnic Interests," www.vdare.com, October 27, 2004.
[1] Huntington 2005.
[2] Borjas 1999.

but would presumably harm the interests of European-Americans. Jewish organizations, in the forefront of the intellectual and political battle to pathologize the ethnic interests of European Americans, have simultaneously been deeply involved in organizing coalitions of minority ethnic groups to assert their political interests in Congress and in the workplace. Plus Jewish efforts on behalf of their ethnic brethren in Israel are famous—and remarkably effective.

I believe we should get rid of the hypocrisy and discuss ethnic interests openly and honestly.

Until recently, ethnic interests were understood intuitively by everyone. People have an interest, or "stake" in their ethnic group in exactly the same way that parents have a genetic interest in raising their children. By bringing up my children, I ensure that my unique genes are passed on to the next generation. This is the fundamental principle of Darwin's theory of evolution. But in defending my ethnic interests, I am doing the same thing—ensuring that the genetic uniqueness of my ethnic group is passed into the next generation.

And this is the case even if I don't have children myself: I succeed genetically when my ethnic group as a whole prospers.

A major step forward in the scientific analysis of ethnicity is Frank Salter's book *On Genetic Interests: Family, Ethny, and Humanity in an Age of Mass Migration*.[3] Salter's basic purpose is to quantify how much genetic overlap people in the same ethnic group or race share, as compared to people from different ethnic groups or races.

Different human ethnic groups and races have been separated for thousands of years. During this period, they have evolved some genetic distinctiveness.

But, Salter notes, measuring these differences is now a straightforward process, thanks to the work of researchers like Luigi Cavalli-Sforza, whose book *The History and Geography of Human Genes* documents the genetic distances between human groups.[4]

It turns out that the distances between human populations correspond approximately to what a reasonably well-informed historian or demographer or tourist would expect. For instance, Scandinavians have greater overlap of genetic interests with other Scandinavians than other Europeans. Europeans have a greater genetic interest in other Europeans than in Africans.

In fact, on average, people are as closely related to other members

---

[3] Salter 2003/2006.
[4] Cavalli-Sforza 1999.

of their ethnic group, versus the rest of the world, as they are closely related to their grandchildren, versus the rest of their ethnic group.

Salter suggests we think of it this way: citing authors like Garrett Hardin and E. O. Wilson, he argues that we can't just keep on expanding our numbers and usage of resources indefinitely. If immigrants contribute to the economy in ways that the native population cannot, the national carrying capacity is raised. But if they are a drain on resources or even of average productivity, they must take the place of potential native-born in the ultimate total population. It's a zero-sum game.

Let's suppose that immigrants have equal capacities to the native born. Then if 10,000 Danes emigrate to England and ultimately substitute for 10,000 English natives, the average Englishman loses the genetic equivalent of 167 children (or siblings) in the ultimate total population. Because of the close genetic relationship between Denmark and England, this is not a great loss.

However, if 10,000 Bantu emigrate to England and substitute for 10,000 English natives, the average Englishman loses the genetic equivalent of 10,854 children (or siblings).

And, of course, it works the opposite way as well: If 10,000 English emigrate to a Bantu territory and substitute for 10,000 Bantu natives, the average Bantu loses the equivalent of 10,854 children (or siblings).

This is a staggering loss. Small wonder that people tend to resist the immigration of others into their territory. At stake is an enormous family of close relatives. And history is replete with examples of displacement migration—for example, Europeans displacing Native Americans, Jews displacing Palestinians in Israel, Albanians displacing Serbs from Kosovo.

All of the losers in these struggles would have been better off genetically and every other way if they had prevented the immigration of the group that eventually came to dominate the area.

Nevertheless, the big story of immigration since World War II is that wealthy Western societies, with economic opportunities and a high level of public goods such as medical care and education, have become magnets for immigration from around the world. Because of this immigration, and high fertility among many immigrant ethnic groups, the result is rapid displacement of the founding populations, not only in the United States, but also in Australia, Belgium, Canada, France, The Netherlands, Germany, and Italy.

If present trends continue, the United States' founding European-derived population is set to become a minority by the middle of this century. In the British Isles, the submergence date is just two generations later, around 2100.

European populations that are allowing themselves to be displaced are playing a very dangerous game—dangerous because the long history of ethnic strife furnishes them no guarantees about the future. Throughout history there has been a propensity for majority ethnic groups to oppress minorities. A glance at Jewish history is sufficient to make clear the dangers faced by an ethnic group that does not have a state and political apparatus to protect its interests.

It does not take an overactive imagination to see how coalitions of minority groups could compromise the interests of formerly dominant European groups. We already see numerous examples where coalitions of minority groups attempt to influence public policy against the interests of the European majority—for example, "affirmative action" hiring quotas and immigration policy.

Besides coalitions of ethnic minorities, the main danger facing Europeans is that wealthy, powerful European elites are often unaware of, or do not value, their own ethnic interests. Frequently, they in effect sell out their own ethnic groups for short-run personal gain. There are many contemporary examples, most notably the efforts by major corporations to import low wage workers and outsource jobs to foreign countries.

Of course, these elite Westerners are the last to suffer personally from ethnic replacement. They are able to live in gated communities and send their children to private schools. They are intensely interested in obtaining wealth and power in order to promote the interests of their immediate family or, sometimes, their social class. But they completely ignore their enormous family of ethnic kin.

This extreme individualism of Western elites is a tragic mistake for all ethnic Europeans—including the elites themselves, who are losing untold millions of ethnic kin by promoting mass immigration of non-Europeans. It is a case of putting short-run class interest and self-interest before long-run ethnic interest.

In the long run, globalism and multiculturalism are a threat to almost everyone's ethnic interest because both ideologies actually legitimize and increase ethnic competition. Globalism results in increased competition because everyone has potential access to everyone else's territory, opening opportunities for plundering another's backyard. Multicultural societies sanction ethnic mobilization because they inevitably become cauldrons of competing ethnic interests.

In this very dangerous game of ethnic competition, some ethnic groups are better prepared than others. Ethnic groups differ in intelligence and ability to control economic resources. They differ in their degree of ethnocentrism, in the extent to which they are mobilized to achieve group interests, and in how aggressively they behave toward other groups. They differ in their numbers and fertility and the extent to which they encourage responsible parenting. They differ in the amount of land and other resources held at any point in time and in their political power.

Given these differences, it is difficult at best to ensure peaceful relations among ethnic groups. Even maintaining a status quo in territory and resource control is very arduous, as can be seen by the ill-fated attempts of Americans to achieve an ethnic status quo with the 1924 immigration law. Accepting a status quo would not be in the interests of groups that have recently lost land or numbers. It would also likely be unacceptable both to groups with relatively low numbers and control of resources and, conversely, to high-fertility groups.

Yet the alternative—that all humans renounce their ethnic group loyalties—seems unrealistic and utopian.

Indeed, given that some ethnic groups, especially ones with high levels of ethnocentrism and mobilization, will undoubtedly continue to function as groups far into the foreseeable future, unilateral renunciation of ethnic loyalties by other groups means only their surrender and defeat and disappearance—the Darwinian dead end of extinction.

The future, then, like the past, will inevitably be a Darwinian competition. And ethnicity will play a crucial role.

Salter's conclusion: the best way to preserve ethnic interests is to defend an ethnostate—a political unit that is explicitly intended to preserve the ethnic interests of its citizens. Promoting ethnostates is not only fair, it also serves the interests of most peoples. All existing nations are vulnerable to displacement by highly mobilized ethnic minorities, especially if the minorities have high fertility.

As Frank Salter argues, a far better solution is to acknowledge everyone's right to live in a state dominated by one's own ethnic group.

This "universal nationalism" would allow people the right to live in an ethnostate that would protect their ethnic interests—and therefore, by extension, the genetic interests of the vast majority of the human race.

Chapter 13

WAS THE 1924 IMMIGRATION CUT-OFF "RACIST"?*

When Dr. Stephen Steinlight first advocated a change in the traditional Jewish support for open borders, his reflexive loathing of the 1920s legislative cut-off that ended the First Great Wave of immigration overwhelmed the logic of his argument.

He described the cut-off as "evil, xenophobic, anti-Semitic," "vilely discriminatory," a "vast moral failure," a "monstrous policy." And he dismissed the vast majority of pre-1965 Americans as a "thoughtless mob" because they supported a near-complete moratorium on immigration.[1]

Three years of arguing with Jewish groups about immigration reform have apparently not changed Steinlight's mind on this point. In his most recent monograph, his only reference to the 1924 Act is that "tens of thousands" of Jews might have been saved from the Holocaust "had the United States not closed its doors . . . ."[2]

The 1924 immigration cut-off enjoys an almost uniquely bad press. For instance, even Governor Richard Lamm, immigration reformer and hero of the Sierra Club insurgency, conceded in a National Public Radio debate that the 1924 legislation was motivated by racial bigotry.[3] In a panel discussion on immigration on MSNBC's Scarborough Country in 2004, Randall Hamud, an Arab-American activist, responded to Pat Buchanan, who had praised the effective 1924–1965 immigration moratorium: "He forgets that the earlier restrictions on immigration were racist-driven." But were the 1920s restrictions "racist-driven"? What, exactly does that mean? And could it be that the opponents of those restrictions had their own ethnic motivations? Motivations still to be found today?

Stephen Steinlight is a useful starting point because he is quite frank in his belief that the only legitimate consideration for immigration policy is his interpretation of Jewish collective interests.

---

* First published at www.vdare.com, June 19, 2004.
[1] Steinlight 2001.
[2] Steinlight 2004.
[3] http://www.vdare.com/letters/tl_032904.htm.

In my research on Jewish involvement in shaping immigration policy, I found that the organized Jewish community has been the most important force favoring unrestricted immigration to the United States. In doing so, the various entities involved have consistently acted to further their own perceived collective interests—interests that are arguably in conflict with those of the majority of Americans.

We shouldn't blanch at the thought of bringing up the issue of ethnic interests. We all accept that African American leaders like Jesse Jackson are pursuing their perceived ethnic interests. No one would deny that the Mexican-American pro-immigration activists advocating open borders are pursuing their ethnic interests. But somehow it's inappropriate or "racist" to bring up the fact that Jews and, yes, Europeans have ethnic interests too. And they are all equally legitimate.

By the time Jewish organizations and Jewish legislators sustained a (temporary) defeat over the 1921 and 1924 legislation, they had been at the forefront of frustrating the immigration restrictionists for over thirty years.

By 1905, a strong element of American opinion had turned against immigration. Even ethnic and religious groups that stood to gain by immigration, such as the Irish, were ambivalent, and anyway were poorly organized and ineffective in influencing policy.

At the time, pro-immigration activism was widely seen as a Jewish movement. University of Wisconsin sociologist Edward A. Ross stated in his 1914 book, *The Old World in the New*:

> The systematic campaign in newspapers and magazines to break down all arguments for restriction and to calm nativist fears is waged by and for one race. Hebrew money is behind the National Liberal Immigration League and its numerous publications. From the paper before the commercial body or the scientific association to the heavy treatise produced with the aid of the Baron de Hirsch Fund, the literature that proves the blessings of immigration to all classes in America emanates from subtle Hebrew brains.[4]

Throughout the entire period from the late nineteenth century to their eventual victory in 1965, Jewish pro-immigration efforts were characterized by strong leadership, generous funding, sophisticated lobbying techniques, well-chosen non-Jewish allies, and good timing. The most visible Jewish activists, such as Louis Marshall, were intel-

---

[4] Ross 1914.

lectually brilliant. They were enormously energetic and resourceful in their crusades on behalf of immigration as well as other Jewish causes.

This full court press exerted by Jewish organizations included intense and chilling scrutiny of immigration opponents, such as Senator Henry Cabot Lodge, and of organizations like the Immigration Restriction League. Lobbyists in Washington also kept a daily scorecard of voting tendencies as immigration bills wended their way through Congress. They engaged in intense and successful efforts to convince Presidents Taft and Wilson to veto restrictive immigration legislation.

Much of the effort was done more or less surreptitiously so as not to fan the flames of anti-Jewish sentiment. (Open anti-Jewish feelings were fairly common during this period, stemming from resentment at Jewish upward mobility, the great numbers of leftist political radicals in the immigrant Jewish community, and dislike of the newcomers' perceived strong ethnic sense.) Jewish organizations supplied the funding for pro-immigration organizations such as the National Liberal Immigration League and the Citizens Committee for Displaced Persons. Non-Jews from Eastern and Southern European countries were recruited to protest the effects of restrictionist legislation on immigration from those areas.

Why members of the Jewish community, which over so many centuries demonstrated such determination to preserve its distinctiveness, should have been so demonstrably active in preventing the preservation of the nation in which they find themselves, is an interesting question.

My hypothesis, advanced in several academic books: it is part of an evolutionary strategy aimed at advancing Jewish interests. As Leonard Glickman of the Hebrew Immigrant Aid Society has put it memorably: "The more diverse American society is, the safer [Jews] are."[5]

Of course, this does not involve all Jews, and some consciously reject it. But positive attitudes and activism aimed at ending the pre-1965 ethnic homogeneity of the United States have been typical of the entire Jewish political spectrum and all of the main Jewish activist organizations. These efforts were the driving force in favor of liberalized immigration up to the 1965 sea change in immigration law. This pattern continues into the present.

In the 1924 debates, the anti-restrictionists invariably alleged that their opponents saw the issue primarily in terms of "Nordic superiority." They complained that restrictionists viewed themselves as a superior ethnic group and argued that this view was immoral, and further-

---

[5] Cattan 2002.

more had no scientific basis.

Imputing motives of racial superiority had some plausibility because such ideas were certainly in the air. For example, in his popular 1916 book *The Passing of the Great Race*, Madison Grant argued that the American colonial stock was derived from superior Nordic racial elements and that immigration of other races would lower the competence level of the society.[6]

But in reality, the contentions the political champions of restriction actually made were quite different—and much more modest. Their basic argument was that, while all ethnic groups in the country had legitimate interests in immigration, the interests of the founding groups made restriction imperative.

The restrictionists actually went out of their way to deny that they believed they were racially superior to other groups. The *Congressional Record* reports the words of Representative William N. Vaile of Colorado, one of the most prominent restrictionists:

> Let me emphasize here that the restrictionists of Congress do not claim that the "Nordic" race, or even the Anglo-Saxon race, is the best race in the world. Let us concede, in all fairness that the Czech is a more sturdy laborer . . . that the Jew is the best businessman in the world, and that the Italian has . . . a spiritual exaltation and an artistic creative sense which the Nordic rarely attains. Nordics need not be vain about their own qualifications. It well behooves them to be humble.
>
> What we do claim is that the Northern European and particularly Anglo-Saxons made this country. Oh, yes; the others helped. But . . . [t]hey came to this country because it was already made as an Anglo-Saxon commonwealth. They added to it, they often enriched it, but they did not make it, and they have not yet greatly changed it.
>
> We are determined that they shall not. . . . It is a good country. It suits us. And what we assert is that we are not going to surrender it to somebody else or allow other people, no matter what their merits, to make it something different. If there is any changing to be done, we will do it ourselves.[7]

One is struck in reading the 1924 Congressional debate that, while virtually all of the anti-restrictionists raised the issue of Nordic racial

---

[6] Grant 1916.
[7] *Congressional Record*, April 8, 1924, 5922.

superiority, those in favor of the legislation rarely did.

After a particularly colorful comment in opposition to the theory of Nordic racial superiority, restrictionist leader Albert Johnson remarked that, "I would like very much to say on behalf of the committee that through the strenuous times of the hearings this committee undertook not to discuss the Nordic proposition or racial matters."[8] Several restrictionists explicitly denounced the theory of Nordic superiority. Clearly, the reformers did not see the concept as helpful to their cause.

What *can* be found in the statements of the reformers is actually fear of inferiority. Several representatives from the far West seem to have viewed the Japanese as racially equal or superior, not inferior. One senator stated, "we admit that [the Japanese] are as able as we are, that they are as progressive as we are, that they are as honest as we are, that they are as brainy as we are, and that they are equal in all that goes to make a great people and nation."[9] A congressman described the Japanese as "a relentless and unconquerable competitor of our people wherever he places himself."[10] Apparently, many restrictionists, far from feeling they were members of a superior ethnic group, worried that their people could not compete with Japanese and Chinese.

Nor did the restrictionists view Jews as intellectually inferior. During the 1920s quotas on Jewish admissions to Ivy League universities had become a controversial issue and a focus of Jewish defense organizations. As noted above, Congressman Vaile noted that Jews were "the best businessman in the world." A. Lawrence Lowell, President of Harvard and the national vice-president of the Immigration Restriction League, advocated quotas on Jewish admission to Harvard.

If anything, restrictionists were worried that the immigration of more Jews from Eastern Europe would result in even more competition between Jews and non-Jews.

And of course subsequent IQ research has shown their concerns to be sound—the average IQ of American Jews is well above the average for whites and is the highest of any known human group.

Restrictionists typically argued that maintaining the ethnic status quo would be fair to all ethnic groups currently in the country. This argument implicitly recognizes that different ethnic groups have different interests in immigration policy.

The restrictionists were concerned that immigration of people of

---

[8] *Congressional Record*, April 8, 1924, 5911.

[9] *Congressional Record*, April 18, 1924, 6614.

[10] *Congressional Record*, April 8, 1924, 5884.

other ethnic groups and cultures would ultimately deprive their own people of political and cultural power. They argued that the interests of other groups to pursue their ethnic interests by expanding their percentage of the population should be weighed against the ethnic interests of the majority, who naturally wanted to retain their ethnic representation in the population.

In the words of the House Majority Report,

> The use of the 1890 census is . . . an effort to preserve as nearly as possible, the racial status quo of the United States. It is hoped to guarantee as best we can at this late date, racial homogeneity in the United States. The use of a later census would discriminate against those who founded the Nation and perpetuated its institutions.[11]

The 1924 law also prescribed that, beginning in 1927, the national origins of the immigrants would match their percentage of the population. For example, if 10 percent of the country in 1920 came from Italy, then 10 percent of the annual quota of 150,000 immigrants would be reserved for Italian immigrants. Clearly this was an attempt to achieve an ethnic status quo.

In other words, in the 1920s, *both* sides were pursuing their perceived ethnic self-interest. Representative Scott Leavitt stated quite bluntly that Jews should respect the desire of other Americans to retain the ethnic status quo:

> The instinct for national and race preservation is not one to be condemned, as has been intimated here. No one should be better able to understand the desire of Americans to keep America American than the gentleman from Illinois [Mr. Sabath], who is leading the attack on this measure, or the gentlemen from New York, Mr. Dickstein, Mr. Jacobstein, Mr. Celler, and Mr. Perlman. They are of the one great historic people who have maintained the identity of their race throughout the centuries because they believe sincerely that they are a chosen people, with certain ideals to maintain, and knowing that the loss of racial identity means a change of ideals. That fact should make it easy for them and the majority of the most active opponents of this measure in the spoken debate to recognize and sympathize with our viewpoint, which is not so extreme as that of their own race, but only demands that the admixture of other peoples shall be

---

[11] *House Report No. 350*, 1924, 16.

only of such kind and proportions and in such quantities as will not alter racial characteristics more rapidly than there can be assimilation as to ideas of government as well as of blood.[12]

The House Committee was clearly annoyed that their motives were continually being cast in terms of Nordic superiority and racial discrimination—an interesting sensitivity to find so many years ago. But the 1924 law was clearly a victory for the Northwestern European peoples of the United States. It halted the substantial transformation of the country which had gotten under way over the previous thirty years.

Because of it, the groups dominant when it passed were still (at least superficially) dominant when the 1924 law was overthrown 41 years later.

Around the time the 1924 victory was won, however, a disaster was occurring elsewhere—on the intellectual front. Beginning in the 1920s, the intellectual and moral high ground in the debate was increasingly claimed by the anti-restrictionists.

This was made possible largely by the influence of Franz Boas and his school of anthropology.[13] The Boasians argued that the only differences among human groups are cultural differences, not biological.

Even in the early 1920s, as I have noted, the restrictionists hesitated to use arguments based on ethnic superiority and they were forced continually to deny that this was their rationale. In terms of my hypothesis, I have argued elsewhere that the Boasian School can be explained in terms of evolutionary strategy as merely another of a series of intellectual movements dominated by Jews and aimed at advancing Jewish interests. These movements were designed to combat anti-Semitism and to de-legitimize the ethnic interests of the European majority of the United States.[14]

What we are seeing now is the long-term consequence of these movements: The displacement of the European majority—and an increase in ethnic conflict.

Since the 1965 law opening up immigration on a large scale to all the peoples of the world, the United States has become a cauldron of competing racial and ethnic interests. Much of the conflict centers immigration and its consequences, ranging from Muslim women having unveiled photos on their drivers' licenses to the survival of Christian

---

[12] *Congressional Record*, April 12, 1924, 6265–66.

[13] *The Culture of Critique*, ch. 2.

[14] This is the thesis established in *The Culture of Critique*.

symbols in public schools.

This shift to "multiculturalism" has been facilitated by an enormous growth of immigration from non-European-derived peoples. Many of these immigrants come from non-Western countries where cultural and ethnic segregation is the norm. In contemporary America, they are now encouraged by public policy to retain their own languages and religions, and may well continue to marry within their group.

The long-term result is, inevitably, increased competition and friction between groups.

The idea that there is no biological reality to race inevitably implies that there is no such thing as ethnic interests at all. The reality, of course, is that race does exist, and different races and ethnic groups do have different and often competing interests. And, indeed, from an evolutionary point of view, ethnic self-interest is not deluded: people have a very large genetic interest in defending their ethnic group (see the previous chapter).

Other non-Western countries seem to understand this. For example, the Japanese feel no need to allow a deluge of non-Japanese immigrants.

It's time to exculpate the 1924 law—a law that succeeded in its aim of preserving the ethnic status quo for over forty years. The law did indeed represent the ethnic self-interest of its proponents—albeit not "racism," if racism is properly understood as irrational prejudice. But the anti-restrictionists also had their own ethnic interests at heart. And their subsequent successful counter-attack has unleashed the far greater, more savage, and more threatening ethnic competition that we see today.

Chapter 14

CAN THE JEWISH MODEL HELP THE WEST SURVIVE?[*]

First I want to thank everyone involved in the award.[1] It means a lot to me. I do think it's important to discuss Jewish issues as openly and honestly as one can and with as much intellectual rigor as one can muster. As a great American, Joe Sobran, once wrote:

> The full story of [Pat Buchanan's 1996 presidential] campaign is impossible to tell as long as it's taboo to discuss Jewish interests as freely as we discuss those of the Christian Right. . . . Not that the Jews are all-powerful, let alone all bad. But they are successful, and therefore powerful enough: and their power is unique in being off-limits to normal criticism even when it's highly visible. They themselves behave as if their success were a guilty secret, and they panic, and resort to accusations, as soon as the subject is raised. Jewish control of the major media in the media age makes the enforced silence both paradoxical and paralyzing. Survival in public life requires that you know all about it, but never refer to it. A hypocritical etiquette forces us to pretend that the Jews are powerless victims; and if you don't respect their victimhood, they'll destroy you. It's a phenomenal display not of wickedness, really, but of fierce ethnocentrism, a sort of furtive racial superpatriotism.[2]

I agree entirely with this. And this last part of Sobran's comments bears directly on the topic of my talk: Is the Jewish model an appropriate model for the survival of the West?—by which I mean not only culturally but ethnically as well. I have at times been accused of being an anti-Semite. But the reality is that I greatly admire Jews as a group that has pursued its interests over thousands of years, while retaining its ethnic coherence and intensity of group commitment. There have been ups and downs in Jewish fortunes, to be sure; but their persistence, at

---

[*] First published in *The Occidental Quarterly* 4 (Winter 2004): 5–14.

[1] Acceptance speech for the first Jack London Literary Prize, awarded October 31, 2004 in Washington, DC.

[2] Sobran 1996, 3.

times in the face of long odds, and their spectacular success at the present time are surely worthy of emulation.

Taking seriously the idea of the Jewish community as a model for ethnic activism is a tall order indeed. What would we have to do that we are not doing now?

First, we would have to develop a strong sense of ourselves as a people with interests—interests that often conflict with the interests of others. The fact is, of course, that any mention of the ethnic interests of European-Americans or even Europeans in Europe or anywhere else is certain to be greeted with scorn and accusations of "racism" and moral depravity. These accusations are effective because if there is one area where the intellectual left has won a complete and decisive victory, it is in pathologizing the ethnic interests of the European majority of the United States. By "pathologizing" I mean not only that people have been taught to believe with utter certainty that there is no biological reality to race or ethnicity, but that the slightest assertion of ethnic self-interest by the European majority of the United States is the sign of a grave moral defect. Indeed, it is a moral defect so grave that it is really more a matter of psychiatric concern than anything else.

Of course, this stance requires a great deal of hypocrisy, because assertions of ethnic interests by Europeans are stigmatized at the same time that assertions of ethnic interest by other groups are utterly commonplace and respectable. As Virginia Abernethy recently wrote:

> The goals of the multicultural game are ethnic separatism, ethnic privilege, and ethnic power. I began to realize not too long ago that I have to play the multicultural game, at least defensively, or I and my family and kin will lose out. It is what every ethnic group except, in the main, European-Americans, does these days.[3]

Indeed, Mexican activists loudly advertise their goal of reconquering the Southwestern United States via immigration from Mexico—an event that would be rather obviously in the ethnic interests of Mexicans but undoubtedly would compromise the interests of European-Americans. Jewish organizations, which were in the forefront leading the intellectual and political battles to pathologize the ethnic interests of European Americans, have also been deeply involved in organizing coalitions of minority ethnic groups to assert their political interests in Congress and in the workplace. The elaborate Jewish effort on behalf

---

[3] Abernethy 2004.

of their ethnic brethren in Israel is legendary and can only be described as awesome in its effectiveness.

So the very first thing that any ethnic group must do is to assert its ethnic interests openly and honestly. Until recently, ethnic interests were understood intuitively by everyone, but not formally analyzed. And of course there has been a major effort by the intellectual left to convince everyone that their commonsense perceptions of race and ethnicity are an illusion. As Frank Salter, Henry Harpending, and William Hamilton have shown, people have an interest in their ethnic group in exactly the same way that parents have a genetic interest in raising their children.[4] When world populations are sampled, genetic differences between groups are significant—on average, they are about the same as the kinship between a grandparent and a grandchild. In other words, on average, people are as closely related to other members of their ethnic group versus the rest of the world as they are related to their grandchildren versus the rest of their ethnic group.

What this means is that it is very rational to make extreme sacrifices for our ethnic group. And I would like to underline that. Because of the large number of ethnic brethren, counted in the hundreds of millions, we are actually far better off from an evolutionary point of view if we have a positive influence on the future of our ethnic group than when we successfully rear our own children. Extreme self-sacrifice is entirely warranted and rational if it has a positive effect on our ethnic survival. I think we should all keep this in mind when planning our future life course.

The best way to defend ethnic interests is to defend a territory against immigration from other ethnic groups. The big story of immigration since World War II is of course that wealthy Western societies with economic opportunities and a high level of public goods, such as medical care and education, are magnets for immigration from around the world. We should never forget and should be immensely proud of the fact that Western societies act as magnets precisely because of the spectacular success of the peoples of European descent in creating the science and technology that are the basis for the incredible explosion of wealth and the breakthroughs in medicine and public health. And it goes without saying that we should also be immensely proud of the extraordinary flowering of European high culture that has repeatedly produced geniuses like Bach, Beethoven, Wagner, and Shakespeare. Jewish pride in their own culture is of course a very important part of the

---

[4] Salter 2003/2004.

Jewish tradition, and it certainly bears emulation. Sadly, a primary effect of the culture of critique has been to produce immense guilt among so many Europeans about their own culture, their own history, and their own people.

However, because Western societies act as very powerful magnets for immigration and because we have not acted to defend ourselves against this onslaught, the result will be displacement of the founding populations, not only in the United States, but also in Australia, Canada, and throughout the European Union. If present trends in the United States continue, the founding European-derived population is set to become a minority by the middle of this century; in the British Isles the submergence date is just two generations later.

In mobilizing a sense of ethnic interest, Europeans are at a very serious disadvantage compared to Jews. A very striking feature of Jewish groups is their intense ethnocentrism—what I call hyperethnocentrism. I have provided a great many examples of this in my writing. Jewish ethnocentrism is a critical component of their success because it is of fundamental importance for their ability to construct highly focused ethnic networks in politics, the arts, the media, and the social sciences—all the critical centers of power in the modern world. Perhaps the main focus of my writing has been simply to describe how these networks operate and the extraordinary effects that they have achieved, from creating the culture of critique and, more recently, the culture of the Holocaust, to the present effort of the United States to transform the politics of the Middle East in the interests of Israel.

We should not forget that the great wellspring of modern Jewish populations was the religious fundamentalist Jewish populations of Eastern Europe in the nineteenth century. These fundamentalists passionately rejected all the assimilatory pressures coming from surrounding governments. Well into the twentieth century the vast majority of Eastern European Jews could not speak the languages of the non-Jews living around them. Corresponding to this intense in-group feeling were attitudes that non-Jews were less than human. "As one famous rabbi put it, 'A Gentile does not have a heart, although he has an organ that resembles a heart.'"[5]

This hotbed of intense ethnocentrism was the origin of all the important modern Jewish movements, including political radicalism and Zionism. Many of the early Zionists had clearly articulated racialist views in which Jews were a unique and superior race. A good example

---

[5] Mahler 1985, 17.

is Vladimir Jabotinsky. Jabotinsky was an important early Zionist and he is the spiritual guide of the Likud party in Israel and its leaders—people like Sharon, Begin, and Shamir. He is also a hero to many American neoconservatives. I just recently learned that the neocon patriarch Leo Strauss was a follower of Jabotinsky. Jabotinsky was deeply ethnocentric, believing that Jews were shaped by their long history as a desert people and that the establishment of Israel as a Jewish state would allow the natural genius of the Jewish race to flourish, stating, for example: "These natural and fundamental distinctions embedded in the race are impossible to eradicate, and are continually being nurtured by the differences in soil and climate."[6] What is striking is that virtually the entire organized Jewish community in the United States is allied to the Likud party and the settler movement in Israel, whose leaders openly idolize Jabotinsky.

As a European in a society that is rapidly becoming non-European, I can sympathize with Jabotinsky's envy of the native Slavic peoples he observed in the early twentieth century. He wrote:

> I look at them with envy. I have never known, and probably never will know, this completely organic feeling: so united and singular [is this] sense of a homeland, in which everything flows together, the past and the present, the legend and the hopes, the individual and the historical.[7]

> Every nation, civilized or primitive, sees its land as its national home, where it wants to stay as the sole landlord forever. Such a nation will never willingly consent to new landlords or even to partnership.[8]

It is the memory of this rapidly disappearing sense of historical rootedness, combined with a sense of impending dispossession, that is at the root of the malaise experienced by many Europeans, not only in the United States but elsewhere. The triumph of Zionism took a mere fifty years from Herzl's inspiration to the founding of the state of Israel. There is a tendency to overlook or ignore the powerful ethnocentrism at the heart of Zionism that motivated people like Jabotinsky, and especially the American Jewish community, which has been dedicated

---

[6] Shavit 1988, 112.
[7] Shavit 1988, 116.
[8] Wheatcroft 1996, 207.

throughout the twentieth century to pathologizing and criminalizing the fragile vestiges of ethnocentrism among Europeans.

But the bottom line is that the Zionists were successful. Israel would not have become a state without a great many deeply ethnocentric Jews willing to engage in any means necessary to bring about their dream: a state that would be a vehicle for their ethnic interests. It would not have come about without the most radical among them—people like Jabotinsky, Begin, Shamir, Netanyahu, Sharon, and their supporters—a group that now includes the entire organized American Jewish community. The impending dispossession of Europeans will only be avoided if people like them can be found among the political class of Europeans.

European populations that are allowing themselves to be displaced are playing a very dangerous game—dangerous because the long history of ethnic strife provides them no guarantees about the future. Throughout history there has been a tendency for majority ethnic groups to oppress minorities. A glance at Jewish history is sufficient to make one realize the dangers faced by an ethnic group not having a state and political apparatus to protect its interests. The organized Jewish community in the United States is well aware of this and has adopted a two-pronged strategy: territorial defense and expansion of Israel as an ethnic homeland, and promoting the displacement and disempowerment of European populations in the Western world. Both of these projects have had a considerable degree of success.

It does not take an overactive imagination to see that coalitions of minority groups could compromise the interests of formerly dominant European groups. We already see numerous examples in which coalitions of minority groups attempt to influence public policy, including immigration policy, against the interests of the European majority. And we must realize that placing ourselves in a position of vulnerability would be extremely risky, given the deep sense of historical grievance harbored by many ethnic activists toward Europeans.

This is especially the case with Jews, and of course Jews have shown a tendency to become part of the elite in Western societies. We have recently seen reports in the press of religious Jews spitting on Christian symbols in Israel, thereby resurrecting an age-old Jewish practice.[9] Indeed, hatred toward all things European is normative among a great many strongly identified Jews. I recently came across the following statement by Dov Fischer, vice-president of the Zionist Organization of America, in the *Forward*, a very prestigious Jewish

---

[9] Barkat 2004.

publication, in 2002:

> Although we appreciate a half-century of West European democracy more than we appreciated the prior millennia of European brutality, we recognize who they are, what they have done—and what's what. We know, if they don't, that they need Arab oil more than they need Jewish philosophy and creativity. We remember that the food they eat is grown from soil fertilized by 2,000 years of Jewish blood they have sprinkled onto it. Atavistic Jew-hatred lingers in the air into which the ashes rose from the crematoria.[10]

Besides coalitions of ethnic minorities, the main danger facing Europeans is that wealthy, powerful European elites are often unaware of or do not value their own ethnic interests. Wealthy and powerful people have much more potential to advance or hinder ethnic interests. In the Western world since 1965, many elite politicians and business interests have acted to subvert the ethnic interests of their own people by allowing and even advocating the mass immigration of non-European peoples. One reason may be that these elite Westerners would be the last to suffer personally from ethnic replacement because they are able to live in gated communities insulated from the rest of the world. Many others have made personal and political alliances with non-European elites that have advanced their interests at the cost of completely ignoring their enormous family of ethnic kin. This extreme individualism of Western elites is a tragic mistake for all ethnic Europeans, including the elites themselves, who are losing untold millions of ethnic kin by promoting mass immigration of non-Europeans.

Wealthy and influential Jews have a strong record of attempting to further the interests of their own ethnic group. And Jews are indeed a very elite group. Although Jews make up less than 3 percent of the population, they constitute more than a quarter of the people on the *Forbes* list of the richest 400 Americans. In general, wealthy Jews have a strong record of donating to Jewish causes.

Jewish organizations are lavishly funded. In 1996, there were approximately 300 national Jewish organizations in the United States, with a combined budget estimated in the range of $6 billion—a sum greater than the gross national product of half the members of the United Nations.[11] The Anti-Defamation League has an annual budget of

---

[10] Fischer 2002.
[11] Goldberg 1996.

over $50 million. Irving Moskowitz not only funds the settler movement and land purchases in Israel, but he also supports the American Enterprise Institute by funding scholars like David Wurmser, who is a prominent member of the very influential neocon group that has turned US foreign policy basically into an arm of the Israeli right wing. Moskowitz provided the money that enabled the 1996 reopening of a tunnel under the Temple Mount, which resulted in seventy deaths due to rioting, started the second intifada, and eventually led to Ariel Sharon's election as prime minister of Israel. He also funds the Jewish Institute for National Security Affairs, a lobbying organization dedicated to establishing close relations between Israel and American military and defense contracting companies. Edgar Bronfman funds the World Jewish Congress, while Charles Bronfman, Ronald Lauder, and the notorious Marc Rich fund Birthright Israel, a program that aims to increase ethnic consciousness among Jews by bringing 20,000 young Jews to Israel every year.

So far as I know, there are no major sources of funding aimed at increasing ethnic consciousness among Europeans or at promoting European ethnic interests. Certainly the major sources of conservative funding in the United States, such as the Bradley and Olin Foundations, are not aimed at this sort of thing. Indeed, these foundations have been a major source of funding for the largely Jewish neoconservative movement and for pro-Israel think tanks such as the Center for Security Policy.

An excellent example of an ethnically conscious wealthy Jew is Haim Saban, who was recently profiled in the *New York Times*. Mr. Saban controls the largest media company in Germany. Saban has stirred controversy in Britain, where he publicly expressed interest in buying ITV, the country's biggest commercial network, while accusing its competitors, including BBC News, of pro-Arab coverage. He views his acquisition of a dominant position in German media as benefiting Israel in the long run. Obviously he thinks of media ownership as not simply a way of making money, but of influencing content by promoting Jewish causes. The *Times* describes him as "perhaps the most politically connected mogul in Hollywood"—and that's saying a lot. He is described as "throwing his weight and money around Washington and, increasingly, the world, trying to influence all things Israeli. 'I'm a one-issue guy and my issue is Israel.'" To that end, he has become one of the largest individual donors to the Democratic Party and its candidates in the country, giving millions over the past decade—$7 million in just one donation to the Democratic National Committee in 2002. He hobnobs with John Kerry and he vacations with Bill Clinton. It is certainly striking that Bill Clinton is on record as expressing very positive attitudes about massive immigration and the impending minority status of his own people, while maintaining a close relationship with a wealthy Jewish ethnic activist intent on advancing the interests of Jews. One could say virtually the same thing about the entire political class in America. This is, I think, a parable of our times.

Saban is far from unique. For example, in Canada, the late Israel Asper, executive chairman of CanWest Global Communications Corp., used his media empire to promote pro-Likud policies and punished journalists for any deviation from its strong pro-Israel editorial policies. In my writing I have tried to show that Jewish involvement in the media has influenced content—that the media in the United States have reflected Jewish attitudes on multiculturalism and all things Jewish, especially Israel, and negative attitudes on Christianity, European ethnocentrism, European culture, and especially the culture of the American South and Midwest.[12]

The point is that Jewish elites have been hugely influential in advancing the interests of their people. This is surely a goal to emulate.

The best way to preserve ethnic interests is to defend an ethnostate—a nation that is explicitly intended to preserve the ethnic interests of its citizens. From an ethnic point of view, a major problem with massive immigration is that there is likely to be an increase in ethnic competition. Multicultural societies sanction ethnic mobilization because they inevitably become a cauldron of competing ethnic interests.

In this very dangerous game of ethnic competition, some ethnic groups are better prepared than others. Ethnic groups differ in intelligence and the ability to develop and control economic resources. They differ in their degree of ethnocentrism, in the extent to which they are mobilized to achieve group interests, and in how aggressively they behave toward other groups. They differ in their numbers, fertility, and the extent to which they encourage responsible parenting. And they differ in the amount of land and other resources held at any point in time and in their political power.

Given these differences, it's difficult at best to ensure peaceful relations among ethnic groups. Even maintaining a status quo in territory and resource control is very difficult, as can be seen by the ill-fated attempts of Americans to achieve an ethnic status quo with the 1924 immigration law. And accepting a status quo would not be in the interests of groups that have recently lost land or numbers; nor is it likely to be

---

[12] Sorkin 2004.

acceptable to groups with relatively low numbers and control of resources; nor would a status quo be likely to be acceptable to groups prone to high fertility. Yet the alternative—that all humans renounce their ethnic group loyalties—seems utopian to say the least.

And given that some ethnic groups—especially ones with high levels of ethnocentrism and mobilization—will undoubtedly continue to function as groups far into the foreseeable future, unilateral renunciation of ethnic loyalties by some groups means only their surrender and defeat—the Darwinian dead end of extinction. The future, then, like the past, will inevitably be a Darwinian competition in which ethnicity plays a very large role.

The alternative faced by Europeans throughout the Western world is to place themselves in a position of enormous vulnerability in which their destinies will be determined by other peoples, many of whom hold deep historically conditioned hatreds toward them. Europeans' promotion of their own displacement is the ultimate foolishness—an historical mistake of catastrophic proportions.

BIBLIOGRAPHY

Abernethy, V. D. (2004). "Arizona Illegals," (letter to the editor). *Washington Times*, Oct. 1.

Aboud, F. (1988). *Children and Prejudice.* New York: Blackwell.

Abrams, E. (1997). *Faith or Fear: How Jews Can Survive in a Christian America.* New York: The Free Press.

Ackerman, N. W., and M. Jahoda (1950). *Anti-Semitism and Emotional Disorder,* vol. 5 of the American Jewish Committee Social Studies Series. New York: Harper and Brothers.

Adelman, T. Z. (1999). "Jewish Ethics: Are they Ethical? Are they Jewish?" The Jewish Agency for Israel, Department for Jewish Zionist Education, Aug. 22.

Adorno, T. W., E. Frenkel-Brunswik, D. J. Levinson, and R. N. Sanford. (1950). *The Authoritarian Personality,* vol. 3 of the American Jewish Committee Social Studies Series. New York: Harper and Brothers.

Alderman, G. (1983). *The Jewish Community in British Politics.* Oxford: Clarendon Press.

Alexander, R. (1979). *Darwinism and Human Affairs.* Seattle: University of Washington Press.

Alterman, E. (2002). "Intractable Foes, Warring Narratives: While Much of the World sees Mideast Conflict Through Palestinian Eyes, in America, Israel's View Prevails." www.msnbc.com, Mar. 28.

Amann, P. (2000). "Jews, Latinos Explore Common Ground." *Jewish World Review*, Aug.

American Jewish Committee. (2003). Press release. www.ajc.org, Feb. 7.

Anderson, S. W., A. Bechara, H. Damasio, D. Tranel, and A. R. Damasio. (1999). "Impairment of Social and Moral Behavior Related to Early Damage in Human Prefrontal Cortex." *Nature Neuroscience* 2: 1032–37.

Anti-Defamation League. (1998). "Which Americans are Most Likely to Hold Anti-Semitic Views." Nov. http://www.adl.org/antisemitism_survey.

———. (1999). Press release. www.adl.org, May 28.

———. (2003). Press release. www.adl.org, June 23.

———. (2004). Press release. "ADL Urges Senator Hollings to Disavow Statements on Jews and the Iraq War." www.adl.org, May 14.

Aruri, N. H. (1986). Preface to this edition. In L. Rokach, *Israel's Sacred Terrorism,* 3rd ed. Belmont, Mass.: Association of Arab-American University Graduates, Inc.

Aschheim, S. E. (1982). *Brothers and Strangers: The East European Jew in Germany and German Jewish Consciousness, 1800–1923.* Madison: University of Wisconsin Press.

Ashburn-Nardo, L., M. L. Knowles, and M. J. Monteith. (2003). "Black Americans' Implicit Racial Associations and their Implications for Intergroup

Judgment." *Social Cognition* 21: 61–87.
Augoustinos, M., and D. L. Rosewarne. (2001). "Stereotype Knowledge and Prejudice in Children." *British Journal of Developmental Psychology* 19: 143–56.
Auster, L. (2002). "View from the Right." http://amnation.com/vfr/, December 9.
Baldwin, N. (2001). *Henry Ford and the Jews: The Mass Production of Hate.* New York: Public Affairs.
Ball, G., and D. Ball. (1992). *The Passionate Attachment: American's Involvement with Israel, 1947 to the Present.* New York: W.W. Norton.
Bamford, J. (2004). *A Pretext for War: 9/11, Iraq, and the Abuse of America's Intelligence Agencies.* New York: Doubleday.
Bargh, J. A., and T. L. Chartrand. (1999). "The Unbearable Automaticity of Being." *American Psychologist* 54: 462–79.
Bar-Haim, Y., T. Ziv, D. Lamy, and R. M. Hodes. (2006). "Nature-Nurture and Own-Race Face Processing." *Psychological Science* 17: 159–63.
Barkat, A. (2004). "Armenian Archbishop Quizzed over Spat with Yeshiva Student." *Ha'artez*, Oct. 11.
Barthelemy, D. (1988). "Kinship." In *A History of Private Life*, vol. 2., ed. P. Aries and G. Duby. Cambridge: Harvard University Press.
Beauregard, M., J. Lévesque, and P. Bourgouvin. (2001). "The Neural Correlates of Selfconscious Control of Emotion." *Journal of Neuroscience* 21 (R165): 1–6.
Bellow, S. (2000). *Ravelstein.* New York: Viking.
Bendersky, J. W. (2000). *The "Jewish Threat": Anti-Semitic Politics of the U.S. Army.* New York: Basic Books.
Benjamin, W. (1968). *Illuminations*, trans. H. Zohn. New York: Harcourt, Brace and World.
Bereczkei, T. (1993). "R-Selected Reproductive Strategies among Hungarian Gypsies: A Preliminary Analysis." *Ethology and Sociobiology* 14: 71–88.
Besharov, D. J., and T. S. Sullivan. (1996). "One Flesh." *New Democrat* 8 (4): 19–21.
Biale, D. (1982). *Gershom Scholem: Kabbalah and Counter-History*, 2nd ed. Cambridge: Harvard University Press.
Bible. References to the Book of Jubilees are from *Apocrypha and Pseudepigrapha of the Old Testament II*, ed. R. H. Charles. Oxford: Clarendon Press, 1966.
_____. References to the Book of Maccabees are to *The New English Bible: The Apocrypha.* London: Oxford University Press and Cambridge University Press, 1970.
Bin Laden, Osama. (1998). Interview. PBS Frontline. http://www.pbs.org/wgbh/pages/frontline/shows/binladen/who/interview.html.
Bloom, Allan. (1987). *The Closing of the American Mind: How Higher Education Has Failed Democracy and Impoverished the Souls of Today's Stu-*

dents. New York: Simon and Schuster.
Bookman, M. Z. (1997). *The Demographic Struggle for Power: The Political Economy of Demographic Engineering in the Modern World.* London and Portland, Ore. Frank Cass.
Borjas, G. J. (1999). *Heaven's Door: Immigration Policy and the American Economy.* Princeton: Princeton University Press.
Borowitz, E. B. (1973). *The Mask Jews Wear: Self-Deceptions of American Jewry.* New York: Simon and Schuster.
Bothwell, R. K., J. C. Brigham, and R. S. Malpass. (1989). "Cross-Racial Identification." *Personality and Social Psychology Bulletin* 15: 19–25.
Bouchard, C. B. (1981). "Consanguinity and Noble Marriages in the Tenth and Eleventh Century." *Speculum* 56: 268–87.
Bourhis, R. Y. (1994). "Power, Gender, and Intergroup Discrimination: Some Minimal Group Experiments." In *The Psychology of Prejudice: The Ontario Symposium,* vol. 7, ed. M. P. Zanna and J. M. Olson. Hillsdale, N.J.: Erlbaum.
Boyle, S. S. (2001). *The Betrayal of Palestine: The Story of George Antonius.* Boulder, Colo.: Westview Press.
Brenner, L. (1997). "The *Forward* is Backward: New York's Unclassifiable Jewish Weekly." *Washington Report on Middle East Affairs,* June/July: 79–80.
Brewer, M. B., and R. J. Brown. (1998). "Intergroup Relations." In *The Handbook of Social Psychology,* 4th ed., vol. 2., ed. D. T. Gilbert, S. T. Fiske, and G. Lindzey. Boston: McGraw-Hill.
Brown, P. (1987). "Late Antiquity." In *A History of Private Life,* vol. 1., ed. P. Veyne. Cambridge: Harvard University Press.
Brownfield, A. C. (2003). "Examining the Role of Israel and its American Friends in Promoting War on Iraq." *Washington Report on Middle East Affairs,* May: 54, 57.
Brubacher, M. (2002). "From War on Terror to Plain War. Israel: Walled in, but Never Secure." *Le Monde diplomatique,* Nov.
Brundage, J. A. (1975). "Concubinage and Marriage in Medieval Canon Law." *Journal of Medieval History* 1: 1–17.
Bruzonsky, M. (1980). "The Mentor Who Shaped Begin's Thinking: Jabotinsky." *Washington Post.* Outlook Section. Nov. 16.
Buchanan, P. J. (2003). "Whose War? A Neoconservative Clique Seeks to Ensnare our Country in a Series of Wars that are not in America's Interest." *American Conservative,* Mar. 24.
———. (2004). "Going Back Where They Came From." www.antiwar.com, Apr. 23.
Burton, M. L., C. C. Moore, J. W. M. Whiting, and A. K. Romney. (1996). "Regions Based on Social Structure." *Current Anthropology* 37: 87–123.
Buss, D. M. (2005). *The Murderer Next Door: Why the Mind is Designed to Kill.* New York: Penguin.

Campbell, J. (1959). *The Masks of God*, 4 vols. New York: Viking.
Canadian Journalists for Free Expression. (2002). "Not in the Newsroom: CanWest, Global and Freedom of Expression in Canada." http://www.cjfe.org/specials/canwest/ canw2.html.
Castro, A. (1954). *The Structure of Spanish History*, trans. E. L. King. Princeton: Princeton University Press.
Cattan, N. (2002). "Community Questioning 'Open Door': Debate Raging on Immigration." *Forward*, Nov. 29.
Cavalli-Sforza, L. and W. F. Bodmer. (1999). *The Genetics of Human Populations*, unabridged ed. New York: Dover.
Ceci, S. J., W. M. Williams, and K. Mueller-Johnson. (2006). "Is Tenure Justified? An Experimental Study of Faculty Beliefs about Tenure, Promotion, and Academic Freedom." *Behavioral and Brain Sciences*, in press.
Chanes, J. A. (1997). "Affirmative Action: Jewish Ideals, Jewish Interests." In *Struggles in the Promised Land: Toward a History of Black-Jewish Relations in the United States*, ed. J. Salzman and C. West. New York: Oxford University Press.
Chazan, R. (1973). *Medieval Jewry in Northern France: A Political and Social History*. Baltimore: The Johns Hopkins University Press.
_____. (1987). *European Jewry and the First Crusade*. Berkeley: University of California Press.
Checinski, M. (1982). *Poland: Communism, Nationalism, Anti-Semitism*, trans. (in part) T. Szafar. New York. Karz-Chol Publishing.
Chernin, K. (2002). "The Seven Pillars of Jewish Denial." *Tikkun*. Sept./Oct..
Chicago Model United Nations. (2001). United States National Security Background Guide. University of Chicago: Chicago Model United Nations VI. Feb. 13.
http://chomun.uchicago.edu/committees/NSC_back.pdf
Chomsky, N. (1999). *The Fateful Triangle: The United States, Israel and the Palestinians*, 2nd ed. Boston: South End Press.
Christison, K., and B. Christison. (2003). "A Rose by Another Other Name: The Bush Administration's Dual Loyalties." *Counterpunch*, December 13.
Chua, A. (2003). *World on Fire: How Exporting Free Market Democracy Breeds Ethnic Hatred and Global Instability*. New York: Doubleday.
Churchill, W. (1920). "Zionism versus Bolshevism: A Struggle for the Soul of the Jewish People." *Illustrated Sunday Herald*, Feb. 8: 5.
Clarke, R. (2004). *Against All Enemies*. New York: Free Press.
Cockburn, A. (2002). "No Respite for West Bank Locals." *National Geographic*. http://magma.nationalgeographic.com/ngm/0210/feature5/online_extra.html.
_____. (2003). "My Life as an Anti-Semite." In *The Politics of Anti-Semitism*, ed. A. Cockburn and J. St. Clair. Oakland, Calif.: Counterpunch/AK Press.
Cohen, J. (1982). *The Friars and the Jews: The Emergence of Medieval Anti-Judaism*. Ithaca, N.Y.: Cornell University Press.

Cohen, M. (1994). *Under Crescent and Cross: The Jews in the Middle Ages.* Princeton: Princeton University Press.

Cohen, N. W. (1972). *Not Free to Desist: The American Jewish Committee 1906–1966.* Philadelphia: Jewish Publication Society of America.

Cohen, P. S. (1980). *Jewish Radicals and Radical Jews.* London: Academic Press.

Cohn, W. (1958). "The Politics of American Jews." In *The Jews: Social Patterns of an American Group*, ed. M. Sklare. Glencoe, Ill.: Free Press.

Coleman, M. S. (2006). "Diversity Matters at Michigan." University of Michigan News Service, Nov. 8.

Coon, C. (1958). *Caravan: The Story of the Middle East*, 2nd ed. New York: Holt, Rinehart, and Winston.

Cooperman, A. (2006). "GOP's Hold on Evangelicals Weakening." *The Washington Post*, Oct. 6.

Corbett, P. E. (1930). *The Roman Law of Marriage.* Oxford: Clarendon Press.

Corbin, A. (1990). "Intimate Relations." In *A History of Private Life*, vol. 4., *From the Fires of the Revolution to the Great War*, ed. M. Perrot. Cambridge: Harvard University Press.

Cosmides, L., J. Tooby, and R. Kurzban. (2003). "Perceptions of Race." *Trends in Cognitive Science* 7: 173–79.

Coughlin, R. J. (1960). *Double Identity: The Chinese in Modern Thailand.* Hong Kong and London: Hong Kong University Press and Oxford University Press.

Courtois, S. (1999). Introduction: The Crimes of Communism. In *The Black Book of Communism: Crimes, Terror, Repression*, ed. S. Courtois, N. Werth, J. Panné, A. Paczkowski, K. Bartosek, and J. Margolin, trans. J. Murphy and M. Kramer. Cambridge: Harvard University Press.

Croll, P. C., D. Hartmann, J. Gerteis. (2006). *Putting Whiteness Theory to the Test: An Empirical Assessment of Core Theoretical Propositions.* Department of Sociology, University of Minnesota.

Cruse, H. (1967/1992). "Negroes and Jews—The Two Nationalisms and the Bloc(ked) Plurality." In *Bridges and Boundaries: African Americans and American Jews*, ed. J. Salzman with A. Back and G. Sullivan Sorin. New York: George Braziller in association with the Jewish Museum, 1992. (Originally published as a chapter in Cruse's *The Crisis of the Negro Intellectual.* New York: William Morrow, 1967.)

_____. (1987). *Plural but Equal: A Critical Study of Blacks and Minorities and America's Plural Society.* New York: William Morrow.

Cuddihy, J. M. (1974). *The Ordeal of Civility: Freud, Marx, Levi-Strauss, and the Jewish Struggle with Modernity.* New York: Basic Books.

_____. (1978). *No Offense: Civil Religion and Protestant Taste.* New York: Seabury Press.

Cunningham, W. A., M. K. Johnson, C. L. Raye, J. C. Gatenby, J. C. Gore, and M. Banaji. (2004). "Separable Neural Components in the Processing of Black and White Faces." *Psychological Science* 15: 806–13.

Cunningham, W. A., J. B. Nezlek, and M. R. Banaji. (2004). "Implicit and Explicit Ethnocentrism: Revisiting the Ideologies of Prejudice." *Personality and Social Psychology Bulletin* 30: 1332–46.
Curtiss, R. (1998). "The Cost of Israel to the American People." Talk presented at the Al-Hewar Center in Vienna, Virginia, May 20.
Curtiss, R. H. (2003). "The Pentagon's Dynamic Duo: Richard Perle and Paul Wolfowitz." *Washington Report on Middle East Affairs*, Apr., 14–15: 90.
Cvorovic, J. (2004). "Sexual and Reproductive Strategies among Serbian Gypsies." *Population and Environment* 25: 217–42.

Damasio, A. R. (1994/2000). *Descartes' Error: Emotion, Reason, and the Human Brain.* New York: Quill.
Dana, R., and P. Carlson. (2003). "Harry Truman's Forgotten Diary: 1947 Writings Offer Fresh Insight on the President." *Washington Post*, July 11.
Dannhauser, W. J. (1996). "Athens and Jerusalem or Jerusalem and Athens?" In *Leo Strauss and Judaism: Jerusalem and Athens Critically Revisited*, ed. D. Novak. Lanham, Md.: Rowman and Littlefield.
Davies, N. (1981). *God's Playground: A History of Poland*, 2 vols. New York: Columbia University Press.
Dawidowicz, L. (1976). *A Holocaust Reader.* New York: Behrman.
Decter, M. (2003). *Rumsfeld: A Personal Portrait.* New York: Regan Books.
Degler, C. (1991). *In Search of Human Nature: The Decline and Revival of Darwinism in American Social Thought.* New York: Oxford University Press.
Dershowitz, A. (1994). "The Betrayals of Jonathan Pollard." *Penthouse*, June.
Diggins, J. P. (2004). "How Reagan Beat the Neocons." *New York Times*, June 11.
Diner, H. R. (1977/1995). *In the Almost Promised Land: American Jews and Blacks, 1915–1935.* Baltimore: Johns Hopkins University Press.
_____. (1998). "Drawn Together by Self-Interest: Jewish Representation of Race and Race Relations in the Early Twentieth Century." In *African Americans and Jews in the Twentieth Century*, ed. V. P. Franklin, N. L. Grant, H. M. Kletnick, and G. R. McNeil. Columbia: University of Missouri Press.
Dizard, J. (2004). "How Ahmed Chalabi Conned the Neocons." www.salon.com, May 4.
Draper, H. (1956). "Israel's Arab Minority: The Beginning of a Tragedy." *New International* 22: 86–106.
_____. (1957). "The Great Land Robbery." *New International* 23: 7–30.
_____. (1997). *Zionism, Israel, and the Arabs: Notes on the Historical Background of the Middle East Tragedy.* Preface to the 1997 ed. Alameda, California: Center for Socialist History. (Originally published in 1967.)
Draper, P. and H. Harpending. (1988). "A Sociobiological Perspective on Human Reproductive Strategies." In *Sociobiological Perspectives on Human Development*, ed. K. MacDonald. New York: Springer-Verlag.

Drew, E. (2003). "The Neocons in Power." *New York Review of Books* 50 (10), June 12.
Drucker, P. (1994). *Max Shachtman and His Left: A Socialist's Odyssey through the "American Century."* Atlantic Highlands, N.J.: Humanities Press.
Drury, S. (1997). *Leo Strauss and the American Right.* New York: St. Martin's Press.
Duby, G. (1983). *The Knight, the Lady, and the Priest*, trans. Barbara Bray. London: Penguin Books.
Dumont, P. (1982). "Jewish Communities in Turkey During the Last Decades of the Nineteenth Century in Light of the Archives of the Alliance Israélite Universelle." In *Christians and Jews in the Ottoman Empire: The Functioning of a Plural Society*, ed. B. Braude and B. Lewis. New York: Holmes and Meier Publishers.
Dunham, Y., A. S. Baron, and M. R. Banaji. (2005). "From American City to Japanese Village: The Omnipresence of Implicit Race Attitudes." Unpublished MS, Harvard Graduate School of Education.
Duntley, J. D., and D. M. Buss. (2005). "The Plausibility of Adaptations for Homicide." In *The Innate Mind: Structure and Contents*, ed. P. Carruthers, S. Laurence, and S. Stich. Oxford: Oxford University Press.

Easton, N. J. (2000). *Gang of Five: Leaders at the Center of the Conservative Crusade.* New York: Simon and Schuster.
Ebrey, P. (1986). "Concubines in Sung China." *Journal of Family History* 11: 1–24.
Ediev, D. (2001). "Application of the Demographic Potential Concept to Understanding the Russian Population History and Prospects: 1897–2100." *Demographic Research* 4: 287–333.
Editors of *Fortune*. (1936). *Jews in America.* New York: Random House.
Efron, J. M. (1994). *Defenders of the Race: Jewish Doctors and Race Science in Fin-de-Siècle Europe.* New Haven: Yale University Press.
Ehrman, J. (1995). *The Rise of Neoconservatism: Intellectuals and Foreign Affairs, 1945–1994.* New Haven: Yale University Press.
Eickelman, D. F. (1981). *The Middle East: An Anthropological Approach.* Englewood Cliffs, N.J.: Prentice-Hall.
Elazar, D. J. (1980). *Community and Polity: Organizational Dynamics of American Jewry.* Philadelphia: Jewish Publication Society.
Emerson, M. O., R. T. Kimbro, and G. Yancey. (2002). "Contact Theory Extended: The Effects of Prior Racial Contact on Current Social Ties." *Social Science Quarterly* 83: 745–61.
Emerson, M. O., and D. Sikkink. (2006). "Does Education Help Breed Segregation?" *Rice Sallyport* 61, Fall.
Endelman, T. M. (1991). "The Legitimization of the Diaspora Experience in Recent Jewish Historiography." *Modern Judaism* 11: 195–209.
Ephron, D. and T. Lipper. (2002). "Sharansky's Quiet Role." *Newsweek*, July

15.
Epstein, L. M. (1942). *Marriage Laws in the Bible and the Talmud.* Cambridge: Harvard University Press.
Eysenck, H. J. (1962). *The Uses and Abuses of Psychology.* Baltimore: Penguin Books.
Fairbanks, E. (2006). "A Hot Paper Muzzles Academia." *Los Angeles Times,* May 14.
Fehr, E., and S. Gächter. (2002). "Altruistic Punishment in Humans." *Nature* 415: 137–40.
Findley, P. (1989). *They Dare to Speak Out: People and Institutions Confront Israel's Lobby,* 2nd ed. Chicago: Lawrence Hill Books.
Fischer, D. (2002). "We're Right, the Whole World's Wrong." *Forward,* Apr. 19.
Fischer, D. H. (1989). *Albion's Seed: Four British Folkways in America.* New York: Oxford University Press.
Fiske, S. T. (1998). "Stereotyping, Prejudice, and Discrimination." In *The Handbook of Social Psychology,* 4th ed., vol. 2., ed. D. T. Gilbert, S. T. Fiske, and G. Lindzey. Boston: McGraw-Hill.
Flinn, M. V., and B. S. Low. (1986). "Resource Distribution, Social Competition, and Mating Patterns in Human Societies." In *Ecological Aspects of Social Evolution,* ed. D. I. Rubenstein and R. W. Wrangham. Princeton: Princeton University Press.
Ford, H. (1920–1922). *The International Jew: The World's Foremost Problem,* 4 vols. Dearborn, Michigan: Dearborn Publishing Co.
Foxman, A. (2003). "Anti-Semitism, Pure and Simple." *Jerusalem Report,* May 5.
Francis, S. (1999). *Thinkers of Our Time: James Burnham.* London: Claridge Press.
⸺. (2002). "Poll Exposes Elite-Public Clash on Immigration." www.vdare.com, Oct. 24.
⸺. (2004). "The Neoconservative Subversion." In *Neoconservatism,* ed. B. Nelson. *Occasional Papers of the Conservative Citizens' Foundation,* no. 6. St. Louis: Conservative Citizens' Foundation.
Frank, G. (1997). "Jews, Multiculturalism, and Boasian Anthropology." *American Anthropologist* 99: 731–45.
Frankel, J. (1981). *Prophecy and Politics: Socialism, Nationalism, and the Russian Jews, 1862–1917.* Cambridge: Cambridge University Press.
Friedman, M. (1995). *What Went Wrong? The Creation and Collapse of the Black-Jewish Alliance.* New York: Free Press.
⸺. (2002). "Democrats, Maybe, but Fewer Liberals." *Forward,* June 7.
Frison, G. C. (1998). "Paleoindian Large Mammal Hunters of the Plains of North America." *Proceedings of the National Academy of Science* 95: 14575–83.

Frommer, M. (1978). "The American Jewish Congress: A History 1914–1950," 2 vols. Ph.D. Dissertation. Ohio State University.
Frum, D., and R. Perle. (2003). *An End to Evil: How to Win the War on Terror.* New York: Random House.
Fukuyama, F. (1995). *Trust: The Social Virtues and the Creation of Prosperity.* New York: Free Press.

Gabler, N. (1988). *An Empire of Their Own: How the Jews Invented Hollywood.* New York: Crown Publishers.
Gay, P. (1988). *Freud: A Life for Our Time.* New York: W. W. Norton.
Geary, D. (2005). *The Origin of Mind: Evolution of Brain, Cognition, and General Intelligence.* Washington, D.C.: American Psychological Association.
Gershman, C. (2003a). "A Democracy Strategy for the Middle East." National Endowment for Democracy. www.ned.org/about/carl/dec1203.html, Dec. 12.
_____. (2003b). "After the Bombings: My Visit to Turkey and Istanbul's Jewish Community." National Endowment for Democracy. www.ned.org/about/carl/dec2703.html, Dec. 27.
Gerson, M. (1996). "Security and Freedom: Making the World Safe with Ronald Reagan." In *The Essential Neoconservative Reader*, ed. M. Gerson. Reading, Mass.: Addison-Wesley, 1996.
Getlin, J. (2002). "Violence in Mideast Galvanizes U.S. Jews." *Los Angeles Times,* Apr. 28.
Gibbon, E. (1909). *The Decline and Fall of the Roman Empire*, 7 vols., ed. J. B. Bury. London: Methuen.
Gilbar, G. (1997). *Population Dilemmas in the Middle East: Essays in Political Demography and Economy.* London and Portland, Ore.: Frank Cass.
Gilchrist, J. (1969). *The Church and Economic Policy in the Middle Ages,* New York: St. Martin's Press.
Gilman, S. L. (1993). *Freud, Race, and Gender.* Princeton: Princeton University Press.
Gilwhite, F. J. (2001). "Are Ethnic Groups Biological 'Species' to the Human Brain? Essentialism in our Cognition of Some Social Categories." *Current Anthropology* 42: 515–54.
Glazer, N. (1969). "Blacks, Jews and Intellectuals." *Commentary,* Apr.
Goldberg, J. (2003). "Jews and the War." *National Review Online,* Mar. 13.
Goldberg, J. J. (1996). *Jewish Power: Inside the American Jewish Establishment.* Reading, Mass.: Addison-Wesley.
Goldmann, N. (1978). *The Jewish Paradox.* New York: Fred Jordan Books/ Grosset and Dunlap.
Goldschmidt, W., and E. J. Kunkel. (1971). "The Structure of the Peasant Family." *American Anthropologist* 73: 1058–76.
Goldstein, J. (1990). *The Politics of Ethnic Pressure: The American Jewish Committee Fight against Immigration Restriction, 1906–1917.* New York:

Garland Publishing.
Gonen, J. Y. (1975). *A Psychohistory of Zionism*. New York: Mason/Charter.
Goody, J. (1983). *The Development of the Family and Marriage in Europe*. Cambridge: Cambridge University Press.
Graham, H. D. (1990). *The Civil Rights Era: Origins and Development of National Policy, 1960–1972*. New York: Oxford University Press.
_____. (2002). *Collision Course: The Strange Convergence of Affirmative Action and Immigration Policy in America*. New York: Oxford University Press.
Grant, M. (1916). *The Passing of the Great Race, or, The Racial Basis of European History*. New York: Charles Scribner's Sons.
Green, S. (2004). "Serving Two Flags: Neo-Cons, Israel and the Bush Administration." www.counterpunch.org, Feb. 28–29.
Greenberg, C. (1998). "The Southern Jewish Community and the Struggle for Civil Rights." In *African Americans and Jews in the Twentieth Century*, ed. V. P. Franklin, N. L. Grant, H. M. Kletnick, and G. R. McNeil. Columbia: University of Missouri Press.
Guttentag, M., and P. F. Secord. (1983). *"Too Many Women?"* Beverly Hills: Sage Publications.
Guttman, N. (2004). "Prominent U.S. Jews, Israel Blamed for Start of Iraq War." *Ha'aretz*, May 31.
Guzzardi, J. (2004). "Attend First Data's Meetings—Put Shoe on Other Foot!" www.vdare.com, Aug. 4.

HaCohen, R. (2002). "Palestinian Enslavement Entering a New Phase." www.antiwar.com, May 24.
Haffner, S. (1979). *The Meaning of Hitler*. New York: Macmillan Publishing Co.
Hagen, W. W. (1996). "Before the 'Final Solution': Toward a Comparative Analysis of Political Anti-Semitism in Interwar Germany and Poland." *Journal of Modern History* 68: 351–81.
Hajnal, J. (1965). "European Marriage Patterns in Perspective." In *Population in History*, ed. D. V. Glass and D. E. C. Eversley. Hawthorne, N.Y.: Aldine.
_____. (1983). "Two Kinds of Pre-Industrial Household Formation System." In *Family Forms in Historic Europe*, ed. R. Wall, J. Robin, and P. Laslett. Cambridge: Cambridge University Press.
Hamilton, W. D. (2001). "At the World's Crossroads: Instability and Cycling of two Competing Hosts with Two Parasites." In *Narrow Roads of Gene Land: The Collected Papers of W. D. Hamilton*, vol. 2, *The Evolution of Sex*. Oxford: Oxford University Press.
Hammer, M. F., A. J. Redd, E. T. Wood, M. R. Bonner, H. Jarjanazi, T. Karafet, S. Santachiara-Benerecetti, A. Oppenheim, M. A. Jobling, T. Jenkins, H. Ostrer, and B. Bonné-Tamir. (2000). "Jewish and Middle Eastern Non-Jewish Populations Share a Common Pool of Y-Chromosome Bialle-

lic Haplotypes." *Proceedings of the National Academy of Sciences*, May 9.
Hanawalt, B. (1986). *The Ties that Bound: Peasant Families in Medieval England*. New York: Oxford University Press.
Harris, J. F. (1994). *The People Speak! Anti-Semitism and Emancipation in Nineteenth-Century Bavaria*. Ann Arbor: University of Michigan Press.
Henrich, J., R. Boyd, S. Bowles, C. Camerer, E. Fehr, H. Gintis, and R. McElreath. (2001). "In Search of *Homo economicus*: Behavioral Experiments in 15 Small-Scale Societies." *Economics and Social Behavior* 91: 73–78.
Herlihy, D. (1985). *Medieval Households*. Cambridge: Harvard University Press.
Herrnstein, R. J. and C. Murray. (1994). *The Bell Curve: Intelligence and Class Structure in American Life*. New York: The Free Press.
Hersh, S. M. (1982). "Kissinger and Nixon in the White House." *Atlantic Monthly* 249 (5): 35–58.
_____. (2003). "Selective Intelligence." *New Yorker*, May 12.
_____. (2004). "Plan B: As June 30th Approaches, Israel Looks to the Kurds." *New Yorker,* June 28.
Hertzberg, A. (1979). *Being Jewish in America*. New York: Schocken Books.
Herzl, T. (1960). *The Complete Diaries of Theodor Herzl*, vol. 2, ed. R. Patai. New York and London: Herzl Press and Thomas Yoseloff.
_____. (1970). *The Jewish State*, trans. H. Zohn. New York: Herzl Press.
Hewstone, M., M. Rubin, and H. Willis. (2002). "Intergroup Bias." *Annual Review of Psychology* 53: 575–604.
Higham, J. (1984). *Send These to Me: Immigrants in Urban America*, rev. ed. Baltimore: Johns Hopkins University Press.
Hill, J. E. C. (1967). *Society and Puritanism in Pre-Revolutionary England*, 2nd ed. New York: Schocken Books.
Hilzenrath, D. S. (2004). "The Ultimate Insider." *Washington Post*, May 24: E1.
Himmelfarb, M. (1974). "On Leo Strauss." *Commentary*, Aug.
Hirschfeld, L. A. (1996). *Race in the Making: Cognition, Culture, and the Child's Construction of Human Kinds*. Cambridge: The MIT Press.
Hirsh, M. (2003). "The Mideast: Neocons on the Line." *Newsweek*, June 23.
Hitler, A. (1943). *Mein Kampf*, trans. R. Manheim. Boston: Houghton Mifflin.
Hogg, M. A., and D. Abrams. (1987). *Social Identifications*. New York: Routledge.
Hollinger, D. A. (1996). *Science, Jews, and Secular Culture: Studies in Mid-Twentieth-Century American Intellectual History*. Princeton: Princeton University Press.
Holmes, S. (1993). *The Anatomy of Anti-Liberalism*. Cambridge: Harvard University Press.
Hook, S. (1987). *Out of Step: An Unquiet Life in the 20th Century*. New York: Harper and Row.
_____. (1989). "On Being a Jew." *Commentary*, Oct.

Horowitz, D. L. (1985). *Ethnic Groups in Conflict*. Berkeley: University of California Press.

Horowitz, D. (1997). *Radical Son: A Journey through Our Time*. New York: Free Press.

_____. (2002a). "American Conservatism: An Argument with the Racial Right." www.FrontPageMagazine.com, Aug. 27.

_____. (2002b). www.FrontPageMagazine.com, December 12.

Horrigan, J. (2004). "Bush increases margins with AIPAC." United Press International, May 18.

Huntington, S. (2005). *Who We Are: Challenges to America's National Identity*. New York: Simon and Schuster.

Institute for Advanced Strategic and Political Studies. (1996). "A Clean Break: A New Strategy for Securing the Realm." www.iasps.org.

Jaffa, H. (1999). "Strauss at One Hundred." In *Leo Strauss, the Straussians, and the American Regime*, ed. K. L. Deutsch and J. A. Murley. Lanham, Md.: Rowman and Littlefield.

Jewish Virtual Library (undated). Jewish vote in presidential elections. www.jewishvirtuallibrary.org.

John, O. P., and S. Srivastava. (1999). "The Big Five Trait Taxonomy: History, Measurement, and Theoretical Perspectives." In *Handbook of Personality: Theory and Research*, ed. L. A. Pervin and O. P. John, 2nd ed. New York: Guilford Press.

John, R., and S. Hadawi. (1970a). *The Palestine Diary, 1914–1945: Britain's Involvement*. New York: The New World Press.

_____. (1970b). *The Palestine Diary, 1945–1948: United States, United Nations Intervention*. New York: The New World Press.

Johnson, G. (1995). "The Evolutionary Origins of Government and Politics." In *Human Nature and Politics*, ed. J. Losco and A. Somit. Greenwich, Conn.: JAI Press.

Johnson, P. (1987). *A History of the Jews*. New York: Harper and Row.

Jones, N. (1996). "U.S. Jewish Leaders Decry Clinton Refusal to Free Pollard." *Washington Report on Middle East Affairs*, Oct.

Jordan, D. S. (1912). *Unseen Empire: A Study of the Plight of Nations that Do Not Pay Their Debts*. Boston: American Unitarian Association.

Jordan, W. C. (1989). *The French Monarchy and the Jews: From Philip Augustus to the Last Capetians*. Philadelphia: University of Pennsylvania Press.

Judge, E. H. (1992). *Easter in Kishinev: Anatomy of a Pogrom*. New York: New York University Press.

Juster, J. (1914). *Les Juifs dans l'empire romain: Leur condition juridique, économique et sociale*, 2 vols. New York: Burt Franklin.

Kamen, A. (2003). "Feith-based Initiative." *Washington Post*, Sept. 10: A17.

Kampelman, M. (Undated). "Trust the United Nations?" http://www.socialdemocrats.org/kampelmanhtml.html.
Kanter, K. A. (1982). *The Jews on Tin Pan Alley: The Jewish Contribution to American Popular Music, 1830–1940*. New York: KTAV Publishing.
Kaplan, L. F. (2003). "Toxic Talk on War." *Washington Post*, Feb. 18.
Katz, J. (1986). *Jewish Emancipation and Self-Emancipation*. Philadelphia: Jewish Publication Society of America.
Kaufman, J. (1997). "Blacks and Jews: The Struggle in the Cities." In *Struggles in the Promised Land: Toward a History of Black-Jewish Relations in the United States*, ed. J. Salzman and C. West. New York: Oxford University Press.
Kaufman, R. G. (2000). *Henry M. Jackson: A Life in Politics*. Seattle: University of Washington Press.
Keller, B. (2002). "The Sunshine Warrior." *New York Times Magazine*, Sept. 22.
Kellogg, M. (2005). *The Russian Roots of Nazism: White Émigrés and the Making of National Socialism, 1917–1945*. Cambridge: Cambridge University Press.
Kelly, D. J., et al. (2005). "Three-Month-Olds, but not Newborns, Prefer Own-race Faces." *Developmental Science* 8: F31–F36.
Kessler, E. J. (2004). "Campaign Confidential." *Forward*, Mar. 19.
Kirkpatrick, J. (1979/1996). "Dictatorships and Double Standards." *Commentary*, Nov. Reprinted in *The Essential Neoconservative Reader*, ed. M. Gerson. Reading, Mass.: Addison-Wesley, 1996.
Klehr, H. (1978). *Communist Cadre: The Social Background of the American Communist Party Elite*. Stanford: Hoover Institution Press.
Klehr, H., J. E. Haynes, and F. I. Firsov. (1995). *The Secret World of American Communism*. Russian documents trans. T. D. Sergay. New Haven: Yale University Press.
Kornberg, R. (1993). *Theodor Herzl: From Assimilation to Zionism*. Bloomington: Indiana University Press.
Kostyrchenko, G. (1995). *Out of the Red Shadows: Anti-Semitism in Stalin's Russia*. Amherst, N.Y.: Prometheus Books.
Kotkin, J. (2002). "The Christian Right, Conservatism, and the Jews." *The Jewish Journal of Greater Los Angeles*, June 6.
Krauthammer, C. (2002a). "Please Excuse the Jews for Living." *Jerusalem Post*, Apr. 29.
———. (2002b). "He Tarries: Jewish Messianism and the Oslo Peace." Lecture given at Bar-Ilan University, June 10. www.biu.ac.il/Spokesman/Krauthammer-text.html.
———. (2004a). "Gibson's Blood Libel." *Washington Post*, Mar. 5: A23.
———. (2004b). *Democratic Realism: An American Foreign Policy for a Unipolar World*. Washington, D.C.: The AEI Press.
Kristol, I. (2003). "The Neoconservative Persuasion." *Weekly Standard*, Aug. 25.

Kruse, K. M. (2005). *White Flight: Atlanta and the Making of Modern Conservatism*. Princeton: Princeton University Press.
Kwiatkowski, K. (2004a). "Open Door Policy." *American Conservative,* Jan. 19.
_____. (2004b). "The New Pentagon Papers." www.salon.com, Mar. 10.

Ladurie, E. L. (1987). *The French Peasantry 1450–1660*, trans. A. Sheridan. Berkeley: University of California Press. (Originally published in 1977.)
Lamb, B. (1990). Interview with Judith Miller. www.booknotes.org, June 17. www.booknotes.org/Transcript/?ProgramID=1008
Landa, J. T. (1994). *Trust, Ethnicity, and Identity: Beyond the New Institutional Economics of Ethnic Trading Networks, Contract Law, and Gift-exchange*. Ann Arbor: University of Michigan Press.
Laqueur, W. (1972). *A History of Zionism*. New York: Holt, Rinehart, and Winston.
Larsen, R. J., and E. Diener. (1987). "Affect Intensity as an Individual Difference Characteristic: A Review." *Journal of Research in Personality* 21: 1–39.
Laslett, P. (1977). *Family Life and Illicit Love in Earlier Generations*. Cambridge: Cambridge University Press.
_____. "Family and Household as Work Group and Kin Group: Areas of Traditional Europe Compared." In *Family Forms in Historic Europe*, ed. R. Wall, J. Robin, and P. Laslett. Cambridge: Cambridge University Press.
_____. (1984). *The World We Have Lost,* 3rd ed. New York: Scribners.
Laughland, J. (2003). "Flirting with Fascism: Neocon Theorist Michael Ledeen Draws more from Italian Fascism than from the American Right." *American Conservative,* June 30.
Lawrence, C. H. (1994). *The Friars: The Impact of the Early Mendicant Movement on Western Culture*. London: Longman.
Ledeen, M. (2002). *War on the Terror Masters: Why It Happened, Where We Are Now, Why We'll Win*. New York: St. Martin's Press.
Lenz, F. (1931). "The Inheritance of Intellectual Gifts," in *Human Heredity*, trans. E. Paul and C. Paul, ed. E. Baur, E. Fischer, and F. Lenz. New York: Macmillan.
Lerner, M. (2002). Editor's note. www.tikkun.com. Sept.
Levering-Lewis, D. (1984). "Shortcuts to the Mainstream: Afro-American and Jewish Notables in the 1920s and 1930s." In *Jews in Black Perspective: A Dialogue*, ed. J. R. Washington. Rutherford, N.J.: Fairleigh Dickinson University; London and Cranbury, N.J.: Associated University Presses.
Levin, D. T. (1996). "Classifying Faces by Race: The Structure of Face Categories." *Journal of Experimental Psychology: Learning, Memory, and Cognition* 22: 1364–82.
Levine, D. L. (1994). "Without Malice but with Forethought." In *Leo Strauss: Political Philosopher and Jewish Thinker*, ed. K. Deutsch and W. Nicgorski. Lanham, Md.: Rowman and Littlefield.
Lewis, B. (1984). *The Jews of Islam*. Princeton: Princeton University Press.

Lewis, B. (2002). *What Went Wrong? The Clash between Islam and Modernity in the Middle East*. New York: Oxford University Press.

Leyser, K. J. (1979). *Rule and Conflict in Early Medieval Society*. London: E. Arnold.

Liebman, A. (1979). *Jews and the Left*. New York: John Wiley and Sons.

Liebman, C. (1973). *The Ambivalent American Jew: Politics, Religion, and Family in American Jewish Life*. Philadelphia: Jewish Publication Society.

Lilienthal, A. M. (1953). *What Price Israel?* Chicago: Henry Regnery Co.

_____. (1978). *The Zionist Connection: What Price Peace?* New York: Dodd, Mead.

Lind, M. (2003). "I Was Smeared." *History News Network*, June 30. http://hnn.us/articles/1530.html

Lindbergh, A. M. (1980). *War Within and Without: Diaries and Letters of Anne Morrow Lindbergh*. New York: Harcourt Brace Jovanovich.

Lindemann, A. S. (1991). *The Jew Accused: Three Anti-Semitic Affairs (Dreyfus, Beilis, Frank), 1894–1915*. New York: Cambridge University Press.

_____. (1997). *Esau's Tears: Modern Anti-Semitism and the Rise of the Jews*. New York: Cambridge University Press.

Lipset, S. M. (1988). *Revolution and Counterrevolution: Change and Persistence in Social Structures*, rev. ed. New Brunswick, N.J.: Transaction. (Originally published in 1968 and 1970.)

Lipset, S. M., and E. Raab. (1995). *Jews and the New American Scene*. Cambridge: Harvard University Press.

Lloyd, J. (2006). "Research Presents Disturbing Picture of Modern Life." *Financial Times*, Oct. 8.

Lobe, J. (2002a). "The Anniversary of a Neo-Imperial Moment." www.AlterNet.org, Sept. 12.

_____. (2002b). "Bush's Trusty New Mideast Point Man." *Asia Times*, Dec. 19. www.atimes.com/atimes/Middle_East/DL19Ak01.html

_____. (2003a). "All in the Family." Inter Press Service News Agency, Mar. 7.

_____. (2003b). "Pentagon Office Home to Neo-con Network." Inter Press Service News Agency, Aug. 7.

_____. (2003c). "What is a Neoconservative Anyway?" Inter Press Service News Agency, Aug. 12.

Locke, R. (2002). "Leo Strauss, Conservative Mastermind." www.FrontPageMagazine.com. May 31.

Luchaire, A. (1912). *Social France at the Time of Philip Augustus*. New York: Frederick Ungar.

Lustick, I. A. (1987). "Israel's Dangerous Fundamentalists." *Foreign Policy* 68 (Fall): 123–24.

Lynch, J. E. (1972a, b). "Marriage and Celibacy of the Clergy: The Discipline of the Western Church: An Historical-Canonical Synopsis." *Jurist* 23: 14–38; 189–212.

Lynch, J. H. (1992). *The Medieval Church*. London: Longman.

Lynn, R. (1992). "Intelligence: Ethnicity and Culture." In *Cultural Diversity and the Schools*, ed. J. Lynch, C. Modgil, and S. Modgil. London: Falmer Press.

MacDonald, K. B. (1983). "Production, Social Controls and Ideology: Toward a Sociobiology of the Phenotype." *Journal of Social and Biological Structures* 6: 297–317.

_____. (1990). "Mechanisms of Sexual Egalitarianism in Western Europe." *Ethology and Sociobiology* 11: 195–238.

_____. (1991). "A Perspective on Darwinian Psychology: The Importance of Domain-General Mechanisms, Plasticity, and Individual Differences." *Ethology and Sociobiology* 12: 449–80.

_____. (1992). "Warmth as a Developmental Construct: An Evolutionary Analysis." *Child Development* 63: 753–73.

_____. (1994/2002). *A People That Shall Dwell Alone: Judaism as a Group Evolutionary Strategy with Diaspora Peoples.* Lincoln, Nebr.: iUniverse. (Originally published in 1994 by Praeger, Westport, Conn.)

_____. (1995a). "The Establishment and Maintenance of Socially Imposed Monogamy in Western Europe." *Politics and the Life Sciences* 14: 3–23.

_____. (1995b). "Focusing on the Group: Further Issues Related to Western Monogamy." *Politics and the Life Sciences* 14: 38–46.

_____. (1997). "Life History Theory and Human Reproductive Behavior: Environmental/Contextual Influences and Heritable Variation." *Human Nature* 8: 327–59.

_____. (1998/2002). *The Culture of Critique: An Evolutionary Analysis of Jewish Involvement in Twentieth-Century Intellectual and Political Movements.* Bloomington, Ind.: 1stbooks Library. (Originally published in 1998 by Praeger, Westport, Conn. Paperback ed. with new Preface.)

_____. (1998/2004). *Separation and Its Discontents: Toward an Evolutionary Theory of Anti-Semitism.* Bloomington, Ind.: 1stbooks Library. (Originally published in 1998 by Praeger, Westport, Conn.)

_____. (1999). "Jewish Involvement in Shaping American Immigration Policy, 1881–1965: A Historical Review." *Population and Environment* 19: 295–357.

_____. (2000). "The Numbers Game: Ethnic Conflict in the Contemporary World." *Population and Environment* 21: 413–25.

_____. (2001). "An Integrative Evolutionary Perspective on Ethnicity." *Politics and the Life Sciences* 21: 67–79.

_____. (2002). "The Education of a Midwestern Industrialist." *The Occidental Quarterly* 2: 69–77.

_____. (2003a). "The Conservatism of Fools: A Response to John Derbyshire." www.kevinmacdonald.net/derb.htm, Mar.

_____. (2003b). "Thinking about Neoconservatism." www.vdare.com, Sept. 18.

_____. (2004a). "Evolutionary Strategies of Enthocentric Behavior."

The Occidental Quarterly 4: 69–83.

———. (2004b). "Jews and the Democrats: Reflections on the 2004 Election." Unpublished MS.

———. (2005). "A Revisionist View of Anti-Semitism." *The Occidental Quarterly* 5: 77–83.

———. (2006a). "The Frankfurt School of Social Research and the Origins of the Therapeutic State." *The Occidental Quarterly* 6: 7–36.

———. (2006b). "Heidi does Long Beach: The SPLC vs. Academic Freedom." www.vdare.com, Nov. 14.

———. (2007). "MidEast Policy—Immigration Policy: Is the Other Boot about to Drop?" www.vdare.com, Jan. 31.

MacFarlane, A. (1986). *Marriage and Love in England: Modes of Reproduction, 1300–1840*. London: Basil Blackwell.

Mahler, R. (1985). *Hasidism and the Jewish Enlightenment: Their Confrontation in Galicia and Poland in the First Half of the Nineteenth Century*. Philadelphia: Jewish Publication Society of America.

Malthus, T. R. (1976). *An Essay on the Principle of Population*. New York: W. W. Norton. (Originally published in 1798.)

Mann, J. (2004). *Rise of the Vulcans*. New York: Viking.

Marchant, R. A. (1969). *The Church under the Law*. Cambridge: Cambridge University Press.

Marcus, S. (1973). *Father Coughlin: The Tumultuous Life of the Priest of the Little Flower*. Boston: Little, Brown and Company.

Margolis, E. (2001). "Sharon Won the Battle, but Does it Mean More War?" *Toronto Sun*, Feb. 11.

Marshall, R. (2004). "Sharon Offers the Palestinians a Prison Camp and Calls it Peace." *Washington Report on Middle Eastern Affairs*, Mar. 6–8.

Masalha, N. (1992). *Expulsion of the Palestinians: The Concept of "Transfer" in Zionist Political Thought, 1882–1948*. Washington, D.C.: Institute for Palestine Studies.

Massing, M. (1987). "Trotsky's Orphans." *New Republic*, June 22.

———. (2002). "Deal Breakers." *American Prospect*, Mar. 11.

Mayer, A. J. (1988). *Why Did the Heavens Not Darken? The "Final Solution" in History*. New York: Pantheon.

McDowell, W. C. (1998). "Keeping Them 'In the Same Boat Together.'" In *African Americans and Jews in the Twentieth Century,* ed. V. P. Franklin, N. L. Grant, H. M. Kletnick, and G. R. McNeil. Columbia: University of Missouri Press.

Mearsheimer, J. J., and S. M. Walt. (2006). "The Israel Lobby and U.S. Foreign Policy." Harvard University Kennedy School of Government, Faculty Research Working Papers Series.

Medved, M. (1992/1993). *Hollywood vs. America*. New York: Harper Perennial.

Meyer, M. A. (1988). *Response to Modernity: A History of the Reform Movement in Judaism*. New York: Oxford University Press.

Miele, F. (2002). *Intelligence, Race, and Genetics: Conversations with Arthur Jensen.* Boulder, Colo.: Westview.

Milbank, D. (2002). "A Sound Bite so Good, the President Wishes He Said It." *Washington Post,* July 2: A13.

Miles, J. (2005). "NASCAR Nation." *The New York Times Book Review,* May 22.

Milinski, M., D. Semmann, and H. Krambeck. (2002). "Reputation Helps Solve the 'Tragedy of the Commons.'" *Nature* 415: 424–26.

Miller, J. G., and D. M. Bersoff. (1992). "Culture and moral judgment: How are conflicts between justice and interpersonal responsibilities resolved?" *Journal of Personality and Social Psychology* 62: 541–54.

Milstein, M. H. (1991). "Strategic Ties or Tentacles? Institute for National Security Affairs." *Washington Report on Middle East Affairs,* Oct. 27.

Mohtashemi, M., and L. Mui. (2003). "Evolution of Indirect Reciprocity by Social Information: The Role of Trust and Reputation in Evolution of Altruism." *Journal of Theoretical Biology* 223: 523–31.

Money, J. (1980). *Love, and Love Sickness: The Science of Sex, Gender Differences, and Pair Bonding.* Baltimore: Johns Hopkins University Press.

Monteith, M. J., L. Ashburn-Nardo, C. I. Voils, and A. M. Czopp. (2002). "Putting the Brakes on Prejudice: On the Development and Operation of Cues for Control." *Journal of Personality and Social Psychology* 83: 1029–50.

Moody, J. (2002). "Race, School Integration and Friendship Segregation in America." *American Journal of Sociology* 107: 679–716.

Moore, J. (2004). "How Chalabi and the White House Held the Front Page: The *New York Times* has Burned its Reputation on a Pyre of Lies about Iraq." *Guardian,* May 29.

Morris, S. L. (2003). "Shipwrecked: Swimming with Sharks in a Sea of Arts Funding." *LA Weekly,* June 27–July 3.

Mosse, G. L. (1970). *Germans and Jews: The Right, the Left, and the Search for a "Third Force" in Pre-Nazi Germany.* New York: Howard Fertig.

Moynihan, D. P. (1975/1996). Statement by Ambassador Daniel P. Moynihan, United States Representative to the United Nations, in Plenary, in Response to the United Nations Resolution Equating Zionism and Racial Discrimination, Nov. 10, 1975. Reprinted in *The Essential Neoconservative Reader,* ed. M. Gerson. Reading, Mass.: Addison-Wesley, 1996.

Mundill, R. R. (1998). *England's Jewish Solution: Experiment and Expulsion, 1262–1290.* New York: Cambridge University Press.

Muravchik, J. (2002). *Heaven on Earth: The Rise and Fall of Socialism.* San Francisco: Encounter Books.

Muravchik, J. (2003). "The Neoconservative Cabal." *Commentary,* Sept.

Murray, S. (2005). "Dean's Words Draw Democratic Rebukes." *The Washington Post,* June 9.

Neuringer, S. M. (1980). *American Jewry and United States Immigration Pol-*

icy, 1881–1953. New York: Arno Press.
Neusner, J. (1987). *Judaism and Christianity in the Age of Constantine: History, Messiah, Israel, and the Initial Confrontation*. Chicago: University of Chicago Press.
New York Times Editors. (2002). "The Times and Iraq." *New York Times*, May 26.
Nicosia, F. R. (1985). *The Third Reich and the Palestine Question*. Austin: University of Texas Press.
Niewyk, D. L. (1980). *The Jews in Weimar Germany*. Baton Rouge: Louisiana State University Press.
Noakes, J. and G. Pridham. (1984). *Nazism, 1919–1945*, vol. 2: *State, Economy, and Society, 1933–1939*. Exeter: University of Exeter.
Nolte, E. (1965). *Three Faces of Fascism*, trans. L. Vennowitz. New York: Holt, Rinehart and Winston.
Noonan, J. T. (1973). "Power to Choose," *Viator* 4: 419–34.
Norden, E. (1995). "An Unsung Jewish Prophet." *Commentary* 99 (4): 37–43.
North, G. (2003). "An Introduction to Neoconservatism." www.LewRockwell.com, June 10.
Nosek, B. A., M. R. Banaji, and A. G. Greenwald. (2002). "Harvesting Intergroup Attitudes and Stereotypes from a Demonstration Website." *Group Dynamics* 6: 101–15.
Novick, P. (1999). *The Holocaust in American Life*. Boston: Houghton Mifflin.

Oberg, J. (2003). "Do You Want to Know Who the Americans Running Iraq Really Are?" The Transnational Foundation for Peace and Future Research, May 14. www.transnational.org.
Öhman, A. (2005). "Conditioned Fear of a Face: A Prelude to Ethnic Enmity?" *Science* 309: 711–13.
Okrent, D. (2004). "Weapons of Mass Destruction? Or Mass Distraction?" *New York Times*, May 30.
Olsson, A., J. P. Ebert, M. R. Banaji, and E. A. Phelps. (2005). "The Role of Social Groups in the Persistence of Learned Fear." *Science* 309: 785–87.

Panchanathan K., and R. Boyd. (2003). "A Tale of Two Defectors: The Importance of Standing for Evolution of Indirect Reciprocity." *Journal of Theoretical Biology* 224: 115–26.
Parkes, J. (1976). *The Jew in the Medieval Community*, 2nd ed. New York: Hermon Press.
Parsons, J. (1998). *Human Population Competition: A Study of the Pursuit of Power through Numbers*. Lewiston, N.Y.: The Edwin Mellen Press.
Patai, R., and J. Patai, (1989). *The Myth of the Jewish Race*. Detroit: Wayne State University Press. (First published in 1975.)
Paul, R. (2003). "National Endowment for Democracy: Paying to Make Enemies for America." www.antiwar.com, Oct. 11.

Petersen, W. (1955). "The 'Scientific' Basis of our Immigration Policy." *Commentary* 20 (July): 77–86.
Peterson, G. (2006). "Brawl Puts Glaring Spotlight on NBA." *Contra Costa Times,* Dec. 22.
Peukert, D. J. K. (1982). *Inside Nazi Germany: Conformity, Opposition, and Racism in Everyday Life.* New Haven: Yale University Press.
Pew Forum on Religion and Public Life. (2006). *Religious Voters and the Midterm Elections.* Washington, D.C., Nov. 13.
Pfennig, D. W., and P. W. Sherman. (1995). "Kin Recognition." *Scientific American*, 272: 98–103.
Phelps, E. A., K. J. O'Connor, W. A. Cunningham, E. S. Funayama, J. C. Gatenby, J. C. Gore, and M. R. Banaji. (2000). "Performance on Indirect Measure of Race Evaluation Predicts Amygdala Activation." *Journal of Cognitive Neuroscience* 12: 729–38.
Phillips, K. P. (1999). *The Cousins' Wars: Religion, Politics, and the Triumph of Anglo-America.* New York: Basic Books.
Pincus, W., and D. Priest. (2003). "Some Iraq Analysts Felt Pressure from Cheney Visits." *Washington Post,* June 5.
Pipes, D. (2001). "The Danger Within: Militant Islam in America." *Commentary,* Nov.
Pipes, R. (1990). *The Russian Revolution.* New York: Knopf.
Platz, S. G., and H. M. Hosch (1988). "Cross-Racial/Ethnic Eyewitness Identification." *Journal of Applied Social Psychology*: 972–84.
Podhoretz, N. (1986). "The Hate that Dare not Speak Its Name." *Commentary,* Nov.
_____. (2000). *My Love Affair with America: A Cautionary Tale of a Cheerful Conservative.* New York: Free Press.
_____. (2002). "In Praise of the Bush Doctrine." *Commentary,* Sept.
Porter, R. (1982). "Mixed feelings: The Enlightenment and Sexuality in Eighteenth-Century Britain." In *Sexuality in Eighteenth-Century Britain,* ed. P. Bouce. Manchester: Manchester University Press.
Prinz, J. (1934). *Wir Juden.* Berlin: Erich Press.
Project for the New American Century. (1998a). Letter to President Clinton. Jan. 26. www.newamericancentury.org/iraqclintonletter.htm.
_____. (1998b). Letter to Speaker of the House Newt Gingrich and Senate Majority Leader Trent Lott. May 29. www.new-americancentury.org/iraqletter/1998.htm
_____. (2002). Letter to President George W. Bush. Apr. 3. www.newamericancentury.org/Bushletter-040302.htm.
Prometheus Research Library. (2002). *Dog Days: James P. Cannon vs. Max Shachtman in the Communist League of America 1931–1933.* New York: Prometheus Research Library.

Raaflaub, K. A. (1986a). "The Conflict of the Orders in Archaic Rome: A Comprehensive and Comparative Approach." In *Social Struggles in Ar-*

chaic Rome: New Perspectives on the Conflict of the Orders, ed. K. A. Raaflaub. Berkeley: University of California Press.

———. (1986b). "From Protection and Defense to Offense and Participation: Stages in the Conflict of the Orders." In *Social Struggles in Archaic Rome: New Perspectives on the Conflict of the Orders,* ed. K. A. Raaflaub. Berkeley: University of California Press.

Raine, A., J. R. Meloy, S. Buhrle, J., Stoddard, L. LaCasse, and M. S. Muchsbaum. (1998). "Reduced Prefrontal and Increased Subcortical Brain Functioning Assessed Using Positron Emission Tomography in Predatory and Affective Murderers." *Behavioral Sciences and the Law* 16: 319–32.

Reich, R. (1997). *Locked in the Cabinet.* New York: Scribner.

Reznikoff, C., ed. (1957). *Louis Marshall: Champion of Liberty. Selected Papers and Addresses,* vol. 1. Philadelphia: Jewish Publication Society.

Riga, L. (2006). "Ethnonationalism, Assimilation, and the Social Worlds of the Jewish Bolsheviks in Fin de Siècle Tsarist Russia." *Comparative Studies in Society and History* 48: 72–97.

Risen, J. (2004). "How Pair's Finding on Terror Led to Clash on Shaping Intelligence." *New York Times,* Apr. 28.

Roberts, B. W., O. S. Chernyshenko, S. Stark, and L. S. Goldberg. (2005). "The Structure of Conscientiousness: An Empirical Investigation Based on Seven Major Personality Questionnaires." *Personnel Psychology* 58: 103–39.

Roebroeks, W. (2001). "Hominid Behaviour and the Earliest Occupation of Europe: An Exploration." *Journal of Human Evolution* 41: 437–61.

Rokach, L. (1986). *Israel's Sacred Terrorism,* 3rd ed. Belmont, Mass.: Association of Arab-American University Graduates, Inc. (Originally published in 1980.)

Rose, P. L. (1992). *Wagner: Race and Revolution.* New Haven: Yale University Press.

Rosenblum, J. (2002). "The Power of an Idea." *Jewish Media Resources,* July 5.

———. (2003). "A Vision in Tatters." *Jewish Media Resources,* June 20.

Ross, E. A. (1914). *The Old World and the New: The Significance of Past and Present Immigration to the American People.* New York: The Century Co.

Ross, O. (2003). "Power Struggle Crisis Worries Jewish Groups." *Toronto Star,* Oct. 4.

Rothbart, M., and M. Taylor. (2001). Commentary on Gilwhite's "Are ethnic groups biological 'species' to the human brain? Essentialism in our cognition of some social categories." *Current Anthropology* 42: 544–45.

Rothman, S., and S. R. Lichter. (1982). *Roots of Radicalism: Jews, Christians, and the New Left.* New York: Oxford University Press.

Rubenstein, J. (1996). *Tangled Loyalties: The Life and Times of Ilya Ehrenburg.* New York: Basic Books.

Ruppin, A. (1971). *Arthur Ruppin: Memoirs, Diaries, Letters,* ed. A. Bein, trans. K. Gershon. London: Weidenfeld and Nicholson.

Ruppin, A. (1973). *The Jews in the Modern World.* London: Macmillan.
Rushton, J. P. (1989). "Genetic Similarity, Human Altruism, and Group Selection." *Behavioral and Brain Sciences* 12: 503–59.
_____. (1999). "Genetic Similarity Theory and the Nature of Ethnocentrism." In *In-group/Out-group Behavior in Modern Societies*, ed. K. Thienpont and R. Cliquet. The Hague: Vlaamse Gemeenschap/CBGS.
Rushton, J. P., and T. A. Bons. (2005). "Mate Choice and Friendship in Twins: Evidence for Genetic Similarity." *Psychological Science*, 16: 555–59.
Russell, J. C. (1994). *The Germanization of Early Medieval Christianity.* New York: Oxford University Press.

Saba, M. P. (1984). *The Armageddon Network.* Brattleboro, N.H.: Amana Books.
Sachar, H. M. (1992). *A History of Jews in America.* New York: Alfred A. Knopf.
Sacks, J. (1993). *One People? Tradition, Modernity, and Jewish Unity.* London: The Littman Library of Jewish Civilization.
Sailer, S. (2004). "Ethnic Electorate: Myths and Realities." *The American Conservative*, Oct. 25: 7–11.
_____. (2005a). "Calling GOP! Sailer Vindicated on Marriage Gap . . . and Immigration?" www.vdare.com, Jan. 23.
_____. (2005b). "The Dirt Gap: The Fundamental Cause of Red vs. Blue States." *The American Conservative*, Feb. 14.
_____. (2005c). "Don't Worry, Democrats! This Hispanic Hype is Hogwash." www.vdare.com, May 29.
_____. (2006). "The Incredible Latino Supervote, the Invisible White Majority: Tales from Election '06." www.vdare.com, Nov. 12.
_____. (2007). "Fragmented Future: Multiculturalism Doesn't Make Vibrant Communities but Defensive Ones." *The American Conservative,* Jan. 15.
Salter, F. K. (1994). "Does Female Beauty Increase Male Confidence of Paternity? A Blank Slate Hypothesis." *Ethology and Sociobiology*.
_____. (1998). *Ethnic Infrastructures USA: An Evolutionary Analysis of Ethnic Hierarchy in a Liberal Democracy.* MS in prep. Forschungsstelle für Humanethologie in der Max-Planck-Gesellschaft, Andechs, Germany.
_____. (2002a). "Estimating Ethnic Genetic Interests: Is it Adaptive to Resist Replacement Migration?" *Population and Environment* 24: 111–40.
_____. (2002b). "Fuzzy but Real: America's Ethnic Hierarchy." Paper presented at the meetings of the Association for Politics and the Life Sciences, Montreal, Aug. 9.
_____. (2003/2006). *On Genetic Interests: Family, Ethny, and Humanity in an Age of Mass Migration.* New Brunswick, N.J.: Transaction. (Originally published in 2003 by Peter Lang, Bern, Switzerland.)
_____., ed. (2004). *Welfare, Ethnicity, and Altruism.* London: Routledge.

Samber, S. (2000). "Cheney has Earned Jewish Leaders' Respect." *Jewish World Review*, July 26.
Samuel, M. *You Gentiles*. (1924). New York: Harcourt, Brace.
Schatz, J. (1991). *The Generation: The Rise and Fall of the Jewish Communists of Poland*. Berkeley: University of California Press.
Schlesinger, A. (1947). *The Vital Center: The Politics of Freedom*. Boston: Houghton Mifflin.
Schneier, M. (1999). *Shared Dreams: Martin Luther King, Jr. and the Jewish Community*. Woodstock, Vt.: Jewish Lights Pub.
Scholem, G. (1971). *The Messianic Idea in Judaism*. New York: Schocken Books.
Semmann, D., H. Krambeck, and M. Milinski. (2005). "Reputation is Valuable Within and Outside One's Own Social Group." *Behavioral Ecology and Sociobiology* 57: 611–16.
Shafarevich, I. (1989). "Russophobia." *Nash Sovremennik* (Moscow) (June and Nov.): 167–92. Trans. *JPRS-UPA-90-115* (Mar. 22, 1990): 2–37.
Shahak, I. (1993). "Relations between Israel and Organized American Jews." *Middle East Policy Council Journal* 2 (3).
_____. (1994). *Jewish History, Jewish Religion: The Weight of Three Thousand Years*. Boulder, Colo.: Pluto Press.
Shahak, I., and N. Mezvinsky. (1999). *Jewish Fundamentalism in Israel*. London: Pluto Press.
Shamir, I. (2001). *Mamilla Pool*. http://www.israelshamir.net, 4/24.
Shavit, Y. (1988). *Jabotinsky and the Revisionist Movement, 1925–1948*. London: Frank Cass and Co.
Shimoni, G. (2003). *Community and Conscience: The Jews in Apartheid South Africa*. Hanover, N.H.: University Press of New England.
Silbiger, S. (2000). *The Jewish Phenomenon: Seven Keys to the Enduring Wealth of a People*. Atlanta, Ga.: Longstreet Press.
Simon Wiesenthal Center. (2002). Press Release. http://www.wiesenthal.com, Nov. 10.
_____. (2003). Press Release. "Buchanan: War in Iraq Fault of Israel and the Jews." http://www.wiesenthal.com, Mar. 12.
Sims, B. (1992). *Workers of the World Undermined: American Labor's Role in U.S. Foreign Policy*. Boston: South End Press.
Skube, M. (2006). "Duke's Recovery from a Rush to Judgment." *Los Angeles Times*, December 31.
Slezkine, Y. (2004). *The Jewish Century*. Princeton: Princeton University Press.
Smith, R. M. (1988). "The 'American Creed' and American Identity: The Limits of Liberal Citizenship in the United States." *Western Political Science Quarterly* 41: 225–52.
Sobel, B. Z. (1986). "Exodus from Israel." In *Voices from Israel: Understanding the Israeli Mind*, ed. E. Levine. New York: Herzl Press.
Sobran, J. (1996). "The Buchanan Frenzy." *Sobran's*, Mar.

_____. (2002). "A Call for World War IV." *Sobran's*, Sept.
Social Democrats, USA. (2003). "For Democracy in Iraq and the Middle East." http://www.socialdemocrats.org/Iraq.html.
Sokolovsky, J. (2003). "For Portugal's Crypto-Jews, New Rabbi tries to Blend Tradition and Custom." *Jewish Telegraph Agency*, Oct. 13.
Soloveichik, M. Y. (2003). "The Virtue of Hate." *First Things* 129: 41–46.
Sombart, W. (1913/1982). *Jews and Modern Capitalism*, trans. M. Epstein. New Brunswick, N.J.: Transaction Books.
Sorkin, A. R. (2004). "Schlepping to Moguldom." *New York Times*, Sept. 5.
Southwood, T. R. E. (1977). "Habitat, the Temple for Ecological Strategies?" *Journal of Animal Ecology* 46: 337–66.
_____. (1981). "Bionomic Strategies and Population Parameters." In *Theoretical Ecology: Principles and Applications*, ed. R. M. May. Sunderland, Mass.: Sinauer Associates.
Sowell, T. (1983). *The Economics and Politics of Race: An International Perspective*. New York: W. Morrow.
_____. (1998). *Conquests and Cultures: An International History*. New York: Basic Books.
Stanovich, K. E. (1999). *Who is Rational?: Individual Differences in Reasoning*. Hillsdale, N.J.: Erlbaum.
Steinlight, S. (2001). *The Jewish Stake in America's Changing Demography: Reconsidering a Misguided Immigration Policy*. Washington D.C.: Center for Immigration Studies.
_____. (2004). "High Noon to Midnight: Why Current Immigration Policy Dooms American Jewry." Center for Immigration Studies, Apr.
Stocking, G. W. (1968). *Race, Evolution, and Culture: Essays in the History of Anthropology*. New York: Free Press.
_____. (1989). "The Ethnographic Sensibility of the 1920s and the Dualism of the Anthropological Tradition." *History of Anthropology* 6: 208–76.
Stoddard, L. (1922). *The Revolt against Civilization: The Menace of the Under-Man*. New York: Scribner and Sons.
Stone, L. (1977). *The Family, Sex, and Marriage in England: 1500–1800*. New York: Harper and Row.
Stone, L. (1980). *The Road to Divorce*. Oxford: Oxford University Press.
Stone, R. (1992). "Random Samples." *Science* 257: 743.
Strauss, L. (1952). *Persecution and the Art of Writing*. Westport, Conn.: Greenwood.
_____. (1962/1994). "Why We Remain Jews: Can Jewish Faith and History Still Speak to Us?" In *Leo Strauss: Political Philosopher and Jewish Thinker*, ed. K. L. Deutsch and W. Nicgorski. Lanham, Md.: Rowman and Littlefield.
Subtelny, O. (1988). *Ukraine: A History*. Toronto: University of Toronto Press.
Sumner, W. G. (1906). *Folkways*. New York: Ginn.

Svonkin, S. (1997). *Jews Against Prejudice: American Jews and the Fight for Civil Liberties*. New York: Columbia University Press.
Sykes, B. (2001). *The Seven Daughters of Eve*. New York: Norton.
Szajkowski, Z. (1967). "Paul Nathan, Lucien Wolf, Jacob H. Schiff and the Jewish Revolutionary Movements in Eastern Europe." *Jewish Social Studies* 29: 1–19.
_____. (1974). *Jews, Wars, and Communism: The Impact of the 1919–1920 Red Scare on American Jewish Life*. New York: KTAV Publishing.
_____. (1977). *Kolchak, Jews and the American Intervention in Northern Russia and Siberia, 1918–1920*. Privately published, copyright S. Frydman.

Tacitus, C. (1942). *The History*. In *The Complete Works of Tacitus*, ed. M. Hadas, trans. A. J. Church and W. J. Broadribb. New York: Modern Library.
Tannenhaus, S. (2003). Interview with Paul Wolfowitz. United States Department of Defense News Transcript, May 9. http://www.defenselink.mil/transcripts/2003/tr20030509-depsecdef0223.html
Tarcov, N., and T. L. Pangle. (1987). Epilogue: "Leo Strauss and the History of Political Philosophy." In *History of Political Philosophy*, 3rd ed., ed. L. Strauss and J. Cropsey. Chicago: University of Chicago Press.
Taylor, J. (2002). Reply to David Horowitz. *American Renaissance*. http:// www.amren.com/inthenews/horowitz_reply.htm
Teitelbaum, M. S., and J. Winter. (1998). *A Question of Numbers: High Migration, Low Fertility, and the Politics of National Identity*. New York: Hill and Wang.
Tellenbach, G. (1993). *The Church in Western Europe from the Tenth to the Early Twelfth Century*. Cambridge: Cambridge University Press.
Thernstrom, S., and A. Thernstrom. (1997). *America in Black and White: One Nation, Indivisible*. New York: Simon and Schuster.
Tifft, S. E., and A. S. Jones. (1999). *The Trust: The Private and Powerful Family behind the New York Times*. Boston: Little Brown and Co.
Triandis, H. C. (1990). "Cross-Cultural Studies of Individualism and Collectivism." *Nebraska Symposium on Motivation 1989: Cross Cultural Perspectives*. Lincoln: University of Nebraska Press.
_____. (1991). "Cross-Cultural Differences in Assertiveness/Competition vs. Group Loyalty/Cohesiveness. In *Cooperation and Prosocial Behavior*, ed. R. A. Hinde and J. Groebel. Cambridge: Cambridge University Press.
Trivers, R. (1986). *Social Evolution*. Cambridge: Harvard University Press.
Trotter, J. W. (1998). "African Americans, Jews, and the City: Perspectives from the Industrial Era, 1900–1950." In *African Americans and Jews in the Twentieth Century*, ed. V. P. Franklin, N. L. Grant, H. M. Kletnick, and G. R. McNeil. Columbia: University of Missouri Press.

Tucker, K. (2007). "Country Radio Grapples with Changing Demographics." *Reuters/ Billboard*, Jan. 7.
Tucker, R. W. (1999). "Alone or with Others: The Temptations of Post-Cold War Power." *Foreign Affairs* 78 (6).
Tucker, T. (2006). "Racing Ratings go Flat." *Atlanta Journal Constitution*, Oct. 27.
Tullberg, J., and B. S. Tullberg. (1997). "Separation or Unity? A Model for Solving Ethnic Conflicts." *Politics and the Life Sciences* 16: 237–48.

Ullman, W. (1970). *The Growth of Papal Government in the Middle Ages: A Study in the Ideological Relation of Clerical to Lay Power*, 3rd ed. London: Methuen.

Vaksberg, A. (1994). *Stalin Against the Jews*, trans. A. W. Bouis. New York: Knopf.
Valentine, T., and M. Endo. (1992). "Towards an Exemplar Model of Face Processing: The Effects of Race and Distinctiveness." *Quarterly Journal of Experimental Psychology* (44A): 671–703.
Van Creveld, M. (2003). "Wir vernichten uns selbst." Interview. http://de.indymedia.org/2003/01/39170.shtml, Jan. 30.
Van den Berghe, P. L. (1999). "Racism, Ethnocentrism, and Xenophobia: In Our Genes or in our Memes?" In *In-group/Out-group Behavior in Modern Societies*, ed. K. Thienpont and R. Cliquet. The Hague: NIDI CBGS Publications.
Van der Dennen, J. M. G. (1999). "Of Badges, Bonds, and Boundaries: In-Group/Out-Group Differentiation and Ethnocentrism Revisited." In *In-group/Out-group Behavior in Modern Societies*, ed. K. Thienpont and R. Cliquet. The Hague: Vlaamse Gemeenschap/CBGS.
Vann, B. (2003). "The Historical Roots of Neoconservatism: A Reply to a Slanderous Attack on Trotskyism." *World Socialist Website*, May 23.
Vaughn, A. T. (1997). *The Puritan Tradition in America, 1620–1730*, revised ed. Hanover, N.H.: University Press of New England.
Ventre, M. (2006). "Two Years Later, a Brawl that's Worse." MSNBC, December 18. www.msnbc.msn.com.
Vest, J. (2002). "The Men from JINSA and CSP." *Nation*, Aug. 15.
Veyne, P. (1987). "The Roman Empire." In *A History of Private Life*, vol. 1., ed. P. Veyne. Cambridge: Harvard University Press.
Vine, I. (1987). "Inclusive Fitness and the Self-System: The Roles of Human Nature and Sociocultural Processes in Intergroup Discrimination. In *The Sociobiology of Ethnocentrism*, ed. V. Reynolds, V. Falger, and I. Vine. Athens, Ga.: The University of Georgia Press.
Vital, D. (1975). *The Origins of Zionism*. Oxford: Oxford University Press.

Wald, A. (2003). "Are Trotskyites Running the Pentagon?" *History News Network*, June 23.

Waldman, P. (2004). "An Historian's Take on Islam Steers U.S. in Terrorism Fight: Bernard Lewis' Blueprint—Sowing Arab Democracy—Is Facing a Test in Iraq." *Wall Street Journal*, Feb. 3.
Walsh, W. T. (1930). *Isabella of Spain: The Last Crusader*. New York: Robert M. McBride.
Walzer, M. (1994). "Toward a New Realization of Jewishness." *Congress Monthly* 61 (4): 3–6.
———. (1997). "Blacks and Jews: A Personal Reflection." In *Struggles in the Promised Land: Toward a History of Black-Jewish Relations in the United States*, ed. J. Salzman and C. West. New York: Oxford University Press.
Warren, D. (1996). *Radio Priest: Charles Coughlin, the Father of Hate Radio*. New York: The Free Press.
Watanabe, T. (2003). "Assyrians Hope for U.S. Protection." *Los Angeles Times* (Orange County Edition), Feb. 17.
Watson, A. (1975). *Rome of the XII Tables*. Princeton: Princeton University Press.
Wattenberg, B. (1984). *The Good News is the Bad News is Wrong*. Washington, D.C.: AEI Press.
———. (2001). "Melt. Melting. Melted." *Jewish World Review*, Mar. 19.
———. (2002). Interview with Richard Perle. PBS, Nov. 14. www.pbs.org/ thinktank/transcript1017.html).
Weiss, P. (2002). "Holy or Unholy, Jews and Right in an Alliance." *New York Observer*, Sept. 19.
Westermarck, G. (1922). *The History of Human Marriage*, 5th ed. New York: Allerton.
Weyl, N., and W. Marına (1971). *American Statesmen on Slavery and the Negro*. New Rochelle, N.Y.: Arlington House.
Wheatcroft, G. (1996). *The Controversy of Zion: Jewish Nationalism, the Jewish State, and the Unresolved Jewish Dilemma*. Reading, Mass.: Addison-Wesley.
Whitaker, B. (2002). "U.S. Thinktanks Give Lessons in Foreign Policy." *Guardian*, Aug. 19.
Wiesel, E. (1985). *Against Silence: The Voice and Vision of Elie Wiesel*. Selected and edited by I. Abrahamson, vol. 1. New York: Holocaust Library.
Williams, V. J. (1998). "Franz Boas's Paradox and the African American Intelligentsia." In *African Americans and Jews in the Twentieth Century*, ed. V. P. Franklin, N. L. Grant, H. M. Kletnick, and G. R. McNeil. Columbia: University of Missouri Press.
Wilson, E. O. (1975). *Sociobiology: The New Synthesis*. Cambridge, Mass.: Belknap Press.
Wilson, J. C. (2004). *The Politics of Truth: Inside the Lies that Led to War and Betrayed My Wife's CIA Identity—A Diplomat's Memoir*. New York: Carroll and Graf.
Wilson, T. D. (2002). *Strangers to Ourselves: Discovering the Adaptive Un-*

conscious. Cambridge: Harvard University Press.
Wisse, R. (1981/1996). "The Delegitimation of Israel." *Commentary,* Oct. Reprinted in *The Essential Neoconservative Reader*, ed. M. Gerson. Reading, Mass.: Addison-Wesley.
Wistrich, R. (1998). "Blaming the Victim." *Commentary*, Feb.
Woodward, B. (2004). *Plan of Attack*. New York: Simon and Schuster.
Wrezin, M. (1994). *A Rebel in Defense of Tradition: The Life and Politics of Dwight Macdonald*. New York: Basic Books.
Wright, J. (2002). *Fixin' to Git: One Fan's Love Affair with NASCAR's Winston Cup*. Durham, N.C.: Duke University Press.
Wrigley, E. A. and R. Schofield (1981). *The Population History of England, 1541–1871*. Cambridge: Harvard University Press.

Yaffe, J. (1968). *The American Jews: Portrait of a Split Personality*. New York: Random House.
Yinon, O. (1982). *A Strategy for Israel in the 1980s*, trans. and ed. I. Shahak. Belmont, Mass.: Association of Arab-American University Graduates, Inc.

Zacharia, J. (2004). "Jews Fear Being Blamed for Iraq War." *Jerusalem Post*, May 29.
Zionist Organization of America. (2002). Press release. Aug. 7.

INDEX

Numbers in **bold** indicate an entire chapter or section of a chapter devoted to a given topic.

A

A. Philip Randolph Institute, 140
Abernethy, Virginia, 356
abortion, 48, 95, 150, 166, 196, 279, 314
Abraham (patriarch), 18, 41, 112, 170
Abrams, Elliot, 86, 135, 144, 154–55, 159, **179–80**, 183–84, 186
academia, 58, 224, 314, 320, 322–23, 328–29
ACLU (American Civil Liberties Union), 199
Adelman, Carol, 190
Adelman, Kenneth, 155, 188–90
ADL: see Anti-Defamation League
Adorno, T. W., 202 (see also: *The Authoritarian Personality*)
adultery, 280–81
AEI: see American Enterprise Institute
affirmative action
  in the United States, 146–47, 150, 166, 197, 207, 212, 320, 345
  in the USSR, 79, 81
Afghanistan, 175
AFL-CIO, 138–40
Africa
  North, 343
  sub-Saharan, 24, 208–10, 215, 272, 294, 326, 335
Africans: see blacks
African Americans: see blacks
aggressiveness, 346, 363
  as Jewish trait, 2–3, 7, 13–14, 40–41, **41–47**, 51, 55, 64, 66, 79, 84, 107–109, 120, 158, 165, 211–12, 241, 252
  psychological basis, 307–309
AIPAC: see American Israel Public Affairs Committee
AJCommittee: see American Jewish Committee
AJCongress: See American Jewish Congress

Albanians, 344
Alexander II, Tsar, 69, 258
Alexander III, Tsar, 3, 55, 69, 258
Alexander, Richard, 272
Alliance Israélite Universelle (France), 104
Al Qaeda, 140
altruism, 275–78
altruistic punishment, 295–98
Amador de los Rios, José, 26
Amalgamated Clothing Workers of America, 246
America: see United States of America
American Board of Rabbis, 133
American Civil Liberties Union (ACLU), 199
American Enterprise Institute (AEI), 123, 129–30, 139, 141, 159, 167–68, 172, 177, 179–80, 184, 187, 190, 194, 362
American Federation of Teachers, 151
American Hebrew, 245
American Indians, 272, 274, 344
American Israel Public Affairs Committee (AIPAC), 22–23, 36, 40, 122–24, 129, 132, 167, 174
American Jewish Committee (AJCommittee), 22, 34, 37, 43, 90, 116, 142, 146–47, 149, 192, 198–204, 206, 212–13, 215, 235, 246, 258
American Jewish Congress (AJCongress), 100, 102, 116, 132, 146, 192, 199–202, 204, 212, 246–47, 262–63
Americans for Democratic Action, 142
amygdala, 339
Anglo-Saxons, 225 n1, 228, 232, 256, 350
Annual Black/Jewish Congressional Awards Ceremony, 215
Annual Interethnic Congressional Leadership Forum, 215
Annual Latino/Jewish Congressional Awards Ceremony, 215
anti-communism, 123, 138, 142, 150,

152, 200, 247, 262
Anti-Defamation League (ADL), 30–32, 34–35, 132–33, 146, 187, 192, 199–200, 202–203, 205, 207, 209, 212–13, 234, 361
anti-Jewish attitudes and actions: see anti-Semitism
anti-Semitism (see also: holocaust, pogroms, quotas), vii, 2–4, **6–8**, 20–22, 27, 39, 44, 92–100, 133–34 n10, 143, 145–47, 160–61, 166, 170, 180, 201–203, 216, **225–54, 255–68**, 353, 355
  and blacks, 147, 153, 197, 209–11, 213–14, 222
  and Christianity, 13, 239, 277
  and "dual" loyalty, 4, 114
  and Jewish behavior, 43, 98–100, 158, 239
  and Jewish cultural influence, 60–61, 227–30, 252–54
  and Jewish economic competition with non-Jews, 13, 42–43, 93–96, 100, 208, 225–27, **247–48**, 252
  and Jewish radicalism, 49, 235–36, **244–47**, 253, **257–60**, 261
  and the non-Jewish Left, 147–48, 213, 222
  and Zionism, 4, **103–106**, 114–15, **243–44**
  charges of as form of intimidation, 45–46, 228–29, 231, 328
  in Russia and the USSR, **49–88**, 161, 165–66, 216, 219, 255
  in the United States, **6–8**, 22, 27, 86, 180, 196, 200, 217–18, **225–54, 255–68**, 347
Anti-Semitism and Emotional Disorder (Marie Jahoda et al.), 203
Antoninus Pius, Roman Emperor, 25
apartheid, 30, 47, 110, 140, 209–11
Arab world and Arabs (see also: Palestine and Palestinians, Muslim world, Islam), 3, 17–20, 22, 28, 38, 46, 90, 106, 108–109, 111–14, 124, 129, 132, 140, 143, 145–47, 153, 168–70, 176, 178, 181–83, 185–87, 194, 244, 267, 347, 361–62
Arafat, Yasser, 38, 90, 141, 172, 188
Armenians (Crimean), 80

Arms Control and Disarmament Agency (ACDA), 159, 174
aristocracy
  European, 8, 55, 273–78, 284–85, 293
  Leo Strauss on, 161–63
Ashkenazi Jews, vi, 35, 82, 101, 196
Asian voters in United States, 315
Asper family, 39, 129
Asper, Israel, 117–18, 129, 363
assimilationism, 59, 214, 353
  Jewish, 3, 89–91, 96–98, 101–103, 114, 145
  Jewish resistance to (see also: Zionism), 89–91, 96–98, 101–103, 114, 161, 204, 214, 241, 255, 353
Assyria and Assyrians, 25
Ateret Cohanim, 194
Atlanta Journal-Constitution, 316
Atlantic Monthly, 243
Auerbach, Elias, 101
Auster, Lawrence, 23
Australia, 1, 344, 358
Austria, 59–60
Austro-Hungarian Empire, 95
The Authoritarian Personality (T. W. Adorno et al.), 202, 204
Aviner, Shlomo, 19
Aztecs, 274

B
Baker, James A., 157, 174
Bakke, Allan, 146, 212
Baldwin, Neal, 239, 247, 249
Balfour Declaration, 103, 105, 111
Ball, George, 45
Banking, 59, 226
  Federal Reserve, **247–48**
Bantu, 344
Baron de Hirsch Fund, 348
Baruch, Bernard, 236, 267
Basic Books, 129, 135
basketball, 318–20
Bauer, Gary, 189 n121
Bavaria, 246
BBC (British Broadcasting Corporation), 362
Beaconsfield, Earl of (Benjamin Disraeli), 246
Beecher, Henry Ward, 297
Begin, Menachem, 105, 108, 110, 112,

116, 119, 145, 154 n117, 359, 360
Beizer, Mikhail, 73
Belgium, 344
Bell, Daniel, 150
Bell, Jeffrey, 189 n121
Bellow, Saul, 128
  Ravelstein, 172–74
Bendersky, Joseph, 7–8, **256–68**
Benedict, Ruth, 127
Ben-Gurion, David, 110–13
Ben Hur (play), 227
Benjamin, Walter, 61–62,
Bennett, James Gordon, 233
Bennett, William, 148, 189 n121
Berlin, Irving (Israel Baline), 230
Besharov, Douglas J., 179–80
Betar, 182
Bible: see Old Testament
Bikerman, I. L., 75
bilateral kinship patterns, 15, 288, 335
Birthright Israel, 35, 362
Black, Conrad, 129
Blacks, iv, 6, 35, 66 n35, 110, 146–47, 153, 179–80, **196–222**, 296, 304, 309–23, 343–44, 348
  alliance with Jews, 6, 146–47, **196–222**
  anti-Semitism of, 147, 153, 197, 209–11, 213–14, 222
  black Jews, 144
  civil rights movement, vii, 6, 124, 140, 146–47, 150, 152, 158, **196–222**
  ethnocentrism of, 310
  intelligence of, 197
  and NASCAR, 317–18
  and the NBA, 318–20
  white attitudes toward, 304, 309–23, 339–40
Bloom, Allan, 128, 161, 163, 172–74, 176
Blumrosen, Alfred W., 207
B'nai B'rith (see also: Anti-Defamation League), 139, 198–99
Board of Rabbis of Southern California, 115
Boas, Franz (see also: Boasian anthopology) 67–68, 121, 163, 201, 265, 353
Boasian anthropology, 8, 77, 201–202, 205, 353

and cultural relativism, 202
and denial of biological race, 201–202
Boeing Corporation, 151, 195
Bolshevism (communism in the Russian Empire, USSR, and Eastern and Central Europe) (see also: communism), 10, **49–88**, 240, 243–47, 253, 254, 257, 260, 264
  and Jews, vii, 3–4, 10, 14, 29–30, **49–88**, 135–41, 199–201, 209–10, 235, **244–47**, 250, 253, **257–63**, 265, 267
Bolshoi Theater, 65
Bolton, John, 189
Boot, Max, 122, 134
Boniface, Saint, 275
Borjas, George, 342
Bork, Ellen, 189 n121
Borowitz, Eugene, 33
Bradford, M. E., 148
Bradley Foundation, 36, 362
Brandeis, Louis, 105, 198, 238, 263
Breen, Joseph, 228
Breger, Marshall, 187
Britain and the British (see also: England and the English), 49, 103, 105, 108, 235–37, 243, 254, 256, 260, 266, 289, 344–45, 358, 362
British Broadcasting Corporation (BBC), 362
British Mandate of Palestine (see also: Palestine and Palestinians), 108, 113, 186
Brom, Shlomo, 183 n101
Bromberg, I. A., 75
Bronfman, Charles, 35, 362
Bronfman, Edgar, 362
Brotherhood of Man (film), 202
Brown v. Board of Education of Topeka, 198, 203
Bruce, Robert the, 300
Bryen, Stephen, 152, **167–68**, 184, 193
Buber, Martin, 102
Buchanan, Patrick, 125, 132–33, 148, 150, 347, 355
Buchenwald concentration camp, 151
Bulgakov, Mikhail, 78
Bulgars, 80
Bundism (Zionist socialist movement),

68
Burnham, James, 126–37
Buruma, Ian, 132
Bush, George H. W., 151, 157, 174–76, 187, 189
Bush, George W., 5, 14, 89–90, 124–26, 128, 130, 132–33, 139, 153, 167, 174–75, 177–79, 181, 183–84, 187–90, 207, 315–16
Buss, David, 307
Byelorussia, 54

C
Caesar, Irving, 230
Cameron, Billy (see also: *The International Jew*), 225 n1
Campbell, Joseph, 287
Campus Watch, 129, 192
Canaanites, 41, 113, 241
Canada and Canadians, 39, 117–18, 129, 240, 344, 358, 363
Canada-Israel Committee, 118
Canadian Jewish Congress, 117–18
Cannon, James P., 135–36
CanWest Global Communications, 39, 117–18, 129, 363
capitalism, 62–63, 67, 69, 77, 282, 292, 325
Carmichael, Stokely (Kwame Touré), 147, 213
Carter, Jimmy, 22, 38, 153–54, 156, 176
Catholic Church and Catholics, iii, 23, 27, 37, 218, 228–29, 238–39, 252, 271–86
  altruism of, 275–77
  clerical celibacy, 275–76
  and concubinage, **279, 279–80**
  and extended kinship relationships, **283–86**
  and Medieval Western European society, 274–78
  and monogamy, iii, 273–74, 278–83
  monasticism, 275–76
  mendicants, 275–77
Cavalli-Sforza, Luigi, 343
celibacy, 275–76, 281–82
Celler, Emanuel, 352
Center for Security Policy, 36, 123, 128, 362
Central Intelligence Agency: see CIA

Cervantes, Miguel de, 287
Chabad Lubavitch, 17–18, 170
Chalabi, Ahmed, 126, 130, 132, 182–84
Chalabi, Salem, 183
Chamberlain, Houston Stewart, 60, 101, 144
charitable donations, 315
Charles Martel, 300
chastity, 275
Chavez, Linda, 189 n121
Chechens, 80
Cheka (Soviet secret police organization), Jewish involvement in, 73, 82
Cheney, Dick, 5, 90, 125–26 n10, 128, 181, **187–90**, 193, 195
Central Europe, 255
Chernin, Kim, 20–21, 27–28
Chicago, University of, 128, 153, 160, 171–72, 176, 183, 191
Chicago Sun-Times, 129
Chicago Tribune, 38, 254
China and the Chinese, iv, vii, 136, 168, 174, 266, 272–74, 292, 335, 351
  overseas Chinese, 44, 50–53, 55–56
  US Chinese, 298, 351
China Commission, 168, 184
Chomsky, Noam, 109, 147
Christian Identity movement, 225 n1
Christian Science Monitor, 254
Christianity and Christians (see also: Catholic Church, Christian Identity movement, Evangelical Christianity, Orthodox Christianity, Protestantism, Puritans, Reformation), 7–9, 13, 16, 24, 27, 31, 38, 42–44, 48, 54–55, 60, 75–76, 78, 81, 83–86, 114, 127, 145, 149, 151, 196, 202, 205, 208, 218, 220, 225 n1, 229–32, 239, 241–43, 252–53, 256, 267, 271–94, 297, 353–54, 355, 360, 363
  and anti-Semitism, 127, 171, 239, 256, 277
  Jewish anti-Christian attitudes and activities, 7, 27, 31, 38, 43–44, 55, 60, 75–76, 78, 81, 83–86, 196, 205, 218, 229–32, 241, 243, 252, 254, 353–54, 360, 363
Christison, Bill, 175

Christison, Kathleen, 175
Churba, Joseph, 182
Church Fathers, 13
church-state separation (US), 31, 48, 196
Churchill, Winston, 49, 74, 161
CIA (Central Intelligence Agency), 46, 131, 142, 175, 179 n82, 183–84, 189, 193
Citizens Committee for Displaced Persons, 44, 349
civil liberties, 48, 196, 199
civil rights movement (US), vii, 6, 124, 140, 146–47, 150, 152, 158, **196–222**
    Jewish involvement in, vii, 124, 140, 146–47, 150, 152, **197–206**
    Jewish motives in promoting, **205–21**
Civil society, 326, 329, 335–36
Civil War, American, 296–97
Clark, Kenneth, 203
Clarke, Richard, 175
Clinton, Bill, 33, 38, 128, 155, 168, 174–75, 181, 362–63
Cohen, Eliot, 128, 189 n121
Cohen, Hermann, 161
Cohen, Richard, 116
Colbert, James, 177
Cold War, 4, 30, 104–105, 137, 142–50, 154–56, 166, 191, 193, 257
Coleman, Mary Sue, 323–24
collective guilt: see guilt
collectivism (see also: individualism), 2–3, 4, 8, 14–16, 136, 292–299, 309, 325–26, **335–37**, 340
    Jewish, 8, 14–16, 59, 94–95, 204, 244, 267–68, 294–99
    Medieval Christian, 276–78, 287–90
Collier's, 264
Columbus Platform of the Guiding Principles of Reform Judaism, 104
Commentary, 22, 38, 89, 129, 134–35, 142–143, 145, 147, 150, 155–56, 159
Commission on Community Interrelations (AJCongress), 202–203
Committee for a Democratic Majority, 150
Committee on the Present Danger, 140, 153, 188

communism (see also: radicalism, socialism), vii, 3–4, 10, 14, 29–30, **49–88**, 123, **135–41**, 142, 152, 160, 163, 165, 169, 180, 199–201, 209–210, 235, **244–47**, 250–51, 253, 259, 262, 265, 267
    and Jews, vii, 3–4, 10, 14, 29–30, **49–88**, 135–41, 199–201, 209–10, 235, **244–47**, 250, 253, **257–63**, 265, 267
    and unions, 246–48
The Communist, 246
Communist Party USA (CPUSA), 29–30, 199–201, 246–47, 262
community involvement, 315
concubinage, iv, **279**, **279–80**, 282, 292
Confederate battle flag, 317–18
Confederate States of America, 296–97
Conference of Presidents of Major Jewish Organizations, 132
conflict, ethnic, 287–88, 314–15, **332–41**, 344–46, 353–54, 356, 360, 363–64
conformity (psychological mechanisms), 323–30
Congress for Cultural Freedom, 142
Congressional Asian Pacific American Caucus, 215
Congressional Black Caucus, 215
Congressional Hispanic Caucus, 215
Congressional Jewish/Black Caucus, 215
consanguinity, 14–15, 102, 273, **285–86**, 292
conscientiousness, 306–309, 324–30
conscious mind: see explicit processing
consensual marriage, **285–86**, **292–94**
conservatism and conservatives (see also: neoconservatism and paleoconservatism), 87
    American political, 2, 36, 120–22, 124, 129, 135, 147–50, 162, 362
    American religious, 86
    Jewish political, 118
    and race, 258, 311, 313, 320–22
Conservative Judaism, 144
Coon, Carleton, 15
Cornell University, 172, 183
Corporate Diversity Award, 215
Cortez, Hernán, 274

Cossacks, 80, 218–19
Coughlin, Charles, 254
country music, 314, 316, 318, 333
courtship, 293–94
Crimea, 54, 80
criminality, 306–308, 330
criticism (social and revolutionary), 1
 (see also culture of critique)
crusades, 274, 277
Cruse, Harold, 206, 213–14
CSP: see Center for Security Policy
Cuba, 137
Cuddihy, John Murray, 173, 217, 238
cultural relativism (tenet of Boasian anthropology), 202
"culture of critique" (concept) (see also: "pathologization" of European ethnocentrism), vi, 1, 6, 60–61, 77, 81, 180, 320–23, 326, 330–31, 358
The Culture of Critique (Kevin MacDonald) iii, vi–viii, 1, 4–8, 10, 31, 36, 66, 120, 122, 142, 180, 193, 201, 297, 299
Cyprus, 25
Cyrene, 25
Czechs, 60, 140, 350

D

Daily Telegraph, 129–30
Daily Worker, 200, 247
Dannhauser, Werner, 160
Darwinism, 205, 251, 256–57, 265, 299, 343, 346, 364
Davenport, Charles, 256
Dean, Howard, 315
Dearborn Independent, 6, 225, 233
Decter, Midge, 134, 139, 149–50, 154, 159, 189 n121
Defender of Israel Award, 139
Defense Department (US) (see also: War Department), 37–38, 40, 90, 106, 130, 134, 155, 159, 167, 174, 176–77, 181, 183–84, 187, 189–91, 195
Defense Intelligence Agency (US), 183
Deir Yasin massacre, 108
democracy, 136–38, 140–45, 149, 155–56, 163–64, 166–70, 185–88, 193, 240
Democratic National Committee, 362

Democratic Party
 and blacks, 315
 and Jews, 36, 106, 117, 124–25, 207, 315, 362
 and neoconservatives, 121, 138–39, 142–55
 and non-whites, 315
 and white fertility, 316
demographics
 European, 94, 164, 201, 222, 281–82
 Jewish, 93–96, 99, 201
Denmark and Danes, 344
department stores, 233–34, 253
Dershowitz, Alan, 168
Dewey, John, 127, 165–66
Diamond, Mark, 115
Diaspora, 19, 50, 57, 59, 72, 74, 91, 95, 101, 114, 159, 161, 187
Dickstein, Samuel, 352
Diner, Hasia, 221
Disraeli, Benjamin (Lord Beaconsfield), 246
Dissent, 138
diversity: see multiculturalism
divorce, 273, **278–79**
Dominican Order, 275
Donnelly, Thomas, 189 n121
double standards (ethical): see moral particularism
Drake, Sir Francis, 300
Draper, Hal, 138 n54
Drury, Shadia, 163
"dual" loyalty (Jewish), 4, 100, 103, 105, 114, 126, 175–76
dual moral codes: see moral particularism
DuBois, W. E. B., 198
Duke University, 323
Duranty, Walter, 165

E

Eastern Europe and Eastern Europeans (see also: Eastern European Jews), 52–54, 59–60, 70, 80, 87, 137, 156, 208, 238, 240, 253, 255, 262, 264
Eastern European Jews (*Ostjuden*), 4, 6–7, 27, **49–88**, 89, **92–103**, 118, 200–201, 208, 210, 215–16, 218–19, 221, 232, 238, 240, 247, 253, 255, 262, 264, 351, 358

Eastman, Max, 136–37
Eberstadt, Nicholas, 189 n121
Edney, Leon, 194
Edward I, King of England, 54
Egypt
  ancient, 25, 112, 272
  modern, 40, 90, 106, 112–13, 175
Ehrman, John, 168
Eisenhower, Dwight, 40, 267
Eisner, Kurt, 246, 253
Elba, Ido, 18
Eleanor of Aquitaine, 278
elites (see also: aristocracy), 1, 13, 205–208, 222, 241, 245, 272
  emulation by masses, 323–24
  European, 6–8, 10, 215, 273–74, 277, **279–80**, 313–14, 320–24, 329, 345, 361
  Germans in the Russian Empire, 54–56
  Jewish, 1–3, 10, **49–88**, 97, 196, 208, 215–16, 221–22, 256–57, 261, 324, 360, 363
  Leo Strauss on, 161–64, 183
  Overseas Chinese, 44, 50–53, 55–56
Emerson, Michael, 313
An Empire of Their Own: How the Jews Invented Hollywood (Neal Gabler), 228
endogamy (vs. exogamy), 14–15, 285 n31, 288
England and the English (see also: Britain and the British), 25, 54, 99, 103, 129, 196, 216, 234, 236, 258, 275, 278–80, 282, 285–86, 291, 294, 196, 300, 317, 344
Enlightenment
  European, 17, 51, 59, 102–103, 161, 164–65, 204
  Jewish (*Haskalah*) (see also: assimilationism), 98, 103
Equal Employment Opportunity Commission, 207
Esau's Tears (Albert Lindemann), 71
Esther, 26
Ethics and Public Policy Center, 159
ethnic conflict (see also: multiculturalism), 287–88, 314–15, **332–41**, 344–46, 353–54, 356, 360, 363–64
ethnic interests (see also: ethnocentrism, genetic interests), 1, 6, 9–10, 24, 298, 300–301, 321–24, 330–31, **332–41, 342–46**, 348, 352–54, **355–64**
  self-sacrifice for one's ethnic group, 300, 357
ethnocentrism (see also: ethnic interests, genetic interests, racism)
  biological roots, **332–41, 342–46**
  black, 310
  European, vii–viii, 8–9, 14–15, 31, 36, 57, 201, 271, 287–88, 291, **294–99, 300–31**, 335–37, 344–46, 355–64
  Jewish, 2–3, 6, 13, **14–34**, 50, 56–57, 89, 92, 115, 117, 119–20, 158, 160, 216–17, 295, 310, 355, 358–60
  Jewish "pathologization" of European ethnocentrism (see also: "culture of critique" [concept]), 6, 31, 34, 57, 61–62, 119, 201–204, 298–99, 321, 343, 356, 359–60, 363
ethnostates, 346, 357, 360, 363
Europe and Europeans (see also specific European regions, countries, and peoples), iv, vi–viii, 1–10, 14–15, 22–27, 30–31, 34–36, 43, 47, 164, 167, 170–71, 173, 186, 205, 208, 222, 225, 232, 243, 247, 253, 255–57, 262–66, **271–99, 300–31**, 335–37, 343–45, 348–54, **355–64**
  culture, 8–10, 14–15, **271–99, 300–31, 335–37**
  demographic displacement through non-white immigration, vi, 3, 6, 9–10, 14, 23–24, 31–32, 35–37, 44, 47–48, 87–88, 180, 124, 158, 222, 237, 253, 262, 264, 297–98, 315–16, 320–23, 344–46, 353–54, 356–58, 360–61, 363–64
  ethnic interests of, vii–viii, 8–9, 14–15, 31, 36, 57, 201, 271, 287–88, 291, **294–99, 300–31, 332–41**, 344–46, 355–64
  ethnic self-defense of, vii–viii, 300–301, **320–322, 322–31**, 332, 340–41, **342–46, 347–54, 355–64**
  evolution of, 8, 14–15, **271–99, 300–**

31, 340
Jewish model for ethnic self-defense, **355–64**
Jewish promotion of non-white immigration to European nations, 3, 6, 14, 23–24, 27, 31–32, 35–37, 44, 47–48, 87–88, 121, 124, 127, 149, 158, 180, 196, 200, 203, 206–207, 214–15, 232, 235, 237, 253, 297–298, 347–49, 353
Jewish role in "pathologizing" ethnocentrism of, 6, 31, 34, 57, 61–62, 119, 201–204, 298–99, 321, 343, 356, 359–60, 363
eugenics, 264–65, 276
Eurasia, 278, 282, 288–89, 291–92, 294
European Union (EU), 24, 358
Evangelical Christians, 314–17
evolutionary biology (see also: Darwinism), iii-v, 16-17, 201,
Evsektsiya (the Jewish section of the Soviet Communist Party), 67, 76
exogamy (vs. endogamy) (see also: consanguinity), 14–15, 285 n31, 288
explicit processing (conscious mental processes) (see also: implicit processing), 301, **304–309**, **322–30**
extended kinship relationships (vs. simple or nuclear family), 8, 14–15, 271, 273, **283–86**, 287–91, 294–96, 335
Eysenck, Hans, 41

F
Fairchild, Henry Pratt, 256
Fallon, William, 195
family (see also: extended kinship relationships, illegitimacy, joint family, marriage, nuclear family, parental investment, sexuality), 8, 14–15, 50, 100, 156, 186, 202, **271–99**, 323, 325–26, 335–36, 343–45, 356, 361
Farrakhan, Louis, 147, 210, 213
Farrell, James. T., 127
fascism, 32, 137, 160, 163, 165, 173, 267
 communist anti-fascism, 66, 72
 Italian, 185
Faustian man (Oswald Spengler), 287

FBI (Federal Bureau of Investigation), 152, 157, 176, 265
Fedeev, A., 76
Federal Bureau of Investigation: see FBI
Federal Communications Commission, 46
Federal Reserve, **247–48**
Feist, Leo, 230
Feith, Douglas, 123, 152, 155, 159, 177, **181–83**, 184, 189–90, 193
Feith and Zell (Law Firm), 181–83
fertility, 19, 51, 94–95, 216, 316, 344, 346, 363–64
Findley, Paul, 36, 46, 174
Finland, 289
First Data Corporation, 323
Fischer, Dov, 360–61
fMRI: see Functional Magnetic Resonance Imaging
football, 318
Ford, Gerald, 38, 188, 190
Ford, Henry (see also: *The International Jew*), vii, 6–7, 41, 43, 49, **225–54**
Ford Foundation, 199
Forbes, 35, 361
Forrestal, James, 106
Forward, 38, 118–19, 133 n33, 360
Foundation for Ethnic Understanding, 215
Foundation for Jewish Studies, 182
Fox News Channel, 129–30, 191
Foxman, Abraham, 31, 132–33, 187
Fradkin, Hillel, 189
France and the French, 24, 49, 60, 104, 248, 266–67, 274–75, 277–79, 285, 289–90, 344
Francis, Samuel, 6, 134, 148, 158 n137, 195 n137, 196 n
Franciscan Order, 275
Frankfurt School, 61–62, 77, 202, 204, 298
Frankfurter, Felix, 198, 263–64, 266–67
Franks, 300
Fraser, Simon, 300
Freud, Sigmund, 34, 121–22, 127, 142, 163, 217
 psychoanalysis, 61–62, 77, 134, 202–

203, 299
Friedlander, Israel, 238
Friedlander, Paul, 151
Friedman, Murray, 206
Friend of Zion Award, 139
Fromm, Erich, 202
FrontPageMag, 29
Frum, David, 122, 129, 134, 168
Frumkina, Esther, 76
Fukuyama, Francis, 325
Fulbright, J. William, 106
Functional Magnetic Resonance Imaging (fMRI), 308–9, 311, 339
fundamentalism
   Christian, 314–16
   Jewish, 4, 17–19, 24, 34, 70–71, 89–96, 108, 111, 113, 118, 212, 216, 358
   Muslim, 131

G

Gabler, Neal (*An Empire of Their Own: How the Jews Invented Hollywood*), 228
Gaffney, Frank, 123, 128, 152, 155, 186, 189 n121
Galicia, 95–96, 98
Gandhi, Mohandas K., 116
Garfinkel, Harold, 217
Garner, Jay, 193
Garvey, Marcus, 198, 210
Gaza, 22, 109–12, 190
Gedmin, Jeffrey, 189 n121
genetic interests (see also: ethnocentrism, racism), 9–10, 284, 323, 332, **342–46**, 354, 357
   self-sacrifice for one's ethnic group, 300, 357
Genetic Similarity Theory (GST), 9–10, 32–34, 284, 309, **333**, 340
Gentleman's Agreement (movie), 203
Gerecht, Reul Marc, 130, 179, 189 n121
German Jews, 54, 59–60, 63, 91, 96, 102–104, 161, 197–98, 200, 208, 215–16, 221, 247–48, 253, 268
Germanic peoples, 263, 284, 289–91
Germany and Germans, 21, 26, 27, 31–32, 42, 59–60, 63, 87, 91, 94, 96, 100, 104, 161, 205, 236, 248–49, 253–54, 256, 260, 268, 297, 344,

362
Germans in Russia, 54–56, 80
Jews in and from, 54, 59–60, 63, 91, 96, 102–104, 161, 197–98, 200, 208, 215–16, 221, 247–48, 253, 268
Third Reich (National Socialism), 3, 14, 17, 24, 26–27, 31, 49, 57, 59–61, 64, 66–67, 78, 82, 87, 102–103, 151, 160, 180, 209, 214, 219, 264–66, 268
Weimar Republic, 100, 160–61, 163–64
Gershman, Carl, 138–41, 155
Gershwin, George and Ira, 230
Gerson, Mark, 145
Getlin, Josh, 115
Gibbon, Edward, 25
Gibson, Mel, 171
Ginzburg, Yitzhak, 18
Giscard d'Estang, Valéry, 24
Glazer, Nathan, 147
Glickman, Leonard S., 24, 214, 349
globalism, 168–70, 345
Goethe, Johann Wolfgang von, 60, 63, 287
Goffman, Erving, 217
Goldberg, J. J., 118–19
Goldberg, Jonah, 122, 129, 134
Goldhagen, Daniel Jonah, 27
Goldsborough, James O., 132
Goldstein, Baruch, 17
Goldstein, Mortiz, 60
Goldwin, Robert A., 190
Golub, Stan, 151
Gorbachev, Mikhail, 81
Gordon, Frank, 229
Gore, Al, 124, 207, 315
Gorky, Maxim, 69, 71–72, 75–76, 84
Goths, 26
Grant, Madison, 58, 205, 256, 350
Great Terror, Jewish involvement in, 73, 78–79
Greece and Greeks
   ancient, 90, 160, 273
   in USSR, 80
Green, Mark, 174
Greenberg, Jack, 198–99, 209 n64
Greenspan, Alan, 33–34
Gruening, Martha, 198

GST: see Genetic Similarity Theory
guilt (collective) (see also: shame)
   Jewish, 81, 82–88
   white, 9, 45–46, 268, 301, 308, **322–30**, 358
Gulag, Jewish involvement in, 73, 81
Gulf War, 128, 157, 174
Gush Emunim, 18–19, 113, 170
Gypsies, 50–51, 56

H
Ha'aretz (Jerusalem), 38, 133 n33
HaCohen, Ram, 109
Haman, 26
Hamilton, William, 16–17, 357
Hammer, Michael, 32
Hammerstein, Oscar, 203, 230
Hamud, Randall, 347
Hardin, Garrett, 344
Harding, Warren, 236
Harms, T. B., 230
Harpending, Henry, 357
Harrington, Michael, 138
Harrington, Tom, 138
Harris, Charles, 230
Hart, Lorenz, 230
Harvard University, 153, 191, 328, 351
Hasidism, 70, 93–98, 107, 118
Haskalah (Jewish Enlightenment), 98, 103
hate, 2, 7, 24–27, 63, 84, 98–99, 203, 239, 327, 342
hate crime statutes, 320
Hays, Will, 228
Hebrew (language), 67, 91, 138, 170–71, 244, 267
Hebrew Immigrant Aid Society, 24, 34, 214, 349
Heine, Heinrich, 60, 310 n19
Helsinki Human Rights Conference, 155
Henry I, King of England, 280
Henry VIII, King of England, 278
Henry Ford and the Jews: The Mass Production of Hate (Neal Baldwin), 239–40
Hentoff, Nat, 116
Heritage Foundation, 134
Hertzberg, Arthur, 101, 114, 145–46 n89
Herzl, Theodor, 42, 100–101, 110, 112, 119, 217, 239–40, 250, 359
Hess, Moses, 238
Heymann, Philip, 167–68
Hier, Marvin, 115, 134
Hill, Charles, 189 n121
Hilliard, Earl, 36
History and Geography of Human Genes (Luigi Cavalli-Sforza and W. F. Bodmer), 343
Hitler, Adolf, 22, 26, 49, 60, 87, 102, 104, 148, 161, 163, 210, 266
Hollinger, David, 201
Hollinger Corporation, 129, 133 n33
Hollings, Ernest F., 133
Hollywood: see movie business
Holmes, Stephen, 161–63
holocaust, 18, 21–24, 27, 31, 44–47, 57–59, 95, 107, 117, 131, 140–45, 151, 171, 173, 176, 347, 358
The Holocaust (television miniseries), 22–23
Holy Land, 274, 277
homosexuality, 150, 314
Hook, Sidney, 127, 136–37, 142, **165–67**
Horkheimer, Max, 202
Horowitz, D. L., 334
Horowitz, David, 22, 28–31
The House I Live In (movie), 203
Howe, Irving, 138
Hudson Institute, 177, 189
"human kinds module," 302, 309, **337–40**, 341
Humanitarian Award of B'nai B'rith, 139
Humphrey, Hubert, 139–40, 142, 150
Huneker, James Gibbons, 242
Hungary, 37, 59–60, 63, 80, 244, 253
hunter-gatherers, northern, 8, 15, 283–85, 288, 292, 295–96, 336–37, 340
Huntington, Samuel, 342
Hussein, Saddam, 89, 125–26 n10, 129–30, 175, 178, 183, 188–89

I
Ice Ages, 287–88, 340
Ignatiev, Noel, 36
illegitimacy, iv, 272–73, **279**, 280
immigration
   1924 immigration restriction, 10, 27,

58, 86, 158, 196, 218, 237, **347–54**, 363
Israel's restrictive immigration laws, 32
Jewish immigration to Palestine and Israel, **76–79**, 81–82, 104–105, 151, 176
Jewish immigration to the US, 27, 57–58, **76–79**, 99, 196, 215–16, 218, 221, 232–33, 256, 264
Jewish immigration within the USSR, **76–79**, 83
Jewish promotion of non-white immigration to European nations, 3, 6, 14, 23–24, 27, 31–32, 35–37, 44, 47–48, 87–88, 121, 124, 127, 149, 158, 180, 196, 200, 203, 206–207, 214–15, 232, 235, 237, 253, 297–98, 347–49, 353
literacy tests, 233–35
McCarran-Walter immigration act of 1952, 298
non-white immigration and ethnic displacement of European peoples, 3, 6, 9–10, 14, 23–24, 31–32, 35–37, 44, 47–48, 87–88, 180, 124, 158, 222, 237, 253, 262, 264, 297–98, 315–16, 320–23, 344–46, 353–54, 356–58, 360–61, 363–64
and race, 9–10, **342–46**, **347–54**, **355–64**
Immigration Restriction League, 37, 349, 351
Implicit Attitudes Test, 310
implicit processing (unconscious mental processes) (see also: explicit processing), 8–9, 301, **302–304**, 331
and explicit processing, **304–309**
and racial attitudes, 309–11, **337–40**
and white communities, vii, 9, 301, **313–20**, **320–22**, 333, 340
incest, 280, 285
India and Indians, 103, 272, 335–36
overseas Indians, 50
individual rights, 8, 156, 204, 271, 287, 292, 294
individualism (vs. collectivism) (see also: collectivism), vii, 8–10, 14–15, 30, 58–59, 77, 94, 160, 204, 214, 271, 277, **286–92**, **292–94**, **294–299**, 309, 320, 325–26, 329–30, **335–37**, 340, 345, 361
Indonesia, 44
infant mortality, 51, 279
infanticide, 279
ingroups (vs. outgroups), 15, 23, 28, 59, 71, 77–78, 94, 96, 118, 121, 162, 211, 221, 242, 277, 310, 313, **332–41**
Inquisition (in Spain), 13, 218
Institute for Advanced Strategic and Political Studies (IASPS), 177
Intercollegiate Studies Institute, 148
The International Jew (Henry Ford et al.), vii, 6–7, 41, 43, **225–54**
intelligence (IQ), 1–2, 49–51, 58, 287, 289, 292, 304–6, 321, 330–31, 345–46, 363
black, 197
Jewish, vi, 2, 13–14, 35–39, 55, 57, 65, 120, 158, 196–97, 206, 351, 363
White, 197, 289
intergroup relations movement, 203–205, 214
intifadas, 92
second intifada, 109, 117, 194, 362
IQ: see intelligence
Iraq, 28, 89–90, 125–126, 128, 130–34, 140–41, 149–50, 156, 164, 172, 174–76, 178–79, 181–87, 189–91, 193, 316
Iraq War (2003–), 28, 89, 125–26, 130–34, 140–41, 149–50, 156, 164, 175–90, 193, 316
Irgun, 108
Irish Americans, 348
Irish Travelers, 50–51
Islam (see also Muslim world), 27, 131, 141, 147, 169–70, 175, 191
fundamentalism, 131
Islamists, 27
Israel, ancient, 25–26, 41, 90–91, 225 n1, 238, 241, 272
Israel, modern (see also: Jews, neoconservatism, United States of America, Zionism), vi, 4–6, 17–20, 22–32, 35–41, 45–48, 56–58, 64, 66, 69, 76–77, 81–82, 84–85, 87–88,

89–119, **120–58**, **159–95**, 196, 204, 211, 213, 243–44, 260, 263, 267–68, 315–16, 328, 343–44, 357–60, 362–63
aggressiveness of, 40–41, 47
Deir Yasin massacre, 108
immigration laws of, 32
Jewish fundamentalism in, 4, 17–20, 24, 34, 70–71, 89–96, 108, 111, 113, 118, 212, 216, 358
Jewish reluctance to criticize, 20–22
King David Hotel massacre, 105, 108, 170
military of, 5, 19, 22, 25, 28, 40–41, 108–109, 111–13, 123, 157, 179, 181, 190–95, 244, 362
nuclear weapons of, 24–25, 113
occupied territories of (see also: Gaza, West Bank), 4, 22, 32, 47, 88, 111–17, 190
and Palestinians, 4–5, 7, 17–20, 22, 30, 32, 39–40, 45, 47, 77, 88–90, 95, 104–105, 108–18, 141, 146–47, 153–54, 157, 176, 182, 185–88, 193–94, 211–13, 222, 243–44, 344
Qibya massacre, 47, 111
settler movement in, 4–5, 28, 35, 45, 89, 91–92, 94, 96, 106–107, 109, 111–16, 130, 144–46, 165, 170, 172, 182, 194, 212, 359, 362
Six-Day War (1967), 40, 57, 81, 107, 112, 114–15, 118, 153–54, 190, 211
terrorism against, 185, 191, 243
terrorism by, 47, 105, 108, 111, 170, 243–44
US policy towards (see also: neoconservatism), 4–6, 22–23, 35–40, 47–48, 89–90, 92, 105–107, 114, **120–58**, 159–95, 196, 267–68, 315–16, 328–29, 358, 362
Yom Kippur War (1973), 57, 114–15
Italy and Italians, 37, 185, 344, 350, 352
ITV (Independent Television), 362

J
Jabotinsky, Vladimir (Ze'ev), 4, 89, 107–109, 119, 144, 182, 243–44, 359–60
Jabotinskyists, 4, 89, 243, 359
Jack London Literary Prize, 355 n1
Jackson, Bruce P., 189 n121
Jackson, Henry, 5, 82, 128, 138–40, **150–55**, 174, 176, 183, 186, 195
Jackson, Jesse, 147, 213, 348
Jackson-Vanik Amendment, 82, 151, 176
Jacobstein, Meyer, 352
Jaffa, Harry V., 163
Jaffe Center for Strategic Studies, 183 n101
Janka, Les, 37–38
Japan and the Japanese, 8, 247, 259, 338, 351, 354
Jenin massacre, 115–16
Jensen, Arthur, 144
Jeremiah, David, 194
Jerusalem Post, 38, 129, 133 n33, 170, 191
Jewish Anti-Fascist Committee, 66, 72
Jewish Board of Guardians, 236
The Jewish Century (by Yuri Slezkine), 3, **49–88**
Jewish Chronicle (Canada), 240
Jewish Chronicle (London), 245–46
Jewish Community Council of Greater Washington, 215
Jewish Congressional Delegation, 215
Jewish Defense League, 182
Jewish Fundamentalism in Israel (Israel Shahak and Norton Mezvinsky), 17
Jewish Institute for National Security Affairs (JINSA), 122–23, 132, 139, 141, 167, 177, 179, 184, 187, 192–95, 362
Jewish Peoples Fraternal Order, 200, 246
Jewish Telegraph Agency, 243
The "Jewish Threat" (Joseph Bendersky), 7–8, **255–68**

JEWS

See also: anti-Semitism, assimilationism, Bolshevism, Christianity and Christians, civil rights movement, communism, Democratic Party, demographics, elites, Europe and Europeans, guilt, holocaust, immigration, Israel, Judaism, Labor Party, Likud Party, marriage, messianism, neoconservatism, particularism (moral), race, racism, radicalism (Leftist), Republican Party, south (US region), United States of America, universalism (moral), Zionism, and the names of Jewish individuals and organizations.

JEWS: CHARACTERISTICS

aggressiveness, 2–3, 7, 13–14, 40–41, **41–47**, 51, 55, 64, 66, 79, 84, 107–109, 120, 158, 165, 211–12, 241, 252
authoritarian, cultish, and charismatic religious and intellectual movements, 2–3, 15, 71, 94–97, 121, 136
charity (financial support for Jewish organizations and communal aims), 10, 25, 35–36, 98, 122, 130, 194–98, 259, 361–63
collectivism, 8, 14–16, 59, 94–95, 204, 244, 267–68, 294–99
"dual" loyalty, 4, 100, 103, 105, 114, 126, 175–76
ethnocentrism, 2–3, 6, 13, **14–34**, 50, 56–57, 89, 92, 115, 117, 119–20, 158, 160, 216–17, 295, 310, 355, 358–60
extremist political tendencies, 4, 19–20, 70, 89, **92–103**, **106–16**, 243
evolutionary history, 14–15, 287–88, 294–96
fanaticism, 6, 16, 25–26, 28, **92–103**, **106–16**, 120, 123, 165, 216, 243
genetic relatedness of, vi, 32–34, 143–45, **237–38**
historical grievances against non-Jews, 2–3, 21–26, 55, 218, 236–38
hostility to non-Jews, 1–3, 7, 14–34, 36, 55, 62–63, 72, 76, 83, 85–87, 97, 204, 216–19, 221–22, 252, 360–61
intelligence (IQ), vi, 2, 13–14, 35–39, 55, 57, 65, 120, 158, 196–97, 206, 351, 363

intolerance of opposition, 45–46, 231–34, 254
lack of objectivity, 242
marriage attitudes, including marriage with non-Jews, vi, 13, 34, 53, 59, 95, 101–103, 179
messianism, 62, 70, 91, 93–95, 99, 118, 170, 216, 221, 255
networking skills, 10, 13, 32–34, 36, 53, 55, 59, 65, 71, 120, 122, 150, 157, 164, 181, 184, 192, 358
psychological intensity, 2, 7, 13–14, **39–41**, 120, 136, 158, 216–19, 221, 252, 358–59
self-deception, 2, 27–30, 64, 67, 92, 220, 245–46
superiority (moral, intellectual, and racial), conviction of, 29, 50, **58–62**, 83, 85, 101–102, 121, 221, 241, 245–46, 256, 297
superstition, 25, 70–71, 96
vengefulness, 26, 84–85, 97, 220, 267–68
victimhood, sense of, 3, 27–28, 49–79, 82, 85–87, 127, 146, 218, 297, 301, 355
wealth, 2–3, 13, **35–39**, 50, 59–60, 97–98, 107, 117–18, 122, 130, 158, 194–98, 259, 361–63
women's status, 15, 95

JEWS: INFLUENCE

alliances with oppressive elites in non-Jewish societies, 53, 208, 241
anti-Christian attitudes and activities, 7, 27, 31, 38, 43–44, 55, 60, 75–76, 78, 81, 83–86, 196, 205, 218, 229–32, 241, 243, 252, 254, 353–54, 360, 363
boycotts and other economic pressure tactics, 7, 46, 233–34, 253
intellectual movements (see also: Boasian anthropology, Bolshevism, communism, Marxism, neoconservatism, psychoanalysis, radicalism, Zionism), 6, 36, 62, 77, 107, 120–22, 124, 129, 136, 159, 180, 186, 193, 201–205, 297–99, 353

lobbying, 5–7, 14, 22–23, 36–37, 40, 45–46, 48, 106, **120–58, 159–95, 196–222, 230–34,** 234–**37, 243–44,** 252–53, 266–67, 348–53, 356–57, 362
media, 5–7, 10, 13–14, 30, 36–39, 44–48, 51, 78, 80, 82, 117–18, 120–21, 123, 128–30, 133–35, 157–58, 163–64, 193, 203, 206, 214, 221, 225–30, 233–34, 243, 252–54, 257, 260, 266, 354–55, 358, 362–63
multiculturalism, 6, 23–24, 28–29, 31, 87–88, 117, 170, 204, 319, 345–46, 353–54, 356, 363
"pathologization" of ethnocentrism of European peoples, 6, 31, 34, 57, 61–62, 119, 201–204, 298–99, 321, 343, 356, 359–60, 363
promotion of interracial marriage among non-Jews, 179–80, 203
promotion of non-white immigration to European nations, 3, 6, 14, 23–24, 27, 31–32, 35–37, 44, 47–48, 87–88, 121, 124, 127, 149, 158, 180, 196, 200, 203, 206–207, 214–15, 232, 235, 237, 253, 297–298, 347–49, 353

JEWS: SUB-GROUPS

Ashkenazi, vi, 35, 82, 101, 196
black, 144
Conservative, 144
Diaspora, 19, 50, 57, 59, 72, 74, 91, 95, 101, 114, 159, 161, 187
Eastern European Jewry (*Ostjuden*), 4, 6–7, 27, 52–54, 60, 70, 80–81, 83, 86–87, 89, **92–103,** 118, 200–201, 208, 210, 215–16, 218–19, 221, 232, 238, 240, 247, 253, 255, 262, 264, 351, 358
fundamentalist, 4, 17–20, 24, 34, 70–71, 89–96, 108, 111, 113, 118, 212, 216, 358
German, 54, 59–60, 63, 91, 96, 102–104, 161, 197–98, 200, 208, 215–16, 221, 247–48, 253, 268
Hasidic, 70, 93–98, 107, 118
Oriental, 101, 144
Orthodox, 26, 34, 99, 133 n32, 144, 216
Reform, 34, 38, 91, 104
Sephardic, vi, 101
settler movement, 4–5, 28, 35, 45, 89, 91–92, 94, 96, 106–107, 109, 111–16, 130, 144–46, 165, 170, 172, 182, 194, 212, 359, 362

Jews and Modern Capitalism (Werner Sombart), 26
JINSA: see Jewish Institute for National Security Affairs
Johnson, Albert, 351
Johnson, Lyndon, 40
Johnston, David, 131
joint family structure (see also: extended kinship relationships), 15, 284 n29, 289–90, 294
Jones, Ernest, 127
Jordan, 108, 110, 113, 182
Jordan, Michael, 319
journalism: see media
Joyce, Kenyon A., 262
Judaism (religion), 32, 93–99, 144, 207–208, **237–39,** 252 (see also entries on Conservative, Fundamentalist, Hasidic, Orthodox, and Reform Judaism)

K
Kabbala, 17, 70–71, 93, 96
Kadish, Lawrence, 194
Kagan, Donald, 189 n121
Kagan, Robert, 189 n121
Kaganovich, Lazar, 3–4, 63
Kahan Commission, 109
Kahane, Meir, 182
Kahn, Otto, 248
Kahn, Tom, 138
Kallen, Horace, 7, 30, 77, 164, 201–202, 204
Kampelman, Max, 139, 141, 150, 153–55, 193
Kant, Immanuel, 42–43
Kanter, Kenneth, 230
Kaplan, Lawrence F., 134
Karsner, Rose, 136 n44
Katz, Jacob, 238
Keane, John, 195

Kehillah, 231, 233, 246
Keller, Bill, 175–76
Kemble, Penn, 139, 150, 154–55
Kennedy, Teddy, 150, 154
Kern, Jerome, 230
Kerry, John, 124–25, 150, 315–16, 362
Khomeini, Ruholla (Ayatollah), 169–70
Khrushchev, Nikita, 80
King, Martin Luther, 116, 201, 207
King David Hotel massacre, 105, 108, 170
Kirk, Russell, 134, 148
Kirkland, Irena (née Neumann), 140
Kirkland, Lane, 140, 153
Kirkpatrick, Evron, 140
Kirkpatrick, Jeane, 139–40, 143, 150, 153–56, 179, 193
Kissinger, Henry, 41, 46–47, 151, 154
Klein, Morton A., 38, 190 n127
Klotz, probably Louis-Lucien, 246
Koch, Christof, 302–303
Koch, Noel, 184
Kopelev, Lev, 63–64, 78
Korea (North), 90
Koreans, 211
Kosovo, 344
Kotkin, Joel, 86
Kramer, Martin, 191–92
Krauthammer, Charles, 30, 155–57, **168–71**
Kristol, Irving, 140, 142–43, 148, 170
Kristol, William, 30, 123, 129, 149–50, 157, 159, 162, 168, 175, 179, 187, 189 n121, 191–92
Kuhn, Loeb and Co., 247–48
kulaks, 78, 81, 85, 165
Kun (Kohn), Béla, 244, 253
Kruse, Kevin, 314
Kurds and Kurdistan, 29, 80, 178–79
Kwiatkowski, Karen, 181

L
La Raza, 215
labor movement, labor unions, 138–41, 146, 150, 212, 219, 246–49
Labor Party (Israel), 4
Ladurie, E. L., 290
Lamm, Richard, 347
Landau, G. A., 75
Landy, Keith, 117

Langer, William, 266
Laqueur, Walter, 142
Larin, Yuri, 64–65
Laski, Harold, 217
Lassalle, Ferdinand, 217
Latin America, 156
latinos, 215, 304, 315, 321
Latvia, Latvians, 60
Lauder, Ronald, 35, 362
Lawrence, David, 236
Le Bon, Gustav, 256
League for Industrial Democracy, 138
League of United Latin American Citizens (LULAC), 215
Leavitt, Scott, 352
Lebanon and Lebanese, 18–19, 90, 109, 113, 116, 184, 191
overseas Lebanese, 50
Ledeen, Michael, 130, 152, 168, 179, **184–85**, 193
Legion of Decency, 228
LEHI (the Stern Group), 108
Lehman, Herbert, 198
Lehman, John, 154–55, 189 n121
Lenin, Vladimir, 72, 84, 260
Lenz, Fritz, 287
Leonidas, King of Sparta, 300
Lerner, Michael, 114–16
Lester, Julius, 210
Levison, Stanley, 201
Lewin, Kurt, 202
Lewin, Nathan, 168
Lewitt, Nathan, 186
Lewis, Anthony, 145
Lewis, Bernard, 152–53, **185–86**
Libby, I. Lewis ("Scooter"), 179 n82, 188–89
Libya, 90
Lieberman, Joseph, 155
Liebold, Ernest (see also: *The International Jew*), 225 n1
Likud Party, 4, 19, 38, 66, 89, 91, 107–10, 118, 124–25, 132–34, 144, 146, 154 n117, 157, 165, 179, 182, 187, 194, 211–12, 359, 363
Lilienblum, Moshe Leib, 100
Lindberg, Tod, 189 n121
Lindbergh, Anne Morrow, 326–27, 329
Lindbergh, Charles, 254, 264, 266–67, 327

Lindemann, Albert, 71–72, 127, 238
Lipset, Seymour Martin, 150, 153, 180 n86, 219–20
liquor trade, 226–27
literacy tests (immigration), 233, 235
Lithuania, 54
Lloyd George, David, 49
Locke, Robert, 172
Lodge, Henry Cabot, 37, 237, 349
Lord, Lance, 195
Los Angeles Times, 38
Lott, Trent, 206
Louis VII, King of France, 278
Louis IX, King of France (Saint Louis), 274, 277
Louis, Saint: see Louis IX
Low Countries, 289
Lowell, A. Lawrence, 351
Lowry, Rich, 189 n121
Lubavitchers, 17–18, 170
Lubin, David, 127
Luckovich, Mike, 316
Lukács, Georg, 63, 68, 69
Luxemburg, Rosa, 68

M

Maariv (Jerusalem), 38
Maccabeans, 90–91
Macdonald, Dwight, 127, 136–37
MacDonald, Kevin, **iii–viii**, 300, 327–28
 A People That Shall Dwell Alone, iii
 The Culture of Critique, iii, vi–viii, 1, 4–8, 10, 31, 36, 66, 120, 122, 142, 180, 193, 201, 297, 299
 Separation and Its Discontents, iii, 4, 6, 27, 34
 (Note: Only discussions of MacDonald's books in the text, and not mere citations in the footnotes, are indexed.)
Mafia, 56
"Magian man" (Oswald Spengler), 286
Magyars, 63
Maimon, Solomon, 217
Malcolm X, 210
MALDEF (Mexican American Legal Defense and Education Fund), 199
Malthus, Thomas Robert, 294
Mamilla Pond/Pool, 243
Mandela, Nelson, 116

Maor, Ron, 177
Marcuse, Herbert, 122, 202
Margold, Nathan, 198
marriage (see also: divorce, concubinage, family, monogamy, sexuality), 333, 336, 340
 age of partners, 281–83, 289, 293–94
 Ancient Roman, 273–74, 278, 281
 arranged, 286, **292–94**
 and Catholic Church, 273–74, 278–81
 companionate, 8, 14–15, 271, **292–94**
 consanguineous, 14–15, 102, 273, **285–86**, 292
 consensual, **285–86, 292–94**
 and courtship, 293–94
 endogamous, 14–15, 285 n31, 288
 exogamous, 14–15, 285 n31, 288
 and individualism, **292–94**
 interracial, 179–80, 203
 Jewish attitudes and practices towards, vi, 13–15, 34, 53, 59, 95, 101–103, 179
 monogamous, 8, 14–15, 156, 271–74, **278–81, 281–83**, 287–89, **292–94**, 335
 polygynous, 14–15, 271–74, 281–83, 288
 and Republican Party, 316, 319
 and Romantic love, **292–94**
Marshall, George C., 267
Marshall, Louis, 37, 198, 212, 258, 263, 348–49
Marx, Karl, 185, 271 (see also: Marxism)
Marxism, 61–63, 68, 70, 77, 93, 136–37, 165, 202, 251
Maslow, Will, 200, 212
Matalo, Rolando, 115
Matthews, Chris, 132
Maxwell, Robert (Ján Ludvík Hoch), 17
May, Charles, 194
May, Clifford, 189 n121
Mazor, Gadi, 177
McCarran-Walter immigration act of 1952, 298
McCarthy, Joseph, 76, 88, 94, 149, 262
McCarthy, Mary, 127
McDougall, William, 256

McFarlane, Robert C., 184
McGovern, George, 142, 150, 155
McKinney, Cynthia, 36
Mead, Margaret, 127
Mearsheimer, John, 5, 328–29
media (news and entertainment), 3, 5–7, 10, 13–14, 30, 36–39, 44–46, 48, 51, 78, 80, 82, 115, 117–18, 120–21, 123, **128–31**, 133–35, 157–58, 163–64, 188 n118, 193, 203, 206, 214, 221, 225–30, 233–34, 252–54, 257, 260, 263–66, 304, 314, 320–22, 328, 330–31, 340, 355, 358, 362–63
medieval period: see Middle Ages
MEF: see Middle East Forum
MEF Wire, 131
Meir, Golda, 64, 105, 113, 186
Meir of Opatów, 97
Mendel of Rymanów, 96
Mendelssohn, Moses, 217
mendicants, 275–77
The Merchant of Venice, 234, 242
messianism (Jewish), 62, 70, 91, 93–95, 99, 118, 170, 216, 221, 255
Mexico and Mexicans, 136, 179, 199, 248, 342–43, 348, 356
Mezvinsky, Norton, 18, 173
Miami Herald, 38
Michael the Archangel Russian People's Union, 55
Michigan, University of, 146–47 n93, 213, 323–24
Mickiewicz, Adam, 63
Middle Ages, European, iv, 8, 21, 42, 54, 208, 273–81, 283–86, 289, 293–94
Middle East, 2, 4, 14–16, 20–22, 24, 28, 39, 45, 47, 64, 66, 78, 88, 105, 123–24, 129–30, 141, 149, 151, 153–56, 168, 172, 176, 179, 182–87, 191–93, 237, 237, 287, 358
Middle East Forum, 123, 129–31, 149, 184, 191–92
Middle East Quarterly, 130, 184, 191
Middle East Initiative, 130
Middle East Intelligence Bulletin, 191
Middle Eastern culture, 14–16, 156, 185–86, 287, 293, 326, 335
Middle Old World culture area (see also: Middle Eastern culture), 15, 288, 295
Midwest (US region), 148, 363
Mikhoels, Paul, 72
military
 Israeli, 5, 19, 22, 25, 28, 40–41, 108–109, 111–13, 123, 157, 179, 181, 190–95, 244, 362
 US, 7–8, 22, 40–41, 64, 106, 123, 128, 130, 153–54, 174, 181, 189–95, 253, **255–68**, 316, 362
Miller, Judith, 130–31
The Mind of Primitive Man (Franz Boas), 201
miscegenation, 179–80, 203
Modern Racism Scale, 310 n16
modernization (Western), 8, 50, 54, 156, **281–83**, 292–4, **335–37**, 340
Moldavians, 80
Moment, 38
monasticism, 275–77
Money, John, 293
Monogamy (see also: family, marriage, nuclear family, pair bonding, sexuality, simple family), iv-v, 8, 14–15, 271–94, 335
Montagu, Edwin, 103–104
Montagu, Samuel, 246
moral particularism: see particularism
moral universalism: see universalism
Moran, James, 132–33
Morgenthau, Henry, Jr., 266–68
Morgenthau, Henry, Sr., 235
Morgenthau Plan, 268
Morning Freiheit, 200, 247
Morocco and Moroccans, iii, 267, 272
Moseley, George van Horn, 264-65, 268
Moshe Dayan Center for Middle Eastern and African Studies, 191
Moskowitz, Irving, 35, 362
Mossad, 46, 167
motion picture industry: see movie business
Motion Picture Producers and Distributors of America, 228
Motivation to Respond without Prejudice Scale, 310 n16
Moulay Ismail the Bloodthirsty, iv, 272
movie business, 45, 78, 82, 203, 226–

30, 253, 264, 362
Moynihan, Daniel P., 143–44, 152 n113, 154, 183, 186
Mubarak, Hosni, 90
Muhammad, Khalid, 210
multiculturalism (see also: ethnic conflict), 6, 9, 16, 23–24, 29, 31, 87–88, 117, 138, 170, 201, 204, 314–15, 321, 326, 344–45, 354, 356, 363
Murdoch, Rupert, 129
music business, 226, 230, 253
Muslims and Muslim world (see also Islam), 8, 14–16, 23–24, 26, 28, 30, 52, 66, 89–90, 113–14, 130, 149, 168–70, 184–85, 208, 213, 222, 237, 272, 274, 277, 300, 353
Myerson, Bess, 203

N

NAACP (National Association for the Advancement of Colored People), 197–99, 209, 212, 215
NASCAR (National Association for Stock Car Auto Racing), 9, 314–20, 333
Nasser, Gamal Abdel, 112
National Asian Pacific American Legal Consortium, 215
National Association of Broadcasters, 254
National Endowment for Democracy (NED), 138–41
National Endowment for the Humanities (NEH), 148
National Jewish Community Relations Advisory Council, 212
National Lawyers Guild, 199
National Liberal Immigration League, 44, 348–49
National Post, 129
National Review, 129, 137, 147
National Security Council (US), 152, 159, 181
National Socialism, 3, 14, 17, 24, 26–27, 31, 49, 57, 59–61 64, 66–67, 78, 82, 87, 102–03, 151, 160, 180, 209, 214, 219, 264–66, 268
National Urban League, 198
nationalism (see also: Zionism), 60–61, 202, 240, 346
Native Americans: see American Indians
NBA (National Basketball Association), 318–20
Near East: see Middle East
Near East Report, 38
negroes: see blacks
neoconservatism and neoconservatives (see also: Israel, Jews, Zionism, and the names of specific neoconservative individuals, organizations, and publications), vii, 2, 5, 22–23, 34–36, 64, 66, 82, 89, **120–58**, **159–95**, 197, 207, 222, 316, 359, 362
nepotism, 56, 275
Nero, 25
Netanyahu, Benjamin, 110, 177, 360
Netherlands, 344
"New Christians," 13
New Deal, 137, 152, 265
New England, 296
New Left, 138–39, 146–48, 166, 213, 220
New Politics, 138–39, 142
New Republic, 38, 130, 165
New York Herald, 233
New York Intellectuals, 127, 137, 218
New York Post, 129, 191, 264
New York Times, 38, 129–31, 145–46, 157, 165, 233–34, 264, 266
New Yorker, 38
New Zealand, 1
NFL (National Football League), 318
NKVD (Soviet secret police organization), Jewish involvement in, 73, 78
Nicaragua, 139
Nicholas II, Tsar, 3, 55, 69, 84–85, 165, 245, 248, 258–60
Niebuhr, Reinhold, 142
Nietzsche, Friedrich, 251
Nisbet, Robert, 135
Nissan, William, 25
Nitze, Paul, 153
Nixon, Richard, 38, 82, 137, 144, 148, 151, 190
Nordic peoples: see Northern Europeans
Nordic superiority thesis, 263–64, 349–51, 353

North, Gary, 134–35
North American Boards of Rabbis, 215
North Eurasian and Circumpolar culture area (see also: Europe and Europeans, Western civilization), 288
Northern Europeans (see also: Germanic peoples, Scandinavians), 8, 15, 287–93, 298, 336–37, 340, 349–51, 353
　in the United States, 58, 205, 155–57, 263–64, 349–51, 353
Northrop Grumman Corporation, 194–95
Northwestern Europeans: see Northern Europeans
Norway, 248
Novak, Michael, 150
Novak, Robert, 132
Novick, Peter, 45–46, 107
nuclear family (or simple family structure, vs. extended kinship), 8, 14–15, 271–94, 325, 335
Nye, Victor, 116

O

occupied territories (see also: Gaza, Palestine and Palestinians, Palestinian Authority, settler movement, West Bank), 4, 22, 32, 47, 88, 111–17, 190
Ochs, Adolph S., 131, 233
Office of Special Plans, 130, 181, 183
OGPU (Soviet secret police organization), Jewish involvement in, 73
O'Keefe, Ted, 158 n137, 195 n137
Old Testament, 14, 18, 19, 26, 41–42, 62, 90, 112–13, 238, 241
Olin Foundation, 36, 362
On Genetic Interests (Frank Salter), 9–10, 343 (see also: genetic interests)
One Jerusalem, 182
Onset Technology, 177
Oppenheimer, J. Robert, 217
oriental Jews, 101, 144
Orthodox Christianity (Russian), 85
Orthodox Judaism, 26, 34, 99, 133 n32, 144, 216
Oslo Accords, 38, 170
Ostjuden: see Eastern European Jewry
Ostrowicz, Yaankely, 242

Ottoman Empire (see also: Turkey), 93
outgroups: see Ingroups
Ozick, Cynthia, 217

P

Pahlavi, Mohammed, Shah of Iran, 132
Pahlavi, Reza, 132
pair bonding (see also: marriage, monogamy), 51, 289, 294
Pakistan, 169
Pale of Settlement, 54, 74, 78, 83, 234
paleoconservatism, 148
Palestine and Palestinians (see also: British Mandate of Palestine, Intifadas, PLO, Palestinian Authority), 4–5, 7, 17–20, 22, 30, 32, 39–40, 45, 47, 77, 88–90, 95, 104–105, 108–18, 141, 146–47, 153–54, 157, 176, 182, 185–88, 193–94, 211–13, 222, 243–44, 344
Palestinian Authority, 90, 193
papacy, 24, 275, 277–78
parental investment (see also: family, marriage, monogamy, sexuality), 51, 272, **283**, 289, 346, 363
particularism, moral (vs. moral universalism) (see also: universalism), 1–3, 15, 18–20, 23–24, 27–31, 92, 121, 163, 165, 211, 242–43, 295, 297, 326, 335–36
　Jewish use of moral universalist rhetoric to defend moral particularist agendas, 17–18, 29–31, 37, 121, 162–64, 185, 192–93, 211, 220–21, 235
Partisan Review, 127, 137
Passing of the Great Race (Madison Grant), 58, 256, 350
Patai, Jennifer, 145
Patai, Raphael, 145
"pathologization" of European ethnocentrism, (see also: "culture of critique" [concept]), 6, 31, 34, 57, 61–62, 119, 201–204, 298–99, 321, 343, 356, 359–60, 363
Patton, George C., 267
patriarchy, 14–15, 62
Paul, Ron, 140–41
A People That Shall Dwell Alone (Kevin MacDonald), iii

Percy, Charles, 40
Peres, Shimon, 170, 184
Peretz, Martin, 130, 189 n121
Perle, Richard, 82, 125–26, 129–30, 152, 154–55, 157, 159, 167–68, 172, 174, **176–79**, 181, 183–84, 186–87, 189 n121, 193
Perlman, Nathan, 352
Perry, Eustace, 240
Persia and Persians, 243
Persian Gulf, 176
Peterson, Gary, 319
Petőfi, Sandór, 63
PFC: see prefrontal cortex
Philadelphia Inquirer, 38, 264
Philadelphia Society, 148
Philip II Augustus, King of France, 278
Pipes, Daniel, 123, 130, 149, 184, 189 n121, **191–92**
Pipes, Richard, 151, 153, 155, 191
Plame, Valerie, 179 n82
PLO (Palestine Liberation Organization), 40, 45, 133 n32
PNAC: see Project for the New American Century
Podhoretz, John, 159
Podhoretz, Norman, 21–23, 28, 30, 89, 134, 139, 142–43, 145, 147, 150, 153–54, 159, 168, 189 n121, 217
pogroms, 55, 69, 83, 85, 99, 218, 243, 255
Poland and Poles, 29, 53–54, 60, 63, 68–69, 80, 83, 92, 98, 135, 218, 234–35, 238, 253, 259, 261
"political correctness," iii, vii, 2, 6–7, 9–10, 314, 317, 326–27, 337–38
Pollard, Jonathan, 168
Polo, Marco, 273–74
polygamy: see polygyny
polygyny (vs. monogamy), iv, 14–15, 271–74, 281–83, 287–88
Portugal, 13, 208
Powell, Colin, 125 n10, 128, 174, 193
power, desire for, 274–75
prefrontal cortex (PFC), 9, 301, 307–309, 311, 321, 325, 332
Prinz, Joachim, 102
Prodemca, 139
Production Code Administration, 228
progress: see modernization

Project for the New American Century (PNAC), 123, 128, 130, 175, 179, 187–89
Protestantism and Protestants (see also: WASPs), 6, 40, 58, 206, 209, 215, 229, 238, 252
Protocols of the Elders of Zion, 6–7, 227, 229–30, 241, **248–52**, 252, 260
Prussia, 60
psychoanalysis/Freudianism, 61–62, 77, 134, 202–203, 299 (see also: Freud, Sigmund)
public goods, 295, 314, 344, 357
The Public Interest, 129, 142
publishing, 129, 135, 226, 230
purdah, 293
Purishkevich, Vladimir, 55
Puritanism, 279, 296–97
Pushkin, Alexander, 60, 63, 84
Pushkin House (Soviet Academy of Science Institute of Literature), 65
Putnam, Robert D., 315

Q
Qibya massacre, 47, 111
quotas (to limit Jewish upward mobility)
in the Russian Empire, 55
in the United States, 22, 207, 351
in the USSR and Eastern Block, 55, 68

R
Rabin, Yitzak, 47, 110
race, 1–2, 6–10, 29, 36, 58, **196–222**, 256–58, 261–62, 265–67, 299, **300–31**, **332–41**, **342–46**, **347–54**, 356–59
fear of other races, 339–40
innate recognition of racial differences, 302, 307, **337–40**, 341
and intelligence, 144, 197, 287, 321
Jews as a race, 101–103, 108, 143–45, **237–38**, 241, 246, 358–59
Race and the American Prospect (ed. Samuel Francis), 6, 196 n
"Race Traitor," 36
racism, vi–vii, 10, 85, 148, **196–222**, 258, 262, 265, 298, **300–31**, 332–

41, **342–46**, **347–54**, 356
Zionism as racism, 57, 89, 101–103, 108, 141, 143–5, 147, 213, **237–38**, 267–68, 358–59
Radical Son (David Horowitz), 29
radicalism (Leftist), iii, 1, 7, 146–47, 213, 216, 240, 313
  and Jews, 3–4, 7, 29–30, **49–88**, 93–94, 99, 100, 103, 118, **135–41**, 146–47, 166, 200, **205–221**, 240, 244–47, 252–56, **257–60**, 262–64, 349, 358
Raine, Adrian, 308
Rand, Ayn, 217
Ravelstein (Saul Bellow), 172–74
Raven's Progressive Matrices, 304–305
Reader's Digest, 264
Reagan, Ronald, 138–40, 148, 151, 153–55, 166–67, 176–77, 183–84, 187–89
reciprocity, 291–92
Reform Judaism, 34, 38, 91, 104
Reform Judaism, 38
Reformation, 275
Reich, Charles, 217
Reich, Robert, 33–34
Reich, Ronnie, 243
Reich, Wilhelm, 217
Reno, Janet, 168
representative government, 8, 156, 271, 287, 292, 294, 325–26
Republican Party (see also: neoconservatism), 106, 124, 137
  and implicit white communities, 9, 314–16, 319
  and Jews, 106–107, 124, 187, 194, (see also: neoconservatism)
  and marriage, 316, 319
  and neoconservatism, **150–55**, 187, 194
  and non-White voters, 315
  and white fertility, 316, 319
republicanism, 15, 205, 240, 292, 298, 325
reputation (see also: trust), 324–30, 335
Rice, Condoleezza, 125 n10
Rich, Marc, 35, 181, 189, 362
Riga, Liliana, 3–4
Ripley, William, 256
Risen, James, 131

Rockford Institute, 148
Rodgers, Richard, 203, 230
Romania and Romanians, 60, 80, 99
romantic love, **292–94**
romanticism, 293
Rome, ancient, iv, 25, 208, 263, 273–74, 278, 281, 284, 287
Roosevelt, Franklin, 254, 264, 266–67
Rosen, Jack, 132
Rosen, Stephen P., 189 n121
Rosenker, Mark, 195
Rosenman, Samuel I., 266
Rosenwald, Julius, 198
Ross, Dennis, 174
Ross, Edward A., 43, 348
Rostow, Eugene, 153
Rubin, Michael, 130, 148, 157
Rubin, Vitaly, 64
Rumsfeld, Donald, 125–26 n10, 134, 159, 181, 187–88, **190**
Ruppin, Arthur, 59, 144
Rushton, J. Philippe (see also: Genetic Similarity Theory), 32, 309, 333, 340
Russia and Russians (see also: Soviet Union), 3, 10, 38, **49–88**, 93–99, 127, 136, 169, 176, 179, 205, 214, 233–37, **244–47**, 248, 250–51, 253, 255, 258–60, 262
Russian Trade Agreement, **234–37**, 253, 259
Russo-Japanese War (1905), 247–48
Rustin, Bayard, 139–40, 153

S
Saban, Haim, 362–63
Sabath, Adolph, 352
Sachs, Walter, 198
Sadat, Anwar, 175
Safire, William, 30, 157
Salter, Frank, 9–10, 35, 103, 293, 323, 332, 343–46, 357
Samaritans, 238
Samuel, Herbert, 243
Samuel, Maurice, 240
Samuel, Stuart, 235
San Diego Union-Tribune, 132
Sandler, Aron, 101
Satloff, Robert, 157
Saturday Evening Post, 264

Saudi Arabia, 22–23, 90, 113, 151, 176, 193
Scandinavia and Scandinavians, 256, 289, 343
Schapiro, Leonard, 73
Schatz, Jaff, 62, 68
Schenker, David, 184
Scheunemann, Randy, 189 n121
Schiff, Jacob, 131, 198, 235, 247–48, 259
Schiller, Friedrich, 60
Schlesinger, Arthur M., Jr., 142
Schmitt, Gary, 189 n121
Schneerson, Menachem Mendel, 17–18, 170
Schneider, William, Jr., 189 n121, 195
Schneier, Marc, 215
School of Advanced International Studies (SAIS), 128
science, viii, 8–9, 15, 44, 156, 162, 256–57, 264–65, 271, 287, 292, 294, 320, 325, 335, 357–58
and individualism 271, 287, 292, 294
Scotland and Scots, 300
Scots-Irish, 317
Scripps Howard News Service, 130
SD/USA: see Social Democrats/USA
self-deception (Jewish), 2, 27–30, 64, 67, 92, 165, 220, 245–46
self-sacrifice for one's kin (see also: genetic interests), 300, 357
Selgin, Clare, 172
Seligman, Herbert, 198
Separation and Its Discontents (Kevin MacDonald), iii, 4, 6, 27, 34
Sephardic Jews, vi, 101
Serbia and Serbs, 344
servants, 289–92
settler movement (see also: Gaza, occupied territories, West Bank), 4–5, 28, 35, 45, 89, 91–92, 94, 96, 106–107, 109, 111–16, 130, 144–46, 165, 170, 172, 182, 194, 212, 359, 362
sexuality (see also: divorce, concubinage, family, marriage, monogamy), iii-iv, 51, 253–54, 271–94, 302, 307–309, 338
Shachtman, Max, **135–41**, 142, 150, 165

Shahak, Israel, 17–18, 84, 113
Shakespeare, William, 63, 287, 357
The Merchant of Venice, 234, 242
shame (see also: guilt), 171, 327, 330
Shamir, Yitzhak, 108, 118, 359, 360
Shanker, Albert, 151
Shapiro and Bernstein (music publishers), 230
Sharansky, Natan, 172, 187–88
Sharett, Moshe, 111–12, 114
Sharon, Ariel, 19, 47, 108–11, 114–15, 119, 133 n32, 177, 186, 359, 360, 362
Sheean, Vincent, 32
Shiite Islam (see also: Islam, Sunni Islam), 126, 178
Shils, Edward, 128
Shternberg, Lev, 62
Shubert family, 227
Shulgin, V. V., 74
Shulsky, Abraham (Abram), 181, **183–84**
Sicily, 56
Sierra Club, 347
Sinai Peninsula, 40, 112–13
Simon, Leon, 238
Simon Wiesenthal Center (SWC), 24, 25, 115, 132–33, 143
simony, 275
simple family structure: see nuclear family, extended kinship relationships
Six-Day War (1967), 40, 57, 81, 107, 112, 114–15, 118, 153–54, 190, 211
slavery, 13, 41, 197, 208, 219, 241, 296
Slavs, 53, 72, 86, 119, 235, 359
Slawson, John, 200
Slezkine, Yuri, 3, **49–88**
Sobel, B. Z., 47
Sobran, Joe, 28, 132, 140, 355
social democracy, 123, 137, 139, 141
Social Democrats/USA (SD/USA), 123, 139–41, 150, 153, 165–66,
social identity theory, 56, 92, 309, **333–35**, 340
socialism (see also: communism, National Socialism), 53, 85–86, 123, **135–41**, 166
Socialist Party (US), 259
Socialist Party USA, 138–39

sociobiology, iii, v
sociopathy, 325, 330
Solarz, Stephen, 193
Soloveichik, Meir Y., 26–27
Soltan (Israeli munitions company), 177
Solzhenitsyn, Alexander, 82
Sombart, Werner, 26
Sonnenfeldt, Helmut, 152
Soros, George, 35–36
south (US region), 137, 148, 197, 199, 208–209, 216–19, 316–18, 363
  Jewish perceptions of South, 218–19
  Jews in the South, 208–209
South Africa, 110, 140, 209–10
South Pacific (musical), 203
Southeast Asia, 44, 51–53
Southern Europe and Southern Europeans, 262, 264, 290–91, 349
Southern Poverty Law Center, iii, vi–vii
southwest (US region), 342–43, 356
Soviet Academy of Science Institute of Literature (Pushkin House), 65, 80
Soviet Union: see USSR
Spain, 13, 26, 88, 100, 208, 218, 236
Spanish Armada, 300
Spanish Inquisition, 13, 218
Sparta and Spartans, 300
Spengler, Oswald, 286–87
Speyer family, 248
Spingarn, Arthur, 198
Spingarn, Joel, 198
sports (see also: NASCAR, NBA, NFL), 9
Stalin, Josef, 3, 53, 63–64, 73, 79, 81, 87, 104–105, 161
Stalinism (and anti-Stalinism), 63, 127, 136–37, 165–66
State Department (US), 38, 40, 105–107, 141 n69, 153, 155, 157, 174, 177, 184, 188–89, 191, 193, 267
Stein, Edith, 27
Stein, Gertrude, 217
Steinlight, Stephen, 86, 149, 347–48
stereotypes (group), 115, 302–304, 309–10, 320–21, 334
Stern, David, 319
Stern, Joseph, 230
Stern Group (LEHI), 108
Stevenson, Adlai III, 45
Stimson, Henry, 267

Stock Exchange, New York, 226–27
Stoddard, Lothrop, 1, 58, 205, 256, 261, 264–65
Stoicism, 293
Stone, I. F., 147
Strategius of St. Sabas, 243
Strauss, Leo, 122, 128, 155, **159–65**, 166, 172–74, 176, 180, 183, 190, 195 n137, 359
Strauss, Robert, 15
Student Non-Violent Coordinating Committee (SNCC), 147, 213
Studies in Prejudice (book series), 202–204
suburbanization, 314–16
Sudoplatov, Pavel, 72
Suez Canal, 106
Sumner, William Graham, 333–34
Sunni Islam (see also: Islam, Shiite Islam), 178
SWC (Simon Wiesenthal Center), 24–25, 115, 132–33, 143
sweatshops, 229
Switzerland, 290
Syria, 90, 113, 178–79, 185, 191, 193, 248
Svonkin, Stuart, 214

T

Tacitus, Gaius Cornelius, 25, 86
Taft, Robert, 37, 234–35, 253, 349
Talbott, Strobe, 38
Talmud, 18, 261
Tamam (Israeli Aircraft Industries), 194
Taylor, Jared, 28–29
Team B, 153
tenure, 328–29
terrorism
  anti-Zionist, 185, 191, 243
  Communist 73, 78, 79, 253
  Zionist, 47, 105, 108, 111, 170, 243–44
Thailand, 51
theater business, 226–30, 253
Theatrical Trust, 227
Theilhaber, Felix, 101
Thermopylae, Battle of, 300
Third World, 137, 142–43, 213, 222, 290

Thurmond, Strom, 206
Tijerina, Pete, 199
Tikkun, 20, 114, 116
Tilzer, Harry von, 230
"Tin Pan Alley," 230
Tolstoy, Leo, 63
Torah, 18, 78
Torop, Jonathan, 177
Touré, Kwame (Stokely Carmichael), 147, 213
Transjordan (see also: Jordan), 108, 113
Treitschke, Heinrich Gotthard von, 60
Trilling, Lionel, 217
Trivers, Robert, iii–iv, 330
Trotsky, Leon, 53, 68, 73, 79, 83, 121–22, 135–37, 165–66, 185, 246, 248, 254, 260
Trotskyism, and neoconservatism, 122, 122 n3, **135–41**, 165
Truman, Harry S., 106, 142, 154, 267
truth (see also: science), 286, 292, 328
trust, 315, 325–26, 329–30, 335
Tsar and Tsarism: see Alexander II, Alexander III, and Nicholas II
Tucker, Robert W., 142
Turgenev, Ivan, 63
Turkey and Turks (see also: Ottoman Empire), 16, 24, 105, 140, 177, 179, 235
  Meshketian Turks, 80
tzadik, 71, 96–97

U

Ukraine and Ukrainians, 3–4, 54, 72, 78, 82, 84, 98, 200
  Ukrainian famine, 63, 78, 82
unconscious mind: see implicit processing
unions (labor and trade), 80, 246–49
United Nations, 139, 213

UNITED STATES OF AMERICA

iii, vi–vii, 4–10, 14, 21–48, 47, 57–59, 61–62, 64, 66–67, 69–70, 76–77, 81–82, 85–90, 92, 94, 99–100, 102–107, 111–12, 114–19, **120–58**, **159–95**, **196–222**, **225–54**, **255–68**, 296–99, 301, 310–22, 329, 333, 335–36, 342–44, 346, 347–54, **355–64**

USA: ETHNICITY AND RACE

1924 immigration restriction, 10, 27, 58, 86, 158, 196, 218, 237, **347–54**, 363
anti-Semitism in, **6–8**, 22, 27, 86, 180, 196, 200, 217–18, **225–54**, **255–68**, 347
Asians in, 315
black civil rights movement, vii, 6, 124, 140, 146–47, 150, 152, 158, **196–222**
blacks in, 6, 35, 66 n35, 146–47, 153, 179–80, 304, 309–23, 343–44, 348
demographic displacement of European majority through non-white immigration, vi, 3, 6, 9–10, 14, 23–24, 31–32, 35–37, 44, 47–48, 87–88, 180, 124, 158, 222, 237, 253, 262, 264, 297–98, 315–16, 320–23, 344–46, 353–54, 356–58, 360–61, 363–64
implicit white communities in, **313–20**
Jewish attitudes toward, 86, 180, 217–18, 232
Jewish immigration to, 27, 57–58, **76–79**, 99, 196, 215–16, 218, 221, 232–33, 256, 264
Jewish promotion of open immigration to, 3, 6, 14, 23–24, 27, 31–32, 35–37, 44, 47–48, 87–88, 121, 124, 127, 149, 158, 180, 196, 200, 203, 206–207, 214–15, 232, 235, 237, 253, 297–298, 347–49, 353
McCarran-Walter immigration act of 1952, 298
non-white voters in, 315
Northwestern European ethnic identity of, 58, 205, 155–57, 263–64, 349–51, 353
as "proposition nation" lacking any specific ethnic and religious identity, 7, 28–29, 30–31, 57–58, 76–77, 164, 169–70, 204–205, 232, 298, 321

USA: GOVERNMENT

Defense Department, 37–38, 40, 90, 106, 130, 134, 155, 159, 167, 174, 176–77, 181, 183–84, 187, 189–91, 195
Jewish influence on Middle East policy (see also: neoconservatism), 4–6, 22–23, 35–40, 47–48, 89–90, 92, 105–107, 114, **120–58**, **159–95**, 196, 267–68, 315–16, 328–29, 358, 362
Jewish influence on other areas of foreign policy, **234–37**, 238, 253
Jewish promotion of US involvement in World War II, 265–67, 327
military, 7–8, 22, 40–41, 64, 106, 123, 128, 130, 153–54, 174, 181, 189–95, 253, **255–68**, 316, 362
republican tradition in, 205
State Department, 38, 40, 105–107, 141 n69, 153, 155, 157, 174, 177, 184, 188–89, 191, 193, 267
War Department, 107, 255, 267

USA: REGIONS

Midwest, 148, 363
"Red States," 86
South, 137, 148, 197, 199, 208–209, 216–19, 316–18, 363
Southwest, 342–43, 356

United Way of America, 315
universalism, moral (vs. particularism) (see also: particularism), 1, 3, 8, 15, 62, 83, 148, 156, 185, 204, 271, 287, 294, 298, 320, 325–26, 335–36, 346
Jewish use of moral universalist rhetoric to defend moral particularist agendas, 17–18, 29–31, 37, 121, 162–64, 185, 192–93, 211, 220–21, 235
US: see United States of America
USS *Liberty*, 40
USSR (see also: Bolshevism, Cold War, communism), vii, 165–66
Jewish elite status in, 3–4, **49–88**, **244–47**, 253, 261
usury, 42–43, 242

V
Vaile, William N., 350–51
Van Creveld, Martin, 25 n29
Varnhagen, Rachel, 217
Veblen, Thorsten, 62
vengefulness (as Jewish trait), 26, 84–85, 97, 220, 267–68
Ventre, Michael, 319
Versailles Peace Conference, 236
Vesti, 38
Vietnam War, 137–38
"Vital Center," **142–49**, 151

W
Wagner, Richard, 60, 357
Wald, Alan, 134
Wald, Lillian, 198
Wall Street Journal, 38, 129–30, 157, 188, 191
Wallace, John, 300
Wallace, William, 300
Walt, Stephen, 5, 328–29
Walzer, Michael, 218–19
War Department (US) (see also: Defense Department), 107, 255, 267
War Industries Board, 236
Warburg, Max, 248
Warburg, Paul, 198, 247–48
Washington, George, 66 n35
Washington Institute for Near East Policy (WINEP), 122–23, 129, 141, 174, 177, 184
Washington Post, 38, 46, 116, 188, 164
Washington Times, 130
WASPs (White Anglo-Saxon Protestants) (see also: Protestantism and Protestants), 117, 173
Wattenberg, Ben, 125–26 n10, 149–50, 154–55, 180
Weber, Max, 58
Wedemeyer, Albert C., 268
Weekly Standard, 129–30, 175, 191
Weimar Republic (Germany), 100, 160–61, 163–64
Weiss, Philip, 117
Weiss, Seymour, 153
Weizmann, Chaim, 110
welfare state, 124, 127, 152, 166, 197, 314–15
West Bank (see also: Gaza, occupied

territories, settler movement), 4–5, 22, 89, 91–92, 109–112, 114–15, 154 n117, 182, 192, 244
Western civilization: see Europe and Europeans
white communities (implicit), vii, 9, 301, **313–20**, 333, 340
"white flight," 314–16
whites: see European peoples
Wiesel, Eli, 18
Williams, Michael, 195
Wilson, E. O., iii, 344
Wilson, Joseph C., 178–79
Wilson, Woodrow, 37, 49, 105, 236, 253, 349
WINEP: see Washington Institute for Near East Policy
Wise, Stephen S., 100
Wisse, Ruth, 145–46
Wittmann, Marshall, 189 n121
Wohlstetter, Albert, 126, 128, 130, 153, 171–72
Wolf, Lucien, 258
Wolf, Simon, 236
Wolfowitz, Paul, 128, 152–53, 155, 159, 168, **171–76**, 179, 183–84, 186, 188–90, 195
Wolfram von Eschenbach, 287
Women
 cultural status, 15, 117, 186
 sexuality, reproduction, and marriage, 95, **271–99**, 316
Woodward, Robert, 190
Woolsey, R. James, 189 n121
working memory, 301, 306
World Jewish Congress, 215, 362
WORLD OF DIFFERENCE Institute (ADL), 205
World War I, 236, 238, 248, 253, 260
World War II, 56, 87, 136, 151, 173, 196, 254, 266–68, 327, 334
 as cultural watershed, 3, 4, 6, 14, 27, 45, 49, 57, 63–64, 67, 69, 77, 80, 83, 85, 87, 104, 106–107, 144, 196, 198–200, 202, 206–208, 210, 214, 218, 221, 257, 262, 314, 320, 344, 357
Wrezin, Michael, 127
Wright, Jim, 316–18
Wright, P., 235–36

Wurmser, David, 130, 177, 181, 184, 362
Wurmser, Meyrav, 177

X
Xenophobia, 15, 31–32, 295, 339–40

Y
Yaroslavsky, Emilian, 64–65
"*Yemach shemo*" ("May his name be erased"), 26
Yiddish (language and culture), 43, 64, 67, 68, 92, 95–96, 103, 180, 200, 218, 236, 247, 252
Yinon, Oded, 178
Yom Kippur War (1973), 57, 114–15
Young, Andrew, 147, 153, 213,
Young, John, 195

Z
Zakheim, Dov, 195
Zangwill, Israel, 232, 244, 246, 298
Ze'evi, Rehavam, 111
Zell, L. Marc, 181–82
Zionism (see also: Israel, Jews, Judaism, neoconservatism, occupied territories, settler movement), vii, 4–5, 7, 32, 42, 57, **89–119**, 138, 200, 236–37, 240, **243–44**, 252, 260, 263, 268, 358–60
 and "dual" loyalties, 4, **103–106**
 Eastern European origins, **92–103**, 200, 210 n68, 215–16, 221, 256
 and Jewish propensity to extremism, 4, 19, 57, 89–92, **106–18**
 racism, 57, 89, 101–103, 108, 141, 143–45, 147, 213, **237–38**, 267–68, 358
 terrorism, 47, 105, 108, 111, 170, 243–44
Zionist Federation of Germany, 102
Zionist Organization of America (ZOA), 38, 122–23, 182, 190, 241, 360
ZOA: see Zionist Organization of America
Zogby, Joe, 38
Zollschan, Ignaz, 101
"zombie mechanisms," 302–303
Zumwalt, Elmo, 153